WORLDWIDE INFLATION

LAWRENCE B. KRAUSE AND WALTER S. SALANT

Editors

WORLDWIDE INFLATION

Theory and Recent Experience

ODD AUKRUST

WILLIAM H. BRANSON

LARS CALMFORS

GERHARD FELS

WYNNE A. H. GODLEY

RYUTARO KOMIYA AND YOSHIO SUZUKI

LAWRENCE B. KRAUSE

ANTONIO C. LEMGRUBER

JOHN D. PITCHFORD

WALTER S. SALANT

PASCAL SALIN AND GEORGES LANE

HAROLD T. SHAPIRO

ALEXANDER K. SWOBODA

THE BROOKINGS INSTITUTION

Washington, D.C.

Library of Congress Cataloging in Publication Data:
Main entry under title:
Worldwide inflation.
Includes index.
1. Inflation (Finance)—Addresses, essays, lectures.
I. Krause, Lawrence B.
II. Salant, Walter S.
HG229.W664   332.4'1   76-51580
ISBN 0-8157-5030-7
ISBN 0-8157-5029-3 pbk.

THE BROOKINGS INSTITUTION is an independent organization devoted to nonpartisan research, education, and publication in economics, government, foreign policy, and the social sciences generally. Its principal purposes are to aid in the development of sound public policies and to promote public understanding of issues of national importance.

The Institution was founded on December 8, 1927, to merge the activities of the Institute for Government Research, founded in 1916, the Institute of Economics, founded in 1922, and the Robert Brookings Graduate School of Economics and Government, founded in 1924.

The Board of Trustees is responsible for the general administration of the Institution, while the immediate direction of the policies, program, and staff is vested in the President, assisted by an advisory committee of the officers and staff. The bylaws of the Institution state: "It is the function of the Trustees to make possible the conduct of scientific research, and publication, under the most favorable conditions, and to safeguard the independence of the research staff in the pursuit of their studies and in the publication of the results of such studies. It is not a part of their function to determine, control, or influence the conduct of particular investigation or the conclusions reached."

The President bears final responsibility for the decision to publish a manuscript as a Brookings book. In reaching his judgment on the competence, accuracy, and objectivity of each study, the President is advised by the director of the appropriate research program and weighs the views of a panel of expert outside readers who report to him in confidence on the quality of the work. Publication of a work signifies that it is deemed a competent treatment worthy of public consideration but does not imply endorsement of conclusions or recommendations.

The Institution maintains its position of neutrality on issues of public policy in order to safeguard the intellectual freedom of the staff. Hence interpretations or conclusions in Brookings publications should be understood to be solely those of the authors and should not be attributed to the Institution, to its trustees, officers, or other staff members, or to the organizations that support its research.

Foreword

INFLATION, an ancient affliction, has hardly been ignored by economists in the past. Yet the inflationary surge of the 1970s, which reached a peak in mid-1974, seemed different from most earlier peacetime episodes. It was both more virulent and more widespread, permeating industrialized and developing countries alike. Inflation continues at a high rate in many countries even though economic activity is sluggish and unemployment is high.

These developments have prompted much broad-based research. Economists have increasingly recognized that recent inflation has been a global and not merely a national disease, but much of their research still tends to reflect a national approach and to prescribe parochial, temporary, and often self-defeating remedies. The search for a more comprehensive diagnosis and for anti-inflationary policies that really work has suffered from the continued proclivity to view inflation almost solely from national perspectives.

Accordingly, in November 1974, the Brookings Institution organized a conference of international experts from the United States, Asia, Latin America, and Europe to review the state of knowledge concerning the causes and possible cures for inflation and to study the attempts of different countries to deal with it. Lawrence B. Krause and Walter S. Salant, both senior fellows in the Brookings Economic Studies program, and C. Fred Bergsten, a senior fellow in the Brookings Foreign Policy Studies program, served as cochairmen of the conference. This volume, the first of a Brookings series on worldwide inflation, includes the thirteen papers prepared for the conference, along with formal comments on the papers and summaries of the conference discussion. The papers have been extensively revised and updated to reflect debate at the conference and subsequent developments.

To define the issues as clearly as possible, the contributors of the first four papers restricted themselves to expositions of different theories of inflation and its transmission, without emphasizing their personal preferences or views. The contributors of the eight country studies that follow shared a common orientation, but were given considerable leeway in carrying out their assignments. A more rigid structure might have yielded better comparability of data, but there was little assurance that the same analytical structure would be appropriate for all countries. To have forced explanations of inflation into a common mold might have undermined the validity of national comparisons. The contributors made their own judgments as to the importance of variables, directions of causation, and interpretation of results. The volume ends with a presentation of one supranational approach to the study of inflation and suggestions for further research.

Mark Duvall, Marion Layton, and Leo Simon assisted the editors in preparing the papers for publication by verifying data and sources. Barbara P. Haskins was responsible for editing the manuscript and was assisted by other members of the Brookings publications staff. Florence Robinson prepared the indexes.

The conference was undertaken with financial support from the German Marshall Fund and the Toyota Motor Sales, U.S.A., Inc. Preparation of this volume has been supported by a grant from the Sloan Foundation. The views expressed in this volume are the authors' alone and should not be attributed to the organizations that helped finance the project, or to the trustees, officers, or other staff members of the Brookings Institution.

GILBERT Y. STEINER
Acting President

January 1977
Washington, D.C.

Contents

PART THREE. FUTURE RESEARCH:
A SUPRANATIONAL APPROACH AND SPECIFIC TOPICS

WORLDWIDE
INFLATION

PART ONE

Theories of Inflation

LAWRENCE B. KRAUSE
WALTER S. SALANT

Summary

No SUBJECT of inquiry is older and yet fresher than that of inflation. It has bedeviled governments and their economic advisers ever since the invention of money. Despite all efforts to understand inflation, there are always surprises when a new bout appears. So it was with the upsurge of inflation of 1972–74. Its most striking characteristic was its virulence, as inflation rates reached a "double-digit" range in an increasing number of countries—and in some countries the first of the two digits became two or three. The 1972–74 inflation was also widespread; all advanced countries and most developing countries suffered from it. Moreover, the disease struck nearly all countries simultaneously. Thus, there was reason enough to describe the inflation as worldwide, to try to find a common source for it, and to pay increased attention to the process by which it spread among countries.

This book is devoted to the study of world inflation. The first part examines the theory of inflation. The second part presents descriptions and analyses of inflation in eight countries. A summary that precedes the country studies draws attention to some similarities and differences in national experiences of inflations. The book concludes with a paper on a supranational approach to world inflation and contributors' suggestions for further research that emerged from the conference at which the original drafts of all papers were presented and discussed.

Theories of Inflation

Theories of inflation are addressed in four papers. In the first, Alexander Swoboda considers monetary approaches to inflation. Next, the Keynesian approach is covered by William Branson. A theory of inflation in small open economies is presented by Odd Aukrust. And, finally, Walter Salant reviews theories of international transmission.

Swoboda notes three elements that are common to monetary approaches to world inflation under a regime of fixed exchange rates: one stresses the link between the money stock in the world and the level of money incomes; a second the role of goods arbitrage among countries in the setting of prices, and a third the monetary theory of the balance of payments, which links changes in the stock of national moneys to the world money stock. By use of a simple model incorporating these three elements, Swoboda is able to demonstrate that under fixed exchange rates, national inflation rates may be expected to converge. Inflation rates may differ, nevertheless, because exchange rates do not stay fixed, because productivity increases at different rates in different countries, and to a lesser extent because of barriers to international trade and the existence of nontraded goods and services. Swoboda also examines the transmission mechanism and draws attention to the complications that capital flows among countries bring to the adjustment process. In conclusion, Swoboda emphasizes the importance of viewing world inflation as the outcome of an interacting world system and of recognizing the complexity of adjustment mechanisms.

The implications of the Keynesian approach to world inflation are drawn out by Branson through manipulating a variant of the standard (IS-LM) model depicting the equilibrium of output and interest rates as determined by investment, the relation of consumption to income, and the demand for and supply of money. Branson modifies the standard model by substituting the price level for output as one of the variables to be determined and is thus able to use the model to solve for the price level and the interest rate in order to determine the rate of inflation. A Phillips curve analysis is added to link inflation and real output. Effects on the trade balance are also derived through the relations between real output and the foreign-trade multiplier. Using the methodology of comparative statics, Branson is able to derive the consequences of shifts of the exogenous variables on the price level and the balance of payments. A notable finding is that while shifts in certain exogenous variables, such as government expenditures, have determinate effects on the price level, it is impossible to determine, a priori, the direction of their effects on the balance of payments because the current account and the capital account change in opposite directions. Branson points out that since this model can explain convergence of changes in price levels among countries through adjustments of real output and unemployment, such convergence does not imply support for monetary approaches to world inflation. In conclusion, Branson warns that the findings of the model rest on comparative statics, but he notes that a beginning has been made in solving the complicated problems of a dynamic system.

Aukrust analyzes the Norwegian model of inflation, which is meant to describe one type of small open economy. The economy is viewed as having two sectors, one exposed to world markets and the other sheltered from them. According to this theory, under fixed exchange rates and in the long run the domestic price level is determined by prices in world markets through direct and indirect linkages to international trade and by the relation between productivity in the exposed and sheltered sectors. The prices of exposed industries are set in world markets through direct competition. These prices, combined with existing technology, determine value added in the exposed industries, and this determines wages in those industries. Wages in the exposed industries, in turn, set the pattern for wages in sheltered industries as workers in the one sector bargain to sustain their wages relative to those of workers in the other. Furthermore, since wages in sheltered industries, along with productivity, determine costs, and entrepreneurs in those industries set prices as a markup over costs, the price-setting mechanism is completed, with world prices and the exchange rate being the only exogenous variables. With exchange rates fixed and some simplifying assumptions, the inflation rate of a small open economy is shown to differ in the long run from the world inflation rate only to the degree that the increase in productivity in its sheltered industries differs from that in the sheltered industries of the rest of the world. Short-run deviations from this relationship may occur, but they are reduced in the long run through wage negotiation, through labor market forces, and through macroeconomic policy. In this model, demand has little direct influence on commodity prices, these being determined by the world market or costs (through cost-plus pricing). In the labor market, however, demand plays an important role and, through its effects on wages, influences prices indirectly. Aukrust observes that in small countries there is little scope for a national price policy if a fixed exchange rate is maintained. Indeed, the success of incomes policy in moderating the fight over income shares rests on the ability of entrepreneurs in exposed industries to resist claims for wage increases. The only transmission mechanism that is important in this analysis occurs through the prices of internationally traded goods. Aukrust notes that some empirical tests of the model have been attempted with promising results, but more research is required to verify the assumptions of the analysis.

Salant introduces his theoretical review of the international transmission mechanism by calling attention to the decline in the dispersion of inflation rates among industrial countries as the rates of inflation have been rising. He shows that the conventional views that such a decrease or dispersion implies increased transmission and that increased transmission reduces dispersion are not necessarily correct, but concludes that the presumption that the transmission mechanism has become more important than ever still holds. Salant examines a number of transmission mechanisms that operate under fixed exchange rates, including increases in prices of internationally traded goods, increases in aggregate demand arising from increases in a country's international balance of goods and services, and increases in the money supply that occur from surpluses in the overall balance of payments. He also examines other mechanisms, such as wage links among countries. Shifting to a floating exchange rate assumption alters the analysis, however. In general, floating rates dampen and may even prevent transmission of inflation from the outside world. An exception would be the transmission of inflation into countries whose demand for imports is inelastic to increases in prices of imports and in which the rise in import prices sets off a depreciation of the currency that in turn sets off a cumulative increase in wages and depreciation. Another would be where outside inflation gives rise to capital outflows. Salant examines the question whether fixed or flexible rates are inherently more inflationary for the world as a whole and concludes that there is no determinate answer if monetary policy is not specified. He concludes by reviewing existing econometric studies of the transmission process, pointing out the pitfalls that such work entails and the need for further empirical work.

The State of the Art

The theoretical papers review the state of the art and make some headway in advancing understanding of inflation, especially in revealing the compatibility of various theoretical approaches. It is still true that economists do not possess a fully satisfactory or general theory of inflation that accurately describes the inflationary process in all countries and fully serves the needs of policymakers. Theories of inflation are not mutually exclusive but overlap and must interact in a dynamic model in ways that are still incompletely understood. Authors of the country studies, while usually resting their analyses more heavily on one particular theory than the others, in the main are eclectic in their use of theory, which under the circumstances seems appropriate. Although it may be foolhardy to expect that a single theory of inflation will ever be discovered or be applicable to all countries, further progress toward greater understanding appears possible.

ALEXANDER K. SWOBODA

Monetary Approaches to Worldwide Inflation

9

Figures

Several of the issues surveyed in this essay by Alexander K. Swoboda, Graduate Institute of International Studies, Geneva, are the object of both theoretical and empirical research in two projects with which he is associated: "National Economic Policy and the International Monetary System" at the Graduate Institute of International Studies (Geneva) under a grant from the Ford Foundation and "International Monetary Theory and Policy" at the London School of Economics under a grant from the British Social Science Research Council. In revising this paper Alexander Swoboda has benefited greatly from the editors' detailed and very helpful comments.

INFLATION has spread to the number of theories and models purporting to explain and analyze worldwide price increases. Specialized versions of the "monetary," "Keynesian," "cost-push," and "sociological" approaches to the generation and transmission of international inflation abound. This paper delineates the main features of the monetary approach though, in the process, the contrast with competing hypotheses should become apparent.

There is no single all-purpose model of the monetary variety that can claim to embody the quintessence of *the* monetary theory of worldwide inflation. Nevertheless, common elements characterize the writings of practitioners of this approach—be they self-proclaimed apostles of the method or damned to those ranks by their opponents.

Common Elements of Monetary Approaches

A wide variety of macroeconomic models of the open economy incorporates elements of what might be called the monetary approach to international adjustment. These models are usually developed for the fixed exchange rate case and their focus is often an analysis of the determinants of the balance of payments and of its adjustment. Three main elements common to many of these models can be distinguished.

First, they incorporate the essentials of what has come to be called "the monetary theory of the balance of payments." This theory stresses the fact that the balance of payments, under fixed exchange rates, is "an essentially monetary phenomenon." This, in a sense, is a truism since the net balance of international payments is defined as the rate of change of the stock of international reserves of the monetary authorities. It is, however, a truism worth emphasizing since it immediately draws attention to the importance of money-market equilibrium and disequilibrium for analysis of the overall balance of payments (as distinct from the latter's composition). It emphasizes that there is a direct link between the balance of payments and the supply of money since international reserves are one of the components of the monetary base. Furthermore, continuing payments surpluses or deficits

11

are, in the absence of continuous policy interventions such as systematic neutralization, incompatible with general equilibrium in a stationary economy. This point is emphasized by Johnson in his celebrated 1958 paper.[1] As a consequence, in a stable economy in which the authorities confine their interventions to stabilizing the exchange rate, there will be an automatic tendency for payments equilibrium—in the "narrow" sense of no excess demand or supply of foreign exchange—to be established.[2] A necessary condition for stability often turns out to be that, other things being equal, an increase in the money stock worsens the balance of payments—and that, in turn, depends on the existence of a stable demand-for-money function.[3] With an automatic payments adjustment mechanism, the money stock in an open economy is seen to be an endogenous variable and an equilibrium distribution of the world money stock asserts itself, in Humean or Ricardian fashion, in the long run when full adjustment has taken place and neutralization operations do not, or can no longer, take place.

Second, monetary approaches to worldwide inflation stress the link between the money stock and the level of money income. The existence of a "stable" demand-for-money function is asserted to motivate this link. In secular or longer-run analyses of worldwide inflation, the growth of real income is often treated as exogenous, or as responding only slightly or in the short run to changes in the rate of monetary expansion. Monetary expansion then becomes the main determinant (or concomitant) of the rate of inflation, however complicated the dynamics of interaction may be in the short run. Note that this implies a steady rate of price *de*flation if the rate of growth of real income should exceed that of monetary expansion by a sufficient margin and suggests that the assumption of exogenous real growth

1. Harry G. Johnson, "Towards a General Theory of the Balance of Payments"; reprinted in his *International Trade and Economic Growth* (London: Allen and Unwin, 1958), pp. 153–68.

2. The "proper" definition of payments equilibrium was the subject of much debate in the postwar period, with Fritz Machlup, James Meade, Ragnar Nurkse, and the International Monetary Fund as main protagonists in the discussion. Though there is no unique "proper" definition, the one adopted here is the most convenient for analytical purposes. It does not prevent one from examining the problems of substance raised by Nurkse (essentially, what if payments equilibrium occurs with unemployment and a high level of exchange restrictions?) while avoiding useless semantic debate (should one still want to call equality of demand and supply "equilibrium" if it is associated with an undesired value of some variable, say, a high rate of unemployment?) and analytical confusions (for instance, *assuming* that if foreign exchange market equilibrium occurs at some exchange rate with unemployment, it cannot occur at that same rate without unemployment).

3. See, for example, Alexander K. Swoboda, "Monetary Policy under Fixed Exchange Rates: Effectiveness, the Speed of Adjustment, and Proper Use," *Economica*, vol. 40 (May 1973), pp. 136–54.

could hardly be maintained in such a case for the purpose of short-run analysis.

Finally, and especially in more recent work, heavy stress is laid on the role of goods arbitrage as a direct link between commodity markets and money prices under fixed exchange rates.

In brief, monetary models of adjustment under fixed exchange rates emphasize the link between the balance of payments and the money stock and between the money stock and money income; they point to the international equalization of money prices (translated into a common currency unit at existing exchange rates) of similar goods, except for any impediments to trade; and they usually incorporate neutrality of money in the long run in some version of the natural distribution of specie. These common features allow, of course, for a wide variety of models, both with respect to static' structure (level of disaggregation, behavioral specification, and the like) and dynamic structure (in particular, specification of the transmission process).

At least three broad strands of analysis, particularly relevant to the process of transmission of inflation, may be usefully distinguished at the outset.

The first derives directly from closed economy monetarist theorizing and, not surprisingly, originates mainly in the United States, the Western industrialized country closest to being large enough to create the illusion that it can be analyzed as a closed economy. The direction of causation is seen as running entirely from the money stock to money income. Some allowances for external influences are made by recognizing that the foreign source component of the monetary base is determined by past balance of payments developments. These are, however, for the purposes of the analysis, treated as exogenous.[4] Feedbacks through the impact of money income on the balance of payments, though acknowledged, are rarely incorporated in formal models. Most important, in dynamic analysis, the direction of causation is always from money stock to money income.

The interaction of money and external payments is taken into much more explicit account in the second strand of analysis that traces its roots to classical analysis and reemerges in the work of Dutch monetary theorists and researchers at the International Monetary Fund.[5] These theorists, especially those at the Fund, postulate simple models where, in the most

4. Most of the traditional money multiplier analysis is of this type. For a convenient summary and references, see, for instance, J. L. Jordan, "Elements of Money Stock Determination," *Federal Reserve Bank of St. Louis Review,* vol. 51 (October 1969), pp. 10–19.

5. For references to Dutch monetary analysis see Frits J. de Jong, *Developments of Monetary Theory in the Netherlands* (Rotterdam: Rotterdam University Press, 1973). For the IMF approach, see, among others, J. J. Polak, "Monetary Analysis of Income

stripped-down version, the balance of payments is equal to the balance of trade plus capital flows, assumed to be exogenous for the purpose at hand (that is, independent of the money stock and of money income), the trade balance depends on income, nominal income is determined by the money stock, and the latter can change either because of a change in domestic credit creation or in foreign exchange reserves. Domestic inflationary impulses originate in either exogenous changes in spending or domestic credit creation, external inflationary impulses in exogenously determined increases in capital inflows or exports. With the exception of the work of Prais, however, the implicit or explicit dynamics of the transmission process stress the influence of the money stock on the level of money income. An increase in domestic credit raises the money stock and, hence, income; this leads to a trade deficit that decreases the money stock and, hence, income until the initial equilibrium is reestablished. Increased exports do affect income directly (in the first round and in some models), but the main effects issue from inflows of reserves and consequent increases in the money supply and income. Furthermore, again with the exception of Prais, the balance of trade depends, through the propensity to import, on income and not on expenditure. This implies that, as stock monetary equilibrium is assumed to prevail continuously, the direction of causation must be as outlined above, and internal growth must lead to a payments deficit. An increase in money income cannot create an excess demand for money reflected in a fall in domestic expenditure and a trade surplus, a mechanism stressed in the third approach.

Mundell's early work incorporates many elements of the last strand of analysis to be discussed but also provides the most sophisticated and complete version of the second one.[6] Mundell, however, stresses the general equilibrium nature of adjustment in open economies, introduces a bond market and interest rates, and his comparative statics are compatible with a wide variety of transmission mechanisms, setting the stage for the most recent developments in the analysis of the transmission mechanism.

In that third variety, the direction of causation between money income and the money stock tends to be reversed for the case of the single small

---

Formation and Payments Problems," *IMF Staff Papers,* vol. 6 (November 1957), pp. 1–50; J. J. Polak and Lorette Boissonneault, "Monetary Analysis of Income and Imports and Its Statistical Application," *IMF Staff Papers,* vol. 7 (April 1960), pp. 349–415; S. J. Prais, "Some Mathematical Notes on the Quantity Theory of Money in an Open Economy," *IMF Staff Papers,* vol. 8 (May 1961), pp. 212–26; and J. J. Polak and Victor Argy, "Credit Policy and the Balance of Payments," *IMF Staff Papers,* vol. 18 (March 1971), pp. 1–24.

6. These papers are conveniently collected in Robert A. Mundell, *International Economics* (Macmillan, 1968). See especially chaps. 11 and 15–20.

open economy. Consider an increase in money income brought about by either an increase in the prices of traded goods or exogenous domestic growth. This increase creates an excess demand for money which in turn depresses expenditure relative to income as economic agents attempt to rebuild their real cash balances. The resulting balance of trade surplus implies an inflow of reserves and an increase in the nominal stock of money. Since the causation, for a small open economy runs from income to the stock of money, one may well ask in what sense this last type of model is "monetary" or "monetarist." The answer is that the world money stock is considered to be exogenous and to determine the world price level, national money supplies to be endogenous. This type of model, then, analyzes the world economy as a closed economy, and it treats transmission problems and individual country payments adjustment as problems of distribution of the world money stock. It is thus analogous to the classic analysis of distribution problems in closed economy monetary theory propounded by Archibald and Lipsey.[7] Probably the most original analysis of this type in an international context is in Mundell's *Monetary Theory,* and Johnson provides a comprehensive survey of the theory and its extension to an *n*-country world.[8]

This last framework, which emphasizes the role of goods arbitrage, the exogeneity of the price level and endogeneity of the money stock for an individual small economy, the exogeneity of the money stock and endogeneity of the price level for the *world* economy, provides a convenient starting point for an examination of why one should expect inflation rates to converge in a world of fixed exchange rates.

However, a word may usefully be said at the outset about the method of presentation adopted in this paper. Main results are presented first in as

---

7. G. C. Archibald and R. G. Lipsey, "Monetary and Value Theory: A Critique of Lange and Patinkin," *Review of Economic Studies,* vol. 26 (October 1958), pp. 1–22. Frenkel has recently argued that this view of the adjustment process is what classical writers "really" had in mind. (See Jacob Frenkel, "Adjustment Mechanisms and the Monetary Approach to the Balance of Payments: A Doctrinal Perspective," in Emil Claasen and Pascal Salin, eds., *Recent Issues in International Monetary Economics* [Amsterdam: North-Holland, 1976; distributed in the United States and Canada by American Elsevier, 1976].) Johnson recasts the monetary theory of the balance of payments in terms of an extension of the Archibald and Lipsey geometry. (See Harry G. Johnson, "The Monetary Approach to Balance of Payments Theory: A Diagrammatic Analysis," *The Manchester School,* vol. 43 [September 1975], pp. 220–74.)

8. Robert A. Mundell, "The International Distribution of Money in a Growing World Economy," in Mundell, *Monetary Theory: Inflation, Interest, and Growth in the World Economy* (Pacific Palisades: Goodyear, 1971), pp. 147–60; and Harry G. Johnson, "The Monetary Approach to the Balance-of-Payments Theory," in Michael B. Connolly and Alexander K. Swoboda, eds., *International Trade and Money* (London: Allen and Unwin, 1973).

simple a fashion as possible, that is, whenever feasible within the framework of a very simple model, although the same conclusion may also be deduced from a more general and complete analytical framework. Allowance for additional elements of the analysis is made by discussing the modifications or qualifications they entail later in the paper. For instance, early sections use, in the main, variants of simple two-country models incorporating only money and goods explicitly as objects of exchange. It is assumed, either explicitly or implicitly, that there are no holdings of securities, or at least of traded securities (no capital movements take place). The justification for this procedure is that in equilibrium, in a stationary economy with flexible prices, the domestic real interest rate will be invariant to monetary disturbances, and its role can be neglected at first in the review of the issues at hand. The role of interest rate variations in both domestic adjustment and in the context of trade in securities is brought up later in connection with capital movements. Furthermore, in much of the discussion it is assumed that neutralization operations by monetary authorities do not take place. This does not reflect a belief that this assumption is empirically correct; far from it. The motivation is, instead, that the consequences of neutralization operations are easily traced—and in some respects can only be traced—after results assuming their absence have been established.

In addition, the analysis often assumes an exogenously given level or rate of growth of real income, so that those elements of the adjustment and transmission process most relevant to periods of rapid inflation are emphasized. This is not to deny that changes in the stock of money or in the rate of monetary expansion have significant employment effects in the short run. Nor is it to deny that policy reactions to such short-run effects may, in fact, help explain variations in the rate of monetary expansion in the longer run. Note, too, that variations in the level of real income and employment play an important—in some cases the central—role in many "monetary" models of adjustment and international transmission. Indeed, the broad variety of short-run adjustment mechanisms compatible with "monetary" approaches is one of the important characteristics of the literature surveyed in this paper. To gain a better feeling for its richness, there is, of course, no substitute for sampling that literature itself.

Why Inflation Rates Converge

The simplest theory yielding convergence in inflation rates states that goods arbitrage will equate prices of goods produced in Country 1, P, with foreign goods prices, P', multiplied by the exchange rate, e, the domestic currency price of one unit of foreign currency, barring transport cost and other impediments to trade. Assuming the latter to be a constant proportion, t, of foreign prices (duties are levied on an ad valorem basis), this implies that[9]

$$(1) \qquad\qquad P = eP'(1 + t).$$

Differentiating both sides of equation 1 with respect to time, denoting the time derivative of a variable by "dotting" it, and the proportional rate of change of a variable by the superscript, $\hat{\ }$, and assuming t constant, yields[10]

$$(2) \qquad\qquad \hat{P} = \hat{e} + \hat{P}'.$$

Using equation 2, with fixed exchange rates, $\hat{e} = 0$, the percentage rate of change in domestic and foreign prices will be equalized. This simplest "theory" of convergence of inflation requires further comment.

In the first place, there is nothing "monetary" about the theory except that it is concerned with equalizing money prices and their rate of change.

Second, and more important, there is no definition of the goods to which P and P' refer. Four main analytical definitions can be offered. The first and almost trivial one is to state that there is only one good produced in the world economy and that good is traded. Equalization of inflation rates follows by assumption. Second, P_i and P_i' can be interpreted as the domestic and foreign prices of any single homogeneous commodity, i, that is traded internationally; there are as many equations of types 1 and 2 as there are commodities. This is a strict statement of the hypothesis of goods arbitrage but it does not imply that inflation rates, as measured by some general price index, will be equalized unless (a) goods enter the national indexes with constant weights, and either (b) all goods enter trade and no change in the terms of trade occurs, or (c) there is no change in either the terms of trade or in the relative price of traded and nontraded goods.

---

9. Actually, equation 1 assumes that the good is imported into Country 1. As Viner emphasizes, assuming the impediment to trade, t (for example, transport cost), to be equal whether the good is imported by Country 1 or another country, equation 1 becomes a pair of inequalities, (a) $P \leqslant P'(1 + t)$ for the case where the good is imported into Country 1 or not traded, (b) $P(1 + t) \geqslant P'$ for the case where the good is exported by Country 1 or not traded. (Jacob Viner, *Studies in the Theory of International Trade* [Harper, 1937], p. 317.) This point and Viner's discussion was brought to my attention by Walter Salant.

10. Throughout the text I follow the convention of denoting the derivative of some variable with respect to time by putting a dot above that variable, the proportional rate of change of that variable by adding a hat above the dot. Thus, for instance,

$$\dot{x} = \frac{dx}{dt}, \ \hat{\dot{x}} = \frac{1}{x}\frac{dx}{dt}.$$

Third, as a special version of the preceding case (which is discussed in more detail in subsequent sections of this paper), P and P' can be taken to be the price of a composite good, all traded goods, and variations in the relative price of the traded and nontraded goods examined separately.

Fourth, appeal can be made to economic theory to demonstrate, as Archibald and Lipsey suggest, that, *in full equilibrium* and in the absence of "real" changes in tastes or production technology, equation 1 must hold even if P and P' represent price indexes, provided that at least one of the goods entering the national indexes is traded internationally.[11] The reason is simple. Assuming all real excess demand functions to be homogeneous of degree zero in money prices and the nominal stock of money, only changes in tastes, endowments, or technology can change relative prices in equilibrium. Therefore, if a monetary shock changes one price by X percent in long-run equilibrium it must change all prices by X percent in long-run equilibrium. In fact, provided that either all goods enter trade (or are sufficiently close substitutes in excess demand for no significant change in relative prices to occur) or that one is concerned only with long-run monetary equilibria (which may actually be brought about in a chronologically short time), goods arbitrage will ensure convergence of inflation rates.

It is convenient to adopt this last assumption below (although not in later discussion). So far, however, I have only demonstrated (or assumed) that, under some restrictive assumptions, inflation rates tend to converge under fixed exchange rates; I have not determined what the inflation rate will be nor how adjustment will take place. As an introduction to later discussion, the comparative statics, the comparative dynamics, and the adjustment process in a simple one-good, or long-run, world are briefly reviewed below.

The comparative statics model

The simplest monetary model of the determination of the world price level is uncommonly simple, not to say "simpliste." It relates the price of the one good produced in the world (the world price level) to the sum of the money stocks of the countries composing the world (the world money stock). It can be illustrated formally with the help of a simple two-country model (the home country and the rest of the world).[12]

11. This is demonstrated for the case of devaluation in a dynamic general-equilibrium model in E. A. Kuska, "The Pure Theory of Devaluation," *Economica*, vol. 39 (August 1972), pp. 309–15.

12. No essential complication arises in this context from using an n-country model. (The two-country version, however, saves adding signs and subscripts.)

Figure 1. *Distribution of the World Money Stock in a One-Good Model*

World price level

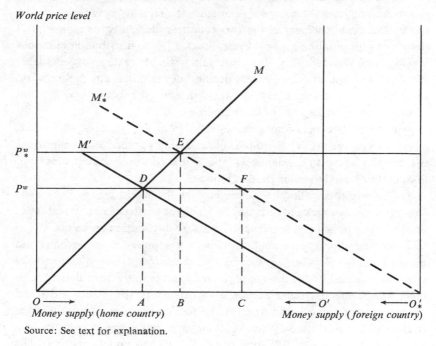

Source: See text for explanation.

The model states that in equilibrium the demand for money must be equal to the supply in each country, as expressed in equations 3 and 4 below:

(3) $$M = kyP,$$

(4) $$M' = k'y'P',$$

where variables without primes refer to the home country and those with primes to the rest of the world. M is the money stock; k is the "Cambridge k," that is, the stock of real money balances the public wants to hold as a proportion of real income; y is real income; and P represents the domestic currency price of "goods." Add to this the goods arbitrage equation, $P = eP'$ (neglecting impediments to trade), set for simplicity the exchange rate, e, equal to 1 by appropriate choice of units to obtain:

(5) $$M^w = M + M' = (ky + k'y')P^w,$$

where M^w and P^w are the world money stock and price level, respectively.

This model is illustrated in figure 1. The world money stock (assumed to be fixed or exogenous) is measured by the horizontal distance between O and

O'. The two countries' demand-for-money schedules, OM and $O'M'$, are drawn starting from their respective origins. The equality between the world money stock and the sum of the two countries' demands for money at D determines the equilibrium world price level, P^w, and distribution of money supplies, OA and AO'. Any other distribution would create an excess supply of one money and matching excess demand of the other; any higher world price level would create an excess world demand for money and a corresponding world excess supply of commodities.

A number of conclusions emerge, even from this simplest of models. These conclusions, which are quite robust to any number of complications that may be added to the model as long as one concerns oneself with equilibrium states, can be summarized as follows:

1. The world price level is determined by the world money stock. The world is treated as a closed economy in which the existence of national states and monetary policies is viewed as giving rise to distribution problems.

2. The equilibrium distribution of money supplies is endogenous and proportional to *effective* size, ky and $k'y'$; the above size is equal to size of GNP, y, weighted by the inverse of the income velocity of circulation, k. In other words, effective size reflects the importance of the country's demand for real money balances. In figure 1 the foreign country receives a larger fraction of the world money stock; its larger effective size is reflected in a lower absolute value of the slope of $O'M'$, which is equal to $1/k'y'$. The equilibrium distribution of the world money stock is algebraically:

$$(6) \qquad \beta = \frac{M}{M^w} = \frac{ky}{ky + k'y'}.$$

3. A corollary of the preceding two points is that, as far as the world price level is concerned, national monetary policy is internationalized by the payments adjustment process. In other words, the effect of a given increase in the world money stock on the world price level is independent of its national origin. Graphically, consider an increase of $O'O'_* = AC$ in the foreign money stock. The origin of the foreign demand-for-money schedule is shifted to O'_* resulting, at the previous world price level, in an excess supply of the foreign country's money equal to AC. Equilibrium requires that the world price level rise to P^w_* and that the equilibrium distribution of the world money stock be reestablished, which will occur when residents of the home country hold OB and foreign residents hold BO'_*, AB of the world money stock having been redistributed to the home country through the payments adjustment process. Note that exactly the same final result would have been obtained had the money stock of the home country been increased by AC

originally: the final result is entirely determined by the size of the world money stock (the length of the line segment linking the two origins on the abcissa of the diagram) and the slopes of the money demand schedules.

4. The model has assumed the world money stock to be fixed so far and has had little to say about the equilibrium distribution of reserves. To justify the former assumption and derive the latter distribution, the nature of the domestic money supply process and its relation to the world stock of money needs to be specified. The simplest specification for this purpose here is to state that the money stock in each country is equal to the liabilities in the consolidated balance sheet of the banking system, whose corresponding assets are divided into foreign reserves, R, and other claims ("domestic credit"), D:[13]

(7) $$M = D + R,$$

(8) $$M' = D' + R'.$$

If, in addition it is assumed that only an outside asset such as gold is held as foreign reserves (or that the quantity of inside assets held as reserves is fixed or exogenous) and that its quantity is given and equal to R^w, one obtains:[14]

(9) $$M^w = M + M' = D + D' + R^w.$$

From equations 6 and 7, the equilibrium distribution of reserves is easily derived by substitution to yield:

(10) $$\frac{R}{R^w} = \frac{\beta M^w - D}{R^w}.$$

Graphically, an increase in the domestic assets of the foreign country by $O'O'_*$ in figure 1 leads to a decrease in its foreign reserves of AB, which are gained by the home country. Had the latter initiated the money supply

13. As securities have not been introduced explicitly into the model, a word of explanation on the meaning of D is in order: (a) one can treat D as a bookkeeping entry, which is a counterpart to currency printed by the government without the backing of international reserves; (b) D may represent the counterpart of stocks of goods acquired by authorities through past fiscal deficits; or (c) one can identify D with securities acquired by monetary authorities and consider the analysis to be relevant only to equilibrium states in which the interest rate is invariant with respect to monetary disturbances (a classical result) or in which spending is invariant with respect to the interest rate; in the latter case, one must rule out the existence of a liquidity trap and, if there are tradable securities, add some restrictions (see the discussion on pages 39–43, and note 40) to validate the results in the text.

14. Some of the complications arising from a more complete consideration of the money-supply process and, in particular, of inside reserve-asset holdings are analyzed below (pages 44–47).

change by creating $O'O'_*$ of additional domestic assets, it would have lost BC of international reserves to the foreign country. The international distribution of reserves, unlike that of money supplies, is not independent of the origin of monetary disturbances.[15]

The comparative equilibrium dynamics model

So far, I have dealt only with the determination of the price level and of once-and-for-all changes in that level. Although, for several purposes, many issues connected with inflation can be treated as similar to a succession of such changes in the upward direction, it is desirable to examine the behavior of rates of change in variables directly for both theoretical and practical reasons. Unfortunately, international monetary theory shares with general monetary theory the lack of a generally agreed-upon framework for analyzing the dynamics of inflation at every point in the adjustment process. It can, however, say something precise about equilibrium rates of change under somewhat restrictive assumptions.

Assuming that actual and expected rates of inflation are equal and that exogenous variables grow at constant and given percentage rates, the equilibrium rates of inflation and of redistribution of the world money stock can easily be established. Domestic credit creation, world reserves, and real income in the two countries are assumed to be growing exogenously. Equality of actual and expected rates of inflation means that in equilibrium the money rate of interest is given and, hence, that one can neglect stock adjustments to lower ratios of real balances to real income as the rate of inflation increases (k and k' can be treated as constants, implying a unitary elasticity of the demand for real balances with respect to real income). Taking time derivatives of the logarithm of equation 5, one obtains the following equation for the world rate of inflation in terms of proportional rates of change:

$$(11) \qquad\qquad \hat{P}^w = \hat{M}^w - \beta\hat{y} - (1 - \beta)\hat{y}'.$$

Equation 11 states simply that the world rate of inflation is equal to the world rate of monetary expansion minus the rate of growth of the demand for world money in the two countries, the latter being determined by the exogenous rate of growth of real income in the two countries, remembering that β changes over time when the two real incomes grow at different rates. Equation 11 is the two-country counterpart of n-country equations devel-

---

15. The results in the text are derived under the assumption that monetary authorities do not neutralize reserve flows. If they did so systematically, no stock equilibrium could take place; a flow "quasi-equilibrium" formula can be established, however, by setting $\dot{D} = -\dot{R}$ for the case of complete neutralization.

oped by Johnson—on the assumption of unit elasticity of the demand for money with respect to income—and by Mundell—neglecting stock adjustments and interest rate effects.[16]

Similarly, well-known results for the balance of payments of an individual country in inflationary and growth equilibrium can be obtained by time differentiation of equation 10 to yield:

$$(12) \quad \hat{R} = \frac{M}{R}(1 - \beta)(\hat{Y} - \hat{Y'}) + \beta \frac{D'\hat{D'}}{R} + \beta \frac{R^w}{R}\hat{R}^w - (1 - \beta)\frac{D}{R}\hat{D}.$$

Equation 12 states the heretic or classic results—depending on when and where one went to school—that the rate of accumulation of reserves of a country, other things being equal, will be higher: (1) the higher the rate of growth of its real income; (2) the higher the rate of domestic credit creation abroad; (3) the higher the rate of growth of outside international reserves; (4) the lower the foreign rate of growth; and (5) the lower its own rate of domestic credit expansion.

Adjustment

No explicit mention has been made above of the process by which a single country adjusts to a higher world price level or rate of inflation, or by which the world price level or rate of inflation adjusts to an excess supply of money (excess demand for goods) in these simplest of monetary models.

Adjustment processes are notoriously difficult to model in a theoretically meaningful, complete dynamic fashion. The reason is, of course, that the adjustment process is determined by the particular dynamic postulates that one chooses to use, and that such postulates are rarely, except for the simplest ones, firmly rooted in a theory of rational economic behavior. This is one reason why economists have typically tried to capture slices of the adjustment process by means of comparative statics analysis under various assumptions, all too often implicit, as to which market is allowed to clear and which is not.[17]

16. Harry G. Johnson, "The Monetary Approach to Balance-of-Payments Theory," and Robert A. Mundell, *Monetary Theory: Inflation, Interest and Growth in the World Economy* (see note 8 for full citations).

17. For a brief survey of devices used to capture the dynamic process of balance of payments adjustment, see Alexander K. Swoboda, "Monetary Approaches to Balance-of-Payments Theory," in Claassen and Salin, eds., *Recent Issues in International Monetary Economics* (see note 7). In addition to the difficulties mentioned in the text, there is a strong temptation to use postulates derived for "tâtonnement" processes in analysis of *actual* changes in economic variables, converting (or often perverting) these postulates, as it were, into reduced form versions of some nonspecified non-"tâtonnement" process.

A simple model of adjustment of the small open economy to a rise in foreign prices, however, is not difficult to provide. Supposing real income to be given in the short run, the balance of trade (and, hence, the rate of change of reserves and of the money stock) is equal to the difference between the given level of real income and domestic expenditure, dubbed absorption and denoted by A. The expenditure function can be written as follows:[18]

$$(13) \qquad A = \bar{y} + \alpha(\frac{M}{P} - ky).$$

Equation 13 states that real absorption, A, is equal to the given level of real income, $\bar{y}$, plus an amount per unit of time that is proportional to the stock excess supply of real balances, $M/P - ky$, the factor of proportionality being denoted by α. Combining equation 13 with a specification of the money supply process, which states that the rate of change of the stock of real balances for a given price level is equal to the balance of payments, the latter being in turn equal to the difference between income and absorption, leads to a very simple model illustrated in figure 2.[19] Equilibrium obtains at that level of real balances for which income is equal to expenditure, that is, at $(M/P)_0$. At any other level of real balances, payments imbalances would set up changes in the nominal supply of money (remembering that the domestic price level is obtained by given foreign prices multiplied by the given exchange rate) to restore the equilibrium level of real balances.

Consider the effect of a rise in foreign prices. Translated at the given exchange rate, this means an immediate rise in domestic prices through goods arbitrage. At the initial level of the nominal stock of money, real balances fall to $(M/P)_1$; as a result, the public reduces expenditure to $(M/P)_1 B$ in order to rebuild its real money stock. The corresponding balance of trade surplus of $\overline{BC}$ leads to a gradual increase in the stock of money until equilibrium is reestablished at D. The dynamics of the process are given by equation 14 below:

$$(14) \qquad M(t) = ky(P_0 - P_1) e^{-\alpha t} + M_1,$$

where $M(t)$ is the money stock at time t, P_0 is the initial price level, P_1 the new price level after the rise in foreign prices, M_1 is the equilibrium money

---

18. This form of expenditure-adjustment function can be derived from maximizing behavior over time as shown in Michael Mussa and Rudiger Dornbusch, "Consumption, Real Balances, and the Hoarding Function," *International Economic Review*, vol. 16 (June 1975), pp. 415–21.

19. For a fuller discussion of this model and its implications see Swoboda, "Monetary Approaches to Balance-of-Payments Theory."

Figure 2. *Income and Absorption as a Function of the Real Money Stock*

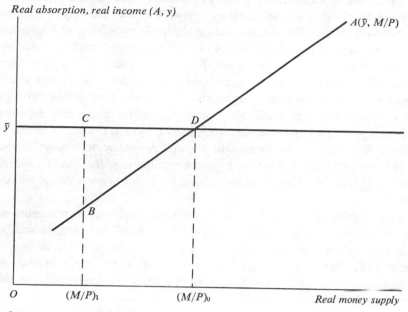

Source: See text for explanation.

supply after the rise in prices, and e is the base of the natural logarithm system and not, of course, the exchange rate.[20]

Adjustment to a rise in the money supply in one country within the framework of an explicit two-country model is more difficult to formalize. Its essential features are, however, readily understood intuitively. At the initial equilibrium price level, the increase in, say, the foreign country's money stock creates an excess supply of money in that country; the home country, however, is still in monetary equilibrium and the excess supply of foreign money is used to bid up the price of goods. As the latter rises, the home country experiences, at the old level of nominal money balances, an excess demand for real balances and a reduction in expenditure leading to a payments surplus at home and deficit abroad. The process will continue with the world price level rising and the world money stock being redistributed

20. Adjustment to a rise in the *rate* of foreign inflation is more difficult to formalize as the ratio of real balances to real income presumably changes over the adjustment period.

toward the home country until prices reach that level at which there is equilibrium in the goods market and payments balance.[21]

This may be an appropriate point at which to take stock of the lessons carried by the very simple monetary approach expounded above. The approach emphasizes the role of goods arbitrage in explaining why inflation rates converge. It focuses on the role of the world money stock in determining the price level in the world and its changes. The fixed exchange rate assumption allows one to define meaningfully both the concept of a world price level and that of a world money stock; it also provides the link, through the required exchange stabilization operations of the authorities, between changes in reserves and national money stocks. Finally, the approach draws attention to the role of changes in absorption relative to income in the adjustment of prices and money balances required to redistribute the world money stock in the face of excess demand for goods or for national money stocks.

The approach, as caricatured so far, however, suffers from a number of defects. First, it is most fully developed in terms of comparative statics. Second, it allows for only one asset (money) and one good. Third, goods arbitrage under fixed exchange rates "does it all" as far as convergence of inflation rates is concerned: with only one composite commodity in the world, inflation rates cannot differ.

21. The reader should be warned, if need be, that far-from-trivial problems in monetary dynamics are swept under an apparently innocuous rug in the text above. In particular, in a simple one-good, two-country model with exogenous real income the requirement that one country's excess of expenditure over income be equal to the other's excess of income over expenditure also implies that world income is equal to world expenditure. Given the total and distribution of money in the world it is the price level that adjusts to bring the equilibrium level of world expenditure to equality with the given exogenously determined level of world income. With these assumptions and using expenditure functions of the equation 13 type, a discrete exogenous increase in, say, M' results in an instantaneous discrete increase in the price level. Further adjustments then take place to redistribute the world money stock through the payments adjustment mechanism. If the speed-of-adjustment coefficients in the two countries, α and α', are equal this redistribution brings no further change in world nominal expenditure and, hence, no further change in the price level, which will have jumped instantaneously to its new equilibrium level. The issue is discussed in a slightly different context and another formulation, in G. C. Archibald and R. G. Lipsey, "Monetary and Value Theory: A Critique of Lange and Patinkin" (see note 7). If $\alpha < \alpha'$, an increase in M' results in an overshooting of the price level and later continuous fall to its equilibrium value, and vice versa if $\alpha > \alpha'$. The reason is that in order to make the home country absorb an amount of money equal to the excess in the foreign country, the price level has to rise a great deal when the home country is relatively sluggish in its reactions ($\alpha < \alpha'$); as adjustment takes place through time, however, the price level falls back to its new equilibrium value. I am indebted to Henryk Kierzkowski for providing a possible mathematical formulation of the latter point (which I hope to discuss in another paper).

Why Inflation Rates Differ

Looking at the world and at statistics, one does of course observe that inflation rates differ from country to country. On an analytical level, one can distinguish four main reasons why inflation rates may differ: (1) exchange rates are not truly fixed; (2) there are impediments to trade or failure of goods arbitrage; (3) there are nontraded goods whose rate of price change differs among countries;[22] and (4) there are errors of measurement in the data.

Nonfixity of exchange rates

Exchange rates can change because of margins of intervention around parities or central rates, devaluations or revaluations, or outright exchange rate flexibility. Only the last of these can explain large and systematic differences in inflation rates.

Intervention margins may cause inflation rates to diverge by the rate of change of the exchange rate while the latter stays within the margins. Once the exchange rate hits the margin and stays there the results under fixed exchange rates obtain once more. This means in practice that inflation rates can differ from each other in the short run but that they cannot do so systematically for very long spans of time. To put it another way, any country's rate of inflation may be either above or below the average rate of inflation of the fixed exchange rate world but the difference between the two rates cannot exceed the size of its exchange rate margins, and it cannot stay forever in either the upper or lower part of the band. Note also that to the extent that arbitrage takes time, the domestic currency price of traded goods is equated to their foreign currency price multiplied by the forward, or expected, rate of exchange for the relevant period.[23]

A once-and-for-all devaluation, or revaluation, causes, other things being equal, a once-and-for-all rise, or fall, in domestic relative to foreign money prices. Adjustment on other grounds (see below) may not be instantaneous so that a once-and-for-all change in the price level will appear as, or manifest

22. Note that goods that are nontraded at one point in time may be traded at others. This may occur if relative prices change enough and must be borne in mind both when examining data and in analysis of adjustment processes.

23. In fact, the situation is more complicated than the sentence in the text implies. At the least, an adjustment for storage cost of the commodities involved should be taken into account.

itself as, a higher-than-average rate of inflation for the devaluing country and a lower-than-average rate for the revaluing country. Continuously higher-than-average rates of inflation in one country over long periods of time, however, require that that country devalue at frequent intervals: its behavior would approximate that which it would follow under flexible exchange rates.

With entirely flexible exchange rates inflation can diverge by the rate of depreciation of the currency of the country that inflates more rapidly. The exchange rate adapts to domestic rates of inflation rather than the other way around, though the dynamics of the process may be much more complicated than this simple statement would seem to imply.

Impediments to trade and sluggish arbitrage

That impediments to trade may cause national money prices of the same good to differ when converted at current exchange rates is obvious. Such impediments take the form of transport costs, duties, quotas, and nontariff barriers; and cartel arrangements, formal and informal, private or governmental, that lead to discrimination among markets. However, such impediments do not cause divergence of inflation *rates* if they are ad valorem, that is, represent a constant percentage of the landed price of traded goods. If impediments to trade represent a constant nominal charge per unit, inflation rates can differ by a factor proportional to the given nominal size of the impediment as a proportion of the price of the good.[24] In fact, as inflation proceeds abroad, the existence of a given nominal "impediment charge" creates a change in relative prices that tends to disappear as the charge becomes negligible in relation to the price of the good. The general import of these remarks, though, is that it is necessary to raise the ad valorem "rate of impediments" by X percent per unit of time in order to obtain a divergence of X percent per unit of time in inflation rates among two countries.[25]

Sluggishness in goods arbitrage acts like a temporary impediment to trade that dwindles over time and thus has a decreasing effect on the convergence of inflation rates. Suppose that an individual country faces a sudden increase in world prices of traded goods. For various reasons (lumpiness of transactions costs, uncertainty, inertia, and the like) arbitrage opportunities may

24. If $P = eP' + T$ where T is the given nominal amount representing impediments to trade:
$$\hat{P} = [eP'/(eP' + T)][\hat{e} + \hat{P}'].$$
25. Let $P = (1 + t)eP'$ and e be fixed. Then:
$$\hat{P} = [t/(1 + t)]\hat{t} + \hat{P}'.$$

not be exploited instantaneously; that is, in the presence of adjustment costs associated with the supply of arbitrage activities, the domestic price of traded goods may adjust only slowly to their foreign price. In addition, adjustment may not proceed at the same rate for all goods. This delayed response can be captured formally in a small economy model, especially for empirical purposes, by a partial adjustment equation of the type:

$$(15) \qquad\qquad \dot{P} = \lambda(eP' - P),$$

where eP' is given parametrically.[26]

Sluggishness in arbitrage can be attributed to a variety of reasons. Among these, one may mention lumpiness of transport costs (which implies the need for investment in transport activities and may result in delayed response for the same reasons as those advocated for noninstantaneous adjustment of actual to desired capital stocks), costs of gathering information, and uncertainty. On the last of these, economic agents may wish to delay response to arbitrage opportunities until they are recognized as not being purely transitory.

Empirical evidence, however, suggests that arbitrage in individual homogeneous traded commodities is rapid enough for sluggishness of response (but not impediments to trade) to be ignored for many practical applications. (This point is discussed briefly at the end of this section.)

Nontraded goods

In one sense, slowness in arbitrage is equivalent to the temporary existence of nontraded goods. Nontraded goods prices are by definition *not* directly equated by arbitrage across national boundaries (though one should always allow for the possibility of nontraded goods becoming traded). If nontraded goods prices change at different rates among different countries, national inflation rates need, of course, not converge. There are, however, limits to the possible divergence of the rates of change in nontraded goods prices among countries as long as some goods are traded and their prices change at common rates. To measure the divergence between national inflation rates as a function of both the rates of change in the prices of traded and nontraded goods and of the weights of these two categories of goods in price indexes,

26. For use of such an adjustment function in the context of devaluation analysis, see M. B. Connolly and D. Taylor, "The Path of Adjustment Following Devaluation," in Claassen and Salin, eds., *Recent Issues in International Monetary Economics* (see note 7).

a mechanistic formula can easily be derived from the following three expressions:

(16) $$P = \gamma P_N + (1 - \gamma)P_T$$

(17) $$P' = \gamma'P_N' + (1 - \gamma')P_T'$$

(18) $$P_T = eP_T',$$

where γ and γ' are the weights of nontraded goods prices, P_N and P_N', in the two national price indexes, P and P'; and P_T and P_T' are the national currency prices of the traded good. Assuming the exchange rate to be fixed, the divergence between the two (absolute) rates of inflation is given by equation 19:

(19) $$\dot{P} - \dot{P}' = \gamma\dot{P}_N - \gamma'\dot{P}_N' + [e(1 - \gamma) - (1 - \gamma')]\dot{P}_T'.$$

Equation 19 indicates that the excess of domestic over foreign inflation will be the higher, the higher the rise in nontraded goods prices at home and their weight in the index; the lower the rise in nontraded goods prices abroad and their weight in the foreign index, the higher the share of traded goods in the domestic relative to the foreign index for a given rate of change in the prices of traded goods and nontraded goods. When the shares of nontraded goods fall to zero, equation 19 reduces to $\dot{P} = e\dot{P}'$, that is, inflation rates cannot diverge.

The extent to which the rates of change of nontraded and traded goods can diverge is, however, limited by a number of economic factors. In the first place, goods that were originally nontraded become traded when relative prices change enough. Second, substitutions will occur in both production and consumption; when the price of nontraded goods increases in terms of that of traded goods, the demand for nontraded goods decreases and their supply increases. Third, the monetary mechanism of adjustment will contribute to equating rates of change in the prices of all goods in the long run (discussed in the following section, which deals with the transmission mechanism in more detail). This is not to deny that there may be long-term trends producing a secular change in the relative price of nontraded goods. Thus, as Balassa has shown in a pioneering article, there will be a secular increase in the relative price of nontraded goods if the growth of productivity is higher in the traded goods sector or/and if the income elasticity of the demand for nontraded goods is greater than unity.[27] This secular increase need not occur

27. Bela Balassa, "The Purchasing-Power Parity Doctrine: A Reappraisal," *Journal of Political Economy*, vol. 52 (December 1964), pp. 584–96. The Balassa argument sets out the framework for deriving the conditions under which the so-called Swedish

at the same rate in different countries and, hence, measured inflation rates may differ even in the long run. In a fundamental sense, however, this phenomenon does not reflect differences in rates of inflation but changes in relative prices and assimilating the latter to the former constitutes an error of identification.

Errors of measurement and identification

One can distinguish two main types of errors of measurement when comparing the evolution of prices in several countries. The first concerns errors in recording individual prices and price changes, including problems of data comparability. The second, which might be called an error of identification, concerns differences introduced into the measurement of general price indexes and their rate of change by differences in weights or changes in relative prices.

Sources of errors of the first type abound. Goods classifications differ from country to country. So do the bases for valuation, which range from market prices to unit values, include or exclude indirect taxes, and differ in how they allow for quality changes, if at all. The timing of price-change recording also varies, with large discrepancies arising in some areas as, for instance, both the frequency and manner of recording actual and imputed rent. In addition, countries use different weighting schemes (for example, using expenditure rather than production data); these are revised frequently in some cases, not for periods of up to ten years in others. Quite obviously, these differences can be responsible for both systematic biases in recorded price levels and rates of inflation and for substantial short-run variations. In view of these discrepancies, it is not surprising that inflation rates diverge from country to country.

The second source of bias is the impact of relative price changes on national price indexes. Supposing that all prices change at the same rate because of generalized inflation, the particular weighting scheme used in the indexes does not matter since the rate of change of any single price will serve as a proxy for a proper index. But suppose that prices of individual goods change at different rates because of changes in relative prices, this will mean, if na-

---

or Aukrust-EFO model is correct in general equilibrium terms. For a description of the Aukrust-EFO model for Norway see Odd Aukrust, "PRIM I: A Model of the Price and Income Distribution of an Open Economy," *Review of Income and Wealth,* series 16 (March 1970), pp. 51–78. For Sweden see Gösta Edgren, Karl-Olof Faxén, and Clas-Erik Odhner, *Wage Formation and the Economy* (London: Allen and Unwin, 1973). Both, however, neglect short-term monetary conditions. These are discussed in Henryk I. Kierzkowski, "Theoretical Foundations of the Scandinavian Model of Inflation" (London School of Economics, International Monetary Research Programme, September 1974; processed).

tional weights differ, that national indexes will indicate different rates of inflation even if the proper scheme of weighting is used. Whether one chooses to call such differences diverging trends in relative prices (mainly of imports and exports and of traded and nontraded goods) or differences in inflation rates is perhaps a matter of semantics, but it should at least be clear that inflation rates do not differ in the sense that the prices of all individual traded goods rise at the same rate in every country. If, in addition, weighting schemes are inappropriate and not comparable, differences in inflation rates as measured by particular price indexes lose much of their meaning—they reflect errors of measurement in the data.

In fact, certain recent empirical findings indicate that, whatever the influence of the four factors mentioned above, inflation rates do seem to converge in the actual fixed exchange rate world. The empirical and analytical work that is most thorough and clearly relevant to the discussion above is probably that of Hans Genberg.[28]

One of the many tests he conducted concludes that there is almost perfect goods arbitrage for a number of individual homogeneous commodities. Another analyzes the variance of inflation rates (as measured by the rate of change of the CPI) in sixteen countries of the Organisation for Economic Co-operation and Development, and compares the results with those yielded by a similar analysis for fifteen large U.S. cities. Two conclusions emerge. First, the hypothesis that inflation rates have differed between countries over two of the sample's three subperiods can be rejected; during the third (mild inflation) significant differences can be accounted for by the higher-than-average Japanese inflation and by exchange rate changes. Second, the differences in rates of inflation among OECD countries are no greater than those between cities within the United States. A third experiment is a principal component analysis of price levels (CPIs) and changes therein in OECD countries. The first principal component accounts for well over 90 percent of the variance in levels, and loading factors compare favorably with those obtained in examining changes in components of the U.S. price level. Statistically, it makes at least as much sense to construct a world price level index under fixed exchange rates as it does to construct an overall price index (aggregated over products and individuals) for the United States.

28. Hans Genberg, "The Concept and Measurement of the World Price Level and Rate of Inflation," in Genberg, *World Inflation and the Small Economy* (Stockholm: Swedish Industrial Publications, 1975), and Hans Genberg, "A Note on Inflation Rates under Fixed Exchange Rates," in Michael Parkin and George Zis, eds., *Inflation in the World Economy* (Toronto: Toronto University Press, and Manchester: Manchester University Press, 1976).

The Transmission Mechanism

The fact that inflation rates tend to converge under fixed exchange rates (even if there were any) does not rob an examination of the transmission mechanism of its interest, nor does it mean that whatever freedom subsists for national differences in inflation rates is not worth having. This section examines elements in the transmission process and emphasizes its monetary aspects under fixed exchange rates.

The transmission mechanism is a subject in economic dynamics and dynamics are difficult to model sensibly. In what follows, I often try to capture the process of adjustment through comparative statics and intuitive dynamic reasoning. Furthermore, abundant use is made of the small country assumption and of the formal analogy between an X percent increase in the foreign price of traded goods and an X percent rise in the price of foreign exchange through devaluation.[29] This analogy makes much of the recent work on devaluation theory relevant to the issue of transmission of inflation under fixed exchange rates. As the transmission of inflation in a one-good and money world is discussed above, this section allows briefly, and in turn, for non-traded goods, variations in the international terms of trade, adjustment in interest rates and capital movements, and miscellaneous elements in the transmission mechanism.

Traded versus nontraded goods

Assume a small country facing given world prices of traded goods (the terms of trade are constant and imports and exports can be lumped together into a composite commodity for the purpose here). The country also produces and consumes a nontraded good. Assume again that there are no traded securities. Equilibrium in the nontraded goods market requires the price of the nontraded good to be such that, since there is no foreign demand for the nontraded good by definition, domestic demand be equal to domestic supply. Given the foreign price of traded goods, the exchange rate, and assuming goods arbitrage, this implies a given relative price of nontraded goods in terms

29. This formal analogy is noted in Alexander K. Swoboda, "Monetary Policy under Fixed Exchange Rates: Effectiveness, the Speed of Adjustment and Proper Use," and exploited, heuristically, in terms of rates of change in Alexander K. Swoboda, "Dual Exchange Rate Systems and Monetary Independence," in Robert Z. Aliber, ed., *National Monetary Policies and the International Financial System* (University of Chicago Press, 1974), pp. 258–72.

of traded goods. In addition, external balance requires that there be no excess domestic demand or supply of the traded good. This, in turn, means that income is equal to expenditure and, hence, the balance of trade is equal to zero. If, at the existing level of the money stock, the relative price of nontraded to traded goods, P_N/P_T, that clears the domestic goods market is different from that which would yield trade equilibrium, the money stock will change to restore both internal and external balance. This monetary version of the Australian or "Salter-Swan-Meade-Corden" model has been developed and used extensively in Dornbusch's work on devaluation. An early "Hicksian" version of the model in its monetary version was first presented by Mundell.[30]

The model is illustrated in figure 3, which is borrowed from a paper by Jonson and Kierzkowski that deals with devaluation analysis.[31] Full equilibrium is at A where the demand and supply for both traded, T, and nontraded, N, goods are equal and the relative price, P_N/P_T, is given by the tangent to the production possibility curve (and to one of a family of homothetic indifference curves) at A. Income is equal to expenditure.

Suppose now that the price of traded goods rises abroad and that the home country is small. With instantaneous goods arbitrage the domestic price of traded goods rises by the same percentage. This creates a tendency for the relative price of nontraded goods to fall, for real balances to fall at the existing nominal stock of money, and hence for expenditure to fall relative to income. The impact effect of the rise in foreign prices (or of a devaluation resulting in the same rise in P_T) can be represented in the diagram. The impact effect is obtained, at the initial nominal stock of money, by requiring the price of nontraded goods to be such as to equate domestic demand and supply of these goods. This will occur, geometrically, at that point on the production frontier above A (since P_T/P_N rises), which has the same slope as an indifference curve that is lower than the initial one (since expenditure is lower through the real-balance effect), that is, at B and B_* in figure 3. Production takes place at B with OD of nontraded goods and OF of traded goods produced. Consumption takes place at B_* with demand for nontraded goods, OD, equal to the supply and domestic consumption of traded goods equal to OE.

30. See Rudiger Dornbusch, "Devaluation, Money, and Nontraded Goods," *American Economic Review*, vol. 43 (December 1973), pp. 871–80, and Rudiger Dornbusch, "Real and Monetary Aspects of the Effect of Exchange Rate Changes," in Robert Z. Aliber, ed., *National Monetary Policies and the International Financial System*, pp. 64–81, for development of the model and for references to the literature; and Robert A. Mundell, "Devaluation," in Mundell, *Monetary Theory: Inflation, Interest, and Growth in the World Economy*, pp. 86–97 (see note 8 for full citation).

31. P. D. Jonson and H. I. Kierzkowski, "The Balance of Payments: An Analytic Exercise," *The Manchester School*, vol. 43 (June 1975), pp. 105–33.

Figure 3. *Income and Absorption with Traded and Nontraded Goods*

Traded goods (T)

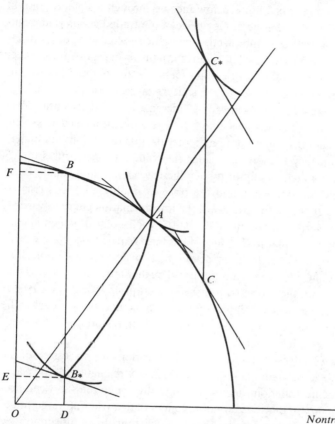

Source: See text for explanation.

The difference between production and consumption of traded goods is EF and is equal to the excess of income over expenditure and, hence, the balance of trade at the point of impact.[32]

32. Geometric derivation of this impact effect is provided in Rudiger Dornbusch, "Real and Monetary Aspects of the Effects of Exchange Rate Changes." Jonson and Kierzkowski, "The Balance of Payments," add a derivation of the path of adjustment through time (B_*AC_*). Mussa in his excellent paper on the effects of tariffs provides a similar description of a path of adjustment to a tariff change. (See Michael Mussa, "Tariffs and the Balance of Payments: A Monetary Approach," in Jacob A. Frenkel and Harry G. Johnson, eds., *The Monetary Approach to the Balance of Payments* [University of Toronto Press, 1976].)

The *short-run* (impact) effect of a rise in the foreign price of traded goods, then, is to increase their relative price at home and to shift production toward these goods, to decrease their domestic consumption and to generate a trade surplus by depressing expenditure below income through a squeeze on real cash balances. The effect on the money price of nontraded goods is ambiguous, as Russell Boyer has emphasized,[33] though one would expect it to increase on intuitive grounds; this will occur, formally, if the substitution effect of the reduction in their relative price on excess demand dominates the general fall in demand brought about by the squeeze on real cash balances.

The *long-run* effect of a once-and-for-all increase in the foreign price level is the restoration of the status quo ante for all real magnitudes. The system cannot stay at B and B_* (unless systematic sterilization operations are undertaken by the monetary authorities), since the trade balance surplus of EF implies that the nominal supply of money increases. As real balances build up again, expenditure increases and the price of nontraded goods rises to clear the market. B begins to slide down the transformation curve toward A, and B_* moves toward A along the path B_*AC_* each point of which is constructed in a manner similar to B_*. Once A has been reached the relative price P_N/P_T returns to its initial level as do production and consumption. The money price of nontraded goods has increased by the same percentage as that of traded goods and, therefore, so has the general price index; the stock of international reserves has increased by the amount necessary to raise the money stock by the same percentage as the price level, restoring real balances to their initial equilibrium level.

The preceding analysis has a number of implications for discussion of the scope for divergence of national inflation rates and of the nature of the transmission mechanism. Inflation rates will tend to diverge in the short run provided that monetary authorities do not accommodate a rise in foreign prices by an immediate expansion of the money stock that drives up nontraded goods prices in concert. The extent of the divergence depends, in this simplified analysis, on the elasticity of substitution of traded for nontraded goods in both production and consumption and on the strength of the real-balance effect. The higher the elasticity of substitution, the smaller the fall in the relative price of nontraded goods required to clear the nontraded goods market, and hence the smaller the scope for the general price index, given expenditure shares, to rise initially by less than the increase in P_T. The lower the share of

33. Russell M. Boyer, "Commodity Markets and Bond Markets in a Small, Fixed-Exchange-Rate Economy," *Canadian Journal of Economics,* vol. 8 (February 1975), pp. 1–23.

expenditure on nontraded goods, the less will be the effect of the change in relative prices on the general price index. And the smaller the real-balance effect (or, in dynamic terms, the α used in preceding sections) the less the impact effect of the fall in real balances will be on the price of nontraded goods. Note, however, in this last case, that the lower the α the lower the speed of return to equilibrium.

The analysis also states that there is no scope for divergence of inflation rates in the long run when monetary equilibrium has been reestablished. In the long run, then, the simple model developed above in the second section is applicable. Importation of money through the balance of trade restores the homogeneity properties of the model over time. The mechanism of transmission sketched above is, indeed, although not exclusively, monetary. In the first place, the size of the impact effect is determined in part by monetary considerations, that is, the domestic price level falls relative to that abroad because of the real-balance effect. Second, the speed at which the rise in traded goods prices is transmitted to nontraded goods prices depends on the rate at which the public rebuilds its real balances, importing the money needed to finance the increased money value of expenditure in the process. Third, recessionary tendencies may develop in the economy if the fall in expenditure caused by the initial rise in prices is strong enough to depress the money price of nontraded goods and wage rigidities exist or resources are immobile between sectors in the short run. Finally, the adjustment process depends crucially on the behavior of monetary authorities: had they increased the money stock by the same percentage foreign prices rose, no changes in P_N/P_T and no payments disequilibrium would have arisen.

As a matter of fact, the preceding analysis suggests that a trade surplus combined with a fall in the *relative* price of nontraded goods constitutes, other things being equal, one symptom of imported inflation. Conversely, a payments deficit combined with a rise in the relative price of nontraded goods reflects domestic inflation at a higher level than the foreign rate. This case can again be illustrated with the help of figure 3. Suppose the monetary authorities engineer a once-and-for-all increase in the money supply above the level compatible with equilibrium at A. The increase in expenditure that results requires that P_N rise for the nontraded goods market to clear. The impact effect of the increase in the money stock is to move production to C, consumption to C_*, and to generate a payments deficit measured by the vertical distance between C and C_*. As the deficit reduces the nominal supply of money, the system moves back to A along the path C_*A. At A, the initial price level is reestablished (in contrast to the previously analyzed case of a rise in foreign prices, or world inflation, where all prices rose in the same proportion), the only change being a cumulative loss of reserves equal to the initial increase in the money stock.

In a world of large countries, the mechanism of transmission is more difficult to formalize but may be described intuitively here. Suppose two countries to be initially in equilibrium and that the foreign country then increases its money stock. This creates an excess demand for both traded and nontraded goods. As the price of traded goods rises, however, part of the foreign country's excess demand for traded goods is matched by an excess supply in the home country brought about by the decrease in real cash balances at the initial domestic money stock. Assuming that the expenditure elasticity of demand for both types of goods is equal to unity, the relative price of nontraded goods must rise abroad and fall at home in order to clear the traded goods market, equating the foreign country's deficit with the home country's surplus. As it were, the foreign country moves to points like C and C_* and the home country to points like B and B_* in figure 3 whereas the world price level rises, both moving back toward A as the process comes to an end at a higher absolute price level but at the same relative prices.[34]

Exports versus imports

The most popular model of international trade theory assumes a different disaggregation of goods than that into traded and nontraded goods, namely, that into exportables and importables. The latter model is sometimes simplified further by assuming that countries specialize in the production of their exportables, which they both export and consume, and that they consume but do not produce imports. The dynamics of transmission in such a model differ slightly from those of the traded versus nontraded goods model, though the same general principles apply.

Consider, first, a "truly small" country in that framework. Such a country faces given world prices for both its exports and its imports. The terms of trade are given to the country and cannot change except through a change in *relative* prices abroad. This case thus reduces to the "one-traded-goods-only" case described in the second section since imports and exports can be lumped into one composite commodity. In order to give the exports versus imports model some differentiated life of its own in the present context, the terms of trade must be allowed to change through some mechanism. One possible way to achieve this is to assume that the country has some monopoly power in the

34. The same warning as that raised on page 26, note 21, is issued here.

market for the export good in which it specializes but is a price taker in the market for its imports.

A model of imported inflation for a pseudo-small country of that type has been constructed by Yoichi Shinkai.[35] Inflation is generated by an increase in the foreign price of importables. The domestic price of the import good rises, expenditure is depressed by the real-balance effect, export supply under certain assumptions rises, resulting in a fall of the foreign price of the export good (which is in less than perfectly elastic demand abroad), that is, the terms of trade deteriorate. If the increase in the foreign price of imports proceeds at a constant rate and the monetary authorities do not increase the money supply through domestic credit creation, the country experiences a permanent deterioration in its terms of trade in addition to paying an inflation tax by acquiring the cash balances needed to finance the imported inflation through a payments surplus.

This model does not explain why export demand, and hence export prices, should not grow at the same rate as import prices, if the source of the increase in the latter is generalized inflation abroad. The model would thus seem most useful in analyzing certain types of short-run changes to which the analysis developed by Dornbusch for the case of devaluation might also fruitfully be applied.[36] The traded versus nontraded goods model of the preceding section would, however, seem a more appropriate one for analyzing the transmission of inflation that finds its origin in a general rise in expenditure and/or the money stock.

Interest rate adjustments and capital movements

Assets other than money have been largely neglected in the discussion so far. Yet they are likely to play a very important role in the analysis of adjustment within the economy, the transmission process, and policy. Even when capital is immobile internationally, interest rate variations will play a significant part in the internal adjustment of an economy to foreign inflation.

A downward adjustment of expenditure in response to a rise in foreign prices can be brought about not only through a direct effect of real balances on expenditure but also as a result of a rise in interest rates due to the requirements of short-run portfolio adjustment. This mechanism has been empha-

35. Yoichi Shinkai, "A Model of Imported Inflation," *Journal of Political Economy*, vol. 81 (July/August 1973), pp. 962–71.
36. Rudiger Dornbusch, "Currency Depreciation, Hoarding, and Relative Prices," ibid., pp. 893–915.

sized by Michael Mussa in the case of capital immobility;[37] it can be shown to lead to a path of adjustment quite similar to that illustrated in figure 3, though the speed of adjustment will be governed by different behavior parameters. This is also the type of mechanism implicit in Mundell's early work and in the analysis of so-called quasi-equilibrium points.[38]

Taking capital movements into account entails no basic change in the long-run effects of monetary expansion; it does, however, impinge on the transmission process. As discussed below, capital mobility will tend to spread the inflationary process more evenly across countries and among goods and thus to moderate the differential impact of an increase in monetary expansion in one country on the relative price of traded to nontraded goods in that country and the rest of the world. Capital accounts bear part of the burden of adjustment needed to reestablish the equilibrium distribution of the world money stock in the short run, mitigating the need for trade balances, and hence relative prices, to adjust as rapidly in the short run.

To illustrate, suppose portfolios are adjusted very rapidly relative to flows of spending. Consider the effect of a rise in the money supply in the foreign country assuming that there is only one bond in the world economy and that it can be freely traded among the residents of the two countries, that is, there is perfect capital mobility. The expansionary foreign monetary policy creates an excess supply of foreign money at the previous interest rate and an excess demand for bonds by foreigners. Bond prices are bid up as foreigners buy these assets from domestic residents, creating a domestic excess demand for money, which is satisfied by the home payments surplus generated by the exchange stabilization operations of the domestic monetary authorities.

The process can be illustrated with the help of figure 4 which is constructed in a manner analogous to figure 1.[39] As before, OO' measures the initial world money stock. LL and $L'L'$ are standard liquidity preference schedules drawn from their respective origins. Each schedule is drawn for a given level of real income or wealth, assumed not to change over the time span relevant to the analysis. Equilibrium obtains at a rate of interest, i, and distribution of the world money stock $B = OA/OO'$. A higher rate of interest would create a

37. Michael Mussa, "Tariffs and the Balance of Payments: A Monetary Approach" (see note 32).

38. Alexander K. Swoboda, "Equilibrium, Quasi-equilibrium, and Macroeconomic Policy under Fixed Exchange Rates," *Quarterly Journal of Economics,* vol. 86 (February 1972), pp. 162–71.

39. Dornbusch provides a somewhat similar figure and algebraic analysis of the case discussed in the text. In addition, and more important, he extends the analysis to nontraded assets and the forward market. (See Rudiger Dornbusch, "Capital Mobility and Portfolio Balance," in Robert Z. Aliber, ed., *The Political Economy of Reform* (Macmillan, 1976), pp. 64–81.

Figure 4. *The Transmission of Inflation with Mobility of Capital*

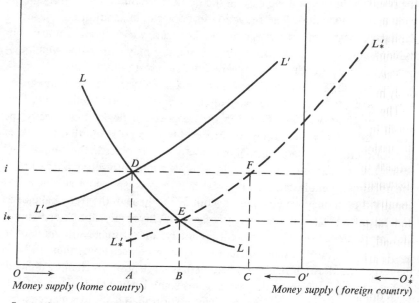

Source: See text for explanation.

world excess supply of money (excess demand for bonds); a different distribution of the world money stock would create an excess supply of one currency and excess demand for the other. Consider, now, the effect of an increase in the foreign money stock $O'O'_* = AC$. This both expands the world money-supply box and shifts the $L'L'$ curve to the right by AC. There is now an excess world supply of money (excess demand for bonds) at the old interest rate and an excess supply of the foreign currency at the new distribution of the world money stock OA/OO'_*. Equilibrium is reestablished when the interest rate has fallen to i_* and the distribution of the money stock has become OB/OO'_*.[40] The home country gains AB of reserves lost by the foreign country.

40. If the interest elasticity of the demand for money is the same in the two countries, the equilibrium distribution of money supplies is invariant with respect to the size of the world money stock. This result is similar to the proposition developed in Swoboda and Dornbusch that the equilibrium interest rate differential, under the same conditions, is invariant to the origin of a money supply change for any given degree of capital mobility in a Keynesian two-country model of *income* determination incorporating monetary equilibrium. (Alexander K. Swoboda and Rudiger Dornbusch, "Adjustment Policy and Monetary Equilibrium in a Two-Country Model," in Connolly and Swoboda, eds., *International Trade and Money*, pp. 225–61 [see note 8].)

If portfolio adjustment is very rapid relative to goods market adjustment the result of foreign monetary expansion is a rapid fall in interest rates worldwide and an immediate increase in the domestic money supply through the capital-account inflow. The reduction in domestic expenditure discussed in the context of the traded versus nontraded goods model without capital mobility need not occur; on the contrary, expenditure may start rising simultaneously in all countries due to the general fall in interest rates.

The spreading of inflation through capital flows is the transmission mechanism most often stressed in early discussions of imported inflation.[41] That discussion, however, is deficient in two respects: it neglects to specify the process that generates the capital flows and fails to point out that the rest of the world must be inflating also if inflation is to take place in the "importing" country. For, suppose that capital flows into a country lowering interest rates and raising expenditure and prices without a corresponding rise in prices abroad, then money would soon flow out again through the trade balance as goods arbitrage takes place. The discussion did, however, capture one important consequence of capital mobility, namely, that it makes the attempt to keep domestic interest rates higher than, and price rises lower than, those in the rest of the world through sterilization of reserve flows much more difficult.

The existence of nontraded assets gives some leeway to domestic interest rate policy even in the small-country case. Nontraded assets were extensively discussed by Scitovsky in 1969 and are explicitly introduced into a number of recent models, notably those of Boyer, Branson, Dornbusch, and Girton and Henderson.[42] These are all short-run models concentrating chiefly on portfolio adjustment. Their main message in the present context can be grasped intuitively. Suppose the home country conducts an expansionary open market operation by buying nontraded rather than traded bonds. In a manner analogous to the case of nontraded goods, the domestic interest rate

---

41. See, for instance, Ira O. Scott, Jr., and Wilson E. Schmidt, "Imported Inflation and Monetary Policy," *Banca Nazionale del Lavoro Quarterly Review*, no. 71 (December 1964), pp. 390–403, and the ensuing discussion with Peter M. Oppenheimer, "Imported Inflation and Monetary Policy: A Comment," ibid., no. 73 (June 1965), pp. 191–97.

42. Tibor Scitovsky, *Money and the Balance of Payments* (London: Allen and Unwin, 1969); Russell S. Boyer, "Commodity Markets and Bond Markets in a Small Fixed-Exchange-Rate Economy"; William H. Branson, "Macroeconomic Equilibrium with Portfolio Balance in Open Economies," Seminar Paper 22 (Stockholm: Institute for International Economic Studies, November 1972; processed); Rudiger Dornbusch, "Capital Mobility and Portfolio Balance"; and Lance Girton and Dale W. Henderson, "Financial Capital Movements and Central Bank Behavior in a Two-Country, Short-Run Portfolio Balance Model," *Journal of Monetary Economics*, vol. 2 (January 1976), pp. 33–61.

must adjust to clear the domestic bonds market to which foreigners have no access. Although this will induce some domestic residents to shift their holdings from domestic to foreign bonds, it creates a rise in domestic relative to foreign bond prices, stimulating expenditure at home without stimulating expenditure abroad to the same extent and thus increasing the scope for differential inflation rates through differential short-run impacts on the price of nontraded versus traded goods.

Other elements in the transmission mechanism

The preceding discussion makes it clear that a monetary approach to the transmission of inflation under fixed exchange rates is compatible with a wide variety of specifications of the exact adjustment mechanisms involved.

As a matter of fact, the strands of analysis presented so far incorporate elements of all three of the main schools of payments adjustment theory. The analysis stresses the role of changes in absorption (expenditure) in determining money income changes at the world level, and the balance of payments of individual countries. It is monetary in the sense that changes in the quantity of money play a crucial role in explaining changes in expenditure either directly or through an interest rate effect in models incorporating portfolio balance requirements. It incorporates elasticity effects since the effect of changes in expenditure on relative prices depend on elasticities. Finally, it is general equilibrium in the sense that both short- and long-run conclusions depend on the interaction of money, expenditure, and relative-price changes.

Clearly, many other elements in the transmission mechanism could and should be distinguished. For instance, expectations will affect the path and speed of adjustment. As in other branches of economics, however, no generally accepted theory of expectation formation and of behavior in response to expectations is available in the present context. For the world economy as a whole, the same types of models as those developed for closed economies are relevant. Furthermore, if home residents build their price expectations partly on the basis of the actual behavior of foreign prices, as has recently been suggested by Cross and Laidler, the transmission mechanism is likely to be speeded up.[43] This might provide one additional reason why it may be appropriate to look at the trade-off between unemployment and inflation for the fixed exchange rate world as a whole rather than in single economies—

---

43. Rodney Cross and David Laidler, "Inflation, Excess Demand and Expectations in Fixed Exchange Rate Economies: Some Preliminary Empirical Results," in Parkin and Zis, eds., *Inflation in the World Economy* (see note 28 for full citation).

as is done, with a good deal of empirical success, by Duck, Parkin, Rose, and Zis.[44]

The division of money income changes into output and price changes, especially during the adjustment process, has not yet been analyzed in a theoretically satisfactory way. Recourse can be had to rigid money wages and Keynesian aggregate supply curves but this is not an entirely convincing device in inflationary or stagflationary times. The assumption that one factor (usually capital) is specific to each sector (for example, traded and nontraded goods) combined with some rigidity in factor returns provides a more elegant alternative for some purposes.[45] In all static models, with the possible exception noted above of perverse effects on the money price of nontraded goods, foreign inflation should tend to lead to an expansion of both output and prices in the short run, though resource reallocation between traded and nontraded goods sectors may create some frictional unemployment problems during the adjustment process. There is some hope that contemporary developments in the theory of the microeconomic foundations of unemployment and inflation and in analysis of expectation formation can be applied to the distribution of unemployment and inflation in the world economy.

The Generation of World Inflation

Discussion of imported inflation often treats the world rate of inflation as given or exogenous and studies the process by which a single small open economy imports it. This begs the question of what determines the world rate of inflation or, to put it in other words, of which countries export inflation. This paper has repeatedly stressed the role of expansion in the world money stock in generating world inflation. The concept of a world money stock as the sum of national money stocks is justified under fixed exchange rates by the fact that fixity of the price of one currency in terms of another allows one to lump all national moneys together into one Hicksian composite commodity.

This suggests that analyzing the determinants of the world money stock is crucial to an explanation of worldwide inflation. Two recent studies bear directly on this question. The first, a paper by Parkin, Richards, and Zis is largely empirical and attempts with some success to relate the growth of the

44. Nigel Duck, Michael Parkin, David Rose, and George Zis, "The Determination of the Rate of Change of Wages and Prices in the Fixed Exchange Rate World Economy, 1956–71," in ibid.

45. See, for example, Rudiger Dornbusch, "Real and Monetary Aspects of the Effects of Exchange Rate Changes" (see note 30).

world money stock to the growth in the sum of high-powered (reserve) money in the world economy (actually, the Group of Ten countries); they conclude that the money multiplier is stable though it shows an upward trend through time that is not easily explained except by very slow adjustment of banks to their desired excess reserve position.[46] The second is my own 1973 theoretical paper.[47]

My analysis identifies three exogenous variables that interact with behavioral parameters of the public, commercial banks, and central banks to determine the world stock of money in a two-country model, the United States and the rest of the fixed exchange rate world (Europe, for short). The exogenous variables are the domestic assets of the U.S. central bank, A^1, and of the European central bank, A^2, and the world stock of gold, G. The European central bank chooses the proportions of its total reserves it holds in gold, Eurodollars, dollar deposits with the Federal Reserve System, and dollar deposits with U.S. commercial banks (or treasury bills). European commercial banks receive domestic currency deposits from residents and dollar deposits from the U.S. public, the European public, and the European central bank. They keep reserves against domestic currency liabilities with their central bank and reserves against Eurodollar liabilities with U.S. commercial banks. The U.S. public divides its total money holdings between U.S. and Eurodollar deposits, the European public between domestic-currency and Eurodollar deposits.

This is not the place to give in detail the conclusions that can be reached with models of this kind, but some of the more important results can be summarized. The main one is that the size of the world money stock multiplier applicable to an increase in A^1, A^2, or G will differ in general both for (1) different patterns of asset holdings, and (2) different origins of the increase in base money, that is, depending on whether it is A^1, A^2, or G that is increased. The pristine simplicity of the world money stock model of the second section above is lost as soon as inside assets are held as reserves. In particular, the practice of European central banks of keeping their foreign exchange re-

46. Michael Parkin, Ian Richards, and George Zis, "The Determination and Control of the World Money Supply under Fixed Exchange Rates 1961–71," *The Manchester School,* vol. 43 (September 1975), pp. 293–316.

47. Alexander K. Swoboda, "Gold, Dollars, Eurodollars, and the World Money Stock" (November 1974; processed), a discussion paper for the research project, "National Economic Policy and the International Monetary System" (see page 10, note). For an early nonmathematical presentation of some of the ideas contained in the paper, see Alexander K. Swoboda, "Eurodollars and the World Money Supply: Implications and Control," in Swoboda, ed., *Europe and the Evolution of the International Monetary System* (Geneva: Graduate Institute of International Studies, 1973), pp. 149–68.

serves in dollar deposits with U.S. commercial banks or in treasury bills increases significantly the impact of U.S. monetary policy on the world money stock. According to one back-of-the-envelope calculation based on not entirely unrealistic numbers, the effect of a $1 increase in A^2 produces only a $1.7 increase in M^w. The basic symmetry of the fixed outside reserve standards illustrated in the second section disappears.

These asymmetries in response to the origin of monetary expansion may be one of the implicit reasons for a tendency in the literature to blame worldwide inflation on the United States.[48] This reviling is often not legitimate but it does raise the question of which countries are responsible for worldwide inflation and that question should be answered in a system-wide framework. The analysis thus far indicates that continuous generation of worldwide inflation through monetary creation can be maintained only as long as the country or countries that create domestic assets do not run out of reserves. This means essentially that worldwide inflation will be generated (a) if monetary expansion of domestic origin occurs simultaneously in most countries, (b) if it occurs in a very large country whose monetary expansion has a substantial effect on the world price level and whose reserves are large enough to sustain the resulting payments deficit, and (c) if the expanding country does not have to face a reserve constraint. The United States clearly fulfills the first part of condition (b) and condition (c), the latter under the dollar standard. In addition, the dollar standard also implies that (as noted in the above paragraph) the impact of monetary expansion in the United States on the world money stock and, hence, world prices is greatly amplified.

The symptoms attached to the exportation of inflation are a deficit in payments, accompanied by a large capital outflow and/or a rise in the price of nontraded relative to traded goods (and a trade deficit). The United States again fills the bill on some of those accounts for part of the period extending from 1966 to 1971. The story, however, is obviously far more complicated than that, with "Europe" probably bearing some part of the responsibility for inflation in the late 1960s. To give a more precise explanation of the dynamics of the generation of world inflation requires empirical estimation that takes adequate account of the interactions, time lags, and policy responses involved.

One further issue in the dynamics of inflation will be left unresolved here. Though a majority of economists would recognize that there is a close association between inflation and monetary growth, many would argue that the

48. See, for instance, Harry G. Johnson, *Inflation and the Monetarist Controversy* (Amsterdam: North-Holland, 1972; distributed in Canada and the United States by American Elsevier).

question is begged until one explains *why* there is monetary expansion in the first place. They often ask monetarists to consider the following argument: suppose there is a recurring cost-push continuously financed by monetary growth in order to prevent incipient unemployment, then inflation is, in an important sense, not a monetary phenomenon. A monetarist would probably not object to stating that *if* there was continuous cost-push and *if* it was continuously financed, *then* there would be inflation. He would, however, deem it unlikely that recurring cost-pushes would occur continuously if they were not systematically financed. Cost-pushes would not occur continuously if their perpetrators (and, unfortunately, society at large) had to bear the consequences. That is, while fully recognizing that real disturbances such as droughts, cost-pushes, or oil crises may occur autonomously on occasion, continuous cost-pushes, if they exist, are, in the sense mentioned above, quite likely to have a monetary origin. One is, of course, free to question this use of the word "origin."[49]

Some Policy Implications

Most of the policy implications of the analysis above are obvious and well known. The briefest summary suffices here.

At a national level, the implications of the small country model are obvious. Domestic inflation rates will tend to converge toward international rates under a fixed-rate system. Monetary policy can exert some moderating influence on the price of nontraded goods. This can be done by sterilizing reserve inflows in order to keep real money balances below and the domestic interest rate above their (payments) equilibrium level. How effective this policy is in preventing the price index from rising at the same rate as the foreign rate of inflation through a fall in the relative price of nontraded goods depends directly on the share of nontraded goods in expenditure and inversely on the elasticity of substitution of traded and nontraded goods in excess de-

49. I would imagine that at least part of current debates between monetarists and Keynesians about the origins of inflation would appear as slightly absurd and largely semantic to the well-worn man from Mars. It seems to me that, once it is recognized that money has an important role to play in inflationary phenomena, the task at hand is to bring existing analytical categories and knowledge to bear on theoretical and empirical research into (a) the interaction between monetary and real phenomena in a market setting, and (b) the motivation behind the actual use of macroeconomic instruments (such as monetary policy). Work along this last line, incorporating policy reaction functions into macroeconomic models, is currently proceeding in the two research projects mentioned in the note on page 10.

mand. The feasibility of carrying out such a divergent price policy hinges on the required flow of neutralization operations, which depends in turn on the degree of capital mobility; the lower that degree, the easier it is to keep the domestic above the foreign rate of interest.

This suggests that monetary policy as an instrument geared to a national price-level target has, at best, a short-run, though not necessarily negligible, role under fixed exchange rates. In the longer run inflation rates will differ only if productivity and taste conditions create a diverging trend in the relative price of traded and nontraded goods. Note, in addition, that goods arbitrage also robs fiscal policy of the traditional expenditure-changing variety of much of its impact on the level of prices and output in the country pursuing that policy unless it can be carried out in nontraded goods and the latter represent a large, not easily substitutable, fraction of output and expenditure. The clear implication is that a country which, other things being equal, feels it cannot live with the foreign rate of inflation in traded goods prices should adopt flexible exchange rates. (Recent experience, though, suggests, to me at least, that most countries would have been satisfied if the world rate of inflation of the 1960s had continued in the 1970s.)

At an international level, control of worldwide inflation under fixed rates requires control of fiscal policies and of the rate of world monetary expansion. To the extent that the coefficients entering the world money supply formula alluded to in the preceding section are stable, this requires simply control of domestic credit creation by monetary authorities and of growth in outside international reserves. It also requires that special attention be paid to the policies of reserve-issuing countries. It requires, finally, that the rate of world monetary expansion be such as to create a rate of inflation that is widely acceptable. These prescriptions are simple in theory; they may even be relatively easy to put in practice in quiet times; after all, they were broadly followed for much of postwar history. They require a basic change in attitudes toward policy at present when inflation has taken hold. Without such a change inflation will not be brought under control, flex the exchange rate as one wishes.

World Inflation under Flexible Exchange Rates

One of the strongest arguments for flexible exchange rates is that they allow countries to choose their own rate of inflation by insulating them, or by allowing them to insulate themselves through monetary policy, from foreign inflation. Yet, since greater flexibility of exchange rates has been introduced, there has been, in general, an increase in inflation rates throughout the world, although the variance of inflation rates around the mean also seems to have increased.[50] This has been puzzling to many analysts who, as a consequence, have been searching for a transmission mechanism under flexible rates.

International monetary theory provides only three main instances that cause transmission of cycles under flexible rates. Laursen and Metzler have argued that fiscal expansion in one country may cause contraction abroad, using a Keynesian model in which infinite elasticity of output with respect to the price level expressed in domestic currency keeps that price level fixed.[51] This assumption implies that devaluation worsens the domestic terms of trade and vice versa for revaluation. Domestic fiscal expansion is assumed to lead to depreciation of the home currency and, hence, by definition to appreciation of foreign countries' currencies and to improvement in their terms of trade. With a Keynesian saving function (the average propensity to save out of real income rises with a rise in real income), the resulting increase in real income abroad results, at the original level of foreign nominal income, in an increase in saving and a "multiple" fall in foreign real income.

Mundell, in contrast, stresses the role of the capital account in demonstrating that monetary expansion at home may cause contraction abroad under perfect capital mobility.[52] Expansion in the money stock results, in the short run, in an outflow of capital from the home country, a capital inflow, and deterioration of the balance of trade with contractionary effects on income abroad. (In contrast, fiscal expansion at home, as it causes a capital inflow under perfect capital mobility, tends to raise income abroad.)

Finally, Dornbusch argues in a recent paper that an increase in the steady-state rate of inflation abroad may result in a lower equilibrium rate of inflation at home.[53] He assumes that there is perfect capital mobility and, for the purposes at hand, that variations in real government expenditure have to be

50. There is some dispute whether this dispersion should be measured by the standard deviation or by the coefficient of variation (the standard deviation divided by the mean). My casual calculation indicates an increase in the standard deviation; as inflation rates have risen the coefficient of variation has tended to fall. However, it increases again in the most recent period. In any event, the issue here is the scope for divergence of national inflation rates from each other and the standard deviation is the appropriate measure to use.

51. Svend Laursen and Lloyd Metzler, "Flexible Exchange Rates and the Theory of Employment," *Review of Economics and Statistics,* vol. 32 (November 1950), pp. 281–99.

52. Robert A. Mundell, "Capital Mobility and Stabilization Policy under Fixed and Flexible Exchange Rates," in Mundell, *International Economics,* pp. 250–71 (see note 6).

53. Rudiger Dornbusch, "Flexible Exchange Rates, Capital Mobility, and Macroeconomic Equilibrium," Discussion Paper 74-6 (University of Rochester, Department of Economics, April 1974; processed).

financed out of variations in the inflation tax on real balances. An increase in the foreign rate of inflation creates an excess demand for securities and a fall in the real rate of interest; the demand for real balances rises at home and, with it, the home government's tax base; as government expenditure at home is given in real terms, a lower rate of monetary expansion and inflation is now required to keep the budget balanced.

These analytical descriptions of possible links between domestic and foreign economic activity under flexible exchange rates do not solve the puzzle of continuation and acceleration of worldwide inflation in recent times as they emphasize reverse rather than direct transmission. Furthermore, as is often emphasized, domestic monetary policies could, in principle at least, nullify these transmission effects.[54]

Two ad hoc explanations of transmission have been offered recently to explain the worldwide increase in inflation under flexible rates. The first is that the breakdown of convertibility has brought about a breakdown in monetary discipline, an argument to which I would subscribe, although others would emphasize the reverse causal chain. (The two views are not incompatible and I would also subscribe to the latter.) The second centers on an international ratchet effect. One not entirely unlikely version of that argument, partly endorsed by Kindleberger and attributed in the press in an unintelligible version to Laffer and Mundell, is as follows. Suppose exchange rates are free to float and that prices are rigid downward but not upward. Suppose that something occurs that causes occasional changes in capital movements and, hence, occasional changes in exchange rates. The incipient and/or actual changes in capital movements are crucial since, otherwise, there would be no reason for the exchange rate to change. The capital inflow exerts some downward pressure on prices and output in the appreciating country and the monetary authorities attempt to "inflate" the economy to ease the country's unemployment . . . and so on in an unending ratchet.

More simply, the recent increase in inflation rates can be attributed in part to three factors. The first, which concerns transmission, is that exchange rates are not truly flexible either because of outright foreign exchange market intervention or because authorities select an exchange rate target that they achieve through monetary policy. Second, the economic history of the 1960s left most

54. Boyer has recently emphasized another transmission channel through the effect on wealth of a change in the domestic currency value of holdings of foreign bonds brought about by an exchange rate change. The effect may go either way depending on whether the country is a net creditor or a net debtor. (See Russell S. Boyer, "Fixed Rates, Flexible Rates, and the International Transmission of Inflation," in Michael J. Artis and A. R. Nobay, eds., *Essays in Economic Analysis* (Cambridge: Cambridge University Press, 1976).

countries with a common heritage of woes at the beginning of the 1970s—
and policy reactions have been quite similar, with a proliferation, at least for
a while, of attempts to "inflate away" decreases in real income even in times
of crisis. Third, most economies have been recently subjected to common
shocks, in particular that of the rise in oil prices. The associated decrease in
output and real income in the face of expanding monetary aggregates was
bound to lead to renewed inflation.

Conclusions

Only two final remarks are offered.

First, worldwide inflation must be analyzed at a "system" level as well as
at a national level. The various strands in the monetary approach surveyed
in this paper seem to provide an appropriate framework for doing so; in particular, they do carry basic lessons for the long-run equilibrium of the world
monetary system and for policy.

Second, the great variety of adjustment mechanisms compatible with the
approach suggests the need for more research, both theoretical and empirical.

Comments by James S. Duesenberry

SWOBODA'S paper is very interesting, technically competent, and I agree
with some of its conclusions, but I do have a few problems with it. I agree
that "worldwide inflation must be analyzed at a 'system' level, as well as at
a national level"; that the "various strands in the monetary approach in this
paper seem to provide an appropriate framework for doing so"; and that "the
great variety of adjustment mechanisms compatible with the approach suggest the need for more research, both theoretical and empirical."

After that, we part company. Take, first, Swoboda's comment about one
still unresolved issue. He says that many economists would agree that there
is a close association between inflation and monetary growth but would argue
that the question is begged if one does not explain why there is monetary expansion in the first place. Other economists often ask monetarists to consider
the following scenario: suppose there is continuous cost-push financed by
monetary expansion in order to prevent incipient unemployment. Then inflation is in an important sense not a monetary phenomenon. The monetarists

would not object to stating that if there were continuous cost-push, and if it were continuously financed, then there would be inflation. They would deem it unlikely, however, that continuous cost-push would occur if it were not continuously financed. Cost-pushes would not continue if the perpetrators had to bear the consequences.

I think that that sentence is very, very important, because the question of whether one attributes inflation to monetary policies and monetary events has been interpreted in two different ways. In one interpretation monetary policy is, so to speak, an active, deliberate villain in the piece. In the other, monetary policy may be permissive, and the reasons for its permissiveness may be political, such as attachment to full employment or some similar goal; but there is an underlying problem that is *not* related to monetary matters to which I refer in my final remarks, and which I consider to be one of the crucial aspects of the whole theme of the paper.

In regard to the substance of the paper, it seems to me that the paper deals with the theory of inflation rather sketchily. Even allowing for the study's brevity, a number of points are not mentioned that are essential in any realistic discussion of inflation.

First, something is involved that is a little more complicated than what is usually called cost-push: some villainous monopolistic society deciding to push up prices arbitrarily. Most industrial economies have some bias that makes it easier for prices to respond to upward pressures—from either demand relative to capacity or from cost—than to pressures in the reverse direction. It may be only a matter of the time rates of response, but time rates will be essential. The mechanisms may partly be market imperfections, but they are also often political; an entrepreneur suffering from downward pressure on his goods' price may seek government help. That is a phenomenon well observed in the United States. But my small acquaintance with foreign countries suggests that it is not a uniquely American custom.

Second, there is a good deal of evidence—of which the most recent episodes are only the most spectacular—to show that surges of demand that push up prices very quickly over the short period have disproportionate effects on the prices of raw materials, which are then reflected in the prices of final goods and the cost of living.

The same kind of rapid surge in demand has some tendency to distort the wage structure by pushing up wages in the more competitive, less well-organized labor markets than in others, better organized, that tend to move slowly. This results in feedbacks to the cost of living and expectations, and, in addition, a second set of feedbacks, which one might call wage linkages, that are really the response of the more highly organized sectors to the wage distortions generated in the first place. John Dunlop could continue indefinitely on this subject, but I also think that it is an important feature of the world. Those points are part of the microeconomic side of the analysis.

On the demand side, two points ought to have been mentioned in Swoboda's paper.

First, fiscal policy seems to have completely disappeared from the scene. His treatment of demand is purely monetarist, since nothing really happens to affect aggregate demand except movements of real balances. Even variations in components of private demand that might be generated by something other than a change in real balances are ignored, including changes in the volume of trade. That seems to me to be going a little too far.

Second, however important one considers monetary influences to be, they involve significant time lags. Imagine, for example, that there is a surge of demand from a fiscal or any other source and the monetary authority is not accommodating in that it does not respond by handing out more money to keep pace with the price level. Short-term interest rates will be driven up, and so will the velocity of money, for some considerable time, which will eventually affect the long-term interest rates and later economic activity.

Meanwhile, if the monetary authority has remained on some fixed monetary track, much of that inflationary surge will have been absorbed by the economy. Even for a monetarist, if he is at all realistic about the way the economy operates, the presence of those time lags may turn out to be very important.

Part of my message (and I say more about this later) is that it is inappropriate to treat inflation on the basis of comparative statics, or long-run equilibrium rates of growth, because a great deal of inflation is caused by a government's inability to deal with such short-run surges, which then trigger a whole chain of reactions that may last for many years.

It is a better understanding of these processes that will help monetary authorities to handle inflation rather than analysis of what would happen if some particular monetary authority kept on increasing the rate of money supply by, say, 10 percent a year indefinitely, or some similar exercise.

Then there is the complicated question of the financial transmission mechanism, on which I wrote a paper in 1974 that I attempt to summarize below.[55]

The United States has a financial structure that permits it to insulate the financial system to a very large extent from the effects of balance of payments

55. James S. Duesenberry, "Worldwide Inflation: A Fiscalist View," in David I. Meiselman and Arthur B. Laffer, eds., The Phenomenon of Worldwide Inflation (Washington, D.C.: American Enterprise Institute for Public Policy Research, 1975), pp. 113–24.

fluctuation. It may choose to respond to the balance of payments, but as a technical matter it can control the money supply without any reference at all to the balance of payments.

There are other elements in the financial market that may be influenced by interest differentials elsewhere that the United States cannot control so readily. Most other countries do not have the kind of open market for securities that Americans have, which permits such large-scale open market operations. They do not have the same degree of control over bank reserves or over the form of bank reserves. They have to resort to all kinds of alternatives— special accounts, various kinds of loan ceilings, and the like. This is not entirely by chance. I do not think it is a necessary feature of the world system that other countries have as low a degree of monetary control as they sometimes appear to have.

All industrial countries suffer from the same kind of biases and problems as the United States; there are the same conflicts between unemployment and inflation. But very often, when some country increases its money supply because of monetary expansion or a U.S. balance of payments deficit, what appears to result from their primitive methods of control may actually reflect their permissiveness in dealing with domestic inflation, for the same reasons that Americans have been permissive in the past. If they were a little more unhappy about how much money they were creating and how much inflation they were having, they would take more stringent measures—although, of course, at various times it may be convenient for them to blame inflation on the United States.

So far as control of money supply is concerned, I suspect that over any decade (although not in the very short run) countries probably manage to have as much control over monetary supply to control domestic inflation as they wish to have.

A final word about the trade transmission: Swoboda's view derives from the neoclassical price theory in which the relative prices depend on one's resources, technology, and the like. If these are given, then there is a given set of relative prices. My impression is that in the real world naturally there is a price system and it hangs together to some degree, but there is a great deal of slack and slippage. When prices of tradable goods rise abroad and one attempts to determine the effect on prices in the home country, if the industries that produce these tradable goods are concentrated in one sector, as they often are, there is a great deal of leeway in what may happen to those prices. Whether the industries producing those tradable goods raise prices by the same amount or choose to increase output will partly depend on their capacity, on domestic competitive restraints, and on long-run domestic price policy. There is no way of knowing exactly how much their prices are going to change. Whatever price changes do occur, when those effects are communicated to nontradable goods industries, exactly the same slippages and uncertainties occur.

There is, in fact, a very wide range of possible responses in the price level of one country to changes in the prices of traded goods elsewhere. In the long run and if prices change greatly, say, doubling or tripling, then such slippages as occur may become of minor importance. However, if what is really taking place is an inflationary process in which from time to time there are surges of demand, such as those caused by the Vietnam War, or supply shifts that kick off a short-run dynamic process, it may make a great deal of difference whether the goods-price arbitrage is very sharp and price changes pass quickly from one country to another, or whether it is attenuated because of all of the circumstances mentioned above. How much inflation there is going to be may depend, really, on the strength of those feedbacks in the very short period.

This brings me back to my opening comment quoted from Swoboda about whether one should regard the monetary aspects of inflation as something caused by crazy central bankers, or as something caused by central bankers forced to deal with nonmonetary forces that tend to produce some inflation and to which they have to adjust in a political world that is averse to unemployment. It seems to me that the real problem is *not* arriving at a reasonable growth in the world money supply once all those special microeconomic problems that tend to generate inflation at any reasonably acceptable level of employment are solved. The real problem is that those forces exist. There is a continuing conflict between employment objectives and price stability objectives. The central banks are in the situation of always making an uneasy compromise, so in the end the money supply does accommodate a good deal of inflation, which is generated by other processes. The real issue, then, is what to do about those microeconomic processes. Improving them would make the monetary choices much easier.

The point on which Swoboda and I appear to be in closest agreement is the delay in reacting to inflationary signals. At the beginning of some of the upward surges of demand, such as at the beginning of the Vietnam War or some other recent expansion, the monetary authorities probably waited too long before they foresaw any inflation problem at all. Without implying that they should have been hardhearted enough to tolerate very high unemployment to solve that problem, I think they could have implemented restraints much faster. That would have been quite effective in choking off the dynamic processes discussed above. I suspect that unwillingness to face the fact that they have a difficult potential inflation to deal with has, sometimes at least, been the fault of monetary authorities, and is therefore one monetary explanation of inflation.

Comments by James Tobin

I FOUND Swoboda's approach both valuable and useful. That approach, basically, is to regard movements of the world price level as endogenous adjustments that take place in order to reconcile exogenously determined world money supply to exogenously determined demand for real money balances.

If the world monetary authorities expanded the money supply, and if all the determinants of the demand for real money balances are fixed, as they are in Swoboda's model, then the only variable that can bring nominal supply and real demand into equality is the world price level. It must fall or rise to adjust the real value of the exogenous money stock to world demand. Balance of payments deficits and surpluses are just transient incidents in this process of adjustment.

I have six queries on aspects of this model.

First, is the price level the only variable that can adjust in this process? Is the real demand for money holdings exogenous, even in the long run? A necessary condition is that real income in every country is fixed, that employment and output are everywhere and always supply-determined. The model allows no output adjustment, either in aggregate real demand and capacity utilization in the short run or in capital accumulation and capacity to produce in the long run.

Evidently the model assumes that the real rate of return on capital is fixed independently of monetary policies all over the world. The assumption is not explicit, but I get the impression that capital stocks are assumed not to vary endogenously even in the long run. Otherwise, the demand for real balances would depend on the real interest rates on capital and on money itself. Although standard growth models show that these real rates vary with rates of inflation and money creation, the "monetary" model of the world ignores these relationships altogether.

Second, does it make sense to regard national money stocks as exogenous? I find such an assumption unrealistic for a closed economy, and even more so in a world setting with *n* different money creators. I doubt that central banks are arbitrarily, blindly, and mindlessly throwing money into the world system. They create money for good reasons, or for what they think are good reasons. They must compromise among incompatible objectives, such as price stability, full employment, and stocks of international reserves in their respective countries.

In the Swoboda model prices and wages are flexible in every economy, and world prices prevail everywhere. Within each nation, wages are sufficiently flexible to maintain full employment whatever the level of world prices. Real output is not affected by domestic or foreign changes in money stocks. In these circumstances, it is hard to see why any central bank would care about the size of its nominal money stock or have any occasion to alter it.

In the real world central banks do care, and they do alter money stocks. Money supplies change as a result of endogenous adjustments of policymakers and their economies. They are not well modeled as arbitrary exogenous Ms, which stay put for decades and to which prices eventually adjust.

Third, does this monetarist approach explain or illuminate the major disturbances in the international monetary system over the last fifty years? I asked myself, and I thought back to the disturbances that I, as a casual, closed-economy-oriented newspaper reader, could recall.

In the twenties, the disturbances had to do with reparations and war debts, the transfer problem, protectionism in the United States, and such matters. They had monetary consequences, but they were not monetary in origin. Then came the Great Depression, for which a model that assumes real output and employment to be constant in every country at full employment levels is not particularly helpful. My mind jumped to the dollar shortage of the 1950s, and I tried to think how that was monetarily determined.

Next was the structural disequilibrium between the United States and Europe and Japan, which characterized the late fifties and early sixties, the dollar glut following the dollar shortage. The dollar glut produced virtually no inflation, even in the United States. The "monetary" model did not seem to illuminate this balance of payments disequilibrium any better than it did previous disturbances. The inflation set off by the financing of the Vietnam War seems at least equally the result of bad fiscal policy as of monetary policy.

Finally, there are the oil and food crises. At a 1974 conference on monetarism—domestic monetarism—somebody asked how I knew that the quadrupling of oil prices by the Organization of Petroleum Exporting Countries was not a response to increases in the world money supply. I suppose I do not!

A brief digression on Swoboda's comments on most countries' common heritage of woes at the beginning of the 1970s: Swoboda says, "policy reactions have been quite similar, with a proliferation, at least for a while, of attempts to 'inflate away' decreases in real income. . . ." When I observed Federal Reserve policy in this country in 1974, I thought that the illusion under which U.S. policymakers were acting was that it is possible to "*de*flate away" decreases in real income due to changes in terms of trade. The Federal

Reserve Board's reaction has been that when the terms of trade turn against the United States the best one can do is to work less hard.

Fourth, to return to the Swoboda model, is it useful to model the world as a global United States with a single price level and single interest rate, only with the difference that every state has its own dollar printing press, and I suppose its own independent fiscal policy—and to endow every state with flexible wages within its borders, so that they all maintain full employment all the time? I don't think it is a very convincing description of an international regime of fixed exchange rates.

There is, for one thing, a difference between exchange rates with adjustable pegs and a true common currency. For a second, the process of equalization of real interest rates, which has occurred within the United States to a considerable degree, would take decades, maybe even centuries, internationally.

The paper deals in detail with goods arbitrage and portfolio asset arbitrage. There is considerable use of Hicks's theorem that, if real demand-supply conditions remain unchanged, and if for some reason one nominal price rises, the only possible way of returning to equilibrium is that all other prices move up in proportion. This is how nontraded goods prices become as international as prices of traded goods. I think the argument is overworked.

Why, too, does the theorem not apply to labor? Why not labor arbitrage? Suppose that a few economists from various countries are in the international labor market, subject to an international wage rate rather than an insulated one. Increases in their international wage will be transmitted to the domestic wage structure of every economy by the same processes that Swoboda describes for traded and nontraded goods. With this logical extension, there could be a common wage level, a common price level, a common interest rate level all over the world.

Fifth, I had trouble with the facile assumption that one can name some asset "money" within every country, add up all the quantities of this "money," and obtain a meaningful world money stock. What is the criterion for choosing M in each country? Is it the means of payment used in the country? Or is it, as it also must be to make sense of the model, some liability of the banking system that moves dollar for dollar or pound for pound with reserve changes? This is essential to meet the condition that each money supply be a sum of international reserves and internally monetized assets. It is not true in the U.S. system, and I do not think it is generally true of other countries, that the set of bank liabilities that moves up and down with international reserve changes coincides with the set used as means of payment.

It seems, in any case, quite arbitrary that Swoboda should exclude a whole host of domestic near-moneys and cash substitutes while telling his readers that money created by the Bank of England or the Central Bank of Uganda is a perfect substitute for dollar currency and dollar deposits in meeting transaction requirements.

A striking feature of Swoboda's additive model is that money supply and demand do not have to be equated in individual countries. The only balance requirement is that the *sum* of world money supplies should equal the *sum* of world money demands. It could be that a country creates no money whatsoever itself and yet satisfies its transactions needs by the money creation of its neighbors and trading partners. That is supposed to occur in the model through the transmission of international reserves from one country to another, so that the creation of pounds sterling in the United Kingdom or the creation of shillings in Uganda will eventually result in the creation of some dollars in the United States, whether Americans like it or not. Americans will get the money they want, even though their central bank does not supply it to them. This mechanism requires a tight connection between international reserves and domestic money supplies.

That connection just does not exist. It has certainly not characterized U.S. policy during the last quarter-century or more. The world does not have a specie system, although the model seems really to wish that it did, that everyone was using gold coins and nothing else as a means of payment.

The theory is meant to explain, among other things, distribution of international reserves. But there cannot be any determinate distribution of international reserves in the model unless there is a fixed connection between international reserves and domestic monetization in every country. Since the connection is not fixed but a matter of policy or an endogenous response of countries to their situations, including their reserve stocks, I do not find the model convincing.

An alternative theory about the distribution of reserves is that countries have reserve targets. One could explain the targets, in a regime of fixed exchange rates, by use of the theory of precautionary holdings of cash as related to the desynchronization of receipts and expenditures, and to the risks and costs of being caught short and forced to borrow. Reserve stocks are targets of national policies. Changes in actual reserves are not automatic, passive incidents to the satisfaction of demands for real balances. They are forced compromises between efforts to hit reserve targets and the complicated and often incompatible domestic objectives of central banks and governments.

Sixth, why does the model throw away as irrelevant the whole apparatus explaining the balance of trade in terms of marginal propensities to import, price elasticities, and so on? One is left with the proposition that if there should be a gap within a country between its capacity to produce and its domestic aggregate demand, the gap would be completely filled tomorrow morning by a flood of export orders. In other words, the only explanation of imports and exports is the temporary emergence of slight differences between domestic and world price levels. National tastes and capacities to supply particular goods, movements of income levels and relative prices are considerations to forget.

ANALYSIS of long-run consequences is the main contribution of the paper and of the approach, so far as I can see. Even as a long-run theory, the model appears to be somewhat underdeveloped. A more complete integration of the so-called monetary approach in long-run growth models would be an important thing to develop. I think it would lead to somewhat different results from those of the paper's simple model.

I conclude that for most of the problems that concern statesmen and pragmatic economists, this approach to world inflation and balance of payments deficits and surpluses is not "the appropriate framework." I do agree that it is worthwhile to consider the long-run consequences of a series of short-run policies and events. But this does not justify policy advice predicated on the assumption that the world is always in long-run equilibrium.

General Comments

HARRY JOHNSON said that some economists who began several years ago working on the problem of rapid world inflation have come to the conclusion that it is not a world inflation; it is a series of accidents occurring in each country. Appeals to the details of microeconomic or sectoral developments might provide satisfactory explanations for inflations in the neighborhood of 1 percent a year, but the rate of the 1973–75 inflation cannot be explained by such details. It is essentially a monetary phenomenon. If economists focus attention not on the microeconomic phenomena, which are the foliage surrounding the economic propositions, but on the application of those propositions themselves, they might well conclude that no government wants to check inflation. That conclusion was already beginning to emerge, when both the United Kingdom and the United States took off the brakes before there was any evidence whatsoever that inflation was even slowing down. Inflation may be the popular choice for a long time to come, but that does not mean that it is not understood. People who do not agree with the monetary approach should present an alternative theory of world inflation or some reason for thinking there is not a world inflation or show why the elements they think are important make a big difference in the rate of inflation.

Arthur Okun interpreted the message of the Swoboda paper to be that no country can swim against the tide of world price trends in an environment of fixed exchange rates. But the paper appears to assume the fixity of those rates as absolute. That ignores the option of a country to change its exchange rate—an option that it has even in a fixed-rate system. Swoboda cites research by Genberg, which concludes that there is no systematic difference between inflation rates among countries any greater than within sectors of a country. Those results are astounding; most economists have the impression that the inflation rates in different countries have been very different (for example, those between Germany and Italy) and that the differences reflect differences in domestic strategies during the past twenty years and differences in countries' attitudes toward the trade-off between unemployment and inflation.

George Perry asked, in connection with these comparisons of inflation rates, whether those rates in different countries had been measured in terms of domestic price levels or after adjustment for exchange rate changes.

Alexander Swoboda answered that Genberg had used two tests, one for a period in which exchange rates did not change so that the question did not arise, and the other covering a longer period, in which domestic inflation rates were used without correction for exchange rate changes.

Max Corden thought the model presented in Swoboda's paper can provide a guide for the sort of research that is needed. The essential point is that worldwide inflation is generated by increases in domestic credit by individual countries and is then spread around the world if other countries do not counteract it by decreasing their domestic credit or by exchange rate adjustments. That is a cause that can be observed statistically, but it is not the deep cause. One must ask why domestic credit increased in some countries and why other countries do not counteract the increases in those countries. There are four reasons. First, the governments find inflation a convenient method of taxation. Second, it is a means of reducing unemployment in the face of increases in employment targets, increases in real wages demanded, or shifts in the curve of the value of labor's marginal product. All these can motivate efforts to cut unemployment below the natural rate hypothesized by Milton Friedman. Third, countries fail to appreciate their currencies and thereby avoid inflation because they wish to maintain incomes in the export sector. Fourth, institutional rigidity makes fiscal policy less able to counteract inflation in some countries, such as the United States and Germany, than in other countries where fiscal policy is more flexible, as in the United Kingdom.

The above are questions of positive analysis. In addition, there are two normative issues. First, what is the optimal way of shifting resources into the public sector, and is explicit taxation better than inflation or not? Second, any attempt to reduce the rate of inflation at the cost of unemployment creates a conflict between long-term gains and short-term losses. However, in some countries institutional changes could make it easier to counteract imported inflation. Research could be done on all of these topics for each of the eight countries studied in this volume.

Alexander Swoboda said that his paper attempted to outline central tendencies, not details. One might want to do much more than that but it must be done within a framework that recognizes that a rise in the general price level has something to do with money. The analysis incorporates elements of all three of the main theories of balance of payments adjustment. It stresses the role of changes in expenditure in determining world changes in money income and the balance of payments of individual countries. It is monetary in the sense that changes in the quantity of money play a crucial role in explaining changes in expenditures, either directly or through interest rates. Finally, it invokes general equilibrium in the sense that both short- and long-run conclusions depend on the interaction of money expenditure and relative price changes. There is no quarrel with the view that relative price changes are important; any detailed discussion of the transmission mechanism must put great stress on the role of relative price changes. In the short run one should not assume that velocity is constant, and the monetary approach does not yet have a convincing general theory of how changes of money income are divided between changes in output and changes in prices. And it is important to stress that this approach is quite compatible with a Keynesian approach.

WILLIAM H. BRANSON

A "Keynesian" Approach to Worldwide Inflation

Tables

Figures

MY ASSIGNMENT is to expound a Keynesian view of the international transmission mechanism, including in this view a Phillips curve approach to explaining wage inflation. The Phillips curve is a development that came after publication of Keynes's *General Theory,* so the first task is to develop a working definition of the Keynesian approach that embraces it. The concept I use here is that the typical Keynesian model focuses on income-expenditure relationships and multipliers based on these relationships, particularly the consumption function. This is the Keynesian model of the standard macroeconomic texts.[1] On this view, changes in assets (money stock, for example) affect equilibrium income only through their effects on expenditures.

I develop a basic Keynesian IS-LM model with a supply side that assumes rigidity of nominal wages, both upward and downward.[2] I take this to represent the standard Keynesian view. The model takes asset stocks as given, and includes a balance of payments with both capital and current accounts. Since the focus of this study is inflation, solutions of the model as exogenous variables change are given in terms of the home price level and interest rate, rather than in terms of output and the interest rate as is usual. These solutions are summarized below in table 3 and in the IS-LM picture of figure 3.

Using the static Keynesian model developed in the next section, the paper then draws some implications for relationships among movements in domestic fiscal and monetary policy, external variables, the price level, and the balance of payments. An interesting contrast to the monetary approach appears, in which movements in the domestic price level have no necessary correlation with changes in the overall balance of payments. Various disturbances have predictable implications for both the price level and the

1. This follows the useful distinction that Leijonhufvud made between "Keynesian economics," which I am discussing in this paper, and the "economics of Keynes." (See Axel Leijonhufvud, *On Keynesian Economics and the Economics of Keynes: A Study in Monetary Theory* [Oxford University Press, 1968].)

2. An IS-LM model conveniently summarizes the determination of equilibrium values of national income and the interest rate. One of the curves (IS) is derived from the real side of the economy including consumption, investment, government expenditures, and so on; the other (LM) is derived from the monetary sector.

balance of payments, but there is no particular correlation between these two endogenous variables.

Later, I add the Phillips curve to a summary form of the static model. The Phillips curve ultimately links the domestic rate of inflation to real output, and thus to the trade balance through the foreign-trade multiplier. These links provide a stable dynamic mechanism causing domestic rates of inflation to tend to converge toward the average world rate. An interesting implication of this result is that such convergence is not unique to the monetary approach and that evidence on such convergence provides equal support for a "Keynesian-Phillips" view.

Throughout the paper I take the exchange rate as an exogenous variable, available for use as an instrument of policy. If the exchange rate were considered freely floating, it would become a recursively determined endogenous variable, with no feedback to other variables, and disappear from the analysis.[3] This view would have little interest for this study. Nor would it be relevant to the real world, because in fact there is considerable intervention by central banks in the exchange markets, making the rate an exogenous policy instrument that changes frequently, much like, say, government purchases. So in the static model I take the exchange rate as exogenous and changeable. The role of the exchange rate as a transmitter of inflation is then examined, and the paper concludes with a brief discussion of the static Keynesian model as part of a more general stock-adjustment system.

A Static "Keynesian" Model of Price Determination

In this section I develop a basic Keynesian model of income determination in an open economy, with particular emphasis on relationships between the price level and the balance of payments. This model brings out the basic Keynesian focus on the relationship between the current-account balance and the price level, as contrasted with the way the monetary approach focuses on the relationship between the overall balance of payments and the price level. I begin with the supply side of the model, which yields a relationship between the price level and output that can be used in the IS-LM analysis of the demand side to replace income (=output) with the price level. The model extends the usual textbook model to include variables of particular interest in a

---

3. William H. Branson, "The Dual Roles of the Government Budget and the Balance of Payments in the Movement from Short-Run to Long-Run Equilibrium," *Quarterly Journal of Economics,* vol. 90 (August 1976), pp. 345–67.

study of the international transmission of inflation. The basic framework can be seen in Sohmen, Takayama, and Blinder and Solow, for example. A recent extension along the present lines is provided by Turnovsky and Kaspura.[4]

The supply side

The model starts with an aggregate production function, a rigid money wage, and a marginal-product condition for employment of labor.[5] The production function gives output as an increasing function of labor and capital inputs, and can be written as:

$$(1) \qquad y = y(N, \bar{K}),$$

where y is real output (GNP), N is employment (man-hours per year), and K is the capital stock, held fixed throughout.[6] The marginal product of labor, y_n, is positive ($y_n > 0$) and declines with additional employment.

I assume that the money wage rate, W, is fixed at $\bar{W}$. The marginal product condition that the money wage equals the value of the marginal product is:

$$(2) \qquad \bar{W} = Py_n,$$

where P is the price of aggregate output (GNP deflator). An increase in the price level (due to an increase in aggregate demand) will raise the value of the marginal product, increasing employment and output at the existing money wage rate.[7] This yields an implicit aggregate supply relationship between output and the price level:

$$(3) \qquad y = y(P).$$

As the price level rises with rigid money wages, the real wage falls, and employment and output rise. The supply function, 3, is used below to replace income, y, by price, P, in the IS-LM analysis, permitting a focus on short-run determination of the price level.

4. See Egon Sohmen, *Flexible Exchange Rates* (rev. ed., University of Chicago Press, 1969); Akira Takayama, *International Trade: An Approach to the Theory* (Holt, Rinehart, and Winston, 1972), chaps. 9–10; Alan S. Blinder and Robert M. Solow, "Analytical Foundations of Fiscal Policy," in Alan Blinder and others, *The Economics of Public Finance* (Brookings Institution, 1974), pp. 3–115. S. J. Turnovsky and André Kaspura, "An Analysis of Imported Inflation in a Short-Run Macroeconomic Model," *Canadian Journal of Economics,* vol. 7 (August 1974), pp. 355–80.

5. For a model with a flexible money wage but money illusion, and a discussion of wage rigidity and unemployment, see William H. Branson, *Macroeconomic Theory and Policy* (Harper and Row, 1972), chaps. 7, 8.

6. See appendix A for a complete list of symbols and their definitions.

7. From equation 1, $dy = y_n dN$; and from 2, with $\bar{W}$ fixed, $0 = Py_{nn}dN + y_n dP$. Combining these expressions gives the implicit supply curve $dy = -(y_n^2/Py_{nn})dP$, with $dy/dP > 0$.

Financial markets: the LM sector

The demand side is a "textbook" IS-LM specification, with asset equilibrium equations (LM) that extend the analyses of Metzler and Tobin[8] to include a foreign asset and a commodity-flow equation (IS) that includes foreign trade.[9] There are only three assets in the model: money, M, government bonds, B, and foreign securities, S. Each of these symbols represents the nominal value of the stock of these assets in private portfolios; their sum is private-sector wealth, V. Holders of domestic assets have demand functions for these three imperfectly substitutable assets. The demand for each is a function of the rates of return on bonds, r_b, and on foreign securities, r_s, and of nominal income, Y. The latter is included to represent the transactions demand for money, which I assume has a fixed—zero—rate of interest. The demand for government bonds is a function of their interest rate, the rate of return on foreign securities, the level of nominal income, and the value of private-sector wealth. These demand functions can be writen as:

$$(4) \qquad\qquad B = F^b(r_b, r_s, Y, V);$$

the demand for foreign securities is a function of the same four variables:

$$(5) \qquad\qquad S = F^s(r_b, r_s, Y, V);$$

and the demand for money is a function of the first three of these variables:

$$(6) \qquad\qquad M = F^m(r_b, r_s, Y),$$

where nominal income, Y, is defined as the product of real income and the price level, $P \cdot [y(P)]$.

My assumption that government bonds, foreign securities, and money are substitutes implies that the demands for bonds and foreign securities increase when their own rates go up ($F^b_b, F^s_s > 0$) and that the demand for each asset falls with a rise in rates on the other assets. Also, since wealth is fixed, the sum of the effects on demand in response to a change in any rate must be zero.[10] Since I model a system in which the exchange rate is exogenously

8. Lloyd A. Metzler, "Wealth, Saving, and the Rate of Interest," *Journal of Political Economy,* vol. 59 (April 1951), pp. 93–116; and James Tobin, "A General Equilibrium Approach to Monetary Theory," *Journal of Money, Credit, and Banking,* vol. 1 (February 1969), pp. 15–29.

9. The IS-LM specification is essentially the same as presented in William H. Branson, "Flow and Stock Equilibrium in a Traditional Macro Model."

10. Formally, $F^b_s + F^m_s = - F^s_s$ and $F^s_b + F^m_b = - F^b_b$. In specifying equations 4 to 6, capital gains effects on V are ignored. If they were included they would complicate the calculations without changing the qualitative results.

determined by the monetary authorities, I do not include expected changes in the exchange rate in the asset demand functions. The demand for money is an interest-sensitive transactions demand, and thus the demand for money should rise if the price level rises.[11] With wealth fixed, this implies that as the price level, P, and real income, y, rise, the combined demand for bonds and foreign securities must fall. Finally, wealth, V, enters the demand functions directly only for the income-earning assets, government bonds, and foreign securities, so that if wealth changes, it must be reflected in these two assets;[12] money is held strictly for transactions purposes.

To use this model to study the questions at hand, I assume that bonds, B, are not internationally tradable assets, and that domestic-asset holders face a supply of foreign securities, S, that is infinitely elastic at the world interest rate, r_s. Domestic-asset holders must hold the given stock of bonds but are free to trade between money and foreign securities. Any purchases of foreign securities implicitly reduce foreign exchange reserves by that amount since foreign securities can be purchased only with foreign moneys. These assumptions yield a two-part wealth, or balance-sheet, constraint.

Private wealth is the sum of the stock of domestic government bonds and the stock of domestically held internationally tradable assets, H:

(7) $$V = B + H,$$

where internationally tradable assets are the sum of money and foreign securities:

(8) $$H = M + S.$$

One can imagine private domestic-asset holders having an initial endowment of government bonds and internationally tradable assets and then trading some of their money stock for foreign securities to reach equilibrium, leaving the balance as the domestically held money stock.

The domestic demand for internationally tradable assets is seen as the sum of the demand functions for money and foreign securities.

(9) $$H = F^s(r_b, r_s, Y, V) + F^m(r_b, r_s, Y).$$

The two portfolio balance equations, 4 and 9, are constrained by 7, so they contain only one independent equation determining the rate of return on government bonds, r_b, given their stock, the amount of internationally trad-

---

11. $F_p^m > 0$. Since y is a function of P on the supply side,

$$F_p^m = \frac{\partial F^m}{\partial Y} [y + P \cdot y_p].$$

12. $F_v^b + F_v^s = 1$.

Figure 1. *Asset-Market Equilibrium: The LM Sector*

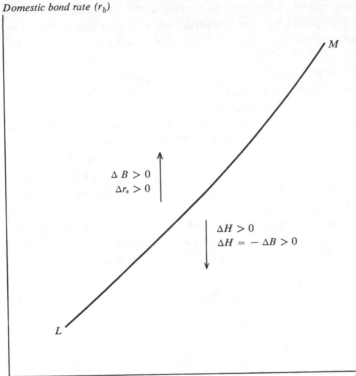

Source: Text equations 4 and 9.

able assets, the rate of return on foreign securities, and the price level.[13] With the rate on foreign securities fixed in the world market, the financial sector is recursive in the sense that equation 9 or 4 can be solved for the rate of return on government bonds, r_b, and then equation 5 can be solved for the stock of domestically held foreign securities, S, with no feedback onto r_b.

Equation 4 or 9 represents the LM curve in figure 1. With nominal income, Y, a function of the price level, P, from the supply side, as the price level rises the demand for money rises and the demand for bonds falls. This

---

13. Here Walras's Law is being applied separately across the stock-equilibrium equations. This is appropriate in a continuous-time model, in which reallocations of existing stocks can be made instantaneously but accumulation (saving) takes time. On the separate application of Walras's Law to the stock and flow equations, see Josef May, "Period Analysis and Continuous Analysis in Patinkin's Macroeconomic Model," *Journal of Economic Theory*, vol. 2 (March 1970), pp. 1–9.

reduces bond prices and increases the rate of return, r_b, that clears the bond market. The LM curve shows the movement of r_b that maintains equilibrium in the financial market as the price level changes.

For any given price level, an exogenous increase in domestically held internationally tradable assets would increase the demand for bonds and shift the LM curve down. An exogenous increase in the bond supply would create an excess supply, shifting the LM curve up. An increase in the rate of return on foreign securities would also shift the LM curve up. Finally, an open market purchase increasing the stock of domestically held internationally tradable assets and decreasing the stock of government bonds by the same amount, would shift the LM curve down.[14] The directions of these shifts are indicated by the arrows in figure 1.[15] A change in the stock of either government bonds, B, or domestically held internationally tradable assets, H, other things being equal, changes private-sector wealth. In economic terms, these changes would come from windfall gains or losses in one or the other asset stock that would violate normal accounting rules. These are called "helicopter" changes in the literature: it is as if the central bank ran a helicopter (with a vacuum cleaner attachment) over the country, dropping (or absorbing) money or bonds. There are two technical reasons for studying such changes. First, they give comparative-statics results for two economies that are identical in structure and in the values of all exogenous variables except one, B or H. Second, since the effects are linearly additive, the two helicopter operations (or one helicopter and one vacuum cleaner) sum to an open market operation in which the change in government bonds outstanding is exactly offset by a change in internationally tradable assets ($dB = - dH$). The separate effects of dB and $-dH$ permit separate analysis of each of the two sides of an open market operation and determination of the direction of change.[16]

The next two subsections introduce the commodity-flow equilibrium

14. Throughout the paper, open market operations are analyzed as purchases of bonds on the open market, with $dH = - dB > 0$, from the point of view of the private sector.

15. Formally, to study the effects of changes in F, P, r_s, and P on r_b in the financial sector, one must totally differentiate equation 4 to obtain the LM curve:

(4a) $$\text{LM}: F_b^b dr_b = - F_p^b dP - F_v^b dH + (1 - F_v^b)dB - F_s^b dr_s.$$

This equation gives the effects on r_b of changes in each of the right-hand variables, holding the others constant.

16. The coefficient of dr_b in equation 4a is positive. Thus the sign of a change in each of the right-hand variables is given by the sign of the coefficient. Since F_v^b is positive, $-F_v^b < 0$, $dr_b/dH < 0$, as shown in figure 1. With $(1 - F_v^b)$ and $-F_s^b$ both positive, dr_b/dB and dr_b/dr_s are both positive. Since F_p^b is negative, $dr_b/dP > 0$, as indicated by the slope of the LM curve of figure 1. So the signs of the coefficients in equation 4a give the direction of the effect of a change in each variable, shifting the LM curve in figure 1.

condition—the IS curve—and show that short-run equilibrium values for the rate of return on government bonds, r_b, and the price level, P, are determined by the intersection of the IS and LM curves, given values for the rate of return on foreign securities, r_s, and the value of private wealth, V. Then, with V, r_s, r_b, and P (and thus real income, y, and nominal income, Y) fixed, equation 5 gives the equilibrium holdings of foreign assets. With a change in any of the exogenous variables, the total differential of equation 5 reflects the short-run effect on the capital account. Changing one variable at a time, an increase in either H or B will spill over into purchases of foreign securities, S (holding r_b and P constant). An interesting question addressed just below is whether *all* such increases of domestic assets flow out through the capital account. A rise in the rate of return on foreign securities, everything else constant, will cause domestic holdings of foreign securities to rise as portfolio balancers substitute foreign securities for bonds and money.

An increase in the price level raises the transactions demand for money, leading to sales of bonds and foreign securities in an attempt to increase money balances. This will occur even if income does not enter directly into the demand equation for foreign securities (that is, if $F_p^s = 0$), so that offsetting shifts occur between government bonds and money as a result of changes in price level ($F_p^b = -F_p^m$). In this case, bond sales to build money balances will raise the rate of return on bonds relative to that of foreign securities, leading to sales of foreign securities by domestic holders and a capital-account inflow.

Once equilibrium values of the rate of return on government bonds and the price level are determined by the IS-LM intersection (see figure 3), precise expressions are obtainable for the net effects of changes in the sum of money and domestically held foreign securities, H, the stock of government bonds, B, the rate of return on foreign securities, r_s, and the price level, P, on holdings of foreign securities, S.[17] Domestic holdings of foreign securities are increased, for example, as a result of a rise in internationally tradable assets,

---

17. The expressions are obtained by totally differentiating equation 5 and substituting 4a for dr_b, the total differential of changes in interest rates, r_b and r_s, income, Y, and wealth, V. Through the supply relationship between the price level and real income (equation 3), the nominal income term can be replaced with P. And since 4a gives the relationship between changes in r_b and the other exogenous variables, it can be used to eliminate the term in r_b. The result for changes in S is

(5a)
$$ dS = \left[F_v^s - F_v^b \frac{F_b^s}{F_b^b} \right] dH + \left[F_v^s + F_b^s \frac{F_v^s}{F_b^b} \right] dB $$
$$ + \left[F_s^s - F_b^s \frac{F_s^b}{F_b^b} \right] dr_s + \left[F_p^s - F_b^s \frac{F_p^b}{F_b^b} \right] dP. $$

Since $F_v^s + F_v^b = 1$, and $-F_b^s < F_b^b$, the coefficient of dH is less than unity.

government bonds, or the rate of return on foreign securities, and are reduced if the rate of return on government bonds should rise. One interesting implication of this financial-sector model with a nontraded asset and less-than-perfect substitutability is that with the price level and real income held constant, less than all of an increase in internationally tradable assets, H, flows into foreign securities, S, leaving the domestic private sector with some increase in money holdings. Only if government bonds and foreign securities were perfect substitutes (so that $-F_b^s = F_b^b$) would all of the increase in H flow into S (that is, $dS/dH = 1$).

The next question is the effects of open market operations in which the monetary authorities swap internationally tradable assets, H, for government bonds, B.[18] As the bond rate, r_b, falls with an open market purchase, the demand for money increases, so that part of the increase in H remains in domestic portfolios, and part, but less than the original increases in H, flows into foreign securities. Thus an expansionary open market operation will *not* result in a one-for-one increase in holdings of foreign securities per unit increase in the money supply in this model with a nontraded asset. Some of the increase in the money stock remains in domestic portfolios. This is consistent with the recent empirical results of Kouri and Porter, which are based on a portfolio-adjustment model of capital movements similar to the one developed here.[19] These authors estimated capital-flow equations for Germany, the Netherlands, Australia, and Italy on data from the 1960s and found that an increase in the monetary base induced by domestic policy led to the following capital outflows (increases in S, in terms of the model here) as

18. If $dB = -dH$ in equations 4a and 5a, and $dr_s = dP = 0$, then equation 4a gives the effect of an open market purchase on r_b, holding r_s and P constant:

$$\left. \frac{dr_b}{dH} \right|_{\substack{dB = -dH \\ dP = 0 \\ dr_s = 0}} = -\frac{1}{F_b^b} < 0,$$

since F_b^b is positive. Similarly, equation 5a gives the effect of the open market purchase on S:

$$\left. \frac{dS}{dH} \right|_{\substack{dB = -dH \\ dP = 0 \\ dr_s = 0}} = -\frac{F_b^s}{F_b^b}.$$

Since $F_b^s + F_b^m = -F_b^b$, if money demand is sensitive to the bond rate ($F_b^m < 0$), F_b^s will be negative but smaller than F_b^b in absolute value. This means that $0 < -F_b^s/F_b^b < 1$, and dS/dH in an open market operation is less than unity.

19. Pentti J. K. Kouri and Michael G. Porter, "International Capital Flows and Portfolio Equilibrium," *Journal of Political Economy*, vol. 82 (May/June 1974), pp. 443–67.

Table 1. *Effects of Increases in Variables Exogenous to the Financial Sector on the Rate of Return of Government Bonds and on Domestically Held Stocks of Foreign Securities*

	Effect on endogenous variable	
Exogenous variable	*Rate of return of government bonds* (r_b)[a]	*Domestic holdings*[b] *of foreign securities* (S)
The price level (P)	Increase	Decrease
Stock of government bonds (B)	Increase	Increase
Stock of internationally tradable assets (H)	Decrease	Increase (but less than the full amount)
Rate of return on foreign securities (r_s)	Increase	Increase
Open market operations[c] $(dB = -dH)$	Decrease	Increase (but less than the full amount)

Sources: Text equations 4a and 5a.
a. From equation 4a.
b. From equation 5a.
c. Government purchases of outstanding government bonds held by the public.

percentages of the initial increase in the base: Germany, 77; the Netherlands, 59; Australia, 47; Italy, 43. In an article surveying the topic and covering some large industrial countries, Thygesen also finds that domestic monetary expansion, or contraction, does not lead to one-for-one offset via the capital account.[20] Thus there is room for an independent monetary policy in the Keynesian model, even with fixed exchange rates and free capital movements, and this independence appears in the empirical estimates.

How changes in the variables exogenous to the financial sector affect the rate of return on government bonds, r_b, and domestic holdings of foreign securities, S, is summarized in table 1. Each cell in the table gives the effect of a change in the relevant exogenous variable on the value of the relevant endogenous variable. Note that the effects on domestic holdings of foreign securities, S, are *shifts* in a given stock of wealth in response to changes in exogenous variables—one-shot "stock-shift" capital movements.

Commodity-flow equilibrium: the IS sector

The LM sector yields equation 9 as an equilibrium condition. This is the LM curve of figure 1. The other equilibrium condition jointly to determine the rate of return on government bonds, r_b, and the price level, P, is the familiar equilibrium condition of real flows in the commodity market, the IS

20. Niels Thygesen, "Monetary Policy, Capital Flows and Internal Stability: Some Experiences from Large Industrial Countries," *Swedish Journal of Economics*, vol. 75 (March 1973), pp. 83–99.

curve: the sum of saving, s, imports, m, and net tax payments, $\phi(y)$, equals the sum of investment, i, government purchases, g, and exports, x:

$$(10) \quad s[y(P) - \phi(y), \frac{V}{P}] + m(y,e) + \phi(y) = i(r_b) + g + x(e,\alpha),$$

where e is the exchange rate (defined as the domestic price of a unit of foreign currency) and a change in α represents a shift in foreign demand. From the supply side, $y = y(P)$, so the IS equation is one equation in the rate of return on government bonds, r_b, and the price level, P, given the values of private wealth, V, government purchases, g, the price of foreign currency, and the shift in foreign demand.

A few comments on the functions in equation 10 may be useful. The saving function relates saving positively to real disposable income and negatively to real wealth. Imports are related positively to income and negatively to the exchange rate. Investment, i, depends on the interest rate, r_b, and exports on foreign demand and the domestic price of the foreign currency unit, e, so that $x_e > 0$. I include a shift parameter, α, in the export function to represent shifts in foreign demand.[21]

Equation 10 is the usual IS curve seen in figure 2. The IS equation can be conceived as determining the price level, P, given the values of the exogenous variables and the rate of return on government bonds, r_b, from the LM sector. As the interest rate, r_b, falls, investment increases and aggregate demand increases, pulling up the price level, P, and real income, y, along the supply curve. Thus the slope of the IS curve is negative. For a given value of r_b, an increase in government purchases, g, in the domestic price of foreign currency, e, or in foreign demand, α, which expands net exports, raises aggregate demand and the price level, shifting the IS curve to the right. An increase in private domestic assets, V, reduces saving and stimulates consumption demand, also shifting IS to the right. These directions are indicated by the arrow in figure 2.[22] The signs of the other coefficients are summarized

---

21. In general, a "shift parameter" represents a change but is customarily measured from a base of zero, and is therefore equivalent to the level of foreign demand; but in the argument of this paper only the change in level matters.

Net interest income on capital assets held abroad is included in x and is assumed to be constant for the short-run analysis below. For the complications that inclusion of interest payments introduce into dynamic stock-adjustment analysis, see Alan S. Blinder and Robert M. Solow, "Analytical Foundations of Fiscal Policy," in Alan Blinder and others, *The Economics of Public Finance* (see note 4).

22. Substitution of the wealth definition from equation 7 into the saving function, and total differentiation of equation 10 yields the IS equation:

$$(10a) \quad dP\{[\overbrace{s_y(1 - \phi_y) + \phi_y + m_y}^{s_p}]y_p - s_v \frac{V}{P^2}\} = - \frac{s_v}{P} dH - \frac{s_v}{P} dB + (x_e - m_e) de$$
$$+ i_r dr_b + dg + x_\alpha d\alpha.$$

Figure 2. *Commodity-Market Flow Equilibrium: The IS Sector*

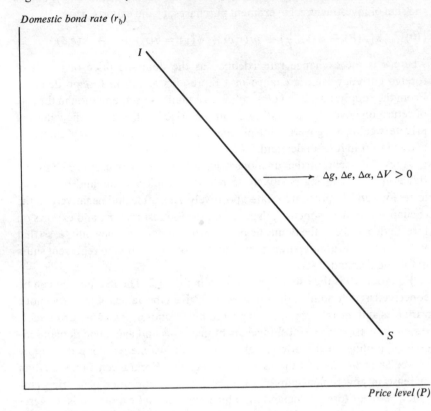

Domestic bond rate (r_b)

$\Delta g, \Delta e, \Delta \alpha, \Delta V > 0$

Price level (P)

Source: Text equation 10.

in table 2 (note that $s_v < 0$), giving the direction of shift of the IS curve when one of the variables changes.

Instantaneous-flow equilibrium with a fixed exchange rate

The IS equation and the LM equation determine equilibrium values for the rate of return on government bonds, r_b, and the price level, P, given the stock of government bonds, B, the stock of internationally tradable assets, H, the rate of return on foreign securities, r_s, government purchases, g, the domestic price of foreign currency, e, and foreign demand, α, as shown in

---

For convenience I have labeled the dP coefficient s_p, as indicated. The coefficient of dP is positive, and that of dr_b is negative, giving the slope of the IS curve of figure 2.

Table 2. *Effects on the Price Level of Changes in Exogenous Variables Underlying the IS Curve*

Exogenous variable and change	Effect on the price level
Increase in rate of return on government bonds (r_b)	Decrease
Increase in stock of government bonds outstanding (B)	Increase
Increase in stock of domestically held, internationally tradable assets (H)	Increase
Increase in government purchases (g)	Increase
Increase in foreign demand (α)	Increase
Increase in domestic currency price of a unit of foreign exchange (e)	Increase

Source: Text equation 10a.

figure 3. Given r_b and P, the stock of domestically held foreign securities is determined through equation 5. Following Blinder and Solow, these values of the price level and the rate of return on government bonds can be interpreted at any point in time $[P(t)$ and $r_b(t)]$ as an *instantaneous equilibrium* that moves through time.[23] Equations 9 and 10 adjust r_b and P to values at which (1) savers are willing to hold existing stocks of assets in their portfolios, and (2) desired saving plus imports plus tax revenue equal desired investment plus exports plus exogenous government purchases. This is not, of course, a long-run equilibrium position, because non-zero values of saving, investment, and the sum of government purchases minus tax receipts plus exports minus imports $[g - \phi(y) + x(e,\alpha) - m(y,e)]$ in instantaneous equilibrium continuously change wealth, the capital stock, and the composite money stock $(H = M + S)$. A long-run equilibrium could be reached only when these variables had reached a final resting place, or growth path, as discussed below.

EFFECTS ON THE RATE OF RETURN OF GOVERNMENT BONDS AND ON THE PRICE LEVEL. The effects of a change in one of the exogenous variables, the stock of domestic government bonds, B, the stock of internationally tradable assets held by domestic residents, H, the rate of return on foreign securities, r_s, government purchases, g, foreign demand for exports, α, and the domestic price of foreign currencies, e, can be analyzed by shifting the relevant curves in figure 3.[24] An increase in government purchases, the price of foreign currency, or exports shifts only the IS curve, pulling the price level, P, out-

23. Alan S. Blinder and Robert M. Solow, "Does Fiscal Policy Matter?" *Journal of Public Economics*, vol. 2 (November 1973), p. 326.
24. The comparative statics of figure 3 are summarized in matrix form in appendix B.

Figure 3. *The IS-LM Determination of Instantaneous-Flow Equilibrium of the Rate of Return on Government Bonds and the Price Level*

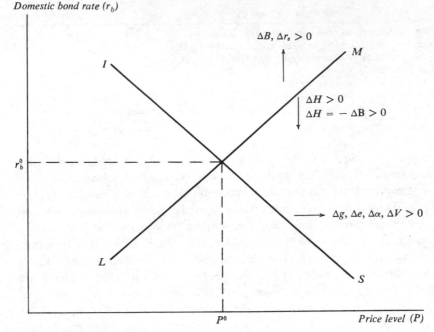

Sources: Derived from figures 1 and 2.

put, y, and the yield on government bonds, r_b, up along the LM curve. An increase in the yield of foreign securities, r_s, shifts the LM curve up, raising the yield on domestic government bonds, r_b, and reducing the domestic price level and output by reducing aggregate demand. An expansionary open market operation shifts the LM curve down along a fixed IS curve, since private sector wealth, V, is unaffected by the swap of internationally tradable assets for domestic government bonds. This open market operation reduces government bond yield, r_b, and increases the price level, P, as well as output, y.

Increases in the stock of domestic government bonds, B, or the stock of outside money, H, by exogenous helicopter operations that also increase private sector wealth, V, have ambiguous effects on one of the variables because they shift both the IS and the LM curves. The ambiguity comes from the wealth effect on the saving function. An increase in either B or H shifts the IS curve to the right. An increase in H also shifts the LM curve to the right,

Table 3. *Effects of Increases in Exogenous Variables on the Price Level, the Rate of Return of Government Bonds, and Domestically Held Stocks of Foreign Securities, as Determined by the IS-LM Curves in Instantaneous Equilibrium*

	Effect on endogenous variables		
Increases in exogenous variables	Price level (1)	Rate of return of government bonds (r_b) (2)	Stock of domestically held foreign securities (S)[a] (3)
Stock of internationally tradable assets (H)	Increase	Ambiguous	Ambiguous
Stock of government bonds outstanding (B)	Ambiguous (likely decrease)	Increase	Ambiguous (likely increase)
Rate of return on foreign securities (r_s)	Decrease	Increase	Increase
Government purchases (g)	Increase	Increase	Decrease
Foreign demand (α)	Increase	Increase	Decrease
Domestic currency price of a unit of foreign exchange (e)	Increase	Increase	Decrease
Open market operations[b] (purchase of outstanding bonds by government, $dB = -dH$)	Increase	Decrease	Ambiguous (likely increase)

Sources: Text equations 4a, 5a, and 10a.

a. The signs in column 3 can be obtained from equation 5a, which is the S column in table 1, combined with the P effects in table 3. To be precise, the effect of a change in B, H, r_s, g, α, or e, or S is given by the sum of the coefficient of that variable in equation 5a and the dP coefficient in 5a times the relevant multiplier in table 3, column 1.

b. Government purchases of outstanding government bonds held by the public.

increasing the price level, P, but its effect on the yield on government bonds, r_b, is ambiguous. The increase in the stock of internationally tradable assets, H, has an expansionary effect on spending through the effect of an increase in assets on saving, and it also eases financial markets. The increase in the stock of domestic government bonds, B, shifts the LM curve to the left, raising r_b, but has an ambiguous effect on the price level. In this case the direct expansionary effect on spending is counteracted by a tightening of financial markets, raising r_b and reducing investment. Thus, while the direction of effects of open market operations is clear, the effect of shifts in wealth on the IS curve makes the effects of helicopter operations ambiguous.

The effects of exogenous changes are summarized in table 3, which follows from tables 1 and 2 just as figure 3 follows from figures 1 and 2. Columns 1 and 2 of table 3 give the effects of changes in the exogenous variables on the price level, P, and the yield on government bonds, r_b. The third column of table 3 gives the effects of changes in the exogenous variables on domestic holdings of foreign securities, S, in the short run. Again, these are "stock-shift" effects.[25] As before, the system is recursive, with no feedback from the stock of domestically held securities to the price level and the yield on government bonds when the stock of total internationally tradable assets, H, is fixed.

Table 3 shows the effects of changes in the stock variables in exogenously given r_s, g, α, and e on the short-run instantaneous equilibrium values of r_b, P, and S. The entries in parentheses in table 3 give, where it is possible to establish it, the presumed direction of effects that are ambiguous. The entries in table 3 give the signs of the results of a comparative-static analysis of the instantaneous-flow equilibrium. This analysis alters each exogenous variable in turn and indicates the change in r_b, P, and S when all other exogenous variables are held constant. The procedure is equivalent to observing two different economies that have the same structure and history, including the same H and B, and differ, for example, only in the current value of g—the *instantaneous* rate of flow of government purchases—and determining the resulting differences in r_b and P. It is not, strictly speaking, the same as *period analysis,* in which either H or B would also have to be changed to allow for the initial impact of financing the additional government purchases.

EFFECTS ON DOMESTICALLY HELD STOCKS OF FOREIGN SECURITIES. Table 3, column 3, gives the effects of changes in the short-run exogenous variables on the stock of foreign securities, S, held by the domestic private sector, given existing wealth. These differ from the S effects shown in table 1 in one important way. That table gives the effects coming from the asset sector (LM) on S, holding constant real variables, represented by P. Table 3 includes the IS curve and simultaneous determination of P, allowing for additional effects on S through the transactions demand for money.

For example, an increase in r_s, holding the price level constant, raises S and pulls up r_b as domestic-asset holders shift their portfolios toward foreign securities. These effects are shown in table 1. The rise in the bond rate reduces investment and aggregate demand, putting downward pressure on the price level, as shown in table 2. The drop in the price level then reduces the demand for nominal money balances, resulting in an additional movement into foreign securities. Thus the entry for r_s in table 3, column 3, includes both

25. The entries in column 3 are obtained from the total differential equation for S, equation 5a, which already includes the effects on S through r_b, plus the result in the first column of table 3.

the financial-market effect of table 1 and the repercussions through the real sector and the transactions demand for money.

When any of the stock variables changes, the effect on S, *holding* P *and* y *constant,* is given in table 1. But in all cases, when the IS sector is introduced so that P is allowed to vary, transactions-demand effects on S (people trading S for M to increase transactions balances, or vice versa) appear. The complications caused by this influence of transactions demand are in the effects of helicopter operations and open market operations on H and B. An increase in H leads directly to leakage into S, but also pulls up the price level. The latter effect increases the transactions demand for money, reducing (partially) the demand for S. Thus the net effect is indeterminate, but is presumably to increase S. An increase in B has an indeterminate effect on P, and thus on the transactions-demand effect on S. The direct effect from table 1 is a spillover into S, but the possibility of an increase in P reducing S cannot be ruled out.

Implications for the Price Level and the Balance of Payments

The last column of table 3 gives the effects of changes in various exogenous variables on the stock of domestically held foreign securities. In table 3 an increase is a capital outflow, that is, a purchase of foreign securities. The effects of changes in the exogenous variables on the current account can be obtained as follows. Increases in the stocks of internationally tradable assets and government bonds, in the rate of return on foreign securities, and in government purchases operate on the current account only through the price level. If P rises, imports increase and the trade surplus decreases. The current account is directly affected by an increase in foreign demand, α, and a currency depreciation, e, and I assume that the direct effect outweighs the induced effect through P, so an increase in α or e increases the current-account surplus.

The effects of changes in the exogenous variables on the balance of payments with fixed exchange rates can be obtained by summing the current-account and capital-account effects. This is done in table 4 where the capital-account entries come from table 3, column 3 (the increase indicated in table 3 is an outflow, which is a decrease in the [positive] international account in table 4), and the current-account entries are as summarized just above.[26] Combining the results for the current and capital accounts, one sees

26. Here the current-account effects are changes in flows, while the capital-account effects are stock shifts spread over some short period. A better label for column 3 in table 4 might be "change in reserves" to avoid the suggestion that pure flow effects are involved.

Table 4. *Effect of Increases in Exogenous Variables on the Balance of Payments Surplus*

Increase in exogenous variables	Effect on endogenous variables		
	Current account (1)	Capital account (2)	Payments balance (3)
Stock of internationally tradable assets (*H*)	Decrease	Ambiguous	Ambiguous
Stock of government bonds outstanding (*B*)	Ambiguous (likely increase)	Ambiguous (likely decrease)	Ambiguous
Rate of return on foreign securities (r_s)	Increase	Decrease	Ambiguous
Government purchases (*g*)	Decrease	Increase	Ambiguous
Foreign demand (α)	Increase	Increase	Increase
Domestic currency price of a unit of foreign exchange (*e*)	Increase	Increase	Increase
Open market operations (purchase of outstanding government bonds, $dB = -dH$)	Decrease	Ambiguous (likely decrease)	Ambiguous (likely decrease)

Sources: Current account, see text discussion; capital, table 3, column 3.

that only the exogenous shift in foreign demand for imports, α, and the exchange rate have unambiguous effects on the balance of payments. When all the feedbacks—just in the simple model used here—are taken into account, the effects of all the other variables on the balance of payments are indeterminate, although there is a presumption that expansionary monetary policy will generate a payments deficit.

The ambiguity concerning the balance of payments outcome of exogenous changes was discussed by Fleming,[27] and can be illustrated in the IS-LM diagram of figure 4. In figure 4, I add a balance of payments (BP) line through r_b^o, P^o, the point of initial equilibrium. This line gives the trade-off that maintains the balance of payments constant as r_b and P change. If an exogenous shock moves the IS-LM intersection below (to the right of) the BP line, it generates a payments deficit. For a given r_b, P becomes too high for external balance. A shift that moves the IS-LM intersection above the BP line generates a payments surplus.

For example, an exogenous increase in expenditure shifts the IS curve up along the LM curve of figure 4, raising both P and r_b. This reduces both the current-account surplus and the capital-account deficit. The result for the

27. J. Marcus Fleming, "Domestic Financial Policies Under Fixed and Under Floating Exchange Rates," *IMF Staff Papers,* vol. 9 (November 1962), pp. 369–80.

Figure 4. *Internal (IS-LM) and External (BP) Balance*

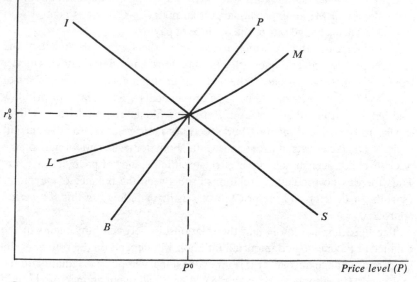

Source: See text discussion.

balance of payments depends on how much P and r_b change and on the various elasticities involved in the current and capital accounts. This information is summarized in the location of the new IS-LM intersection relative to the BP line.

It may be seen from figure 4 that a crucial question is whether the BP line is steeper than LM. With no capital mobility it would be vertical; with complete mobility, as discussed by Mundell,[28] it would be horizontal at the rate of return on foreign securities with the rate of return on government bonds equal to the rate of return on foreign securities. If the BP line is steeper than LM, a fiscal policy increase in g would lead to an external deficit; if it is flatter, an increase in g would yield a surplus.

The empirical results on the slope of the BP line generally tend to favor the case of relative capital immobility: BP is steeper than LM. For example, my calculations using the Kwack current-account model and the Branson-Hill capital-account equations for the United States show a BP line significantly

28. Robert A. Mundell, "Capital Mobility and Stabilization Policy under Fixed and Flexible Exchange Rates," in Richard E. Caves and Harry G. Johnson, eds., *Readings in International Economics* (Irwin, 1968), pp. 487–99; originally published in *Canadian Journal of Economics and Political Science,* vol. 29 (November 1963), pp. 475–85.

steeper than LM.[29] Helliwell reports simulations based on a linking of the MIT-Penn-SSRC (MPS) model of the United States and the RDX2 model of Canada.[30] These simulations show a BP curve for Canada with about the same slope as LM; an expansionary fiscal policy in Canada is neutral with respect to the exchange rate or the balance of payments.

The results in table 4, which follow from the Keynesian model of the first section, have several interesting implications that differentiate this model from the monetary approach. The first has just been discussed; the effects of many exogenous shifts on the balance of payments are unclear a priori; they could change it in either direction. But in the monetarist model their effects can be in only one direction. The second is more relevant for the current topic. While the effects of exogenous shifts, both domestic and foreign, on the price level are determinate, their effects on the balance of payments are not. Thus there is no predictable relationship between the balance of payments (surplus or deficit) and the price level (rising or falling) in this Keynesian approach.

The third implication is that the relationship between movements in the balance of payments and imported inflation will depend on the source of the exogenous change abroad. If it is an expansionary impulse originating in the real sector (fiscal policy, for example), then it will mean an increase both in foreign demand, α, and in the rate of return on foreign securities, r_s, from the point of view of the inflation-importing country. This will increase the home price level through current-account multiplier effects, but the effect on the balance of payments is unclear.

29. See Sung Y. Kwack and George R. Schink, "A Disaggregated Quarterly Model of United States Trade and Capital Flows: Simulations and Tests of Policy Effectiveness," in Gary Fromm and Lawrence R. Klein, eds., *The Brookings Model: Perspectives and Recent Developments* (Amsterdam: North-Holland, 1975; distributed in the United States and Canada by American Elsevier), pp. 95–168; my "Discussion" of their paper, pp. 169–73; and William H. Branson and Raymond D. Hill, Jr., *Capital Movements in the OECD Area: An Econometric Analysis,* published as *OECD Economic Outlook: Occasional Studies* (December 1971).

30. The MPS model is a quarterly econometric model of the United States economy developed over the years in a number of versions by econometricians from the Massachusetts Institute of Technology and the University of Pennsylvania under the auspices of the Social Science Research Council. The RDX2 model is a version of a quarterly econometric model of the Canadian economy developed by the Bank of Canada, also continuously over several years, with the cooperation of econometricians from various Canadian universities. For references to both models and their linkage, see the text, appendixes, and list of references in John F. Helliwell, "Trade, Capital Flows, and Migration as Channels for International Transmission of Stabilization Policies," in Albert Ando, Richard Herring, and Richard Marston, eds., *International Aspects of Stabilization Policies,* Proceedings of a 1974 Conference (Federal Reserve Bank of Boston, n.d.), pp. 241–78.

As an example, consider the effect on foreign countries of the increase in federal purchases of goods and services in the United States from $58 billion in 1965 to $78 billion in 1968, a substantial shift in the IS curve of figure 4. This shift in demand increased U.S. imports and raised U.S. interest rates. The import increase appeared as an increase in demand abroad, putting upward pressure on foreign countries' prices. At the same time, rising U.S. interest rates tended to reduce the U.S. capital-account deficit, making the outcome for the balance of payments unclear. Thus the inflationary impulse felt by the rest of the world could have come through the current-account effects of the expansion of aggregate demand in the United States, with no necessary relationship to the total balance of payments.

On the other hand, from the rest of the world's point of view, if the impulse in the United States had appeared on the monetary side (expansionary monetary policy), it would have meant an increase in demand for exports, α, but a fall in the rate of return on internationally tradable securities, r_s. This would have raised the rest of the world's price level and increased the net balance in its current account. But it is not the increase in the net balance that generates the price increase; it is the impulse abroad (that is, in the United States) that generates both.

The message of this simplest Keynesian model is that relationships between the balance of payments and the price level are complicated and that they can be either positive or negative. If the source of an exogenous shock is known, then one can probably determine what it will do both to the domestic price level and to the balance of payments. But knowing what it does to the balance of payments does not indicate what it does to the price level; one has to know the model and the source of the shock for that.

The Phillips Curve and the Equilibrium Rate of Inflation

The static Keynesian model described in the second section begins with a rigid money wage and includes the usual foreign-trade multipliers, which are taken into account in table 3. The other major strand of "Keynesian" theory about inflation is the relationship between the rate of wage increase and the unemployment rate depicted by the Phillips curve. This can be combined with the foreign-trade multiplier to yield a simple dynamic model that explains convergence of national rates of inflation toward the average "world rate."

Monetarist writing on the international transmission of inflation internationally focuses on the mechanism of price arbitrage with fixed exchange rates.[31] Empirical studies of the convergence of national inflation rates then have taken the presence or absence of such convergence as a test of the monetarist hypothesis. Here a good example is Hines and Nussey,[32] who found little evidence of such convergence. This section sketches another mechanism, consistent with the "Keynesian" view of the world, which also leads to such convergence. The purpose here is to isolate one alternative mechanism, not to elaborate an entire theory of inflation.

I begin with a standard pair of price and wage equations, as developed by Gordon or Smith, for example.[33] The percentage rate of wage increase, $\dot{W}$, is a function of the unemployment rate, u, and the rate of price increase, $\dot{P}$:

$$(11) \qquad\qquad \dot{W} = f(u) + \beta\dot{P} \qquad f_u < 0.$$

This is the usual price-augmented Phillips curve. I assume that the unemployment rate, u, is a decreasing function of the level of real output, y, given the value of potential output:

$$u = u(y) \qquad u_y < 0.$$

These two equations imply a Phillips curve relationship between the percentage increase in wage rates, $\dot{W}$, and real output, substituting $u(y)$ for u, which gives equation 12:

$$(12) \qquad\qquad \dot{W} = g(y) + \beta\dot{P} \qquad g_y > 0, \quad 0 \leqq \beta < 1.$$

The next step is development of the price equation from the labor market equilibrium condition, equation 2 in the first section, where it is recognized that the money wage equals the value of the marginal product:

$$W = Py_n.$$

This implies a rate of inflation, $\dot{P}$, given by:

$$(13) \qquad\qquad \dot{P} = \dot{W} - \dot{y}_n,$$

where $\dot{y}_n$ is the rate of growth of (marginal) labor productivity. This equation for the inflation rate, $\dot{P}$, is consistent with labor market equilibrium as in equation 2; it also could come from a constant markup price model or an

31. A good example is chapter 3 in Harry G. Johnson, *Inflation and the Monetarist Controversy* (Amsterdam: North-Holland, 1972; distributed in the United States and Canada by American Elsevier), pp. 75–108.

32. A. G. Hines and C. Nussey, "The International Monetarist Theory of Inflation: The Story of a Mare's Nest," University of London Discussion Paper 23 (Birkbeck College, Department of Economics, April 1974; processed).

33. See Robert J. Gordon, "Inflation in Recession and Recovery," *Brookings Papers on Economic Activity, 1:1971*, pp. 105–58; and Warren L. Smith, "On Some Current Issues in Monetary Economics: An Interpretation," *Journal of Economic Literature*, vol. 8 (September 1970), pp. 767–82.

assumption of constant relative shares of income between profits and wages. Substituting equation 12 for $\dot{W}$ in equation 13 gives:

$$(14) \qquad \dot{P} = \frac{1}{1-\beta}\,[g(y) - \dot{y}_n].$$

With exogenous growth in labor productivity, this equation can be summarized as saying that the rate of inflation is a function of the level of real output and the rate of growth of productivity:

$$(15) \qquad \dot{P} = h(y, \dot{y}_n) \qquad h_y > 0.$$

Holding the growth rate of productivity constant, an increase in real output (relative to potential) increases the rate of inflation.

With exchange rates fixed, the current-account balance can be written as $b(= x - m)$, a function of the home price level, P, relative to the world price level, P_w:

$$(16) \qquad x - m = b = b(P/P_w) \qquad b_p < 0.$$

As the home price level rises faster than the world rate of inflation, $\dot{P} > \dot{P}_w$, the current-account surplus declines, and vice versa.[34]

Finally, holding other exogenous variables (such as government purchases and the real value of the money stock) constant, the foreign-trade multiplier implicit in the model of the second section can be summarized as:[35]

$$(17) \qquad y = y(b) \qquad y_b > 0.$$

This completes the dynamic system. The trade balance depends on P, y depends on the trade balance, and y drives $\dot{P}$. Combining equations 15, 16, and 17, the rate of inflation as a function of the domestic price level relative to world prices and the rate of growth of productivity is:

$$(18) \qquad \dot{P} = h\{y[b(P/P_w)], \dot{y}_n\} = \lambda(P/P_w, \dot{y}_n),$$

with

$$\overset{+}{}\ \overset{+}{}\ \overset{-}{}$$
$$\lambda_p = (h_y)\,(y_b)\,(b_p) < 0,$$

as required for stability.

The system is described in the simple phase diagram of figure 5, in which

34. In a full dynamic model of inflation, dependence of imports on income, and the like, would be included. Here I analyze the basic elements in only one transmission mechanism of inflation.

35. Using the supply equation $y = y(P)$, $dy = y_p dP$. Thus effects on y in table 3 would be given by y_p times the P effects for all variables. Thus in general the foreign-trade multiplier would be

$$\frac{dy}{db} = y_p\left(\frac{dP}{db}\right),$$

where b is the current-account balance and dP/db comes from table 3.

the horizontal axis measures y and b in suitable units, and the rate of infla-tions, $\dot{P}$, is on the vertical axis. First, the y^*, b^* values are located that yield $\dot{P} = \dot{P}_w$; these are equilibrium values. Then an initial point with y_0, $b_0 < y^*$, b^* is considered. At that point $\dot{P}_0 < \dot{P}_w$, so the trade balance is increasing, pulling y and P up toward the equilibrium point, as shown in figure 5. If one begins with y, $b > y^*$, b^*, one would see movement back down the phase line. Thus, in the absence of policy action, the Keynesian-Phillips model would predict that national inflation rates would tend to converge toward the average world rate through the action of the foreign-trade multiplier alone.

This line of analysis yields two interesting implications. First, implicit in the Keynesian-Phillips view of inflation is a tendency (a) for rates of inflation to converge, and (b) for real output and unemployment rates to adjust so that rates of inflation converge. This happens through the foreign-trade multi-plier, with given rates of productivity and real-asset growth. Second, since inflation rates tend to converge in the Keynesian-Phillips view, evidence that they are converging, taken alone, does not necessarily support the monetarist view. Research designed to distinguish between Keynesian and monetary ad-justment mechanisms must go beyond the study of convergence of rates of inflation; it must model the actual mechanism behind such convergence—if it, in fact, occurs.

Conclusion: Stock Adjustment in the Keynesian Model

The static Keynesian model of the first section is a pure flow equilibrium model. Given values of the initial stocks of money and bonds (and implicitly capital) and values for exogenous variables, such as government purchases and the foreign interest rate, values are determined for the rate of return on government bonds, the price level, and the rate of flow of output and income. This equilibrium is an instantaneous moving equilibrium in a system with continuous adjustment of stocks.

Along with equilibrium values for the rate of return on government bonds, the price level, and real output, the model determines instantaneous equilib-rium values for investment, the government deficit, and the external balance. These variables *are* the rate of change of the stock variables that were initially held constant. Investment is the rate of change of the capital stock, $I = dK/dt$, and the sum of the government deficit, $g - \phi$, and the external surplus, $x - m$, is the sum of the rates of change of the money stock, dM/dt, and the bond stock, dB/dt:

$$(19) \qquad \frac{dM}{dt} + \frac{dB}{dt} = P[(g - \phi) + (x - m)] - \frac{dS}{dt}.$$

Figure 5. *Convergence of Domestic and World Rates of Inflation*

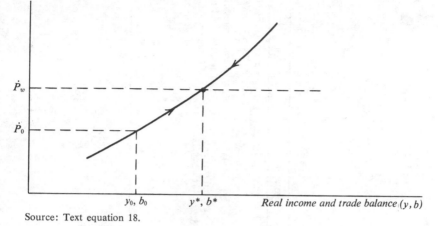

Home and world rates of inflation $(\dot{P}, \dot{P}_w)$

$\dot{P}_w$

$\dot{P}_0$

y_0, b_0 y^*, b^* *Real income and trade balance* (y, b)

Source: Text equation 18.

Thus the instantaneous equilibrium solution includes values for the rates of change of the stocks, which are in turn functions of the stocks themselves. This exposes the system as a set of differential equations in which rates of change of the stocks depend on levels of the stocks themselves; it is shown schematically in table 5.

The Keynesian model of the second section takes an arbitrarily given set of stocks and solves for equilibrium flows. These flows then move the stocks through time, presumably to a final stock equilibrium represented by a balanced growth path. The actual solution of this dynamic system is a complicated problem, on which a beginning has been made recently by Blinder and Solow, Branson, and Dornbusch.[36] But the point to be noted in conclusion here is that the Keynesian model of the first section is consistent with and part of this stock-adjustment system, giving the instantaneous-flow solutions at any point in time, based on the stocks inherited from the last point in time.

36. See Alan S. Blinder and Robert M. Solow, "Analytical Foundations of Fiscal Policy," in Alan Blinder and others, *The Economics of Public Finance;* Rudiger Dornbusch, "A Portfolio Balance Model in the Open Economy," *Journal of Monetary Economics,* vol. 1 (January 1975), pp. 3–20; and the following three articles by William H. Branson: "Macroeconomic Equilibrium with Portfolio Balance in Open Economies," University of Stockholm, Institute for International Economic Studies, Seminar Paper 22 (November 1972; processed); "The Dual Roles of the Government Budget and the Balance of Payments . . ." (see note 3 for full citation); and "Stocks and Flows in International Monetary Analysis," in Albert Ando, Richard Herring, and Richard Marston, eds., *International Aspects of Stabilization Policies* (see note 30).

Table 5. *Structure of the Stock-Adjustment System*

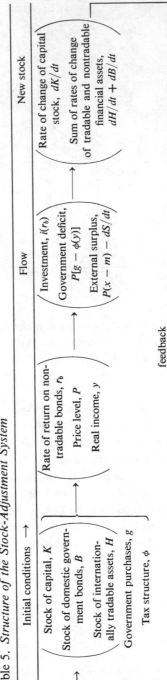

Initial conditions →	Flow	New stock
$\left(\begin{array}{l}\text{Stock of capital, } K \\ \text{Stock of domestic govern-}\\ \text{ment bonds, } B \\ \text{Stock of internation-}\\ \text{ally tradable assets, } H\end{array}\right.$ Government purchases, g Tax structure, ϕ	$\left(\begin{array}{l}\text{Rate of return on non-}\\ \text{tradable bonds, } r_b \\ \text{Price level, } P \\ \text{Real income, } y\end{array}\right) \rightarrow \left(\begin{array}{l}\text{Investment, } i(r_b) \\ \text{Government deficit,}\\ P[g - \phi(y)] \\ \text{External surplus,}\\ P(x - m) - dS/dt\end{array}\right) \rightarrow$	$\left(\begin{array}{l}\text{Rate of change of capital}\\ \text{stock, } dK/dt \\ \text{Sum of rates of change}\\ \text{of tradable and nontradable}\\ \text{financial assets,}\\ dH/dt + dB/dt\end{array}\right.$

feedback

Appendix A: Symbols and Definitions

Assets

B = stock of domestic government bonds (in dollars) (held only by domestic residents).

K = capital stock in constant dollars.

M = stock of domestically held outside money equal to central bank holdings of government debt and foreign exchange (in dollars).

S = stock of domestically held foreign securities (in dollars).

V = private sector wealth (in dollars).

$H = (M + S)$ (internationally tradable assets held domestically) (in dollars).

Prices and Employment

r_b, r_s = financial market rates of return on bonds and foreign securities.

$\overline{W}$ = rigid money wage rate.

P = price level.

e = exchange rate in units of domestic currency per unit of foreign currency.

N = employment (man-hours per year).

u = unemployment rate.

Flows

Y = nominal income.

y = income and output in constant dollars.

s = saving in constant dollars.

i = investment in constant dollars.

g = government purchases in constant dollars.

x = exports and other current-account credits in constant dollars.

m = imports and other current-account debits in constant dollars.

b = balance on current account ($b = x - m$).

ϕ = tax function.

α = shift parameter for foreign demand.

Operators

$$\dot{X} = \frac{\frac{dX(t)}{dt}}{X(t)};$$

a dot over a variable denotes a proportional time rate of change.

$$f_i = \frac{\partial f(X_1, \ldots, X_n)}{\partial X_i};$$

a subscript to a function denotes its partial derivative with respect to the relevant variables including functions of one variable. For readability, all subscripts are lower case.

All variables have a time dimension that is omitted in the text on the assumption that it is understood.

Appendix B: Derivation of the Results of Table 3

To obtain the effects of changes in the stock variables, and in g, e, and α, on instantaneous equilibrium price level and interest rate, the LM and IS total differentials can be combined:

$$
\begin{array}{c} A \\ \text{(4a)} \quad \text{LM:} \\ \text{(10a)} \quad \text{IS:} \end{array}
\begin{bmatrix} -F_p^b & -F_b^b \\ s_p & -i_r \end{bmatrix}
\begin{pmatrix} dP \\ dr_b \end{pmatrix} =
$$

$$
\begin{bmatrix} F_v^b & -(1 - F_v^b) & +F_s^b & 0 & 0 & 0 \\ -\dfrac{s_v}{P} & -\dfrac{s_v}{P} & 0 & 1 & x_\alpha & x_e - m_e \end{bmatrix}
\begin{pmatrix} dH \\ dB \\ dr_s \\ dg \\ d\alpha \\ de \end{pmatrix}
$$

The sign patterns of the A and B coefficient matrices are as follows:

$$
\begin{bmatrix} + & - \\ a_{11} & a_{12} \\ + & + \\ a_{21} & a_{22} \end{bmatrix}
\begin{pmatrix} dP \\ dr_b \end{pmatrix} =
\begin{bmatrix} + & - & - & 0 & 0 & 0 \\ b_{11} & b_{12} & b_{13} & & & \\ + & + & 0 & 1 & + & + \\ b_{21} & b_{22} & & & b_{25} & b_{26} \end{bmatrix}
\begin{pmatrix} dH \\ dB \\ dr_s \\ dg \\ d\alpha \\ de \end{pmatrix}
$$

with the a_{ij} and b_{ij} coefficients representing the entries in equations 4a and 10a. The determinant of A is positive. Inversion of A and solution for dP, dr_b gives the sign pattern of effects of changes in exogenous variables shown in table 3. The inverted solution is:

$$
\begin{pmatrix} dP \\ dr_b \end{pmatrix} = \frac{1}{|A|}
\begin{bmatrix} a_{22} & -a_{12} \\ -a_{21} & a_{11} \end{bmatrix}
\begin{bmatrix} b_{ij} \end{bmatrix}
\begin{pmatrix} dH \\ dB \\ dr_s \\ dg \\ d\alpha \\ de \end{pmatrix}
$$

The determinant of A is positive, and the dP, dr_b solutions of table 3—the short-run instantaneous multipliers—are the appropriate cross-products of the inverted A matrix and the B matrix given above.

Comments by Rudiger Dornbusch

BRANSON'S paper constitutes an interesting and successful attempt to combine elements of various macroeconomic approaches in analyzing the determination of short-run output and prices in a "small" open economy. The main elements on the commodity demand side are the Keynesian model of two commodities—relative demands that depend on the terms of trade and aggregate demand that depends on real income and the rate of interest. On the production side, output depends on the level of prices, given the money wage rate or the expected price level. In the asset markets the formulation follows the portfolio balance literature in formulating consistent asset demands and adopts a distinction between traded and nontraded securities.[37]

The model calls for an emphasis on both the role of aggregate demand and relative prices. The level of prices is central since it determines, via the level and composition of aggregate demand, the trade balance and the level of output. The level of prices determines, too, the composition of assets between money and securities.

I first discuss the Branson model from the perspective of the channels of transmission of foreign impulses, and later discuss particular properties of that model and the extent to which the model in its implications differs from the monetary approach.

Channels of transmission

The basic model can be developed in terms of the market for domestic output and the market for domestic (nontraded) securities. Equilibrium in the market for domestic output requires that demand for domestic goods equal their supply:

$$(20) \qquad y(P) = d(\bar{y}, r, V/P) + g + b(q, \bar{y}, \alpha),$$

where

$y, \bar{y}$ = domestic output and disposable real income
r = the yield on domestic debt
V/P = real wealth

37. See, too, William H. Branson, "Macroeconomic Equilibrium with Portfolio Balance in Open Economies," Seminar Paper 22 (Stockholm: Institute for International Economic Studies, November 1972; processed); Rudiger Dornbusch, "A Portfolio Balance Model in the Open Economy," *Journal of Monetary Economics,* vol. 1 (January 1975), pp. 3–20; Rudiger Dornbusch, "Capital Mobility and Portfolio Balance" in Robert Z. Aliber, ed., *The Political Economy of Monetary Reform* (Macmillan, 1976), pp. 64–81.

g = real government spending
b = the trade balance surplus
q = the relative price of domestic output in terms of foreign goods
P = the nominal price of domestic output
α = a shift parameter in the foreign demand for domestic goods.

The market for domestic debt is in equilibrium when the nominal stock of debt outstanding, B, is equal to the demand for domestic debt:

(21) $B = F(r, Y, V; r^*),$

where

Y = nominal income
V = nominal wealth
r^* = the given rate of interest in the world market.

The equilibrium condition in the asset market can be solved for the interest rate in terms of nominal income and the parameters:

(22) $r = \tilde{r}(Y, V; r^*, B); \; \tilde{r}_1 > 0; \; \tilde{r}_2 < 0; \; \tilde{r}_3 > 0; \; \tilde{r}_4 > 0.$

(Here and throughout, a tilde over a function denotes that it is a reduced form embodying the condition of asset-market equilibrium and taking nominal and real income along the supply function of output, that is, $Y = Py(P)$.)

In equation 22 an increase in money income raises the equilibrium interest rate as does a decrease in wealth. A rise in the foreign interest rate spills over, via substitution, into an increase in the domestic rate. Finally, an increase in the stock of debt outstanding will require an increase in the yield to induce the public to hold a larger stock.

The equilibrium interest rate in equation 22 can be substituted into the aggregate demand function in equation 20, and permits a definition of the excess of income over absorption, z:

(23) $z = y(P) - d(r, \bar{y}, V/P) - g = \tilde{z}(P; B, V, g; r^*).$

For given values of the parameters, B, V, g, and r^*, the excess of income over domestic absorption will be an increasing function of the domestic price level. There are three factors that combine in generating this relation. One is the increase in output that is associated with an increase in the level of prices. With a marginal propensity to spend less than unity this will cause output to rise relative to aggregate demand as prices increase. Second, the increase in the level of prices raises money demand, lowers the demand for debt and thereby raises the equilibrium interest rate, which in turn depresses aggregate expenditure at each level of output. The third factor is the reduction in the real value of money and debt arising from an increase in the level of prices.

Figure 6. *The Equilibrium Price Level and the Balance of Trade*

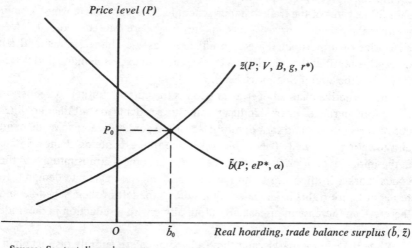

Source: See text discussion.

Given these considerations, figure 6 shows the excess of income over domestic absorption, $\tilde{z}$, as an increasing function of the price level.

The trade balance surplus, $\tilde{b}$, is a decreasing function of the domestic price level for two reasons. An increase in the domestic price level improves the terms of trade and therefore by the substitution effect lowers exports and raises imports.[38] The increase in output and therefore import demand associated with the increase in the price of domestic goods further reinforces this effect. The trade surplus is therefore shown in figure 6 as a decreasing function of the domestic price level. The schedule is drawn for a given exchange rate and price of foreign goods.

Equilibrium in the domestic goods market obtains in figure 6 at the intersection of the two schedules where the excess of output over domestic absorption equals the trade surplus. By construction the domestic securities market is in equilibrium, too.

Figure 6 is a useful summary of the channels through which foreign disturbances can affect the equilibrium domestic level of prices and output. One channel of transmission is the trade balance. Variations in the foreign demand for domestic output—represented by variations in α—will at the initial

---

38. The terms of trade are defined as $q = P/eP^*$ where e is the domestic currency price of foreign exchange and P^* the foreign currency price of imports. The statement in the text assumes that the Marshall-Lerner condition is satisfied.

price of domestic output create an excess demand and therefore raise the equilibrium price level and rate of output. In figure 6 this corresponds to a shift to the right of the trade balance schedule. The same effect would obtain if either the domestic price of foreign currency were depreciated or the foreign price of imports increased. In all three cases a change in demand for domestic output at the initial price level creates an excess demand and therefore raises the equilibrium price level.

An alternative channel of transmission is the capital market. A reduction in the foreign rate of interest induces domestic residents to shift their holdings out of foreign debt and into domestic securities, creating an excess demand and lowering the yield. This reduction in the interest rate on domestic debt at the initial level of prices, and hence money income, is transmitted into the goods market in the form of an increase in domestic aggregate demand. In terms of figure 6 this is indicated by a shift to the left of the $\bar{z}$ schedule and therefore an increase in prices and output along with a reduction in the trade surplus.

While the capital market and the trade balance are entirely distinct channels of transmission, the two have in common that they ultimately affect the demand for domestic output and therefore the equilibrium level of prices. Branson is correct in emphasizing that both channels of transmission have the distinct flavor of the Keynesian approach to the open economy in their emphasis on the interest rate as a determinant of aggregate demand, and aggregate demand as a determinant of the level of output and prices.

The role of money in this formulation is distinctly subsidiary. The supply of money plays no active role in the transmission mechanism. To see the reason for this perhaps surprising result, one must consider the monetary aspects of the model. The demand for nominal balances will depend on interest rates and nominal income:

(24) $$L = L(r, r^*, Y).$$

In equilibrium the demand will equal the supply of money where the latter is equal to domestic credit plus foreign reserves of the central bank:

(25) $$R + D = L(r, r^*, Y),$$

where

  R = foreign reserves
  D = domestic credit.

Combining equations 25 and 22 and noting that money income is a function only of the price level, one can write the equilibrium stock of foreign reserves as a function of the factors determining the demand for money, P, V, B, r^*, and domestic credit where the latter is a policy variable:

$$(26) \qquad R = \tilde{L}(P; V, B, r^*) - D.$$

Under fixed exchange rates and given the opportunity to lend and borrow *instantaneously* in the world capital market the private sector will always be in portfolio equilibrium. This implies that the private sector will always hold the desired quantity of money, and the desired position is attained by buying or selling domestic money for securities in the world market. The counterpart of the private sector's dealing is the changes in reserves of the central bank. Since the money supply is entirely endogenous and determined by demand, it cannot serve as a vehicle of transmission. In fact, monetary policy affects variables other than the central bank's balance sheet only to the extent that it affects the quantity of domestic debt outstanding or wealth.

Some implications of the model

Branson develops from his model propositions that are designed to shed light on the subject of transmission of expansionary impulses and on the difference between the proposed Keynesian approach and an alternative "monetary approach." Among the propositions is the suggestion that the relationship between the price level and the balance of payments, when influenced by exogenous disturbances, will depend on the nature of the disturbance:

... the relationship between movements in the balance of payments and imported inflation will depend on the source of the exogenous change abroad. ... [Furthermore,] it is not the increase in the net balance that generates the price increase; it is the impulse abroad (that is, in the United States) that generates both.

The proposition is not entirely correct within the framework of the Branson model. Nor is it correct, I believe, to assert or imply that the monetary approach could not be construed, in some of its variants, to predict the correct versions of the above propositions. This would lead to the perhaps obvious suggestion that in a well-specified, general-equilibrium model it will be hard to distinguish Keynesian and monetary approaches. This is not to say, however, that in judging the empirical relevance or magnitude of some effects a Keynesian might not want to give emphasis to some considerations in preference to others that he might discount as "monetary snubbings."[39]

39. For a discussion of "monetary snubbings" and the difficulty of distinguishing between "eclectic Keynesians" and "soft monetarists," see Alan S. Blinder and Robert M. Solow, "Analytical Foundations of Fiscal Policy," in Alan Blinder and others, *The Economics of Public Finance* (see note 4).

Figure 7. *International Reserves and the Balance of Payments*

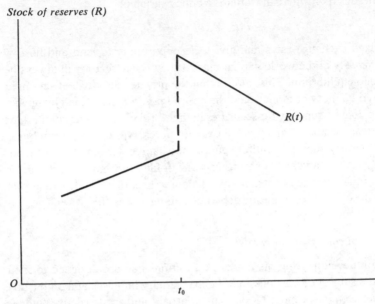

Stock of reserves (R)

$R(t)$

O

t_0

Time (t)

Source: See text discussion.

Consider now the specific objections to the proposition. Branson asserts that the effects of a foreign impulse on the relationship between price changes and changes in the balance of payments are ambiguous. This ambiguity arises, I believe, from a failure to distinguish between discrete changes in the stock of reserves at a point in time and the rate of change of reserves or the balance of payments. While this distinction is clearly recognized at some points in the Branson paper, it is glossed over when stock changes in reserves are added to the trade-account effects of various disturbances.

The point at issue can be clarified with a simple picture developed by Wallace.[40] Figure 7 shows the stock of reserves, $R(t)$, as a function of time. Up to t_0 the stock grows at the rate of the balance of payments given by the slope of the graph. At point t_0 reserves jump to a higher level and the balance of payments turns negative, as seen from the negative slope of the graph. It is important to recognize that at point t_0 there is both a change in the stock of reserves—a jump—and a change in the balance of payments from a surplus to a deficit.

40. Neil Wallace, "The Determination of the Stock of Reserves and the Balance of Payments in a Neo-Keynesian Model," *Journal of Money, Credit, and Banking*, vol. 2 (August 1970), pp. 269–90.

Branson makes predictions about changes in the stock of reserves and *not* about the balance of payments. The endogeneity of the money supply at a point in time that is implied by the ability to buy and sell money for securities in the world market at a given interest rate is reflected in discrete changes in the stock of reserves whenever a disturbance changes the demand for money (or domestic credit). To treat these discrete changes in reserves as the balance of payments and their counterpart as the capital account is conceptually incorrect.

The impact effect of a disturbance in the Branson model involves three considerations:

1. The change in the stock of reserves induced by the disturbance.
2. The change in the trade balance or current account.
3. The change in the balance of payments.

Items 1 and 2 can readily be determined from the model and are in fact laid out in table 4 where the second column should properly be labeled "reserve change," as Branson recognizes in note 26. The third item is considerably harder and requires consideration of the dynamic elements of the economy that are introduced in the concluding section of Branson's paper. In particular, assumptions are needed about the manner in which investment is financed and about the rate of creation of debt and money in the process of financing the budget. All one can say at a general level is that the balance of payments will be affected to the extent that the rate of domestic credit creation changes relative to the flow demand for money.[41]

The foregoing discussion might be criticized on the ground that portfolio adjustment internationally does not proceed in an instantaneous manner but rather as a flow adjustment to stock disequilibrium. If this is correct, the portfolio problem cannot be formulated as above, and in particular equation 9 of Branson's paper, where it is quite explicitly assumed that the public can trade debt for money instantaneously. What are required rather for this alternative approach are asset demand functions constrained by the actual holdings of foreign securities and an explicit theory of the adjustment mechanism.

The above point has been developed at some length since it is the byproduct of the correct specification of asset markets and capital mobility and is therefore one of the more interesting implications of Branson's model. The point can be summarized as follows: at a point in time reserve behavior is governed by the *stock* demand for money, given domestic credit. Over time reserve behavior is governed by the stock demand for money and the *flow* supply of assets.

41. See Rudiger Dornbusch, "Capital Mobility and Portfolio Balance," and William H. Branson, "Macroeconomic Equilibrium with Portfolio Balance in Open Economies."

Branson is entirely correct in pointing out that the foreign impulse or disturbance determines all endogenous variables and that it is not the surplus that causes the price change. This property of the impact effect of a disturbance on the price level and the balance of payments (in the absence of capital mobility and domestic credit creation) is a property of any reasonable model and is certainly a feature that is shared by the monetary approach.

To support the above suggestion, consider the following simple story: there is a reduction in the foreign demand for real balances, which, at current prices, causes an increase in real expenditure by the foreign country and leads, therefore, to an excess demand for goods in all markets. The excess demand causes prices to rise, thereby depressing the home country's real spending or, equivalently, raising its domestic real hoarding. The net effect of the disturbance is therefore an increase in the price level and a trade and balance of payments surplus for the home country. Over time the home country accumulates real balances and the price level rises further until expenditure equals income again in both countries, with lower real balances abroad and unchanged real balances at home. It is true that the path from the impact effect to the long-run effect is governed by how monetary redistribution affects real spending and thereby prices. But in regard to the impact effect itself, the price level jumps concurrently with the change in the balance of payments.

The introduction of capital mobility—one of the important aspects of Branson's paper—significantly complicates the story. Now the foreign shift out of money will be directed to securities, and at unchanged interest rates and prices there will be an excess demand for debt and an excess supply of money. The equilibrium interest rate will fall and the price level will rise, which will encourage the world to hold the existing stocks of assets. These changes imply, however, that the home country will have purchased money from the foreign country since, at lower interest rates and higher prices, the demand for nominal balances will be higher. The effects on trade and balance of payments accounts will be indeterminate and depend on the nature of the saving function and flow supplies of assets.

The Phillips curve

An imaginative extension of the analysis is offered in the third section of Branson's paper in which inflation is introduced by way of a wage-price equation. The argument assumes that wage increases depend both on the rate of price increase and unemployment where the latter is inversely related to ag-

Figure 8. *Inflation and the Terms of Trade*

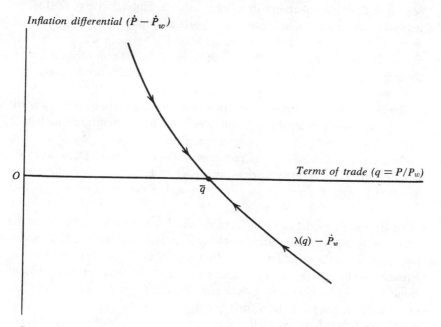

gregate demand. Aggregate demand in turn—given all other determinants—depends on the trade balance, which depends on the terms of trade. This chain allows one to write the rate of inflation as a decreasing function of the relative price of domestic goods in terms of foreign goods:

(27) $\dot{P} = \lambda(P/P_w); \quad \lambda < 0,$

where

$\dot{P}$ = domestic rate of inflation
P_w = domestic currency price of foreign goods.

The foreign rate of inflation can be subtracted from both sides of equation 27 to obtain the difference in inflation rates as a function of the relative price, given the foreign inflation rate $\dot{P}_w$:

(28) $\dot{P} - \dot{P}_w = \lambda(P/P_w) - \dot{P}_w.$

This relation is shown in figure 8 for a given foreign inflation rate, $\dot{P}_w^0$. It is readily seen from figure 8 that beginning with terms of trade that are too low the trade balance surplus, and hence demand pressure, will be high. As a consequence, domestic inflation will be high—that is, high relative to the foreign inflation rate so that the terms of trade begin to improve. As a consequence of the improvement in the terms of trade, the trade balance progressively worsens, demand pressure declines and so does the rate of inflation until it becomes equal to the foreign rate of inflation. At that point a steady-state trade balance, income, and employment level are achieved.

Branson notes that "national inflation rates would tend to converge toward the average world rate, through the action of the foreign-trade multiplier alone," independent of any monetary adjustment process. While it is entirely correct that inflation rates converge in Branson's model and do so via the effect of changing relative prices on aggregate demand for domestic output and thereby on inflation, it is not correct to neglect the monetary policies that will sustain this inflationary process.

In Branson's model one can focus on the foreign-trade multiplier to the exclusion of all other considerations only if, in fact, real income and *relative* prices are the sole variables. This condition, in turn, requires that the real interest rate be constant and that real wealth be held constant, as is obvious from inspection of equation 20. Such constancy of the real rate of interest and real wealth requires, in turn, that the authorities pursue an asset-market policy that involves an expansion in the nominal quantity of money. It is important to recognize this point since it eliminates most of the possible disagreement between monetarist and alternative approaches in this context.

A further aspect of this model that is not entirely fortunate arises when one considers changes in the foreign rate of inflation. Specifically, consider an increase in the foreign rate of inflation. In figure 9 the schedule relating the difference in inflation rates to the terms of trade shifts down and to the left. The impact effect of the higher foreign inflation rate is to generate an equal difference in inflation rates. Over time the domestic inflation rate catches up under the influence of the worsening in the terms of trade and the resulting rise of aggregate demand. The long-run effect is to worsen the home country's terms of trade, improve the trade balance, and raise income, employment, and inflation. The long-run effect on the terms of trade and the trade balance is not desirable as a theoretical feature of the model since it would be impossible to sustain it in a two-country model. Not everybody's trade balance can improve as a consequence of a higher rate of world inflation.

The problem is easily remedied by introducing long-run neutrality into Branson's wage-price equation. This is achieved by adding in equation 12 the term $(1 - \beta)\dot{P}_w$, with the consequence that the difference in inflation rates becomes independent of the foreign rate of inflation or the level of steady-

Figure 9. *Adjustment to Higher Inflation*

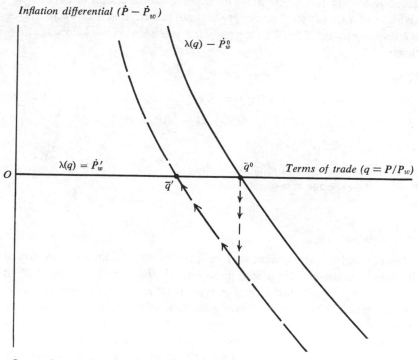

Source: See text discussion.

state world inflation. In terms of my equations this implies that equation 28 now becomes 28a:

(28a) $$\dot{P} - \dot{P}_w = \lambda(P/P_w).$$

This reformulation has the property that in the long run the terms of trade, and indeed all real variables, are independent of the world rate of inflation. Furthermore, a jump in the foreign rate of inflation now causes an instantaneous adjustment in the domestic rate of inflation. This latter feature is perhaps not entirely desirable but can be easily remedied by introducing the expected rate of inflation as the relevant argument in the wage-price equation.[42] Such

42. For a discussion of the role of import prices and expectational variables in the wage equation, see Michael Parkin, Michael Sumner, and Robert Ward, "The Effects of Excess Demand, Generalized Expectations and Wage-Price Controls on Wage Inflation in the UK: 1956–71," in Karl Brunner and Allan H. Meltzer, eds., *The Economics of Price and Wage Controls,* Carnegie-Rochester Conference Series on Public Policy, vol. 2 (Amsterdam: North-Holland, 1976; distributed in the United States and Canada by American Elsevier), pp. 193–221.

a formulation together with an expectations formation mechanism of the adaptive variety will assure long-run neutrality of the level of inflation together with a transition period of gradual adjustment that is characteristic of the Branson model. Such a reformulation is presented in the following equations:

(28b)
$$\dot{P} = \lambda(P/P_w) + \pi^e$$

(29)
$$\dot{\pi}^e = \theta(\pi - \pi^e)$$

(30)
$$\pi = \sigma\dot{P} + (1 - \sigma)\dot{P}_w$$

where

π = the actual rate of inflation of the *price level*
π^e = the expected rate of inflation.

Conclusion

In concluding these comments I wish to draw attention to two aspects of Branson's model that are indeed important for the transmission-of-inflation issue and that have quite certainly received insufficient emphasis in the monetary approach. These are respectively the concurrent variation in output and prices, including the multiplier process as an adjustment mechanism, and the explicit interaction of capital markets. Branson's treatment of these issues is very suggestive and should, along with the dynamic extensions he suggests, prove a valuable starting point for further work. Two points seem to stand out as particularly important. The first is an integration of the Phillips curve analysis with the asset markets. The second is the development of a two-country model of the asset-market interaction and the Phillips curve process. The step to a two-country model is likely to restore more endogeneity to the model and concede to monetary considerations a more central role then they require in the present treatment.

Comments by Hendrik Houthakker

THIS is a very stimulating paper. Let me just make a few points that have not already been raised by Dornbusch.

First, the treatment of the exchange rate strikes me as a little peculiar. Branson says that the exchange rate is exogenous. It is not fixed, but it is exogenous. I really do not know how this is to be interpreted. If exchange rates are, in fact, a variable because of policy rather than because of floating, some of the equations need to be revised. In particular, I am bothered by equations 4, 5, and 6 in the asset model. If there is a possibility of exchange rate changes, then presumably the interest rate, r_s, should be adjusted by the forward rate. That leads me to believe that the exchange rate is really not regarded as an exogenous variable, but is just held fixed. However, even if the exchange rate is held fixed a problem remains because the bonds that are a domestic and nontraded asset are denominated, usually, in a different currency from the foreign assets. Branson's paper, after all, does use the small-country assumption throughout. Therefore, it is perhaps logical to assume that the foreign assets are denominated in a foreign currency. This means, further, that one should be looking at the real rates of return, both on domestic and on foreign assets. Therefore, a correction should be made in r_b and r_s for changes in the price level, both at home and abroad. This changes the equations to an extent that I have not fully investigated. I would like to see this incorporated in the analysis, if my observation is valid.

Another point, which is perhaps of less quantitative importance, is that the current account is defined, apparently, to coincide with the trade balance; no allowance is made anywhere as far as I can see for interest flows. Yet interest flows will change if r_s changes. Therefore, I believe that the phrase "current account" is a misnomer. More important, some allowance should be made for the effect of changes in the foreign interest rate on interest flows, and therefore on the balance of payments as a whole.

Third, I share some of the questions that have already been raised about the conclusion that the Phillips curve mechanism, combined with the foreign-trade multiplier, will give the same convergence of inflation rates that follows from certain other models. But I think my objections are somewhat different from those of Dornbusch. They relate primarily to equation 16: the seemingly innocuous equation that says that the trade balance (which Branson calls the current-account balance but really is not) is a function only of the home price level relative to the world price level. That, I think, is very odd, because presumably the trade balance also depends on income, both in the home country and abroad.

If the dependence on income in the home country is included in the foreign-trade multiplier, is the trade balance independent of the growth of income abroad? It is, after all, a dynamic system, in which one cannot assume that income or output in the rest of the world is constant; but that seems to be assumed here. In a dynamic situation, one has to have a term representing the growth of foreign income. It was pointed out in the important papers that Harry Johnson wrote in the 1950s on the relation between growth and the balance of payments that the income elasticities have a very important effect on the trade balance in a growth situation, as one essentially has here.

It is quite possible that foreign income grows rapidly enough to improve the trade balance of the home country, even though the inflation rate in the home country is higher than the inflation rate in the rest of the world. In that case, there would be no convergence, because the arrows no longer go the way Branson draws them in figure 5. I believe it is important to correct this and to make clear that the convergence that Branson observes holds only when certain elasticity conditions are satisfied.

These may be relatively minor changes, but without them, the conclusions do not really follow.

General Comments

ALEXANDER SWOBODA noted that in Branson's formulation the trade balance depends only on real income, assuming that the exchange rate is fixed, but that Branson nevertheless obtains a relationship between the trade balance and the price level from the monotonic relationship postulated between real income and the price level. If some disturbance changes the aggregate supply curve and shifts the relationship between real output and the price level in such a way that when real income returns to its original value the price level does not, then, given foreign prices, the model would leave the trade balance unchanged. With the trade balance depending solely on real income, it too would be unchanged, yet one would expect that if there is any price elasticity of demand for the goods in question, then the trade balance should change. Relating the trade balance to the price level only through the relationship that both bear to real income appears unsatisfactory. Branson makes the point that the introduction of assets that are not internationally traded implies that an increase of domestic credit does not necessarily cause an equal outflow of international reserves. Mundell has also obtained this result in the short run for models with imperfect capital mobility, but Branson's model is an improvement in that it specifies the stock portfolio equilibrium correctly.

Rudiger Dornbusch said that Branson has also shown that the specific domestic effect of open market or foreign exchange market operations depends on what asset is used as a medium of intervention.

William Branson agreed that exchange rates should be included in the account of what happens in the asset markets and that interest income should be included in the current account. These could both probably be incorporated but had been omitted from the paper because of its emphasis on the exposition of asset changes that are often neglected in the literature.

ODD AUKRUST

Inflation in the
Open Economy:
A Norwegian Model

Odd Aukrust, Statistisk Sentralbyrå, points out that the ideas contained in the models
of this paper grew out of research work undertaken at the Central Bureau of Statistics
of Norway during the early 1960s. Thus the distinction between sheltered and exposed
industries was introduced for the first time in the Bureau's *Economic Survey 1962*. The
models themselves were formulated and published in 1966 in two reports by a group
of three economists who were called upon to provide background material for that
year's round of negotiations on wages and agricultural prices. Members of the committee (Utredningsutvalget for inntektsoppgjørene 1966) were Chairman Odd Aukrust,
Fritz C. Holte, Agricultural College of Norway, and Gerhard Stoltz, Norwegian School
of Economics and Business Administration. The committee produced two reports. The
first of these contained the multisector, short-term model summarized on pages 113–17
(see also note 16). The second report, which was a study of the causes of long-run price
developments in Norway, contained the two-sector, long-term model described on pages
117–22 (see also *Innstilling II fra Utredningsutvalget for inntektsoppgjørene i 1966,
avgitt 20. oktober 1966* [Second Report of October 20, 1966, by the Reporting Committee for the 1966 Income Settlement] Oslo: Office of the Prime Minister, 1967).

Two considerations have determined the direction of this paper. One is a recognition that the developments of prices and incomes in small and medium-sized economies are strongly affected by events in the outside world and that, for this reason, price theory, more than hitherto, should address itself explicitly to the problems of open economies. The other is a belief that a disaggregated type of analysis is needed if one is to understand better the network through which exogenous price impulses, whether originating at home or abroad, are propagated through the economy.

Work in the Nordic countries on problems of price trends and income distribution has recognized the need for disaggregating the analyses and, in particular, that price impulses from abroad may affect individual industries very differently, depending upon their ties with the international market. Consequently, a two-sector model distinguishing between "sheltered" industries and "exposed" (or "competitive") industries has been found indispensable, even in the simplest of analyses aiming at understanding the mechanism of price and income distribution.

The Norwegian Model: A Brief Presentation

I shall begin by outlining two variants of such disaggregated models—a two-sector version for the long run and a multisector version for the short run—that have been in use in Norway since 1966. The ideas contained in these models grew out of research undertaken at the Central Bureau of Statistics of Norway during the early 1960s.

Sheltered and exposed industries

In Norwegian economic thought a fundamental distinction is drawn between sheltered and exposed industries.

Exposed industries (E industries) are those that are exposed to strong competition from abroad, either because they export most of their products or because they sell their products on the domestic market under strong foreign competition. Mining, most manufacturing industries, shipping, and, in some countries, agriculture are typical examples of this category.

Sheltered industries (S industries), on the other hand, are those whose products are marketed at home under conditions that leave them relatively free of foreign competition.[1] Building and construction, power generation, a few manufacturing industries, and most service industries belong to this category. Because no clear-cut line of division exists between exposed and sheltered industries, arbitrary decisions are unavoidable when distinguishing between the two groups in actual model building. According to the classification used at present in Norway, the exposed industries contribute approximately 30 percent of net national product and employ some 22 percent of the labor force.[2]

There are two reasons why a distinction between sheltered and exposed industries is crucial in an analysis of prices and incomes. First, the two groups of industries show marked differences in price behavior. The output prices of the exposed industries will be largely determined in the world market. These industries, therefore, cannot compensate for a cost increase through an upward adjustment of prices; if their costs increase, they must absorb the whole effect in the form of reduced profits and perhaps reduced production.[3] The sheltered industries are in a different position. Because they do not risk losing their market to foreign competitors they tend to compensate for cost increases by raising output prices. There is considerable evidence that in Norway at least increasing costs (for example, as a result of higher wages) are passed on quickly by the sheltered industries in a way that leaves the share of profits

1. Either because of the physical nature of their products or because of government protection. The fact that they are relatively free of foreign competition does not mean, of course, that firms within these industries do not compete on prices among themselves. It does mean, however, that as a group they may raise prices when costs go up without having to fear a loss of market to foreign firms.

2. Because the exposed industries will typically consist of nonsubsistence agriculture, mining, and part of manufacturing, the contribution to total product of these industries in most developed and semideveloped economies may be expected to be of the order of magnitude of 30 percent, as was found for Norway. One would expect the share of the exposed industries in total employment to be about the same size, whereas in Norway it is in fact significantly smaller; this is probably because the exposed industries in Norway (including basic metals and shipping) happen to be rather capital-intensive. Indeed, data for Sweden put the contribution of the exposed industries in 1967 at 28.5 percent of total product and their share in total employment at 30 percent. (See Gösta Edgren, Karl-Olof Faxén, and Clas-Erik Odhner, "Wages, Growth and the Distribution of Income," *Swedish Journal of Economics,* vol. 71 [September 1969] pp. 133–60.)

3. Throughout this paper the word "profits" is used as a synonym for "operating surplus" as defined in the U.N. Present System of National Accounts. Hence, for any single industry (or group of industries), wages plus profits equal net value added equals factor income originating in that industry (or group of industries).

Figure 1. *The Share of Profits in Total Factor Income
(Wages plus Profits), Norway, 1953–73*

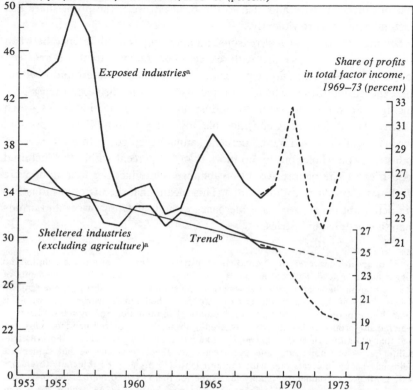

Source: Adapted from Odd Aukrust, "PRIM I: A Model of the Price and Income Distribution Mechanism of an Open Economy," *Artikler*, no. 35 (Oslo: Statistisk Sentralbyrå), p. 25.

a. Solid line: data based on the old national accounts data for 1953–69 and the old sector classification used in PRIM I (scale to the left). Broken line: revised national accounts data and modified sector classification used in PRIM II (scale to the right).

b. The trend line is estimated from the old national accounts data and is based on the old sector classification used in PRIM I. The dotted line is an extrapolation of this trend.

in factor income largely unaffected.[4] It can be seen from figure 1, that for the sheltered industries as a group this share has fluctuated only moderately from one year to the next, following a downward trend that may be taken to reflect

4. The same observation has been made for Sweden (Edgren and others, "Wages, Growth and the Distribution of Income"), and for Finland (Hannu Halttunen and Ahti Molander, "The Input-Output Framework as a Part of a Macroeconomic Model: Production-Price-Income Block in the Bank of Finland Quarterly Econometric Model," *Kansantaloudellinen aikakauskirja* [*Finnish Economic Journal*], vol. 68, no. 3 [1972], pp. 219–39.) Fluctuations of the profit share around the trend may be due to fluctuations in capacity utilization, a point that has been explicity built into the Finnish model.

the decreasing number of employers and self-employed relative to the number of employees within the group.[5] In the exposed industries, which are much more sensitive to the movements of the national cost level relative to that of other countries and also to the business cycle, the profit share has fluctuated much more violently.

Second, for technological reasons, another important difference between the two industry groups exists with respect to productivity trends. It has been found in Norway that output per man has risen much more rapidly within the exposed industries, which are typically capital-intensive and mass-producing, than within the sheltered industries where service industries weigh heavily. The difference is considerable: over the period 1957–69, product per man-year increased by 6.3 percent (annual average) within the exposed industries as a whole, but by no more than 2.4 percent within the sheltered industries.[6] (The picture would not change if product per man-hour were used as the productivity measure.) This means that the exposed industries are better able to absorb wage increases without affecting prices and profits than the sheltered industries.[7]

5. In regard, however, to individual industries within the group the relation no longer holds. Instead, national accounts data show considerable erratic movements of the relationship between profits and wages for most industries. In this light the remarkable stability of the relationship for the group of sheltered industries as a whole is difficult to explain. It may be that (1) fluctuations in output caused by the trade cycle, which cause profits to deviate from the trend, are not synchronized beween industries, and that (2) although most firms apply some variant of the cost-plus pricing principle, selling prices are not continuously corrected as direct costs change but rather are adjusted at long intervals and with random lags. (Firms may be reluctant to change selling prices too frequently; it may take time for them even to realize that costs have changed; sometimes a small increase in costs may be used as an excuse for a long contemplated and considerable increase in prices; and so on.) Such randomness would explain observations made in the past but would not, of course, guarantee indefinitely the future stability of the profit-wage ratio of the group of sheltered industries as a whole.

6. In Sweden (1960–68) product per man-hour (not man-year) increased by 8.2 percent and 3.8 percent (trend values) within the exposed and sheltered industries, respectively (see Gösta Edgren, Karl-Olof Faxén, and Clas-Erik Odhner, *Wage Formation and the Economy* [London: Allen and Unwin, 1973], p. 74). The same source quotes Finnish data (1960–68) showing productivity increases of 4.6 and 3.0 percent for exposed and sheltered industries, respectively (annual averages), and German data (1960–65) showing labor productivity increases (annual averages) of 4.6 percent for the export sector and 2.9 percent for the total economy.

7. This statement holds as a generalization. It is not necessarily the case, however, that the rate of productivity increase in exposed industries is uniformly high and in sheltered industries uniformly low. For instance, inland transport, although classified as a sheltered industry, has productivity increases comparing favorably with those of many exposed industries.

The two-sector, long-run model

A simple two-sector model based on these characteristic properties of sheltered and exposed industries purports to describe the mechanism determining the long-term movement of wages and prices in an economy where, because of foreign trade, national wage and price trends are subject to strong price impulses from abroad. The main argument may be sketched as follows:

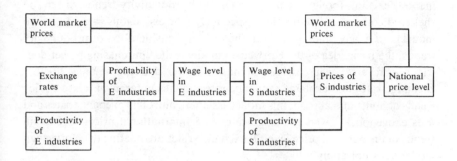

Put into words the argument may be summed up in five propositions:

1. World market prices for products of the E industries, together with existing foreign exchange rates, determine the output prices the E industries can ask, measured in national currency. These prices, together with the existing technology (the productivity of E industries) are key factors in determining the profitability of the E industries, meaning by "profitability" the ability of the E industries to earn a surplus available for distribution as wages or profits.

2. The profitability of the E industries is a key factor in determining the wage level of the E industries: mechanisms are assumed to exist which ensure that the higher the profitability of the E industries, the higher their wage level; there will be a tendency for wages in the E industries to adjust so as to leave actual profits within the E industries close to a "normal" level (for which, however, there is no formal definition).

3. The wage level that establishes itself within the E industries determines the wage level within the S industries: mechanisms are assumed to exist (for example, market forces or the solidaristic trade union policy under the centralized wage bargaining system of Norway) that tend to keep wages in the two industry groups in a normal relation to each other.

4. The wage level within the S industries together with the existing technology (productivity of S industries) determines the output prices of these

industries: mechanisms (for example, some type of cost-plus pricing) are assumed to exist that will cause the S industries to adjust output prices so that a normal relation between wages and prices is maintained.

5. Output prices of E industries, output prices of S industries, and world market prices for goods not produced at home, each appropriately weighted, determine the national price level.

Taken as a whole, then, the model explains national wage and price trends (the endogenous variables of the model) in terms of price trends in the world market, existing foreign exchange rates, and productivity trends within the sheltered and exposed industries respectively (the exogenous variables of the model). In a way, and apart from the explicit consideration of productivity trends, the basic idea of the Norwegian model is the "purchasing power doctrine" in reverse: whereas the purchasing power doctrine assumes floating exchange rates and explains exchange rate changes in terms of relative price trends at home and abroad, this model assumes controlled exchange rates and uses exogenously given exchange rates and international prices to explain trends in the national price level. If exchange rates are floating the Norwegian model does not apply.

Critical to the validity of the model are the controlling mechanisms postulated by propositions (2), (3), and (4) above. Do such controlling mechanisms in fact exist, and how exact are the relationships dictated by them? In answer to these questions there is no need to say much about (3) and (4): there is plenty of evidence, both in Norway and Sweden, that the relation between wages in S industries and E industries have remained remarkably stable through time,[8] and the observed stability of the profit share within the S industries (figure 1) supports the view that some mechanisms of the kind assumed by propositions (3) and (4) do in fact exist.[9]

The truth of proposition (2)—that wages in the E industries tend to adjust so as to leave the E industries with normal profits—is much more doubtful. In fact, historical data show profits of the E industries to have fluctuated considerably (figure 1). The relation between "the profitability of E industries" and "the wage level of E industries" that the model postulates, therefore, is certainly not a relation that holds on a year-to-year basis. At best, it is valid only as a long-term tendency and even so only with considerable slack. It is equally obvious, however, that the wage level in the E industries is not com-

8. See, for example, Lars Calmfors's paper in this volume, and Edgren and others, *Wage Formation and the Economy,* chap. 6.

9. Some of the models described in the last section are explicit in suggesting mechanisms that may result in a normal level of relative profits establishing itself within sheltered sectors.

pletely free to assume any value irrespective of what happens to profits in these industries. Indeed, if actual profits in the E industries deviate much from normal profits, it must be expected that sooner or later forces will be set in motion that will tend to close the gap.

There are at least three corrective mechanisms that may be counted upon to have this effect:

First, the system of *wage negotiations* will tend to correct deviations. Abnormally high, or low, profits will be taken as a sign by the trade unions to ask for larger, or smaller, wage increases than usual and at the same time weaken, or strengthen, the tendency of entrepreneurs to resist the claims. Negotiated wage increases will therefore be higher, or lower, the higher, or lower, the actual profits of the E industries.

Second, *market forces* will tend to work in the same direction as organized negotiations through the mechanism of the wage drift. Abnormally high, or low, profits will motivate higher, or lower, demand for labor by entrepreneurs for production and investment purposes. High, or low, profits will therefore lead to a tighter, or less tight, labor market and ultimately influence the size of the wage drift. In extreme situations, if actual wages are kept low enough (for example, through some "successful" incomes policy) to generate extraordinarily high profits in the exposed industries, and consequently excess demand for labor, a wage explosion may follow that will quickly reduce profits to more normal levels.[10]

Third, *economic policy* will aim to keep profits of the E industries at a reasonable or normal level. In particular, economic policy tends to step in whenever wages become so high (and the competitiveness of E industries so low) as to endanger full employment and the balance of payments. In such cases deflationary measures are resorted to in order to slow down wage increases and thus restore profits to normal levels.[11]

This leads to the hypothesis that mechanisms exist which tend to make the

10. One wonders whether economic events in the Netherlands during the early 1960s are not more easily explained through this mechanism than through some variant of a monetary theory such as that of M. W. Holtrop (in "On the Effectiveness of Monetary Policy: The Experience of the Netherlands in the Years 1954–69," *Journal of Money, Credit, and Banking,* vol. 4 [May 1972] pp. 283–311). The hypothesis is that the Dutch incomes policy, which had been successful for a number of years in keeping the rate of increase in wages and prices in the Netherlands below the rates of other countries, but which too long left the rate of the guilder unchanged, simply had to break down in the end because of tensions building up in the labor market.

11. Richard E. Caves points out (in "Looking at Inflation in the Open Economy," in David A. Belsley and others, eds., *Inflation, Trade and Taxes* [Ohio State University Press, 1976], p. 84), rightly in my mind, that this part of the model has the implication of making macroeconomic policy to some degree endogenous.

Figure 2. *The "Wage Corridor"*

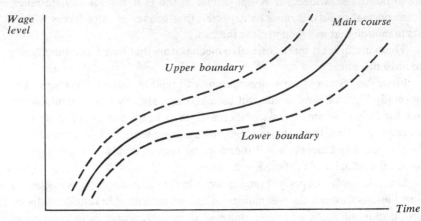

Source: See text for explanation.

national wage level follow a course through time set ultimately by price trends abroad, by the chosen exchange rates, and by the productivity trends of the E industries. Such a course is referred to in Norwegian studies as the "main course" of wages. It is defined as the level of wages consistent, at any point of time, with normal profits of the E industries. Because of the slack in the system, however, wages are free to diverge, within bounds, from either side of the main course, but the further they diverge the stronger will be the forces pulling them back. Wages are in fact free to move within "a corridor with elastic borders" as illustrated by figure 2. If wages are near the upper border of the corridor, profits of the E industries will be abnormally low, and vice versa.

Corresponding to the main course of wages there will be a "main course" through time that the national price level will have to follow, again with an allowable margin on either side ("a price corridor"). The main course of prices will depend, in part, on the factors determining the position of the main course of wages. But it will depend also on the productivity trend of the S industries since this determines the extent to which S industries have to raise output prices in response to higher wages in order to maintain a normal relation between profits and wages.[12]

12. Inasmuch as productivity increases faster in the E industries than in the S industries, the model implies that the national price level will tend to rise even though foreign trade prices remain constant. This does not mean, as is sometimes believed, that the country in question will have a higher rate of inflation than its trading partners. The question of possible intercountry differences in inflation rates is discussed later in this paper.

So far, constant foreign exchange rates have been assumed. A devaluation will abruptly shift the wage corridor upward and lead to a steeper rise of actual wages and therefore prices in the years following the devaluation. A revaluation, on the other hand, will shift the wage corridor downward and cause the wage and price increase to slow down. Therefore, other things being equal, countries that have devalued their currencies (France and the United Kingdom) would be expected to have witnessed higher price increases than others, whereas countries that have revalued (West Germany and the Netherlands) would be expected to have had less inflation than others. (Of course, although some correlation undoubtedly exists between exchange rate changes and price trends, the direction of causation may sometimes be subject to dispute.)

The many-sector, short-run model

More insight into the mechanisms that determine price and income trends within an economy may be gained by disaggregating further the two-sector model sketched above. An example is the Norwegian multisector price income model.[13] PRIM may be characterized briefly as a short-term, cost-push, input-output model. It is *short term* in that it takes wage rates to be given, that is, fixed by negotiations; because the model does not attempt to explain wage trends, it is useless as a theory of long-term price movements. It is *cost-push* in that it explains prices entirely in terms of costs. There is no reference to demand as a possible source of price increases; the model derives changes in prices and income shares (the unknowns) from changes in wage rates, agricultural prices, productivities, world market prices, and a few other given variables assumed to affect costs. It is an *input-output* type of model in that it takes into account that higher output prices in one industry mean higher input prices, that is, higher costs, in other industries. Price interrelationships can therefore be examined using an input-output technique somewhat similar to that used in the study of quantitative interrelationships.

The structure of PRIM in its early versions has been described in detail

13. PRIM has been designed primarily as an instrument to help in negotiations on wages and prices. In Norway, such negotiations are strongly centralized and take place biennially. In advance of each round of negotiations the model is used to provide the negotiating parties with forecasts of the developments to be expected in the coming two years in prices and income shares. The forecasts are prepared in alternatives, each alternative representing one possible outcome of the negotiations that are about to start. Through such forecasts, it is intended that the negotiating parties be in a better position to anticipate the consequences, for themselves and for the national economy, of alternative courses open to them.

elsewhere.[14] All that needs to be repeated here is that the main endogenous variables of the model are the national price level and various categories of income such as total wages and the profits of various industry groups. The model takes as exogenous those variables that, within the time horizon of the model, are supposed to be important in influencing prices and/or incomes. They include the wage rate and agricultural prices (both assumed to be set through negotiations), prices of different categories of exported and imported goods as given in the world market, indirect taxes, and, finally, two variables that together determine output: labor productivities and employment. Repercussions on productivities and employment from incomes through demand are neglected. The model simply assumes that there is always sufficient demand somewhere for the products of the industries. The original version of PRIM (PRIM I, 1966) distinguished six industry groups that were later extended to seven (PRIM II, 1972):[15] three sheltered industry groups (agriculture, building and construction, other) and four exposed industry groups (fisheries, import-competing manufacturing, shipping, other export-oriented industries).[16]

Crucial to the working of the model are the assumptions made with respect to price behavior:

• Output prices of the agricultural and fishing industries are assumed to be exogenous, stipulated through income settlements negotiated with the government.

• Output prices of sheltered industries apart from agriculture are assumed to be endogenous and determined through some variant of cost-plus pricing in such a way that the profit share in these industries (profits as a share of factor income) will assume a predetermined value (either a trend value or, if a better guess is available, some other value stipulated by the user of the model).

• Import and export prices are supposed to be given, determined by the world market.

• Output prices of import-competing manufacturing are assumed to follow the (given) prices of similar imported goods. (In the practical use of

14. Odd Aukrust, "PRIM I: A Model of the Price and Income Distribution Mechanism of an Open Economy," *Review of Income and Wealth,* series 16 (March 1970), pp. 51–78; also published, with additional statistical material, as *Artikler,* no. 35 (Oslo: Statistisk Sentralbyrå [Central Bureau of Statistics], 1970).

15. Vidar Ringstad, "PRIM II: A Revised Version of the Price and Income Model," published as *Artikler,* no. 44 (Oslo: Statistisk Sentralbyra, 1972).

16. *Innstilling fra Utredningsutvalget for inntektsoppgjørene 1966, avgitt 22. januar 1966* [Report by the Reporting Committee for the 1966 Income Settlement, January 22, 1966] (Oslo: Office of the Prime Minister, 1966).

the model they may be considered exogenous and stipulated in some other way if a better guess is available.)

• Output prices of shipping and other export-oriented industries are assumed to follow the (given) export prices.[17]

Throughout, percentage changes in output prices are assumed to be the same for all deliveries from any one industry, for example, the same for sales at home and on the export market.[18]

One way in which PRIM can be used to shed light on the working of the economy appears in table 1.[19] A selected number of important exogenous variables of the model are listed vertically on this table along with the share of profits earned in sheltered industries other than agriculture. The table

17. To treat export prices as exogenously given, independently of costs, may be justifiable as a first approximation. Even a small country like Norway, however, obviously has price-setting power in certain industries, for example, shipping. If, therefore, a set of national models of the PRIM type were to be combined into a world model, a different solution would have to be chosen. In such a model world market prices would become endogenous variables to be determined through some price-setting mechanism, involving supply and demand relationships.

18. The description in the text applies to a version of PRIM which was in use until lately. The more recent version, termed PRIM II, appears as an aggregated variant of the submodel for prices contained in the much bigger and more general model MODIS IV. In this version of PRIM some new features have been added that complicate the model structure but do not change much the basic ideas:

• The input-output structure of the model has been changed from a sector-by-sector to a commodity-by-sector basis.

• The number of sectors has been kept flexible.

• The price of a given commodity flow is no longer assumed to be the same in all uses but may differ depending on origin and destination; accordingly, each commodity may have one import price, one export price, and one domestic price.

• Import and export prices are determined on the world market and are therefore exogenous.

• Domestic prices are either exposed or sheltered. If they are exposed, they are normally assumed to follow corresponding import prices. If they are sheltered, they are either regulated (subject to price control or stipulated by publicly controlled enterprise) or negotiated (prices of agricultural products) or cost-determined through cost-plus pricing.

The new version of PRIM offers more flexibility than the old one in that it can handle more sophisticated hypotheses about price behavior than the crude dichotomy between prices that are either sheltered or exposed. For the time being, however, far too little is known about how prices are actually determined to be able to make much use of these potentialities of the model.

19. The table of effects reproduced here is for 1967. It was computed on the basis of PRIM I in which construction was included with "sheltered industries other than agriculture," and is not shown separately in the table. A PRIM type of analysis of U.S. inflation for the 1970–73 period is presented by William Nordhaus and John Shoven in "Inflation 1973: The Year of Infamy," Challenge, vol. 17 (May/June 1974), pp. 14–22.

Table 1. *Effects of a 1 Percent Change in Wages, Agricultural Prices, Productivity, Other than Agriculture on Prices, Income, and the Distribution of Income, 1967*

Exogenous variable that is increased 1 percent	Price changes (percent)		Income changes			
	Products from sheltered industries[a]	Consumer price level	Total factor income	Total wages income[b]	Income from	
					Agriculture	Fisheries
Wages and salaries						
All industries[d]	0.68	0.47	270	307	−13	−3
Sheltered industries[a]	0.68	0.47	270	217	−13	−3
Import-competing industries	...	...	...	40	...	...
Shipping	...	...	...	23	...	...
Export-oriented industries[c]	...	...	...	28	...	...
Prices						
Agricultural	0.03	0.08	37	...	39	e
Fish	0.01	0.01	7	...	−1	13
Productivity						
Agriculture	...	...	21	...	21	...
Sheltered industries[a]	−0.83	−0.57	49	...	16	4
Import-competing industries	...	...	59	...	...	...
Fisheries	...	...	11	...	...	11
Shipping	...	...	70	...	...	...
Export-oriented industries[c]	...	...	57	...	...	...
Total employment						
Agriculture	...	...	21	...	21	...
Sheltered industries[a,f]	−0.15	−0.10	320	217	3	1
Import-competing industries[f]	...	...	59	40	...	...
Fisheries	...	...	11	...	...	11
Shipping[f]	...	...	70	23	...	...
Export-oriented industries[c,f]	...	...	57	28	...	...
Export prices						
Shipping	0.01	0.01	106	...	e	e
Export-oriented industries[c]	0.05	0.05	97	...	−3	e
Sector prices of imported intermediate goods						
Agriculture	...	...	−2	...	−2	...
Sheltered industries[a]	0.08	0.05	−5	...	−2	e
Import-competing industries	...	...	−35	...	...	...
Fisheries	...	...	−1	...	...	−1
Shipping	...	...	−30	...	...	...
Export-oriented industries[c]	...	...	−28	...	...	...
Sector prices for imported final goods						
Imported consumer goods[g]	...	0.13	...	...	...	...
Competing imports[h]	0.05	0.12	106	...	−1	−1
Imported capital goods (excluding ships)[i]	0.05	0.03	−19	...	−4	e
Imported ships[g]	...	...	−38	...	...	...
Share of profits						
Effect of a percentage-point change in share of profits in sheltered industries (r_2)[j]	1.00	0.68	393	...	−19	−5

Source: Odd Aukrust, "PRIM I: A model of the Price and Income Distribution Mechanism of an Open Economy," *Artikler*, no. 35 (Oslo: Statistisk Sentralbyrå, 1970), pp. 18–19.

    a. Excluding agriculture.
    b. Excluding agriculture and fisheries.
    c. Excluding shipping.
    d. This is to be understood as a proportional increase in W_j ($j = 2, 3, 5, 6$).
    e. Negligible effect.
    f. Proportional increase of 1 percent in total employment (N) and number of wage and salary earners (L) implying a 1 percent increase in the number of self-employed.

Employment, Foreign Prices, and the Share of Profits in Sheltered Industries

| (millions of kroner) | | | | Income changes (percent) | | | | | | | |
| Profits | | | | | | | | Profits | | | |
Sheltered industries[a]	Import-competing industries	Shipping	Export-oriented industries[c]	Total factor income	Total wages income[b]	Income from Agriculture	Fisheries	Sheltered industries[a]	Import-competing industries	Shipping	Export-oriented industries[c]
94	−48	−27	−40	0.57	1.00	−0.61	−0.45	1.00	−3.54	−2.79	−2.05
94	−8	−4	−12	0.57	0.71	−0.61	−0.45	1.00	−0.62	−0.37	−0.64
...	−40	...	...	...	0.13	...	...	...	−2.92	...	...
...	...	−23	...	...	0.08	...	...	...	...	−2.43	...
...	...	...	−28	...	0.09	...	...	...	...	...	−1.42
...	−1	e	−1	0.08	...	1.76	−0.02	...	−0.05	−0.01	−0.06
...	e	e	−5	0.01	...	−0.04	1.77	...	−0.01	−0.02	−0.26
...	...	...	...	0.04	...	0.94	...	...	...	...	...
...	10	4	15	0.10	...	0.73	0.54	...	0.74	0.44	0.77
...	59	...	...	0.12	...	...	...	...	4.34	...	...
...	...	...	...	0.02	...	...	1.50	...	...	...	...
...	...	70	...	0.15	...	...	...	...	...	7.34	...
...	...	...	57	0.12	...	...	...	...	...	...	2.92
...	...	...	...	0.04	...	0.94	...	...	...	...	...
94	2	1	3	0.68	0.71	0.13	0.10	1.00	0.13	0.08	0.14
...	19	...	...	0.12	0.13	...	...	...	1.42	...	...
...	...	...	...	0.02	...	...	1.50	...	...	...	...
...	...	47	...	0.15	0.08	...	...	...	...	4.91	...
...	...	...	29	0.12	0.09	...	...	...	...	...	1.50
...	e	107	e	0.22	...	−0.01	−0.01	...	−0.01	11.20	−0.01
...	−6	−1	108	0.21	...	−0.16	−0.04	...	−0.46	−0.08	5.56
...	...	...	...	...	...	−0.07	...	...	...	...	...
...	−1	e	−1	−0.01	...	−0.07	−0.05	...	−0.07	−0.04	−0.07
...	−35	...	...	−0.07	...	...	...	...	−2.53	...	...
...	...	...	...	...	...	...	−0.10	...	...	...	...
...	...	−30	...	−0.06	...	...	...	...	...	−3.19	...
...	...	...	−28	−0.06	...	...	...	...	...	...	−1.42
...	...	...	...	...	...	...	...	...	...	...	...
...	112	−1	−3	0.22	...	−0.05	−0.07	...	8.20	−0.09	−0.17
...	−5	e	−10	−0.04	...	−0.18	−0.03	...	−0.36	−0.02	−0.51
...	...	−38	...	−0.08	...	...	...	...	...	−3.98	...
453	−12	−5	−18	0.83	...	−0.88	−0.65	4.81	−0.90	−0.54	−0.92

g. Goods imported directly for consumption.

h. The price of imported goods that compete on the Norwegian market with products from "import-competing industries."

i. Increase in the price of capital goods leads to an increase in depreciation calculated in current prices. This immediately reduces income from agriculture and profits in the exposed industries and causes "sheltered industries other than agriculture" to raise output prices.

j. The share of profits in "sheltered industries other than agriculture" in 1967 was 30.3 percent (of total factor income). The figures in this row show what the effects would have been if this share, other things being equal, had risen by 1 percentage point, that is, to 31.3 percent.

shows the expected effects of a partial 1 percent change of the exogenous variable of each row on each of the endogenous variables listed at the top. The effects are expressed partly as percentages and, in the case of income variables, in kroner as well. The first row indicates, for instance, that a 1 percent increase in the wage level, other things being equal, may be expected to raise the level of consumer prices by 0.47 percent, to increase the total of nominal factor incomes by 0.57 percent, to decrease income from agriculture by 0.61 percent, and to decrease profits of "import-competing industries" by 3.54 percent. If one reads down the columns, on the other hand, table 1 gives information for each endogenous variable on the effect of changes in exogenous variables. All effects specified in the table may be considered as additive for small changes in the exogenous variables. The combined effect, therefore, of a simultaneous change in two or more exogenous variables may be gauged by adding the effects of each variable taken separately. For instance, a parallel increase of all import prices by 1 percent, if other factors remain the same, may be expected to raise the level of consumer prices by 0.33 percent (0.05 + 0.13 + 0.12 + 0.03, second column).

Some Policy Implications

Some of the policy implications of these models, which may be applicable to other economies as well, are pointed out below. The models, if correct, hold a message of great relevance to the choice of targets for an incomes policy.

The scope for a national price policy

Granted that the models give a reasonably accurate description of the price and income distribution mechanism of small to medium-sized open economies, what scope is there in such countries for a national price policy? To what extent, and through what instruments, can national price trends be influenced by government actions? The answers depend on the time horizon of the analysis.

In the very long run, say, for periods of from five to fifteen years or more, according to the long-run model the trends of national wages and prices are determined by international trends modified by the exchange rate. If the model is correct, it is impossible for national prices, measured in international currency units, to deviate from world market prices. The conclusion drawn from the long-term model is that national authorities have little or no room for influencing the long-run trend of the price level of their countries if foreign exchange rates are kept stable.[20] Contrarily, manipulating the exchange rate (disregarding, for the moment, possible balance of payments problems) may be expected to be a very potent long-run price policy instrument; for example, a country that revalues by 10 percent is virtually guaranteed over the ensuing years to experience 10 percent less inflation than other countries, and less than it would otherwise have had. The trouble is that foreign exchange rate changes cannot always be manipulated freely, nor are they well suited as regular instruments of a price policy because exchange rate changes, when they are foreseen and expected, are bound to create unwanted speculation.

In the short run, say, over periods of from one to two years, lasting from the conclusion of one round of wage negotiations until the conclusion of the next, the short-run model suggests that the ability of national authorities to influence price developments is again very limited. Under Scandinavian circumstances, where wage negotiations take place for most groups of wage earners simultaneously, the outcome of the negotiations will determine the course of wages (apart from the wage drift) for a period ahead. The authorities can do little under such circumstances. They may try to slow down the wage drift through a policy of demand management or monetary policy, but such measures will probably be ineffective in the short run. They may try to counter the price increases triggered by the wage increases by resorting to the use of subsidies, price controls, and similar devices. These may delay—but cannot indefinitely hold back—the price increases to be expected as a consequence of the wage settlement. Yet such policies may have limited success in cases where tariff settlement contains an escalation clause tying wages during the tariff period to the index of consumer prices; should an escalation clause be part of the tariff agreement, a slowing down of the price increase

20. In Norway, over the period 1951–71, the level of wages (labor costs per man-year) increased by 7.9 percent on an annual average. Prices, measured by the gross domestic product deflator, increased by 3.9 percent a year. The model asserts that these wage and price increases were unavoidable, given world market price trends and the prevailing exchange rates. A different wage increase, say 8.9 percent or 6.9 percent a year instead of 7.9 percent (which would have led to a somewhat higher or lower price increase than 3.9 percent a year), if it had been possible, would have meant a wage level in 1971 some 20 percent above or below the actual level. At a wage level 20 percent above the actual, Norwegian industries would certainly not have remained competitive. At a wage level 20 percent below the actual, E industries in 1971 would have shown enormous profits. None of these could have happened without triggering the correction mechanisms assumed by the long-term model.

may serve to slow down the wage increase and thus reduce the rise in wages and prices in the course of the tariff period.

In the medium run, however, say, over a period of from two to five years, the scope for a national price policy should be considerable. According to the long-term model, it is perfectly possible for wages to rise more or less steeply within the boundaries set by the wage corridor: actual wages may move from a position near the lower boundary of the corridor toward the upper boundary, or from the upper boundary toward the lower boundary, depending in part on the outcome of wage negotiations taking place during the period and in part on the size of the wage drift. Because the outcome of wage negotiations and the size of the wage drift presumably depend to some extent on the general economic climate (for instance, the tightness of the labor market) it should be possible for policy authorities to influence wage and price developments in the medium run through demand management or monetary policies, supplemented perhaps by an incomes policy. Note, however, that such a course of action, to the extent that it succeeds in holding back price increases, will have achieved this through holding back wage increases, thus shifting the distribution of the national income in favor of the owners of enterprises in the E industries. (This points to the existence of a latent conflict between price and income distribution targets, a subject discussed further below.) Observe, moreover, that the scope for such a policy is limited by the need for actual wages to remain always within the boundaries of the wage corridor. In a world with rising prices, where the wage corridor will point steeply upward at stable exchange rates, a national policy aiming at stable prices, however successful in the short and medium run, cannot succeed in the long run unless it is backed by repeated revaluations of the national currency.

Implications for an incomes policy

The Norwegian models, if correct, also hold a message of great relevance for the choice of targets for an incomes policy: with foreign exchange rates given, the national price level is determined through simultaneous developments in wages, agricultural prices, indirect taxes and subsidies, prices of exports and imports, and productivities. Since this is so, no simple formula can serve as a guidepost, once and for all, for an incomes policy aiming at stable prices. The assertion often heard, for instance, that a necessary and sufficient condition for price stability is that wages should rise in step with average productivity, is a false statement. An incomes policy adhering strictly to this principle might lead to a falling, stable, or increasing national price level depending on what happens simultaneously to the other exogenous variables of the model; in particular, the resulting national price trend would depend strongly on the trend of world market prices (although price impulses from abroad might conceivably be counteracted through exchange rate adjustments).

According to PRIM, the national price level and the distribution of the national income are determined through the same set of exogenous variables. But the ways in which the price level and the individual income shares are affected by the exogenous variables are not identical, as is seen in the entries in the columns of table 1 or the equations of PRIM in reduced form.[21] It is most improbable, therefore, that a set of values for the exogenous variables can be found that will result in a desired development of prices and at the same time in a desired distribution of incomes: only by chance will world market prices and productivities (which society does not control) change in such a way that an incomes policy can be designed that will ensure stable prices without having undesired effects for the (pretax) distribution of income, or maintain the established distribution of income without allowing unwanted changes in the price level. In other words, society's targets for prices and for income distribution may very well be in conflict. Those who aspire to an intelligent price and incomes policy must start by facing this fact squarely.

Incidentally, one has to give up the popular belief that the struggle over income shares may be viewed simply as a confrontation between wage earners and employers. Instead, wage earners and owners of enterprises in the sheltered industries may well have a common interest in rising wages since, according to the model, a rise in wages will lead automatically, by means of price adjustments, to a proportionate increase in profits of the sheltered industries. Together these groups may be able to obtain a (short-run) gain in real incomes at the expense of other groups (farmers and owners of enterprises in the exposed industries). The parties confronting each other in the struggle over income shares, therefore, may be said to be (1) the farmers, (2) the owners of enterprises in the sheltered industries and the wage earners, and (3) owners of enterprises in the exposed industries.[22]

Farmers can work actively to increase their share of the national income through demanding higher prices for agricultural output. Wage earners and owners of enterprises in the sheltered industries can work actively to increase

21. Reproduced in Aukrust, "PRIM I," pp. 77–78.

22. The reasoning in this paragraph is based on the short-run version of the Norwegian model and describes possible outcomes of the fight over income shares in the short run. In the long run one would expect a tendency for wages, profits in S industries, and profits in E industries to remain in a normal relation to each other, in conformity with the long-run model described above.

their share of the national income through demanding or allowing higher wages. Owners of enterprises in the exposed industries, on the other hand, can work actively to increase their share of the national income only through opposing the price and wage claims of the other groups. The implication is far-reaching: the whole burden of holding back on wage increases and avoiding cost-push inflation is seen to rest with a small group of enterprises in the exposed industries, since all other groups (wage earners, farmers, enterprises in the sheltered industries) may increase their income in the short run by allowing the national cost and price level to be inflated. It should perhaps not be surprising that modern society has shown itself prone to inflation.[23]

Properties of the Norwegian Model

A number of questions about the Norwegian model need further consideration. To what extent does it provide a theory of inflation? What are its shortcomings? By what mechanism are inflationary pressures transmitted from abroad? What is the role of demand in the model? What light does it throw on the differences in rates of inflation among countries?

General and national theories of inflation

For a body of ideas to qualify as "a theory of inflation" it must be able to explain both prices and wages; that is, prices and wages should both enter the reasoning as endogenous variables. Judged by this criterion it is clear that the Norwegian approach does not qualify as an inflation theory in the same sense as some competing approaches, such as the monetary approach or the excess demand–Phillips curve approach originated by Keynes.

This is quite obvious in the case of the short-run (PRIM) variant of the model. PRIM says nothing about how the wage level is determined; it simply takes the wage level (or rather changes in it) as given. What it purports to do is to describe in some detail how changes in national prices and income shares follow from ("are determined by") given changes in wages and other predetermined variables such as world market prices. Although the model may contribute to a better understanding of the way in which inflationary

23. It is conceivable that entrepreneurs in E industries might try to protect their interests by working to get the exchange rate changed rather than by opposing wage claims, although this possibility has not been considered in the text. To the extent that they succeed in obtaining a devaluation of the national currency the inflationary trend will be increased.

impulses work their way through the economy, it has nothing to say about the origin of these impulses. It contributes nothing to an understanding of what the propelling forces of inflation are.

With respect to the long-run variant of the model the position is different. The key element here is a mechanism making the national wage level dependent mainly on international prices, the foreign exchange rate, and productivities of the exposed industries. Other components of the model are assumptions (the same as in PRIM) about the price behavior of different categories of industries. The total outcome is a theory that, for an open economy, explains wages and prices in terms of technology (productivities), the use of policy instruments (choice of exchange rate, measures designed to influence the position of actual wages within the wage corridor), and factors outside national control (international prices). At the national level, therefore, the Norwegian model has the necessary formal properties of a theory of inflation. It is no theory of world inflation, however, because it does not attempt to explain world market prices. Unlike the monetary and Keynesian approaches it is not a general theory capable of explaining the phenomenon of inflation as such.

Shortcomings of the Norwegian model

From a formal point of view the Norwegian model suffers from weaknesses that limit its usefulness even at the national level. Two in particular should be noted. First, both the short-run and long-run variants of the model, in their present formulation, are static rather than dynamic. Therefore they ignore the time dimension of the inflationary process. Second, the long-run model is nonoperative since, so far, no operational definition has been given of "normal profits," a key variable in the model. It follows that the concepts of "the main course" of wages and "the wage corridor" are also nonoperational concepts. It may not be possible, therefore, to tell whether, at any particular point of time, actual wages are "high" or "low" in the wage corridor. Nor can the degree to which actual wages deviate from their main course be indicated. For this reason the model is not helpful in the formulation of quantitative statements about the implications of wage trends, past and present.

The transmission mechanism of the inflationary process

According to the Norwegian model, inflationary tendencies are imported into one country from others solely through foreign trade prices. These price effects are of various kinds. Three classes may be distinguished.

DIRECT EFFECTS OF IMPORT PRICES. The effects under this heading are the following:

1. Price increases of imported consumer goods. Such increases will almost immediately be reflected in the level of consumer prices of the importing country. According to PRIM, a proportionate increase of 1 percent in the prices of all imported consumer goods may be expected in Norway ultimately to raise the level of consumer prices by 0.13 percent, as table 1 indicates.

2. Price increases of supplementary imports of raw materials and capital goods. Such increases are passed on by the producers into prices of final goods, presumably with some time lag. The ultimate effect, according to PRIM, of a proportionate increase of 1 percent in the prices of these goods will be in Norway a rise in the level of consumer prices of 0.08 percent.

3. Price increases of competitive imports. Such increases affect the national price level by inducing producers in the exposed industries to raise their selling prices for similar commodities. (If the goods in question are consumer goods, the price increase will at the same time affect the national price level through the channel described under (1) above.) Again some time lag has to be reckoned with. Assuming that a 1 percent increase in the prices of competitive imports will cause a 1 percent increase in the selling prices of national producers of similar commodities, the effect on the level of consumer prices will be 0.12 percent, according to PRIM, under Norwegian conditions.

To summarize, the total direct price effect to be expected, under Norwegian conditions, from a proportionate increase of 1 percent of all import prices can be put at 0.33 percent (0.13 + 0.08 + 0.12).

DIRECT EXPORT PRICE EFFECTS. When prices of exported goods rise on the world market, prices charged for these goods on the national market will also tend to rise. Whether the goods in question are consumer goods or intermediate goods, the level of consumer prices will be affected, possibly with a time lag. The direct price effect to be expected, under Norwegian conditions, from a proportionate increase of 1 percent of all export prices has been calculated by PRIM to be 0.06 percent.

INDIRECT EFFECTS THROUGH THE WAGE LEVEL. Under this heading comes the complex mechanism described above whereby rising export and import prices will lead, as a result of improved profitability of the exposed industries, to a rise in the national wage level that in turn causes the sheltered industries to raise their selling prices. The magnitude of this effect is difficult to calculate exactly; however, in the long run, national prices might be expected to move roughly parallel to prices in other countries. The time needed for this transmission mechanism to work will be rather long.

The direct effects of changes in import and export prices have been well recognized in the literature. Less attention has been given to what may be the main contribution of the Norwegian model: the central role that it ascribes to the wage level in the transmission mechanism. This role is derived from the view that changes in the level of wages in a national economy are strongly related to economic developments in other countries. Not only this idea but the far-reaching conclusions that follow from it appear to have been overlooked or given insufficient emphasis in the literature so far.

While emphasizing the transmission of inflationary impulses through foreign trade prices and wages, however, the Norwegian approach neglects the transmission mechanisms assumed by the monetary and Keynesian approaches. According to the monetary approach, inflationary tendencies are transmitted from one country to another chiefly through the liquidity effects arising from a surplus or a deficit on the current balance, plus or minus net capital flows. According to the Keynesian approach, the transmission mechanism is to be sought in the demand effects arising from increased exports to countries already experiencing demand inflation. The Norwegian approach tends to dismiss both of these effects as of secondary importance compared with the direct and indirect price effects.

It should be pointed out, perhaps, that although the monetary, Keynesian, and Norwegian approaches each stresses different aspects of the transmission mechanism of inflation while suppressing others, the three approaches are not mutually exclusive. Rather they are complementary in showing that inflation can travel along many routes.[24] Within a more generalized framework all approaches could, in principle, be accommodated.

The role of demand

In judging the role played by demand in the Norwegian approach a distinction should be made between commodity markets and the labor market. In the commodity markets demand is not supposed to matter much (except indirectly through the effect that demand for commodities has on demand for labor as discussed below). PRIM, in its crudest formulation, assumes commodity prices to be either exogenous or determined by cost-plus pricing. Thus, these are supposed to be completely unaffected by demand. In actual use of PRIM for prognostic purposes, however, it is sometimes recognized,

24. For an attempt to give a complete list of possible routes, see "The International Transmission of Inflation," *OECD Economic Outlook*, no. 13 (July 1973), pp. 81–96.

by ad hoc reasoning "outside the model," that the percentage markup may depend on the general state of demand. Of course, this reasoning could be made an inherent part of the model: whereas the markup percentage at present is considered a parameter of the model it could be considered, alternatively, a variable whose magnitude would be related to some indicator of the pressure of demand through a new relation to be added to the model.[25]

In the labor market, in contrast, the Norwegian approach assumes the balance between supply and demand to play a crucial role. According to the long-term model this balance is a key element in the correction mechanisms that are supposed to guarantee that actual wages will not deviate far from the main course of wages. I have already mentioned that one such mechanism is the system of wage negotiations. There can be little doubt that the size of the wage increases that are demanded and granted during wage negotiations will be influenced, among other things, by the state of the labor market. A related correction mechanism is the phenomenon of the wage drift. There is plenty of evidence that the state of the labor market also influences the amount of the wage drift that will take place between wage negotiations.

There is no disagreement, therefore, as to the ultimate effect that demand is supposed to have on prices between the Norwegian approach on the one hand and the monetary and Keynesian approaches on the other. All agree that excess demand will cause commodity prices to rise, but they differ in the assumptions made about the mechanism producing this result. The monetary and Keynesian approaches focus primarily on commodity markets and stress the pull on commodity prices exerted by excess demand for commodities. The Norwegian approach focuses on the labor market and stresses the pull that excess demand for labor exerts on wages, assuming rising wages, in turn, to exert a push effect on commodity prices. Since all these mechanisms, however, may be operating together and since excess demand for labor is hardly possible without excess demand for commodities, the difference is more one of emphasis than of principle. Although the short-run model PRIM, which considers the wage level as exogenously given, may justly be referred to as a cost-push model, such a description is inadequate to the Norwegian approach as a whole: if there is excess demand pushing up wages, with firms raising prices as a result, the situation may well be characterized as demand inflation.

The various approaches differ more fundamentally when it comes to listing and evaluating factors that may cause demand to become excessive. The monetary and Keynesian approaches tend to look for these causes in faulty monetary or budgetary policies. The Norwegian approach in addition allows

25. For example, see the way in which this was done in the Finnish companion to PRIM described below.

for another potent source of trouble, that is, the possibility of a faulty combination of incomes policy and foreign exchange rate policy, causing the wage level to be set too low relative to wages in other countries. The result will be abnormally high profits in the exposed industries, inducing them to expand their demand for commodities and labor.

Note one implication of these remarks for the possibilities of testing the three approaches. One may find, and indeed many studies show, a significant negative correlation between wage-price increases and the level of unemployment. Such findings do not necessarily confirm the validity of the Phillips curve, nor do they necessarily refute the thesis of the Norwegian approach: the observed fluctuations in prices and wages on the one hand and in demand for labor on the other may both have been caused by events abroad that have affected the economy in the manner assumed by the long-term Norwegian model.[26]

Small and large economies

Two key assumptions of the Norwegian model are, first, that exposed industries are pacesetting in the wage determination process, and, second, that exposed industries are price takers and accept output prices as given on the world market and have no ability to influence them. These assumptions may be reasonably realistic in the case of a small economy with a relatively large exposed sector. Assumption (1), in particular, and perhaps assumption (2) are less realistic in a relatively closed economy that is at the same time big enough for its demand and supply of some commodities to affect world market prices.

To such an economy the Norwegian model may not apply. Still, the dis-

26. Caves makes the same point in the following words: "The structure of the Aukrust model indeed raises a statistical question about applying a simple Phillips-type relation to highly open economies. Suppose that the Aukrust model is correct about the prevalent source of price disturbances, namely, movements in the world prices of traded goods. Suppose also that the nation manages its macroeconomic policy with one eye on external balance. An increase in traded-goods prices raises profits and induces expansion and wage increases in this sector, and the fiscal authorities permit aggregate demand to expand and unemployment to fall because of the favorable external balance. The price increase thus leads to greater demand pressure and reduced unemployment, rather than the other way around! Faster wage increases and lower unemployment result from common ultimate causes. The curve-fitters should at least seek assurance that they have the direction of causation right. . . . The apparent prevalence of 'Phillips curve' relations suggests the sufficiency of a closed-economy model of inflationary processes, but international linkages could generate a spurious Phillips relation with the causality reversed." ("Looking at Inflation in the Open Economy," pp. 94, 95; see note 11 for full citation.)

tinction between sheltered and exposed industries may help to explain the inflationary process, although the chain of causation may be found to be very different from what it is in the small and open economy. Assume the pace-setting industries in the wage determination process to be contained in the sheltered sector. Then the trend of national wages would be determined by national factors independent of developments abroad, for instance, through some process consistent with, say, the monetarist approach or the Keynesian-Phillips curve approach. From the sheltered industries the wage increases would be passed on to the exposed industries. The result might be a profit squeeze in the exposed industries and a deterioration of the trade balance. Or it might be exactly the opposite, depending on whether national wages went up more quickly or more slowly than wages in other countries. Then the well-known adjustment processes of the monetarist-Keynesian approaches would begin to apply.[27]

Intercountry differences in rates of inflation

The implications of the Norwegian model for intercountry differences in rates of inflation should be clearly understood. They may be conveniently analyzed by means of a two-country, four-commodity model. Constant exchange rates are assumed.

Let the two countries be denoted i and j. For country i the (percentage) rate of price inflation p^i is:

$$\text{(1)} \qquad p^i = \alpha^i p_S^i + \beta^i p_E^i + \gamma^i p_E^j,$$

where

p_S^i = the rate of price inflation of (nontraded) output of country i's S industries

p_E^i = the rate of price inflation of (home-consumed) output of country i's E industries

p_E^j = the rate of price inflation of output of country j's E industries (country i's import)

α^i, β^i, and γ^i = the appropriate weights reflecting the combination in which the three kinds of output are sold in country i.

Similarly, the rate of price inflation of country j is:

$$\text{(2)} \qquad p^j = \alpha^j p_S^j + \beta^j p_E^i + \gamma^j p_E^j,$$

27. I owe this point to Caves who suggests: "The model in this guise may hold some interest for explaining developments in the United States, where several large industries that appear to be important wage-setters are only marginally exposed to international competition." (Ibid., p. 85.)

where

$$\dot{p}_S^j = \text{the rate of price inflation of (nontraded) output of country}$$
$$j\text{'s S industries}$$

α^j, β^j, and γ^j = the appropriate weights reflecting the combination in which
the three kinds of output are sold in country j.

Assume for each country, in accordance with the long-run Norwegian model, that the wage level is determined by the productivity of the E industries and the prices obtainable internationally for the output of the E industries in such a way that the wage share of the E industries remains constant. Then, as a long-run tendency,[28]

(3)
$$\dot{w}^i = \dot{p}_E^i + \dot{q}_E^i$$

and

(4)
$$\dot{w}^j = \dot{p}_E^j + \dot{q}_E^j,$$

where

$\dot{w}^i$ and $\dot{w}^j$ = the rates of wage inflation in countries i and j, respectively
$\dot{q}_E^i$ and $\dot{q}_E^j$ = the rates of productivity change in E industries of countries
i and j, respectively.

I assume, furthermore—again in accordance with the Norwegian model—that prices in the S industries are determined through cost-plus pricing. Then

(5)
$$\dot{p}_S^i = \dot{w}^i - \dot{q}_S^i$$

and

(6)
$$\dot{p}_S^j = \dot{w}^j - \dot{q}_S^j,$$

where

$\dot{q}_S^i$ and $\dot{q}_S^j$ = the rates of productivity change in S industries of countries
i and j, respectively.

In general, the product (or product mix) of the E industries in country i will be different from the product (or product mix) of the E industries in country j. Therefore, the prices of these products will not, in general, have identical price trends. I assume, in a Marshallian way, that the prices of two goods will tend to move in inverse proportion to the productivities in the industries producing them. Then, as a long-run tendency,

---

28. Here, as well as in equations 5 and 6, I neglect the price effects of cross-deliveries of commodities (materials) between industries. To take such cross-deliveries into account would complicate the reasoning considerably without much changing the conclusion.

(7) $$\dot{p}_E^i - \dot{p}_E^j = -(\dot{q}_E^i - \dot{q}_E^j).$$

Where do equations 1 to 7 lead?

Note that, by definition, the difference in price inflation between countries i and j may be derived from equations 1 and 2 as

(8) $$\dot{p}^i - \dot{p}^j = (\alpha^i \dot{p}_S^i - \alpha^j \dot{p}_S^j) + (\beta^i - \beta^j)\dot{p}_E^i + (\gamma^i - \gamma^j)\dot{p}_E^j.$$

In order to simplify, assume that commodities are demanded in the same proportion in the two countries; this will approximately be the case in countries with reasonably similar income levels and standards of living. This means that $\alpha^i = \alpha^j \ (= \alpha)$, $\beta^i = \beta^j$, and $\gamma^i = \gamma^j$. Then equation 8 is reduced to

(8a) $$\dot{p}^i - \dot{p}^j = \alpha(\dot{p}_S^i - \dot{p}_S^j),$$

or, because of equations 5 and 6,

$$= \alpha(\dot{w}^i - \dot{q}_S^i - \dot{w}^j + \dot{q}_S^j).$$

Inserting equations 3 and 4 in equation 8a and rearranging gives

(9) $$\dot{p}^i - \dot{p}^j = \alpha[(\dot{p}_E^i + \dot{q}_E^i) - \dot{q}_S^i - (\dot{p}_E^j + \dot{q}_E^j) + \dot{q}_S^j]$$
$$= \alpha[(\dot{p}_E^i - \dot{p}_E^j) + (\dot{q}_E^i - \dot{q}_E^j) - (\dot{q}_S^i - \dot{q}_S^j)]$$

which because of equation 7 reduces to

(10) $$\dot{p}^i - \dot{p}^j = -\alpha(\dot{q}_S^i - \dot{q}_S^j).$$

Equation 10 shows that, under the simplifying assumptions made, differences in the rates of price inflation among countries will reflect differences in the rate of productivity increases in their sheltered industries, and only such differences. The higher the productivity increase in the sheltered industries of one country relative to that of other countries, the lower relatively will be the rate of price inflation of that country.

Note that rates of productivity increases in the exposed industries do not enter into equation 10. Therefore differences in these rates cannot be a source of differences in rates of price inflation under the assumptions made in the model. This result was obtained because it was assumed, first, that different countries produce different commodities for export and, second, that the prices of these commodities change over time in inverse proportion to productivities. Together these assumptions imply that wages have to change at the same rate in all countries. (Equations 3 and 4 together with 7 imply $\dot{w}^i = \dot{w}^j$.) If the model had been specified so as to allow nominal wages to change at different rates in different countries (for example, allowing countries to produce partly identical commodities for export and assuming productivities in the export industries to increase at different rates in different countries), the simple equation 10 would no longer hold.

Testing the Norwegian Model

An economic model may be tested in various ways. One possibility is to study the validity of the individual behavioral relations that are part of the model. Another possibility is to study the ability of the model to account for actual developments. Attempts along both these lines are described below.

Testing the price behavior relations

The assumptions made in the Norwegian model about the price behavior of industries are listed on pages 113–14. My early attempt to compare these assumptions with facts has been reported in detail.[29] Among the conclusions reached the following may be worth repeating here:

• The assumption made for the sheltered industries, namely, that they tend to adjust output prices through some cost-plus pricing principle in such a way that the relation between wages and profits conforms with a certain trend value, stood up well against the data. It was noted, however, that profits tended to fall short of the trend value in years when production was unfavorably influenced by the trade cycle. This seemed consistent with a pricing principle according to which the markup percentage was chosen so as to give the firm normal profits in years with normal output.

• The assumption made for competing manufacturers, namely, that output prices tended to follow import prices of similar goods imported by Norway, appeared to be doubtful. During the 1960s these industries seemed to have had considerably more scope for raising output prices than the model assumed.[30]

• The assumption made that percentage changes in output prices are the same for all entries along one industry row of the input table (that is, for all deliveries of an industry irrespective of their uses, as in table 1) was clearly not consistent with the data. Although this is a standard assumption in input-output analysis it may not be well founded when the model distinguishes only a small number of industries, each of them turning out a wide variety of prod-

29. Aukrust, "PRIM I." (See note 14 for full citation.)
30. The explanation could be that the sector is "exposed" with respect only to some of its output and "sheltered" so far as other output prices are concerned. It appears that a Canadian model described by Gigantes and Hoffman has been constructed to allow for this possibility. (See T. Gigantes and R. Hoffman, "A Price-Output Nucleus for Simulation Models," in A. Brody and A. P. Carter, eds., Input-Output Techniques [Amsterdam: North-Holland, 1972; distributed in the United States and Canada by American Elsevier], pp. 319–39.)

ucts that are unlikely to be sold in the same proportions to all categories of users. The practical importance of this for the model, however, was not found to be serious.

A more rigorous testing of the price behavior assumptions of the model was recently undertaken by Vidar Ringstad. Ringstad applied econometric methods to Norwegian data in order to test a large number of alternative hypotheses about pricing behavior of industries. The data available to him consisted of annual national accounts data for the 1961–69 period on prices and other relevant variables for about 120 individual industries classified according to market orientation.[31]

It is impossible here to give more than a sample of Ringstad's computations. Of particular interest is his attempt to estimate, for various industry groups, the parameters of the relation

(11) $P_H = aC + bP_E + cP_I + u,$

where P_H is the seller's price of home-produced goods delivered to the home market, C represents the unit variable costs (actual costs not normalized for business cycle effects), P_E is the price of exports, P_I is the price of competing imports, and u is a residual error with zero mean and constant variance.

On the assumption that the Norwegian model is correct and that home market prices adjust to world market prices without time lag (an assumption not necessarily made by the model) it might be expected that for sheltered industries

$$a > 0, b = c = 0;$$

for export-oriented industries

$$b = 1, a = c = 0;$$

and for import-competing industries

$$c = 1, a = b = 0.$$

These expectations are not supported by Ringstad's findings, as table 2 shows. Ringstad finds unit value costs to be the dominating explanatory variable for the home market price in all groups of industries. Prices of competing imports are found to have had a significant but small impact on home market prices of import-competing industries, an impact in the direction expected

31. Vidar Ringstad, *Prisutvikling og prisatferd i 1960-årene: En presentasjon og analyse av nasjonalregskapets prisdata, 1961–1969* [*The Development and Behaviour of Prices in the 1960's: Presentation and Analysis of the Price-Data of the Norwegian National Accounts, 1961–1969*], Samfunnsøkonomiske Studier no. 23 (summary in English) (Oslo: Statistisk Sentralbyrå [Central Bureau of Statistics], 1974).

Table 2. *Estimated Parameters of a Simple Price Behavior Relation, by Industry Group*[a]

Group	Number of industries in group	$\hat{a}$	$\hat{b}$	$\hat{c}$	$\hat{\sigma}$
Sheltered industries	23	1.095 (0.041)	0.081 (0.043)	0.127 (0.048)	0.068
Exported-oriented industries	16	0.770 (0.155)	0.079 (0.107)	0.111 (0.075)	0.091
Import-competing industries	31	0.854 (0.056)	−0.116 (0.044)	0.283 (0.044)	0.065

Source: Vidar Ringstad, *The Development and Behaviour of Prices in the 1960's*, tables 4.1, A.2, B.2, C.2, pp. 166, 171–73. (See note 31 for full citation.)
a. The numbers in parentheses are standard errors of estimates.

and, understandably, a slight positive impact also on home market prices of sheltered industries. The price of exports seems to have had a small positive impact on sheltered industries, a small negative impact on import-competing industries, and no significant impact whatsoever on home market prices of export-oriented industries, which is indeed surprising.

It is obvious that Ringstad's findings do not support the price behavior assumptions of the Norwegian model. His attempts to test many alternative hypotheses about price behavior, however, have not given more acceptable results. (One possible explanation could be that his various formulas have failed to capture properly the time structure of the price determination process.) Seen as a whole, Ringstad's findings are not encouraging. Perhaps the main conclusion to be drawn is that the problem of how prices are actually determined in various industry groups cannot be studied successfully using the kind of data available to him (annual data for implied price indexes of the national accounts).

At least two possible sources of data error are to be noted. First, the price data in question are aggregated to such a degree that there is no assurance that price indexes observed for sales on the home market, for exports, and for competitive imports refer to "identical commodities" (or a given commodity mix). Second, as Ringstad carefully points out, the alleged output price indexes of the national accounts are in a large measure based on cost indexes, namely, input price indexes and wage indexes.[32] This means that

32. Because this source of error may be important in other countries as well, Ringstad's figures deserve to be quoted as a warning, especially since the national accounts data of Norway are presumably no worse than those of most other countries. He finds input price indexes or wage indexes to be the empirical basis of "output price

there is spurious correlation between the observations available for the variable P_H of equation 11 and its explanatory variables.[33]

Testing the wage relation

According to the Norwegian model the national wage level is determined by the profitability of the exposed industries (defined above as the ability of these industries to pay out wages and profits), which in turn depends on world market prices, foreign exchange rates, and productivities. Indirectly, therefore, the model assumes the national wage level to depend on world market prices expressed in the national currency. The precise form of this relation has not been spelled out, however. It is difficult, therefore, to test this particular part of the model and no such test has been attempted in Norway.

But the extensive research undertaken for a number of years in many countries to determine a "wage relation" is clearly relevant to the issue. Studies that find wage changes to be strongly related to rates of profits in the exposed industries (or to total profits, since fluctuations in total profits tend to mirror fluctuations of profits in exposed industries) may be said to support the Norwegian hypothesis, whereas findings that changes in the wage level depend on past price changes, the balance of demand and supply in the labor market, or both might seem to speak against it. The latter conclusion, however, may not always be well founded since, as it was pointed out above, observed price changes and the state of the labor market in the past may have had a common root in developments abroad.

This is not the place to attempt a summary of the vast literature devoted to the wage relation; nevertheless, reference should be made to the study by Nordhaus presenting estimates for seven countries of alternative wage equa-

---

indexes" used to deflate no less than 43 percent of total domestic output. Another 12 percent of total domestic output was deflated by consumer price indexes and 17 percent by wholesale price indexes; these indexes are based on directly observed prices for goods and services but are nevertheless unsuitable for the purpose because they reflect the prices of imported as well as domestically produced goods. Only for the remaining 28 percent of total domestic output were price indexes available which, although not always of good quality, were at least conceptually suited for the purpose. To this category belonged unit price indexes, sector price indexes constructed especially for the national accounts, and implicit sector price indexes resulting from estimates at constant prices.

33. This could be a serious source of error. To minimize its effects Ringstad omitted from his calculations no less than forty-seven industries where he knew cost indexes to dominate the empirical basis of the output price indexes. To some extent, however, the same source of error may also have affected the price indexes of some of the seventy industries actually retained in his study.

tions based on competing theories of inflation.[34] One of the alternatives studied is supposed to represent the Norwegian-Scandinavian approach which, in Nordhaus's formulation, is termed the export-constrained theory of wage determination.[35] Nordhaus assumes wages, w_t, to be related to current and past import prices, p_t, by

$$(12) \qquad \Delta \ln w_t = m_0 + m_1 (0.5 \, \Delta \ln p_t + 0.33 \, \Delta \ln p_{t-1} + 0.17 \, \Delta \ln p_{t-2}).$$

He finds the import price coefficient, m_1, to be large and significant for Japan, Sweden, and the United Kingdom, "indicating that it could have a large effect on wages,"[36] but small and sometimes insignificant for Canada, France, West Germany, and the United States. When comparing equation 12 with some other equations, including those based on the monetarist viewpoint and the Phillips curve, Nordhaus finds the export-constrained theory of wage determination to outperform the monetarist theory in all cases and the Phillips curve approach in all cases except Canada and the United States, and possibly West Germany. For small-to-medium open economies, therefore, Nordhaus's study gives considerable support to a vital part of the Norwegian model.

Testing the model as a whole

No attempt has been made, so far, to make the Norwegian long-run model as a whole the subject of a formal econometric test. One reason is that the model has not been given the strict mathematical formulation required by such a test.[37] In particular, the wage equation implied by the model has not been explicitly spelled out. Furthermore, for the time being a test would be hampered by lack of data since an ongoing revision of the national accounts has caused a serious break in all relevant time series in 1967.

The postwar Norwegian history of wages and prices, however, seems to suggest that the model might be expected to survive an empirical test reasonably well. There are clear indications that the chain of causation in the past has run from world market prices and exchange rate policy, by means of the wage determination process, to the national price level. Thus the assumed

34. William D. Nordhaus, "The Worldwide Wage Explosion," *Brookings Papers on Economic Activity, 2:1972*, pp. 431–64.

35. Ibid., pp. 451–55.

36. Ibid., p. 454.

37. The mathematical formulation of the long-run model given by Holte is intended to serve pedagogical purposes. It is too simplified to provide a starting point for a serious testing of the Norwegian approach. (See Fritz C. Holte, "A Model for Estimating the Consequences of an Income Settlement," *Economics of Planning* [Oslo], vol. 8, no. 1-2 [1968], pp. 57–69.)

Figure 3. *Foreign Trade Prices and Average Wages, Norway, 1949–73*

Three-year moving average of annual percentage
change in prices of traded goods

Annual percentage change
in wage costs

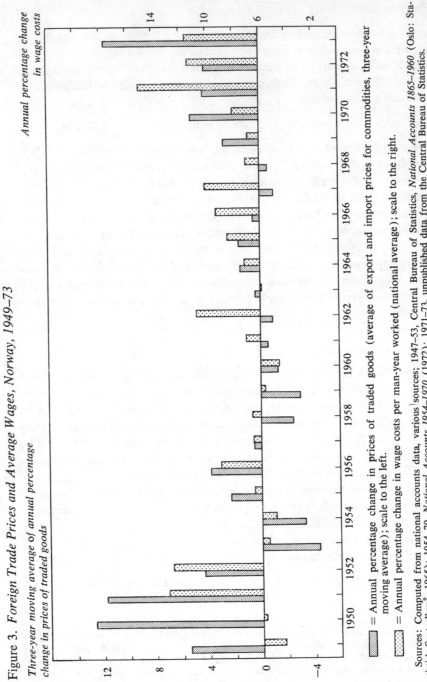

= Annual percentage change in prices of traded goods (average of export and import prices for commodities, three-year moving average); scale to the left.

= Annual percentage change in wage costs per man-year worked (national average); scale to the right.

Sources: Computed from national accounts data, various sources; 1947–53, Central Bureau of Statistics, *National Accounts 1865–1960* (Oslo: Statistisk Sentralbyrå, 1965); 1954–70, *National Accounts 1954–1970* (1972); 1971–73, unpublished data from the Central Bureau of Statistics.

relation between foreign trade prices and the wage level shows up quite well in figure 3, and the relation between wages and prices is obvious from other material. Of particular note are:

• The devaluation of the Norwegian krone in 1949, together with the international inflation following the Korean War shortly afterwards, caused Norwegian import and export prices for commodities, expressed in kroner, to rise some 40 percent from 1949 to 1952. There seems to be an obvious link between these developments on the one hand, and, on the other, the extremely high profits of the exposed industries in 1951 and 1952, and the steep rise of wages and prices (annual averages of approximately 13 and 10 percent, respectively), during the three years following the devaluation.

• In only one period during the postwar years has the trend of export and import prices been downward for any length of time and that was in 1957–63 when prices of commodity exports and imports fell by approximately 2 percent a year on average. During this period the rate of postwar wage and price inflation was at its minimum (annual averages of 8 percent and 2.5 percent, respectively).

• After some years (1963–70) of moderate increases in import and export prices and in the national wage and price level, world market prices rose more steeply in 1970 and 1971 and soared in 1973 and 1974; import and export prices, expressed in kroner, rose 25 to 30 percent between early 1973 and the middle of 1974. The profitability of the exposed industries improved greatly and the wage and price inflation accelerated.[38] On a year-to-year basis

38. But the chain of causation in this case has been disputed. The Organisation for Economic Co-operation and Development, in its country report on Norway published in 1973, concluded that the recent price history of Norway did not support the Norwegian theory of inflation as interpreted (in a much too restricted and simplified way, I think) by OECD: "The analysis . . . leads to the conclusion that, at least in the past two years, the rate of domestic cost and price inflation has been well in excess of anything that could be ascribed to import of inflation from abroad. . . . The explanation therefore needs to be sought primarily in domestic factors." (*OECD Economic Surveys: Norway* [Paris: OECD, 1973], p. 14.) However, in the OECD country report for Norway published in 1974 the authors seem to have come around to the view argued in the present paper, at least as far as 1973 is concerned: "Given the absence of excessive demand pressures and 'aggressive' wage policies at home, it seems that the transmission of inflation from abroad was the key element behind the high rate of price and cost increases in 1973. . . . The strong inflationary tendencies abroad have, thus, not only directly raised the level of prices in Norway but could also have indirectly added to cost and, hence, price pressure through weakening the resistance of employers to higher wage claims in the export and import-competing industries and inducing higher wage demand in the sheltered sector of the economy. An important part of the 1973 wagedrift can probably be explained by this form of international transmission of inflation." (*OECD Economic Surveys: Norway* [Paris: OECD, 1974], pp. 15, 19.)

the increase in wage costs (the average for all industries) was 13.5 percent in 1974 and reached 18.1 percent in 1975; the corresponding figures for consumer prices were 9.4 percent for 1974 and 12.2 percent for 1975, according to the national accounts. Yet the recent rate of inflation in Norway has been somewhat lower than in the majority of European countries, a fact that may have been an effect of the appreciation since 1972 of the Norwegian krone by somewhat more than 10 percent relative to other countries.

The short-run model PRIM was tested against historical data for 1961–68 in my previous study.[39] Because PRIM takes changes in the wage level to be given, a test of this model can neither confirm nor refute the central thesis of the Norwegian approach, which is that world inflation is imported by means of the wage level. The tests did throw light, however, on other aspects of the model: they showed, for instance, that PRIM tended systematically to under-estimate the price increase from one year to the next by some tenths of 1 per-cent. The underestimation occurred because prices of competing manufac-turers did not, in fact, follow prices of similar imported goods, as is assumed by the model, but rose somewhat more steeply; this is consistent with Ring-stad's later finding, quoted above, that output prices of competing manufac-turers seem to depend as much, or more, on costs than on import prices. The tests showed also that non-negligible prediction errors were the result of the postulated stability of the ratio of profits to wages in the sheltered industries. These errors were not systematic, however, and may simply mean that the assumption made about cost-plus pricing in the sheltered industries could be represented in the model by a better operational specification.

Testing the model in other countries

A considerable amount of empirical data on which to test the Norwegian approach when applied to the Swedish economy is available in the two pub-lications of Edgren, Faxén, and Odhner.[40] Their findings are not easily sum-marized. It is obvious, however, that their study of recent wage and price experience in Sweden has convinced them that the approach has considerable explanatory power. Work to construct a model along the same lines as PRIM has been undertaken in Finland and some results are reported in Halttunen and Molander[41] (see below). It is also known that research on the applica-

39. Aukrust, "PRIM I." (See note 14 for full citation.)
40. "Wages, Growth and the Distribution of Income," and *Wage Formation and the Economy*. (See notes 2 and 6 for full citations.)
41. "The Input-Output Framework." (See note 4 for full citation.)

bility of the Norwegian approach to other economies is under way in other small European countries. Results from these studies will be of great interest as they become available.

Disaggregated Models of Other Countries

Disaggregated models intended for the analysis of wages and prices, often with an input-output basis, have become available for many countries during the last few years. Although not a complete survey, this section reviews a few of the models, focusing on the assumptions that they make with respect to price behavior and wage determination.[42]

The Swedish EFO model[43]

In Sweden the well-known EFO model follows the Norwegian precedent of a two-way classification of sheltered and exposed industries, with further subdivisions.[44] Output prices of the exposed sectors are assumed to follow world market prices although data show the relation not to be an exact one. Output prices of the sheltered sectors result from cost-plus pricing: "In industries sheltered against foreign competition, pricing is mainly determined by the development of costs. . . . Our estimates show a striking constancy in the share of the operating surplus in the sector product of the sheltered sector as a whole."[45] This constancy implies a constant rate of profit. An interesting suggestion, which is also seen in models for other countries, is that the

42. In addition to the models described in the text, a disaggregated model intended for the study of intersectoral wage and price interdependencies is being developed for the Netherlands. (See W. Driehuis and P. de Wolff, "A Sectoral Wage Price Model for the Netherlands' Economy," in H. Frisch, ed., *Inflation in Small Countries* [Springer-Verlag, 1976], pp. 283–339.) Four sectors are distinguished, namely, manufacturing, services, building, and agriculture.

43. In Sweden the work of the Aukrust Committee in Norway in 1966 soon inspired research along similar lines. The brief 1969 report by the chief economists of the labor market organizations, Edgren, Faxén, and Odhner, "Wages, Growth and the Distribution of Income," was followed by the extended report by the same authors in their 1970 book, *Wage Formation and the Economy*.

44. Within the sheltered sector group, five subsectors are distinguished: (1) sheltered goods production, (2) government services or services under strict governmental control, (3) building, (4) private services, and (5) government sector. Within the exposed sector group there are four subsectors: (6) raw material production exposed to competition, (7) semimanufactured goods production for export, (8) import-competing production, and (9) finished goods production.

45. Edgren and others, *Wage Formation and the Economy*, pp. 10–11.

normal rate of profit of the sheltered industries is the rate necessary to maintain investment, production, and employment in these industries.

The wage level is assumed, as in the Norwegian model, to be determined through a mechanism geared to developments in other countries: "The industries exposed to competition have long been wage leaders in the Swedish labour market. . . . The whole wage level in the country therefore has depended strongly on what the competing industries have been able and willing to pay. . . . From the competing sector wage impulses proceed to the sheltered industries, both through the market mechanism . . . and through the wage policy based on the solidarity principle. The market mechanism makes itself felt both in wage negotiations and through wage drift."[46] This description is very similar to the argument above (pages 113–17). But in its discussion both of the wage determination mechanism and of other parts of the model, the Swedish study is much more detailed than its Norwegian predecessor; in particular, fluctuations in quantities are considered explicitly. The Swedish study is very useful, therefore, in pointing out modifications that could be made to the basic assumptions of the two models.

A quarterly model for Finland

A quarterly model for Finland, constructed at the Bank of Finland, contains as a central feature a production-price-income block built around an input-output framework.[47] The structure of the block is similar to the structure of PRIM, which inspired it. Two of the four sectors distinguished are sheltered sectors: agriculture and noncompetitive production (services, a few branches of manufacturing); two are exposed sectors: forestry and competitive production (bulk of manufacturing). Agricultural prices are stipulated in income negotiations between organizations of farmers and government and are exogenous. Prices of noncompetitive industries are endogenous and result from a markup policy: "In the non-competitive industries it is assumed that the share of nonwage income of all factor incomes [my phrase, 'share in total factor income'] is left unchanged apart from the long-run decreasing trend and fluctuations caused by changes in capacity utilization.[48]

46. Ibid., p. 22.
47. Halttunen and Molander, "The Input-Output Framework."
48. Ibid., p. 227. Note that if the unemployment rate (LUR) is used as a rough indicator of capacity utilization, the percentage share of nonwage income in factor income is expressed as a function of time (T) and LUR by the equation in Halttunen and Molander (ibid.):

$$\frac{\text{nonwage income}}{\text{factor income}} = 45.693 - 0.160T - 0.507LUR,$$

which means that the nonwage share falls (and the wage share increases) when unemployment rises (implying lower capacity utilization). This may be an improvement

Prices of forest industries are exogenous, reflecting world market conditions for wood products. Prices of competitive production are also assumed to be mainly determined by world market prices, that is, export and import prices. No significant effect, however, of import prices on the output price of this sector was found in the estimations attempted. On the other hand, unit labor cost was found to have a positive effect, indicating, as Ringstad found for Norway, that the output prices of exposed industries even in a small country are influenced in part by costs and not entirely by prices given on the world market. The wage relation of the Finnish model appears to rely on past prices and the unemployment rate in the tradition of the Phillips curve.

The French Fi-Fi model

In French planning a distinction between sheltered and exposed industries was introduced for the first time in 1965 by Raymond Courbis (who was obviously not aware that the same distinction was already in use in Norway). Since then it has been a permanent feature of French models.[49]

The distinction is also made in the French planning model, Fi-Fi, which is used at present in preparing projections for the medium term. Fi-Fi distinguishes seven sectors, classified in three broad groups that are supposed to differ with respect to determination of prices and production. The following assumptions are made about prices.

Sectors under public control (agriculture, energy, transport, housing): output prices are assumed to be exogenous to the model. They are fixed either as part of the agricultural policy of the European Common Market or as instruments of the economic policy of the French state.

Sheltered sectors (agricultural and foodstuffs industries, building, services, and trades): these sectors are subject to weak competition from abroad. Therefore, "production is determined by demand (which is, of course, a function of the price level) and prices adjust themselves to a level such that there is compatibility between available self-financing and the requisite investments."[50] There is an idea here that is in the Swedish approach and that

---

compared with PRIM in which the nonwage share is supposed to depend on time only. The Finnish refinement is possible because the Finnish model, in contrast to the early versions of PRIM, determines production and employment simultaneously with prices and incomes.

49. The literature on French planning and the models on which it is based is extensive, most of it, however, in French. The information given in the present paper is based on Raymond Courbis, "The Physio-Financial Medium-Term Economic-Projection Model Fi-Fi" (paper presented at the First Seminar on Mathematical Methods and Computer Techniques, Varna, Bulgaria, 1970; United Nations, Economic Commission for Europe [MATHECO 1970/s—1/VAR/C.2]).

50. Ibid., p. 36.

is also present in Eichner's model for the United States, discussed below, namely, that the profit rate (the percentage markup on costs) used by the sheltered industries in calculating their output prices depends, somehow, on the need of these industries to finance their investments.

Exposed industries (the majority of manufacturing industries): "Domestic producers exposed to keen foreign competition must bring their prices into line with those of their keenest foreign competitors or lose their customers."[51] This being so, "price is a fixed datum for exposed enterprises; the latter have to fall into line with the prices laid down by their more competitive foreign rivals."[52]

The rate of increase of the average wage level is supposed in Fi-Fi to depend on (1) the unemployment rate, (2) the rate of rise in prices, and (3) something called, for short, "the financial situation of enterprises."[53] Courbis gives the following relation, estimated from annual data 1957–67:

$$(13) \quad TXH_t = 8.10 + 0.53\ TPG_t - 0.15\ TPG_{t-1} - 3.68 \left(\frac{DENS}{PA_t}\right)$$
$$ (1.22) \quad (0.09) \qquad\quad (0.12) \qquad\qquad\quad (1.61)$$

$$+\ 2.67\ RAP_t + 0.04\ (A_{t-1} - \bar{A}_{t-1}),$$
$$ (1.31) \qquad\quad (0.05)$$

$r = 0.972$; numbers in parentheses are standard errors.

where TXH and TPG, respectively, stand for the growth rate (in percent) of the hourly wage rate and for that of the general level of prices in relation to the previous year; $DENS/PA$ is a measure of relative unemployment ($DENS$ is the number of job seekers, PA is the total available working population); RAP is a dummy variable intended to take into account the arrival of repatriates from Algeria in 1962–63; and the last term represents the financial situation of enterprises (A is the effective rate of self-financing and $\bar{A}$ the trend-oriented rate of self-financing of private-law corporations; and t is the year considered).[54]

Equation 13 indicates that the rate of growth of the wage level is sensitive to unemployment and past price changes and little affected by the financial situation of enterprises. It therefore seems to uphold the Phillips curve approach to inflation. But unemployment may itself depend on wages because high wages may mean low competitiveness and a low demand for labor. The French approach, if I have understood it correctly, interprets equation 13 as

51. Ibid., p. 10.
52. Ibid., p. 39.
53. This somewhat loose concept apparently plays about the same role in Fi-Fi as does the equally loose concept of "profitability" in the Norwegian long-run model.
54. Courbis, " 'Fi-Fi,' " p. 29.

part of a larger equilibrium model establishing a link between the wage level and the given output prices of the exposed industries (and, of course, all other exogenous variables of the model).[55]

A three-sector model of the United States

The process of wage and price determination in a big economy with little dependence on foreign trade—the United States—is analyzed by Eichner[56] in terms of three broad sectors called the competitive sector, the oligopolistic sector, and the (private and public) services sector, respectively. Prices are assumed to be determined differently in the three sectors. In the competitive sector (agriculture and a minority portion of manufacturing) output prices are determined through the interplay of supply and demand. In this sector fluctuations in aggregate demand conditions are quickly reflected in fluctuations in prices. In the oligopolistic sector (comprising industries dominated by a few large corporations) output prices are "administered prices"; they are set by the producers to cover their costs as well as a certain margin above those costs. Costs generally depend on prevailing wage rates. The margin above costs is chosen to generate an income high enough to cover dividend payments and, in addition, "the funds out of which the megacorp is able to finance its own internal rate of growth."[57] Thus, as was the case with the sheltered sectors in the French model, the margin chosen depends on the amount of investment needed to allow the industry in question to expand as required by the general growth rate of the economy. Prices are virtually

---

55. "The French data thus confirm the results of Phillips analysis according to which there is a negative link between an increase in the wage rate and the unemployment rate. This assumed link, determined for high and low unemployment rates alike, expresses the fact that the labor market is not in equilibrium. It plays a part in regulating wages and the level of employment: any increase in unemployment tends to put a brake on wage growth; this lowers costs and consequently boosts the output of the 'exposed' sectors, checks the rise in prices and increases the demand in 'sheltered' sectors; the new jobs created by this additional activity counteract the upward trend of unemployment and the brake put on wages. The opposite effects occur where the trend is towards over-employment. Since the prices of 'exposed' enterprises are dictated by more competitive foreign producers, the *ex post* wage trend is in fact determined by this price constraint, account being taken of vulnerable enterprises' costs other than wage costs; this being so, everything happens as though relation (1) given above did in fact determine the rate of unemployment in a state of equilibrium; if the unemployment rate was lower (higher) there would be a quicker (slower) rise in wages, which would weaken (strengthen) the competitive position of exposed enterprises and depress (stimulate) employment." (Ibid., p. 31.)

56. Alfred S. Eichner, "Price Policies of Oligopolistic Companies," in *OECD Regional Trade Union Seminar on Prices Policy*, November 1972. Final Report (Paris: OECD, 1974).

57. Ibid., p. 81.

unaffected by short-run changes in aggregate demand conditions, contrary to the situation in the competitive sector. In the services sector, where inputs other than labor are likely to be insignificant, prices are determined largely by the prevailing wage rate; again they are unaffected by aggregate demand conditions.

The model does not explicitly set out a wage relationship. Roughly, the wage determination mechanism appears to work as follows. The oligopolistic sector is wage leader. In this sector "trade unions have the predominant voice in determining wage rates—at least in nominal terms" (for example, in steel and automobile production).[58] The basic wage rate established by trade unions in the oligopolistic sector spills over to other sectors and governs the basic wage rate in the competitive and service sectors.[59] Taken as a whole, the model seems to consider the basic wage rate of the economy an administered price that is set at the discretion of the trade unions. There is nothing in the model to restrict the power of the trade unions either upward or downward since wage changes are reflected in the prices of all sectors. As it stands at present, therefore, the model would seem to leave the level of wages and prices, and the rate of inflation as well, totally undetermined.

A dynamic Australian model

All models considered so far have been static. A noteworthy attempt to construct a dynamic, disaggregated model of wages and prices has recently been made by Haig and Wood for the Australian economy.[60] The model is basically a closed input-output system that describes the transmission of price changes between different industry sectors, and in addition relates changes in costs of production to changes in final prices. Prices are either exogenous or determined by a markup on historical costs of production, and prices of outputs of industries are, therefore, based on costs of production in a previous period. This results in a dynamic input-output system in which increases in costs are passed on, after a delay, as increases in selling prices of industries. The model is closed by equations that relate changes in wages and profits to previous changes in prices of sales to final buyers. Some allowance is also made, however, for the influence of demand factors on wages and prices.

The model distinguishes twenty-three industries that, with respect to price

58. Ibid., p. 89.
59. Ibid., p. 84.
60. B. D. Haig and M. P. Wood in Karen R. Polenske and Jiri V. Skolka, eds., *Advance in Input-Output Analysis* (Ballinger, forthcoming).

behavior, are divided into four broad groups. In primary industries (agriculture, pastoral and mining industries), which in Australia are strongly export-oriented, output prices are assumed to be exogenous and determined by world prices or seasonal conditions. In manufacturing industries prices are obtained by applying a constant percentage markup on the historical cost of the goods sold. Costs of material are assumed to be passed on by the period of stock turnover (estimated at from two to eight months for different industries) and costs of wages by the period of turnover of work-in-progress (one to two months). In trade selling prices are obtained by applying a constant percentage markup on the price of goods for resale. The turnover period for sales to final buyers (estimated at from two to eight months depending on the product) is assumed to represent the lag in passing on increases in costs to consumers. In other services output prices are also obtained by applying a constant markup on historical costs, assuming increases in costs to be passed on with a lag of one month.[61]

The model contains two equations that together determine the wage rate. One equation makes "nominal" (that is, negotiated) wages a function of prices and thus, according to the authors, completes the wage-price spiral; the best fit was obtained by assuming a two-quarter lag between changes in retail prices and nominal wages. The second equation explains the wage drift (the excess of actual over nominal, or negotiated, wages) in terms of excess demand for final goods, thus introducing demand elements into the explanation of inflation. The reasoning, as I understand it, is along the following lines. Assume an initial increase in nominal (negotiated) wages. This will immediately increase the money value of the demand from employees for consumer goods, but be reflected in the prices of such goods only with some delay. Therefore real demand will have gone up, sales will increase in volume terms, producers will hire more labor, and thereby perhaps (depending on the state of the labor market) bid up wages. The model consequently assumes the size of the wage drift to be positively related to the real wage in past quarters (representing demand for final goods) and negatively related to the unemployment rate (representing the state of the labor market). Actual wages are

---

61. In commenting on some of their test results the authors point out possibilities for improving the assumptions made. For instance, they make the point that since the transport industry is largely government owned, prices of this industry should perhaps be considered an exogenous variable determined by policy decisions. Similarly, they argue, the output prices of some manufacturing industries, which in the 1970s were subject to intense competition from overseas (for example, household appliances), should perhaps also be considered exogenous variables, determined in this case by world market prices.

Table 3. *Assumptions about Price Behavior in Selected Disaggregated Models*

		Prices exogenous, and given by:			Prices endogenous, and related to:	
Model	*Country*	*World market*	*Oligopolistic pricing*	*Government agreement*	*Markup on costs*	*Domestic demand*
PRIM	Norway	Shipping Forestry Manufacturing[a]	...	Agriculture Fishing	Sheltered (excluding agriculture)	...
EFO	Sweden	Manufacturing[a]	...	...	Sheltered (including agriculture)	...
Bank of Finland	Finland	Forestry Manufacturing[a]	...	Agriculture	Sheltered (excluding agriculture)	...
Fi-Fi	France	Manufacturing[a]	...	Agriculture Energy Transport Housing	Sheltered (excluding agriculture)	...
Eichner	United States	...	Oligopolistic sector[b]	...	Services sector	Competitive sector (including agriculture)
Haig and Wood	Australia	Primary sector (including agriculture)[c]		...	Manufacturing Trade Services	...

Source: See text for explanation.
a. Mining included, but excluding a small part of manufacturing industries that is classified among sheltered industries.
b. Part of manufacturing, in other models classified as exposed.
c. Agriculture, forestry, mining including base metals.

supposed to change at the same rate in all sectors. No sector, apparently, is considered more important than any other in the wage determination process.

Summary of assumptions on price behavior

Table 3 presents in summary form the assumptions made about price behavior in the various models that have been surveyed. The main impression is of considerable diversity, yet certain features are noteworthy.

Most striking, perhaps, is the fact that in only one model—Eichner's for the United States—is it assumed that demand in commodity markets has a significant effect on output prices, and even in this model it is supposed to be the case for only a few of the industries. In the majority of cases prices are assumed to be determined either on the world market and not influenced by the national economy or through some process of markup pricing. Some of the models explicitly acknowledge that output prices of some industries—notably agriculture and government services—are fixed through a process of negotiations or by government decree and, consequently, treat these prices as exogenous, whereas the same prices in most other models are treated as cost-determined. (This difference in approach, however, is unlikely to be of importance in practice inasmuch as these output prices will presumably be fixed with close reference to costs, even though they are formally subject to negotiations or government decisions.)

Agricultural prices are treated as determined by market demand and supply forces in only the models for Australia and the United States, which are big exporters of agricultural products.

A final point is the differences in assumptions made about the price behavior of manufacturing in the model for the United States and the remaining models. In the model for the large, almost closed, U.S. economy the output price of this sector is assumed to result from oligopolistic pricing, and there is no reference whatsoever to the existence of a world market. For all the smaller open economies (except Australia, where cost-plus pricing is taken to be the rule) the models assume the output prices of manufacturing to be determined mainly on the world market. In the models for these countries there is no reference to the possible oligopolistic power of national industries. This asymmetrical treatment of manufacturing may be assumed to be more than accidental. Presumably the assumptions made are useful first-order approximations to reality in large and small economies, respectively. Yet one suspects that, if a more realistic multinational model is to be constructed, some assumption midway between the two extremes should be adopted.

Suggestions for Further Research

No country can avoid being affected by price impulses from abroad. I have argued that these price impulses are sometimes so strong as to dominate the trend of wages and prices at the national level. The conclusion I draw is that future research on inflation should be oriented more explicitly toward the problems of the open economy and the transmission mechanism of international inflation. I believe, furthermore, that continued work based on highly aggregated models will give rapidly diminishing returns. Rather, a disaggregated approach seems a necessity if a deeper insight into the inflationary process is to be gained.

At the national level a natural point of departure for research on inflation may be to take international developments of wages and prices as a datum. The aim will be to design models that will explain national price trends in terms of national policies and price impulses reaching the economy from outside. At the international level, however, this will not do. Instead, to understand world inflation, one must develop models that reflect fully the interdependencies of the economies of the world and that explain world prices in terms of policy decisions taken simultaneously, but independently, in many economies.[62]

The ultimate goal might conceivably be to design a family of partly dependent, interlocked, national models of inflation. Used separately, each model would allow partial analysis at the national level, assuming world market prices to be given. Used together, the models would form a world model allowing a general analysis of world prices as determined through independent national policy decisions. As I foresee them, the national models will all have to incorporate an input-output element.

Empirical research should be undertaken in the following three areas so

62. Research along these lines has already begun in some quarters. Particularly well known is the continuously developing project LINK on which quite a large literature exists. Two other projects, both explicitly addressing themselves to the problem of generation and international transmission of inflation and covering the member countries of the European Common Market, were reported at a conference held in November 1974 in Vienna by the Institut für Volkswirtschaftslehre [Institute for Advanced Studies], Technische Universität. (See Guy Carrin and A. P. Barten, "International Aspects of Cost Push Inflation," in H. Frisch, ed., *Inflation in Small Countries*, pp. 243–81, and Jean Waelbroeck and A. Dramais, "DESMOS: A Model for the Coordination of Economic Policies in the ECE Countries" in Albert Ando, Richard Herring, and Richard Marston, eds., *International Aspects of Stabilization Policies*, Federal Reserve Bank of Boston, Conference Series 12 [June 1974 conference], pp. 285–347.)

that national models can be gradually improved and international comparisons made easier.

Attempts to design a suitable sector-sector (or sector-commodity) classification for use in disaggregated price models. It may well be that the optimal classification of sectors will be different for different countries. There are a number of considerations to be taken into account. Some are: (1) the sector classification should reflect existing differences in price behavior among industries, in particular, the varying degree to which industries are exposed to foreign competition. (2) It should be suitable for analysis of the wage determination process (for example, those industries considered wage leaders should be singled out for special study). (3) It should be suitable for analysis of the different routes (price effect, demand effect, liquidity effects) through which foreign inflation hits the economy. And (4), since the national model is to be part of a larger world model it may be useful to distinguish in the national model between, on the one hand, industries whose output prices are determined on the world market through forces of demand and supply, and, on the other, those characterized by oligopolistic pricing. There is no guarantee that these considerations do not conflict. Consequently, an analytically suitable classification can be selected only after much experimentation.

Empirical studies of price behavior. Current understanding of how commodity prices are determined in the real world is insufficient. It is not certain, for instance, to what extent commodity prices are the result of forces of demand and supply operating "in a free market" and to what extent they are "administered," resulting from cost-plus pricing. Nor is it known, in the latter case, how prices are calculated. A realistic formulation of price behavior relationships requires more research to provide the answers to these questions.

Empirical studies of the wage-determining process. Perhaps the greatest hindrance at present for the construction of a realistic model of inflation is the inability to formulate a reliable wage relation (or set of wage relations). For reasons set out in the text I find the Phillips curve explanation of wages (linking wages to some employment indicator and, perhaps, past prices) highly unsatisfactory. If one is to be realistic, one must consider the wage rate to be determined, simultaneously with employment and other variables, through a process that only a very complicated model could describe. At the national level, the exogenous variables of such models, on which wages like everything else would be seen to depend, would include national policy variables and world market variables. Again, a disaggregated approach could be attempted, with the focus primarily on the forces operating within the wage leading industries.

Comments by Johan Myhrman

AUKRUST'S PAPER is a good example of very scholarly work and the best presentation I have seen of this type of model.

I like, too, the honesty of the author when he says that he has no full theory of inflation. To have a full theory of inflation a theory of a dominant impulse is needed, and a transmission mechanism. What he has is one type of transmission mechanism, putting aside the explanation of the dominant impulse that determines world prices.

It is important to distinguish between the short-run and long-run uses of this model. I shall discuss, first, the long-run use, which is said to produce a cost-push theory of the transmission of international inflation. The cost-push comes about by assuming that prices in the sheltered sector are markups on the wage increases.

Although Aukrust asserts that this is a cost-push model, there are statements in the paper about demand influences. I refer to one on page 130: "In the labor market, in contrast, the Norwegian approach assumes the balance between supply and demand to play a crucial role." That brings me to an important question, the definition of cost-push. I would like to define a pure cost-push situation where wages, for instance, are increased independently of market conditions. If wages react to supply and demand, I would not call that cost-push.

Then there is a second question relating to the distinction between demand and cost-push theories of inflation. I do not find that classification very useful. Essentially, demand for labor is a derived demand from the commodity market. If it is said that an excess demand for labor pushes up wages, and that firms then mark up prices because their costs have risen, it is more useful to characterize the whole situation as a demand inflation.

Still another question is: what is the difference between this model and other types of models, such as the monetary theory of the balance of payments? Here, Aukrust has taken one point of mine by admitting that there is no inconsistency between the two. Everything in the Norwegian model might be explained as the long-run monetary theory of the balance of payments, if one does not insist on saying that it is cost-push. If the model is expressed in equations and the prices in the sheltered sector are set by markup it can be said that those prices are raised by cost-push, but the inflation itself is not cost-push because the following might be another interpretation. Assume that one starts with an increase in world demand that raises world prices. Then demand for the products of the exposed sector increases, their prices increase, profits increase, demand for labor increases, and wages increase. But at the same time, if one begins from an equilibrium in the balance of payments, there is money coming into the economy as a result of the balance of payments surplus. That will increase domestic demand. It will increase demand for sheltered sector products and will increase prices and wages in the sheltered sector. As far as I can see, the same result would be obtained by that kind of experiment. That is why I do not object to the form of the model. I really object more to some of the interpretations.

So much for the long-run model. Aukrust also has a short-term model, which is an input-output, cost-push model that he thinks is a reasonable explanation of what goes on in the short run. I am not sure that I would agree with that, either, unless there is a perfectly accommodating monetary policy, for instance, such as there may be in Norway, but which there certainly is not in Sweden. As a short-run explanation demand policy, whether fiscal or monetary policy, must be taken into account. It seems obvious that the developments in Sweden between 1971 and 1973 would be very difficult to explain without taking into consideration monetary and fiscal policy actions.

It is of interest to note, incidentally, that Aukrust suggests that demand management has the greatest effect over a period of between two and five years, whereas Faxén, in the Swedish version of this model, says that there is no use in formulating demand policy for less than five years.

Another point raised in the paper, and which is not part of the model, concerns the formulation of wage behavior in an open economy, especially in the form of a Phillips curve. It seems to me that, in the long run, the Phillips curve in a small open economy would be reduced to a dot. In the short run, however, in the specification of equations that are to be estimated for the Phillips curve, information on the behavior of international wages and prices must be considered. That is one of the points I think Aukrust wants to take up.

Finally, in the discussion of the income distribution between sectors a number of important factors are not considered. I have read no comment, for example, on automatic forces working to adjust sectors over time, through different price elasticities in the two sectors and through entry and exit of different firms between the two sectors. For instance, in Sweden, in a situation of excess demand, there would be a more rapid rise in wages and prices in the sheltered sector. If those wage increases were forced into the exposed sector, firms would fail and have to leave the sector. That is a kind of natural economic adjustment.

Comments by Charles S. Maier

AS A HISTORIAN I am not sure that I shall be able to give Aukrust's paper the technical economic commentary that it deserves. But as a historian who has been concerned with inflation, not as Public Enemy No. 1 but as an index of social conflict and as a means of expressing collective preferences, I find this paper useful. Furthermore, since social scientists in America rarely think about small countries, it has been doubly useful.

Let me spotlight both what I believe are Aukrust's contributions and those questions that I think he left unanswered. The major argument in the paper is that the Norwegian model shows the transmission of inflation in an economy that is buffeted by the general currents of the world market and world pricing. According to the paper, the exposed industries in Norway produce 30 percent of the net national product and engage 22 percent of the labor force. That does not seem to me an inordinately large sector oriented toward exports or the world market, especially for a small open economy like that of Norway.

My major question in looking at figure 1, which illustrates a causal chain for price increases, relates to the mechanism by which wages in the exposed industry sector, employing 22 percent of the labor force, actually become the accepted wage standard for the sheltered activities as well. From the point of view of social factors, I think that link is obviously very important. Perhaps it is the system of highly centralized wage bargaining in Scandinavia that is crucial. Still, the government must face some different constituencies in negotiating wages. I am surprised that the sheltered sector wages become so readily determined by the wages in the exposed industries.

According to this model there is obviously an upward bias for prices. It must lead to inflation because of the difference in productivity of the two sectors. Aukrust points out that productivity has risen more than twice as fast in the exposed industries, thus allowing wage increases without inflationary pressure, but that the wage increases are transmitted to the sheltered industries. Because these tend to operate on a cost-plus pricing basis, the effort to keep a "normal" relation between profits and wages will tend to raise output prices (see page 116, note 12).

I do have a further question about the tendency for wages in the exposed industries to adjust so as to maintain or restore profits in these industries to a normal share of factor income. Aukrust admits that such a tendency is hard to demonstrate in view of the oscillation of the percentage from year to year (see figure 1). Nonetheless, the existence of the trend is crucial to his explanation of how price impulses are transmitted in the Norwegian economy, for the model postulates that the wage level in the exposed industries, and thereafter in the sheltered industries, tends to follow the productivity gains in the most efficient sector of the economy. I would like to know more about this tendency to move toward normal profits and the justification for the argument.

It would also be informative to specify further how wage increases slacken when profitability falls. (The greatest slowdown in wage inflation that has been adduced for Norway in this paper occurred in the 1950s, when wage demands moderated during a period of slowdown in world commodity prices.) The only way to hold down wage increases, Aukrust suggests, is by general deflationary measures applied to the economy as a whole. Is there no chance for selective wage stabilization or even a reduction in the relative share of wages to respond to declining sectoral profitability without a general deflationary policy?

The model also presents testing difficulties, as Aukrust admits. One possibility for testing would be to look at how wages follow prices in the world sector. This generally confirms the model. On the other hand, according to Ringstad, whom Aukrust cites, the parameters of table 2—especially the second row of the table relating to export industry prices at home—do not apparently yield the sensitivity to export prices abroad or to import-competing prices that the model would warrant. A problem arises with autocorrelation, which is detailed in the paper and which I am not qualified to resolve. Nonetheless, the result is that the Aukrust model tests positively by one method and indeterminately by another.

Aukrust's model has been termed a "third" causal model to place alongside the monetarist and the Keynesian models, although Aukrust himself has not made that claim. Is one not dealing, though, with a Keynesian model that has certain limiting conditions created by the large export sector? I am not sure that this affects the validity of the model, but it may affect the way causal typologies of inflation are considered. Aukrust discusses the difficulty (on pages 124–26) of finding any economic policy that can simultaneously solve two different dilemmas, that can deal with the price pressures imposed by the world market and yet not prevent a regressive distribution of income on behalf of those in the exposed industries. Is not this argument just a restatement under Norwegian conditions of the general Phillips curve dilemma, if instead of considering the trade-off as one of unemployment against inflation, it is seen as one of income or sectoral factor shares against inflation?

Perhaps this dilemma represents part of the more general trade-off faced in the West. As I have said, my own major interest in inflation centers on its role in revealing and defining group conflict. The paper suggests that 30 percent of the economy has an interest in price stability, while the 70 percent in sheltered industries has a virtual interest in creeping inflation. Thus an open economy may produce social divisions along different lines than those suggested, say, by Bach and Stephenson who divide economic interests between households and corporations and examine the transfer of incomes and assets from the former to the latter.[63] Does the Norwegian type of open economy thus tend to crystallize different constellations of interests or classes from the large and more self-sufficient economy? This is the kind of question that Aukrust's paper poses for noneconomists.

It further raises the issue of how bargaining actually occurs in society. Why does the government supervise a process by which the wages of the sheltered industries so ineluctably follow the wages of the exposed industries? Is it a question of public employees? If the country under discussion were Sweden, I would look to see whether state bargaining with public employees forms a major contribution to the inflationary tendency in the sheltered sector. But the state seems to play a smaller role as employer in the Norwegian model, and thus perhaps its role in inflationary wage settlements matters less in proportion to the influence of the exposed sector, as stressed by Aukrust.

Aukrust invites further thought on the political economy of world market-oriented systems. Both the left and the right in today's policy debates converge on the role of the state in trying to mediate between the needs of capital accumulation on one side and the demands of social peace—to be secured through irreversible wage increases and extensive welfare provisions—on the other. The Norwegian case suggests that these countervailing pressures force crucial domestic decisionmaking, even when an economy seems dependent upon the larger price movements of the world economy. At the very least, adjustment of the exchange rate will have great sociopolitical consequences: too great a revaluation may increase unemployment; even an adjustment that does not inhibit exposed-industry competitiveness and manages to slow inflation may have undesirable redistributive effects. Resolution of the trade-offs will ultimately require political as well as economic bargaining. Here Aukrust underlines the need to study not only the international economic determinants but the social forces within the individual country to probe how bargains are struck, to learn who is supervising them, and how the responsible authority answers to different constituencies.

63. G. L. Bach and James B. Stephenson, "Inflation and the Redistribution of Wealth," *Review of Economics and Statistics,* vol. 56 (February 1974), pp. 1–13.

General Comments

Wynne Godley noted that a key mechanism in the Aukrust model is the increase of wages in export industries associated with the receipt of higher prices by producers for export. This sequence should be easy to observe, but Aukrust's paper does not say whether larger-than-average wage increases in the export sector associated with big increases in profit shares were actually observed.

John Pinder questioned why trade unions in the sheltered industries limited their demands to what was required for parity with wages in the exposed industries: if they had enough power to push for parity why did they not push for more? One answer is that they might expect pushing for more to cause a balance of payments deficit and could foresee, looking two or three years ahead, that this would make everyone worse off. But if these trade unions are so enlightened when the circumstances create risk of a balance of payments deficit, why do they continue to be so restrained when everyone in the rest of the world is pushing as hard as possible, so that an equally strong push by them would not cause such a deficit? Has the current freedom of a country to float its currency not altered the situation from that described in the Aukrust paper, so that the threat of a deficit would cease to be an inhibition on the trade unions in the sheltered industries? Furthermore, the prospect that Norway will become an oil exporter has also changed the situation by making it unnecessary for Norway to have any other export industries, so one could say that workers in the sheltered industries would be doing their patriotic duty if they drove other export industries into bankruptcy. In other words, why do they not push harder than they do, now that the patriotic incentive not to push too hard has been removed? The question of why they do not push harder is worth study; so, too, is the behavior of workers in the sheltered industries with respect to wages, if such a review is not already being undertaken.

Giorgio Basevi questioned whether the assumed causal relation between the increase of wage levels in the exposed sector of the economy and the wage level in the sheltered sector is valid generally. For some countries, such as Switzerland, the sheltered sector has an elastic supply of labor arising from the availability of foreign labor. For that reason, wages in the sheltered sector were kept lower than they would be if immigrant labor were not available, with the result that the general price level in such a country is lower, or rises less than it otherwise would. Caution is therefore indicated in the use of models like the Aukrust model for countries other than those, such as Norway or Sweden, where foreign labor is not available.

Helen Junz considered the basic assumption of the Norwegian model to be that the markets are free so that in the long run the sheltered sector is just as exposed as the so-called exposed sector. The structure of markets probably has much to do with the creation of an inflationary climate, and the proposed future work on this point, referred to in the Aukrust paper, should not be confined to study of commodity markets.

Robert Gordon questioned Aukrust's statement that the monetary theory of the balance of payments took no account of the wage level. That theory has been worked out in detail for a two-sector economy with a special assumption that there is only one wage rate and labor is mobile between sectors. This assumption is well borne out in American statistics; they show that no matter how the labor force is disaggregated, whether demographically, industrially, or by occupation, wages have accelerated and decelerated together, so that the assumption of high substitutability across all these sectors dominates any other assumption, even in periods as short as one year or so. The only exception to this is that there has been some divergence between the wage rates of experienced adult males on the one hand, and teenagers on the other. Also, even if it is conceded that nominal wages in the traded and nontraded goods sectors do move together, it is cause for concern that the model attempts to determine how an impulse toward higher prices in the traded goods sector will affect nominal prices in the nontraded goods sector without specifying anything about policy, especially monetary policy. Without such a specification anything can be obtained, from no response in nontraded goods prices to complete elimination of the initial fall in their relative prices, depending on whether the balance of payments surplus is raising the domestic money supply (it may or may not be), on whether sterilization is possible, and on whether the country is large enough to control its own money supply. It is not useful, therefore, to talk about the nominal prices of traded goods and the overall rate of inflation without specifying some monetary constraints.

George Perry, referring to the treatment of wages in the Aukrust model, thought it was very similar to the old American idea that wage changes were led by a strong, presumably unionized, sector that was the first to raise wages, either autonomously or in response to demand, and then dragged other wages up with it. But this view of wage developments in the United States has not been supported by research. There are systematic differences in the timing of wage changes in the United States. Wages in the highly unionized sectors lag rather than lead other wages in response to unemployment or other measures of labor market tightness. An expansion of demand in the sector where people prefer to work at the given wage, generally the unionized sector, results in an expansion of output in that sector and an expanding demand for labor in it. Because these are preferred jobs, this labor is readily available and prices and wages do not rise in this sector. But the process does bid labor away from other industries, causing wages and prices to rise in them. Thus while the preferred sector is central in this explanation, just as in the Aukrust model, its wage changes do not lead wage changes in other sectors. This view provides a plausible linkage and might be more consistent with the empirical evidence in Norway, which Aukrust states is inconsistent with his own model.

James Duesenberry noted that the trade union explanation of inflation is more incomplete than incorrect in that it centers on one out of a number of possible initiating sectors. Analysis of wage making has to take account of the basic structure of the labor market and of forces that might disrupt it. The fundamental idea is that the labor market structure is tightly knit and has several sectors, of which unions are only one. A second sector is the large part of the labor force that is not unionized but has a highly structured and classified compensation system in which relative wages are always monitored very closely to maintain or attain specified relations between grades of labor, skills, and other characteristics. Because there are many such relations and they interlock in a complicated way, it is a whole structural network. A third sector is a secondary labor market consisting of people in more or less casual employment. Fourth, and at the other end of the scale, is what might be called a free professional market with high mobility consisting of professors, accountants, lawyers, and others who may be employed sometimes in one of the above-mentioned systems but for whom there is a separate market that operates in a different manner from the labor markets in general. The two largest of these four sectors are the union markets and the classified employees' markets, the latter including the federal, state, and local government labor force, and almost every employer with more than 500 employees. Those systems are not rigid, but they move slowly.

Given that kind of structure, the initiating force that can start the whole process in motion and produce secondary reactions will be different at different times. In 1955, which was a good automobile year, people thought the process began with the United Automobile Workers' settlement. But in 1966, when no contracts were coming up for renewal, the big wage pressure was on the bottom of the labor market, with people being drawn out of gas stations and warehouses into factories at higher wages, which pulled up the wage structure. At the same time, there was a shortage of skilled workers in the markets where wages could rise with relative freedom, so those wages went up, and later the unions tried to restore their previous relative wages. At still other times there was a construction boom and construction workers were able to raise wages, at least in some trades, and these spread from one trade to another throughout the industry, and finally into other industries.

There is no general rule as to where impulses that will initiate a general wage movement will originate. They are generally associated with increased profits and higher employment somewhere but not always in the same sector. Nevertheless, the original notion that there is an initiating sector is a powerful one, and the Aukrust paper shows that there are countries other than the United States that have a highly structured and interconnected wage system. It is not entirely independent of supply and demand but operates in ways different from what would be expected from such forces; wages can go up within a sector despite the presence of much unemployment in it. The total system also has a positive correlation of responses to supply and demand conditions.

What is really needed is a general approach, which must then be supplemented by drawing on particular characteristics of the wage structure of a given country, and some indication of where the initiating forces will most probably occur.

George Perry, in agreeing with the above analysis, said that he had intended to distinguish between wage increases that are independent of expansion of aggregate demand and those resulting from such expansion. If a rise in world market prices raised export prices and this, in turn, directly raised wages in the export sector, then policy could not be blamed for the domestic inflation; in that case world prices would cause domestic price and wage increases without raising domestic aggregate demand. But if, instead, the expanded demand for exports operated through raising aggregate demand and the wage responses followed from that, then domestic policy would be much more responsible for the rise in the wage level because policy could have offset the expansion in demand for exports. The contrast was between a shift in the Phillips curve and a movement along it.

William Branson noted that although the national price level is a weighted average of prices of sheltered and exposed goods, nothing is said about where the weights come from. In the model, the price of sheltered goods is always rising in relation to the price of traded goods, but this would imply a downward trend in their output unless one made some special assumptions about price and income elasticities of demand. Such assumptions are not stated. Also, it is ambiguous whether the assumption that income shares are constant in the short run is intended to be simply an instrument to help in negotiation about wages and prices by telling labor and others how wage and price decisions would affect their shares, or whether it is a theory about why shares will in fact remain constant. If it is the latter, something should be said about production functions, elasticities of substitution, and similar factors, and also about whether the theory is true. In the latter connection, there has been substantial fluctuation of shares in Sweden and also trends in the profit share in the United States, as shown by William Nordhaus (see page 139, note 34). Finally, the statement in Aukrust's paper that "in the commodity markets, demand is not supposed to matter much" is surprising, because it runs counter to the general tendency of the paper to discuss only supply-side or cost conditions, holding demand constant. This partial equilibrium analysis is different from a general equilibrium analysis in which it is also assumed that demand does not matter.

Assar Lindbeck observed that Aukrust offered an explanation not only of why countries have similar rates of inflation but a framework for discussing differences in their rates of inflation. These differences could be accounted for by three factors: first, differences in the rate of productivity growth in the exposed sectors of two countries that have the same exposed industries; second, differences in the rate of productivity growth in the sheltered sectors of the two countries; and third, differences in the behavior of export prices in the two countries owing to differences in the composition of their exports.

It has often been said, especially with reference to the United Kingdom, that inflation should be fought by increasing the relative importance of manufacturing because productivity increases are most rapid in that sector. The Aukrust model comes to the opposite conclusion; if productivity increases more in the exposed sector while it remains unchanged in the sheltered sector, inflation would accelerate because wage rates would increase more rapidly and cause greater cost-push in the sheltered sector.

The model demonstrates why the exchange rate is the only instrument that permits a country to determine its own price trend. The short-term part of the model also gives some explanation, or at least a framework for discussion, of what determines variation in the profit share of national income. The profit share of the exposed sector is determined approximately by the relations between international prices and unit labor costs. If variations in the profit margins of the sheltered sector are very small, it is basically the relation between world market prices and unit labor costs in the exposed sector that determines the distribution between profits and labor in the country as a whole. This inference from the model is realistic for small countries. In Finland, for example, which has more rapid inflation than the outside world, the profit share goes down when it revalues its currency. A period of unemployment follows, it devalues, and the profit share goes up. Further inflation reduces the share again. Its behavior is like that of a seesaw. Thus the short-term behavior of the model gives some indication of the determination of distribution of income between labor and capital not only in the exposed sector but in the economy as a whole.

One difficulty with the model, however, is that it is hard to distinguish between the exposed and sheltered sectors; nearly all sectors are exposed to some extent, even building activity. Where the line is drawn is important because different predictions for the aggregate price trend can be made depending on whether it is assumed that the sheltered sector is very small or very large. The group working on a similar model for Sweden has been very indecisive about the fraction of the Swedish economy that is exposed, sometimes saying it was one-third sheltered and sometimes that it was one-third exposed. This decision greatly affects the forecast of the price trend.

Alexander Swoboda agreed that the model did not specify what determined aggregate demand for nontraded goods and therefore did not enable one to derive the average price of nontraded goods from the average price of traded goods. To determine their relative prices some hypothesis about monetary portfolio equilibrium is necessary as well as some assumptions about the nature of fiscal policy and monetary policy in relation to the demand for traded and nontraded goods. Without that, what is happening to prices cannot be determined, and only with such knowledge, supplemented by what is known about productivity, can the demand for labor in the two sectors be derived. Then, to derive wages, some kind of supply curve for labor is needed, either a neoclassical curve or something else. This would give a more complete model, but that model would be indistinguishable from the Australian model of traded and nontraded goods, which incorporates money and specifies the production sectors, for example, by postulating that capital is specific to each of the two sectors and that labor moves between them.

It is both important and difficult to know how to distinguish between sheltered and nonsheltered goods. The analytical purpose of making the distinction is essentially to identify goods that respond quickly and those that respond more sluggishly to excess demand or supply. The distinction is useful in accounting for facts in the short run, even though what is not traded becomes tradable in the long run or has a high degree of substitution with tradable goods. But it is difficult to apply to actual statistics.

Gerhard Fels noted that the Aukrust model is in many respects similar to a model used by the German Expert Council on Overall Economic Development during the 1960s. That model operated by means of an increase in export demand, an increase of profits in the export sector, a wage increase in that sector, and a consequent wage and price increase in the domestic sector. It explained the economy fairly well up to the end of the 1960s, especially of how inflation came in from abroad. But in the early 1970s the conditions upon which the model was based changed. For instance, several revaluations of the deutsche mark dampened export demand and increases in export prices. Inflation was still imported, but mainly by inflows of liquidity that were often encouraged by expectations of changes in the exchange rate. Another change was the shift in wage leadership from the export sector to the public sector. The domestic sector continued to inflate whereas in the export sector the rate of price increase was rather moderate because of the direct price stabilizing effects of the revaluations. The terms of trade of the export sector vis-à-vis the domestic sector deteriorated.

Walter Salant remarked that the model is referred to as a two-sector model and exposed industries are treated as one sector. This raises the question whether the model makes any distinction between exports and import-competing industries. To treat them as part of a single sector prevents the model from dealing with the impact on the domestic economy of a change in the terms of trade. That might be why the model broke down in 1973–74; the rise in food and oil prices involved the very deterioration in the terms of trade which, if he understood it correctly, the model could not take into account. An adverse change in the terms of trade is equivalent to a fall in the productivity of the export sector, and perhaps could be worked into the model by treating it in that way. Such a change is like a fall in the productivity of the export sector because it reduces the quantity of goods available for consumption and investment per unit of domestic output; if aggregate nominal demand were to remain unchanged, the reduction in output available for consumption and investment would be inflationary. If the model cannot currently take into account a change in the terms of trade, it should be modified, either in the way suggested or in some other way, to enable it to deal with such changes. Perhaps a modification of this kind would give better results for the last few years.

Odd Aukrust, confining his response to a few general remarks, suggested first that the model might work better for countries like Sweden and Norway than for others because the former have a very centralized trade union movement and centralized wage negotiations that take place more or less at the same time for all workers. That partly explains why the wage level spills over so easily from the exposed to the sheltered industries. The trade union leadership, which negotiates on behalf of both groups, is responsible and does not want to destroy the firms that employ the workers. The union leaders tend to look at the profitability of the exposed industries.

As to the many questions raised about the role of demand, it is agreed that the "real" side of the economy is not spelled out in the Norwegian model and that it presupposes that demand adapts itself. But this is basically what happens; the only ultimate prices found that explained the movement of prices and wages in Norway over a twenty-year period have been world market prices and the exchange rate, which had been kept stable. That is a cost-push type of explanation. When wage negotiations had been concluded—and it was reasonably well known what the wage level would be over the next two years—prices during those two years could be forecast by applying some of the principles relating to cost-push pricing. Within such a two-year period one had to consider labor market developments to explain wage drift, that is, the portion of the wage change that was not negotiated and which might be 4 percent, more or less. Demand did not have to be taken into consideration anywhere else to explain price developments over such a period. In explaining what would happen over a five-year period, however, during which a number of wage negotiations occur, demand management would be important because it would influence the demand for labor in two years' time, which in turn would influence wage negotiations at that time and have further effects on price trends.

As to whether the model is a third explanation of inflation, that is, in addition to the monetary and Keynesian explanations, there is no way to respond except to say that it does point to certain aspects of inflation not highlighted in alternative explanations. Moreover, this difference in diagnosis might on occasion lead to different remedies. Although the reasoning in each instance is in different modes, each seems to come to similar conclusions. It might be that the monetary theory is the most useful to explain the very long-run trend of the world price level, that the Aukrust model is an important explanation of the mechanism that operates to tie things together in a short period, and that there is plenty of room for the Phillips curve.

In regard to the statement that foreign exchange rates cannot be manipulated freely and that they are not well suited for use as regular instruments of price policy, there is at least one difficulty: every time a change in exchange rates is proposed, there are pressure groups that oppose it. The effect of currency appreciation on exposed industries is immediately seen by everyone, and these groups are strong and put pressure on the policymakers. If the world comes to expect a change in Norway's exchange rate every year or two, the resulting unfavorable speculation might cause trouble.

WALTER S. SALANT

International Transmission
of Inflation

Walter S. Salant is greatly indebted both to Mark Duvall for his careful and conscientious assistance in putting together the basic data underlying the tables in this paper, for making the necessary computations, and for his energy and initiative in filling the many gaps in standard sources of the data underlying the appendix tables, and to Marion Layton, his successor, as research assistant, for her excellent work in completing the tables and reviewing and revising them in accordance with revisions of the basic data.

THE RISE of national price levels and the acceleration of their rise has become generally recognized in recent years to be a world phenomenon. Since 1961 the annual rate of increase in consumer price indexes climbed steadily through 1974, at least in twenty member countries of the Organisation for Economic Co-operation and Development. As figure 1 and table 1, column 1, show, the unweighted average of their percentage increases over the preceding year rose from 2.4 percent in 1960 to 10.2 percent in 1973 and 16.3 percent in 1974.[1] This rise in the average annual increase is not the result merely of an acceleration of increases in a few countries; the dispersion of annual inflation rates from their mean, expressed in percentage points, was lower in all but three years of the 1960s than in the lowest year of the 1954–59 period and showed no persistent movement until it rose in 1973 and then nearly doubled in 1974. When expressed as a percentage of the mean changes, the average deviation of national rates from their mean has fallen greatly since the early 1950s and more or less steadily since 1959; despite increases in 1973 and 1974, this average deviation remained well below that of any year from 1954 to 1964, indicating that the increases have become less diverse, at least in the advanced countries of OECD (see table 1, columns 2 and 3). The evidence of both the acceleration of the increases in consumer price indexes and the reduction in their dispersion is reinforced by corresponding data for the GNP deflators of all the advanced countries in OECD and for the European members alone (see figure 1 and table 1, columns 4, 5, and 6). The impression that the decline in dispersion has been great may be exaggerated by the very large dispersion in 1958 and the high, although smaller, dispersion in 1959 (presumably part of the same economic episode), but there is little doubt that some moderate reduction of the dispersion occurred over most of the period as a whole.[2]

1. Price statistics used in this paper have been revised to include new data made available since November 1974.

2. The dispersion of changes in both consumer price indexes and GNP deflators is here measured by an unweighted average of the national deviations. The OECD, using the coefficient of variation to measure the dispersion of GNP deflators for seventeen OECD members and thirteen northern European members, found a more or less steady decline in it from 1958 to 1971, except for a sharp rise in 1968, and an approxi-

Figure 1. *Average Rates of Change and Dispersion of Prices in Twenty OECD Countries, 1954–74*

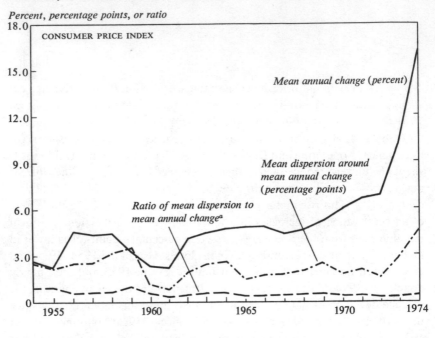

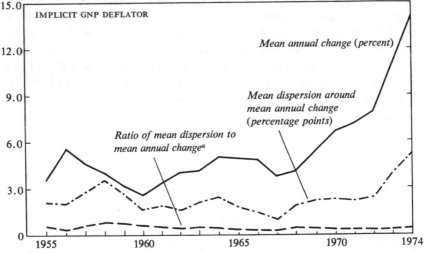

Source: Table 10.
a. See table 1, note b, for explanation.

Table 1. *Average Rates of Inflation and Their Dispersion in Twenty OECD Countries, 1954–74*[a]

	Consumer price indexes			Implicit GNP deflator		
		Mean dispersion[b]			Mean dispersion[b]	
Year	Mean annual change[c] (percent) (1)	Percentage points (2)	Rates of mean dispersion to mean annual rates (3)	Mean annual change[c] (percent) (4)	Percentage points (5)	Rates of mean dispersion to mean annual rates (6)
1954	2.62	2.55	0.973	n.a.	n.a.	n.a.
1955	2.31	2.26	0.977	3.63	2.08	0.575
1956	4.64	2.51	0.540	5.53	2.01	0.363
1957	4.41	2.54	0.576	4.66	2.74	0.589
1958	4.51	3.18	0.704	4.09	3.56	0.871
1959	3.22	3.53	1.098	3.20	2.75	0.860
1960	2.35	1.25	0.533	2.64	1.74	0.658
1961	2.33	0.89	0.382	3.39	1.82	0.537
1962	4.18	1.91	0.456	4.09	1.74	0.425
1963	4.52	2.47	0.546	4.19	2.10	0.501
1964	4.74	2.66	0.562	5.06	2.46	0.487
1965	4.83	1.55	0.321	4.96	1.79	0.360
1966	4.86	1.78	0.367	4.85	1.42	0.293
1967	4.39	1.79	0.409	3.78	0.99	0.261
1968	4.62	2.01	0.436	4.10	1.87	0.455
1969	5.26	2.58	0.491	5.44	2.26	0.415
1970	6.00	1.89	0.315	6.71	2.29	0.341
1971	6.73	2.16	0.321	7.17	2.25	0.314
1972	6.89	1.65	0.239	7.87	2.42	0.307
1973	10.18	2.87	0.282	10.98	3.92	0.357
1974	16.28	5.61	0.344	14.13[d]	5.20	0.368

Sources: *Consumer price index:* International Monetary Fund, *International Financial Statistics*, vol. 27 (June 1974), vol. 28 (March 1975), vol. 29 (May 1976); and IMF, *International Financial Statistics*, 1972 Supplement (n.d.). *GNP deflators*, Organisation for Economic Co-operation and Development, *Statistics of National Accounts, 1950–1961* (Paris: OECD, 1964); OECD, *National Accounts of OECD Countries, 1960–1970* (Paris: OECD, 1972), and ibid., *1953–1969* (Paris: OECD, 1971); *OECD Economic Surveys*, selected issues for various countries; IMF, *Annual Report, 1974*; IMF, *International Financial Statistics*, issues for June 1974, March and April 1975, and May 1976; Bank of Greece, *Summary of the Statement of Governor Xenophon Zolotas at the Annual Meeting of Shareholders, 24 April 1975* (Athens: 1975), p. 16.

n.a. Not available.

a. The OECD member countries included are Austria, Belgium, Canada, Denmark, Finland, France, Germany, Greece, Iceland, Ireland, Italy, Japan, Netherlands, Norway, Portugal, Spain, Sweden, Turkey, United Kingdom, and United States. Those omitted are Australia, Luxembourg, New Zealand, and Switzerland.

b. The mean dispersion expressed in percentage points is the unweighted arithmetic average of the absolute values of the differences of the individual percentage increases from the mean for the twenty OECD countries. The ratio is the mean dispersion in percentage points divided by the mean annual percentage changes.

c. The mean annual change is the unweighted arithmetic average of percentage increases from the previous year for the twenty OECD countries.

d. Based on seventeen countries for which GNP data are available.

The widespread character of the inflation and of its acceleration, and especially the reduction in its dispersion, has led to a rather general acceptance of the view that it is being transmitted among countries to a greater extent than before, to expositions of various possible mechanisms of transmission, and to econometric testing of the relative importance of these mechanisms. Although this paper is mainly about the process of international transmission itself, it examines the interrelations between dispersion of national inflation rates and transmission before describing and commenting on the mechanisms of transmission. It does not attempt to present a finished set of answers to questions about the transmission of inflation or to test hypotheses. Rather it reviews these hypotheses, brings together some appraisals of them, offers comments on them, and makes suggestions for further studies that appear to be needed. What is said about mechanisms of international transmission of inflation is for the most part not new; the hypotheses stated are the conventional ones and are presented only to be examined so that light may be thrown on their implications and on problems requiring further empirical work.

Interrelations between Dispersion of National Inflation Rates and International Transmission of Inflation

It is tempting to assume that the reason changes in national price levels are similar is that such changes begin in one or a few countries and are transmitted to others, and to infer that a reduction in the dispersion of national rates of change results from greater international transmission of inflationary

---

mate leveling in 1971 to 1973 for both groups of countries. (See "The International Transmission of Inflation," *OECD Economic Outlook,* no. 13 [July 1973], pp. 82–83.) Michael Parkin, in "World Inflation, International Relative Prices and Monetary Equilibrium under Fixed Exchange Rates" (in Robert Z. Aliber, ed., *The Political Economy of Monetary Reform* [Macmillan, 1976]), using the consumer price indexes of sixteen OECD countries from 1950 to 1973 and the standard deviation to measure the dispersion of their increases, found no clear tendency for any change in dispersion of increases in those prices between 1954 and 1973. He preferred to measure dispersion by the standard deviation, an absolute measure, rather than one relating dispersion to the level of mean changes, such as the coefficient of variation, because "one wants to know about movements in the dispersion of relative price levels. Since the rate of inflation is a (logarithmic) first difference of the price level, only a zero standard deviation of the inflation distribution implies constant relative prices" (note 2). The difference between the measures of dispersion that OECD and Parkin use accounts for some, perhaps most, of the difference in their conclusions about the trend of dispersion; as noted later, however, some of it may reflect differences in the behavior of consumer price indexes and GNP deflators, especially from year to year. Data on both indexes are shown in figure 1 and table 1.

pressures through market forces than occurred in the earlier post–World War II period. Similarly, it is natural to make the converse inference: that an increase in international transmission of inflationary pressures will reduce the dispersion of inflation rates. The validity of these two inferences are considered below.

Does a decrease in dispersion of inflation rates necessarily imply increase in transmission?

The greater prevalence of increases in national price levels and a convergence of their rates of increase suggest that international transmission has increased. The inference is not necessarily correct: other explanations are equally logical and sufficiently important to be worth serious consideration. Many countries might experience inflation at the same time without international transmission of inflationary forces because they respond in the same way to common causes. A substantial increase since World War II in intellectual exchange between nations led to increased diffusion of views about both economic policy objectives and the means of achieving them. One result has been a change of the modal view (and probably also a coalescence of national views) toward less tolerance of unemployment. Consequently nearly all national economies were kept running at levels closer to their potential outputs than they were before the war, and were therefore more vulnerable to inflation as a response to shocks.

Moreover, nearly all countries have undergone long-period institutional and structural changes which, although not in themselves inflationary, have made them more vulnerable to inflation. One of these changes is a widespread increase in the resistance to reductions of nominal prices and wages. Another is the growing role of the public sector in most national economies, a development that may increase the vulnerability to inflation in a number of different ways, which are discussed in the appendix to this paper.

Another possible cause of a decrease in the dispersion of rates of change in consumer prices and other comprehensive price indexes, such as gross national product deflators, is a convergence in the rates of productivity growth of different countries. These comprehensive price indexes tend to diverge from the corresponding national indexes of wholesale prices in degrees related to the growth in a country's productivity. If changes in national wholesale prices continue to be tied together, a convergence of national rates of productivity growth would cause a convergence of changes in their consumer price indexes and GNP deflators.

Other changes, not associated with any one or a few countries, also may directly release inflationary forces. In the monetary field, the development and expansion of the Eurocurrency market, even if it has not greatly increased the supply of what one chooses to call "money," has increased the supply of liquidity or reduced the demand for it. (See appendix for a fuller discussion.) Similarly, the establishment of special drawing rights has provided a non-national addition to the international reserve assets of the recipient countries without increasing the liabilities of other countries. Although reserve creation through SDRs has been small, it illustrates the potential if not the past actual importance of one type of common cause.

The above points relate to common factors that make national economies more vulnerable to inflationary pressures or shocks without actually generating such pressures or shocks. Other explanations of a decrease in dispersion of inflation rates are also possible. For example, inflation rates may have been generated in many countries at the same time merely because cyclical expansion in a number of important countries coincided to an unusual degree. Although the probability that such similarity of movement in several large countries occurred by sheer coincidence may not be high, it is not so low as to be negligible; such synchronization has occurred at times in the past when the world economy is widely regarded as having been less integrated than it is now, and it occurred then to a greater extent than in some subsequent periods, as is indicated by the evidence cited in the appendix.

Does an increase in transmission necessarily reduce dispersion of inflation rates?

Just as national inflation rates may converge without increased international transmission through market forces, so may such transmission increase without making inflation rates converge. Indeed, an increase in such transmission may even increase the dispersion of some measures of inflation. This may be more than a possibility with regard to dispersion of consumer price indexes. It is now widely recognized that the more rapidly a country's productivity in producing tradable output grows, the greater tends to be the excess of the rise in its consumer prices over the rise in its wholesale prices. If consumer prices in countries with differing rates of productivity growth happened to be changing at similar rates when the world economy was not very highly integrated, their wholesale price indexes would be changing at different rates. If the world economy then became more integrated so that influences on prices were more completely transmitted from one country to another, the tightening of the linkage would reduce the dispersion of changes of wholesale prices, but the relationship between consumer prices and wholesale prices within each country would generally not be much changed, so that the dispersion of changes in consumer prices would increase. Thus the increase in transmission would increase rather than reduce the dispersion of changes in consumer price indexes.

It is also possible, although less probable, that increased transmission would not reduce dispersion of changes in GNP deflators. GNP deflators do not directly include changes in import prices, because they measure the average amount of value added per unit of national output. If, when import prices rise, the absolute margins added by domestic sellers of imported goods remain unchanged or nearly so, and if there is little rise in prices of import-competing output, there is little relationship between changes in average import prices and a properly calculated GNP deflator.

Despite all the foregoing cautionary observations about the relation between dispersion of changes in national price indexes and international transmission of inflationary pressures through market forces, the extension of inflation in recent years to virtually every country strongly suggests that international transmission, whether greater than in earlier years or not, has played a large role. Various possible mechanisms of transmission are examined below.

Mechanisms of International Transmission

Nearly all the mechanisms contributing to the international transmission of inflation have their basis in the economic integration of the world economy. In specifying *economic* integration, I use the word mainly in a narrow sense of markets and market responses, which excludes similarities in the policy responses of governments and large groups in the private sector caused by the spreading of common knowledge, opinions, technology, and decisions following upon increased international communication and travel.

Integration in the narrower sense of markets and market responses results from the international mobility (with or without actual movement) of goods and services, of labor, and of capital. Such mobility limits the degree to which prices, wages, and interest rates can differ in different countries. It also limits the degree to which their changes may diverge, an effect that is more relevant to the transmission of inflation. It is often said that the world economy has become more integrated as a result of reductions in the barriers to international movement of goods, labor, and capital. Although scattered evidence suggests that integration has increased since the end of World War II, it probably diminished between the two world wars, so it is less clear that it has in-

creased over the past half century. Considering that the international movements of capital in the decades preceding World War I were large relative
to total capital, the proposition that integration has increased should probably
not be fully accepted without more systematic examination than has been
made to date. Direct evidence would be reduction in the difference among
prices of identical or similar and therefore highly substitutable goods in different markets, including yields on financial assets. Less direct evidence is the
greater increase in international than in intranational trade, in international
travel, and in international movement of workers and capital. This increased
international mobility springs from the greater reduction of international than
of intranational barriers to movement as a result of technological changes.
Reduction in the cost of communication has increased the spread of information within a country about market and other conditions in other countries
and has facilitated business and other international negotiations. Improved
and increased teaching of foreign languages, the reduction (with scattered
interruptions) of government-imposed barriers to international trade and
capital movements, and other long-term changes also have contributed to
increasing the degree of world economic integration during the period since
World War II, if not over a longer period.

There is conflicting evidence, however, concerning even a postwar increase
in integration. Kravis and Lipsey state, on the basis of their new indexes of
export prices of selected manufactured goods and nonferrous metals: "It is
difficult to make any broad generalization about alterations in the degree of
market fragmentation in the world as a whole during 1953–64. International
diplomacy was bent toward the reduction of barriers through negotiations
under the General Agreement on Tariffs and Trade (GATT) and other
means; but the Cold War, domestic pressures in the developed countries, and
import substitution and related policies in developing countries worked in the
other direction." In a footnote they add: "Despite the common view that
trade barriers were diminishing, closer study of individual commodity sectors
discloses some tendencies in the opposite direction."[3]

An analysis of levels and changes of spot prices of fifteen primary commodities in different markets, presented in the first two lines of table 2, shows
that the average dispersion in levels of prices nearly doubled from 1957–59
to 1967–69. The dispersion of their annual changes was almost the same in
these two periods but in 1972 was more than four times as great.

The evidence concerning financial integration, based on two measures of

3. Irving B. Kravis and Robert E. Lipsey, *Price Competitiveness in World Trade*
(Columbia University Press for the National Bureau of Economic Research, 1971),
p. 55.

the dispersion of short-term interest rates calculated by Argy and Hodjera for ten industrial countries, indicates that it declined after 1958. The reductions, however, occurred mainly before 1966, and they found no evidence of any continuing decline between 1966 and 1971.[4] The standard deviation of these rates rose sharply from 1967–69 to 1972 and their coefficient of variation rose slightly.

Even the dispersion of movements of money wages, which one might suppose would be least likely to fall owing to the presumed obstacles to labor mobility, appears to have diminished, probably in part because of reductions in those obstacles and in part because of the indirect effects on factor prices of increased mobility of goods.

Less direct evidence of increasing integration is the fact that international trade has grown more rapidly than output during the postwar period, both in the world as a whole, whether measured in current prices (as shown in table 2, item 4) or, according to such measures as are available, in physical quantity, and in individual countries (as summarized in table 2, item 5, and for individual countries in table 3).[5] International trade has grown in relation to output not only during the postwar period but since 1938. Taking the 1967–69 average of trade ratios for individual OECD countries as representative of the recent postwar period, table 3 shows that, in comparison with 1938, they are higher by more than half of a percentage point for thirteen of the nineteen countries, lower by more than half a point for only five countries, and changed by less than that for one country. Similarly, in comparison with the 1947–49 average trade ratios, the averages for 1967–69 are higher for sixteen of twenty-one countries by more than 0.5 percent of GNP, lower by more than that for only three, and different by less for two. Between 1957–59 and 1967–69, however, the ratios rose for thirteen countries but fell for eight countries and changed hardly at all for one. These data suggest that by this measure the integration of the world economy increased substantially be-

4. See Victor Argy and Zoran Hodjera, "Financial Integration and Interest Rate Linkages in Industrial Countries, 1958–71," International Monetary Fund, *IMF Staff Papers*, vol. 20 (March 1973), especially pp. 28–35, and unpublished calculations for 1972 kindly made for me by Hodjera. Argy and Hodjera used U.S. Treasury bill rates and Eurodollar deposit rates as alternatives for the rate of return on dollar-denominated assets and measured dispersion by both the standard deviation and the coefficient of variation. The standard deviations were lowest in the period 1965–67 and then rose in the next three and one-half years, while the coefficients of variation showed no clear tendency to change.

5. It is worth mentioning, since it is almost universally ignored in discussions of this increase, that some of these increases must be attributable to multiplication of the number of countries, which converted some trade that was domestic into international trade. It is unlikely, however, that this change accounts for much of the increase.

Table 2. *Indicators of World Economic Integration,*
Selected Periods, 1929–72

Indicator	1929	1938	Average 1947–49	Average 1957–59	Average 1967–69	1972
1. Average percent deviation of prices of fifteen world-traded commodities in different markets from their averages in all markets[a]	n.a.	n.a.	n.a.	7.22	13.13	13.49
2. Average of deviations of annual percent changes in prices of fifteen world-traded commodities from their average changes in all markets[b]	n.a.	n.a.	n.a.	4.17	3.97	19.31
3. *Dispersion of short-term interest rates in ten industrial countries*						
Standard deviation	n.a.	n.a.	n.a.	2.37[e]	1.44	2.39
Coefficient of variation	n.a.	n.a.	n.a.	0.63[e]	0.27	0.33
4. *Noncommunist world trade as percent of output*						
Noncommunist trade (billions of dollars)	n.a.	n.a.	57[d]	116[d]	288[d]	525
Noncommunist output (billions of dollars)	n.a.	n.a.	705[d]	1,395[d]	2,939[d]	3,409
Trade as percent of output	n.a.	n.a.	8.1[d]	8.3[d]	9.8[d]	15.4
5. *Average of exports and imports of goods and services as percent of GNP, current prices, OECD countries*						
Eighteen countries[e]	n.a.	20.6	20.2	24.1	26.1	27.6
Five countries[f]	21.4	19.3	19.6	19.7	20.1	20.1

Sources: *Items 1 and 2:* Based on data in International Monetary Fund, *International Financial Statistics*, various issues, which give spot prices of internationally traded commodities in various markets.

Item 3: 1957–69, Victor Argy and Zoran Hodjera, "Financial Integration and Interest Rate Linkages in Industrial Countries, 1958–71," *IMF Staff Papers*, vol. 20 (March 1973), table 1, p. 30 (I have used the column headed "U.S. dollar rate," which includes the rate on three-month U.S. Treasury bills, rather than the column headed "Eurodollar rate," in which the rate on dollars is represented by the rate on three-month Eurodollar deposits); 1972, calculated and supplied by Hodjera in response to my request, for which I am grateful.

Item 4: Noncommunist trade, averages of merchandise exports (f.o.b.) and imports (c.i.f.) based on data in *International Financial Statistics, 1972* Supplement pp. xii–xv, and *International Financial Statistics*, vol. 28 (May 1975), pp. 40–41; noncommunist output, estimates by Herbert Block, U.S. Department of State, Bureau of Intelligence and Research (communication to author, May 22, 1975). Trade output data are in current prices.

Item 5: Based on data in table 3.

n. a. Not available.

a. Item 1 was obtained by calculating (a) the average spot price of each commodity in all markets for which prices were given; (b) the percentage deviation of the price in each market from the average price for that commodity, and (c) the average of these percentage deviations. This measure of percentage dispersion of prices for each commodity was then averaged over all fifteen commodities for which data were available in all years shown to obtain an average of percentage dispersions.

b. The figures in item 2 were obtained by making a calculation similar to that for item 1 for each commodity of percentage changes from the preceding year in each market. The percentage tween 1938 and 1967–69, but that most of this increase had occurred by 1957–59. If, however, the recent ratios of trade to GNP are compared with that for 1929 before the Great Depression (which can be done for only five of the twenty-two OECD countries shown in table 3) the ratio is higher in 1967–69 than in 1929 for only one of the five, Norway. It is less than in 1929 for Australia, Canada, and the United States and little more than half of the 1929 ratio for Japan. This small sample, for whatever it is worth, raises the question whether economic integration, measured by this ratio, has not decreased since the predepression years, and whether the increase since 1938 has done more than restore the degree of integration to or toward where it was before the Great Depression. That possibility is supported by general evidence that openness decreased substantially between 1929 and 1938. Whether the world economy is, as is commonly believed, more integrated than it was a half-century or more ago, and therefore whether inflation really does tend to be a more worldwide phenomenon than ever before, should perhaps be regarded as still open questions.

Turning now to the specific mechanisms of international transmission of inflation it is convenient to distinguish four ways in which inflation may be transmitted from one country to another. These mechanisms are described first as they operate under a regime of more or less fixed exchange rates; the modification necessary for one of freely floating rates is considered later.

Transmission under fixed exchange rates

First, inflation may be transmitted to a country through a rise in the prices of internationally traded goods. Increases in import prices tend to raise the consumer and wholesale price indexes of the importing country, and this tendency is realized if these increases do not cause offsetting decreases in the prices of other goods and services. Increases in the prices of imports also raise the GNP deflator, although only to the degree that they raise the prices of competing domestic output or that the rise in their prices is passed on to

---

changes in each market were averaged and the deviations of the percentage changes in individual markets from the average of their percentage changes, expressed in percentage points, were then calculated and averaged, to obtain the average deviation for each commodity over all markets. These average annual deviations were then averaged to derive a fifteen-commodity average of deviations in percentage changes.

    c. 1958–59 average.

    d. The figures in the third, fourth, and fifth columns are for 1950, 1960, and 1970, respectively.

    e. Unweighted averages of percentages of GNP for eighteen countries (Austria, Belgium, Canada, Denmark, France, Germany, Greece, Iceland, Ireland, Italy, Japan, Netherlands, Norway, Portugal, Sweden, Switzerland, United Kingdom, and United States).

    f. Same as preceding line but including only Australia, Canada, Japan, Norway, and United States, the only countries for which comparable 1929 data are available.

Table 3. *Foreign Trade in Goods and Services as a Percentage of GNP,
Twenty-two OECD Countries, Selected Periods, 1929–72*[a]

Country	1929	1938	Average 1947–49	Average 1957–59	Average 1967–69	1972
Australia[b]	19.3	18.3	22.5	18.0	17.3	16.7
Austria	n.a.	17.6[e]	11.3[d]	24.2	26.3	30.6
Belgium	n.a.	28.2	25.9	33.3	40.6	46.5
Canada	29.0	24.3	25.6	20.1	23.3	24.2
Denmark	n.a.	26.2	22.4	33.2	30.4	30.1
Finland	n.a.	n.a.	19.2[d]	21.9	24.3	28.8
France	n.a.	13.1	13.8	13.9	13.3	17.0
Germany	n.a.	16.5[e]	8.5[f]	19.0	20.0	21.4
Greece	n.a.	17.8	11.7	15.1	15.8	18.9
Iceland	n.a.	46.8	30.1	25.0	39.3	41.1
Ireland	n.a.	25.5	35.7	35.8	42.1	40.3
Italy	n.a.	7.6	11.3	13.4	18.1	21.6
Japan	19.4	19.7	5.8	11.6	10.4	10.5
Netherlands	n.a.	28.1	30.3	43.9	42.3	44.3
New Zealand	n.a.	n.a.	32.3[g]	26.3	22.2	21.7
Norway	33.6	29.2	36.2	43.8	43.5	42.4
Portugal	n.a.	13.0	20.8	21.5	27.6	29.5
Spain	n.a.	n.a.	n.a.	8.9	14.1	16.8
Sweden	n.a.	20.1[h]	22.1	25.9	23.1	25.0
Switzerland	n.a.	17.9	23.5	32.4	33.7	35.0
United Kingdom	n.a.	16.9	19.2	23.0	22.1	23.4
United States	6.3	4.4	5.5	5.2	5.8	6.7
All countries[i]	n.a.	20.6	20.2	24.1	26.1	27.6

Sources: Except as noted below for individual countries, data come from the following sources:
For 1938 and 1947–49, trade data for several countries and GNP are from Organisation for
European Economic Co-operation, *Statistics of National Product and Expenditure, No. 2: 1938
and 1947 to 1955* (Paris: OEEC, 1957). Other 1938 trade data are from International Monetary
Fund, *Balance of Payments Yearbook, 1938, 1946, 1947* (IMF, 1949). Trade data for later years
come from *Balance of Payments Yearbook*, vol. 5 (for 1947–53), and vols. 13, 14, 20, 22, 24 for
other years. GNP data for 1948–59 are from IMF, *International Financial Statistics*, 1972 Supplement; for 1967, from *International Financial Statistics*, vol. 27 (December 1974); for 1968–72,
from ibid., vol. 28 (August 1975).
   Australia: N. G. Butlin, *Australian Domestic Product, Investment and Foreign Borrowing, 1861–
1938/39* (Cambridge: Cambridge University Press, 1962), pp. 442–43 (for trade data, 1929), and
p. 468 (for GNP, 1947); E. A. Boehm, *Twentieth Century Economic Development in Australia*
(Melbourne: Longman Australia, 1971), p. 216 (for GNP, 1939); Benjamin U. Ratchford, *Public Expenditures in Australia* (Duke University Press, 1959), p. 303 (for GNP, 1929 and 1948).
   Belgium: OECD, *National Accounts Statistics, 1956–1965* (Paris: OECD, 1967) (for trade data,
1957–59); OECD, *National Accounts of OECD Countries, 1960–1970* (for trade data, 1967–69);
ibid., *1962–1973* (Paris: OECD, 1975), vol. 2 (for trade data, 1972).
   France: OECD, *National Accounts Statistics, 1956–1965* (for trade data, 1957–59).
   Japan: Kazushi Ohkawa and Henry Rosovsky, *Japanese Economic Growth: Trend Acceleration
in the Twentieth Century* (Stanford University Press, 1973), pp. 278–79 (for GNP, 1929, 1938,
1947–49), and pp. 298–301 (for trade data, 1920, 1938, 1947–49).
   Norway: Odd Aukrust, Central Bureau of Statistics of Norway (correspondence with author,
April 7, 1976) (for GNP, 1929, and trade data, 1929–48); Central Bureau of Statistics of Norway
National Accounts, 1865–1960 (Oslo: 1965), pp. 346–65 (for GNP, 1938–49), and p. 368 (for trade
data, 1949).

immediate or ultimate domestic buyers in greater absolute amount. It may be assumed, however, that in the absence of deflationary pressures or price controls in the importing country, the combination of effects on competing domestic output and net increases in markups on the imports themselves is not negligible, so that a rise in import prices normally increases the GNP deflator, too. The degree and even the direction of further repercussions depend on a variety of factors governing intranational transmission, such as the effects of the initial price increases on wages and thereby on the costs and prices of goods and services not linked to imports through direct or indirect input-output relationships.

One of the influences affecting not only the degree but the direction in which prices of nontradable output are influenced is monetary policy. If it is sufficiently restraining, it may force compensating decreases in prices of nontradable goods. The fact that monetary influences are also a channel for international transmission indicates that the various mechanisms of international transmission are interrelated and that the mechanisms conventionally described as channels of international transmission depend for their operation on assumptions about domestic monetary conditions and about other elements of intranational transmission that are rarely mentioned.

Increases in world prices of a country's exports also generally have pervasive price-raising effects. If they are caused by factors outside the country under consideration, they lead to an increase in the money demand for its exports, whether they result from an increase in foreign demand for the total world supply of such goods or from decreases in the supply functions of foreign competitors. The GNP deflator is directly affected by these increases in price. To the extent that the exports consist of consumer goods the domestic and export prices of which move together, or to the extent that domestically consumed goods are close substitutes for the exports or use them as direct or

---

United States: U.S. Department of Commerce, *The National Income and Product Accounts of the United States, 1929–1965: Statistical Tables* (Government Printing Office, 1966), p. 2 (for GNP, 1929), and p. 74 (for trade data, 1929).

n.a. Not available.

a. Percentages are based on data in current prices. Trade is defined as one-half of the sum of exports and imports of goods and services, including merchandise, nonmonetary gold, freight, other transportation, travel, investment income in gross amounts received and paid, and other current public and private services.

b. Fiscal years ending June 30.

c. 1937.

d. Average of 1948 and 1949, only.

e. 1936.

f. 1949 only.

g. 1948 only.

h. Based on GNP for fiscal year.

i. Unweighted averages of percentages for countries for which 1938 and later data are available.

indirect inputs, export price increases also affect the consumer price index. If the exports that rise in price are neither consumer goods nor inputs into them, they do not affect that index directly, but several possible intranational linkages with other variables can cause them to affect other domestic prices. The model described in Aukrust's paper illustrates one such linkage.[6] In it, wages in the tradable goods industries are tied to the prices of tradable goods, and other wages are tied to those in the tradable goods industries. Here again is an illustration that a full exposition of how an exogenous foreign influence affects a national price level explains not only what is transmitted internationally but how the affected variables in the recipient country affect its national price level; in other words, how changes in the domestic variables that are directly affected are transmitted intranationally. Whatever the exports for which foreign demand increases, that increase raises the net balance of goods and services of the exporting country and the income generated in export production. This effect may be said to illustrate the second mechanism of transmission.

This second mechanism is the tendency for any increase in the nominal goods-and-services balance to generate an increase in aggregate money demand for domestic output. Through this primary increase, further increases in income and demand are generated by means of the familiar multiplier effect. If this tendency is not suppressed by policy measures, it becomes an actuality. In an inflationary external environment such an increase in the balance of goods and services is generally the result of an increase in foreign demand for the total world output of the given country's exports, but, as noted above, it may also be the effect of a decrease in supplies offered at given prices by foreign competitors.

Increases in the demand for a country's exports raise its domestic nominal income and aggregate demand, whether they increase the quantity of exports, export prices, or both. If the demand increases raise export prices but not real domestic output, the improvement in the terms of trade permits an increase in total real expenditure by domestic residents,[7] but nominal aggregate demand does expand, thereby generating inflationary pressures.

Similarly, a rise in the balance on goods and services as the result of an externally caused reduction of imports can bring about inflationary pressure by diverting domestic demand from foreign to domestic output. Such a diver-

6. See pages 109–43.
7. The possibility of an increase in absorption with neither a reduction in the net balance of goods and services nor an increase in output may seem paradoxical, but any appearance of paradox disappears when it is recognized that an increase of real absorption requires neither an increase in output nor a decrease in the balance of goods and services when the terms of trade improve.

sion will occur when prices of imports rise and the demand for them is more elastic than unity.[8]

When import prices rise and the price elasticity of demand for them is less than unity so that the value of imports rises, the two mechanisms operate in conflicting ways. The rise of import prices themselves and of prices of goods that are produced from them or are substitutes for them is inflationary, but the decrease in the net balance of goods and services, to the extent that it is not offset by a decrease in the saving function, reduces aggregate demand and is in that respect deflationary. Whether a rise in import prices that has such effects should be regarded as "inflationary" or "deflationary" is in part a semantic question that arises because the term "inflationary" is used to mean both "tending to raise prices" and "tending to create or increase excess aggregate demand." Inasmuch as excess demand can be reduced by a rise in prices caused otherwise than by excess of demand, a rise in prices can be inflationary in the first sense and deflationary or anti-inflationary in the second.[9]

But the question is only partly semantic; there is also a substantive question. Even if the term "inflationary" is used, as it has been in this paper, to mean "tending to raise the general level of prices," the rise in import prices and the fall in the net balance of goods and services have conflicting effects on the price level. It is not possible to say, a priori, what the net effect on the direction of movement of the general price level will be, since the direction of its effect depends both on the relative sizes of various coefficients of behavior in the mechanism determining prices and on whether the effects being con-

8. An improvement in the balance of goods and services when import prices fall and the demand for them is less than unity may also have an expansionary effect on the importing country, but that case is not one of transmission of inflationary pressure. The decline of world food and raw material prices during the deflation of the early 1930s appears to have been a decided stimulus to recovery in the United Kingdom, and, as has been suggested to me, perhaps also to Japanese expansion from 1953 to the 1960s.

9. The same issue arose during World War II in the United States and the United Kingdom, and presumably also in other countries, in the controversy over the effects of subsidies to hold down prices to consumers in the face of rising prices to producers. It was argued on the one hand that such subsidies were counterinflationary because they they held prices down, and on the other hand that they were inflationary because they increased excess demand by increasing government expenditures and, indeed, by their very effect of holding down prices to consumers. The possibility of having prices rise and excess demand fall at the same time requires that prices be determined at least in part by some influence other than excess demand. In the case of World War II subsidies, this other influence was price control. In the case considered here it is exogenously determined world prices of imports. The quadrupling of the world price of oil in 1973 precisely illustrates this case of a change in the price of an import with an inelastic demand that both raises prices and decreases excess demand.

sidered are those on the average price of gross national product, which includes exports but not imports, or that of gross national expenditure, which includes imports but not exports.

The third major mechanism for the international transmission of inflation is the chain of effects that is or tends to be the result of an inflow of money caused by a surplus in the balance of payments. What is involved here is not the *change* in the balance of goods and services from a level to which the economy had become adjusted but the existence of surplus in the total balance, that is, in the sum of the current and capital accounts, on the official settlements definition. The mechanism is not an externally caused change in the flow of income and expenditure but an increase in the foreign component of the base for the domestic money supply caused by an inflow of international monetary reserves, a consequent increase in the domestic money supply, and a presumed consequent increase in aggregate domestic demand caused by the public's efforts to reduce money holdings that have become excessive. Inflationary influences abroad that are most likely to give rise to such inflows are income expansion and easing of monetary policies in foreign countries, both of which would tend to cause a surplus in the total balance of payments of the country being considered, with the probability that foreign income expansion would work through effects on the current account and that foreign monetary expansion would affect both the current and capital accounts.

One may speculate that this mechanism would have operated weakly or with a long lag, if at all, in the United States during most of the postwar period had the United States been in surplus, because its net total balance was not so much financed by changes in reserve assets as largely by changes in liabilities to foreign monetary authorities that did not affect the reserve base for the domestic money stock. If the United States had had surpluses and large liabilities to foreign monetary authorities, its surpluses probably would have been financed by decreases in these liabilities rather than by increases in reserve assets, and probably would not have increased the reserve base or the money stock for some time. Had such liabilities to foreigners been small (or had they become small by being drawn down), surpluses would have expanded reserve assets. The reserve expansion might have been sterilized for a while, as it was in the 1920s, although it may also be guessed that such sterilization would not have continued indefinitely; in that case the mechanism would have come into operation after a lag.[10]

10. It should be added that the reserve-currency arrangement itself, which in effect gave the United States the power to print international reserves, is regarded by many, perhaps most, economists as making it improbable that the United States would have run surpluses for any protracted period.

It should also be recognized that not every inflow of monetary reserves gives rise to an excess domestic money supply, even in the absence of sterilization. The transmission of inflation through an inflow of monetary reserves requires that the inflow create an excess supply of money or increase an existing excess. Postulation of this result implies that the supply and demand for the stock of money in the country receiving the reserves were initially in equilibrium or that there was already an excess supply. If there was an excess demand that was not being satisfied by the domestic monetary authority, however, the reserve inflow would at first only reduce that excess demand. If the reserve inflow continues, of course, it will sooner or later eliminate the excess demand for money and create an excess supply. Until that point is reached, however, it should be expected only to reduce downward pressure on aggregate demand for output, not actually to raise the domestic price level. The surpluses of other countries corresponding to U.S. deficits were probably of this demand-satisfying character until about the mid-1960s.[11] To the extent that deficits in the U.S. balance of payments reflected unsatisfied demand of foreigners for dollars or for their own currencies, those deficits were not positively inflationary; they merely avoided the deflationary influence abroad of leaving that demand unsatisfied. Insofar as liquid non-money assets are close substitutes for money, a surplus of balance of payments on the net liquidity definition will also have an inflationary effect on the surplus country, even if it involves no increase in monetary reserves, because it increases the stock of liquid assets in the hands of the public.[12]

With the renascence of monetarist views, the monetary channel of international transmission, which was expounded by David Hume in 1752 in his famous essay, "Of the Balance of Trade," has not only been elaborated theoretically but has been assigned increasing importance in explaining the worldwide character of recent inflation by contributors to this volume as well as others.[13] It has been pointed out that the deficits in the U.S. balance of payments have increased the international monetary reserves of other countries and therewith their monetary bases without reducing the monetary base

11. See Emile Despres, Charles P. Kindleberger, and Walter S. Salant, "The Dollar and World Liquidity: A Minority View," *Economist* (London), vol. 218 (February 5, 1966) (Brookings Reprint 115). See also Walter S. Salant, "Capital Markets and the Balance of Payments of a Financial Center," in William Fellner, Fritz Machlup, Robert Triffin, and others, *Maintaining and Restoring Balance in International Payments* (Princeton University Press, 1966), chap. 14 (Brookings Reprint 123).

12. See John G. Gurley and Edward S. Shaw, *Money in a Theory of Finance* (Brookings Institution, 1960), and the literature stimulated by that book.

13. See, for example, the paper by Alexander Swoboda (pages 9–51) and the discussion by Edward Shaw (pages 442–45), as well as various papers by Harry Johnson on the monetary theory of the balance of payments.

Table 4. *Increase in Monetary Aggregates, 1967–72,*[a] *and GNP,*
1968–73, in Six Major Industrialized Countries

Monetary or GNP aggregate	France	Germany	Italy	Japan[b]	United Kingdom[c]	United States
Increase in components of reserve money (billions of national currency units)						
1. Net foreign assets of central bank	15.59	42.8[d]	−22	4,682	641	−1.7[d]
2. Net domestic assets of central bank	29.73	6.7	6,754	2	794	24.2
3. Total reserve money	45.31	49.6	6,734	4,686	1,435	22.4
Increase in components of reserve money (percent)						
4. Net foreign assets of central bank	45.1	121.6[d]	−0.6	644.9	25.0	−11.4[d]
5. Net domestic assets of central bank	69.5	57.8	184.1	...	12.1	45.3
6. Total reserve money	58.5	106.2	93.5	140.0	36.0	32.8
7. Money[e]	54.7	62.8	143.6	156.0	49.9	37.0
8. Money and quasi-money[f]	106.0	92.6	104.1	144.4	75.1	55.6
Increase in gross national product measures (percent)						
9. GNP in current prices	81.6	71.6	72.1[g]	115.2	66.7	49.8
10. Real GNP (1970 prices)	33.7	28.4	23.5[g]	58.0	15.9	18.8
11. GNP deflator (1970 = 100)	35.8	33.6	39.4[g]	36.2	43.8	26.2

Sources: Lines 1–8, IMF, *International Financial Statistics*, vol. 21 (September 1968), and various other relevant issues; lines 9–11, *International Financial Statistics*, vol. 29 (January 1976). Figures are rounded and may not add to totals.

a. Averages of ends of November, December, and succeeding January.

b. Changes in monetary aggregates are based on averages of September, December, and succeeding January; November 1967 figures are not available.

c. Changes in monetary aggregates are based on end-of-year figures only.

d. Gross foreign assets.

e. Money is defined as currency outside banks plus private-sector deposits in the central bank (including deposits in the central bank of official entities that are not part of the government) plus demand deposits at commercial banks.

f. Quasi-money is defined as time, savings, and foreign-currency deposits held by the private sector (residents only) in commercial banks and in the central bank.

g. Gross domestic product.

of the United States, and that this has led to a vast expansion in the aggregate of national money supplies.

In this connection, the data for several major industrialized countries relevant to these monetary influences contained in table 4 are of interest. This table shows the change in the domestic and foreign components of the monetary base of each country, the changes in each country's supply of money, narrowly and broadly defined, and gross national product in current prices, as well as the quantity and price components of that change in GNP. For the monetary aggregates, the change is between the end of 1967 and the end of 1972; for GNP it is the change from 1968 to 1973 (to allow for some lag). Over the whole five-year period, the percentage increase in reserve money was of approximately the same order of magnitude as the increase in the stock of money, either narrowly defined or broadly defined (money or money plus quasi-money, in the terminology of the International Monetary Fund). All six countries experienced increases in reserve money greater than in real GNP. In Germany and Japan, however, where reserve money more than doubled, 85 percent of the increase in Germany and all of the increase in Japan resulted from an inflow of foreign reserves, whereas in Italy, which also came close to doubling its reserve money, the increase came wholly from an increase in the net domestic assets of its central bank. The contrast brings out clearly that an inflow of international reserves was not a necessary condition for an increase in the money supply. Although the Italian currency depreciated substantially beginning early in 1973, the domestically generated increase in reserve money had been going on more or less steadily throughout the preceding five years. In Germany, despite the doubling of reserve money, the rise in GNP in current prices was only about 72 percent, which suggests that an inflow of foreign reserves and a rise in total reserve money does not necessarily lead to a proportional rise in the nominal GNP even in five years. Also, the Italian money supply, narrowly defined, rose 144 percent although reserve money rose by only 94 percent. Thus, table 4 at least suggests that an extraordinary inflow of reserves may persist for quite a few years without an extraordinary price rise, and extraordinary price rises have been generated and persisted for some time independently of an inflow of reserves.

It is noteworthy that the GNP deflators for all the countries, despite the diversity of their monetary experiences, increased substantially over the five-year period. The U.S. deflator rose by 26 percent, the others between 34 and 44 percent.

The monetary channel of transmission introduces the possibility of another conflict between different mechanisms of transmission—one between externally generated income effects and externally generated monetary effects. Expansion of aggregate demand abroad may, by raising the world price of imports, reduce a country's surplus of goods and services (or increase its deficit), which would have a contracting effect on its domestic income, and at the same time, reduce foreign interest rates and thereby stimulate a flow of capital into it. This inflow of capital could cause a surplus in its total balance of payments despite the decline in its balance on goods and services. In that case a decrease in income and in the portion of aggregate demand for domestic output determined by income would be accompanied by a simultaneous increase in the monetary base and (in the absence of sterilization) in the stock of money, and in aggregate demand insofar as it is determined by excess money holdings. This situation would be comparable to simultaneously relaxing monetary policy and increasing the restrictiveness of fiscal policy by cutting government expenditures or raising taxes. Its net effect on the price level depends on answers to the same questions that have been debated between monetarists and fiscalists in recent years. In an economy in which prices have some downward flexibility, no generalization can be made even about the direction of the effect on the price level. Insofar as prices are inflexible downward, the price level is almost certain to increase, whatever the net effect on aggregate demand, since prices will rise in the sectors experiencing increases of demand without falling in others. Uncertainty about the outcome is then confined to how much any specified price level will rise.

The fourth mechanism of transmission, the international linkage of wages other than the indirect linkage through markets for goods, may take several forms. One is through competition between national labor markets, which can operate when labor is mobile between the countries concerned, either directly or via third countries. This linkage is of course limited by immigration laws and differences in language, customs, and other social factors impeding mobility, but it has been a significant influence in recent decades, when there have been large movements of labor into Germany, Switzerland, and France from Italy, Spain, Greece, and some countries of southeastern Europe and North Africa.[14] It was largely the rise of wages in Germany and its potential for drawing labor from the Netherlands that broke Dutch wage policy in 1963.[15] A study by Helliwell found that the relative tightness of the labor markets in the United States and Canada has a substantial effect on both emigration from and immigration into Canada. It presumably would also affect the wage level in Canada.[16] The tightness of the U.S. labor market also affects migration between the United States and islands in the Caribbean.

14. Almost six million foreign workers were employed in Belgium, Denmark, Germany, France, Luxembourg, Netherlands, and Switzerland in 1973. In the same year 28 percent of the Swiss labor force consisted of foreigners. (*Economist* [London], vol. 227 [August 9, 1975], p. 23.)

15. See, for example, Piet de Wolff's survey of incomes policy in the Netherlands in *On Incomes Policy,* Papers and Proceedings from a Conference in Honour of Erik Lundberg (Stockholm: Industrial Council for Social and Economic Studies, 1969), pp. 33, 35; and Anne Romanis Braun, "The Role of Incomes Policy in Industrial Countries Since World War II," *IMF Staff Papers,* vol. 22 (March 1975), especially the citation of A. Kervyn de Lettenhove on p. 33.

16. John Helliwell, "Trade, Capital Flows, and Migration as Channels for International Transmission of Stabilization Policies," in Albert Ando, Richard Herring, and Richard Marston, eds., *International Aspects of Stabilization Policies* (Federal Reserve Bank of Boston Conference Series 12 [June 1974 conference]), pp. 241–78.

In addition to the pressure of competition between national labor markets, other influences on wage linkages often thought to be important generally specify or imply monopoly or oligopoly in the labor market. International trade unions or cooperation between national trade unions have been cited, and so has the effect on wages of transnational pricing policies of multinational corporations. But the most commonly hypothesized effects operating on the supply side of the labor market and thought to be important are the so-called demonstration effect and the price-expectations effect. The demonstration effect refers to pressure by labor unions in one country to obtain wage increases because such increases have been obtained by unions in the same industries of other countries. Whether such wage demands are granted depends to a considerable extent on the resistance of employers, which in turn depends in part on the possibility of passing cost increases on to buyers. That possibility, in turn, is influenced to some extent by conditions in product markets, but in countries where wages are set by government tribunals, it may be determined and is certainly influenced by other factors as well.

One such factor is the change in consumer prices. In small open countries, where prices of consumer goods are greatly influenced by import prices, wages may be linked to foreign export prices and thus indirectly to foreign wages. It has been argued that the expectation of increases in the consumer price index based on past actual price increases also raises the wage level, and this influence, to the extent that it operates, would also be a mechanism for international transmission of inflation or of its acceleration. Perry's analysis of the evidence, however, suggests that if such an effect exists at all, it is small.[17]

It has also been argued that rises in the prices of imported consumer goods raise wages not only through awards made by governmental tribunals setting wages but because of labor union militancy. Specific forms of the latter argument are that labor unions bargain for real wages, so that money wages rise

17. This statement is based on the finding by George L. Perry in his study of influences on money wages in ten industrial countries. (See his "Determinants of Wage Inflation around the World" in *Brookings Papers on Economic Activity (BPEA),* *2:1975,* especially pp. 408–09 and 413–35.) Earlier work on this question was done by Otto Eckstein and Roger Brinner in *The Inflation Process in the United States,* a study prepared for the use of the Joint Economic Committee, 92:2 (Government Printing Office, 1972); by Robert J. Gordon in "Wage-Price Controls and the Shifting Phillips Curve" in *BPEA, 2:1972,* pp. 385–421, and in other papers in subsequent issues of *BPEA;* and by William D. Nordhaus in "The Worldwide Wage Explosion," also in *BPEA, 2:1972,* pp. 431–64. See also further references in Nordhaus's article. Nordhaus's testing of several hypotheses advanced to explain the wage explosion has been criticized as "limited and simplistic" in the OECD's "International Transmission of Inflation," p. 84 (see note 2 for full citation), and by Michael A. Salant and Richard J. Sweeney in an internal Department of the Treasury memorandum of July 2, 1973.

with the consumer price index, and even that they bargain for real wages after income taxes, the effective rates of which rise with nominal wages, so that nominal wages before taxes rise by more than the consumer price index.[18]

The importance of linkages that operate on national price levels through demonstration effects and other domestic cost-push factors has been denied or at least questioned on both theoretical and empirical grounds. The theoretical ground is that cost-push factors could not operate in the absence of other conditions, such as an inflationary monetary environment, and therefore can explain, at most, movements in relative prices. The a priori argument is implied but not elaborated by Johnson, who derides "people naive enough to accept the concept" of cost-push inflation; he states that on the quantity-theoretical or monetarist approach, " 'cost-push' is merely an institutional manifestation of the natural tendency to restore equilibrium in real relative price relationships whose expression in monetary terms has been disrupted by the erosion of the real value of money through inflation."[19] Acceptance of the argument implied by Johnson (and more specifically by his statement quoted in note 19) requires faith that the relative prices appropriate to equilibrium are always restored within the time period relevant to the inflation that is being explained, even when at least one of the parties to the wage bargain is a monopoly. This is a more positive argument than the mere contention that an expansion of the money supply is *necessary* to support a price inflation precipitated by union pressure for higher wages; it states that such a monetary expansion is also *sufficient* to produce that inflation, so that the same rate of inflation would have occurred without the union pressure. It also implies that the rate of monetary expansion is not influenced by the pressure for higher wages.

One might agree that an equal monetary expansion in the absence of

18. The view that unions bargain for real wages after taxes has been put forward, on the basis of evidence drawn from the United Kingdom, by F. Wilkinson and H. Tanner in *Do Trade Unions Cause Inflation?* (Cambridge: Cambridge University Press, 1972).

19. See Harry G. Johnson, *Inflation and the Monetarist Controversy* (Amsterdam: North-Holland, 1972; distributed in the United States and Canada by American Elsevier), pp. 56–57. The passage quoted above is followed by an attack on incomes policy, which, Johnson says, "can only succeed if it is backed up by sufficient monetary restraint to make stability of money prices on the average, and the corresponding behaviour of money wages, rational behaviour in real terms for the individual economic decision-taking units concerned" (page 57). The general hypothesis that trade union militancy is an explanation of inflation is examined for five continental EEC countries and compared with some results for the United Kingdom by R. Ward and G. Zis in "Trade Union Militancy as an Explanation of Inflation: An International Comparison," in *Manchester School,* vol. 42 (March 1974), pp. 46–65, and by some of the other writers cited in that article.

union pressure would suffice to produce the same degree of inflation sooner or later.[20] But this proposition implies only that an increase in the money supply creates disequilibrium in the demand-supply relations for the stock of money and that the disequilibrium will be reduced at *some* rate and the excess supply eliminated at *some* time in the future. It is perfectly consistent with this view to hold at the same time that the *rate* at which an excess supply of money is eliminated—by inflation—is influenced by the strength of wage-push. The argument that a given expansion of the money stock creates a disequilibrium has a bearing on whether wage-push influences how far the price level will ultimately rise but none whatever on whether it influences the time it will take to attain that higher level.

Furthermore, the monetary-theoretical criticism of the wage-push argument assumes that the expansion of the money supply itself is no larger because of wage-push than it would be if union demands were smaller. That is possible, but it is not to be taken for granted. The view may be accepted that market forces would sooner or later eliminate the distortion of relative prices resulting from wage-push in one sector. If the wage-push is resisted, however, and the monetary authorities foresee that this resistance will make elimination of the distortion by market forces a long and painful process, they may decide to help restore equilibrium by easing monetary policy. The conclusion, perhaps a paradoxical one, is that the more the monetary authorities accept the need to restore equilibrium through forcing *relative* decreases in some prices, the more probable it is that wage-push will affect the money supply, and the weaker, therefore, is the argument that it does not contribute to inflation. The response of the monetary authority to wage-push has to be incorporated in the model as an endogenous variable that responds to changes in the level of unemployment, among other things.

The empirical work designed to test whether trade union militancy provides a satisfactory explanation of inflation of money wage rates runs into the difficulty of finding a quantitative measure of union militancy.[21] Ward

20. To deny this, one would have to argue that the money holdings of households and business firms could increase equally without causing an equal increase in the demand for current output, either as a direct result of their larger money holdings or as a result of the holders' bidding down interest rates and thereby stimulating expenditure on current output indirectly. I am not inclined to assert that proposition; I accept that the interest-elasticity of the demand for the money stock is normally not infinite and also that the interest-elasticity and liquid-asset-elasticity of demand for current output are normally not zero. (See Walter S. Salant, "The Demand for Money and the Concept of Income Velocity," *Journal of Political Economy*, vol. 49 [June 1941], especially pp. 395–407, for an early discussion of these issues.)

21. This problem is the subject of the paper by D. L. Purdy and G. Zis, "On the Concept and Measurement of Trade Union Militancy," in D. Laidler and D. Purdy,

and Zis (in "Trade Union Militancy as an Explanation of Inflation"), using three alternative measures of strike activity as a proxy for such militancy, find that in none of six countries that they examined is the coefficient on that variable in any of its three forms statistically significant. In appraising their conclusions, however, it should be recognized that the extent to which militancy causes strikes depends on the degree to which employers resist union demands and that the strength of that resistance is bound to depend partly on the state of aggregate demand and its direction of change.[22] Despite union militancy, strikes may not occur if monetary and fiscal policies are such that market conditions permit wage demands to be met without strikes. From that obvious fact it is sometimes inferred that monetary and fiscal policies are—and that union militancy is not—responsible for wage increases. The negative part of that inference is not necessarily correct. Permissive monetary and fiscal policies may be a necessary condition for unions to get the wage increases they demand without strikes, but they may not be a sufficient condition; if the wage increases demanded by unions had been less,

---

eds., *Inflation and Labour Markets* (Manchester: Manchester University Press, and Toronto: University of Toronto Press, 1974), pp. 38–60, and is considered in other papers in the same volume.

22. There is also empirical work that supports the thesis that union militancy does play an important role. Hines, measuring trade union pushfulness by changes from 1893 to 1961 in the percentage of the labor force unionized, found that in the United Kingdom "trade unions do affect the rate of change of wages *independently* of the demand for labour" (his italics). (See A. G. Hines, "Trade Unions and Wage Inflation in the United Kingdom, 1893–1961," *Review of Economic Studies*, vol. 31 [October 1964], p. 221.) Hines's model has been critically examined by D. L. Purdy and G. Zis, "Trade Unions and Wage Inflation in the U.K.: A Reappraisal," also in Laidler and Purdy, eds., *Inflation and Labour Markets*, pp. 1–37. See also Michael Parkin, Michael T. Sumner, and Robert A. Jones, "A Survey of the Econometric Evidence of the Effects of Incomes Policy on the Rate of Inflation," in Michael Parkin and Michael T. Sumner, eds., *Incomes Policy and Inflation* (Manchester: Manchester University Press, 1972), pp. 1–29, and A. G. Hines, "The Determinants of the Rate of Change of Money Wage Rates and the Effectiveness of Incomes Policy," in H. G. Johnson and A. R. Nobay, eds., *The Current Inflation* (London: Macmillan, 1971), pp. 143–75. Godfrey, although rejecting Hines's view that the percentage of the labor force unionized and the rate of change in this percentage are adequate proxies for union pushfulness in the period 1956 to 1969, and using the number of work stoppages as the proxy, also found evidence, which he called tentative, "that union militancy . . . is an important determinant of the rate of change of money wage rates," and that the unemployment variable was insignificant. (See Leslie Godfrey, "The Phillips Curve: Incomes Policy and Trade Union Effects," in Johnson and Nobay, eds., *The Current Inflation*, pp. 99–124 [p. 118 for the quotation].) Taylor also found significant effects on wages for measures of strike activity. (See Jim Taylor, "Incomes Policy, the Structure of Unemployment and the Phillips Curve: the United Kingdom Experience, 1953–70," in Parkin and Sumner, eds., *Incomes Policy and Inflation*, pp. 182–200.)

laxity in those policies might have led to smaller increases, at least in short periods. Indeed, it may be union militancy that forces an accommodating monetary policy. In using strike activity as a measure of union militancy, therefore, it is necessary to find some method of "holding constant" (in the statistical sense) the degree of employer resistance. A surrogate for that variable might be some measure of the restrictiveness of monetary and fiscal policy or the level and rate of change of the relation between actual and potential GNP.

Transmission under floating exchange rates

The above discussion of mechanisms by which inflation is transmitted among countries assumes that their national moneys are linked by relatively fixed exchange rates. Consider now whether inflation tends to be transmitted internationally when exchange rates are flexible by making the extreme, if unrealistic, assumption that these rates are permitted to float freely.

It is widely accepted that a country whose domestic monetary and fiscal policies are not inflationary can avoid importing inflation from the outside world if the foreign exchange value of its currency is free to change, and that one whose domestic policies are inflationary will not transmit inflationary impulses to others if its currency is similarly free to change. This proposition implies that under floating exchange rates the mechanisms of international transmission do not operate or that their operation in transmitting price changes in national currency to prices expressed in other national currencies is diluted. It may best be examined in relation to the specific mechanisms of transmission previously discussed.

Consider first a rise in the world prices of tradable goods. A general rise in the world prices of a country's exports will tend to raise the value of its exports and thereby create an excess demand for its currency at the initial exchange rate. The appreciation of its currency will prevent or mitigate the rise in prices measured in its own currency. If the world prices of its imports are not rising, import prices in its national currency will fall and domestic demand will shift away from its own import-competing output, thereby putting downward pressure on the prices of that output.[23] If little exportable

23. The statement that the value of exports will rise depends basically on the assumption that changes in the prices of world-traded goods, when expressed in the same currency, change more or less in the same degree in different markets. This proposition asumes that they are highly competitive and are mobile between markets. Robert Dunn, however, in a study of the relation between Canadian and American prices of six traded industrial goods (copper, coal, gasoline, crude oil, window glass, and rolling mill products) during the period 1950–62, when Canada had a flexible exchange rate

output is sold at home and prices of imports and import-competing goods are flexible downward, the average price levels of gross national expenditure and consumer prices may actually decline, because these price levels include prices of imports and import-competing goods but not prices of actual exports, and these prices are likely to fall enough to offset the dampened rise in the prices of exportable output sold to domestic residents. The GNP deflator may change in either direction, however; even though it does not include prices of imports, it includes both prices of exports, which presumably rise, and prices of import-competing output, which fall. If the fall in prices of imports and import-competing goods outweighs the rise in prices of domestically consumed exportable output, there will be no upward pressure on wages from the side of consumer prices. The general wage level may rise in this case only if wages in the export sector share substantially in the rise of export prices and if wages in other sectors of the economy are closely tied to those in the export sector, as is assumed in the Scandinavian model. In any event, it seems clear that whatever the direction of the change in the gross national expenditure (GNE) deflator or the consumer price index and however much the GNP deflator rises, all the price indexes will rise less than they would have done under a fixed exchange rate.

Consider next a rise in the world price of imports as a result of influences outside the country under study. At first, such a rise will tend to increase the consumer price index. If the demand for imports is elastic to prices, the exchange value of the currency will rise and foreign demand for exports will fall, subjecting the prices of exportable outputs to downward pressure, but the rise in import prices will shift domestic demand to import-competing goods and perhaps stimulate demand for other domestic output. Thus there will be conflicting influences directly on both prices and on demand for ex-

---

and its dollar moved over a range of about 14 percent in relation to the U.S. dollar, finds no close relationship between changes in the exchange rate and relative prices over six-month periods in any of the six markets, and that only one market showed even a rough relationship. While Dunn finds that the "price reactions which perfect competition implies did not occur in *any* of the six markets" (his italics), he recognizes that the variation in price relationships has limits and it seems to follow from what he says that the limits become narrower the longer the price discrepancies persist. His results, therefore, do not appear to invalidate the basic proposition that there is a *broad tendency* for prices of traded products in different markets to move together, even in the case of imperfectly competitive markets, and that this tendency will be realized sooner or later when the change in the dominant market is large. (See Robert M. Dunn, Jr., "Flexible Exchange Rates and Traded Goods Prices," in Harry G. Johnson and Alexander K. Swoboda, eds., *The Economics of Common Currencies* [London: Allen and Unwin, 1973], chap. 16 [the quotation is on p. 278].)

ports and imports. Although there is no presumption as to the net outcome, the depressing effects of the rise in the exchange value of the currency on the demand and prices of exports and exportable output and their dampening effect on import prices ensure that there will be less inflationary effect than if the exchange rate had been prevented from changing.

But if, in contrast, the demand for imports is inelastic, the foreign exchange value of the currency will fall, and this will both raise the domestic prices of exportable output and aggravate the rise in the prices of imports. These effects could well set off a wage increase, a further decline in the currency, and further increases in the prices of tradable output. An inflationary process would thus be generated through repetition of the tradable-price, wage, exchange-rate, price, wage, exchange-rate spiral, unless or until it is arrested either by monetary restriction or a rise in import prices relative to other prices to the point where demand for imports became elastic. In this case, the average level of prices may be raised more than under fixed exchange rates because, under fixed exchange rates, deterioration in the current account of the balance of payments has a contracting effect on money income, and the deficit in the total balance of payments of a country (if it is not a reserve-currency country and its monetary authorities do not offset the effects of losses of foreign reserves) reduces the monetary base. These influences may offset or more than offset any tendency for the rise in prices of imports and import-competing goods to raise wages and costs in the economy as a whole.

The appreciation of the currency, while not preventing inflation, ensures that the price level will rise less than if the exchange rate had been fixed. This conclusion also holds true if world prices of exports and imports both rise, assuming that the demand for both is elastic or, even if the demand for imports is inelastic, that the elasticity of demand for exports is high enough to increase the total balance of payments at the initial exchange rate, so that the currency rises in the foreign exchange markets. The effect of appreciation of currency in all these cases is to dampen or prevent the increase in the current account that would occur under fixed exchange rates, and so to prevent or dampen the stimulus to expansion of income and thus of total demand generated by the multiplier process.

As to monetary effects, appreciation of the exchange rate prevents increases in the foreign component of the monetary base that would be forced on a country by a balance of payments surplus under a fixed exchange rate. Such a country would have to sterilize foreign inflows indefinitely to avoid increases in the total monetary base, a policy that would imply accepting indefinitely large quantities of foreign reserves in preference to increasing imports of goods and services or securities and, if continued long enough, would become (and be seen to become) economically irrational. When the external value of the currency is free to appreciate, however, control of the nominal stock of money is easier. But currency appreciation, by holding prices down and in some cases actually reducing them (as in the case mentioned above where a rise in the world prices of exports, by raising the value of the currency, reduces the national currency price of imports), increases the real value of a given nominal money stock above what it would otherwise have been. If the nominal stock of money is, in fact, held constant in such cases, this increase in the real money supply mitigates the decline of prices, but it cannot generate an actual rise of prices, since its occurrence depends on the price level's having fallen.[24]

It is noted above that where the world prices of imports rise and the domestic demand for them is inelastic, the domestic price level may rise more under flexible than under fixed rates. One other case in which a country may be more subject to outside inflationary influences under flexible than under fixed exchange rates is the case where the external inflation increases profit opportunities abroad and so gives rise to an outflow of capital. Under fixed exchange rates, the effect is unambiguously deflationary. Under flexible rates, the currency depreciates and the domestic prices of tradable products rise. This price effect reduces the real value of the monetary stock if its nominal value is kept from rising by more than the rise in the average domestic price level. This reduction, however, may not reduce prices of nontradable output or may reduce them but not by enough to offset the rise in prices of tradable output; part of the effect may take the form of a fall in output and employment. Then the domestic price level as a whole rises. Moreover, the rise in domestic prices of tradable output may cause a rise in money wages. If either the fall in output and employment or the rise in money wages causes the monetary authorities to increase the nominal stock of money, any downward pressure on prices that would otherwise have occurred will be reduced or prevented, so that the balance of forces will be more strongly in the direction of raising the domestic price level. But these may be regarded as either special cases or discretionary policy responses. In

24. An exception to this conclusion would be a situation in which the demand for real money were determined to a substantial degree by its purchasing power over imports. In that case, the appreciation of the currency, by reducing the price of imports, would cause an excess supply of money and could generate a tendency for prices to rise. This tendency would be nullified, however, by a reversal of the currency's appreciation.

general, floating rates block the market mechanisms by which inflation is transmitted internationally.

Presumably the transmission of inflationary pressures also would be less than under fixed rates in a system in which exchange rates, while not floating freely, were subject only to limited official intervention that did not resist pressures of strong and persistent market forces. Such a system has existed, more or less, since March 1973. The principal officially managed restriction on movements of exchange rates among the advanced countries appears to have been limited to countries in the European Community's snake, and even among these countries movements up to 2¼ percent on either side of par values or central rates have been permitted. Despite this fact, almost every country experienced an acceleration of inflation in 1973 and the first few months of 1974.

It is true that in many, perhaps most, countries this acceleration began in 1973 before the floating of exchange rates, which suggests that it did not result from floating and that recognition of a world grain shortage, which became important before exchange rates were floated, might have been the cause. Nevertheless, it might have been expected that floating would have been accompanied by a reduction in the rates of inflation in some countries and an increase in the dispersion of national rates of inflation compared to their dispersion before the period of floating. Because neither change appeared to have occurred by the end of 1974, some observers were led to question whether floating of exchange rates either reduces or makes possible a reduction of inflation rates and whether it permits countries to free their own inflation rates from the influence of inflation in other countries.

One comment in response to this question is that, whatever a comparison of pre-floating and post-floating data turns out to show concerning changes in average of national rates of inflation and in their dispersion, conclusions as to the effects of floating must be drawn in full recognition of the true relation between flexibility of rates and international transmission of inflation. That relation was well and concisely stated by Harry Johnson when he said, "A flexible exchange rate is not of course a panacea; it simply provides [to a country] an extra degree of freedom. . . ." In other words, while it permits a country to protect its national price level against changes in the world price level, it does not ensure that the country will do so. Its effect on the price level depends on whether the governments use the additional freedom well. Some economists think that the additional freedom has not been used well; one group has said, "Unfortunately the system of flexible exchange rates introduced in March 1973 has not succeeded in moderating inflation. Indeed some of us feel that the floating rate system has contributed to inflation by weakening monetary discipline and adding to asymmetrical cost pressures acting through an international ratchet effect."[25]

The second comment is that this one experience of floating was accompanied by other developments so powerful and pervasive in their effects on prices—the sharp increases in the prices of foods in early 1973, in the price of oil later in that year, and the large decline in aggregate real demand in the major countries during 1974—that the effect of floating itself is hard to disentangle from the other influences. A casual inspection of the data, however, seems to indicate that there has been a greater dispersion of percentage changes in national price levels around the mean of such changes in the period since floating than there was before, and that changes in the effective exchange value of currencies have been negatively associated with their rates of inflation. It would take a more careful analysis of the data than it is feasible to make for this paper to determine whether the increased dispersion of inflation rates could be equally attributed to variables other than changes in exchange rates and whether the inflation rates can be equally or better explained by other variables.

The a priori expectations of the results of external inflationary influences suggest that, in general, a country will be less vulnerable to them if its exchange rate is flexible than if it is fixed, except in two cases: (1) where there is a rise in the world prices of imports for which its demand is price-inelastic, and (2) where the external inflation generates a capital outflow. The first case is conventionally regarded as, in general, unlikely, but the rises in the world prices of food and oil may fulfill the conditions of that case. That may explain any reduction in the dispersion of national inflation rates, especially of increases in consumer prices, in 1973 and 1974, when flexibility of exchange rates might have led people to expect the dispersion of inflation rates to increase. This possibility should be borne in mind when the experiences under fixed and flexible rates are compared, lest the peculiarities of the first two years of flexible rates lead to incorrect generalization.

25. The quotation from Johnson comes from "The Case for Flexible Exchange Rates, 1969," first published in Harry G. Johnson and John E. Nash, *U.K. and Floating Exchanges: A Debate on the Theoretical and Practical Implications* (London: Institute of Economic Affairs, 1969), and reprinted in Harry G. Johnson, *Further Essays in Monetary Economics* (Harvard University Press, 1973) and in other collections. (The quotation appears in part V of the paper.) The second quotation comes from "The Santa Colomba Conclusions: 1974" (statement by a group of bankers and economists at the conclusion of the Siena-Santa Colomba Conference on Bank Stability, Recession and the Control of Inflation, jointly sponsored by the Monte dei Paschi di Siena and the International Center for Monetary and Banking Studies, Geneva, August 29–September 1, 1974; processed), p. 3.

Thus far, the international transmission of inflation has been considered from the point of view of how countries with no internally initiated inflationary pressures are affected by external inflationary forces. How inflation in the countries generating the inflationary pressures is affected by its transmission to others should also be considered, but in the interest of space that will have to be omitted; it can be deduced by reasoning parallel to that applied to the country receiving inflationary impulses, with the effects on countries transmitting the impulses generally being mirror images of the effects on those receiving them. What cannot be omitted is consideration of the aggregate effects of economic integration and of the exchange rate system on inflation in the world as a whole. These questions are discussed in the two following sections.

Effects of International Transmission on the Rate of World Inflation

Does the increased transmission of inflation likely to result from greater integration increase inflation in the world as a whole? Whether and how the transmission of given initial inflationary impulses affects the rate of increase of some world price index, such as a gross world product deflator, arises because transmission affects not only the price levels of the countries that receive the inflationary impulses originating elsewhere but may also affect in an opposite direction the price levels of the countries in which those impulses originate. Therefore, it does not necessarily increase the rate of inflation in the world as a whole.[26] Although this transmission generally causes inflation in the countries in which the inflationary pressures do not originate, the very

26. The world price level that is relevant here may be conceived of as an index of GNP deflators expressed in a common currency unit, as in effect they would be automatically under completely fixed exchange rates, or by explicit translation into a common currency unit when exchange rates change. The technical character of a hypothetical world price index need not be examined in detail for purposes of the questions discussed here. Presumably the national deflators should either have fixed weights or be chain indexes that link annual changes, rather than have weights that shift with the composition of money GNP, as do the conventional implicit deflators published by most countries. The world index presumably should combine the component national indexes by weighting them in proportion to GNP (or consumption, if the world index is one of consumer prices). The choice of a common currency unit under flexible rates raises questions that I have posed in the appendix to my paper, "A Supranational Approach to the Analysis of World Inflation," in this volume.

exportation of these pressures may be expected, especially under fixed exchange rates, to reduce the rate of inflation in the initiating countries. The availability of imported goods increases supplies available to the initiating country at given prices. It also constitutes a leakage from the domestic income-expenditure stream and thus reduces the multiplier effects of a given autonomous expansionary influence. And losses of reserves (or reductions in their rates of increase), although they can be offset, have counterinflationary effects on the domestic money supply, except in reserve-currency countries in which acquisition of reserves by foreign monetary authorities does not reduce that country's monetary base.

Exportation of inflationary demand pressures generally dampens the rate of price increase in countries that export them, but that is not the only possibility; it conceivably could aggravate their price increases. That might happen, for example, if the induced inflationary effects in their partner countries were so large that even the feedback from the partners to them more than offset the reduction in the induced domestic effects. In such cases, international transmission clearly would increase inflation in the world as a whole. But the combination of conditions required for this result is improbable; it may be assumed, therefore, that in virtually all instances the effect of openness on income flows through the current account of the balance of payments is to dampen inflation in the countries exporting it.

World economic integration could also accentuate rather than dampen inflation in a country initiating inflationary impulses by facilitating inflows of foreign capital in response to expectations of increasing profits. The availability of foreign capital has accentuated inflationary booms in some countries at various times in the past. In some of these cases, however, these capital flows have had a restraining effect on the capital-exporting country so that the international mobility of capital may not have increased the inflationary effect on the world as a whole.

In short, there appears to be no presumption that the average rate of inflation for the world as a whole is increased by the transmission of inflationary influences among countries. The fact of openness and the consequent transmission of inflationary influences could increase the role of inflation in the world as a whole, reduce it, or leave it unaffected. It would increase world inflation if the reduction of induced effects in the country or countries originating the inflationary influences were smaller than the inflation that openness induced in other countries, or if any increase of induced effects in the originating countries were greater than the induced reduction of effects in others, but it would reduce world inflation if these relationships were reversed.

Effects of the Exchange Rate System on World Inflation

Whether the rate of world inflation is likely to be greater under fixed or flexible exchange rates is a question that involves comparison of the potential inherent in two exchange rate regimes for spreading inflation. The degree of world economic integration must be assumed to be the same, except to the extent that the exchange rate regime itself affects it. Since the question arises because of interest in what happens to national price levels expressed in their own currencies, the measure of world inflation should be an average of the national rates of change or the rate of change in an average of national price indexes expressed in the various countries' own currencies, rather than indexes translated into a common currency.

The comparative inflationary potential of fixed and floating exchange rates for the world as a whole is considered here in two of its aspects. One is confined to those relative effects of the two polar exchange rate systems on the rate of world inflation that operate through the conventionally accepted mechanisms of balance of payments adjustment, which depend on the mechanisms of international transmission of price and income changes already discussed. The other and broader aspect is whether the rate of world inflation may be greater under one or the other system when factors other than international transmission through market mechanisms are taken into account.

Comparative effects on world inflation of mechanisms of adjustment under fixed and flexible rates

Most discussions that I have heard recently purporting to analyze whether a fixed or a flexible rate system is, per se, the more inflationary from the whole world point of view, have not actually done so. Instead, they have generalized from the experience of one country without considering the effects on other countries. On the one hand, I have heard some British economists argue that flexible rates promote inflation, supporting their argument —indeed, apparently deriving it—from the fact that freedom of sterling to float has permitted pursuit of inflationary policies in the United Kingdom. They say, "Just see how the price level of the United Kingdom has been pushed upward by the depreciation of sterling." That argument offers no explanation of why sterling depreciated. On the other hand, I have heard German economists argue that freedom of the deutsche mark to rise has permitted Germany to avoid inflation by enabling it to pursue anti-inflationary policies, or that actual appreciation has restrained increases in the German price level below those of other countries.

Perhaps the oldest argument is that freely floating rates are more inflationary than fixed rates because under them countries that tend to pursue inflationary policies are not constrained by the losses of reserves that would result, under fixed rates, from inflation-induced deficits in the balance of payments. The counterargument is that the fall in the exchange value of an inflating country's currency that occurs when rates are not fixed may be an equal or greater constraint. Whether reserve losses or depreciation of the currency exercises the greater constraint on the pro-inflationary impulses of governments (which both sides take for granted) an economist has no special qualifications to determine. Moreover, there is no reason to suppose that the answer, if it could be known, would be the same for all countries.

It has also been argued that the depreciation of an inflating country's currency, by raising the domestic prices of its imports and tradable output, stimulates increases in the level of its money wages, causing further depreciation, domestic price and wage increases, and so on—the so-called ratchet effect. If the mechanism invoked by this argument does operate, inflation is bottled up within that country when its currency depreciates, and its inflation is greater than it would be under a fixed exchange rate. But the transmission of inflation to other countries presumably would be less than under fixed rates, so it cannot be concluded from this argument that the flexibility of rates would increase inflation in the world as a whole.[27]

More recently Gottfried Haberler has argued that under modern conditions a system of fixed rates has, per se, an inflationary bias for the world as a whole, which clearly implies that the bias is greater than in a system of flexible rates.[28] His view, based primarily on medium-term or long-term con-

---

27. For an early statement of the ratchet effect, see Robert Triffin, *Gold and the Dollar Crisis: The Future of Convertibility* (rev. ed., Yale University Press, 1961), pp. 82–85. See also his *Our International Monetary System: Yesterday, Today, and Tomorrow* (Random, 1968), pp. 72–74. The arguments that flexible rates are more inflationary than fixed rates are stated, in order to be refuted, by Harry G. Johnson, "The Case for Flexible Exchange Rates, 1969," part V, but both the conclusions and their refutations are made from the point of view of inflation in one country, not in the world as a whole.

28. This argument must be distinguished from the more general point that the Bretton Woods system was more inflationary than one of flexible rates, because that system involved not only fixity of rates (subject to adjustment in cases of "fundamental disequilibrium") but use of the U.S. dollar as an international monetary reserve, which permitted the United States to have balance of payments deficits without losing reserve assets or undergoing a reduction in its monetary base. No one has denied that such a reserve system has inflationary potentialities. (For a statement of Gottfried Haberler's argument, see "Prospects for the International Monetary Order," the second

siderations, is that disturbances to balances of payments are always occurring and that under modern conditions deficit countries do not reduce their general price levels, so that the adjustment of payments imbalances must occur entirely through increases in the price level of the surplus countries. In my view, this step of the argument is correct, but the conclusion it establishes is only that adjustment under modern conditions and fixed rates is inflationary, not that it is *more* inflationary than adjustment under modern conditions and flexible rates. Under flexible rates, the deficit country experiences a rise of prices, at the minimum through the direct effect of the fall in the value of its currency on the national currency prices of tradable goods, and—under the modern condition that Haberler has in mind, downward inflexibility of prices—the surplus country, whose currency appreciates, is as likely to resist a compensating decrease in its prices as is the deficit country under fixed rates. Thus it appears that what causes the inflationary bias in an adjustment process, insofar as it depends on the changes in relative prices that are required for equilibrium, is not the fixity of exchange rates but the "modern condition" that makes prices inflexible downward while leaving them flexible upward. Up to this point in the debate, therefore, the opposing sides do not appear even to have faced, let alone resolved, the issue of the relative inflationary biases under the two systems for the world as a whole.

The argument may be carried further, however, by taking into account that the process of international adjustment affects national price levels under the two systems in different ways. Under fixed rates, the inflationary pressure is generally spread from the inflating country mainly through the expansionary income effects on the current account or the effects of increases in monetary reserves, or through both. In theory both of these effects can be fully offset, and in practice they can be offset to at least a limited degree by fiscal and monetary policy if they are not too persistent. The prices that tend to rise under a fixed-rate system are mainly those of nontradable outputs, the prices of tradable output being held down until the rise of external demand is sufficient to raise the world prices of internationally traded goods.

---

of his *Two Essays on the Future of the International Monetary Order,* Reprint 21 [American Enterprise Institute for Public Policy Research, 1974], pp. 9–10, and his paper, "Inflation as a Worldwide Phenomenon—An Overview," in David I. Meiselman and Arthur B. Laffer, eds., *The Phenomenon of Worldwide Inflation* [American Enterprise Institute for Public Policy Research, 1975], pp. 19–21 [also published in *Weltwirtschaftliches Archiv* [*Review of World Economics; Tübingen, West Germany*], vol. 110, no. 2 [1974]. See also Otmar Emminger's *Inflation and the International Monetary System,* Per Jacobsson Memorial Lecture [Washington: Per Jacobsson Foundation, 1973]).

Under flexible rates, the surplus country will be well protected by appreciation of its currency, but the deficit country experiences direct increases in the domestic prices of tradable output because of the fall in the exchange value of its currency. These increases are less likely to be restrained or postponed by policy, given the changes in the exchange rate. Insofar as wage rates and other nominal incomes are adjusted to price increases, it seems on the whole probable that they will be adjusted more promptly in a deficit country under flexible rates than in a surplus country under fixed rates. Thus, while a surplus country is better protected from outside inflation under flexible than under fixed rates, an inflating deficit country experiences more inflation than it would under fixed rates. It seems quite likely, and certainly possible, that the excess inflationary effect of flexibility (through upward adjustment of nominal wages in deficit countries in which the inflationary impulses are assumed to originate) may offset, or more than offset, the greater stability in surplus countries receiving those impulses. To the extent that this actually occurs, the flexible-rate system is more inflationary for the world as a whole.

But the extent to which it occurs is not known. Indeed, that depends on the comparative labor market responses and the policies of the deficit countries, including especially their monetary policies, under the two exchange rate regimes. Thus there may be no general answer to the question that is valid for all countries and all circumstances. I conclude that the question, as posed, involves more variables than equations, so that the answer is indeterminate.

Moreover, since some of the missing information concerns these comparative responses to the fixed-rate and flexible-rate effects of given autonomous inflationary impulses, the process of obtaining the missing information requires incorporating the policy responses of the fiscal and monetary authorities to increases in reserves, changes in the current-account position, and the flow of capital in the case of fixed rates, and incorporating these responses and also those of nominal wages (and other factor returns) in the case of flexible rates. Here again, one sees that some of the responses ordinarily treated as exogenous must be treated as endogenous.

Comparative probability of world inflation
under fixed and floating rates

It is noted above that the mechanisms by which inflationary pressures are transmitted among countries depend on the fixity of exchange rates between their currencies. This is true of increases in the prices of internationally traded goods operating through the law of one market, subject to some possible exceptions when the increases result from changes in supply conditions; of increases in demand for exports; and of changes in money wages operating through the mobility of labor or international trade unionism. The prices of internationally traded goods and services, measured in the currencies of countries other than the one in question, may rise, but if that country pursues stabilizing domestic monetary and fiscal policies, the foreign exchange value of its currency will rise and the rise in the prices of tradable commodities measured in its currency will be damped, while prices of other commodities will be subjected to downward pressure. Similarly, if foreign demand for a country's exports increases, raising the foreign exchange value of its currency, its general national price level need not rise, even if the national currency prices of the directly affected exports do rise. The prices of imports will be reduced, thus tending to depress the national prices of its import-competing goods, and the costs of domestic production in which both imports and import-competing goods are used. Whether price decreases will offset increases in the prices of exports depends mainly on how far the exchange value of the currency rises, which can be more or less well controlled by domestic policy. Changes in nominal money supply operating through changes in international monetary reserves would not occur at all without official exchange rate management. The dependence of these mechanisms on fixity of rates, taken by itself, leads naturally and logically to the conclusions that under freely floating rates a country's general price level need not be influenced by inflationary forces abroad, and that such an exchange rate system enables a country to control its national price level, so that it need have no more inflation than it "wants."

In a narrow economic, almost mechanical, sense these conclusions are undoubtedly correct. It should be recognized, however, that they assume that domestic monetary and fiscal policies are exogenous or are determined solely with a view to avoiding inflation, and that the only mechanisms making for worldwide inflation are those just discussed, which operate through the market. Although the conclusions can be accepted on those assumptions, they reflect a much narrower view than should be taken in any serious effort to analyze the problem of world inflation. Even in the analysis of national inflations, to regard domestic monetary and fiscal policies as exogenous or as determined solely by the effort to avoid inflation of the general price level, and as entirely unresponsive to depressing effects on demand for the outputs of major sectors of the economy and the consequent effects on employment, is to take too narrow a view.

In addition to that consideration is the fact, noted early in this paper, that most countries have become subject to influences that make them more vulnerable to inflation than they were in the prewar world, even apart from mechanical transmission of inflationary impulses among them. These influences include widespread acceptance of the view that governments can and should prevent all but serious lapses from high employment; increased downward rigidity of prices and money wages; reduction in the role of the private sector; and other changes that may have been transmitted internationally by intellectual or sociological communication rather than market forces. There is no reason to expect that free floating of exchange rates would diminish the importance of these common causes. I do not pretend to know how strong an influence they have been compared to the market mechanisms through which inflation has been transmitted, but it must be true that, to whatever degree the worldwide scope of inflation results from them, it would continue to be worldwide, even with freely floating exchange rates. Of course, the reduction in interdependence of national price levels through market mechanisms might make inflation more national than worldwide in *essential character* and would certainly eliminate international transmission through the mechanisms of the market, but it might not make inflation much less worldwide in scope.

Econometric Studies of International Transmission

At least nine studies of the economic linkages among countries have been made and undoubtedly these are being improved and others are being developed.[29] Some of them focus primarily on trade relationships, but increas-

29. Since November 1974, such studies have proliferated. The studies referred to in the text include (1) the major and continuously developing Project LINK, which has already resulted in some dozen theoretical and empirical papers appearing in R. J. Ball, ed., *The International Linkage of National Economic Models* (Amsterdam: North-Holland, 1973; distributed in U.S. and Canada by American Elsevier); (2) the IMF Multilateral Exchange Rate Model, described in Jacques R. Artus and Rudolf R. Rhomberg, "A Multilateral Exchange Rate Model," *IMF Staff Papers,* vol. 20 (November 1973), pp. 591–611 (summarized in ibid., vol. 23 [March 1976], pp. 103–04); (3) the IMF Expanded World Trade Model, which contains more on prices; (4) Lee Samuelson, "A New Model of World Trade," in *OECD Economic Outlook, Occasional Studies* (Paris: OECD, December 1973); (5) J. Waelbroeck, "On the Structure of International Trade Interdependence," in *Cahiers économiques de Bruxelles* (University of Brussels), no. 36 (1967), pp. 495–511; (6) M. Grinwis and Y. Guillaume, "Modèles économétriques simples de cinq pays du Marché Commun," in ibid., no. 50 (1971), pp. 237–77; (7) Michael Beenstock and Patrick Minford, "A Quarterly Econometric Model of World Trade and Prices, 1955–71," in Michael Parkin and George Zis, eds., *Inflation in Open Economies* (Manchester: Manchester University Press; Toronto: Toronto University Press, 1976); (8) Richard Berner and others,

ing attention is being given to the determination of prices and direct and indirect price linkages. Since limitations of time and space prevent me from studying, describing, and appraising most of these models in this paper, I shall confine myself to describing the results of the most recent simulation worked out under Project LINK, which I believe is the most comprehensive of these studies.

Simulation from the LINK model

The multinational model of the transmission mechanism constructed by Project LINK welds together the national econometric models of thirty-one countries or regions through use of a matrix of international trade. One very recent version of this model has been used by Bert Hickman to simulate the transmission of inflation and estimate the quantitative effects of a given percentage increase in real income in each of a number of countries on the price level of the others.[30] This simulation is based on full structural models for twelve developed countries and reduced form equations for import quantities and export prices for thirteen other developed countries. The socialist economies and a few others are treated as a self-contained bloc in the world trade calculations. In most of the structural models for developed market economies, wages are explained by some version of the Phillips curve, output is determined by aggregate demand, employment is determined as a function of output through short-run production functions, and domestic prices are directly determined as a markup on unit labor cost, often with an allowance for demand pressures, as they are reflected in unemployment or utilization rates. In all the national models except those of Australia and Germany domestic prices also are directly determined by import prices. A monetary sector that permits money stock and interest rates to be determined endogenously was used in the simulations only for Italy, the United Kingdom, and the United States, and the national balances of payments so far programmed into the world model include only the current accounts, so some

---

"Simultaneous Determination of the U.S. Balance of Payments and Exchange Rates—An Exploratory Report," International Finance Discussion Paper 59 (Board of Governors of the Federal Reserve System, February 1975; processed); (9) studies at the University of Manchester published in Parkin and Zis, eds., Inflation in the World Economy (Manchester: Manchester University Press; Toronto: Toronto University Press, 1976) and other publications.

30. Bert G. Hickman, "International Transmission of Economic Fluctuations and Inflation," in Albert Ando, Richard Herring, and Richard Marston, eds., International Aspects of Stabilization Policies, pp. 201–31 (see note 16 for full citation).

of the mechanisms of transmission cannot be well simulated yet.[31] The principal connections between national models were therefore through prices and quantities of merchandise imports and exports. Imports, which are divided into four commodity classes, are assumed to be in infinitely elastic supply in each country, and their quantities are assumed to be determined by a homogeneous function of degree zero in prices and incomes but are affected by the relation of their prices to those of domestic goods through close but not perfect substitution. Export prices are endogenously determined in the national models, generally on the basis of markups over labor and raw material costs, but in some national models prices of competing exports and indexes of utilization are also explanatory variables. In only a few national models used in Hickman's simulation are export prices disaggregated, although a four-category disaggregation is being developed.[32]

As this description indicates, the resulting linked model includes in some degree all the mechanisms of transmission except direct wage connections. As Hickman says, "An exogenous change in domestic expenditure, for example, will affect domestic incomes and prices, which in turn will affect incomes and prices abroad directly by changing the export demands and import prices of other countries and indirectly by the consequential induced movements of incomes and prices in those countries. The price linkages include direct effects—prices of imported materials are determinants of domestic prices in many of the models—as well as indirect connections via the influence of aggregate demand on wages and prices through the wage and mark-up equations."[33]

With this model Hickman simulated the percentage effects in each country

31. Hickman reports that bank deposits but not interest rates are endogenous in the national models for Australia and the Netherlands, and interest rates are endogenous but bank deposits are not for Canada and Japan. Complete monetary sectors have recently been developed for the Austrian, German, and British models, and complete models of the balance of payments have been developed for Canada, Japan, the United Kingdom, and the United States, but had not been programmed into the world model in time for use in Hickman's simulation. Results for the Netherlands are not reported, owing to technical programming difficulties.

32. An earlier version of the simulation included four regional models for the developing countries. In these models domestic prices are determined by capacity utilization, import prices, and the ratio of the money stock to GNP. Export prices are a function of the domestic price level and export volume. The money stock is exogenous, and neither interest rates nor an explicit demand function for money is included in the model. Multipliers may be calculated for these models, but none is reported in the Hickman paper because of the absence of country detail and because the models are structured for forecasting rather than for simulation.

33. Bert G. Hickman, "International Transmission of Economic Fluctuations and Inflation," pp. 206–07.

on both income and prices of a given percentage change in real income. A dynamic control solution for 1973–75 was first calculated for the entire system, using 1973 values for the exogenous variables in all years and initial conditions of 1972 and earlier years as far back as was needed to solve the model for 1973. Then the model was shocked by increasing exogenous domestic expenditures in one country and maintaining them at the higher level for three years, and a new solution was obtained. In both the control and shocked solutions exchange rates are exogenous variables, so the solutions represent those of a fixed exchange rate world. As Hickman notes, "the multiplier properties might be very different under a system of floating rates."[34] The difference between the shocked and controlled solutions gives the changes in incomes and prices induced by the shock. This permits calculation of the effects in each country on income and prices of the exogenous increase in expenditure in every country, yielding a set of cross-country-elasticity multipliers (that is, the ratios of the total percentage effects in each country not experiencing the shock to the percentage exogenous change in the country experiencing the shock) and of own-multipliers (that is, the ratios of total percentage effects in the shocked country itself to the percentage shock).[35]

The simulations of effects on national price levels, which are measured by the GNP deflator, have some unexpected results. For example, the simulated exogenous increase in demand in France with its consequent increase in output, actually reduces the French price level for all of the first three years calculated, and the demand-induced increase in output in the United Kingdom reduces the British price level in the first two of the three years.[36] Insofar

34. Ibid., p. 225.

35. The effects of a supply-induced shock from a rise in the price of oil have been simulated, as have several other shocks, in a paper by Keith Johnson and Lawrence Klein, "Stability in the International Economy: The LINK Experience," in Albert Ando, Richard Herring, and Richard Marston, eds., *International Aspects of Stabilization Policies,* pp. 147–88 (see note 16 for full citation). In connection with the effects of the exchange rate system on the multipliers, Hickman cites the comparison of these effects under alternative exchange rate regimes made by Rudolf R. Rhomberg, in "A Model of the Canadian Economy under Fixed and Fluctuating Exchange Rates," *Journal of Political Economy,* vol. 72 (February 1964), pp. 1–31.

36. Hickman points out that in the French model output and wages increase, but a given increase in output involves a relatively small increase in labor input, so that the relatively large increase in output per man-hour (which he thinks the model overestimates) reduces unit labor costs. In the model for the United Kingdom, the straight-time money wage (that is, the wage for standard hours worked) is exogenous and unit labor costs decrease in the first two years, but overtime earnings increase after the first year and rise enough by the third year to increase unit labor costs, despite the assumed fixity of the straight-time wage rate.

as the national models portray the national economies correctly, these differences bring out the dangers of generalizing about inflation. Although price changes induced by disturbances from abroad are found usually to be negligible in the first year and to become somewhat larger later, there is great variance in effects. The highest cross-multiplier found was the third-year effect of a 1 percent increase of income in the United States, which raised the Canadian price level by 0.64 percent. In general, however, the price responses to income increases in other countries were small. In some countries, in fact, they were frequently or always negative. For example, the United Kingdom had negative price responses to income increases in several European countries and in Australia in the first year simulated, to increases in the latter countries and in the United States and Japan in the second year, and to increases in Germany in all three years. These negative responses resulted from the treatment of U.K. wage rates as exogenous.

What may be concluded from these simulations? Hickman's opinions are worth quoting. He says that they

. . . suggest that the observed worldwide inflation of recent years should not be attributed to the spread of demand impulses from one or two dominant countries via foreign trade in merchandise, since the cross-multipliers for prices are generally small. Transmission of cost-push inflation could conceivably be stronger, however, especially if the exogenous shock to wages or prices were accompanied by accommodating demand policies to prevent an induced fall in real income. Unfortunately, the present simulations cast little light on this question, since the observed price responses are normalized on income shocks and are heavily influenced by propagation through income-induced increases in export demands as well as by the concomitant increases in foreign trade prices.

Even the conclusion that the international propagation of inflation from demand impulses is generally weak may be wholly or partly reversed by improvements now underway in the LINK system, including the incorporation of international capital flows and domestic monetary sectors and improved explanations of commodity prices and linkages. There is scope within the present system for at least a partial explanation of worldwide inflation owing to synchronization of disturbances across many countries, however, with induced trade flows serving to amplify and reinforce the common impulses. . . .

Whatever the degree and importance of synchronization of shocks . . . it remains true that their inflationary effects could be offset by restrictive monetary policies. . . . Even allowing for induced variations in income velocity, there is some degree of restraint on the money supply that would prevent the price level from rising. At bottom, then, the explanation for inflation rests on those motivations which determine the unwillingness of monetary authorities to curb inflation. These motivations include, but may not be restricted to, the unwillingness to augment unemployment and reduce real incomes in order to restrain prices.[37]

37. Bert G. Hickman, "International Transmission of Economic Fluctuations and Inflation," pp. 217, 221–22.

Possibilities and pitfalls in further empirical work

A review of the preceding sections and of some of the literature not mentioned earlier prompts a few suggestions for further empirical work on international transmission and warnings about the interpretation of data and analytical results.

1. Decreases in the dispersion of national rates of inflation do not necessarily mean that international transmission through the mechanisms discussed has increased, and increases need not mean that it has decreased.

First, dispersion of inflation rates may decrease because nations are responding more similarly to common world influences not originating in any identifiable country or because domestic expansions are more coincident; it may increase because they are responding less similarly or because their cyclical experiences are diverging. Changes in dispersion for these reasons do not necessarily imply anything about changes in the effectiveness of transmission through market mechanisms.

Second, the significance of dispersion of inflation rates for the degree and type of international transmission also depends partly on the type of price index used to measure inflation. Dispersion of price indexes that measure the average price of domestic value added, such as the GNP or GDP deflator, may change differently than dispersion of indexes that measure the average price of domestic expenditure, such as the deflator for gross national expenditure (GNE) or the consumer price index, because the first two include export prices directly but not import prices, whereas the latter two include import prices directly but not export prices. When the terms of trade change, these two types of indexes can be expected to move at different rates and, in some circumstances, even in opposite directions. In any event, when export and import prices change at different rates, I would expect the differences in movement of these two types of index to be greater, in most cases, the larger is the proportion of foreign trade in GNP. This result is not a necessary one, of course, because the price of exportable output consumed at home presumably moves with, or is at least influenced by, export prices, and the prices of import-competing output are related to prices of competitive imports, and prices of these nontraded domestic outputs are included in both indexes. But my expectation that the difference in movement between the two types of index when the terms of trade change would be related to the importance of foreign trade in GNP is easily testable across countries that have experienced similar movements in their export prices and in their import prices.[38]

38. It should be noted that since every country's export is another country's import, a change in the terms of trade of one country implies an opposite change in those of

This point is likely to prove especially important in any comparison of national inflation rates between 1972 and 1974, owing to the unusually large changes in the terms of trade of most countries resulting from the great rise of food and oil prices. One can predict confidently that the GNP or GDP deflators of oil-exporting countries, especially those that produce little besides oil, such as the Arab oil countries, will be found to have risen far more than those of oil-importing countries. The dispersion will undoubtedly be greater than in prior years, but this will not indicate that international transmission has diminished. At the same time, the GNE deflators of oil exporters may be found to have risen less than those of oil importers, especially those of countries in which oil is an important element of national expenditure and which import most of it, such as Japan and Italy.

Third, another, although longer-run, influence on dispersion that is unrelated to transmission is the difference among countries in rates of growth. As seen above, convergence of changes in their price levels may mean merely that their rates of productivity growth are converging and indicate nothing about the source of the impetus to their inflations.

2. Substantial differences in the increases of national price indexes usually used to measure rates of inflation may seem to imply that the countries with the most rapid rises are the sources of inflation and those with less rapid rises are their innocent victims. This inference would be unjustified. Although the national prices of internationally traded goods tend to change in the same degree when measured in a common currency unit, the link between the prices of a country's tradable and nontradable output is not ordinarily tight in short periods. If relative prices of tradables and nontradables change to the same degree in all countries, the movement of their national indexes may still differ because of differences in the shares of tradables in GNP or GNE and the consequent differences in the weights of tradable and nontradable output in their national price indexes. A country with little average price rise can be the source of inflation if tradable output is very important in its price index. Imagine, for example, that a small country with imports of about 40 percent of GNP has $50 billion or more of reserves. If it embarked on an inflationary policy it could inflate its supplying countries and possibly cause those with lower proportions of foreign trade to GNP to have larger increases in their national price indexes than it has itself.

---

at least one other country (unless it is caused by a change in costs of international transportation and those costs are not included in the measurement). This fact could make the GNP deflator rise more in one country than in another while its GNE deflator rises by less, especially if their bilateral trade is an important part of their total foreign trade.

One general conclusion implied by these considerations is that in empirical work on international transmission, it may make a substantial difference what price indexes one is trying to explain. It is especially important, if one is seeking to distinguish between transmssion via exports and via imports, to distinguish between price indexes of domestic value added and of domestic expenditure. The factor that may cause different indexes to move at different rates and the dispersions of their rates of change to move differently may be important.

Another implication to be drawn from the remarks above is that correct interpretation of data relating to international transmission of inflation requires that data for each country be disaggregated enough to distinguish, at least roughly, the price movements and rates of productivity growth of tradable from nontradable outputs and to take into account their relative importance in the price index that is being explained.

3. Conventional assumptions about the behavior of both the current account and the balance of payments may also lead to incorrect inferences about international transmission.

First, it is often assumed that if inflationary forces come from outside a country, their transmission to it will be reflected in an increase in its (positive) current account. An open and competitive economy, however, may receive inflationary pressures from abroad without experiencing such an increase. Its current account may even decrease, although a decrease is ordinarily taken to indicate that it is inflating faster than the outside world. For example, inflation originating elsewhere may raise world prices of a country's imports and its demand for imports may be inelastic, so that its current-account balance may decrease. Conversely, an improvement in its current balance that may appear to result from a rise in foreign demand may result from a rise of wages in production of exportable output for which the foreign demand is inelastic, or from a rise in domestic demand for that output, as Mintz found was actually the case during cyclical expansions in the United States since 1921.[39]

Second, the absence of a surplus in the total balance of payments and of a consequent inflow of monetary reserves does not necessarily mean that a country is not receiving impulses toward monetary expansion from abroad. If a rise in world prices or an increase of foreign demand for a country's exports is foreseen, a rise in its demand for money should be expected. An increased demand for money can be satisfied as well by domestic credit crea-

---

39. See Ilse Mintz, *Cyclical Fluctuations in the Exports of the United States since 1879* (Columbia University Press for the National Bureau of Economic Research, 1967), chap. 7, especially pp. 252–57.

tion on the part of the central bank as by an inflow of reserves, and the monetary authorities may prefer to satisfy it that way, knowing that by doing so they need not cause an outflow of reserves but merely reduce or prevent an inflow. Johnson, who makes this point in the context of secular inflation, argues that if the monetary authorities recognize and act on this point, they are likely to prefer domestic credit creation if they regard their international reserves as already adequate or excessive. Such action will tend to prevent the surplus and the inflow of reserves.[40]

4. A number of other problems in interpreting observed data are mentioned by Johnson. One is that a rise of prices, wages, or both in the sector producing tradable output that appears to be domestically generated may in fact be an anticipatory response to an expected increase of external demand, and this anticipatory response may prevent the emergence of actual excess demand. "Thus, in an open and competitive international economy, in which prices and wages in the traded goods sector will be adjusted to world price levels and the marginal productivity of labour in terms of world goods respectively, one should not expect inflation to occur only as a lagged adjustment to observed excess demands either in the domestic markets for goods and labour, or in the form of a lagged improvement in the current account balance of the balance of payments."[41]

5. Econometric models of a multinational system need to be made more complete with respect to the internal workings of the individual countries because the mechanisms of intranational transmission are as important as those of international transmission in determining rates of inflationary response to given stimuli. This is recognized by Project LINK. As Hickman points out in "International Transmission of Economic Fluctuations and

---

40. This case may appear unlikely to occur in most situations, but it is a possible and perhaps a probable one in an environment of general reserve abundance. In his paper Johnson made the point seem more plausible than the above bare statement of it. (See Harry G. Johnson, "Secular Inflation and the International Monetary System," *Journal of Money, Credit, and Banking,* vol. 5, pt. 2 [February 1973], p. 516.) There he put it in the context of the situation faced by a country in a reserve-currency system when the reserve-currency country is running a deficit. It should be noted that the point reflects Johnson's view that, so long as the currency is not appreciated, the authorities have no choice between having inflation and avoiding it; they cannot escape creating the money required to finance it. Their only choice is between increasing the domestic component of the monetary base and increasing its foreign component. Johnson also made this and the preceding point in "Inflation: A 'Monetarist' View," chap. 13 of his *Further Essays in Monetary Economics* (Harvard University Press, 1973), pp. 335–36.

41. See Harry G. Johnson, "Secular Inflation and the International Monetary System," p. 515.

Inflation," work is proceeding on the development of fuller models of monetary sectors in all the national models, on complete balance of payments sectors, and on the Eurodollar market, and the participants in Project LINK have recognized the need for commodity models for food, fuels, and raw materials that transcend national boundaries and aggregate international supplies and demands for given products. Hickman also recognizes that transmission of changes in price levels as well as real income might be very different under floating exchange rates, and that the investigation of the properties of such a system requires that international capital flows and exchange rates be endogenized. More work also remains to be done on determinants of money wages and of markups over labor costs, which are not necessarily of the same relative importance in different countries.

6. I save for last one of the most difficult problems of analysis, which arises in connection with international transmission of inflation but which is a much more general scientific problem. Stated most broadly, it is the problem of knowing whether an observed stimulus, operating through an observed mechanism of response, is a "basic cause" of the observed result. I am not referring to the problem of identifying which one of many necessary conditions has changed and is in that sense the "cause" but, rather, to the question of whether an apparently necessary condition really is necessary. This question is whether attributing causality to it is merely a superficial mistaking of appearances for reality, with the basic cause being something else that merely happens to operate through the observed channel under given circumstances and would produce the same result through other channels under different circumstances.

One could have an econometric model that fitted the facts perfectly and therefore appeared to "explain" them, yet one might not correctly identify the basic cause of the observed result. For example, monetarists (and others as well) charge that it is such a misidentification to attribute wage increases resulting from union bargaining to union militancy; to attribute increases in the general price level to cost-push merely because they appear to be caused by it; or to attribute such increases to increases in particular prices, like those of food or oil, merely because those prices are the main statistical component of a rise in price indexes. In connection with international transmission of inflation, the problem arises with the Scandinavian model. That model may fit the facts for, say, Norway perfectly, but that would not justify the conclusion that increases in the world price of Norwegian exports would not produce an equal inflation in Norway even if wages in its export sector were not directly tied to export prices or if wages in other sectors were not tied to wages in the export sector through a nationwide wage bargain. Perhaps, if wages in export industries rose less, the quantity and value of exports would rise more. The greater increase in income from exports or in monetary reserves that would then occur might give rise to equal inflation, because there is no reason to suppose that the given increase in the stock of money would be willingly held at a lower price level.

The only way to resolve questions of this kind by econometric analysis, as contrasted with a priori reasoning with or without the support of casual empirical observation, is to observe situations in which one of the alleged causes operated and the other did not, or in which both operated but the mechanism of response regarded as necessary for one of them to work its effects did not operate, and to see whether the same result was produced in the absence of one of the alleged causes or of the response mechanism through which one of them was alleged to operate. In connection with the monetarist argument, mentioned earlier, that " 'cost-push' is merely an institutional manifestation" of more basic forces, in order to distinguish the superficially apparent from the real causes, situations must be observed in which one of the alleged causes is not present.

The implication is not that little can be accomplished by further econometric work, but quite the opposite. It has been pointed out in this paper that possibilities of conflict exist among transmission mechanisms, that different measures of inflation may be expected to respond to given influences in different ways, and that given measures of inflation may respond differently to given impulses in different countries. This consideration adds importance to the systematic study of the inflation experiences of individual countries. In short, much work remains to be done.

Appendix. Possible Causes of Convergence of National Inflation Rates

The text states that a convergence of inflation rates does not necessarily imply that market forces have led to increased international transmission of inflationary pressures generated in one or a few countries because such a reduction could be the result of other changes. The other possible causes mentioned are common policy responses to common causes, convergence in rates of productivity growth, institutional and structural changes, supranational monetary developments, and the coincidence of cyclical expansions. Some of these possibilities are discussed more fully below and data are presented that bear on some of them.

Almost all of the reasons why countries might experience inflation at the same time without international transmission of inflationary forces reflect common responses of one kind or another to common causes. The sole exception is sheer accident in the sense of an improbable coincidence of random events. Other explanations require an account of what common causes have operated and why they have done so at more nearly the same time in many countries than they formerly did or why many countries apparently respond to them in more similar ways now than in the past. Central to most such explanations is an increase in noneconomic integration of the world in the form of improved communication between and transportation of people, which have brought about increased transmission of both specific factual information and general ideas affecting analysis and policy objectives.

Common policy objectives and instruments

During the period since World War II there has been an increased diffusion of views about macroeconomic theory, policy objectives, and the instruments appropriate to achieving them, which is in striking contrast to the prewar intellectual insularity among both professional economists and policy-making officials. The increased intellectual exchange has led to change of the modal view toward lesser tolerance of unemployment by both electorates and policy officials. Consequently, nearly all governments have tried to run their economies at levels closer to their potential outputs than before the war. This made these economies more vulnerable to inflation as a result of shocks. The bias in public policy toward achieving lower unemployment at the risk of greater and more persistent inflation was forecast and commented upon by a number of writers in the early postwar years.[42]

42. See, for example, M. W. Reder, "The Theoretical Problems of a National Wage-Price Policy," *Canadian Journal of Economics and Political Science,* vol. 14 (February 1948), pp. 46–61; Arthur Smithies, "Reflections on the Work and Influence of John Maynard Keynes," *Quarterly Journal of Economics,* vol. 65 (November 1951), pp. 597–98; and "The Age of Inflation," an anonymous three-part article in *Economist* (London), vol. 161 (August 18, August 25, and September 1, 1951). Whether the realization of the forecast has resulted from the international spread of the Keynesian revolution, the experience of the Great Depression, or other causes is debatable but irrelevant to the present point. For a denial that the Keynesian revolution had anything to do with it, see Harry G. Johnson, *Inflation and the Monetarist Controversy,* pp. 5–6 (see note 19 for full citation). For references to German economists who, in the face of conservative orthodoxy, advocated expansionist monetary policies before publication of *The General Theory,* see George Garvy, "Keynes and the Economic Activists of Pre-Hitler Germany," *Journal of Political Economy,* vol. 83 (April 1975), pp. 391–405.

Common institutional and structural changes

Nearly all countries have also undergone certain long-period institutional and structural changes (that is, changes in the composition of major sectors of output or expenditure) that, although not in themselves inflationary, have made those countries more vulnerable to inflation.

One institutional change that has frequently been noted is a widespread increase in the resistance to reduction of nominal prices and wages. One element in this change is probably a more general expectation of increases in real returns associated with the belief, already mentioned, that recessions have become unnecessary and avoidable and that governments will avoid them. This belief is fortified by, and perhaps really derived in, many countries from the rapidity of actual real growth during the first postwar decades. Another element is the increased size and strength of labor organizations and the increase of social legislation on minimum wages, higher unemployment compensation, and the like, which directly or indirectly sets floors under nominal wage rates or limits reductions in them when the demand for labor declines. There may also have been a widespread increase in concentration of industry, having the result of more oligopolistic setting of prices and increased perception by individual firms that the demand curves for their products are linked, which would make for increased resistance to decreases in their prices. The facts about trends in concentration, however, appear not to be clearly established.

Increased resistance to reductions in nominal prices and wages means that changes in real demand and supply functions requiring declines in *relative* prices and wages have to take the form, to a greater extent than before World War II, of greater increases of other nominal prices and wages than would occur if the prices that needed to fall relatively were more flexible downward. The result is that structural changes, which are always occurring and may have been occurring more rapidly in the postwar world than before, and the changes in relative prices that they require to preserve or establish both equilibrium of relative prices and high total output and employment, can be attained only by increases in the general price level. Clearly, if the price level sometimes rises but falls little if at all, even during cyclical contractions, its long-run trend will necessarily rise.[43]

43. See, for example, Charles L. Schultze, *Recent Inflation in the United States,* Study Paper No. 1 of Materials Prepared in connection with the Study of Employment, Growth, and Price Levels, Joint Economic Committee, 86:1 (Government Printing Office, 1959), and Arthur F. Burns, *Prosperity without Inflation* (Fordham University Press, 1957), pp. 15–18.

Another long-run structural change with several aspects that bear on vulnerability to inflation is the great and widespread increase in the importance of government expenditure and taxation. Data on one variant of such changes for some OECD countries are shown in table 5, and data showing several variants of them are shown in table 6.

One aspect is that increases in government expenditures on goods and services that are not more than matched by increases in *net* tax receipts (that is, tax revenues less transfer expenditures)—as they apparently have not been—augment aggregate demand and keep national economies operating more persistently near their potentials than when the economic role of governments is smaller.

A second relevant aspect of the increased relative importance of government expenditure on goods and services is that its price elasticity, if not zero, is clearly much lower than that of private expenditure, at least in short periods. An increase in the prices of goods and services purchased by governments induces very little reduction in the quantity of the real resources they absorb and larger increases (or smaller decreases) in money demand than would result from a corresponding increase in prices paid by the private sector.[44]

A third aspect of the increase in the public sector is that, apart from extreme situations, most central governments (and perhaps subordinate governments in some countries) are relatively little influenced by the level of interest rates or the availability of credit. As a result, their behavior is not greatly affected by credit controls invoked to restrain inflationary demand pressures. To state the point otherwise, the corresponding shrinkage of the private sector's share has reduced the area of the economy amenable to such control.[45]

Moreover, both the ordinary methods of government contracting and the increase in income taxes associated with the larger role of government have reduced the incentives of all businesses to maximize their operating efficiency. The increase in taxes on net income of business has also reduced the responsiveness of business to increases in interest rates where interest payments are

44. Since the concept of price elasticity is fundamentally concerned with relative prices, its application to changes in nominal prices may appear to be misplaced. This possible objection is not valid, however, because the increases in nominal prices referred to here originate as increases in relative as well as nominal prices. They would cease to be increases in relative prices only insofar as an initial rise of relative prices was converted into a general inflation that raised other nominal prices proportionately.

45. The relative lack of response by government to higher interest rates may be regarded as an aspect of the low price elasticity of demand referred to in the preceding point, since interest rates reflect relative prices of future and present goods. But even if that is true, it is sufficiently different from elasticity of demand for goods in the ordinary sense of that term to justify separate mention.

Table 5. *Expenditures of All Governmental Units as Percentage of GNP, Twenty OECD Countries, Selected Periods, 1929–72*[a]

Country	1929	1938	Average 1948–49	Average 1957–59	Average 1967–69	1972
Australia[b]	20.4[e]	23.1[e,d]	23.3[e]	21.6	26.6	27.7
Austria	n.a.	n.a.	n.a.	31.5	36.4	35.8
Belgium	n.a.	n.a.	24.1	27.6	35.3	39.3
Canada	15.0[e]	20.8[e,d]	22.2[e]	28.8[f]	33.4	38.2
Denmark	n.a.	n.a.	21.3	25.5	36.0	42.9[g]
Finland	n.a.	n.a.	n.a.	29.3	33.7	34.3
France	n.a.	n.a.	n.a.	33.6[h]	37.2	36.9
Germany[h]	n.a.	n.a.	32.9	32.3[f]	36.6	37.8
Greece	n.a.	n.a.	26.7[e]	16.7[f]	24.0	22.5
Iceland	n.a.	n.a.	n.a.	33.1	29.8[i]	n.a.
Ireland	n.a.	n.a.	n.a.	26.5	32.9[j]	37.9[j]
Italy	n.a.	n.a.	n.a.	28.7	33.8	39.9[j]
Japan	n.a.	n.a.	26.9[k]	22.2	19.1	15.8
Netherlands	n.a.	n.a.	27.8[e]	35.2	42.0	46.9
Norway	17.4	18.2	25.4[e]	30.6[f]	38.5	45.5
Portugal	n.a.	n.a.	n.a.	17.7	21.2	22.0
Spain	n.a.	n.a.	n.a.	13.5[e]	17.3[e]	20.0[e]
Sweden	n.a.	n.a.	22.8[l,e]	28.2[e]	41.3	46.7
United Kingdom	n.a.	23.8	31.4[e]	31.8	36.7	37.0
United States[m]	10.0	19.5	20.4[e]	27.9	32.8	34.9

Sources: Fiscal data are from the following sources, except as noted below in the individual country sources: Organisation for European Economic Co-operation, *Statistics of Sources and Uses of Finance, 1948–1958* (Paris: OEEC, 1960); OECD, *Statistics of National Accounts, 1950–1961;* OECD, *National Accounts of OECD Countries, 1953–1969;* ibid., *1960–1971* (Paris: OECD, 1973), and ibid., *1961–1972* (Paris: OECD, 1974).

Australia: Benjamin U. Ratchford, *Public Expenditures in Australia* (Duke University Press, 1959), p. 302 (for 1929–49); Commonwealth Bureau of Census and Statistics, *Australian National Accounts: National Income and Expenditure, 1953–54 to 1966–67* (Canberra: 1968), pp. 25, 27 (for 1957–59).

Canada: Dominion Bureau of Statistics, *The Canada Year Book, 1955* (Ottawa: Queen's Printer and Controller of Stationery, 1955), p. 1176 (for 1929); and *The Canada Year Book, 1957–58* (1958), p. 1126 (for 1939).

France: Economic Commission for Europe, *Economic Survey of Europe in 1949* (Geneva: United Nations, 1950), pp. 273–75 (for 1948–49).

Japan: Bureau of Statistics, Office of the Prime Minister, *Japan Statisical Yearbook, 1961* (Tokyo: 1962), p. 400 (for 1948–49).

Norway: Odd Aukrust (correspondence with author, April 7, 1976) (for 1929); Central Bureau of Statistics of Norway, *National Accounts, 1865–1960*, pp. 104, 194 (for 1938).

United Kingdom: Central Statistical Office, *National Income and Expenditure, 1956* (London: Her Majesty's Stationery Office, 1956), p. 3 (for 1938).

United States: U.S. Department of Commerce, *The National Income and Product Accounts of the United States, 1929–1965*, pp. 52, 54 (for 1929 and 1938).

GNP data are from the following general sources, except as noted below in the individual country sources: OEEC, *Statistics of National Product and Expenditure, No. 2: 1938 and 1947 to 1955* (for 1938 and 1948–49); OECD, *National Accounts of OECD Countries, 1953–1969* (for 1957–59); and IMF, *International Financial Statistics*, vol. 27 (September 1974) and vol. 28 (June 1975) (for 1967–69 and 1972).

Australia: Ratchford, *Public Expenditures in Australia*, p. 303 (for 1929 and 1948); E. A. Boehm, *Twentieth Century Economic Development in Australia* (Melbourne: Longman Australia, deductible from taxable income. As a result, public treasuries now bear larger portions of any increases in interest costs paid by business. The rise of tax rates on individual incomes may also have reduced the responsiveness of individuals to changes in interest rates on mortgages and consumer credit in the United States and other countries in which interest payments are deductible from income in determining tax liability. Higher rates of individual income taxation may also have been a factor in causing business corporations in the United States and some other countries to pay out a smaller portion of earnings as dividends. Increases in retained earnings make business firms less dependent on external funds and thus make private expenditure less susceptible to a given degree of monetary and credit restraint.[46]

Many of these changes in ideas about economic goals and policies and in economic structure have their effects mainly on long-run trends of the price level, but some are relevant to short-run changes. For example, the efforts of all sectors to increase their real consumption and investment at accustomed rates when the total output available rises by less than those rates, or even to maintain such consumption and investment when the total available falls, can set off a rise in the general price level, and that rise will continue so long as total demand continues to be excessive. This influence apparently was at work

46. Some of these specific points, as they apply to the United States, have been effectively expounded by Arthur F. Burns in his discussion of "The New Environment of Monetary Policy" (chap. 3 of his *Prosperity without Inflation*).

1972) p. 216 (for 1938 and 1949); Commonwealth Bureau of Census and Statistics, *Australian National Accounts: National Income and Expenditure, 1953–54 to 1966–67*, p. 22 (for 1957–1959).

    Canada: Canada Year Book, 1955, p. 1173 (for 1929) and *Canada Year Book, 1957–58*, p. 1122 (for 1939).

    Japan: Kazushi Ohkawa and Henry Rosovsky, *Japanese Economic Growth*, p. 278 (for 1929 and 1938); *Japan Statistical Year Book, 1961*, p. 399 (for 1948–49); ibid., *1970* (Tokyo: 1971), p. 489 (for 1957–59 and 1967); *Japan Statistical Yearbook, 1973/74* (Tokyo: 1974), p. 487 (for 1968–69 and 1972).

    Norway: Odd Aukrust (correspondence with author, April 7, 1976) (for 1929); Central Bureau of Statistics of Norway, *National Accounts, 1865–1960*, p. 364 (for 1938).

    n.a. Not available.

    a. Government expenditures include interest on public debt, consumption of goods and services, subsidies, social security benefits, other current internal and external outgoing transfers, and general government gross fixed capital formation. Transfers between governments within a country have been eliminated except where noted.

    b. Fiscal years ending June 30.

    c. Excludes government gross fixed capital formation.

    d. 1939.

    e. Transactions between government units not eliminated.

    f. Excludes gross fixed capital formation of government enterprises.

    g. 1971.

    h. For years before 1960, excludes Saar and West Berlin.

    i. 1967–68 average.

    j. Includes some net purchases of land and intangible assets.

    k. Fiscal years beginning April 1.

    l. Excludes central government interest on public debt.

    m. Excludes expenditure on machinery and equipment.

Table 6. *Frequencies of Direction of Change in Fiscal Totals of Twenty OECD Countries as Percentages of GNP or GDP over Selected Periods, 1938–72*[a]

| | Central government | | | All governmental units | | | |
| | | | | | Expenditure for goods and services[c] | | |
Period and direction of change[b]	Total expenditure (1)	Expenditure for goods and services[c] (2)	Revenue[d] (3)	Total expenditure (4)	Current prices (5)	Constant prices (6)	Revenue[d] (7)
1938 to 1948–49							
Increase	5	3	5	3	7	5	4
No change	0	2	0	2	5	3	0
Decrease	0	0	0	0	5	3	0
1948–49 to 1957–59							
Increase	4	3	2	7	11	11	7
No change	2	3	0	1	4	2	0
Decrease	2	1	6	3	3	2	3
1957–59 to 1967–69							
Increase	14	6	13	18	15	4	18
No change	3	11	4	0	3	7	1
Decrease	2	2	2	2	2	8	1
1967–69 to 1972							
Increase	9	3	7	12	8	1	16
No change	7	13	8	5	12	15	3
Decrease	1	1	2	2	1	4	0
1938 to 1967–69							
Increase	5	5	5	5	10	6	4
No change	0	0	0	0	2	1	0
Decrease	0	0	0	0	5	4	0
1948–49 to 1967–69							
Increase	6	4	1	10	13	7	8
No change	1	2	3	0	3	4	1
Decrease	1	1	4	2	2	3	1

Sources: Column 4 is from table 5; other columns are based on tables available from author.

a. Frequencies are based on data in current prices, except for column 6, which is based on data in constant prices.

b. Change of less than 1 percent of GNP is treated as "no change."

c. Includes defense expenditure, but excludes all expenditure on equipment, construction, and works for civilian purposes, and all expenditure on land.

d. Sum of revenues from direct and indirect taxes, social security contributions, income from property and government enterprises, and current internal and external transfer receipts.

in some oil-importing countries when the quadrupling of the price of imported oil in late 1973 reduced rates of growth in the quantity of goods and services available to the country as a whole.

Convergence of rates of productivity growth

Several writers have found that over periods in which prices have time to adjust to changes in cost (generally at least a year), consumer price indexes and other comprehensive price indexes, such as GNP deflators, tend to rise more rapidly than wholesale price indexes, which are generally more heavily weighted with traded goods, and that their divergence tends to be greater the more rapid the growth in a country's productivity. If wholesale price indexes in different countries move together, therefore, the rate of increase in consumer price indexes or GNP deflators will tend to be positively associated with rates of productivity growth. Under those conditions a convergence in rates of productivity growth would be sufficient to reduce the dispersion of increases in consumer price indexes.[47]

There is some evidence that such a convergence occurred during at least the first part of the postwar period. Denison provides estimates of rates of growth in total productivity for the United States and eight European countries for the period 1950–62. The average deviation of the rates of growth in real national income per person employed from the unweighted mean growth rate of these nine countries fell from 1.6 percentage points for growth from 1950 to 1955 to 1.0 for growth from 1955 to 1962, and the average deviation of their growth rates of output per unit of input fell from 1.5 percentage points from 1950 to 1955 to 0.9 from 1955 to 1962.[48]

Supranational monetary changes

While the institutional and structural changes discussed above merely increase the vulnerability to inflation, some monetary changes, supranational in character, may have directly released inflationary forces. In the years 1970,

---

47. On the relation between rates of productivity growth and the relative movements in wholesale and consumer prices, see, for example, Bela Balassa, "The Purchasing-Power Parity Doctrine: A Reappraisal," *Journal of Political Economy,* vol. 72 (December 1964), pp. 584–96, and Ronald I. McKinnon, *Money and Capital in Economic Development* (Brookings Institution, 1973), p. 96.

48. These measures of dispersion were calculated from the percentage rates of growth given in Edward F. Denison, *Why Growth Rates Differ: Postwar Experience in Nine Western Countries* (Brookings Institution, 1967), tables 2-2, 2-3, and 15-2, pp. 18, 190.

1971, and 1972, additions to international monetary reserves were created in the form of special drawing rights amounting to approximately $9 billion. These reserves were assets to the recipient countries but were not liabilities in the conventional sense to any country, so that they must have reduced the balance of payments constraints on some countries without increasing those on any others. Although this reserve creation was small relative to increases in reserves caused by other influences and did not directly increase demand, it probably had some expansionary effect. In any case, it illustrates the potential, if not the past actual, importance of one type of common cause.[49]

Another monetary influence not associated with any particular country and quantitatively more important than creation of SDRs has been the development and vast expansion of the Eurocurrency market. It is now widely believed that the development of this market has increased the total supply of money, at least on a broad definition, and not merely shifted where it is held. The reasons given are that the banks accepting Eurocurrency deposits are enabled, as a group, to create deposits to a multiple of the primary deposits they receive through their lending operations, and that most of them keep a lower ratio of reserves to deposits than do banks from which their primary deposits are transferred. Moreover, the practice of some central banks of depositing reserves, directly or through the Bank for International Settlements, in the Eurocurrency market also resulted in multiple deposit creation. The Eurocurrency market lent these central bank funds to private borrowers, who in turn sold the Eurocurrencies for their national currencies in the foreign exchange market whence they were bought up by their central banks, which again deposited them in the Eurocurrency markets, where the process was repeated. The central banks of the Group of Ten countries and Switzerland agreed in the spring of 1971 to stop such redepositing because it was believed to be inflationary.[50]

Whether Eurobanks as a group have created deposits has been called "one of the most widely debated questions in the literature on the Euro-dollar market," and estimates of the deposit multiplier associated with initial deposits

49. For a statement of the position that creation of SDRs is likely over the long run to be so inflationary as to leave the real value of international monetary reserves unchanged, see Harry G. Johnson's comments in *International Reserves: Needs and Availability*, Papers and Proceedings, Seminar at the International Monetary Fund, 1970 (IMF, 1970) pp. 150–51. The effect of increases in nominal reserves, as well as on liberalization of international trade, is examined in the analytical paper by J. Marcus Fleming, "Reserve Creation and Real Reserves," in the same volume, pp. 521–52.

50. Fritz Machlup forcefully directed attention to such central bank redepositing as an inflationary influence in "World Inflation: Factual Background," in Randall Hinshaw, ed., *Inflation as a Global Problem* (Johns Hopkins University Press, 1972), pp. 32–34.

in that market have varied greatly.[51] In a more recent contribution to the theory of the Eurodollar market, Niehans and Hewson suggest not only that the Eurodeposit multiplier may be less than unity but that if the Eurodollar market is viewed as a means of increasing the efficiency of credit distribution rather than of creating liquidity, the deposit multiplier ceases to be an indicator of liquidity creation.[52] My preliminary opinion of this new view is that even if, as the authors believe, it implies that Eurobanks are not as subject to liquidity risks as was previously thought, it does not necessarily imply (and the authors do not say) that their operations are not inflationary. Some (although not all) increases in the efficiency of credit distribution reduce the demand for liquidity by reducing the liquid assets that business firms are impelled to hold. If the supply of liquidity remains unchanged, a reduction in the demand for it is as inflationary as an increase in the supply when the demand is unchanged. The question that remains, therefore, is whether the increases in the efficiency of credit distribution attributable to the Eurocurrency markets have been of a kind that has reduced the demand for liquidity, rather than merely, say, distributing credit to more productive users while leaving the demand for liquidity unchanged. It seems unlikely that it could have failed to reduce the demand for liquidity to some degree, so that even in the Niehans-Hewson interpretation it was probably inflationary, although to an extent that is unknown.

Whether one interprets the development of the Eurocurrency market as having increased the supply of liquidity or reduced the demand for it, the effect seems to be the same, and to be an application of a general principle: when creation of a new financial institution offers conveniences not previously available and thereby induces the public to substitute deposits in it for forms of liquid assets that do not offer such conveniences, it will increase the

51. The quotation comes from John Hewson and Eisuke Sakakibara, "The Euro-Dollar Deposit Multiplier: A Portfolio Approach," in *IMF Staff Papers*, vol. 21 (July 1974), p. 307. In that paper the authors are critical of the conventional method of estimating the multiplier for the primary inflow of deposits. Using a portfolio approach, they estimate that the multiplier is between 0 and 1 (that is, that there is no multiple deposit creation) in the absence of central bank redepositing, and that with it the multiplier lies between 0 and the reciprocal of the proportion of central bank foreign reserves not held in the form of Eurodollars. For the period 1968–72, they estimate this multiplier as having had a maximum value of 1.4. Their estimates imply that the deposit-creating effects of this practice may not have been as large as Machlup thought, but those estimates relate to the four years 1969–72, whereas central bank depositing of reserves in the Eurocurrency market evidently became substantial first in 1971 and, because of depositing by central banks of countries outside the Group of Ten, expanded greatly in 1972. (See IMF, *Annual Report 1973*, pp. 37–38.)

52. See Jürg Niehans and John Hewson, "The Eurodollar Market and Monetary Theory," *Journal of Money, Credit, and Banking*, vol. 8 (February 1976), pp. 1–27.

supply of liquid assets relative to the demand for them, regardless of whether liquid assets are defined to include or exclude deposits in that institution.[53]

It has been argued that the Eurocurrency market developed mainly because of restrictions imposed by the United States on certain types of international lending and that in the absence of these restrictions other forms of money or near-money assets would have experienced a similar rapid growth. The ensuing expansion of private liquidity, therefore, should be regarded as a result not of the Eurocurrency market but of whatever gave impetus to the increased demand to acquire international liquidity. However much or little truth there is in this point, it implies merely that the source of the effect has been incorrectly identified, the basic source being the increase in world financial integration and the Eurocurrency market being merely the channel through which that increase happened to have operated.

Coincidence of cyclical expansions

It is noted in the text that while cyclical expansions might coincide because expansion in one or a few countries is transmitted to others, the probability of such expansions coinciding by mere chance is not so low as to be negligible. Expansions did coincide to an unusual degree in 1972 and 1973 and brought real demand to levels that pressed on world resources.[54] That there was at least some element of chance in this synchronization is made plausible by the apparent lack of any long-term trend toward greater synchronization that conforms with the trend toward greater world economic integration that is generally assumed to have occurred; such synchronization has occurred when the world economy is widely regarded as having been less integrated than it is now, and it has been followed by periods of less synchronization when integration is regarded as having increased.

53. Tibor Scitovsky makes this point with reference to creation of a bank that, by offering a convenience not previously available, induces the public to substitute deposits in it for currency. He illustrates it by the case of a bank established in a small community that previously had no bank. If its establishment induces people to hold less currency and more demand deposits than before, this shift increases the supply of money. As Scitovsky also indicates, the point is equally applicable if the new institution merely induces the public to shift deposits from other banks to it but keeps a lower ratio of reserves to deposits than other banks. If the new institution is one whose deposits are not part of the money supply, a shift from demand deposits in other banks to it will not increase the money supply but will reduce the demand for money, with the same economic effect. (See Tibor Scitovsky, *Money and the Balance of Payments* [Rand-McNally, 1969], pp. 34–36.)

54. See, for example, data on annual changes in real product in eleven countries between 1954 and 1973 in Otto Eckstein, "How Deep a Recession?" in American Statistical Association, *1974 Proceedings of the Business and Economic Statistics Section* (1975), table 3, p. 235.

Geoffrey Moore, after recalling that as long ago as 1927 Wesley Mitchell found a long-term trend toward greater international synchronization of business cycles, examined annual growth rates in real GNP, industrial production, and value of exports and imports for the United States and eight other advanced countries during the period 1953–73.[55] Comparing annual growth rates in the United States with the median of the rates for eight other countries, he found that they change in the same direction in about two-thirds of the years, with the correspondence being poor only in 1962–66. Among the eight countries other than the United States, he found eight phases of expansion and contraction and compared the changes in industrial production in each of the eight countries with their median changes. Doing this in each of these phases gives sixty-four opportunities to compare rises and falls in national and median growth rates. Moore found that in fifty-seven of the sixty-four comparisons (that is, 89 percent of them), national rates rose and fell in line with median rates. His evidence does not suggest that conformity of growth cycles increased during the period but it does suggest (to me, at least) that although such conformity was greater after 1966 than in 1962–66 it was also greater before 1962. Similarly, the OECD's calculation of dispersion of potential output gaps in seventeen OECD member countries and thirteen northern European members, although extending from 1955 only to 1971, shows that dispersion in 1964 and 1965 and in 1969 was higher than in 1971 but also that it was higher than in most of the earlier years, and that it shows no downward trend.[56]

Thus, one cannot rule out the possibility that the reason for the greater generality of inflation in the past few years is merely a coincidental greater conformity of cyclical expansion, rather than that inflationary pressures have been more intense in one or a few countries and have been transmitted from them to others in unusually high degree because of an increase of integration.

Comments by Bert G. Hickman

THERE is very little in Walter Salant's paper with which I specifically disagree. He has surveyed a wide range of empirical generalizations and theoretical propositions bearing on the question of international transmission of inflation. The survey is lucid, insightful, and encyclopedic. It would be a disservice to quibble about details, and I will not do so. Instead, I have tried to

55. Geoffrey H. Moore, "The State of the International Business Cycle," *Business Economics,* vol. 9 (September 1974), pp. 21–29.
56. See OECD "International Transmission of Inflation," p. 82 (note 2).

find a few central themes on which to focus my comments and, I hope, to clarify some concepts and issues.

The first part of the paper is devoted to refuting the proposition that the generality and uniformity of inflation throughout the world since the 1960s necessarily implies a greater tendency toward international transmission than existed before. Although I do not disagree with Salant's conclusion that greater uniformity need not necessarily imply increased transmission, I am unsure whether the question has been posed in the most fruitful way. The basic analytical problem is to distinguish between the international transmission mechanism somehow defined and other potential explanations of generalized inflation. By placing this question in a specific historical context—the *recent* acceleration and generalization of inflation—one is led to look for *new* factors in one or the other categories. This occurs especially in Salant's discussion of common policy objectives and common structural changes under the category of other potential explanations, but there is also a brief discussion of increased integration of international trade and finance at the beginning of the section on the mechanism of international transmission. Perhaps important recent changes have occurred in either or both of these respects. Nonetheless, it is well to remind ourselves that inflation is an old story with a very long history, and that there is some danger, when embarking on a search for new structural factors to explain an old phenomenon, of emphasizing superficial novelty rather than fundamental causality. Without undertaking a new study or searching the literature, I am reasonably confident that one could find many earlier historical periods of prolonged and widespread inflation among market economies. Perhaps it is true that the more things change the more they remain the same.

If one nonetheless accepts Salant's arguments that the postwar changes in policy objectives and market structures have made the industrialized nations as a group more vulnerable to inflationary shocks—and I do accept them as far as they go—it does not follow that these changes are independent of "international transmission mechanisms." If one thinks of the world economy as a set of national economies linked by flows of goods, labor, and capital, then the extent to which inflation in one country occurs in response to developments in another depends not only on the degree of international integration between them but also on the internal responses of both countries to inflationary shocks. For this reason, I believe it is preferable to classify the common structural changes in the various national economies as part of the postwar change in the international transmission mechanism rather than as a phenomenon independent of the latter. This would be consistent with Salant's own analysis of the components of the transmission mechanism, as constructed with historical changes therein, when he stresses that "the mechanisms conventionally described as channels of international transmission depend for their operation on assumptions about domestic monetary conditions and about other elements of intranational transmission. . . ."

Notice that I am not questioning the proposition that synchronized shocks may lead to synchronized expansions and inflations, either because of an accidental conjuncture of independent national shocks or because of common supranational shocks due to such events as wars, droughts, or oil embargoes. The basic distinction is between synchronized shocks as a cause of generalized inflation and an international transmission mechanism strong enough to spread inflation from one or a few countries to many others in the absence of synchronized shocks. As part of that distinction, the properties of the transmission mechanism, and changes over time in those properties, depend on the internal structures of the constituent economies as well as on their external economic relationships. For given internal structures, increased integration of international trade and finance may augment the cross-multipliers for incomes and prices, but it is also true that the cross-multipliers may be increased by destabilizing internal structural changes independently of any change in external integration. (My reference to own- and cross-multipliers, incidentally, refers to the total effects on prices from all induced responses built into the models and not merely to the textbook Keynesian income-expenditure multiplier.)

Thus I believe that the crucial question at hand is not whether the international transmission mechanism has changed in either its internal or external aspects, but whether the cross-multipliers for incomes and prices are strong enough to explain generalized inflation in today's world. This is also the central issue which Salant addresses in the main body of his paper dealing with the transmission mechanism.

He organizes the discussion around four principal transmission channels: (1) direct linkages through prices of tradable goods; (2) linkages through the income effects of exogenous changes in export or import demand; (3) the effects of payments imbalances on official reserves and the monetary base; and (4) direct international wage linkages. His discussion of these channels provides a thorough catalog for the potential researcher, disclosing pitfalls to be avoided as well as concepts to be exploited in the search for guiding principles. His discussion of the implications of alternative price measures for the analysis of imported inflation is the subtlest that I have read and repays attentive study. So also does his careful analysis of the direct and indirect effect of exogenous changes in import and export prices on the domestic prices of tradable goods and their substitutes.

One way to view the entire corpus of this section, apart from some of the comments on direct international wage linkages, is as an exercise in the application of the theory of adjustment of balance of payments to draw out its implications for domestic stability in the face of external shocks. Viewed this way, the analysis is a synthesis of the relative price, absorption, and monetary approaches to balance of payments adjustment. It is a synthesis not only in the sense that all these elements are considered in the taxonomy of transmission channels, but also in the sense that Salant emphasizes the interdependence of the elements. One lesson from this literature that Salant emphasizes is that the effects of external increases in the prices of tradable goods on domestic prices depend not only on the direct linkages but also on the income and monetary stimuli from the induced changes in aggregate money demand from exports or imports; the latter in turn depend on the price elasticities of imports and exports as well as on the income multipliers and monetary policy of the country in question.

Given that the direction, magnitude, or both of predicted outcomes to external shocks depends on the numerical values of key elasticities and propensities of the foreign and domestic sectors, what is one to do? The advice implicit in Salant's analysis, as I interpret it, is to model in rather considerable detail both the internal quantitative structures and the external quantitative relationships of the various nations or regions of the world. The economist interested primarily in his own economy ignores the external influences at his peril, and the international specialist who abstracts from domestic structures and intranational transmission mechanisms may be led sadly astray.

Project LINK is just such a system of linked national dynamic econometric models. It includes large-scale structural models for thirteen developed market economies, as well as eighteen other models to fill out the rest of the world. It provides a number of the channels for the international propagation of disturbances discussed by Salant. The magnitude of the indirect responses to internal or external shocks depends on the various numerical elasticities and propensities in the models and cannot be inferred analytically in such a large and interdependent system. They can be estimated by simulation techniques, however, and Salant has quoted some results from simulations that I performed recently with the LINK system. My interpretation of these results, which is reported accurately by Salant, is that the cross-multipliers for prices in response to demand shocks originating in one or another of the nations modeled in the system are generally weak. This conclusion is qualified by the observation that exogenous shocks to wages or prices conceivably could have larger external effects, especially if accompanied by accommodating demand policies to prevent an induced fall of real income in the originating country. I have also stressed—again as accurately reported by Salant—that the LINK system needs improvement with regard to the incorporation of capital flows, monetary sectors, and international commodity markets, and that such improvements are proceeding as fast as research resources permit. Meanwhile, and awaiting further evidence on the transmission mechanism itself, I ventured the suggestion that generalized inflation or inflationary episodes may be due to synchronized shocks.

With regard to the synchronized shock hypothesis, Salant has discussed a number of plausible communication and demonstration linkages that lie outside the sphere of formal economic analysis. Moreover, it is known from quantitative simulations of the LINK system undertaken by Johnson and Klein, that the international trade linkages modeled therein will amplify the effects of synchronized domestic shocks without converting them into unstable endogenous movements.[57] A simultaneous exogenous reduction in real GNP of equal percentage size in all the national models was imposed in one of these simulations. A comparison of the solutions before and after linkage disclosed that international transmission and feedbacks amplified the GNP decline by about 50 percent. A second simulation assumed simultaneous wage shocks sufficient to raise the GNP deflator for each country by approximately 200 basis points. It turned out that the amplification effects of international linkage on the price increases induced by wage shocks were generally small, although differing considerably across countries. A third exercise was to increase the price of Middle Eastern oil exports and observe its effects on the developed market economies. In this case an exogenous increase in oil prices of 25 percent resulted in domestic increases in the GNP deflators or consumer price indexes of the developed economies ranging up to 5 percent for the Netherlands and averaging less than 2 percent. In interpreting these results it is again necessary to remember that the models are incomplete in potentially important respects and that the strength of the trade and price relations which are modeled may be underestimated.

Another important point is that monetary policy was held constant in the Hickman and the Johnson and Klein simulations, on the implicit assumption that exchange reserve flows are sterilized. One must agree with the Keynesians and monetarists that some degree of monetary restraint could prevent exogenous increases in wage rates and food or materials prices from affecting the general domestic price level. This is not a frictionless world, however, and Salant correctly points out that accommodating increases in the money stock may be undertaken by central bankers to ameliorate the adjustment process even at the expense of general inflation.

57. Keith Johnson and Lawrence Klein, "Stability in the International Economy: The LINK Experience," in Albert Ando, Richard Herring, and Richard Marston, eds., *International Aspects of Stabilization Policies*, pp. 147–88 (see note 16 for full citation).

This brings me somewhat tangentially to the final problem raised by Salant. He asks how one can know whether a given system of impulse responses is a true model of the fundamental causal mechanism or merely a superficial rendering of observed channels under given institutional circumstances, citing as an example the contention that the true cause of a general inflation is not cost-push but the accommodating increase in the money supply. On one level, the question may be unanswerable, since even a "true" model will not have causal interpretability unless its structure is recursive. More pragmatically, the distinction between cause and effect may better be replaced by that between instrument and target variables. Then if the model is a valid representation of the given institutional and market structure, causal significance can be attributed to the policy instruments, since policymakers are capable in principle of setting them so as to neutralize the adverse effects of exogenous changes in noncontrollable variables. In the cost-push example, if one assumes that exogenous wage or price increases are not controllable by direct instruments whereas the money supply can be fixed by policy, the latter would be a causal factor in the resulting inflation whereas the former would not be.

As is well known from the theory of economic policy, however, problems may arise because of the incompatibility of instruments and targets or because the economic structure imposes an unsatisfactory trade-off between policy objectives. Given the objective function of the policymakers, the available instruments, and the economic structure, acceptance of inflation may be necessary to avoid more adverse effects on unemployment or income distribution or growth. In those circumstances, saying that an excess supply of money is the cause of inflation may be instrumentally true but may not get one very far toward controlling inflation. The underlying problem is the political one of mediating among various interest groups in the struggle for real income shares and equitably distributing the incidence of inflation control. As the Organization of Petroleum Exporting Countries has sharply reminded the rest of the world, the struggle for income distribution has an international dimension as well. Deeper understanding of the inflationary process will require incorporation of the reaction functions of public and private policymakers in economic models.

Comments by *Robert J. Gordon*

IN GENERAL Salant has written a very good and comprehensive survey paper. There are three more or less independent sections that I will discuss separately. First of all, whether increased transmission or integration implies a reduction in the dispersion of international inflation rates; second, the specific channels by which inflationary impulses are communicated from abroad to the domestic economy; and finally, his comments on the Project LINK simulations.

The relation between dispersion and integration

Does the narrowed dispersion of inflation say anything about the increased importance of the international transmission mechanism? A more important cause, as much of Salant's discussion recognizes, has been the simultaneous adoption by many countries of full employment goals and the simultaneous shift in structure toward more wage and price inflexibility. Administered prices, labor unions, and workers' unwillingness to accept cuts in wage rates can all be viewed as reducing the dispersion of inflation by shifting the position and shape of the short-run Phillips curve, but without any implications for the importance of international transmission, that is, whether countries are moving simultaneously back and forth along the Phillips curve.

Salant suggests that a reduction in the international dispersion of inflation rates could have been observed, if, by some coincidence of history, business cycles have become simultaneous, in contrast to a previous era when they were not. This is a weak position upon which to base conclusions, although I have heard it used to discredit my simulations of the wage-price control era.[58] How does one really know that controls had any effect on prices, despite the effects of the simulation, since there could have been a historical coincidence on August 15, 1971, for example, the sun spot cycle could have suddenly changed its nature? Economists should be prohibited from appealing to historical coincidence. Some specific reason other than international monetary integration should be suggested as an explanation of the simultaneous cyclical movements in the world in the last five years.

Consider the monetary theory in which there is complete goods market integration with one traded goods price in the world. One might observe either an increased or reduced dispersion of nontraded goods prices depending entirely on the reaction of domestic monetary policy to exogenous events. One could have, assuming that a country is large enough to control its own supply of domestic credit, a response of the price of nontraded goods to imported inflation that is almost zero or one substantial enough to eliminate the change in relative prices, depending on the reaction of domestic policy.

58. Robert J. Gordon, "Wage-Price Controls and the Shifting Phillips Curve," *BPEA, 2:1972*, pp. 385–421. See also Robert J. Gordon, "The Response of Wages and Prices to the First Two Years of Controls," *BPEA, 3:1973*, pp. 765–78.

In a world of complete integration shocks might be experienced in one period and not in another. Korean War commodity prices in the early 1950s, and oil and food inflation in the early 1970s, affected all countries at the same time. But in between there were no such major simultaneous shocks, so that changes in statistical measures of dispersion would have depended on domestic policy responses during the transition into and out of the periods of simultaneous shocks. An example is the striking recent contrast of Germany's response with those of Japan and Italy—two types of possible domestic policy reactions to imported inflation.

Salant discusses the effect of integration on dispersion in a particular case with different productivity movements in the traded and nontraded goods sectors. He has an example in which movements in the consumer price index are initially uniform across countries, with a different set of productivity growth rates across countries that convert the uniform growth rates of the consumer price index into divergent rates of the wholesale price index. In his example an increase in world integration would cause convergence of the wholesale price index (a proxy for price of traded goods), with an increased divergence of the consumer price index.

But this result is due entirely to his original assumption that the growth rates of the consumer price index happened for some unspecified reason to be identical in the first instance. In another case the initial wholesale price indexes might be random variables, drawn out of a random number generator, and the consumer price indexes in each country would be equal to that random number plus an adjustment for productivity change. Movement to integration that causes convergence in wholesale price indexes across countries would automatically reduce the divergence of the consumer indexes as well. Everything depends on the initial situation before the world is integrated, and one cannot reach any conclusions from artificial initial assumptions.

The transmission mechanism with demand and supply shocks

The second part of Salant's paper concerns the classification of transmission mechanisms. There are four channels of transmission from a rest-of-the-world inflation shock—direct price effects, income or expenditure effects, monetary effects, and labor mobility effects. The main problem with the analysis is the failure to distinguish two different kinds of external shocks: a "demand shock," which originates in an increase in demand in the rest of the world, raising expenditures and the price of traded goods, and a "supply shock," as in the case of oil prices in 1974, where there is a reduction in supply in the rest of the world, raising the price of traded goods produced outside the local country. Most of the ambiguities and conflicts that Salant finds between the various channels of influence result from his failure to distinguish demand from supply shocks.

In particular, he is concerned about the effect of an inelastic demand for imports, which causes an increased price of imports to raise import expenditures. The problem is simplified if one recognizes that in the case of a demand shock there is no a priori reason to assume a change in the terms of trade. An increase in foreign demand should raise both the price of imports and the price of exports. Without further information, there is no reason to assume that one increase is greater or less than the other. If import prices and export prices rise together, then most of the problems that concern Salant in this section disappear. One no longer needs to worry about which price index is chosen. An expenditure index, including imports, will provide the same answer as a product index, which includes exports. There is no problem with the expenditure channel. In Salant's case, where he allows only the import price to increase with no change in the price of exports, an inelastic demand for imports will raise import expenditures and reduce nominal GNP, leading to a conflict between the imported inflation and the domestic deflation, which results from the fall in expenditure. But if export and import prices rise together, there are no changes in the terms of trade. If the initiating shock from abroad is demand-induced, there must be an increase in domestic demand that reinforces the imported increase in prices. In the case of asset markets, a demand-induced shock causes an increase in import and export prices, a balance of payments surplus, and an inflow of reserves, so that the monetary impulse of capital inflows and increased reserves will work in the same direction as the expenditure channel.

All of Salant's ambiguities return, of course, in the case of a supply shock. An increase in oil prices in a country that does not export oil must shift the terms of trade. This is the situation occurring around the world at the present time, a simultaneous increase in price for an inelastic good imported from overseas, with a decline in real balances and in real expenditures. Recession and inflation occur simultaneously.

The LINK simulations

Let me argue that no attention whatsoever should be paid to the estimates from Project LINK of small cross-multipliers of inflationary impulses on domestic inflation. A number of years ago I wrote a long review article of a volume on the simulations of the Brookings quarterly econometric model of the United States and concluded that we learned absolutely nothing about the real world from these simulations. Instead, the simulations were of value only in providing a long laundry list of improvements needed in the model.[59]

In the LINK simulations are models in which domestic prices depend only on import prices. There are no domestic substitutes for imports, and so this link between foreign and domestic prices is ignored. In addition, there is no substitution between exports and foreign goods; prices of all domestically produced goods are simply marked up over domestic wages. So the construction of the model has constrained the multipliers to be small. Further, there is no monetary sector in several of these models, so that they omit the impetus to domestic expenditure that would occur with a demand-induced external shock as an inflow of reserves raises the domestic money supply.

In addition, there are negative multipliers in several countries, France being one, due to a misspecification of the price equation. Phillips curves slope the wrong way, that is, an increase in expenditure reduces prices, because productivity rises faster than wages in an economic expansion. This occurs because of the failure to distinguish actual productivity from standard productivity. In the United States the historical evidence suggests that only a very small share of changes in actual productivity flows through to prices.

Conclusion

Finally, the conflict should not be exaggerated between the monetary theory of the balance of payments and the apparent Keynesian suggestion that the real cause of inflation is not changes in the world money supply but rather various nonmonetary external shocks. The right way to look at this "conflict" is to distinguish the short run from the long run. Few economists would disagree with the proposition that in the short run the increase in oil prices is going to raise the rate of inflation in the world.[60] But if one looks at the present era from the perspective of the year 2075, the rate of inflation that actually comes out of the present situation in the end will depend very much on the extent to which the oil shock is accommodated by domestic monetary policy.

59. Robert J. Gordon, "The Brookings Model in Action: A Review Article," *Journal of Political Economy,* vol. 78 (May/June 1970), pp. 489–525.

60. One exception is Milton Friedman: "You have to distinguish relative prices from absolute prices and from the average level of prices. If the price of oil and food went up, that meant that consumers had less to spend on other things and that other prices went up less. You mustn't confuse the arithmetic of a price inflation with the economics of price inflation." (Statement by Milton Friedman at AEI Round Table, July 1974, in Eileen Shanahan, moderator, *Indexing and Inflation* [American Enterprise Institute for Public Policy Research, 1974], p. 38.)

General Comments

MICHAEL PARKIN observed that international transmission is perhaps the most difficult subject under consideration, largely because there is no solid guiding theory about transmission, either international or intranational. In explaining how a rise in the money supply causes a change in the price of one or another specific commodity, one is thrown back on undesirably loose analysis. Some insights, however, may be had from the theory of price-setting behavior and by working backward from there. What are the immediate determinants of the prices that individual producers set? They respond partly to their expectations of how others will set their prices and partly to excess demand. If the expectations of price setters are very accurate and the prices they set turn out to be equilibrium prices, then prices will change by the amount required to restore equilibrium and, assuming that technology and taste have not changed, relative prices will also remain unchanged; only the general price level will change. On the more reasonable assumption that people cannot guess future full equilibrium prices correctly, prices will tend to change by the wrong amounts in immediate response to a change in total demand. That gives rise to some excess demands and excess supplies, which will produce a subsequent response. The implication is that if inflation rates are not changing very much and if the initial shock is in nominal spending, then much of the adjustment can be expected to be of the first type rather than through subsequent disequilibrium and adjustment in demand. If, however, nominal world demand were to change massively so that people could not make reasonable guesses, one would expect much more transitional disequilibrium involving substantial excess demands and supplies and flows of money. Alternatively, if the shock were not one of total nominal demand but a large change in the nominal price of one commodity, then uncertainty would be expected about the new equilibrium relationships, not only between the price that had changed and all others in the aggregate but among all, because a major change in one price, such as would be the result of a major change in monopoly power, presumably would affect all relative prices. In this situation one would expect the transmission mechanism to involve substantial excess demands and supplies, and monetary flows associated with them. All this relates to a world of absolutely rigid exchange rates. If to that is added the problem of trying to form expectations of what will happen to nominal price levels in different countries because of exchange rate adjustments, then price setters have to guess not only the nominal behavior of competitors in their own economy but also monetary policy and exchange rate movements; otherwise they cannot adjust their prices accurately. The need for such additional forecasting will occasion more disequilibrium in the adjustment process and tend to make relative price movements less in line with the underlying requirements of technologies and preferences.

In any event, how important is it to discuss transmission mechanisms? The time in which the transmission process operates may be so short that it is more important to focus upon the primary impulses to inflation.

Charles Maier drew a distinction between the question of how the transmission process operates and what he called the question of "why": referring to the underlying institutional factors, such as the new fiscal demands of the state, the extension of collective bargaining, and the effect of wider communication, which makes various groups of society more aware of the windfall gains accruing to other groups, in contrast to the mechanisms working through the banking system, exchange rates, and flows of capital and trade in themselves. But to take the longer view and look at the why: the period 1914–21 was one of substantial inflation induced by the war; from 1936 to 1951 the world experienced another fifteen years of inflation; then, leaving aside the creeping subsequent inflation, the years 1967–68 might be added to these. In short, more than half of the past sixty years has been inflationary. What happened in the inflationary periods that was different from what happened in the periods of price stability? First, the state had to claim a large share of resources quickly and claim it in a way that did not offend powerful industry or organized labor. This entailed a new system of social bargaining. Second, in the periods of price stability the terms of trade favored the manufacturing nations; that was not the situation in the three inflationary periods. Considering that inflation constituted a trend over a long period, one is not inclined to accept the theory of simultaneous shock; what happened over six decades could not be considered continuing shock. From the long-term view, the question of why appears to be the more important.

Gerhard Fels, commenting on the importance of the transmission mechanism for policy, thought it should be analyzed to obtain the correct indicators needed for policy guidance. The right policy decisions require a knowledge of whether inflation is imported or homemade. Salant has pointed out in his paper that the balance of payments mechanism and the mechanism operating through price effects would conflict when the price elasticity of import demand was very low. There is another case of conflict: a foreign economic expansion raises a country's exports and is inflationary through its effects on income and liquidity, but the price and wage effects are still negative, owing to the usual lag in adjustment of wages and prices. Then, when the upswing comes to its peak, the balance of payments is deteriorating because of bottlenecks in domestic supply, but prices and wages are rising to adjust to the international level. That rise suggests that the inflation is imported, but the effects of the balance of payments are negative. The reverse conflict occurs during the downswing of the cycle. Thus, there are conflicting indications as to whether the inflation is imported or not. To resolve the problem of finding the correct indicator, it is very important to discover how inflation is transmitted.

Assar Lindbeck observed that doubts about the importance of the transmission mechanism are expressed by a British contributor and its importance affirmed by a German contributor. This is natural enough, because the United Kingdom does not need a transmission mechanism, being able to generate inflation itself, whereas Germany is in the opposite situation, having an anti-inflationary bias but being a British neighbor. What is meant by the assertion that rates of inflation are becoming more similar? And how best can one measure convergence of rates? During the fifties and sixties the dispersion of rates did not appear to fall if it is measured by variance, but if it is measured by the coefficient of variation it is found to have fallen, the two measures giving different results because the mean rate was rising. The way to measure dispersion depends on the question one is trying to answer—whether one is interested in the consequences for the balance of payments, for income distribution, or for something else. That should probably be the criterion. In a very recent year (for example, 1974) with floating rates, both the variance and the coefficient of variation will be found to have increased, the rate of inflation being 25 percent for Japan and about 7 percent for West Germany.

Alexander Swoboda suggested that perhaps a more important inquiry than whether there is a tendency for inflation rates to converge historically is their failure to diverge more as the general rate of inflation becomes more pronounced, because this raises the question whether the increasing rate of general inflation will not increase the desire of some countries to pursue anti-inflationary policies. One would expect that as the range of inflation rates rose from 1 or 2 percent—which does not worry anyone very much—to 10, 15, and 20 percent, some countries would feel strongly enough about it to make the rates diverge. Whether this is not more important is something that might be considered.

Assar Lindbeck, referring to the possibility mentioned in Salant's paper that the increase of direct investment may have increased monopoly power, expressed doubt that it has had that effect. In fact, the opposite occurred; the internationalization of markets and entrepreneurship in the postwar period had greatly increased competition. Nearly all countries have experienced falling profit margins, and with less monopoly power there is probably less cost-push than there used to be. If national firms were to take over the world this might be reversed, but that has not happened yet, except in the newspapers.

Max Corden pointed out that discussion of transmission mechanisms is chiefly concerned with automatic or market mechanisms; one should also consider transmission through policy. For example, fiscal expansion in the United States had produced a surplus in the Japanese balance of payments. In the paper on Japan Komiya and Suzuki see the result as a big monetary expansion, created by the private sector.[61] It appears to have been internally generated, and not to have been transmitted from abroad. But a careful reading of the paper shows that this monetary expansion occurred because the Bank of Japan hesitated to tighten monetary policy, and the reason they hesitated was that, had they tightened policy, surpluses would have resulted and that would have been inconsistent with cooperation in maintaining the newly realigned network of exchange rates. In short, policy was motivated by external considerations. Purely statistical analysis would not catch that case. The same situation occurred in Australia, which also had a large surplus and ran liberal budgets in 1972 and 1973 under two different governments. The governments had felt free to have such budgets because there was a surplus in the balance of payments. These policy transmissions should be detected as well as the automatic or market ones that are discussed above.

Bert Hickman, referring to the statement that one should pay no attention to the inflation cross-multipliers for inflation in Project LINK's simulations, as reported in the Salant paper, urged that they be examined more carefully than is possible from Salant's quotations. It is a mistake to think that the simulations included no direct links between the prices of tradable goods and other domestic prices. In all but two of the national models prices of imported goods and materials are among the determinants of the consumer or wholesale price index. Moreover, these direct connections permit feedback through consumer prices, wages, and similar relationships. Although they may not be completely and correctly specified and estimated, these relationships are in the models, and they were formulated by good econometric investigations in the different countries. Furthermore, the income propagation mechanisms involved in the multiplier processes arising from changes in merchandise exports and imports are adequately modeled and they are connected to the domestic price level, usually through a Phillips curve mechanism. The results in the French model are peculiar in giving lower unit labor costs with expansions of income, but as already explained, this was occasioned not by a failure of the model

61. See pages 303–48.

to get an induced rise of wages (as implied by Gordon's statement that the Phillips curve sloped the wrong way) but from the combination of an induced rise and a more than offsetting increase in productivity. That result is suspicious, but occurs only in the French model. The monetary sector, as pointed out in Hickman's original paper, was not modeled completely for all countries and even where it was, monetary policy had been held constant in the simulations. The interpretation of that procedure is that the simulation shows what would happen if inflows of reserves were sterilized. That does not mean one should pay no attention to the results, because the effects of sterilizing reserve changes may be of interest. Of course, it is important to develop more complete models, but one should not reject out of hand results that give significant information about the parts already modeled. Whether allowance for additional channels of transmission will turn out to make an overwhelming difference is something one cannot foretell until the work is actually performed; it should not be assumed a priori that the result will be greatly different and, on the basis of that assumption, conclude that the weak transmission shown by an incomplete model is a result that should be totally disregarded.

Robert Gordon said that what he specifically criticized is the lack of direct effect of foreign impulses on domestic imports. To illustrate the general problem, Gordon's own equation for U.S. prices works very well in the sample period but would have given bad results if it had been used to simulate the effect of a U.S. devaluation, because the devaluation raises not only import prices but export prices directly and independently of the state of U.S. demand. The point is that equations that may behave well during a sample period may be inadequate for simulating an external shock unless some sort of a priori structure is imposed on them.

Bert Hickman noted that in the LINK system export prices are systematically related to import prices and there are devices in it by which changes in exchange rates would affect both import and export prices. Thus export prices are not neglected in that system.

Walter Salant, commenting on Gordon's objection to the paper's illustration of how an increase in world economic integration could increase, as well as reduce, the divergence in rates of increase of the consumer price index, agreed that the conclusion in that illustration depends on the assumption that these indexes had moved similarly before integration increased, but that does not make the point invalid. That part of the paper is directed to pointing out how limited are the conclusions one can draw safely from convergence of inflation rates alone. The case in question is only one example of how a generalization frequently made can be upset; the argument does not depend on the initial rates of increase in consumer price indexes being equal. In any event, a special case, even if exceptional, is sufficient to show that a contrary generalization cannot be applied universally; the illustration shows that one cannot properly infer an increase in transmission merely from convergence of inflation rates, since the paper shows that in at least one type of situation increased transmission would cause divergence, and correspondingly, convergence could result from a decrease in transmission. Referring to Gordon's objection that the paper fails to distinguish demand-induced and supply-induced shocks, it would have been desirable to have put "demand" and "supply" labels on the categories to which the illustrative cases belonged, but that is a matter of exposition. The substantive point is that in some cases the mechanisms of transmission may operate in conflicting ways. Gordon agrees with that conclusion. His comment is helpful, however, in making clear that these conflicts occur only in the case of shocks induced by changes in supply. Gordon observes that in the case of inelastic demand for imports where a rise in import prices raises the value of imports, the problem the paper poses of which price index to use to measure convergence of inflation rates is simplified if one recognizes that in the case of a demand shock there is no a priori reason to assume a change in the terms of trade. If import and export prices rise equally there is no problem in choosing between price indexes of domestic output and of domestic expenditure. But to say that there is no reason to assume that one increases more or less than the other suggests that the best a priori assumption is that they rise equally. There is no a priori reason to assume that, either. When it is unknown which of several possibilities actually will occur, the effects of all should be examined. Because export and import prices do not necessarily rise equally, one has to worry about which price index one chooses, even in the case of shocks induced by demand.

PART TWO

Recent Experiences in Eight Countries

LAWRENCE B. KRAUSE

Summary

THE UPSWING of inflation between 1972 and 1974 was a worldwide phenomenon. It was remarkable because of its breadth and it affected all industrial countries, as well as developing countries. It is useful therefore to compare the experiences of a number of countries to identify similarities and differences that shed light on the inflationary process. Eight countries were chosen for this study: the United States, Japan, West Germany, the United Kingdom, France, Sweden, Australia, and Brazil.

The authors of the papers also stress numerous factors and institutions that are of particular importance to their respective countries. The paper on Japan, for instance, explains why monetary policy has been so effective there. The German paper reflects the historical roots of the popular antipathy to inflation. The French paper indicates why the authorities expanded the money supply (M_1) during various periods. Discussion of wage determination in the paper on the United Kingdom differs from that given elsewhere. The paper on Sweden, through its analysis of the interaction of high marginal tax rates and wage-determined price changes, provides an explanation of why there could be a perverse negative relation between changes in money wages and the real income of workers. The role of wage courts is described in the paper on Australia, and attention is drawn to the importance of this institution in reducing male-female differentials. The paper on Brazil analyzes the policy of monetary correction begun in 1964 and extended to the foreign exchange market in 1968. Although these explanations are specific to individual countries, they may provide lessons for other countries.

The Measurement of Inflation

Reference is often made to a rise or fall in the rate of world inflation implying that the concept of world inflation can be measured and have analytical meaning. These country studies call attention to the ambiguity of such a concept. The technical problems involved in forming an index of world inflation are extremely difficult. A reasonable comparable price measure for each of the eight countries—the consumer price index being the

Figure 1. *Annual Percentage Changes in Consumer Price Indexes in Eight Countries, 1953–74*

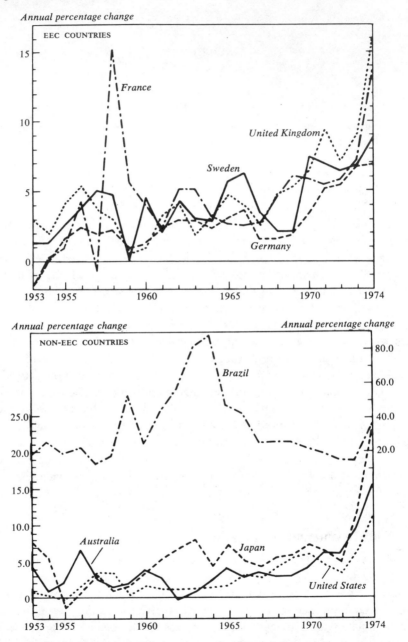

Sources: Brazil, supplied to the author by Antonio C. Lemgruder; other countries, International Monetary Fund, *International Financial Statistics*, various issues. Brazil: scale to the right; other countries: scale to the left.

only feasible possibility—could be combined to form a single world index using gross national product weights or a principal component analysis.[1] But what would be the analytical meaning of changes in such an index? Consumer price indexes have meaning in each of the eight countries, but not necessarily the same meaning. In France the CPI is the only significant and reliable measure of inflation. In the United States, West Germany, Sweden, Australia, and Brazil, the CPI is also recognized as a useful, but not exclusive, measurement of inflation. The CPI in the United Kingdom can be adapted as an indicator of inflation, although a value added index of manufactured prices is thought to be superior. But for Japan the situation is very different. There is a divergence between the consumer price index and the wholesale price index that grows out of the dual nature of the Japanese economy. The CPI to a greater extent than the WPI reflects the traditional economy, which is labor-intensive, small-scale, less productive, and subject to larger wage increases. Japanese policymakers have reacted to inflation as measured by the WPI and not the CPI. Indeed, the economist Osamu Shimomura, influential during the Ikeda administration, denied that increases in the CPI constituted inflation if wholesale prices were stable. Since the increase of the Japanese CPI was higher than many other countries for most of the postwar period (and the WPI below others), the Japanese contribution to a world index of consumer prices would tend to exaggerate inflation.

Even with their limitations, however, one is forced to use consumer price indexes for cross-country comparisons of inflation for a general impression of its quantitative dimensions. As shown in figure 1, the data would not seem to support the proposition that inflation has been constantly accelerating for the last twenty years in most countries. Furthermore, inflation rates vary from country to country although those of European countries seem to be clustered in a rather narrow band. Beginning in 1954, typical experience in one of these countries can be described in the following way:

- Rather high rates of inflation in the late fifties.
- Somewhat slower inflation rates and less year-to-year variance in the early and mid-sixties.
- Increasing inflation again, but generally within the range of preceding years, in the late sixties.
- A sharp upward acceleration of inflation, generally outside the range of previous postwar experience, in the early seventies.

Deviations from the typical inflation pattern are of great interest because

1. See, for example, Hans Genberg, *World Inflation and the Small Open Economy* (Stockholm: Swedish Industrial Publications, 1975).

they point to national differences in the importance of certain variables in the inflation process. The inflation rates for the United States tended to be somewhat below those of most other countries, but began to accelerate earlier (the mid-1960s), an acceleration generally attributed to the Vietnam War. The German inflation rate was also below those of other countries, but tended to rise slightly throughout the entire twenty-year period. This might be attributed to the progressive opening of the German economy to foreign influences, which made Germany less able to maintain its stance as an island of stability in an inflationary ocean. The Japanese inflation position relative to that in other countries was more favorable in the late 1950s than subsequently because of the existence of excess labor supply, which later was absorbed. (These observations say little about international competitiveness that is better reflected in WPI comparisons.) The United Kingdom (before 1974), France, and Sweden more or less fit the typical pattern except for some peculiarities associated with the timing of incomes policy, major devaluations, and the May–June 1968 events in France. The surprise concerning Australia is that it looks so much like the typical pattern despite having an economic structure different from most of the others. The Brazilian experience, however, was almost totally different. The average rate of inflation over the twenty-year period, 30 percent a year, was much above the others and inflation accelerated markedly from 1959 until monetary correction was introduced in 1964. From 1964 a decade of deceleration in the rate of price increases followed. Brazil, like the others, saw inflation rise sharply in 1974, but the rate still fell within the range of previous experience and, because of previous experience, Brazilian institutions may be better designed to cope with the disturbance.

Causes of Inflation: Domestic and Foreign

Conceptually a distinction can be drawn between an inflationary impulse that has its origins in the domestic economy and one that originates abroad. For instance an increase in government expenditures without appropriate increases in taxation can be described as a domestic impulse whereas the quadrupling of oil prices for an oil-importing country caused by the Organization of Petroleum Exporting Countries can be attributed to foreign influences. The internal-external dichotomy is by no means exact. An explosion in a country's money supply fed by an increase in its monetary base that resulted from an inflow of capital from abroad could be considered an external impulse, but if the monetary authorities had the capacity to sterilize the inflow and chose not to do so, then it would seem inappropriate to blame only foreigners for the result. Nevertheless a qualitative judgment can be made whether most of the inflation suffered by a country over a period of time has domestic or foreign origins. Of the eight countries covered in this study, only two (West Germany and Sweden) attribute inflation largely to foreign impulses. The other six countries (the United States, Japan, the United Kingdom, France, Australia, and Brazil) attribute inflation to domestic causes, although foreign influence is recognized in varying degree. All countries attribute much of the acceleration of inflation in the 1972–74 period to foreign impulses.

Countries also differ in their ability to dampen inflationary pressures once they have occurred. Differences arise because of public attitudes that may or may not support vigorous anti-inflation policy, the effectiveness of those policies, and institutional structures in factor and product markets. Of the countries included in this study, Germany would appear to be the best able to dampen inflationary impulses and the United Kingdom the least. The leading contender with Germany for top position is probably the United States. As for the least able, Brazil occupied that dubious position before 1964 and is still short of anti-inflation weapons, both because of and despite monetary correction. The characteristics that determine a country's ability to dampen inflation change with time and experience, and thus their ability to deal with inflation is also likely to change.

Country Studies

The salient characteristics of inflation in each of these eight countries—the United States, Japan, West Germany, the United Kingdom, France, Sweden, Australia, and Brazil—are reviewed below. Common or parallel experiences are alluded to and the authors' suggestions of possible explanations of inflation explored.

United States

An eclectic approach is taken by Harold Shapiro to explain the inflation experience of the United States. Classic excess demand was the root of two inflation episodes, 1956–57 and 1966–69. In the earlier one, the monetary stimulus beginning in 1955 is identified as a possible cause and attention is drawn to the difficulties faced by the monetary authorities in that period. Shapiro also notes that the inflation became pronounced after the increase in output began to slow down or approach zero—a lag common to other episodes as well. The inflation of the 1966–69 period is found to be consistent with the standard explanation that it was caused by fiscal policy failure. Shapiro also draws attention to the overvaluation of the dollar and the consequent importance of foreign competition in controlling U.S. inflation in that period.

The acceleration of inflation beginning in 1971 seems to have been of a different sort. There was little evidence of strong excess demand, but much concern about the efficacy of traditional economic policies that led to experimentation with incomes policy. Some demand pressures did appear and they were compounded by the devaluations of the dollar, which raised the prices of import and export products. Direct inflationary impulses also came from rising food prices and internationally traded raw materials (including oil). Finally, some sort of battle for income shares leading to upward pressure on wages and prices also seemed to be taking place.

Shapiro presents two related structural explanations of the U.S. inflation process. He observes that, in general, the American inflations were widely spread across all goods and services. Periods of price stability, however, were characterized by declines in wholesale prices of farm products and processed food, and there was marked weakness in the price of crude materials. In subsequent periods, the price laggards caught up. Thus price stability obtained by temporary changes in relative prices can lead subsequently to general inflation through a familiar ratchet mechanism. The overvaluation and subsequent devaluations of the dollar can be considered part of this mechanism of relative price changes followed by a catch-up process. Similarly he notes that large relative price changes were required to move resources within the domestic economy, that there was downward rigidity of many prices and wages, that there were wage changes reflecting the desire to maintain or restore relative positions of certain wages in the labor market, and that there was a commitment to full employment. In combination these facts imply that any structural change will lead to inflationary pressures that will be accommodated by the monetary authorities.

He observes further that inflation cannot be considered as solely an economic phenomenon, nor understood with only economic tools of analysis. National and international institutions, attitudes, traditions, political and social objectives should also be considered, and he suggests that a broadly based theory of public policy is needed to explain the inflation process. Indeed, it may be that inflation is the policy preferred to available alternatives rather than an aberration, as implied by traditional economic analysis.

Japan

Ryutaro Komiya and Yoshio Suzuki identify three distinct periods with significantly different inflation experiences for Japan. The first period from 1960 through 1968 did not evidence a trend toward increases in wholesale prices; the second period from 1969 to mid-1972 had creeping inflation; and the third period from mid-1972 through 1974 had galloping inflation. Wholesale prices have risen in Japan during boom periods and, unlike other countries, have fallen during periods of slack. The downward flexibility of Japanese wholesale prices has been attributed to the existence of excess capacity, since each economic expansion was led by growth of business investment; there was vigorous competition in product markets, downward flexibility in wage costs due to cutbacks in overtime work, and lower bonuses during recessions.

Monetary policy has been the prime mover of the economy over the entire time span. During the first period, monetary policy was expansive whenever possible in order to finance maximum plant and equipment investment. When an expansion became pronounced, wholesale prices rose and began to undermine international competitiveness. Combined with the pull of the domestic market, export growth was reduced and a trade deficit occurred in the balance of payments. In response to the deficit, monetary policy would be tightened, slowing the economy, reducing prices, and forcing producers to look abroad for markets. The resulting export push would correct the deficit, permitting monetary policy to be eased again thus triggering another investment boom. Basing monetary policy on the balance of payments led to the determining of wholesale prices that was consistent with international competition, which in the first period implied stability.

During the second period the balance of payments constraint on monetary policy no longer ensured price stability, and Japan experienced imported inflation. Prices in other countries were advancing substantially during this period so Japanese exports rose despite the domestic boom and gave further stimulus to the expansion. The rise in import prices gave a modest upward push to costs adding to the price pressures from rising demand. Also noted are the expansive monetary consequences of the balance of payments surplus, although well within the ability of the monetary authorities to control. Finally, the rising inflation forced the authorities to tighten money despite the balance of payments surplus. The economy did slow down, the price rise was moderated, and exports expanded rapidly increasing the external disequilibrium. Belatedly the yen was revalued as part of the Smithsonian agreement after several months of floating.

The third period, mid-1972 through 1974, witnessed galloping inflation unlike anything seen since the immediate postwar monetary adjustment. Rising prices of imported raw materials were a major cause of the inflation contributing directly and indirectly from one-third to one-half of the total rise of wholesale prices, even though moderated by the rising value of the yen. The monetary root of the inflation cannot be attributed primarily to the balance of payments, except for a possible lagged liquidity effect of the 1971 monetary expansion. Rather, monetary expansion was a deliberate domestic policy to counter the expected recessionary effects of a rising yen and to reduce the balance of payments surplus, thereby forestalling a further yen revaluation; there were also internal political considerations. The monetary expansion was broadly based, which not only led to increases in normal investment but also to speculative behavior of various sorts feeding inflation psychology and possibly raising the price of certain imported raw materials. Furthermore, there was no counter fiscal constraint in 1972–74; unlike other expansions, tax reductions more than offset the growth in tax receipts. Finally, supply restraints were greater than usual during this boom because depression cartels were permitted to operate longer than necessary in 1972, unusual bottlenecks developed early in the expansion and the worldwide synchronization of the expansion meant resources could not be attracted from abroad. The rise in prices in 1972–73 led directly to a wage-push in 1974 when an increase of 33 percent was granted. This outsized increase, however, should not be viewed as aggressive labor behavior but rather as a catching-up measure to parallel previous price increases. Japanese inflations still appear to be demand-determined, which can lead directly to a phase of cost-push.

West Germany

While different explanations have been suggested from time to time for Germany's postwar inflations, it is almost universally accepted by German economists and endorsed by Gerhard Fels that most of the inflations have been imported from abroad. The factors that have kept domestic inflationary pressures weak in Germany include the remembrance of hyperinflation and the desire to avoid a repetition, the existence of easy labor markets resulting from the inflow of refugees and guest workers from other countries, responsible policy attitudes taken by the trade unions, the refusal of the West German government for many years to pursue active fiscal policies that have resulted in budget surpluses, and the gradual liberalization of foreign trade over most of the period. Fels also suggests that entrepreneurs in Germany may have adopted rather longer planning horizons than those in other countries; this constrained them from raising prices when excess demand pressures were expected to be of short duration.

The dynamics of price change in Germany were such that prices followed the domestic business cycle and thus the source of inflationary impulses was sometimes hard to distinguish. Prices seemed to track costs of production rather closely. Since costs did not rise until well after an upswing of the economy, prices lagged behind the production cycle as in the United States. The lag in costs was related to a slow adjustment of wages to better business conditions and also presumably to cyclical variations in productivity gains. Costs continued to rise even after the peak of output was passed. The proximate cause of inflation could be attributed to monetary expansion, but the monetary authorities did not have a free hand in determining monetary policy. Every German expansion since 1958 was marked by a rise in foreign demand for German goods (so that some observers characterized German growth as export-led). This caused rising surpluses in the balance of payments, particularly in 1960, 1964, and 1968–69. The monetary authorities were inhibited from exercising severe monetary restraint lest they aggravate the surplus by attracting capital inflows, and thus monetary policy tolerated inflation. Ultimately the deutsche mark was appreciated to ease the policy dilemma and, indeed, German prices measured in marks went up less than those of their trading partners by the amount of the currency adjustment.

Circumstances have changed, however, so that Germany may have more independence in determining its own inflation rate, but it may also have an inflation rate that will be higher than those experienced hitherto. The most important factor has been the sharp appreciations of the deutsche mark and particularly the movement to floating exchange rates. The more that the mark rate is left to market forces, the greater the independence obtained by the German monetary authorities. Second, greater militancy exhibited by labor unions has already led to a wage explosion in 1970–71. Third, the government has shown increased concern about unemployment that may inhibit its use of anti-inflationary measures. Fourth, new entry of foreign guest workers has been stopped. And, finally, the government is now willing to use public-sector deficits to stimulate the economy as it did in 1974–75. Germany may still be less tolerant of inflation than other countries, but the level of inflation is probably higher on both sides of the comparison (there is more in Germany and more in other countries).

United Kingdom

Two different views are presented concerning the nature of inflation in the United Kingdom: one by Wynne Godley and one by Michael Parkin. Both are plausibly consistent with econometric evidence.

Godley contends that there is no evidence that excess demand has influenced the pricing of manufactured goods except through its effects on

costs, once costs are properly measured. In other words, British manufacturers set prices by adding a markup over costs and these markups have
not been influenced by the state of domestic and foreign demand and the
severity of foreign competition. Thus changes in prices are determined by
changes in normal or standard wages (wages corrected for cyclical variation), prices of imported raw materials, and trend growth of productivity.

Attention is thus centered on the determination of import prices and
wages. The explanation of import prices as put forth by John Llewellyn
is thought to be convincing.[2] Import prices reflect long-run supply and
demand, and deviations from trend are caused by fluctuations in world
industrial production. Britain's own domestic costs per unit of output also
exert some influence on Britain's import prices through both a direct and
indirect linkage. The direct effect occurs because British demand is often
a large part of world demand for certain commodities (such as tea) and
the indirect effect results from British costs being a major determinant of
the sterling exchange rate whose changes are reflected in import prices.

Godley further contends that although a standard Phillips curve explains
movements of British wages before 1969 reasonably well, no general theory of wage determination fits the British 1969–73 experience. Therefore
there is now no equilibrium rate of wage increase. Actual wages are determined by weak inertia (serial correlation), but can be pushed upward by
various events, such as exogenous price increases through imports or a particularly generous wage award won by some union, which upsets established
and accepted wage differentials and spreads to all wages as other unions seek
to restore their own wage differentials. The timing of price changes is affected
by incomes policy and discrete exchange rate changes, but the basic force of
import prices and wages eventually takes over.

The contrasting views of Michael Parkin suggest that excess demand is
indeed important in determining British price changes independent of costs.
He supports this case by econometric methods that measure excess demand
in a different way from that used by Godley. He recognizes, however, that
there is an insoluble identification problem that prevents a clear separation
of a cyclical excess demand variable and a cyclically adjusted standard
wage variable, so that econometric methods cannot settle the issue. Inability
to distinguish international price effects is partially attributed to the "law
of one price" that prevents the prices of traded goods produced in the
United Kingdom (adjusted for changes in exchange rates) from varying
independently of the prices of traded goods produced in other countries.

2. G. E. J. Llewellyn, "The Determinants of United Kingdom Import Prices,"
Economic Journal, vol. 84 (March 1974), pp. 18–31.

Parkin believes that an economic explanation can be found for wage behavior, but that a standard Phillips curve will not provide it. Rather, a variable measuring inflation expectations needs to be added (along with expected tax changes) and then a short-run relationship can be established between changes in wages and unemployment. Over time the explanation must recognize a rising reservation price for labor growing out of more liberal unemployment benefits, which has caused the natural rate of unemployment to rise from 2 percent to around 4 percent.

The openness of the British economy, moreover, makes world excess demand rather than merely domestic demand important for price setting. With excess demand established as important in both goods and factor markets, the major determinant of money demand becomes a significant inflationary influence, and Parkin identifies monetary expansion as that determinant. In a fixed exchange rate world, a "world" concept of money supply is critical, whereas, with floating exchange rates, more traditional domestic measures of money might be appropriate.

France

Pascal Salin and Georges Lane identify two distinct periods in the inflation experience of France since the "Plan de Stabilization" in 1963: mild inflation from 1963 to 1968 and a period of rapid inflation from 1968 to 1974 (with great acceleration in 1974 itself). While France as a middle-sized industrial country is integrated into the world economy, it still is not dominated by external influences. The French inflation rate tends to be consistently above those of its trading partners, indicating some distinctly French source of inflation as well as worldwide inflationary impulses. With higher inflation rates, adjustments have been necessary in the exchange rate of the franc in relation to other currencies and seem to be roughly in line with relative changes in the purchasing power of the franc and other currencies. The causation seems to run primarily from domestic inflation to the exchange rate, although at times such as 1969 the franc may have been undervalued by too great a devaluation.

A number of circumstances combine to explain why France has had a higher inflation rate than some other industrial countries. The proximate cause of price increases can be traced to monetary expansion, but the key question is why the authorities felt the need to provide money in inflationary amounts. One answer, according to the authors, is the form of shallow Keynesianism followed in France whereby fiscal and monetary policies have been focused on unemployment. Second, France has an immobile population that believes in its right to pursue traditional activities and keep existing jobs. Thus any structural change requiring a shift in employment is likely to cause difficulties. Inflation allows some of these old activities to survive. They are subsidized in the form of low interest rates and nonmarket allocations of credit. Third, the existence of five-year plans stands in the way of good stabilization policy since deviations from the plan are perceived as external and self-correcting incidents requiring no policy action, and thus timely responses to inflationary outbursts are not taken. Fourth, until 1974, monetary policy was exercised with reference to interest rate targets, which at times of unexpectedly high credit demand leads to excessive money growth unless these targets are adjusted upward. Furthermore, with a long history of inflation—but with no searing hyperinflation—it is relatively easy to raise inflationary expectations in France with self-fulfilling results. Fifth, social tensions in France between entrepreneurs and wage earners have led the monetary authorities to validate wage demands so as to avoid political difficulties. While these tensions do not explain the entire inflation story—as some observers have suggested—they are of consequence. A strong sense of equality and justice is embedded in French society. Different firms, industries, sectors, and regions consider it their right to advance at the same rate as their peers, despite different growths of productivity. There is constant pressure for the upward alignment of incomes. And, finally, agricultural prices are determined solely in a political setting and add inflationary pressure to the economy.

An examination of the macroeconomic relations of the French economy suggests that real growth and employment are quite independent of inflation, which refutes the conventional wisdom that some inflation is necessary for growth in France. Real growth has remained remarkably stable and unemployment quite low. Unemployment appears to be more the result of demographic rather than economic factors, such as unusually large numbers of young people entering the civilian labor force, a decline in the draft of young men, or an increase in repatriates from other countries. There may also have been some change in the natural rate of unemployment. With little variance of unemployment, a Phillips curve relationship cannot be established. Some short-run trade-offs may exist, but they have probably shifted upward over time with expectations of greater inflation. In reality it is very difficult to distinguish between the consequences of wages on prices and of prices on wages. While there has been constant pressure for wage earners to gain a larger share of output, it is hard to prove that it has had any effect on actual shares. From 1963 to 1974, there seems to have been little change in the distribution of income.

Sweden

Lars Calmfors observes in his paper that the inflation rate in Sweden increased sharply from 1960–69 to 1970–74. It is significant, however, that in the earlier period of lower overall inflation, the Swedish rate was above the average for European members of the Organisation for Economic Co-operation and Development, whereas subsequently it was below it. The importance of such a measurement of Swedish inflation relative to other countries is that inflation in Sweden seems to be overwhelmingly determined by international impulses and thus Sweden's success or failure in dealing with inflation must be judged by deviations from an international trend. The process that determines the overall Swedish inflation is well described by the Aukrust-EFO model. The price of tradable goods in Sweden is determined in world markets, according to this model. Tradable goods prices along with productivity trends in those industries determine producers' profits, which in turn determine wages in the tradable goods sector. Wage changes in this sector spill over to wages in the nontradables sector. Wage costs and productivity trends solely determine the prices of nontradables. Thus the only exogenous variables in this model are prices of tradable goods and productivity trends.

The model does not fully explain Swedish price performance because of the labor market situation. Wages are set in Sweden through centralized bargaining, which allows political considerations to affect the determination. In the late 1960s, political sentiment to reduce income differentials grew in response to a belief that current income distribution was unfair. As a result, the centralized wage bargain raised below-average wages more than those above the average. This narrowing of differentials was resisted by high-wage workers and set off a wage-wage spiral. The mechanism for these wage changes was mainly "wage drift," that is, changes in wages outside those set in the bargain and made possible by labor market conditions. Furthermore, econometric analysis of price increases indicated that there are large autonomous influences not included in the Aukrust-EFO model that make it impossible for the model to provide an adequate explanation for short-run changes.

But, even though the Aukrust-EFO model does not provide a fully satisfactory short-run interpretation of Swedish inflation, it may still be correct for the long run. First, a reconciliation is possible if the assumption of a constant profit share—a necessary condition of the model—is realized in the long run, although not necessarily at every point in time. Conditions that tend to reestablish the constancy of the share of profits include wage bargaining as suggested by the model, but they may operate only after critical values are exceeded, so that adjustments are discrete rather than continuous. Second, unusual profits, through their effect on investment demand and thereby on aggregate expansion, will affect labor markets and through wage drift tend to reestablish the previous relation of wages to profits. Finally, policymakers keep an eye on international competitiveness, which is positively related to the profit share. If competitiveness improves, then policy is likely to be more expansionary, leading to a reversal of competitiveness and ultimately to a decline in profits. Indeed, it was the profit squeeze in the 1960s that undermined competitiveness, caused balance of payments problems, and led to a change of policy.

The goal of macroeconomic policy in Sweden is to give priority to full employment, and monetary and fiscal policies have validated this result. Thus while the quantity of money is highly correlated with prices and therefore seems to support the quantity theory of money as an explanation for Swedish price behavior, causation is still in question. During the 1960–69 period, domestic sources dominated monetary expansion, whereas in 1970–74 foreign exchange reserves were more important. This raises the possibility that external forces affect domestic inflation through a monetary link reinforcing the direct price effect of tradable goods, the dominant force. The monetary link, however, operates only under a fixed exchange rate system. About 40 percent of Swedish trade is within the deutsche mark zone to which fixed exchange rates are now maintained, but the remainder is with countries whose currencies are floating against the krona.

Australia

A complex interaction of external and domestic factors helps explain Australian inflation. John Pitchford, in identifying a number of inflationary episodes, points to only the 1950–51 and the 1972–74 experiences as particularly virulent. During the 1960s, Australia's inflation was rather moderate with no sign of acceleration. Both in 1950–51 and 1972–74, domestic inflation was closely associated with rapidly rising export prices. Australian exports are dominated by primary products and raw materials, and the prices of these products are set in world markets. The domestic sources of inflation relate in part to the labor market. Australia has a unique set of judicial bodies including an arbitration court that has a role in wage setting as well as the usual labor market forces. Aside from the two exceptional episodes, inflation in Australia is well explained by a combination of export prices, import prices, wage pressures adjusted for productivity (including external productivity in the form of changes in the terms of trade), and excess demand for labor.

The 1972–74 price explosion can be attributed to a process that began with the sharp rise in export prices. The corresponding rise of incomes of primary producers led to excess demand in product markets and pulled up prices. Since wage rates did not rise correspondingly, industrial disputes ultimately led to wage increases and cost-push pressures on prices. Monetary and fiscal policies were also very expansionary during these years as a reaction to the 1970–71 slowdown and in anticipation of elections. Thus monetary expansion was doubled, government expenditures were increased sharply, and a budget deficit emerged. Possibly as a result of these measures, a building boom of great dimensions was generated in 1972 and 1973. It would appear to be improper to attribute this inflation to excessive wage demands despite the large national wage award of March 1971, because real wages did not rise above their trend in 1971 and 1972 and declined in 1973. The sharp recovery in real wages in 1974 can be viewed as a catch-up to inflation rather than its cause. Other structural changes, however, were probably taking place in the economy since the average increase in productivity per employed person dropped to 0.6 percent in the early 1970s from 2.0 percent in the later 1960s, despite reaching 3.6 percent in manufacturing in the 1970s.

The 1972–74 inflation differed from the 1950–51 experience in that in the earlier period import price increases were a much more important element. A number of measures were taken in the 1970s to limit the impact of rising import prices on the economy. These included the sterilization of short-term capital inflows in 1971–72, appreciations of the exchange rate in December 1972 and September 1973, and a 25 percent cut in import tariffs in July 1973. The price-restraining impact of the tariff reduction was subsequently reversed as Australian manufacturers sought and obtained government relief from the increased import competition.

The residual effect of the 1972–74 experience may be that Australia is more prone to inflation, high unemployment, or both. Reactions to external inflationary pressures seem to have speeded up, and the trade-off between inflation and unemployment has become weaker. Also, inflationary expectations seem to be greater than in the 1960s.

Brazil

The Brazilian inflation detailed by Antonio Lemgruber was unlike that of the other seven countries in this study. The overall inflation rate in Brazil from 1952 through 1974 was 30 percent, much above that of the others, and the standard deviation of annual rates was 20 percent, which presumably led to greater uncertainty. The inflation rate was moderate from 1952 to 1958, accelerated from 1959 to 1964, decelerated from 1965 to 1973, and accelerated again after September 1973. This pattern differed from other countries except for 1974. In earlier years, real economic growth in Brazil was dominated by developments in agriculture. In recent years, however, rapid and diverse economic growth occurred in all sectors so that the structure of the Brazilian economy now more nearly approaches that of the other countries. Furthermore, Brazil has become a more open economy in the 1970s and is thus likely to reflect world economic developments to a greater extent than in the past.

Lemgruber's evaluation of Brazil's inflation seems to confirm a quantity theory of money determination. He examines macroeconomic relationships and establishes the usual type of explanations, but notes many discrepancies. For instance, excess demand (as measured by the GNP gap) is a significant variable determining price changes, but works badly in the early 1970s. Also the GNP gap is significant in determining prices in a standard Phillips curve form, but recent years suggest that the relationship should be specified in its accelerationist form, that is, with the inclusion of a variable measuring expected future price changes. It is not surprising that macroeconomic relations covering a long span of time are difficult to establish when an economy is undergoing fundamental structural change. In addition, financial relationships were substantially altered following the adoption of monetary correction in 1964. As a direct result there was substantial growth of nonbank financial intermediaries and diversification of financial assets held by Brazilians. Tax and administrative reforms were added in 1966 and 1967. The trotting peg system for adjusting exchange rates, by which the rates maintained by the authorities are adjusted every few weeks, was adopted in 1968. These changes had a cumulative effect on the economy.

Foreign influences have affected Brazilian inflation, although not so greatly as domestic factors. In particular, world real incomes and the world price level were found to be significant variables. The exchange rate is also important and reconciles foreign and domestic prices. The domestic variables of significance include government expenditures (or the fiscal deficit) and the monetary base, along with the GNP gap. It is also noteworthy that the previous history of price change is important, suggesting that price expectations matter a great deal. Many of these factors combined to cause the price acceleration in 1973–74. World incomes and prices rose rapidly and domestic variables were also very expansionary including peak measurements of excess demand.

The Monetary Mechanism and Monetary Policy

In all of the countries studied the monetary mechanism clearly has some role in the process of creating inflation. That role differs from country to country and it is not always clear exactly what it is. In their reaction to the monetary mechanism, three classes of countries seem to emerge from the investigation: those that are continuously very sensitive because the authorities utilized monetary policy as the primary stabilization instrument, those that are occasionally sensitive, and those that are rather insensitive. Germany, Japan, and Brazil fall into the first group; the United States and France into the second; and the United Kingdom, Sweden, and Australia into the third. In the latter, as contrasted with the monetary-sensitive countries, monetary policy is forced to adjust or conform to other economic and social policies.

Japan would appear to have given monetary policy the greatest role in controlling the economy, in part because a strong relationship exists between money growth and money incomes. Some lags were recognized, but they were of relatively short duration (one to three quarters). Furthermore, the Japanese exercised stringent exchange controls to help seal off the economy from international capital flows, giving independence to domestic monetary policy even during the fixed exchange rate period. On the other hand, while Germany is sensitive to monetary factors, foreign developments have frequently affected its domestic monetary goals. Periodic revaluations of the deutsche mark have permitted German divergence from world inflation rates, but not monetary independence under fixed rates. A further consideration in Germany was the rather long lag (up to three years) between money supply changes and industrial product prices. The Brazilian recognition of the importance of the monetary mechanism is not surprising since, under conditions of rapid inflation, it is difficult to ignore. Recognition, of course, did not imply the ending of inflation and thus the adoption of monetary correction was a significant policy accommodation.

At times the monetary mechanism has been identified in the United States as the source of inflation, but at other times it has been overshadowed by other influences. The relationship between money supply and money GNP in the short run is not very close and thus other policy choices are sometimes allowed to dominate monetary decisions. A similar situation has existed in France where even less public attention has been given to monetary policy as a means of controlling inflation.

In the United Kingdom, Sweden, and Australia, there is no semblance of central bank independence from the government. Monetary policy has been made conditional to other policies to achieve a variety of goals and thus had to conform to the need for money. Hence, monetary policy has been made fully endogenous in these economies.

The Transmission of Inflation

All countries were affected by external inflationary impulses to some degree, particularly in the 1972–74 episode. But where did these impulses start? No definitive answer issues from these studies. Of course the OPEC-induced oil price increase is one important factor, but it does not explain the earlier inflation, nor the universal nature of the inflation in the later period.

The explanation of inflation in the United States is consistent with the widely held belief that monetary expansion in the United States spilled over to other countries through balance of payments deficits. Thus the United States may well have been a transmitter of inflation in the last half of the 1960s and up to March 1973. After the breakdown of the Bretton Woods system when countries were no longer obliged to intervene in exchange markets, the United States ceased playing this role, although lagged price increases from earlier monetary expansions may have been taking place.

Japan has also been a transmitter of inflationary impulses through its effect on commodity prices. Japan is such a large importer of raw materials that variations in its demand can have a noticeable impact on world prices.[3] The 1972–74 upswing and the 1974–75 decline in commodity prices may have been particularly influenced by Japan. Furthermore, Japanese direct investment policy in part tends to concentrate investment on raw material development to supply Japanese needs. Thus Japan is influential on both the demand and supply side of the market.

The only other countries mentioned as possible transmitters of inflation are the United Kingdom and France. The United Kingdom may have had an effect on certain raw materials similar to that in Japan, but not to the same extent. In the case of France, its consistently higher inflation rate may have spilled over to its neighbors. The channels may have included international trade in goods, international capital movements, and labor market

3. The inventory policies of the large Japanese trading companies may also be of great importance. (See Lawrence B. Krause and Sueo Sekiguchi, "Japan and the World Economy," in Hugh Patrick and Henry Rosovsky, eds., *Asia's New Giant: How the Japanese Economy Works* [Brookings Institution, 1976], pp. 389–97.)

effects. The pervasiveness of the influence, however, may not have been strong since higher French inflation rates were ultimately reflected in franc devaluations.

Conclusion

How serious was the problem of inflation to the countries in this study? There is little question that the rapid acceleration of inflation in 1972–74 did constitute a major problem and posed a significant challenge to policy-makers. Even in countries such as Japan and Australia, which had been tolerant of rather high rates of consumer price increases, the galloping inflation did foster political resistance. To a somewhat lesser extent, Sweden was also not much concerned with moderate inflation and opposition only grew when the CPI increase exceeded 4 percent, even though the rapid world inflation did not alter the terms of trade of Sweden very much. Indeed, it has been suggested that moderate inflation in the United States may be getting a bad press and be exaggerated—that the real effects may have been quite small. For instance, little change caused by inflation can be noticed in the distribution of national income among major claimants. This is also true in Japan. As noted above, real growth in France seems to have been little affected by moderate inflation.

Germany is the most important counter example. Inflation that is moderate by world standards nurtures strong resistance there. Political opposition is a reality in itself and implies negative economic consequences even if they cannot be observed. But the most damaging case against inflation may come from the experience of Brazil. In Brazil in the later 1960s and early 1970s, real growth accelerated when inflation decelerated. Earlier real growth declined when inflation advanced. It is not argued that direct causation running from high inflation to low growth can be proved, but the experience is suggestive. Brazilian inflation, of course, was very much higher than that found in other countries, and real consequences may occur only at those high levels, but it is also possible that moderate inflation if not vigorously contained will inevitably reach the critical ranges.

HAROLD T. SHAPIRO

Inflation in the United States

Tables

Figures

Harold T. Shapiro, University of Michigan, wishes to thank Gardner Ackley, E. Philip
Howrey, Saul Hymans, Ronald Teigen, Thomas Wilson, and the editors for their very
useful comments on an initial draft of this paper. Discussion at the Brookings Conference on Worldwide Inflation also contributed significantly to the final content.

CONTRARY TO widely held current opinion, I believe that we economists do understand the essential dimensions of the origin, nature, and process of inflation. But our knowledge falls far short of public expectations and demands, the needs of public policy, and the claims contained in our own occasional bursts of immodesty. Nevertheless, we could, by emphasizing what we understand and pointing to the limitations of our knowledge, provide the valuable service of helping to define more appropriate criteria for public policy choices.

In this paper I review critical aspects of the U.S. inflationary experience over the past two decades in a way that may shed some light on matters of current interest. Moreover, I attempt to evaluate current perceptions of the inflationary processes, their limitations, and how our narrowness of vision may prevent progress in understanding. This paper then is not based on the results of original research (the reader will find no new regression equations), but on my own attempts to gather in the evidence and to get a sense of "where we are," both in experience and understanding.

Efforts to explain inflation exclusively in economic terms are not only less than fully satisfying but may in fact work to obscure the nature of some of its important underlying causes. National and international institutions, traditions, politics, and social objectives all play a role in a phenomenon intricately embedded in the economic system. Economic analysis and the insights it provides must be supplemented by a theory of public policy that explains those factors that induce a government to select a certain set of policies. The actions of government must certainly be considered an endogenous consequence of—or response to—the demands of the various political and social groups that enable it to maintain power and to govern. If inflation seems a persistent problem in the United States today, Americans must at least entertain the notion that it is the preferred policy (or at least an acceptable component of the preferred policy) of the dominant political coalition. For example, it may have become the easiest way to resolve the collective decision concerning the sharing of national income. Should this be the case, inflation itself is not the basic crisis, but a manifestation of it. The only alternative hypothesis is that inflation is the un-

269

anticipated consequence of certain public policy actions. Although these issues deserve increased attention, they are not pursued in this study; I simply refer to the set of institutions that characterize the American economy and American society. Whereas my analysis sometimes attributes certain types of behavior to these institutions, I do not always probe the origins of those behavior patterns or make normative judgments about them. I have chosen the easier task of simply trying to understand the implications of *the* system for the process of inflation.

The Inflation Record

The prices of almost all aggregate bundles of final goods and services have risen continuously over the last quarter-century. In the twenty-one-year period 1953–74 (which excludes the Korean War inflation and the subsequent wage-price freeze), the consumer price index rose by 84 percent for an average annual compound growth rate of 2.96 percent.[1] The analogous figures for the overall gross national product price deflator are 93 percent and 3.19 percent, respectively. Not only have such prices increased during business cycle expansions, but they have continued to rise during those periods of substantial excess capacity that have marked all the recessions in economic activity since 1948–49. Indeed, it has become increasingly difficult to notice any marked change in the rate of inflation (as measured by either the implicit GNP deflator, P_{GNP}, or the CPI in the periods classified by the National Bureau of Economic Research as recessions. Beginning with the 1953–54 recession, and during the four ensuing business cycle contractions (1957–58, 1960–61, 1969–70, 1974), the average annual rate of inflation, as measured by the GNP deflator, is 4.5 percent. This compares with an average of 2.9 percent for periods of expansion as a whole, and with 4.4 percent if only later stages of each expansion (the four quarters preceding the

1. Although econometricians have now classified it as ancient history, the period immediately following the Korean War inflation (1951–52) contains a fascinating episode illustrating the behavior of prices. A general price and wage freeze was inaugurated in January 1951, but throughout the period of control, prices of many goods declined to well below their legal ceilings and, when the controls were subsequently lifted (the last at the beginning of 1953), there was hardly a quiver in the overall price level—this despite the very recent memories of both the Korean War inflation and the post–World War II inflation of 1946–48. It now seems apparent that the backlash to the speculative accumulation of commodities and consumer goods, the program of fiscal and monetary restraints (increased taxes and mortgage credit restrictions), and the wage-price controls all played some part in defusing the inflation. Two additional factors were also important. First, profit margins had expanded so quickly in 1950 that there was ample room for upward adjustment in money wages without a corresponding movement in prices. Second, falling prices for imported commodities provided further leeway.

peak) are considered.[2] Although in general the trends are similar for prices at the wholesale level, the evidence is not quite so uniform. Wholesale prices of farm products and processed foods have registered annual declines in ten of the last twenty-five years and there have been similar declines in the prices of crude materials. During certain years in the early 1960s the wholesale price of consumer durables also fell.

The only periods of comparative stability in prices (that is, inflation rates of 1.5 percent), mid-1954 to mid-1955 and mid-1958 through 1964, were characterized by falls in the wholesale prices of farm products and processed foods and by marked weakness in the prices of crude materials and imports. These disparate movements in agricultural and industrial prices reflect shifts in relative prices and cannot by themselves be said to have had any direct causal influence on the overall price level itself. Nevertheless, the correlation between periods of relative overall price stability and the falling relative price of agricultural products may be important in the analysis of price level movements. Food prices, for example, may have a greater relative impact on inflationary expectations than their weight in the CPI would indicate.

Despite the exceptions noted above, over the last decade price rises have occurred in an increasing number of goods and services, and their magnitude has been growing. The raw data from the last decade suggest the possibility that the economy may be evolving toward a state of ever-accelerating inflation. It is such a prospect that is the source of so much current concern. That this inflationary experience of the last two decades has permanently altered the price expectations and therefore the behavior of both firms and households is widely accepted. Although there are few direct measures of this change, existing systematic information[3] indicates that both the level of expected inflation and the degree of uncertainty regarding inflation have steadily increased, particularly in the last decade, and that these trends have important effects on economic behavior.[4] In figures 1 and 2 the course of inflation over the period being examined is measured by the aggregate GNP deflator and by the CPI. Information on annual inflation over the period 1953–74 is given in figure 1. In figure 2 the

2. If the years 1971 through 1974 are eliminated, the relevant averages are: for recessions, 2.76 percent; for expansions, 2.28 percent; and for the last stage of expansion, 3.46 percent.

3. F. Thomas Juster, "Savings Behavior, Uncertainty, and Price Expectations," in *The Economic Outlook for 1974,* Paper presented to the Twenty-first Conference on the Economic Outlook, 1973 (University of Michigan, Research Seminar in Quantitative Economics, 1974), pp. 49–70.

4. Since 1948 data on both the mean and variance of expected price changes by U.S. households have been collected by the Survey Research Center of the University of Michigan. These data have been carefully analyzed by Juster, "Savings Behavior."

Figure 1. *Alternative Measures of Annual Rates of Inflation, 1953–74*

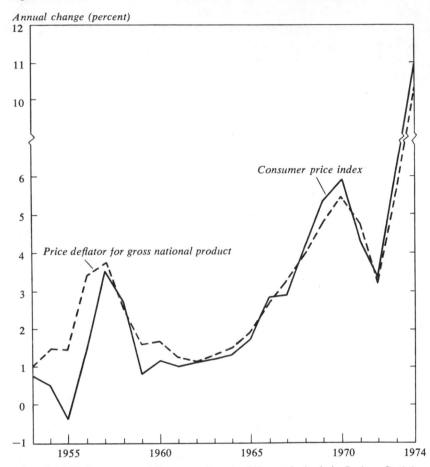

Annual change (percent)

Sources: U.S. Department of Commerce, Bureau of Economic Analysis, *Business Statistics, 1973* (Government Printing Office, 1973), pp. 1, 4, 40; Department of Commerce, BEA, *Survey of Current Business,* vol. 53 (August 1973), pp. S-1, S-8, and vol. 55 (June 1975), pp. S-1, S-8.

quarterly movement in these price indexes over the last three years, 1972–74, is shown.

There is, of course, the much discussed problem of deciding just which of the traditional price indexes is the most appropriate signal in an economy in which some of its parameters are continually changing. Although it would seem advisable to select a price index of final goods and services, the choice of a base-weighted rather than a current-weighted index, an index inclusive or exclusive of excise taxes, and so on, is not a matter of grave

Figure 2. *Alternative Measures of Annual Rates of Inflation, Quarterly Data, 1972:1–1974:4*

Annual change (percent)

Consumer price index

Price deflator for gross national product

Sources: *Survey of Current Business*, various issues. The CPI data are averages of monthly figures.

concern given the limitations of current knowledge about inflation.[5] In any case, this problem will certainly not be very serious if a really significant inflation is going on. Causal definitions of inflation, however, should be

5. The formulation and choice of a price index would, of course, be critical in a sector of the economy where factor payments were tied to the movement of prices. In this paper, however, the complex practical problem of indexing factor payments against inflation is not considered.

Table 1. *Average Annual Compound Rates of Change, Implicit Price Deflators for Gross National Product and Selected Components, Various Periods, 1953–74*

GNP Deflator	1953–58	1959–65	1966–73	1972:4–1973:4[a]	1973:4–1974:4[a]	Entire period, 1953–74
Personal consumption expenditures	1.8	1.2	3.7	8.3	12.5	2.8
Nonresidential fixed investment	3.6	1.0	3.8	4.0	14.7	3.1
Residential structures	1.7	1.9	5.4	11.6	10.1	3.0
Imports of goods and services[b]	0.2	0.5	5.3	24.1	39.9	4.2
Government purchases of goods and services	4.1	2.6	6.1	8.3	12.6	4.7
Total	2.5	1.5	4.2	7.6	12.0	3.2

Sources: U.S. Department of Commerce, Bureau of Economic Analysis, *Business Statistics, 1973* (Government Printing Office, 1973), pp. 202–05; Department of Commerce, BEA, *Survey of Current Business*, vol. 55 (June 1975), p. 9.

a. Fourth quarter to fourth quarter.

b. Since the GNP deflator refers to the price of domestic value added, import prices alone have no direct influence on the overall GNP deflator. The increase in the price of consumer and investment goods is offset, to the extent that they are imported, by the negative impact of the increase in import prices themselves.

avoided. Such definitions as "inflation is too high a rate of growth in the money supply" or "inflation is too large a federal deficit" merely serve to narrow the focus of thought on a very complex and inadequately understood process.

Despite the continuous rise in prices in the last twenty years, U.S. inflationary experience cannot be considered uniform in all of its critical dimensions. First, the inflation rate itself, although always positive, varied considerably. Second, the entire period was one of important changes in relative prices and the movement in the relative price of most goods and services was not generally monotonic. For example, until the mid-1960s the prices of imports, crude materials, and other commodities remained stable despite rises in the overall price level. These same prices, plus food, however, were the most explosive during the recent inflation. There are, of course, cases in which the movement in relative prices is almost monotonic as in government purchases and consumer services. These changes in relative prices are important not only as clues to shifting preferences and technologies and to shifts in the distribution of national income but, for reasons developed below, as essential guides to the diagnosis (and perhaps appropriate remedy) of particular inflationary experiences. Data on the

Table 2. *Average Annual Compound Rates of Change, Selected Price Indexes, Various Periods, 1953–74*

Index	1953–58	1959–65	1966–73	1972:4–1973:4[a]	1973:4–1974:4[a]	Entire period, 1953–74
Consumer price index						
Food	1.3	0.9	5.2	19.5	12.0	3.3
Commodities except food	0.7	0.7	3.2	4.4	13.3	2.1
Housing	1.6	1.1	4.5	6.6	13.6	3.0
Services	3.1	2.3	5.3	5.9	11.0	4.0
All items	1.6	1.2	4.4	8.4	12.1	3.0
Wholesale price index						
Crude materials for further processing	0.0	−0.4	7.8	39.4	6.8	3.5

Sources: *Business Statistics, 1973*, pp. 40–44; *Survey of Current Business*, vol. 54 (June 1974), p. S-8, and vol. 55 (June 1975), p. S-8.
a. Fourth quarter to fourth quarter.

average rate of change of a broader group of price indexes, both for the entire period under study and for particular subperiods, are presented in tables 1 and 2. Somewhat more detail is provided with respect to recent developments because these are of the greatest concern at the moment. Associated data (per capita GNP, money supply, productivity, unemployment rates, government purchases, and the like) covering the same time intervals appear in tables 3 and 4, whereas table 5 presents some evidence on the shifts in relative prices. The figures in table 5 are relative rates of growth in the price of particular sets of goods and services. A score of 1.00 indicates that the price of a particular product is rising at the same rate as the overall price index. A score of less than 1.00 indicates that it is rising more slowly. For example, the data in table 5 indicate that, although for the period as a whole food prices rose by the same amount as other consumer prices (the relative price remaining unchanged), the experience of the last twenty years is better characterized as one of an initial and continuing drop in the relative price of foodstuffs subsequently balanced by a dramatic rise to their former position in 1973 and 1974.[6] A discussion of the role of these changes in relative prices in understanding particular inflationary episodes is resumed in a later section. It is useful here to review more carefully some of the key characteristics of the major inflationary periods in the United States since 1953.

6. For a more detailed analysis, see Dale E. Hathaway, "Food Prices and Inflation," *Brookings Papers on Economic Activity, 1:1974*, pp. 63–109.

Table 3. *Average Annual Compound Rates of Change,*
Selected Economic Indicators, Various Periods, 1953–74

Economic indicator	1953–58	1959–65	1966–73	1972:4– 1973:4[a]	1973:4– 1974:4[a]	Entire period, 1953–74
Per capita GNP[b]	−0.1	3.2	2.9	3.2	−5.5	2.0
Money supply[c]	1.5	2.7	5.9	6.2	5.0	3.8
Private sector						
GNP deflator	2.2	1.2	3.9	7.7	12.4	2.9
Productivity	2.4	3.4	2.5	0.4	−3.7	2.6
Compensation per man-hour	4.6	4.2	6.8	6.11	9.8	5.5

Sources: U.S. Department of Commerce, *The National Income and Product Accounts of the United States, 1929–1965: Statistical Tables* (GPO, 1966), p. 161; *Survey of Current Business,* various issues; U.S. Bureau of Labor Statistics, *Handbook of Labor Statistics 1975—Reference Edition* (GPO, 1975), p. 188; Bureau of Labor Statistics, *Monthly Labor Review,* vol. 98 (November 1975), p. 128, and (December 1975), p. 110; and vol. 99 (January 1976), p. 120; *Business Statistics, 1973,* pp. 4, 68, 101; tabulations, "Revised Money Stock Measures" (Board of Governors of the Federal Reserve System, January 29, 1976; processed).
a. Fourth quarter to fourth quarter.
b. Calculated using 1958 dollars.
c. Demand deposits plus currency outside banks.

Major Inflationary Periods

Expansion that began in 1954 and the early sixties led to two periods of relatively slow and accelerating inflation, respectively. Then, after the 1970 recession began the recent 1971–75 inflation that eventually reached unprecedented dimensions.

The inflation of 1956–57

A period of rapid expansion beginning in 1954 led to an inflation that was less rapid than the two previous post–World War II inflations (1946–48 and 1950–51), but that was the first not associated with various wartime adjustments. The economic expansion was paced by a durable goods boom, initially in consumer automobile purchases, residential construction, and business investment. Prices remained stable during the period of most rapid expansion (mid-1954 through 1955), but began rising quickly during 1956 and continued to rise right through the 1957–58 recession. Thus the inflation began in earnest just as the expansion began to flatten out. Coincidentally at this moment there was also an abrupt reversal of the decline in farm prices. Most analyses of this inflationary episode trace the origin of the inflation to events in 1955. The usual story is that in 1955 the state of actual and expected aggregate demand for durable goods together with the oligop-

Table 4. *Unemployment Rates, Government Purchases, and Federal Surplus, Average for Various Periods, 1953–74*

Economic indicator	1953–58	1958–65	1965–73	1973	1974	Entire period, 1953–74
Unemployment rates (percent)						
All workers	4.7	5.7	4.5	4.9	5.6	4.9
Male workers, 20 years and over	4.1	4.7	3.0	3.2	3.8	3.8
Government purchases of goods and services as percent of GNP[a]						
Total	20.9	19.8	19.2	17.2	17.8	19.8
Federal	12.8	10.8	9.2	6.8	6.9	10.5
Federal surplus (billions of dollars)[b]	−1.9	−2.1	−7.3	−5.5	−8.1	−4.2

Sources: *Handbook of Labor Statistics 1975*, p. 145; *Business Statistics, 1973*, pp. 4, 98; *Survey of Current Business*, vol. 55 (June 1975), pp. S-1, S-19.
a. Calculated using 1958 dollars.
b. National income accounts basis.

olistic nature of the industries producing them led to substantial increases in wages and prices in those industries. Wage and cost linkages to other industries and poor productivity performance then led to another round of more broadly based price increases in the following years. And, as noted above, the decline in farm prices had been reversed. The early years of the expansion (1954–55) were also characterized by a substantial increase in the rate of growth of the money supply (M_1), and the 1955–57 period witnessed persistent increases in velocity. Thus the monetary stimulus too seems to have had its origin in 1955. Interest rates, as usual, rose with the expansion and fell during the 1957–58 recession.

The later years of this period seemed, at the time, to pose a difficult dilemma for monetary policy. After 1955 the economy began to show signs of weakness but prices were still rising rapidly. The Federal Reserve Board was criticized for the effects (particularly on residential construction) of its tight money policy of 1956–57 (interest rates rose and the growth of the money supply declined throughout this period) and for failing to ease conditions early enough in 1957. Nevertheless, although the decline in business activity was sharp, it was short-lived, and by mid-1958 the expansion had resumed again, at least hesitatingly, and inflation rates returned to normal levels (that is, 1.5 to 2.0 percent as measured by the GNP deflator and the consumer price index). The behavior of prices during the 1957–58 recession strongly influenced the thinking of economists on inflationary processes in the U.S. economy. The continuous rise in prices during a period of growing excess capacity (stagflation) induced a new interest in the concept

Table 5. *Rates of Increase of Prices of Selected Items Relative to Total GNP Deflator and Consumer Price Index, Various Periods, 1953–74*

Item	1953–58	1959–65	1966–73	1972:4– 1973:4[a]	1973:4– 1974:4[a]	Entire period, 1953–74
Relative to total GNP deflator						
Personal consumption expenditures	0.72	0.80	0.88	1.09	1.04	0.88
Nonresidential fixed investment	1.44	0.67	0.90	0.53	1.22	0.97
Residential structures	0.68	1.27	1.28	1.53	0.84	1.12
Imports of goods and services	0.08	0.33	1.26	3.17	3.32	1.31
Government purchases of goods and services	1.64	1.73	1.45	1.09	1.05	1.47
Relative to consumer price index						
Food	0.81	0.75	1.18	2.32	0.99	1.10
Commodities except food	0.44	0.58	0.73	0.52	1.10	0.70
Housing	1.00	0.92	1.02	0.78	1.12	1.00
Services	1.94	1.92	1.20	0.70	0.91	1.33

Sources: Same as tables 1 and 2.
a. Fourth quarter to fourth quarter.

of cost-push inflation, or in more general terms a consideration of the nature and origin of the inflationary biases built into the institutions (public and private) of the U.S. economy.[7]

The accelerating inflation of 1966–69

The happy combination of rapidly expanding output, falling unemployment rates, and relative price stability that had characterized the preceding five years came to an abrupt end in 1965–66. The noninflationary expansion of the early 1960s was in many ways a triumph of macroeconomic policy, and as Okun has noted, 1965 probably represented the high watermark of the economist's prestige in Washington.[8] Trouble threatened the profession (and the country), but few heeded Ackley's prophetic warning that, despite recent successes, rough seas were ahead and few reliable charts existed for the high employment economy.[9] By 1965 not only had

7. Charles L. Schultze, *Recent Inflation in the United States,* Study Paper 1, Materials prepared in connection with the Study of Employment, Growth, and Price Levels for consideration by the Joint Economic Committee, 86:1 (Government Printing Office, 1959).

8. Arthur M. Okun, *The Political Economy of Prosperity* (Brookings Institution, 1970).

9. Gardner Ackley, "The Contribution of Economists to Policy Formation," *Journal of Finance,* vol. 21 (May 1966), pp. 169–77.

the 4 percent unemployment target been reached, but strong productivity performance had almost stabilized unit labor costs. At just this moment, however, a new stimulus in spending was injected in the form of an extremely rapid and unexpected (to everyone but the Pentagon) increase in defense spending and in the letting of large defense contracts. The latter element had an important effect on inventory building. Over the next three years military spending was to rise by almost 60 percent. The new stimulus to demand overwhelmed the developing weakness in both the automobile market and residential construction. On the price front, wholesale prices had begun to accelerate early in 1965 after more than six years of stability. The acceleration was particularly rapid in food prices, but the prices of industrial commodities were also rising fast. In 1966 the GNP deflators and consumer prices began a swift advance with only a slight pause during the 1966–67 mini-recession.[10] In addition, during 1966 there was a marked quickening in the rate of wage increases, which continued to rise at a rate considerably in excess of the productivity trend. Unit labor costs therefore also continued to rise at an increasing rate, putting direct pressure on the rate of inflation. The corporate sector, however, was not quite able to pass all these costs on, profits remained under pressure throughout the remainder of the 1960s.[11] In this connection, the overvaluation of the U.S. dollar and the resultant strong foreign competition was an important contributing factor. In the period 1965–69 constant-dollar imports rose at an average annual rate of over 11 percent. Nevertheless, price rises did accelerate and the formal wage-price guideposts established in 1962 were abandoned.[12] During the 1961–65 period the rate of growth of the money supply increased continuously. The rate of growth of real GNP increased irregularly. The 1966 credit crunch saw a sharp drop in the

10. The mini-recession of 1966–67 was associated with a sharp slowdown of inflation rates (attributable in great part to falling interest rates generated by an easing of the credit crunch), but with only a negligible increase in unemployment rates. For a moment the trade-off looked very attractive, a fact that added to the general confusion of policymakers over the succeeding few years.

11. In the postwar period the *profit share* (the share of capital income in corporate income) has declined in two more or less distinct movements, 1948–54 and 1966–70. The explanation of these declines has important implications for the expected rate of inflation. The issue is whether one can expect corporations to exert strong pressure to regain this lost share of national income. Conclusive evidence on this issue is not available, but I am somewhat persuaded by Nordhaus's argument that these movements may be related to declines in the cost of capital and do not therefore represent strong latent pressures for future inflation. (See William D. Nordhaus, "The Falling Share of Profits," *Brookings Papers on Economic Activity, 1:1974*, pp. 169–208.)

12. Despite the abandonment of formal numerical guideposts, "ad hoc jaw-boning" was continued and perhaps even intensified. The details and effects of this informal policy are hard to judge.

growth of the money supply, but an unusually sharp increase in velocity of money. The subsequent years (1967–70), however, saw growth rates in the money stock considerably in excess of the growth rate in real GNP; the overall inflation rate accelerated throughout this period.[13]

The second half of the 1960s was marked by a rather complicated mixture of fiscal and monetary policies (surcharges, investment tax credit, and so on), the effects of which were largely unanticipated. The monetary ease of this period may perhaps be explained in part by incorrect forecasts of the effects of the tax increases in 1968. The boom came to an end in 1969 (as did the fiscal stimulus), but in the price-wage area the legacy of this period is a permanently altered set of price expectations, which in turn affects wage bargains and pricing behavior.[14] This became apparent during the 1970 recession when the unemployment rate rose by 60 percent with hardly a noticeable effect on the rate of increase of wages. Unit labor costs rose at a near peak rate of 6.3 percent, and inflation continued. The rate of growth of the money supply once again advanced after a temporary slowdown during the period of restraint in late 1969.

The story of the recent inflation, 1971–75

This period can perhaps best be told in a number of episodes. First, there is the short period before the New Economic Policy of August 1971 in which recovery from the 1970 recession got under way although with little effect on the unemployment rate, no effect on the rate of increase of wages, and some little deceleration in the rate of increase of final prices. The money supply continued to increase rapidly and the federal deficit rose. The pace of recovery, however, seemed disappointingly slow, and both unemployment rates and inflation rates remained unacceptably high. The country seemed again to be experiencing a type of inflation unrelated to the pressures on capacity; the social costs of lost output were rising. That traditional policies to combat inflation could not be made to work at reasonable costs appeared a strong possibility. Furthermore, confidence in the dollar—undermined by a steady deterioration in the balance on current account—had reached crisis proportions with the balance of payments (by the Official Reserves Transactions definition) registering unprecedentedly large negative amounts during 1971. In any case, by August 1971 the administration had become convinced that the traditional tools of monetary

13. For the whole period 1966–70 (including the 1966 credit crunch), the rate of growth of the money supply outstripped the rate of growth of real GNP by a ratio of well over two to one.

14. See Juster, "Savings Behavior."

and fiscal policy were no longer adequate. The second post–World War II experiment of the United States with an incomes policy involving extensive mandatory controls was therefore inaugurated. This so-called New Economic Policy was introduced with special provisions designed to handle wage-price inflation, the balance of payments, and the disappointingly slow recovery. Although the permanent effects of this policy on the process of inflation will be argued for some time, some of the short-run effects are clearly visible. By the last half of 1972 (Phase II), the wage-price control seems to have caused some slowdown in the rate of wage increases and in the overall rate of price inflation in the nonagricultural sector.[15] At the same time my own view of this period suggests that the end of 1972 and the beginning of 1973 may be analogous to the 1965–66 period when an already expanding economy was overstimulated by easing monetary and fiscal policies. This time the new balance of payments policy also contributed to inflationary pressure. The devaluation of the dollar early in 1973 raised the absolute and relative prices of imports, exports, their close substitutes, and the resources used in their production. In any case, Phase III (1973–74) stands clearly as a period of extraordinary price inflation, the interpretation of which is still not well understood. In the first half of 1973, prices moved up sharply and continued increasing through the beginning of the following year. This acceleration in the rate of inflation can be traced to a number of factors, but arithmetically the primary stimulation came from the near explosion in the retail price of food and the prices of internationally traded commodities. In both these cases, the effects of transition to Phase III undoubtedly played a part, but other factors were equally important, such as capacity pressures, dollar devaluation, and strong worldwide demand and low inventories for food and other commodities. On the whole, built into the inflation of that period were important elements of structural or supply shift; therefore, some forces not likely to contribute to future inflation rates were involved. At the same time, few observers would deny that some battle over income shares inducing a wage-price spiral was a continuing factor and that the inflationary forces generated in this battleground could be expected to persist.

With respect to the monetary environment, growth in the money supply was still very high relative to output during this period, and interest rates, apparently incorporating a new set of price expectations (at least short-run expectations), reached record levels. In general, however, the increas-

15. The evidence through 1972 is consistent with the view that the controls had little influence on wages but did affect the markup over cost. (See, for example, Robert J. Gordon, "The Response of Wages and Prices to the First Two Years of Controls," *Brookings Papers on Economic Activity, 3:1973*, pp. 765–78.)

ing importance of the huge blocks of internationally mobile capital makes the monetary environment of any particular situation harder to define. That is, as bank deposits (and other short-term debts) issued in various countries become closer substitutes for each other in the portfolios of investors, the critical importance of the domestic money supply—for example, in defining or characterizing the monetary environment—is diminished. Unfortunately, it is not yet clear how to define the analogous concept on a new international basis.

The current debate on the transmission of inflation

In the contemporary debate on the causes of the inflation in the United States the influence of foreign prices inevitably enters. This influence is new in post–World War II discussions and consideration of it is clearly appropriate because the extent to which such a phenomenon explains U.S. inflation is important in determining appropriate counterinflationary policies. It is noteworthy, therefore, that the Bronfenbrenner-Holzman survey of inflation theory in the mid-1960s merely raises the issue in a footnote.[16] Otherwise excellent accounts of the cyclical evolution and development of the U.S. economy over the period 1950–71 (for example, Gordon, Okun[17]), which was hardly a period of price stability, occasionally note the effects of certain balance of payments problems and constraints but almost never deal with the issue of imported inflation. The figures in the tables above clearly indicate the reason for this lack of concern. Until the 1970s import prices remained relatively stable, and given the demand for dollars, even the commitment to a regime of fixed exchange rates did not result in the generation of inflationary pressures from abroad—this despite the fact that, over the period as a whole, trend rates of inflation among the chief trading partners of the United States were usually higher than the domestic inflation rate.[18] The recent experience, however, of: (1) rapidly rising domestic prices, (2)

16. Martin Bronfenbrenner and Franklin D. Holzman, "A Survey of Inflation Theory," in *Surveys of Economic Theory*, vol. 1: *Money, Interest, and Welfare* (St. Martin's, 1965) pp. 46–107.

17. Robert Aaron Gordon, *Economic Instability and Growth: The American Record* (Harper and Row, 1974); and Okun, *Political Economy of Prosperity*.

18. In recent years interest in monetarist models of the international transmission of inflation has revived. These, of course, have a long and established tradition dating from Hume. The basic proposition articulated in these models is that in a world of integrated markets operating under a regime of fixed exchange rates the inflation rate in any particular country will tend to converge, *in the long run*, on the world inflation rate. Discrepancies in inflation rates will set off balance of payments adjustments that tend to eliminate these differences. The world inflation rate itself is governed by the rates of increase in the world money supply.

even more spectacular rises in the prices of imported goods, and (3) floating exchange rates has led economists toward a more careful consideration of how domestic inflation is affected by the world prices of internationally traded goods.

No sooner did the opportunity develop to insulate the country from foreign inflation through a floating exchange rate system than the United States put the primary blame for inflation on foreign price movements. Unlike the defunct Bretton Woods arrangements, under a system of flexible exchange rates there need be no world inflation. Each country has an opportunity either to go along with foreign inflationary impulses, or not to do so. Flexible rates, however, do not eliminate the underlying problem of world inflation but simply shift the focus of attention to more basic items such as international transfers of wealth and changing claims to shares of world output. That is, although disturbances from abroad still have important effects, they need not take the form of rising or falling domestic price levels. Of course, in a world of speculative capital flows the neat classroom model of the floating exchange rate system will not quite work (for example, if rising import prices generate a capital outflow), particularly when an excessive amount of dollar liquidity is available to finance, for instance, speculative purchases of securities or commodities. Theories of adjustment under flexible exchange rates really address themselves to a world where trade and comparative advantage dominate the international flow of capital. In addition, floats are, in fact, never quite clean, and in the analysis of events, therefore, it must be considered that in reality there is a mixture of fixed- and floating-rate systems.

I must note, however, that any macroeconomic analysis of this problem is immediately hindered by two important constraints. The first is the lack of data on appropriate prices. The consumer and wholesale price indexes of U.S. trading partners give only indirect and often misleading clues to the price of their exports. Furthermore, as Kravis and Lipsey[19] have effectively pointed out, implicit deflators for imports and unit value indexes are also seriously deficient. The second and perhaps more forbidding constraint is the rather primitive understanding of how capital flows are affected by current and expected differential inflation rates and exchange rate movements. The data problems in this area are most severe and there has been little opportunity to test whatever primitive ideas on these issues there may be. Moreover, theoretical models are highly aggregative, generally designed for a very small open economy with little to say about a world with imperfect

19. Irving B. Kravis and Robert E. Lipsey, *Price Competitiveness in World Trade* (Columbia University Press for National Bureau of Economic Research, 1971).

markets, administered pricing, and the like; they are almost silent on the critical problem of dynamic adjustment (as opposed to steady-state properties).[20] Thus in the case of goods that are not perfectly homogeneous there is almost no way of knowing how a foreign supplier's prices will respond to a domestic devaluation. Indeed, the relation between a particular balance of payments position and movements in the domestic price level is not easily discerned and has yet to be adequately articulated. In short, the channels through which foreign inflation can affect domestic price levels are many and are not mutually exclusive. To test the empirical relevance of each of these would require both a more detailed conceptualization of the processes involved and a much more elaborate set of data.

In my judgment, many of the current explanations of the recent inflation confuse those forces causing changes in relative prices (such as wheat harvest failures or the control of oil prices by the Organization of Petroleum Exporting Countries), and the forces contributing to a rise in the general price level (such as the transition to Phase III or the wage-price spiral). For example, the inflation of the domestic price level may or may not have been a useful way to absorb the real loss that accompanied the worsened terms of trade (especially since imports can no longer be paid for with IOUs) but it was not a necessary consequence of such movements. It was one of the ways the United States chose to respond to these circumstances. For a basic explanation of these rising price levels one has to revert to an analysis that focuses on public policy decisions in the framework of society's changing institutions and goals. It must be said, however, that even after such an analysis, certain important enigmas remain.

Understanding Inflation

Inflation has become embedded in the U.S. economic system in a complicated way that relates not only to the setting of wages and prices itself, but also to the wide spectrum of additional socioeconomic goals that are being pursued in the context of the set of institutions that currently characterize U.S. society. To the extent that inflation is becoming an increasingly difficult problem, therefore, attention must be directed to important changes in society's goals and institutions.

It has become clear that the American economy now contains a built-in inflationary bias that results from the interaction of a range of factors of

20. The role of capital movements is also particularly important in the short-run adjustment process. Their effects on the steady state are minimal.

which the most critical are: (1) required changes in relative prices to induce the necessary reallocation of resources to accommodate change; (2) the downward rigidity of prices and wages in most sectors; (3) strong links between sectors in the wage determination process; and (4) commitment to the maintenance of full employment. As a result of the first three factors, structural change will generally be accompanied by upward pressures on prices, whereas a commitment to full employment induces those charged with the responsibility for public policy to provide the additional money necessary to circulate the national income at the increased prices. While change is occurring (and it seems to be occurring ever more frequently) and wages and prices resist decline, there will be a choice, at least in the short run, between unemployment and some added inflationary pressure. It seems the latter is being chosen.[21]

Proponents of the natural unemployment rate theory maintain that such a choice is not really available. They argue that in the long run the Phillips curve is vertical and the only way traditional monetary and fiscal policies can achieve a lower unemployment rate is through ever-accelerating inflation. They would of course agree that policies aimed at improving the efficiency of labor markets and removing barriers to the accumulation of human capital could lower the natural unemployment rate itself. Their arguments are quite persuasive in the sense that the short-term trade-off between unemployment and inflation, if any, must certainly be based on incorrect perceptions of wage and price movements; surely economic units can distinguish, at least in the long run, between real and nominal values. Otherwise, no one would really know that an inflation was in process.[22] Since, however, the economy is in a perpetual state of disequilibrium as it moves through different stages of the business cycle and attempts to adjust to continuing shifts in demand, the trade-off may last long enough, given political time preferences. In any case, the benefits of lower unemployment now would have to be balanced with the cost of the accelerating inflation

21. A similar but somewhat different inflationary process may be generated in the highly concentrated sectors of the economy. Wage bargains in these sectors involve higher money wages and lower output and employment than would be the case under more competitive conditions. Government policy, responding to slack growth in employment, then allows general price levels to rise. If the leads and lags in expectations and perceptions line up, this could produce not only a once-and-for-all monopoly shift in the price level, but continuing inflationary pressures.

22. It is also true, however, that the source of the observed negative correlation between inflation rates and the unemployment ratio may be caused by the lack of full (instantaneous) information on the prices in diverse markets that prevents individuals from distinguishing between absolute and relative changes in prices.

rates it may release. The accelerationists have made an important contribution to current understanding of this problem not only with respect to how the trade-off might shift in the long run, but in inducing the defenders of the downward-sloping Phillips curve to refine and clarify their position. In this latter regard there has been a growing awareness of the effects of demographic shifts in the labor force on the appropriate interpretation of how aggregate unemployment rates relate to tightness on the labor market. It is now generally recognized, thanks to the work initiated by Perry,[23] that the composition of the labor force has been shifting over time toward groups with higher specific unemployment rates, causing an upward trend in the aggregate unemployment rate (of perhaps 0.5 to 1.0 percentage point a year) that is unrelated to changes in excess demand in the labor market. Thus it has been estimated that whereas in 1956 an inflation rate of 3 percent a year would be accompanied by an aggregate unemployment rate of 4.1 percent, in 1971 the aggregate unemployment rate associated with the same rate of inflation would be about 5.2 percent.[24] Similarly, Hall has estimated that in the period between 1964 and 1973 the unemployment rate that might accompany a particular rate of price inflation had risen by about 0.6 percentage point.[25] To the extent that the unemployment rate is a target of economic policy, the importance of these results cannot be overemphasized. Fixed-weight unemployment rates clearly reveal much tighter labor markets in the early 1970s than does the traditional aggregate unemployment rate.[26] The significance of this fact in the analysis of the current inflation is obvious.[27]

23. George L. Perry, "Changing Labor Markets and Inflation," *Brookings Papers on Economic Activity, 3:1970,* pp. 411–41.

24. Robert J. Gordon, "Inflation in Recession and Recovery," *Brookings Papers on Economic Activity, 1:1971,* pp. 137–39.

25. Robert E. Hall, "The Process of Inflation in the Labor Market," *Brookings Papers on Economic Activity, 2:1974,* pp. 392–93.

26. It has become apparent that empirical studies of the wage-price mechanism in the U.S. economy can benefit not only from the use of fixed-weight unemployment rates, but also from the use of fixed-weight wage indexes (to eliminate the effect of shifts from high- to low-wage industries) and fixed-weight productivity indexes.

27. I have two reservations regarding the above issue. First, it is difficult to distinguish empirically between the hypothesis that the Phillips curve has shifted because of structural shifts in the labor force and the hypothesis that it has shifted because of fundamental revisions in price expectations. Second, from the point of view of the development of knowledge, the work on the development of new unemployment rates has a flavor of "gasping for air" under the deluge of the accelerationist attack. Finally, as Hall (in "The Process of Inflation in the Labor Market") and others have effectively pointed out, the analysis of the problem may well yield greater insights if economists focused more on the wage determination process itself, perhaps

Despite their valuable contribution, I think that at least the extreme policy position implied by the accelerationists—the abandonment of low unemployment as an explicit policy objective of monetary and fiscal policy —is probably inadvisable. A policy position such as this depends on at least two factors: (1) the relevance of the natural rate theory in an economy in perpetual disequilibrium, and (2) evaluation of the costs of an accelerating inflation for some future period compared with the benefits of lower unemployment rates for some immediate period. This involves not only an evaluation of gains and losses and of the duration of misperceptions on wages and prices (how fast expectations adjust), but also a determination of the rate of time preference.

In summary, I believe there is almost certainly a trade-off between inflation and unemployment in any sense that would be relevant for stabilization policy. The quantitative features of this trade-off, however, are not likely to remain stable for a long period of time and there is still uncertainty about the nature of the shifts involved. Although recent studies have refined and clarified understanding of the trade-off, all policies must still rest on a certain amount of guesswork, or at least be conditional on minimizing the effects of errors in judgment.

If the U.S. economy were typified by state control of all prices and factor allocations, if foreign commerce were prohibited, and if the government protected society from the uncomfortable redistributive effects of technological change and shifting preferences by freezing the existing productive relations, inflation would not be a problem. There could be a constant money wage and no unemployment, and productivity gains, if any, could be absorbed by lowering prices. The reality of the goals of U.S. society, however, are quite different, embracing a more complex set of institutions; inflation control is, correspondingly, a more complicated affair. Within the current institutional setup in the United States, simple solutions to the control of inflation are almost certain to be either wrong, too costly, or both. It is known that at any given time, for any given set of supply conditions, the level of aggregate demand will determine the price level. Thus

---

in the direction suggested by the turnover theorists (for example, Holt, Tobin) and paid closer attention to the work of traditional labor economists.

It should also be noted that rising unemployment rates together with increasing inflation rates can also be caused by any set of factors that increase the natural rate of unemployment. It has been suggested, for example, that over the last decade the United States has failed to accumulate enough capital to employ the growing labor force. If this conjecture is justified, the natural rate will certainly have increased, causing at least a temporary worsening of the trade-off.

it will almost always be possible to control the price level through the control of aggregate demand. That solution may, however, mean lost production and the sacrifice of other important goals. The present search is for a cure at reasonable cost. Although in a formal sense it is permissible to think of all inflations as demand-pull inflations (since the purchasers of goods and factors are willingly paying the higher prices), it would often be a misrepresentation of the process in that it would lead to inappropriate diagnosis and remedy. Likewise, the simple alternative to demand-pull inflation—cost-push inflation—although it contains valuable insights, dangerously oversimplifies the process. Complicated and as yet incompletely worked out ideas on inflation in the United States will involve demand-pull and cost-push elements and will specify the interrelations of these sets of forces. They will also contain important dimensions relating to the world economy, technology, and sociopsychological factors. Inflation must be controlled within the constraints imposed by other goals.

A sustainable increase in prices requires as a necessary and sufficient condition either a substantial permanent rise in velocity or a continuing increase in the domestic money supply. Other models of the inflationary process (for example, cost-push, demand-pull, and so on), which I argue are essential to understanding and selection of appropriate anti-inflation policies, cannot be considered independently of the monetary environment within which they must operate. There is no disagreement on the point that, over a suitably defined length of time, the price level is almost by definition tied to the money supply. The real issue is whether this understanding is of any real use in the selection of public policies, for there is little agreement on how the relationship operates within a time period relevant for stabilization policy. Perhaps the major deficiency in the theories (and understanding) of inflationary processes is the lack of any acceptable model of the short-run dynamic adjustment path of prices. Theory perceives only the long-run steady state that is, of course, consistent with many short-run patterns. It is the short-run behavior of prices, however, that has an important bearing on public policy decisions affecting the steady state.

Despite the limitations of its knowledge, I believe that the economics profession has had a very reasonable and useful taxonomy of normal inflations for quite some time. This taxonomy was set out in numerous publications in the late 1950s and early 1960s and was recently restated by James Tobin.[28] Essentially, the classification scheme distinguishes between one-

28. For example, Bronfenbrenner and Holzman, "Survey of Inflation Theory"; Bert G. Hickman, *Growth and Stability in the Postwar Economy* (Brookings Institution, 1960); Harry G. Johnson, *Essays in Monetary Economics* (Harvard University Press, 1967). See also James Tobin in *New York Times,* September 6, 1974.

shot events that lead to a once-and-for-all rise in the price level and those processes that are cumulative in the sense of possibly leading to continuing and perhaps accelerating rates of inflation.[29] All these inflations must be validated by monetary expansion, but the costs and possible success of particular anti-inflationary monetary and fiscal policies will be quite different in the different cases. For example, if an inflation is the result primarily of a shift in demand it may yield somewhat more easily to the traditional tools of monetary and fiscal policy than if it is due to shifts in supply conditions. Unfortunately, the classification, useful for organizing discussion and analysis of events, does not by itself easily enable one to forecast unambiguously, or even to recognize, a particular inflationary experience as being of Type A. Furthermore, as suggested above, these various inflationary processes are not mutually exclusive and most inflationary periods probably reflect the operation of more than one process.

It is critical, however, to distinguish inflationary forces that appear to be one-shot affairs and those that threaten continued or accelerating contributions to the rate of inflation because the benefits of fighting the inflation are quite different. The recent spectacular rise in food, commodity, and oil prices is probably a one-shot affair and there may be little benefit in fighting that battle. Inflation of the domestic urban price level may have been the most useful response to that situation. If, however, that inflation was fed by the wage-price spiral, or what might be called an incomes inflation, during which all groups attempted to enlarge their shares of national output, even a temporarily difficult policy may have large payoffs. Perhaps an incomes policy or a policy of restricting aggregate demand and output (until some group no longer has the power to attempt a change or there is little left to expropriate) may be an appropriate anti-inflation policy.

Conclusion

Although this paper is not concerned with the normative theory of inflation, it seems important to recognize again that there is a basic asymmetry between inflation and unemployment that is often ignored. Prices are a yardstick (a tool of measurement and analysis) and inflation represents—at least at one level—a simple change in calibration. With or without the homogeneity postulate, the money stock and the units of account remain basically a vehicle for facilitating exchange and nothing more. Even a

29. It should be noted, however, that if these one-shot price increases are somehow permanently built into price expectations even they can contribute to continuing inflation.

wage-price spiral by itself causes no collective loss to the groups involved. One person's payment is another's income. Unemployment, on the other hand, represents an actual loss of goods and services. All the attention focused on the Phillips curve during the last decade has somehow encouraged economists to consider these two variables as of equal stature. I believe this is a mistake. It is obvious why society wants to avoid unemployment, but if inflation too should be avoided, it must be because it is believed that it also eventually leads to a loss of goods and services (that is, inflation is deflationary!), or that it works to redistribute income and wealth in some undesirable way.

Unfortunately, there is little hard evidence on the redistributive effects of inflation in the United States. Even with respect to income, the national accounts simply do not provide adequate measures for this purpose. The true share of profits, for example, is difficult to assess in the absence of careful measurement of both true economic depreciation and capital gains —concepts that are largely missing from the national accounts figures for both corporate profits and national income. Additional difficulties in the interpretation of the national accounts data on distributive shares are caused by the shifting relative importance of various production sectors— with their widely different capital-output ratios—as well as the shifts in employment from agriculture to industry and industry to government with their obvious implications for the income shares of unincorporated business, corporate profits, and wages. Even the shifting age distribution of the population may dramatically affect the importance of transfer incomes. In principle, all these effects can be isolated, but the set of data necessary to do so is lacking. Despite these difficulties, some interesting preliminary studies have been made. Bach and Stephenson for example, reach the following tentative conclusions.[30] (1) During inflationary periods current income is redistributed from profits to wages and salaries. This conclusion is based on the evidence that over the last twenty years the proportion of national income accounted for by wages and salaries fell during the period of relative price stability (1959–65) and rose during the more inflationary periods (1954–58, 1966–73). The reverse was true of corporate profits. (2) During inflationary periods there is a transfer of wealth from households to the government, and among households from older persons to younger persons, and from the very poor and rich to the middle-income groups. Inflation, as expected, hurts those in net creditor positions, but there is no uniformity in this respect within the traditional functional income groups.

30. G. L. Bach and James B. Stephenson, "Inflation and the Redistribution of Wealth," *Review of Economics and Statistics*, vol. 56 (February 1974), pp. 1–13.

Although while the Bach-Stephenson results are compatible with the broad movements apparently occurring during relatively inflationary periods, there is a fair amount of important variance within these periods. This is illustrated by a significant development in 1973, when the real hourly wages of urban workers declined. The decline was caused in large part by a deterioration in the terms of trade of the domestic nonfarm sector of the economy (relative rise in import and farm prices), and the growing discrepancy between hourly wages and the cost of labor to the firm (increased social security taxes, and so on). At the same time the share of profit in national income has been growing, though modestly, since 1970. There is some question, therefore, about the soundness of the measures employed in the Bach-Stephenson study. Nordhaus's examination of the postwar movements in the corporate profit share, for example, do not support these findings.[31]

In summary, these types of redistributional effects are quite complex and it is often difficult, with the data available, to classify broad groups of losers and gainers. It is noteworthy, however, that although documentation of any systematic redistribution of real income and wealth caused by inflation is difficult, whatever redistribution does take place bears a relation to the social and/or economic contribution of those affected. The recognition of such arbitrary transfers is certainly perceived as a welfare loss and undoubtedly contributes to social and political tension. Particular anti-inflationary policies (for example, monetary restraint) do, however, have differential impacts on particular sectors such as residential construction.

The question might then be: is it simply that inflation has a bad press, or is it really deflationary in the sense of leading to more unemployment or underemployment of resources? Price stability is often held to be the key to high employment, growth, efficiency, and a strong balance of payments position, yet the evidence for the United States hardly gives overwhelming support to this view. I believe that the bad reputation inflation has among the U.S. public rests in part on not quite relevant historical experiences together with a deep desire for stability, rather than on a convincing demonstration that inflation causes economic slowdowns. The German experience of the early 1920s—the picture of inflation destroying the middle class and causing a general economic breakdown—has had an extraordinary influence on U.S. thinking. The hyperinflation of that time, however, does not teach much about the U.S. inflation of the last two decades. In this respect I am reminded of the old tavern sign, "Remember the Jamestown flood—don't spit on the floor." Consider instead the collection of data

31. Nordhaus, "The Falling Share of Profits."

Table 6. *Average Compound Rate of Growth, Various Periods, 1954–74*

Item	1954–64	1964–73	1964–74
GNP deflator	2.0	4.0	4.6
GNP per capita[a]	2.0	3.1	2.5
Disposable income per capita[a]	2.2	3.7	3.0
Nonresidential fixed investment[a]	4.1	5.8	5.2

Sources: *Business Statistics, 1973*, pp. 4, 68; *Survey of Current Business*, vol. 54 (June 1974), pp. S-1, S-13, and vol. 55 (June 1975), pp. 9, S-1, S-13; *1967 Supplement to Economic Indicators* (GPO, 1967), p. 15; *Economic Indicators, December 1971* (GPO, 1971), p. 5; ibid., *December 1975* (GPO, 1975), p. 5.
a. Calculated using 1958 dollars.

in table 6 relating to the U.S. economy since 1954. The evidence seems clear that the decade of inflation (1964–73) was associated with greater gains in per capita real output, real disposable income, and business capital formation. It certainly does not appear that inflation has been deflationary. Although this evidence is crude and inconclusive, it seems that over the last two decades inflation has not prevented U.S. economic development. During this time inflation in the United States has not, as far as can be determined, led to (a) hyperinflation, (b) monetary collapse, (c) income being redistributed away from savers or real wealth being shifted in some undesirable way, (d) gross inefficiency, or (e) a low growth rate. Contrary to the popular myth that, if the price level were stable, many significant risks would be eliminated from economic activity, such risks are part of a dynamically developing system and bear little relation to the process of inflation.

Inflation is, of course, not without some identifiable costs. First, there is the uncertainty associated with an inflation that is unexpected. Unfulfilled prophecies are costly to the efficient operation of the U.S. economic system, and inflation has undoubtedly caused some inefficiencies in the allocation of resources and loss in production. Although there is little evidence on this issue for the United States, a recent study by Juster shows that consumers respond conservatively to unexpected rates of inflation—by increasing their savings rate.[32] George Katona, also using data from the Survey of Consumer Finances, has been making the same claim for years. Furthermore, uncertainty about the future increases the income insecurity of many households and thereby causes a hard-to-measure but definite welfare loss. In addition, the disappointment of small savers and the resultant feeling of having been cheated represent an actual loss in perceived economic welfare. These feelings, even if unjustified, may have important social consequences. A country with a major world financial role

32. Juster, "Savings Behavior."

to play is further hindered by uncertainty regarding exchange rates and monetary policy. Adjustment to expected rates of inflation is another costly matter requiring the use of scarce resources; the higher the absolute rate of inflation the more complicated and costly are the adjustments. Finally, inflation acts as a tax and like many other taxes is inefficient in that it encourages efforts to economize on cash balances, which is largely unproductive activity. These difficulties are, however, only of secondary concern and can be overcome by allowing market-determined interest rates to be paid on money balances.

However these various costs are weighed, it nevertheless remains true that elected representatives continue to consider inflation social dynamite. Public opinion polls always reflect citizens' deep concern with rising prices. Yet I believe that one of the main reasons for these attitudes concerns a phenomenon not produced by inflation but associated with it in economies like that of the United States. Structural changes in the U.S. economy may be accompanied by a certain amount of inflation. These same structural changes (shifting technologies, preferences, and comparative advantage) are also associated with a redistribution of society's production from the gainers (who may be foreigners) to the losers. In any case, the losers blame the inflation rather than the basic shift in productive relations, whereas the gainers believe they are belatedly getting what is due them. For a number of decades the cumulative number of losers may be quite large. And a policy perfectly successful in ensuring price stability will unfortunately do nothing to eliminate these continuous shifts in resources.

All these points can perhaps be clarified in the context of the recent inflation. The U.S. urban worker suffered an unusual decline in real wages and will undoubtedly demand large increases in money wages in an attempt to catch up. Much of the urban workers' loss reflected a transfer to farmers and foreign and domestic oil producers and to try to recapture it from a broad spectrum of U.S. industry would simply initiate another round of inflationary wage and price increases. It is possible, of course, to fight this income inflation with a demand deflation induced by restrictive monetary and fiscal policies, but the cost in lost output may be significant even without considering the impact of such policies on the world economy. If this cost seems too high and the specter of another round of inflation at the beginning of a business cycle expansion frightening, some type of incomes policy can always be considered. Incomes policies per se are unpopular, but they may be regarded as a tool of last resort, to be used when more traditional policies can no longer be expected to generate acceptable solutions. (Sharp differences of opinion arise, however, as to when a situation of last resort exists.) It is understandable that economists who, more accurately than the rest of society, perceive the inevitable inefficiencies and inequities of such policies, should stand against them longer than the rest of the electorate. Inasmuch as the situation is political (wage bargaining is always a dispute over shares of national output), too much too soon cannot be hoped for from traditional remedies; it may be time to try the damnable solution once again. It may work, it may simply give the economy some breathing space, or it may fail. The dilemma is real: any solution will take time and, given political time preference rates, it is not clear that successive administrations can be prevented from quickly pulling one policy lever after another.

The oil crisis and its repercussions on the international payments mechanism and world inflation are, I believe, an interesting and revealing example of how inflation may be adopted as a public policy. The large surplus being accumulated by various oil-producing countries could be accommodated in various ways, but all of them confront what seem to me important institutional barriers. Somehow the relative price of crude oil must adjust in a downward direction (that is, oil consumers will not accept the deterioration in the terms of trade permanently). The method of solving this problem may certainly have a strong effect on prospects for world inflation.

Comments by Thomas A. Wilson

LET ME begin with some remarks on the U.S. situation. In his paper, Shapiro stresses the difference between a relative price change that supposedly has only a transitory effect on the price level and the process of inflation as determined either by the rate of monetary growth or the wage-price spiral.

Although this distinction is useful in analyzing the sources of inflation, I think it can be overworked. In a number of models, a major inflationary relative price change can have a lasting influence on the inflationary process. Consider the case of a pure accelerationist model, where the policymakers decide to maintain the unemployment rate at the natural level. In that kind of system, if an inflationary relative price change occurs and the policymakers adjust their policy to keep the economy at the natural unemployment rate, a certain amount of that inflationary shock becomes incorporated into inflationary expectations and is hence locked into the wage-price spiral. The only way to erase the inflationary impact of the relative price change is to endure an episode of deflationary demand policies or to administer some kind of direct deflationary shock.

During the 1972–74 period, the United States suffered from a series of major but transient inflationary shocks. A key problem is to determine the extent to which these transient shocks have become incorporated into the expected rate of inflation. If one knew what the natural unemployment rate was in the United States and how to reach it, what rate of inflation would remain? I suspect the resulting inflation rate—the expected rate—would be quite high, probably not double-digit but somewhere between 5 and 10 percent. The important policy issue here is whether anything can be gained by reducing the rate of inflation significantly below this expected rate by restrictive macroeconomic policies. What is particularly interesting to me, as a Canadian looking south, is that Canada and the United States apparently made different choices in this respect.

In the United States policymakers opted for an extraordinary amount of restriction, and as a result the U.S. economy suffered a major loss of real output and very high unemployment. The hope is, of course, that the country will finally emerge from this period with significantly less inflation. But it is clear that a very high price was paid for doing so.

Canada is fortunate in the sense that what is most important for the Canadian price level is what the United States is doing. At a meeting in Ottawa the argument was heard, "The United States is tightening up. Can we afford to do anything different?" Some Canadians maintained that, on the contrary, this was precisely the ideal solution to the problem in Canada, since it would shift the trade-off between inflation and unemployment in a favorable direction. If the United States does succeed in controlling inflation, that would put Canada 75 percent of the way toward controlling its own inflation. Canada could therefore orient its policies toward fuller employment and maintenance of an adequate real rate of growth. Fortunately, the Canadian budget did reveal further major expansionary fiscal moves.[33]

I think that the resulting situation in Canada, therefore, contrasts with what went on in the United States. Canada had a positive rate of growth during 1975 unlike the United States. Yet the price inflation situation was not significantly worsened.

Let me explain briefly why I think that the U.S. solution to its inflation problem helped Canada solve its problem.

---

33. Whereas the November 1974 budget was expansionary, the subsequent budget in June 1975 had a contractionary impact on real aggregate demand, combined with inflationary direct price effects. The latter were the result of oil price increases and the imposition of an excise tax on gasoline.

A few years ago Lester Taylor, Stephen Turnovsky, and I published a study of the inflationary process in Canada and the United States.[34] We found that there are very strong linkages between wages and prices in the two countries. These are direct linkages in multivariate models that include other variables in both the labor market and the product market in order to capture the effects of demand and cost factors. In other words, we have found that there is a significant separate effect of U.S. prices and wages directly impinging on Canadian prices and wages. The effects on Canadian prices of those in corresponding U.S. industries did not occur via the route of cost increases of materials or the route of changing demand conditions because variables measuring these were also included in the models.

As for the wage models, we found evidence that there is little money illusion in the Canadian labor market. The coefficients on consumer price changes in the typical wage equation are close to unity. Changes in employment, as a measure of demand conditions in the labor market, and industry profits were other important domestic variables in these models. Furthermore, in some of the industries where one would expect it to be important, wages in the corresponding U.S. industry had a significant partial effect. In other words, we found that in a number of sectors there were direct wage linkages to the United States.

One of the more important implications of these econometric results is that any reduction in the U.S. rate of inflation benefits the Canadian wage-price system in a very direct way. Given that the coefficient of consumer prices in the wage equation is close to unity, a reduction in inflation in the United States starts to benefit the Canadian economy directly on the price side, then touches off a series of adjustments, working through the wage-price process to damp down Canadian inflation rates.

I think that what one observes then is a short-run trade-off in Canada that, from the political standpoint, is extremely favorable. Canada can focus on employment and on maintaining real output growth because the reduction in inflation that could be achieved by restrictive domestic demand policies is very limited over a two-year horizon—the longest horizon politicians usually consider.[35]

34. Lester D. Taylor, Stephen J. Turnovsky, and Thomas A. Wilson, *The Inflationary Process in North American Manufacturing* (Ottawa: Information Canada, 1973).

35. A recent development in Canada, not incorporated in this analysis, is an upsurge of wage pressures in the public sectors. High wage settlements early in 1975 were a major factor leading the Trudeau government in October of that year to institute a program of wage and price controls.

On the other hand, because of the direct impact of U.S. inflation rates on both wages and prices and the interaction between U.S. and Canadian wages and prices, the success of the United States in dampening its inflation rates by a percentage point or two would translate fairly rapidly into a more favorable situation in Canada.

General Comments

ARTHUR OKUN observed that Shapiro's paper appears receptive to apparently conflicting views on several issues. One such issue is whether a one-shot increase in the price level can set off accelerating inflation. Shapiro sometimes appears to say that the effects of such an event die away, but he then contemplates its continuation as a result of money wage increases designed to maintain real wages in the face of a price rise, which constitutes a chain reaction to the initial shock. If there is no continuing excess demand for labor, a one-shot increase in the price level could not cause acceleration of inflation unless the one-time event did set off a chain reaction. Similarly, Shapiro seems to say that inflation causes welfare losses only if it has a deflationary effect on output, but he also later suggests that inflation might impair the efficiency and longer-term growth of the system. It is implied that the recent inflation was simply a bigger version of earlier inflations, that the one in 1973 differed from that in 1966 only in magnitude. There was a fundamental difference between the two, at least in the ability to explain the 1973 experience. Any model—Keynesian, monetarist, leading-indicator, or any other—could explain the acceleration of inflation in 1965 and 1966, given the fiscal and monetary policies of that period and what was happening to unemployment and utilization of industrial capacity, but no model calculated through the end of 1972 that did not break out farm and oil prices as special factors and that treated monetary and fiscal policies of those years as exogenous predetermined variables could generate anything like the degree of inflation experienced in late 1973 and 1974. Nor could that degree of inflation be explained by the unemployment data, by any labor market indicators, or by utilization of manufacturing capacity, using the relationships that had prevailed through 1972. In that sense, the macroeconomic developments of 1972 to 1974 were a fundamental puzzle; they forced economists to look at special factors, and especially at the international sector.

Robert Gordon agreed that no model specified up to the end of 1972 could capture the behavior of prices. One must recognize, however, that even without the shocks of increases specifically in food and oil prices there would have been price-raising influences in 1973. In particular, with unemployment at 4.5 percent in 1973 there were many shortages, whereas in 1969, when unemployment was 3.5 percent, there seemed to be none. It is useful to disentangle the permanent and transitory reasons for this apparent shift in the natural unemployment rate. The ratio of capital to labor at a given unemployment rate had shifted; between 1969 and 1973 enough capital apparently had not been accumulated to equip the additional workers who entered the labor force. The major permanent element was not the demographic shift in the labor force that many people point to, but the portion of investment that took the form of pollution control and other objectives incapable of producing more GNP. There were also some transitory factors, such as the combination of controls and devaluation, that together led to an increase in exports and a consequent reduction in supplies available for the domestic market. In the absence of these factors, the shortages would have been much less severe. Added to these transitory factors relating to the one-shot problem was an underlying inflation that had continued more or less since the late 1960s and that had not changed fundamentally in character or magnitude. Oil prices, food prices, termination of controls, and devaluation were bubbles superimposed on that inflation and were inherently transitory, with the possible exception of the food price problem. The others would die out, whether the U.S. unemployment rate were 6, 8, or 10 percent. Even if the natural unemployment rate rose substantially because of a shift in the relation of capital to labor, there would still be no acceleration of inflation if unemployment were kept at the natural rate. Although the underlying inflation could not be eliminated, it was not true that there had been a steady acceleration in that underlying inflation rate since 1971 as a result of a recklessly expansive monetary policy; those who maintain that argument are failing to distinguish the bubble from the nonbubble inflation.

Arthur Okun pointed out that George Perry had found that measures of capacity utilization could not explain the upsurge of the price level in 1973. A shortage of capital in the aggregate may not be the explanation of the upsurge, although perhaps shortages of capacity in industries producing basic materials like steel and chemicals might provide a partial explanation. It has not yet been demonstrated, however, that an explanation lies in a shortage of capital and the data must be strained to find support for that viewpoint. This is not to imply that capital shortages in basic industries are of no consequence.

Walter Salant noted that, although Perry had found no evidence of a general capacity shortage, it should be recognized that the growth of the labor force had accelerated very rapidly in the preceding few years; this is a demographic factor different from the change in the composition of the labor force that Gordon has in mind. In a paper published in 1961 John Power points out that if, beginning with an equilibrium situation, the rates of growth of the labor force and the capital stock diverged, unemployment could increase and inflation occur at the same time.[36] This theoretical explanation was written before anyone had thought of stagflation, and it deserves empirical investigation. It might explain increasing shortages of specific capital that may have greatly affected some crucial prices and through them the general price level.

Charles Schultze proposed a conceptual measure of the impact of structural shifts other than those in the labor market. Realizing that certain changes in relative prices were needed to clear markets without inflation of the general price level, he suggested measuring the variance of actual relative prices from those imagined market-clearing relative prices, and then testing the hypothesis that the rate of change in the general price level would be in part a function of that variance, as well as whatever other variables were put into the model. It would be difficult to know how to calculate the variance and such a hypothesis would indicate nothing about the various spirals that might follow from a failure of price relationships to clear the market or about how a change in the variance would affect the length or magnitude of the rate of inflation. But the variance of actual relative prices from the relationships needed to clear markets at zero inflation would explain a large part of the rate of inflation, and notably the difference between the experiences of 1972–74 and 1968–69 in the United States.

Thomas Wilson, referring to Gordon's association of relative price changes with transitory changes in the general price level, thought that, if the oil-exporting countries tried to maintain oil prices permanently at a given relation to the world price level through indexing, the bursting of the transitory bubble would leave some residue in the system that would increase the permanent rate of inflation for any given rate of unemployment.

Assar Lindbeck suggested that Wilson's point—that the rate of Canadian inflation was more influenced by the rate in the United States than by its own macroeconomic policies—could be generalized to some extent. Policymakers in small countries usually believe that inflation is imported from abroad;

---

36. John H. Power, "Laborsaving in Economic Growth," *American Economic Review*, vol. 52 (May 1962, *Papers and Proceedings, 1961*), pp. 39–45.

however, it makes no sense to prevent this happening at the cost of unemployment; the transmission mechanism operates as effectively with low as with high capacity use. Because such inflation cannot be squeezed out by cutting back aggregate demand, more expansionist policies are pursued in small countries than in the large countries. Their only protection against imported inflation is progressive appreciation of exchange rates. Under those circumstances, small countries may as well have high as low use of capacity. In this regard, small countries have a much greater independence in domestic employment policies than large countries.

Fred Bergsten did not agree with Shapiro in doubting that external factors and flexible rates could be blamed for U.S. inflation, because he believed that explanation had some validity. The international monetary system in effect before August 1971 had enabled the United States to avoid importing inflationary impulses during the late 1960s, when the dollar was becoming progressively more overvalued. In August 1971 the United States moved from a system that enabled it to protect itself from imported inflation to one in which it received more inflationary impulses from abroad. It would be interesting to investigate empirically the quantitative importance of the fixity of the dollar exchange rate in enabling the United States, before August 1971, to maintain a rate of inflation below the world average.

Alexander Swoboda pointed out that one reason external influences seemed to have a greater influence on the U.S. price level in recent years was that earlier, with a given monetary policy target and fixed exchange rates, part of the inflationary impulse in the United States spilled over to the rest of the world. But when the fixed-rate system gave way to a flexible-rate system more of that impulse remained bottled up in the American economy. Although one might interpret the change as the result of an increase of foreign inflationary influence under flexible exchange rates, one could also interpret it as involving a decrease in foreign anti-inflationary influence.

According to Lindbeck the traditional distinction between exports and imports was crucial for understanding the role of floating exchange rates in relation to stabilization of the domestic economy. For example, if world prices of both imports and exports rose by 10 percent, a country's exchange rate under a floating system might be expected to appreciate by 10 percent and to shield its economy from world inflation; if import prices rose, however, and the price elasticity were small, the country's balance of payments and the price of its currency would depreciate, aggravating the inflationary impulse. On the other hand, if it were export and not import prices that rose, the currency would appreciate, shielding the economy from the rise in world prices. Whether the floating-rate regime would counteract or exaggerate the external inflation then would depend on whether the terms of trade were deteriorating or improving. In the case of the United States, floating exchange rates exaggerated inflation; not only were domestic inflationary forces bottled up, but floating was begun when the U.S. dollar was overvalued, so that it began to depreciate as soon as it was floated. For another country, movement of the rate toward equilibrium might be in the opposite direction: for example, floating rates meant stabilization for Germany.

Gerhard Fels agreed that an increase of import prices has a deflationary effect when import demand is inelastic, but that is true only when exchange rates are fixed; when they are floating, an increase in import prices with inelastic import demand is inflationary. That explains why floating has had an inflationary effect in the Japanese case, with oil the imported commodity the price of which has risen so steeply and the demand for which is so inelastic.

Harold Shapiro explained that he had not been able to define the monetary environment in his paper; to do so is much more difficult for the 1970s than it is for the 1950s or 1960s, partly because of the development of the Eurodollar markets. The change in the monetary environment is an important factor that deserves more careful analysis; so, too, does the issue of the welfare costs of inflation, about which the paper is indecisive because the problem involves so many unanswered questions.

RYUTARO KOMIYA
YOSHIO SUZUKI

Inflation in Japan

Ryutaro Komiya, University of Tokyo, and Yoshio Suzuki, Bank of Japan, are grateful to staff members of the Economic Research Department of the Bank of Japan, who assisted them greatly in the preparation of the statistical tables. The views expressed in this paper are those of the authors and in no way represent those of the organizations to which they belong.

THIS PAPER attempts to examine the causes of inflation and the relative importance of various factors in the inflationary process. The period under consideration here, 1960 to late 1974, can be divided into three parts. The first, 1960 through 1968 (period I), witnessed a steady and fairly rapid rise in consumer prices, with wholesale prices fluctuating cyclically but remaining quite stable over the period as a whole. The second, 1969 to mid-1972 (period II), saw a "creeping" inflation, in which wholesale and consumer prices rose slightly more than in period I under external inflationary pressures, though the rate of increase in wholesale prices over the period as a whole was very small compared with the rate of increase in other major industrialized countries. Inflation started "galloping" in period III, beginning in the latter half of 1972 and continuing until the end of 1974.

Table 1, which gives a summary of movements in Japanese price indexes, growth rate, and balance of payments, shows that the 1950s, apart from the first few years, saw the most stable prices experienced in postwar Japan. The severe inflation immediately after World War II came to an end around 1950, and the inflationary impact of the Korean War was largely absorbed by 1953. Real income, industrial production, per capita consumption, and other indexes recovered to the prewar level between 1953 and 1955, and it appeared that the Japanese economy was returning to some sort of normalcy. The wholesale price index fluctuated cyclically but remained stable overall during the decade; even the consumer price index was quite flexible and sensitive to business conditions. It continued to rise considerably until 1954, owing to the aftermath of the Korean War boom, but remained stable thereafter until 1959. It was during the fifties that Japan was commented upon as being the only major industrialized country to retain nineteenth century price flexibility.

Table 2 gives a comparison of the rates of inflation of Japan and other major industrialized countries. Until 1972, the rate of increase in Japan's WPI was by far the lowest among the countries compared, whereas its rate of increase in CPI was the highest (except for that of the United Kingdom in 1969–72). The increases in both WPI and CPI in Japan in 1972–74 were among the highest of major industrialized countries.

The fact that until 1972 the rise in WPI was the lowest and the rise in CPI the highest in Japan meant that the annual discrepancy between WPI and CPI was larger for Japan than for any other country. This was a reflection of faster and more extensive structural changes in the pattern of relative prices in Japan, resulting from rapid and widely divergent productivity growth among industries. The rate of growth in real gross national product and the rate of increase in the wage rate in Japan were also the highest among the countries compared. As table 2 shows, both the nominal wage rate and the labor productivity in manufacturing rose rapidly in Japan throughout the whole period under consideration.[1]

Period I: Rising Consumer Prices and Stable Wholesale Prices

From 1960 through 1968, the Japanese economy experienced unprecedented rapid growth and structural changes. The average annual rate of increase in CPI over the period amounted to 5.4 percent. The WPI remained stable, with an average annual rate of increase of only 0.9 percent. The real annual rate of growth of the economy in this period averaged 11.4 percent, substantially higher than in the 1950s.

The balance of payments had often showed a deficit in the 1950s and continued to do so in the first half of period I, constituting one of the most important constraints on economic growth. But it tended to yield more surpluses than deficits toward the end of the period, and ceased to be a constraint on the government's monetary and fiscal policies. The balance of payments indexes in table 1 show that Japan became a net capital exporter after around 1960.

Another characteristic that distinguished this period from the 1950s was a much faster rise in wage rates. The rate of increase in nominal wages in this period was about double that in the later 1950s (see table 3), reflecting the tightening of the labor market. This change in the labor supply situation was one of the basic factors in the rapid and steady rise in consumer prices.

Two major phenomena in the price indexes must be explained. First, it must be asked why there arose such large and persistent discrepancies between the rates of increase of wholesale and consumer prices. Second, since such a large and ever-widening gap between the WPI and the CPI could be compatible with either a stable WPI and a rising CPI, or a stable CPI with a declining WPI, it must be asked why the former existed.

1. Except that in 1973 the wage rate rose slightly more in Italy than in Japan and in 1974 the labor productivity was the lowest in Japan compared with other countries.

The discrepancy between the WPI and the CPI

The reasons why consumer prices rose more than wholesale prices apply not only to period I but also to other periods, as well as to many other countries.

First, goods and services represented by the CPI are more labor-intensive than those represented by the WPI. About one-third of the total weights of the CPI are given to services, most of which are highly labor-intensive (see table 4); none of these services is included in the WPI. Also, perishable foods such as fish, vegetables, and fruits, which are covered by the CPI with far greater weights, are also largely labor-intensive. Among manufactured products the WPI gives much more weight to products of large-scale industries and less to those of small and medium-sized businesses. In fact, the weights in the WPI for products of large firms amount nearly to two-thirds of the total, so that the movement of the WPI is often dominated by the prices of products of large-scale manufacturing industries, which are relatively capital-intensive. The weights given to these products in the CPI are much smaller, whereas the products of labor-intensive small and medium-sized businesses are given greater weight. Moreover, the value added at retail for manufactured and other products implicit in the CPI but not in the WPI are probably more labor-intensive than the goods covered by WPI, on the average.

When the wage rate—that is, the price of labor—rises faster than the prices of other factors of production, even with productivity rising more or less uniformly in various industries, the more labor-intensive CPI is bound to rise relative to WPI. The discrepancy is larger in Japan than in other countries because of its faster annual increase in wages relative to the prices of other factors of production.

In addition to the above general tendency, which is more or less common to other countries, there were two other factors at work in the ever-widening discrepancy between the CPI and WPI in Japan in the period under consideration.

First, the interindustry pattern of technological progress in this period is such that the rise in productivity was heavily concentrated in the large-scale heavy and chemical industries. Productivity in small-business manufacturing, agriculture (especially vegetables and fruits), fishing, services (including not only personal services but also transportation, education, and so forth) and retail trade rose more slowly (see table 5). In order to pay competitive prices to labor and other factors of production, these sectors needed to raise the prices of their products or services relative to the prices of products of large-scale heavy and chemical industries.

Second, wage rates rose faster in small and medium-sized businesses than in large firms (see table 3). It is well known that there has long been, and still is, a large gap between the wage rates of small and medium-sized firms and those of large firms in Japan. As a result of the tightening of the labor market, however, small and medium-sized firms had to raise wages rapidly to attract and keep workers, so the wage differentials between big and small businesses were reduced considerably during this period. As already noted, the WPI largely reflects the prices of products of large-scale manufacturing industries, whereas in the CPI more weight is given to products of small and medium-sized firms as well as to services, a sector in which small firms predominate (see table 4). Thus a faster rise in wages in small and medium-sized businesses than in big business tended to raise the CPI relative to the WPI.[2]

Comparison with the previous period

Why, in view of the persistent tendency of the CPI to rise steadily and considerably relative to the WPI in period I and afterward, was such a trend absent in earlier years? Especially from 1955 through 1959, both indexes remained largely stable, and the discrepancy between their rates of change was almost negligible. The lower rate of growth of the economy and, therefore, slower structural changes appear to have been responsible for this. Also, the labor supply was somewhat more elastic before 1960 than afterward, so that even a relatively small rise in wage rates made it possible to expand employment considerably (see table 3).

The belief that there had existed a pool of surplus labor before 1960, which by that time was absorbed by rapid economic growth, is unfounded. Even before 1960 the annual rise in wage rates was quite substantial according to the standards of other major industrialized countries. In Japan, at least since the mid-1950s, surplus labor was reflected not in a high rate of unemployment but rather in the underutilization of labor in the less productive, low-wage sector, or in the preponderance of low-income proprietors and workers in family-owned agriculture, services, and small manufacturing firms. The mobility of such underutilized labor is low: proprietors and their family members, except those who are newly entering the labor force, are willing to move to higher-productivity sectors only when sufficient incentives are present.

---

2. In period II, when the tendency to narrow wage differentials became less pronounced (see table 3), the discrepancy in the rate of increase between CPI and WPI became somewhat smaller than in period I.

Progressively larger wage increases were necessary to transfer labor from lower-productivity sectors to rapidly growing ones. Especially toward the end of period I, those who still remained in the low-productivity sectors were mostly older people who were more reluctant to move, so that the labor supply became more and more inelastic over time. This necessitated a faster rise in wage rates and faster structural changes in relative prices in period I than in the 1950s.

Flexibility of the WPI

Why, then, did the WPI remain largely stable during period I? In our view, it is because the monetary authorities chose as their policy target balance of payments equilibrium rather than stability of the CPI; since in that period a stable WPI was the only course of price movements compatible with the balance of payments equilibrium, the WPI was stabilized.

Until 1971, the WPI (both the overall average and manufactured products) was subject to cyclical fluctuations: it rose in booms and declined considerably in recessions. The flexibility of the index seems to have been maintained primarily through cyclical movements in the rate of increase in wages and in the price of imports (see the third and fifth columns, table 7).

In Japan a substantial part (from a quarter to one-third) of wages and salaries are bonuses and overtime payments. Bonuses, paid once or twice a year by employers, often amount to several months' salary and are highly dependent on the company's profits and the general business outlook. Overtime work is paid at much higher rates than regular wages and it increases in booms and declines in recessions. Because of the so-called lifetime commitment system, Japanese employers tend to depend on overtime work more heavily than employers in other countries. Moreover, since labor unions are organized on a company-by-company basis, even the annual increase in regular wages and salaries is highly dependent on the company's or industry's profits and on labor market conditions. Thus the labor cost, a major component in the cost of production, is more sensitive to business conditions and fluctuates more cyclically in Japan than in other industrialized countries.

The prices of certain Japanese imports are also quite sensitive to Japanese business conditions (see the third column, table 7). An overwhelmingly large part of Japan's imports consists of raw materials and fuels for industrial production. This was even more true in period I than today, since imports of foodstuffs and consumer goods have been increasing rapidly in recent years. Japan is highly dependent on imports for raw materials and fuels, and its share in world imports of certain raw materials is quite high (see table 6).

Since the amount of Japan's raw material imports is quite sensitive to Japanese business conditions, the import price index goes up during booms and declines in recessions.

It should also be pointed out that, at least until 1970, Japan's domestic as well as export markets were highly competitive. The rate of growth of most industries was high, heavy new investment was undertaken annually, technological changes and innovations were taking place continuously, and new entry was not too difficult in many industries. This appears to be one of the factors that made it possible for prices to remain more flexible in Japan than in other countries.

Effectiveness of monetary policy

In Japan, monetary policy exercises an important and almost determining effect on price movements. This was even more true for period I and earlier than it has been recently. For example, table 8 indicates that the WPI and the GNP deflator respond to changes in the money supply (M_1 or M_2) with a lag of one to three quarters. The correlation coefficient is especially high for years before 1964.

The reasons why monetary policy has been quite effective in influencing price levels can be summarized as follows. (The following applies more to period I than to recent years, but still remains more or less true in Japan today compared with other countries.)

First, large commercial banks (so-called city banks) are normally dependent to a very considerable extent on funds borrowed from the Bank of Japan, and the latter is in a position to exercise discretionary control over commercial banks' lending to their customers as well as over their securities investments. Thus the total amount of the commercial bank credit extended to the private sector can readily be controlled by the Bank of Japan.

Second, the private sector is overwhelmingly the principal recipient of funds supplied by the banking sector in Japan (see table 9), whereas in some other countries, the public sector is much more important as a user of funds. This means that the Bank of Japan can adjust the money supply without much attention to the needs or conditions of the public sector, and thus has more freedom of action for the purpose of monetary policy.

Third, the business sector is much more heavily dependent on funds borrowed from the banking sector in Japan than in other countries (see table 10). Therefore, the change in the rate of money supply from the banking sector affects more directly the level of investment of the business sector. Thus, in a period of monetary tightening, as soon as lending (or its rate of increase) from commercial banks is reduced, the business sector begins to restrain investment in inventories and in plant and equipment (see table 11).

Fourth, business investment constitutes a high proportion of GNP, or of the total of autonomous components of effective demand consisting of government expenditures, exports, and private investment, and is the principal determinant of the cyclical pattern of business fluctuations (see table 12). Thus the changes in commercial banks' lending and in money supply, through their impact on business investment, exert strong influence on the behavior of GNP.

Fifth, the WPI is highly sensitive to the demand-supply conditions of commodity and labor markets and the rate of capacity utilization, which is determined by the course of GNP (see table 13). This is because the commodity markets are generally competitive and wages are sensitive to the business conditions, as explained above.

The pattern of business cycles

Until around 1970, recessions in Japan were caused by the tight money policy demanded by the deterioration of the balance of payments. The typical course of a business cycle in postwar Japan is as follows.

When the balance of payments is not in deficit, the monetary authorities continue to increase money supply, thus sustaining the investment boom and a high rate of growth in GNP. After a while the WPI begins to rise, and this together with the income effect stimulates imports. Manufacturers find the domestic market expanding rapidly so that the growth in exports is halted. Thus during booms the balance of payments deteriorates and turns into deficits, sometimes rather substantial ones.

At this point the monetary authorities decide to tighten money supply, and this is usually the beginning of a recession. Thus every recession shown in table 7 (except the one in 1970:4 to 1971:4) was caused by the monetary tightening following the worsening of the balance of payments. When money supply is tightened—or, more exactly, when the rate of increase in money supply is strongly restrained—the typical pattern is that inventory investment is suppressed, followed by halting of the increase in plant and equipment investment (see table 11); the rate of growth in GNP is then much reduced and the WPI begins to decline (see table 7).

During a recession domestic effective demand is reduced while productive capacity continues to expand as a result of investment in the preceding boom. The rate of capacity utilization, therefore, declines, so manufacturers seek eagerly for overseas markets, and exports rise quickly. This, combined with decreased imports during a recession, causes the balance of payments to improve. When the monetary authorities consider the balance of payments to be sufficiently improved, the tight money policy comes to an end.[3] Once again money is supplied liberally, and a new boom sets in.

The target for monetary policy

Until 1971, the primary target of monetary policy in Japan was balance of payments equilibrium rather than stability in the CPI. The monetary authorities pursued policies compatible with balance of payments equilibrium over the long run and supplied money liberally so long as the balance of payments did not turn into large deficits. As a result, the WPI was stabilized because, roughly speaking, a stable WPI was the only course of price movements compatible with the balance of payments equilibrium until around 1968. In this period, the export and import price indexes and the WPI exhibited very similar movements (see table 7), whereas the CPI, including perishables and services not covered by the WPI, the export, or the import price index, moved divergently.

In the beginning of period I balance of payments equilibrium was barely maintained behind the protective wall of import quotas and other measures restricting payments, and encouraging receipts, of foreign exchange. Thus the fixed exchange rate of ¥360 to a dollar was then an overvalued parity. In view of a gradual rise in the WPI elsewhere in the world, the stability of Japan's WPI made it possible for Japan to remove or relax import quotas and other restrictions without running into balance of payments deficits and to improve the competitiveness of Japanese exports over the period. In order to avoid the balance of payments difficulties in this process of gradual liberalization of import restrictions and exchange controls, it was mandatory, under the fixed exchange rate system, to maintain the stability of the WPI over the long run. In this way the overvaluation of the yen was disappearing toward the end of period I.

The decline in the WPI during recessions was accompanied by a decline in the rate of utilization of productive capacity. In most recessions the index of industrial production and GNP did not decline or declined only slightly; but their rates of growth were substantially reduced (see table 7). Since the potential level of GNP or industrial production was continually pushed up-

3. The role of short-term capital inflows in relieving the balance of payments deficits during this period is another question. Generally speaking, the monetary authorities were reluctant to permit short-term capital inflows even when the balance of payments was in deficit. They viewed such capital inflows as potentially destabilizing and disruptive of the process through which the current-account balance was improved and maintained an elaborate system of stringent exchange controls. The improvement of the current-account balance was considered essential in balance of payments management.

ward by a very high level of investment and by technological progress, a much slower rate of growth in recessions than in booms meant that a certain portion of productive capacity became idle during recessions. In other words, the rate of capacity utilization declined considerably during recessions (see table 13).

Also, although the level of unemployment always remained very low even in recessions, working hours—and hence overtime wage payments—as well as the rate of increase in employment, exhibited cyclical movements. The growth of "regular" employment represents a shift of labor from agriculture and other low-productivity sectors dominated by small proprietors into more productive and remunerative employment.

If prices and wages had been more flexible and labor and other resources more mobile it would have been possible to lower the price level more easily without causing as much underutilization of productive capacity as occurred in past recessions. But because of various degrees of rigidity in prices and wages and of immobility of labor and other resources, some decline in the rate of capacity utilization was unavoidable in order to lower the price level. Thus in period I as well as in period II there was a trade-off between the average rate of utilization of productive capacity over the long run and the degree of price stability. In this situation the monetary authorities chose to stabilize the WPI in period I.

It might have been possible to stabilize the CPI with a downward tendency in the WPI, if the money supply had been increased more slowly. But it would probably have meant a lower level of investment, somewhat shorter booms and more prolonged recessions, and slower growth of the economy. Also, the balance of payments would have yielded chronic surpluses much earlier. Thus it appears that the monetary authorities judged it advisable to give priority to faster economic growth over the stability of the CPI and to continue to supply money unless the balance of payments turned into deficits.

Period II: Creeping Inflation under the Balance of Payments Surplus

The period from 1969 to mid-1972 is more or less a continuation of period I. The average annual rate of increase in the CPI and WPI was only slightly higher than in the previous period. The rate of growth in real GNP declined slightly from period I, due mainly to a monetary tightening in 1967–68, but the rise in wage rates was higher, reflecting tighter labor market conditions.

But an important difference is the large surplus in the balance of payments every year, caused primarily by faster inflation abroad. Thus Japan's balance of payments was in fundamental disequilibrium in the surplus direction. The tight money policy of September 1967 to August 1968 was the last undertaken to overcome the balance of payments deficit. After the second half of 1968, Japan's balance of payments exhibited continuous and substantial surpluses, at the fixed exchange rate of ¥360 to the dollar. Thus the balance of payments equilibrium could no longer be the target for monetary policy, as it had long been in postwar Japan.

Inflationary pressures from abroad

The balance of payments disequilibrium in the surplus direction during period II exerted inflationary pressures upon the Japanese economy. There were three ways in which inflation abroad was imported into Japan.

First, inflation abroad improved the competitiveness of Japanese exports and worked to increase both their volume and prices. The proportion of exports in autonomous effective demand, such as government expenditures and business investment (see table 12), or the share of exports in the annual increase in GNP (see table 15) rose substantially during period II. The multiplier effect made exports an important source of the rise in the total effective demand. But exports were still a much smaller share of the whole than business investment or government expenditures.

Second, the import price index rose 2.3 percent in 1969 and 3.3 percent in 1970 (see table 15). Even though a rise in prices of imports for which the demand elasticity is low can exert a deflationary effect upon domestic production if it is not supported by a monetary expansion, the rise in import prices of raw materials has a cost-push effect, like an aggressive wage hike, and its impact upon the domestic price level is likely to be inflationary.

Third, the share of the total supply of "high-powered money" represented by money supply resulting from the increase in official reserves—that is, from the purchases of foreign exchange assets by the monetary authorities— amounted to 42.2 percent in 1969 and 54.1 percent in 1970. In 1971, the year of the international monetary crisis, the ratio went up to 518.7 percent: this large amount of high-powered money was supplied through a huge balance of payments surplus, and the monetary policy had to absorb most of it through other means (see tables 15 and 22).

Monetary tightening under the surplus balance of payments

Under the pressures of imported inflation, the domestic price level rose substantially in 1969 and 1970. In particular, the increases in both WPI and

CPI in 1970 were the highest ever experienced since the latter half of the 1950s (table 1).

From September 1969 to October 1970, for the first time in postwar Japan a tight money policy was adopted when the balance of payments was in surplus for the purpose of stabilizing the domestic prive level.[4] There followed international complaints that the Japanese government was acting destructively toward international monetary stability. The rise in the WPI was halted in May 1970 and declined thereafter to a low in January 1972. The rise in the CPI was also somewhat arrested in 1971–72; the quarterly rate of increase was the lowest in the last quarter of 1971 and the first quarter of 1972 (see table 17). Thereafter, the rate of price increase over period II as a whole remained at a level more or less comparable with that of the creeping inflation in period I.

Revaluation of the yen in 1971

The recession and the slowing down of the pace of inflation in 1971–72 were initiated by the tight money policy of 1969–70, but the main depressive force in the latter half of 1971 was the revaluation of the yen.

When the large balance of payments surpluses in 1970 and the first half of 1971 awakened expectations of a revaluation of the yen, and when the yen was finally revalued in August 1971, many predicted that Japan's exports would decline substantially. In fact, exports were not affected as much as was feared, but revaluation of the yen gave rise to a pervasive feeling of uncertainty about the general business outlook; many businessmen and government officials expected a rather severe and prolonged recession to follow the revaluation. The decline in exports and slackening business investment caused the rate of capacity utilization to decline substantially in 1971 and 1972. Both the WPI and the import price index declined following the yen revaluation. The latter declined most drastically in the last quarter of 1971 and the first quarter of 1972 (see table 17), partly because of the rise in the external value of the yen, and contributed substantially to the decline in the WPI.

It is clear in retrospect that the yen should have been revalued much earlier to prevent such external inflationary pressures from being imported into Japan. In fact, quite a few academic economists had been advocating revaluation since long before August 1971. A moderate revaluation of the yen or a

4. The tight money policy undertaken in 1960, when the balance of payments was also in surplus, was different, because the monetary authorities intended only to prevent deterioration of the balance of payments in advance, and the implicit objective was still balance of payments equilibrium.

shift to a floating exchange rate system in 1969 or 1970 would have made it much easier to achieve price stability over this period.

Nevertheless, several circumstances made it possible to maintain a reasonable degree of stability in WPI in the face of substantial surpluses in the balance of payments. First, the share of exports in the GNP was still only about half that of business investment (see table 12), so that when business investment was restrained by a tight money policy, the demand-supply condition in the domestic market was slackened. Second, the effect of the changing demand-supply condition in the domestic market on the WPI seems to have been much more powerful in this period than that of the rising costs of imports: in fact, it was the main deflationary agent, especially in 1971, counteracting the cost-push effect of rising wages (see table 16). Moreover, since the impact of Japanese business conditions on the world markets for certain commodities is considerable, the slackening demand-supply condition in Japan induced the import price of such commodities to decline, thus reducing to some extent the pressure of imported inflation. During the twelve months preceding the yen revaluation in August 1971, the import price index rose only 0.5 percent. Third, until the middle of 1971, since the share of the increase in official reserves in the total supply of high-powered money was no more than about half, the total money supply could be readily controlled by the monetary authorities.

Period III: Galloping Inflation

From the last quarter of 1972 through 1974, the WPI rose at an annual rate of at least 10 percent in every quarter and at a much higher rate in many; the CPI also rose continuously since the first quarter of 1973, at a rate even higher than 10 percent. This constitutes galloping inflation, unprecedented for the Japanese economy since around 1950. The rate of inflation accelerated until the first quarter of 1974, and was especially high during the months of the oil crisis in late 1973 and early 1974 (see table 17). The sources of this inflation were both external and domestic.

Impact of external inflationary pressures

THE RISING COSTS OF IMPORTS. From the last quarter of 1972, the import price index (in terms of the yen) rose continuously at annual rates exceeding 20 percent (except in the second quarter of 1973). The exchange rate of the yen remained at approximately ¥300 to the dollar in the latter half of 1972, and moved upward to ¥265 under the floating system after February 1973. After the oil crisis, the yen depreciated gradually, and declined as far as ¥300 for a short period in January 1974. But it recovered soon to ¥285 to 290 and remained largely in that range until May. It then depreciated once again and fluctuated around the rate of ¥300 to a dollar. This means that for the period from the last quarter of 1972 to the second quarter of 1973 the rise in import prices in terms of the dollar is about 12 percent more than indicated in table 17, whereas for the subsequent period only a very small part of the rise in the import price index is accounted for by depreciation of the yen. Over period III as a whole, the change in the yen exchange rate was a dampening factor, the dollar prices of Japan's imports in the world market having risen more rapidly than the Japanese import price index (see table 18).

Among imports, foodstuffs, textile materials, lumber, hides and skins, and scrap iron registered the highest price increase prior to the oil crisis; after the crisis, the price of crude oil rose most markedly (see table 20). The rise in the prices of these commodities seems to have been caused to a considerable extent by export restrictions on the part of exporting countries (see table 19). In view of Japan's significance in the world market as a major importer of some of these commodities, the business recovery in Japan since the beginning of 1972 and the increasing Japanese demand for imports may partly account for the rise in the import prices.

The direct effect of the rise in the import price index on the WPI amounted to 1.6 percent for 1973 and 3.7 percent for the first half of 1974 (against total increases of 15.9 percent and 17.8 percent, respectively). But if indirect effects through increased costs of production or even through the rises in the cost of living and in wage rates were included, the inflationary impact of the rising cost of imports would have been much greater.[5]

According to another estimate (see table 21), based on input-output analysis, the oil price increase between October 1973 and February 1974 should have raised the WPI by 7.3 percent. Since indirect effects through the rises in the cost of living and in wage rates are ignored in this estimate, and since the CIF (cost, insurance, freight) price of crude oil import continued to rise after February 1974, the total effects (including rises in the prices of intermediate products, electricity, gas, transportation costs, and wages) could have been much larger.

5. The magnitude of indirect effects depends on the assumptions used for estimation. According to an estimate prepared by the Bank of Japan (see table 16), the direct and indirect effects of the rising costs of imports accounted for 4.1 percent in 1973 and 9.4 percent in the first half of 1974 of the rise in the WPI; that is, about one-quarter to one-half of the total increase is attributable to imports.

THE MULTIPLIER EFFECT OF EXPORTS. In a typical situation of imported inflation the increase in exports under a fixed exchange rate expands domestic effective demand through the multiplier effect. Also, the rise in the international prices of goods competing with the exports of the country in question has an inflationary effect on the domestic price level. This propagation process through exports occurred in Japan only to a limited extent in period II, however, and even then the increase in exports was not the leading factor in expanding the total effective demand.

In period III, when Japan was experiencing galloping inflation, the increase in exports accounted for a very small part of the increase in effective demand (see table 15). Under the Smithsonian agreement in December 1971, the yen was revalued by about 17 percent, and when the yen shifted to the floating system in 1973 the effect was to revalue it again approximately by 16 percent, and it remained at a level about 35 percent above the pre-1971 parity until it began to depreciate as a result of the oil crisis. Expansion of Japan's exports, which had proceeded at a very high pace since the latter part of period I, was halted in 1972–73, and after the beginning of 1973 the balance of payments was continuously in deficit.

Furthermore, after the second quarter of 1972, when the WPI began to rise after a decline following the yen revaluation in 1971, its rate of increase in each quarter exceeded that of the export price index for two years, with the exception of the last quarter of 1973 and the second quarter of 1974 (see table 17). In other words, export prices were lagging behind wholesale prices to a considerable extent throughout 1972–73. This suggests that the demand-pull inflationary pressures from the rising world prices of Japanese exports were largely absent in period III.

THE LIQUIDITY EFFECT OF THE EXTERNAL BALANCE. In 1971 the incremental supply of high-powered money resulting from the increase in official reserves amounted to ¥4,400 billion, which was about five times the total increase in high-powered money during that year. In 1972 it amounted to ¥1,700 billion, or almost 90 percent of the total increase (see table 22). High-powered money supplied in this way was added to the credit base of the banking sector and undoubtedly expanded its capacity for credit creation.

The liquidity effect of the balance of payments surpluses in 1971 and 1972 was counteracted by other forces, however. In both years a large amount of high-powered money—¥2,000 billion and ¥1,800 billion, respectively—was absorbed through the government sector. This was due partly to surpluses in the general budget and partly to an unexpectedly high rate of increase in savings deposits received by the postal savings system. In 1971 contraction of the Bank of Japan's lending to commercial banks was also an important counteracting factor. On the other hand, in 1972 the Bank of Japan's increased lending added to the supply of liquidity.

In 1973, however, the balance of payments turned into a huge deficit, and the external balance was no longer a positive factor in the supply of liquidity to the economy: it was an important contractionary factor. The Bank of Japan's purchases of bonds and bills took over as the leading source of liquidity supply.

After the beginning of 1971 money supply continued to increase at a very high rate throughout 1971, 1972, and the first half of 1973. As table 17 shows, from the beginning of 1971 the annual rate of increase in M_2 surpassed 20 percent in every quarter until the third quarter of 1973. The Marshallian k went up substantially as a result; in other words, the velocity of circulation of money was substantially reduced.

Table 22 summarizes the ways in which such a rapid and continuous expansion of the money supply took place. The expansion taking place in 1971 may be considered to be caused by the liquidity effect of the external surplus, as already noted. But in 1971, it was offset by the absorption of liquidity through the government sector, and in 1973, because of the huge deficits in the balance of payments, changes in the official holdings of foreign exchange turned into a conspicuous negative factor in the liquidity supply. The increase in money supply in 1972 and 1973 was due to a discretionary expansion of the Bank of Japan's credit—namely its lending to commercial banks and purchases of bonds and bills. For 1971–73 as a whole, the supply of high-powered money through the increase in official reserves was exactly offset by the absorption of funds by the government sector (see the last column of table 22), and the total increase in money supply over the period is entirely accounted for by the credit expansion of the Bank of Japan (tables 22 and 23).

The Bank of Japan lowered the bank rate five times in 1971–72: in January, May, July, and December 1971 and in June 1972. Thus easy money characterizes the monetary policy of the Bank of Japan in this period. It turned to monetary tightening in 1973, but real tightening was begun only from the third quarter of 1973. It may be concluded, therefore, that the rapid and continuous increase in money supply during period III was caused not by the liquidity effect of the external surpluses but by the discretionary easy money policy pursued by the monetary authorities.

Inflationary pressures from domestic sources

EASY MONEY POLICY. When the yen was first floated and then revalued in 1971, the Japanese economy was still in a recession, and many feared the depressive effect of the revaluation. The ¥360 rate had not been altered since

1949, when Japan established a single official exchange rate for the first time after the war. For most Japanese the revaluation meant a venture into a highly uncertain world. It was expected by many, including those who based their prediction on sophisticated econometric models, that Japan's exports would decline substantially following the revaluation.

After the Smithsonian agreement an easy money policy was called for in order to counteract the deflationary impact of the yen revaluation and to stimulate domestic effective demand. It was also thought that easy money would increase imports, thus helping to reduce the balance of payments surplus.

The pace of recovery from the 1970–71 recession accelerated in the latter half of 1972, and the WPI began to rise appreciably during the fourth quarter. It was then thought that a shift to an at least mildly restrictive monetary policy was in order. However, several circumstances made the monetary authorities hesitate: the monthly balance of payments was again recording large surpluses from the middle of 1972, and it was thought that monetary tightening would work destructively against international cooperation if Japan followed a tighter monetary policy, it would work against international cooperative efforts to maintain the realigned multilateral monetary system.[6] Also, in late 1972 the Diet was deliberating an annual supplementary budget bill, the size of which was fairly large. Heated discussions were going on between the government and the opposition parties about whether the supplementary budget would give rise to a strong inflationary pressure. The monetary authorities did not want to take tightening measures until the deliberation of the budget bill was over, in order to remain politically neutral.

The reserve requirements were raised in January 1973 as a step toward shifting to a tight money policy. In February the yen was floated, which in effect meant a revaluation up to the rate of ¥265 to the dollar. The monetary authorities wanted an opportunity to observe the depressive effects of floating the yen, which had by then been appreciated by more than 35 percent above the old parity before August 1971. It soon became evident that the immediate depressive effects were not significant. By that time a rapid increase in wholesale prices was already gaining momentum. The bank rate was raised in April and a series of restrictive measures was adopted.

It is now clear that the shift to tight money occurred much too late. Also, the yen should have been floated much earlier, say, in the early autumn of 1972. Unfortunately, in the critical years of 1971–73 both the pace of infla-

6. It should be noted that although the Ministry of Finance and the Bank of Japan cooperate closely with each other on monetary and exchange policies, the final responsibility for the money supply rests with the Bank of Japan, that for the exchange rate with the Ministry of Finance.

tion abroad and the dynamic power of recovery of the Japanese economy were underestimated. Few expected that investment in plant and equipment would rise after the yen revaluation at such a fast pace as it did. Until late 1972 many feared a prolonged depression resulting from a decline in exports and in investment much more than they feared inflation.

HIGH LEVEL OF LIQUIDITY AND ITS CONSEQUENCES. A major part of the increased money supply supported by the easy money policy in 1971–72 was channeled primarily toward small and medium-sized corporations and proprietors and households (see table 24), whereas before the revaluation increased money supply was channeled primarily toward the large manufacturing corporations that were engaged more actively in exports. As a result the business sector as a whole maintained an unusually high level of liquidity (see table 25). Households also had a high level of liquidity, partly through housing loans and partly through sales of land and stocks to the corporate sector.

The high level of liquidity thus created gave rise to strong inflationary pressures in 1972–73. First, the high level of liquidity expedited an unexpectedly quick recovery in 1972. Plant and equipment investment by small and medium-sized businesses, especially those in nonmanufacturing sectors, housing construction, and household consumption, played a leading role in this recovery in the latter half of 1972. Second, the large firms in manufacturing and certain other industries used their surplus funds to purchase land and stocks, causing these prices to rise sharply in 1972. This aroused inflationary expectations among the public. Third, the rise in world prices of lumber, cereals, natural textile materials, and some other raw materials that occurred from the fall of 1972 generated speculative movements. Such developments spread in Japan to certain intermediate products such as steel, textiles, and some food products in the spring of 1973. The high level of liquidity in the business sector facilitated speculative purchases of raw materials and intermediate products, bringing about speculative price increases.

As noted above, the money supply was increased at an unusually high pace throughout 1971, 1972, and the first half of 1973, which resulted, not surprisingly, in an increase in expenditures and in the prices of some commodities. It appears from table 8 that the time lag between increased money supply and the rise in prices was somewhat greater in period III than earlier. But the rapidly increasing money supply under the conditions prevailing in Japan in the early seventies is bound to result in an eventual rise in price levels.

INCREASED GOVERNMENT EXPENDITURES AND TAX REDUCTION. Another important factor in the quick recovery in 1972–73 and the tightening of the demand-supply condition was the high level of government expenditures and the income tax reduction. In earlier booms and recessions, government expenditures tended to fluctuate in a countercyclical way (see table 14). In the upswing of 1972–73, however, government expenditures continued to increase at a very high rate, almost as high as in the preceding recession, when all other major components of effective demand were increasing rapidly. In addition, reduction in the personal income tax amounting to ¥407 billion (the biggest tax cut till then) was put into force in late 1971, and its expansionary effects were felt through 1972–73.

The government was then under strong pressure from various political groups demanding increased expenditures as well as the tax reduction. Investment in social overhead capital and housing, expansion of public welfare programs, improvement of the national social security system, and reduction in the personal income tax were considered as urgent tasks for the government. The fear that the yen revaluation would cause a prolonged recession helped to loosen the government's purse strings.

RESTRICTIVE BEHAVIOR ON THE SUPPLY SIDE. Thus an extremely easy money policy and increasing government expenditures brought about a rapid expansion in effective demand throughout 1972 and 1973, but the supply side did not respond to rising demand as smoothly as in earlier booms. The level of capacity utilization in 1973 is estimated to have been about as low as in 1966 or 1971 (table 13), but the real output did not expand as elastically as it had in the past (table 26). There were several reasons for this.

First, during the preceding recession of 1970–72, manufacturers in major industries producing basic industrial raw materials such as iron and steel, chemicals, and paper and pulp enacted the so-called depression cartels. These cartels are exempted from the general prohibition of cartels under the antitrust law, when approved by the Fair Trade Commission. Although depression cartels are not new in Japan, many of them enacted during the 1970–72 recession were allowed to restrict production and thereby to support prices until very lately: most of them were in force until the last quarter of 1972, when the recovery was already in full swing (see table 27). Thus the supply of certain key commodities was artificially and unnecessarily restricted throughout 1972. Second, the recovery was led by public investment, housing construction, and plant and equipment investment in nonmanufacturing sectors, as already noted. The price of products closely related to these components of effective demand rose substantially, as a result of a bottleneck situation in the industries producing such products (see table 28). Third, apart from officially approved depression cartels, various types of restrictive behavior or factors caused the supply to respond only sluggishly in the face of increased demand. The shortage of resources on a worldwide scale, antipollution limitations on the operation of plant capacity, difficulties in finding new plant locations because of antipollution laws, and the shortage of labor were among the factors responsible for the sluggish supply response. Also, these factors often contributed to oligopolistic, anticompetitive behavior in industries dominated by a small number of firms, which had previously been relatively competitive. Finally, export restrictions by countries exporting industrial raw materials contributed to the supply lag (see table 19).

WAGE-PUSH. An aggressive wage-push by labor unions did not play an active role in the galloping inflation that developed in late 1972. In fact, wage costs in manufacturing did not rise appreciably until the first quarter of 1974 (see tables 16 and 30). In the annual spring offensive in 1974, the wage base of large firms was raised on the average by 32.9 percent, but this wage hike did not represent an aggressive wage-push.

The galloping inflation of period III in Japan is primarily of the demand-pull type, although a cost-push from rising prices of imports played an important role. In this inflationary process large excess profits had been earned by corporations and independent proprietors. The wage hikes in the springs of 1973 and 1974, shown in table 31, although unusually large, were primarily in order to recover the share of wages (and salaries) in the value added. Without a large wage hike not only the labor share in national income but also the real wage would have declined considerably in view of rapidly rising costs of living.

The ex post rate of increase in the per capita wage in 1974 was considerably below the rate of the wage hike negotiated and agreed upon in the spring offensive. Under monetary tightening industry was subjected to a rather severe profit squeeze. Bonuses and overtime payments were reduced, especially in small and medium-sized businesses.

Propagation process from the WPI to the CPI

So far the analysis has concentrated on the WPI, since it is through the WPI that inflation is felt in the CPI and the GNP deflator. But, as noted above, in contemporary Japan the WPI and the CPI exhibit a tendency to diverge steadily, the latter rising relative to the former. A faster rise in the WPI than in the CPI in 1973, experienced for the first time since the mid-1950s, was caused by strong pressures concentrated first on the WPI, which then propagated to the CPI.

According to an estimate prepared by the Bank of Japan, of the 11.7 percent rise in the CPI in 1973, 3.7 percent may be accounted for by the rise in wholesale prices of manufactured goods, and 2.6 percent by the rise in prices of agricultural products (see table 29). About 5.0 percent may be considered as the normal trend in the CPI when the WPI is stable, so that the part attributable to the rise in the WPI represents a very substantial proportion of the increase. Thus it can be concluded that the factors identified above as causing the rise in the WPI are also responsible for the rise in the CPI, and therefore the galloping inflation in period III.

Tables

Table 1. *Annual Changes in Prices, Wages, Rate of Growth, and the Balance of Payments, Japan, 1953–74*

	Wholesale price index (percent)	Consumer price index (percent)	Nominal wages (percent)	Rate of growth in real GNP (percent)[a]	Balance of payments (millions of U.S. dollars)	
					Current account	Basic balance
1953	0.7	6.7	15.3	5.7	−205	−343
1954	−0.7	6.5	6.5	6.4	−51	−1
1955	−1.8	−1.1	5.1	8.6	227	228
1956	4.4	0.4	7.8	8.3	−34	39
1957	3.0	3.1	4.6	8.2	−620	−579
1958	−6.5	−0.4	2.9	5.3	264	354
1959	1.0	1.1	6.0	9.3	361	414
1953–59[b]	−0.1	2.3	6.8	7.3	−8	16
1960	1.1	3.5	7.0	14.0	143	89
1961	1.0	5.4	11.2	15.6	−982	−993
1962	−1.6	6.8	10.3	6.6	−49	124
1963	1.8	7.5	10.7	10.2	−779	−313
1964	0.2	3.8	9.9	14.0	−480	−373
1965	0.8	7.7	9.7	4.6	932	517
1966	2.4	5.0	10.8	10.1	1,254	446
1967	1.8	4.0	11.9	13.5	−190	−1,002
1968	0.9	5.3	13.5	14.2	1,048	809
1960–68[b]	0.9	5.4	10.5	11.4	100	77
1969	2.1	5.4	15.6	12.1	2,119	1,964
1970	3.7	7.9	17.1	10.6	1,970	379
1971	−0.8	6.2	14.7	6.8	5,797	4,715
1972	0.8	4.6	15.9	8.7	6,624	2,137
1969–72[b]	1.4	6.0	15.8	9.5	4,128	2,299
1973	15.9	11.7	21.7	10.2	−136	−9,886
1974	31.3	24.5	26.3	−1.8	−4,693	−8,574
1973–74[b]	23.4	17.9	24.0	4.0	−2,415	−9,230

Sources: The Bank of Japan, *Economic Statistics Annual*, various issues; Economic Planning Agency, *Annual Report on National Income Statistics*, various issues.
a. Real GNP in 1965 prices.
b. Average.

Table 2. *International Comparison of Prices, Wages, and Productivity, 1960–74*

Percent

Item	Japan	United States	United Kingdom	West Germany	France	Italy
Wholesale price index						
Average annual increase, 1960–68	0.9	0.9	2.4	1.4	1.6	1.8
Average annual increase, 1969–72	1.4	3.8	6.2	4.0	6.2	4.7
Change from previous year, 1973	15.9	13.8	7.3	6.7	14.7	17.0
Change from previous year, 1974	31.3	18.8	23.4	13.2	29.2	40.3
Consumer price index						
Average annual increase, 1960–68	5.4	2.0	3.3	2.4	3.6	3.8
Average annual increase, 1969–72	6.0	4.7	7.1	4.0	5.8	4.5
Change from previous year, 1973	11.7	6.2	9.2	6.8	7.3	10.8
Change from previous year, 1974	24.5	11.0	16.1	7.0	13.6	19.2
Nominal wages (manufacturing)						
Average annual increase, 1960–68	10.9	3.6	6.5	8.1	7.6	8.1
Average annual increase, 1969–72	15.9	6.1	12.3	10.9	11.3	10.8
Change from previous year, 1973	23.6	7.1	12.5	10.1	12.4	24.3
Change from previous year, 1974[a]	26.5	(9.0)	(18.4)	(12.0)	(20.5)	(20.1)
Labor productivity (manufacturing)[b]						
Average annual increase, 1960–68	8.2	3.6	3.0	4.8	5.3	6.5
Average annual increase, 1969–72	8.3	3.3	4.6	4.6	7.5	0.9
Change from previous year, 1973	17.4	4.0	8.0	7.4	2.7	8.0
Change from previous year, 1974[a]	(−2.0)	(−0.6)	(0.6)	(1.4)	(3.0)	(−1.6)

Sources: Organisation for Economic Co-operation and Development, *Main Economic Indicators*, various issues; the Bank of Japan, *Economic Statistics Annual*, various issues.

a. Figures in parentheses are changes from the third quarter of 1973 to the third quarter of 1974.

b. For Japan: ratio of manufacturing production index to employment index of manufacturing industries. For the remaining countries: ratio of mining and manufacturing production index to employment index of manufacturing industries.

Table 3. *Selected Labor Indicators, Japan, 1955–73*
Percent, unless otherwise indicated

Year	Number of regular employees[a] (change from previous year)	Working hours (change from previous year)	Demand-supply ratio of labor[b]	Nominal wages (change from previous year)		Wages, by size of establishment (manufacturing)			Gap between CPI and WPI[d]
				Total[c]	Regular payments	Large businesses (change from previous year)	Small businesses (change from previous year)	Wage differential: small-business as a percent of large-business	
1955	2.4	0.2	n.a.	5.2	4.9	5.5	4.5	58.8	0.7
1956	6.9	2.4	0.33	7.8	5.0	11.6	6.3	56.1	-4.0
1957	10.4	-0.1	0.39	4.6	2.7	4.7	4.1	56.0	0.1
1958	6.3	-0.7	0.32	2.9	4.0	3.4	2.2	54.7	6.1
1959	10.5	1.2	0.44	6.0	4.5	6.3	9.4	56.1	0.1
Average, 1955–59	7.2	0.6	0.37	5.3	4.2	6.3	5.4	56.3	0.6

1960	13.7	1.5	0.59	7.0	4.9	6.3	10.9	58.9	2.4
1961	11.7	−1.3	0.74	11.2	9.3	8.5	14.4	61.7	4.3
1962	8.7	−1.8	0.63	10.4	10.1	6.0	15.0	66.7	8.4
1963	5.9	−0.7	0.70	10.7	9.7	9.2	13.1	68.8	5.7
1964	6.0	−0.3	0.80	9.9	11.3	10.3	10.8	69.5	3.6
1965	3.2	−1.4	0.64	9.6	8.9	7.4	9.2	71.0	6.9
1966	2.7	0.1	0.74	10.9	10.0	12.5	10.6	69.8	2.6
1967	3.6	−0.1	1.00	11.9	11.4	13.7	11.7	67.7	3.2
1968	3.9	−0.3	1.12	13.5	12.5	13.9	15.9	68.9	4.4
Average, 1960–68	6.5	−0.5	0.78	10.5	9.8	9.7	12.3	67.0	4.8
1969	3.7	−1.6	1.30	15.6	13.5	15.9	16.7	69.6	3.3
1970	3.8	−0.8	1.41	17.1	16.4	17.1	17.5	69.6	4.2
1971	1.9	−1.1	1.12	14.7	14.7	13.4	14.0	69.9	7.0
1972	0.4	−0.5	1.16	15.9	15.6	15.3	15.1	69.7	3.8
1973	0.8	−0.9	1.75	21.7	18.7	23.9	24.9	70.3	−4.2
Average, 1969–73	2.1	−0.9	1.35	16.9	15.8	17.1	17.6	69.8	2.9

Sources: The Bank of Japan, *Economic Statistics Annual*, various issues; Ministry of Labor, *Monthly Labor Survey*, various issues.

n.a. Not available.

a. Includes those employed on a permanent basis or for a fixed period of one month or longer, those who worked eighteen days a month or more for the last two months, and full-time directors.

b. Ratio of job offers in the year plus job offers carried over from the previous year to job seekers in the year plus job seekers carried over from the previous year.

c. Includes bonuses and overtime payments.

d. Rate of increase (or decrease) during the year in the consumer price index minus the rate of increase (or decrease) during the year in the wholesale price index.

Table 4. *Distribution of Weights in the Consumer Price Index and the Wholesale Price Index, Japan, 1965 and 1970*

Industry	CPI		WPI	
	1965	1970	1965	1970
Goods	69.50	67.92	100.00	100.00
Manufacturing industries	45.05	46.52	82.00	85.53
Large businesses	n.a.	22.62	59.56	63.32
Small businesses	n.a.	23.90	20.96	20.09
Imports	...	...	1.48	2.12
Nonmanufacturing industries	24.45	21.40	18.00	14.47
Services	30.50	32.08	...	...
Total	100	100	100	100

Source: The Bank of Japan, *Economic Statistics Annual*, various issues.
n.a. Not available.

Table 5. *Increase in Labor Productivity in Japan, by Industry, 1960–73*[a]
Percent

Industry	Average annual increase		
	1960–64	1965–69	1970–73
Manufacturing	9.5	12.4	11.3
Machinery	11.2	15.3	12.8
Iron and steel	13.2	15.4	13.6
Chemicals	10.7	13.9	12.9
Services	−1.1	3.6	4.7
Retail trade	1.5	2.7	5.7

Sources: Japan Productivity Center, *Quarterly Journal of Productivity Statistics*, various issues; Ministry of Finance, *Financial Statements of Corporations*, various issues.
a. Labor productivity is computed as follows: for manufacturing, ratio of manufacturing production index to employment index in the industry; for services, ratio of sales in the service sector divided by the consumer price index to number of employees in service sector; for retail trade, ratio of retail trade sales divided by the CPI to number of employees in retail trade.

Table 6. *Japan's Share in World Imports, Selected Commodities, 1960s*
Percent

Period	Lumber and logs	Wool	Rawhide
Average, 1961–63	...	17.7	...
Average, 1964–66	37.0	19.4	...
1967	45.6	...	22.5
1968	47.4	...	23.4
1969	47.5	...	24.8
Average, 1967–69	...	22.0	...
1970[a]	48.6	24.2	...

Source: The Bank of Japan, *The Japanese Economy in 1972*.
a. Estimates.

Table 7. *Cyclical Flexibility of the Wholesale Price Index and Related Statistics in Japan (Seasonally Adjusted), 1956–74*
Percent (annual rate of change)

| Period | Phase of cycle | Wholesale price index | | Import prices | Export prices | Nominal wages | Real gross national product | Production index (mining and manu-facturing) | Rate of capacity utilization (manu-facturing) |
		All com-modities	Manu-factured goods						
1956:1–1957:1	Upswing	7.1	7.3	3.6	3.2	6.4	5.5	23.3	7.4
1957:2–1958:4	Downswing	−5.3	−6.4	−10.4	−8.0	3.8	7.4	3.7	−6.8
1959:1–1959:4	Upswing	4.4	5.4	1.3	8.8	7.0	9.5	27.3	13.7
1960:1–1960:4	"Minirecession"	−1.2	−2.0	−4.0	−4.7	6.9	15.9	21.5	2.1
1961:1–1961:3	Upswing	2.8	1.6	3.9	−3.6	14.5	13.9	20.1	4.1
1961:4–1962:4	Downswing	−2.2	−2.5	−3.7	−2.5	8.5	6.1	3.7	−8.1
1963:1–1963:4	Upswing	3.2	2.5	6.5	3.7	12.5	14.6	20.8	7.0
1964:1–1965:3	Downswing	0.0	−0.4	−1.8	−0.1	9.1	8.0	6.4	−2.8
1965:4–1967:4	Upswing	2.2	1.5	0.8	0.3	11.9	11.9	17.7	7.8
1968:1–1968:2	"Minirecession"	−0.4	−0.6	−2.4	0.2	14.4	13.0	13.3	0.0
1968:3–1970:3	Upswing	2.7	2.9	2.5	3.4	16.1	12.4	14.8	−0.4
1970:4–1971:4	Downswing	−1.0	−1.3	−2.2	−0.4	13.8	6.2	1.6	−4.6
1972:1–1974:2	Upswing	18.3	17.2	30.7	14.2	22.9	4.9	9.2	0.0

Sources: The Bank of Japan, *Basic Data for Economic Analysis: Seasonally Adjusted by the U.S. Census Method II. X-11*, various issues; the Bank of Japan, *Economic Statistics Annual*, various issues.

Table 8. *Correlation Coefficients of Changes in M_1 and M_2 Outstanding to Changes in the Wholesale Price Index and GNP Deflator,[a] 1957–73*

Price index,[a] money supply,[b] and period calculated	Quarters lagged after change in money supply				
	0	1	2	3	4
	Wholesale price index				
M_1					
1957:2 to 1964:4	0.718	0.825	0.702	0.399	0.030
1965:1 to 1970:4	0.392	0.639	0.539	0.231	−0.136
1971:1 to 1973:4	0.017	0.330	0.326	0.168	−0.062
M_2					
1957:2 to 1964:4	0.501	0.757	0.707	0.440	0.060
1965:1 to 1970:4	0.537	0.694	0.500	0.144	−0.242
1971:1 to 1973:4	−0.131	0.445	0.617	0.624	0.623
	Gross national product deflator				
M_1					
1957:2 to 1964:4	0.577	0.815	0.740	0.559	0.368
1965:1 to 1970:4	0.511	0.702	0.772	0.652	0.467
1971:1 to 1973:4	−0.392	0.121	0.518	0.460	0.119
M_2					
1957:2 to 1964:4	0.375	0.663	0.666	0.509	0.320
1965:1 to 1970:4	0.616	0.803	0.782	0.554	0.293
1971:1 to 1973:4	−0.552	0.047	0.589	0.703	0.605

Sources: The Bank of Japan, *Economic Statistics Annual*; Economic Planning Agency, *Annual Report on National Income Statistics.*
a. Data are rates of change of a weighted moving average (1:2:1), seasonally adjusted.
b. M_1 represents currency and demand deposits; M_2 currency plus demand and time deposits.

Table 9. *Components of Annual Rate of Increase in Money and Quasi-Money in Major Countries, 1956–73*

Country and component	Average, 1956–60	Average, 1961–65	Average, 1966–70	1971	1972	1973
Japan						
Amount of increase (billions of yen)	4,929	15,070	28,841	13,162	16,643	14,148
Components of increase (percent)						
Foreign assets (net)	1.0	−0.5	4.7	14.5	7.4	−23.6
Claims on public sector	−1.9	5.8	8.8	−2.7	3.6	−3.6
Claims on private sector	100.9	94.7	86.5	88.2	89.0	127.2
United States						
Amount of increase (billions of dollars)	29.1	99.0	130.2	54.7	58.3	66.1
Components of increase (percent)						
Foreign assets (net)	−12.6	−2.1	−0.6	−2.6	0.3	1.4
Claims on public sector	22.2	31.1	38.1	49.0	17.5	15.8
Claims on private sector	90.4	71.0	62.5	53.6	82.2	82.8

Table 9 (*continued*)

Country and component	Average, 1956–60	Average, 1961–65	Average, 1966–70	1971	1972	1973
United Kingdom						
Amount of increase						
(millions of pounds)	1,538	2,558	5,013	2,372	5,665	7,110
Components of increase						
(percent)						
Foreign assets (net)	−15.3	−111.4	−3.2	77.5	−16.4	−10.4
Claims on public sector	−13.1	134.6	45.2	−39.4	12.6	23.8
Claims on private sector	128.4	76.8	58.0	61.9	103.8	86.6
West Germany						
Amount of increase						
(billions of marks)	160.3	225.6	160.1	53.8	62.5	53.6
Components of increase						
(percent)						
Foreign assets (net)	23.8	3.3	14.0	7.9	12.3	22.3
Claims on public sector	11.9	9.3	10.0	8.1	7.0	5.9
Claims on private sector	64.3	87.4	76.0	84.0	80.7	71.8
France						
Amount of increase						
(billions of francs)	44.12	98.63	141.19	64.18	77.60	74.00
Components of increase						
(percent)						
Foreign assets (net)	7.9	21.2	−4.8	16.5	1.8	1.4
Claims on public sector	29.7	14.1	7.8	4.8	−3.1	−13.2
Claims on private sector	62.4	64.7	97.0	78.7	101.3	111.8
Italy						
Amount of increase						
(billions of lira)	4,254	12,508	22,643	7,942	12,308	12,595
Components of increase						
(percent)						
Foreign assets (net)	26.4	7.2	1.9	5.6	−6.3	−0.4
Claims on public sector	11.2	21.7	26.2	41.9	38.1	34.8
Claim on private sector	62.4	71.1	71.9	52.5	68.2	65.6

Source: International Monetary Fund, *International Financial Statistics*, various issues.

Table 10. *Composition of Funds Used by the Business Sector in Major Countries, Annual Average, 1968–72*[a]

Percent

Type of funds	Japan	United States	United Kingdom	West Germany[b]	France[c]
Internal	46.4	61.1	66.5	61.4	63.0
External	53.6	38.9	33.5	38.6	37.0
Borrowings	46.0	19.6	24.9	26.2	29.4
Bonds and stock issues	5.4	19.3	8.6	3.9	7.6
Other	2.2	...	...	8.5	...
Total	100.0	100.0	100.0	100.0	100.0

Source: The Bank of Japan, *Japan and the World: A Comparison by Economic and Financial Statistics.*
a. Excludes financial institutions and interbusiness credit.
b. Includes private and public enterprises but excludes construction.
c. Includes private and public enterprises.

Table 11. *Correlation Coefficients of Increase in Loans with GNP and Private Investments*[a]

Item	Quarters lagged after increase in loans				
	0	1	2	3	4
Real GNP	0.498	0.707	0.628	0.464	0.387
Real private investment	0.616	0.787	0.605	0.323	0.138
Investment in plant and equipment (real)	0.460	0.667	0.666	0.596	0.489
Inventory investment (real)	0.414	0.469	0.171	−0.077	−0.176

Sources: Calculated from data in Economic Planning Agency, *Annual Report on National Income Statistics*, various issues; the Bank of Japan, *Economic Statistics Annual*, various issues.
a. Calculated for 1957:2 to 1968:4. All data are in rates of change from previous quarter, seasonally adjusted (weighted moving average of 1:2:1).

Table 12. *Components of Japan's Gross National Product, 1960–73*[a]
Billions of yen

Year	GNP[b]	Government expenditures[c]	Export[d]	Business investment[e]
1960	19,699	3,520	1,799	3,547
	(100)	(17.9)	(9.1)	(18.0)
1961	22,766	3,854	1,924	5,528
	(100)	(16.9)	(8.5)	(24.3)
1962	24,228	4,480	2,244	4,712
	(100)	(18.5)	(9.3)	(19.4)
1963	26,785	4,994	2,410	5,424
	(100)	(18.6)	(9.0)	(20.3)
1964	30,466	5,392	2,908	6,458
	(100)	(17.7)	(9.5)	(21.2)
1965	31,897	5,895	3,563	5,708
	(100)	(18.5)	(11.2)	(17.9)
1966	35,133	6,535	4,114	6,478
	(100)	(18.6)	(11.7)	(18.4)
1967	39,878	6,950	4,374	9,039
	(100)	(17.4)	(11.0)	(22.7)
1968	45,558	7,674	5,356	11,093
	(100)	(16.8)	(11.8)	(24.3)
1969	51,059	8,205	6,430	13,012
	(100)	(16.1)	(12.6)	(25.5)
1970	56,336	8,658	7,453	15,707
	(100)	(15.4)	(13.2)	(27.9)
1971	60,187	9,954	8,788	15,106
	(100)	(16.5)	(14.6)	(25.1)
1972	65,514	11,354	9,448	15,692
	(100)	(17.3)	(14.4)	(24.0)
1973[f]	72,411	12,180	10,065	19,432
	(100)	(16.8)	(13.9)	(26.8)

Source: Economic Planning Agency, *Annual Report on National Income Statistics*, various issues.

a. Figures in parentheses are ratios of items to GNP.
b. Real GNP in 1965 prices.
c. General government expenditures on goods and services plus government fixed capital.
d. Includes factor income received from abroad.
e. Investment in plant and equipment plus inventory investment of the business sector.
f. Preliminary figures.

Table 13. *Changes in the Wholesale Price Index, Capacity Utilization in Mining and Manufacturing Corporations, and the Supply-Demand Gap in Gross National Product, 1957–73*

Percent

Year	Annual change in wholesale price index	Rate of capacity utilization in mining and manufac-turing corporations[a]	Supply-demand gap in gross national product[b]
1957	3.0	94.2	5.5
1958	−6.5	81.6	17.9
1959	1.0	92.3	7.3
1960	1.1	97.3	2.7
1961	1.0	97.3	0.6
1962	−1.6	90.2	7.1
1963	1.8	88.5	8.8
1964	0.2	92.9	5.8
1965	0.8	86.7	9.4
1966	2.4	91.4	6.7
1967	1.8	97.9	2.4
1968	0.9	99.2	−0.6
1969	2.1	99.3	0.1
1970	3.7	96.3	2.7
1971	−0.8	90.1	6.8
1972	0.8	89.7	7.4
1973	15.9	94.5	6.6

Source: The Bank of Japan, *Economic Statistics Annual*, various years.

a. Fourth quarter of 1968 = 100. An upward trend which the index of rate of capacity utilization (published by the Ministry of International Trade and Industry) shows has been removed.

b. Defined as: $1 - \dfrac{\text{real GNP}}{\text{capacity GNP}}$. Capacity GNP is calculated by using the production function estimated by the Economic Research Bureau of the Bank of Japan (see table 26).

Table 14. *Average Annual Rate of Increase in Major Components of Nominal Gross National Product, by Phases of the Investment Cycle, Fiscal Years 1956–73*

Percent

Component of GNP	Phase of the investment cycle				
	Upswing, 1956–61	Downswing, 1962–65	Upswing, 1966–69	Downswing, 1970–71	Upswing, 1972–73
Private investment in plant and equipment	28.0	4.4	26.5	7.7	22.3
Government expenditures	12.9	17.1	13.8	19.5	18.9
Personal consumption	10.9	15.4	14.9	14.3	18.1
Surplus of the nation on current account[a]	(−74)	(192)	(98)	(718)	(−1,636)
Private inventory and housing investment	24.4	17.0	22.1	11.8	39.0
Total	14.4	13.4	17.4	14.5	18.9

Source: Economic Planning Agency, *Annual Report on National Income Statistics*, various issues.

a. Figures in parentheses are the annual average amount (in billions of yen) of increase or decrease.

Table 15. *Measures of Imported Inflation in Japan, 1961–73*

Percent

Year	Contribution of exports to GNP[a]	Rate of change in import price index	Ratio of net official purchases of foreign exchange assets to increase in high-powered money[b]
Average, 1961–65	1.4 (9.7)	−0.2	0.8
1966	1.7 (10.1)	2.0	−10.4
1967	0.7 (13.5)	0.9	− 7.8
1968	2.5 (14.2)	0.4	45.9
1969	2.4 (12.1)	2.3	42.2
1970	2.0 (10.6)	3.3	54.1
1971	2.4 (6.8)	0.0	518.7
1972	1.1 (8.7)	−4.3	87.8
1973	0.9 (10.7)	21.0	−61.7

Sources: The Bank of Japan, *Economic Statistics Annual*; Economic Planning Agency, *Annual Report on National Income Statistics*.

a. Ratio of increase in real exports over the previous year to real GNP in the previous year. Figures in parentheses are rates of growth in real GNP over the previous year.

b. Ratio of net purchases of foreign exchange assets by the Bank of Japan and the government to increase in bank notes plus reserve deposits.

Table 16. Actual and Estimated Changes in the Wholesale Price Index, 1969–74[a]

Percent

Year or quarter	Dependent variable			Independent variable					
				Supply-demand condition of manufactured goods		Increase in wage costs		Increase in the cost of imports	
	Actual change	Estimated change	Percentage of actual change	Annual percentage change	Percentage of actual change in WPI	Annual percentage change	Percentage of actual change in WPI	Annual percentage change	Percentage of actual change in WPI
1969	2.1	2.2	104.8	0.6	28.6	1.1	52.4	0.5	23.8
1970	3.7	3.9	105.4	0.4	10.8	2.8	75.7	0.7	18.9
1971	−0.8	−1.1	137.5	−5.6	700.0	4.6	−575.0	−0.1	12.5
1972	0.8	1.3	162.5	0.1	12.5	2.0	250.0	−0.8	−100.0
1973	15.9	15.6	98.1	9.8	61.6	1.7	10.7	4.1	25.8
1972:3	1.1	1.2	109.1	1.2	109.1	0.0	0.0	0.0	0.0
1972:4	3.0	2.3	76.7	1.4	46.7	−0.1	−3.3	1.0	33.3
1973:1	4.3	4.8	111.6	3.6	83.7	−0.1	−2.3	1.3	30.2
1973:2	3.6	3.6	100.0	2.2	61.1	0.9	25.0	0.5	13.9
1973:3	5.4	5.0	92.6	2.3	42.6	0.9	16.7	1.8	33.3
1973:4	8.6	8.9	103.5	4.6	53.5	2.3	26.7	2.0	23.3
1974:1	14.1	13.4	95.0	6.3	44.7	0.6	4.2	6.5	46.1
1974:2	3.7	4.8	129.7	−3.9	−105.4	5.8	156.7	2.9	78.4

Sources: The Bank of Japan, *Economic Statistics Annual*; the Bank of Japan, *Short-Term Economic Survey of Principal Corporations in Japan*.

a. The following regression equation was used (1965:1–1974:2, seasonally adjusted quarterly data):

$$WPI = 0.1185\ EDJM + 0.3744\ ULCM + 0.1829\ IPIP + 4.9557\ DUM1$$
$$(21.7657)\quad\ \ (28.3179)\qquad\quad (6.7690)\qquad\ (5.7181)$$
$$+ 9.3017\ DUM2 + 45.0303$$
$$(5.4520)\qquad (23.9857)$$

$R^2 = 0.9980$; standard error = 0.6046; Durbin-Watson statistic = 1.2784; *t*-values in parentheses.

WPI = wholesale price index (1970 = 100, seasonally adjusted)

$EDJM$ = diffusion index of supply-demand condition of manufactured goods

$ULCM$ = wage costs in manufacturing industries = $\dfrac{\text{wage index} \times \text{employment index}}{\text{production index}}$

$IPIP$ = import price index for producer goods (1970 = 100, seasonally adjusted)

$DUM1$, $DUM2$ = dummy for the impact of the oil crisis
($DUM1$: 1973:4, 1974:1, 2 = 1.0; other periods = 0.0)
($DUM2$: 1974:1, 2 = 1.0; other periods = 0.0)

Table 17. *Annual Rates of Change in Prices and Money Supply in Japan, 1970–74*[a]

Percent

Year	Whole- sale price index	Con- sumer price index	Import price index	Export price index	M_1 (out- stand- ing)	M_2 (out- stand- ing)	M_1 as a percent of nominal GNP	M_2 as a percent of nominal GNP
1970:1	6.7	13.2	8.4	8.5	13.1	16.2	0.259	0.685
1970:2	2.0	5.4	−0.4	1.6	21.5	19.2	0.259	0.684
1970:3	−0.8	2.0	−2.0	0.0	12.6	15.2	0.258	0.685
1970:4	−1.2	10.8	0.4	1.2	16.7	16.5	0.265	0.703
1971:1	−2.4	6.0	1.2	2.4	31.1	22.7	0.271	0.715
1971:2	0.8	5.1	4.9	2.0	29.7	22.8	0.285	0.734
1971:3	0.4	6.6	0.0	−2.0	39.1	28.0	0.299	0.755
1971:4	−2.4	3.8	−17.9	−6.1	20.4	22.1	0.309	0.782
1972:1	−2.0	2.6	−12.1	−6.1	17.4	21.4	0.312	0.797
1972:2	0.2	4.9	1.7	−1.2	13.6	21.4	0.309	0.800
1972:3	4.1	6.3	−0.8	−0.8	17.3	23.3	0.307	0.805
1972:4	12.6	4.7	23.0	2.9	46.1	29.5	0.320	0.815
1973:1	18.7	13.4	28.8	8.0	30.0	25.6	0.323	0.815
1973:2	15.3	17.1	11.8	10.8	29.9	23.6	0.326	0.812
1973:3	23.4	16.4	40.2	17.9	13.1	15.4	0.323	0.808
1973:4	39.2	19.3	44.0	43.0	7.9	11.3	0.306	0.774
1974:1	69.2	48.2	192.2	69.1	16.1	14.1	0.311	0.782
1974:2	15.7	14.2	62.0	18.6	17.6	11.5	0.306	0.760

Source: The Bank of Japan, *Basic Data for Economic Analysis; Seasonally Adjusted by the U.S. Census Method II. X-11.*

a. Data are seasonally adjusted, except for the last two columns which are actual levels.

Table 18. *Changes in the Import Price Index and the Wholesale Price Index, 1969–74*

Percent

Year or quarter	Rate of change in IPI (all commodities)	Contributions to rate of change in IPI[a]				Rate of change in WPI	
		Mineral fuel	Reuters' commodity index	Yen exchange rate	Residual	All commodities	Contribution change in import prices[b]
1969	2.3	−0.9	2.1	0.0	1.1	2.1	0.2
1970	3.3	0.3	1.3	0.0	1.7	3.7	0.3
1971	−0.0	3.2	−1.8	−1.5	0.1	−0.8	0.1
1972	−4.3	−0.8	4.1	−6.3	−1.3	0.8	−0.3
1973	21.0	1.9	24.8	−4.5	−1.2	15.9	1.6
1972:3	−0.2	−0.5	2.3	−0.3	−1.7	1.1	−0.0
1972:4	5.3	0.1	5.4	0.0	−0.2	3.0	0.4
1973:1	6.6	0.0	7.8	−2.6	1.4	4.3	0.5
1973:2	2.8	−0.1	4.5	−2.2	0.6	3.6	0.2
1973:3	8.9	1.2	10.8	0.0	−3.1	5.4	0.7
1973:4	9.5	4.8	4.9	1.1	−1.3	8.6	0.8
1974:1	30.8	22.3	5.5	1.6	1.4	14.1	2.6
1974:2	11.6	8.2	−3.1	−0.8	7.3	3.7	1.1

Sources: The Bank of Japan, *Economic Statistics Annual*; the Bank of Japan, *Wholesale Price Indexes Annual*.

a. Contributions of Reuters' index and the yen exchange rate to the U.S. dollar are calculated by using the following regression equation (quarterly data; period covered is 1965:1–1974:2):

$$IPI = 0.0671R + 0.1748ER - 1.7088$$
$$\quad\quad (20.3129) \quad\ (6.7645)$$

$R^2 = 0.9519$; standard error = 2.9358; Durbin-Watson statistic = 1.1241; *t*-values in parentheses.

IPI = import price index (excluding mineral fuel), seasonally adjusted
R = Reuters' commodity index
ER = yen exchange rate to U.S. dollar

b. The weight of imported goods in the WPI amounts to approximately 7.5 percent.

Table 19. *Quantitative Export Restrictions Enforced by the Governments of the Exporting Countries*

Item	Date	Content of restrictions
Cotton		
Brazil	August–September 1973	All shipments prohibited.
	October 1973–74	7,000 tons in October 1973 and 10,000 tons in December 1973 were temporarily permitted; permission up to 150,000 tons planned during 1974 (export quantity during 1973, 250,000 tons), but low-price contracts (50,000 tons) were canceled.
Guatemala	December 1973	15 percent of forward export contracts was shifted to domestic consumption by government order.
Pakistan	August 1973	Exports prohibited
	October 1973	A government-owned cotton exporting company was established, and export restrictions were repealed. But actually, export was almost in suspension.
Lumber		
United States	October 1973	Wyatt Act was promulgated to prohibit export of logs from national forests (January to June of 1974)
Philippines		Quantity of logs exported was restricted as follows.
	From 1970	Export of logs restricted within 80 percent of the total lumber export.
	January 1974	Export of logs restricted within 60 percent of lumber export.
	January 1975	Exports of logs restricted within 30 percent of lumber export.
	January 1976	Exports of logs prohibited.
Malaysia	November 1972	Export of logs from western Malaysia prohibited.
Indonesia	January 1972	For lauan (for furniture), export of logs was restricted to 80 percent of the total.
Steel scrap		
United States	July 1973	New export contracts of 500 tons or more were temporarily prohibited. Existing contracts to be shipped in August and afterward were subject to the instructions of the authorities concerned.
	September 1973	Issue of export permit to small-lot of less than 500 tons was suspended.
	November 1973	Export quota was announced for January–March 1974: total of 2.1 million tons, of which 823,300 tons allotted to Japan. For April–June 1974, total of 1.51 million tons, of which 723,000 tons was allotted to Japan.
Soybeans		
United States	June 1973	Temporary prohibition on exports of soybeans and soybean cake announced.
	July 1973	Shift to the export permission system; outstanding contracts as of June 13 were cut by 50 percent for soybeans and by 60 percent for soybean cake.
	October 1973	Restrictions were abolished.

Source: The Bank of Japan, *The Japanese Economy in 1973.*

Table 20. *Increase in Prices of Selected Imports, 1972–74*[a]
Percent

Import	Weight in the wholesale price index[b]	1972		1973		January–June 1974
		January–June	July–December	January–June	July–December	
Soybeans	0.21	2.0	11.7	56.9	2.5	1.3
Beef	0.02	16.2	3.1	71.1	2.8	0.0
Cotton	0.23	−8.6	−1.7	19.0	54.6	−19.5
Wool	0.17	41.6	61.9	49.0	−10.3	−22.6
Raw materials for feed	0.29	−12.2	40.0	18.6	33.0	−2.7
Rawhide	0.05	43.9	32.6	−24.5	15.3	−16.1
Imported lumber	0.66	−4.1	29.7	10.4	22.9	−5.1
Steel scrap	0.16	0.0	9.0	42.5	22.0	55.8
Crude oil	1.23	4.1	−0.9	2.4	54.2	153.4
Coking coal	0.47	−2.7	−2.1	−2.9	17.0	39.5

Source: The Bank of Japan, *Wholesale Price Indexes Annual*.
a. Rate of increase over the previous six-month period.
b. Total of weights is 100.

Table 21. *Impact of Increase in Crude Oil Price on Wholesale Prices*

Period	Crude oil price			Contribution to the increase in the wholesale price index[a]
	Beginning (dollars per barrel)	Ending (dollars per barrel)	Percent change	
September 1973– February 1974	3.305	9.901	199.6	7.3
September 1973– late October 1973	3.305	4.567	38.2	1.8
Late October 1973– February 1974	4.567	9.901	116.8	5.5

Source: The Bank of Japan, *The Japanese Economy in 1973*.
a. Estimated by the input-output table for 1970. For price rises in each sector subsequent to the rise in oil price, an estimation was made by the following:

$$\Delta P_j = \frac{B_{ij}}{B_{ii}} \Delta Pi.$$

B_{ij} is a factor of $(I - A)'$; I is a unit matrix, and A is a matrix on input coefficients. The contribution rate to the rise in WPI is the weighted average of the price rises in each sector caused by the increased crude oil price. The weights are those of WPI in each sector.

Table 22. *Components of the Annual Increase in High-Powered Money,*
1970–73[a]

Billions of yen

Item	1970	1971	1972	1973	1971–73, total
Total increase in high-powered money	825.9 (100.0)	848.2 (100.0)	1,981.2 (100.0)	3,055.6 (100.0)	5,885.0 (100.0)
Increase in foreign exchange assets	446.6 (54.1)	4,399.8 (518.7)	1,739.7 (87.8)	−1,884.0 (−61.7)	4,255.5 (72.3)
Increase in the central bank's claims on government	−933.1 (−113.0)	−2,006.6 (−236.6)	−1,849.8 (−93.3)	−438.4 (−14.3)	−4,294.8 (−73.0)
Increase in the central bank's claims on private sector					
Loans	411.6 (49.8)	−1,672.5 (−197.2)	1,441.3 (72.7)	147.4 (4.8)	−83.8 (−1.4)
Purchases of bonds and bills	923.6 (118.8)	−247.1 (−29.1)	781.0 (39.4)	5,573.0 (182.4)	6,106.9 (103.8)
Other	−22.8 (−2.7)	374.6 (44.2)	−131.0 (−6.6)	−342.4 (−11.2)	−98.8 (−1.7)

Source: The Bank of Japan, *Economic Statistics Annual.*
a. Figures in parentheses are percentages of the total.

Table 23. *Components of the Money Supply, 1970–73*

Billions of yen

Item	1970	1971	1972	1973	1971–73 total
Increase in the money supply (M₂)					
Total	7,837.5	13,160.9	16,642.3	14,148.0	43,951.2
M_1	3,077.0	6,333.6	6,833.0	5,785.4	18,952.0
Time deposits	4,760.5	6,827.3	9,809.3	8,362.6	24,999.2
Net change of assets of banking system					
Foreign assets	557.8	2,797.4	1,557.9	−2,764.9	1,590.4
Claims on nonbank private sector	8,590.9	12,737.5	17,807.2	16,083.0	46,627.7
Claims on central government	185.3	−396.5	735.8	−472.7	−133.4
Claims on local governments	199.5	343.0	515.3	617.3	1,475.6
Other	−1,696.0	−2,320.5	−3,973.9	685.3	−5,609.1
Amount of increase in money supply accounted for by:[a]					
Net change in international monetary reserves[b]	4,240.1	68,265.6	14,611.9	−8,729.3	31,776.7[e]
Net receipt on treasury funds[c]	−8,856.4	−31,138.7	−15,527.3	−2,023.2	32,084.4[e]
Discretionary monetary policies[d]	12,453.8	−23,966.0	17,557.7	24,900.5	44,258.9[e]

Source: The Bank of Japan, *Economic Statistics Annual.*

a. In these calculations increases in the money supply are attributed to the components shown in the last three rows on the assumptions that, in the absence of discretionary monetary action, the changes in money supply would be a constant multiple of nondiscretionary changes in high-powered money and that all deviations of the total change in the money supply from these non-discretionary changes are attributable to discretionary monetary policy. Discretionary changes in the money supply could reflect either discretionary changes in high-powered money or changes in the ratio of the money supply to high-powered money. Nondiscretionary changes in high-powered money consist of changes in official foreign exchange reserves and in net receipts on treasury funds. The calculations are based on the formulas in notes b, c, and d.

b. Increase in money supply

$$\times\ \frac{\text{net payments on Foreign Exchange Fund Special Account}}{\text{increase in high-powered money}}$$

c. Increase in money supply $\times\ \dfrac{\text{net receipts on treasury funds (including government bonds)}}{\text{increase in high-powered money}}$

d. Increase in the money supply (M_2) − (net change in international monetary reserves + net receipt on treasury funds).

e. Since the increase in high-powered money was not in proportion to the increase in money supply each year, the figures for 1971–73 do not equal those of the 1971–73 total.

Table 24. *Rate of Increase in Stock of Lending by Major Financial Institutions,*[a] *1970–73*

Annual rate (percent)

Borrowers	October 1970– June 1971	July 1971– June 1972	July 1972– December 1972	January 1973– December 1973
Corporations	19.5	21.9	9.7	15.4
Large corporations	23.9	21.1	7.2	14.7
Small corporations[b]	13.5	23.2	13.1	16.3
Manufacturing	20.4	14.6	6.6	11.7
Nonmanufacturing	18.8	28.2	12.0	18.0
Proprietors and households	27.8	39.2	20.0	43.1
Local governments	19.7	35.2	22.9	8.7

Source: The Bank of Japan, *Economic Statistics Monthly.*

a. Lenders include all banks (banking and trust accounts), mutual loan and savings banks, and credit associations. Loans to corporations by mutual loan and savings banks and credit associations are all regarded as loans to small corporations. Overdrafts are excluded.

b. Corporations capitalized at ¥50 million or less (for wholesale and retail trade services ¥10 million or less).

Table 25. *Liquidity of the Business Sector, 1955–73*

Period	Ratio of cash on hand and deposits to monthly average sales	Ratio of increase in internal funds to investment in plant and equipment and inventories	Ratio of total savings of business sector to total investment of business sector
Average, 1955–59	0.745	n.a.	61.4
Average, 1960–64	0.926	65.5	59.9
Average, 1965–69	1.116	67.4	75.3
Average, 1970–73	1.270	63.4	74.2
1970	1.089	61.0	70.6
1971	1.273	67.6	77.4
1972	1.400	83.6	87.8
1973	1.281	51.6	64.8[a]

Sources: The Bank of Japan, *Short-Term Economic Survey of Principal Corporations in Japan;* Economic Planning Agency, *Annual Report on National Income Statistics.*

n.a. Not available.

a. Preliminary figure.

Table 26. *Bank of Japan's Estimates of Responsiveness*
of Aggregate Supply and Aggregate Supply-Demand Gap, 1960–73

Year	Responsiveness of aggregate supply[a]	Aggregate supply-demand gap[b]
1960	0.706	2.7
1961	0.672	0.6
1962	0.590	7.1
1963	0.682	8.8
1964	0.755	5.8
1965	0.444	9.4
1966	0.668	6.7
1967	0.740	2.4
1968	0.767	−0.6
1969	0.724	0.1
1970	0.585	2.7
1971	0.578	6.8
1972	0.615	7.4
1973	0.444	6.6

Sources: The Bank of Japan, *Economic Statistics Annual;* the Bank of Japan, *Monthly Bulletin* (June 1974).

a. Defined as ratio of rate of increase in real GNP to rate of increase in nominal GNP.

b. Defined as $1 - \dfrac{\text{real GNP}}{\text{capacity GNP}}$. Capacity GNP is calculated by using the following production function estimated by the Economic Research Bureau of the Bank of Japan (period covered is January–March 1960 to July–September 1973; t-values are in parentheses).

$$\log Y = 0.1567 + 0.6115 \log p \cdot K + 0.411 \log h \cdot L + 0.2541 \log V + 0.00023t.$$
$$\qquad\quad (13.8514) \qquad\quad (3.1695) \qquad\quad (10.3206) \qquad\quad (4.0265)$$

$\bar{R}^2 = 0.9993$; standard error $= 0.0047$; Durbin-Watson statistic $= 1.8890$.

$Y =$ real GNP (based on prices in 1965, seasonally adjusted, in billions of yen).

$p =$ rate of capital utilization in manufacturing industry (the linear time trend was removed from the index of the Ministry of International Trade and Industry, October–December 1968 = 100).

$K =$ gross capital stock of all industries (installation basis, based on prices in 1965, seasonally adjusted, in billions of yen).

$h =$ total working hours per worker in all industries (the index of the Ministry of Labor was multiplied by working hours in the base period (187.7 hours per month); seasonally adjusted; unit, 1,000 hours per month).

$L =$ number of persons employed in all industries (according to the Labor Survey by the Prime Minister's Office, 1,000 persons).

$V =$ equipment vintage (ratio of increase in gross capital stock of all industries during the past three years to gross capital stock outstanding in the latest period).

$t =$ time trend (January–March 1960 = 1).

Table 27. *Depression Cartels Approved by the Fair Trade Commission,*
Selected Years, 1965–72

Period of approval	Number of cartels ended during each quarter					
	1965:4	*1966:1*	*1966:2*	*1966:3*	*1966:4*	*1967:1*
1965–66 recession (trough: 1965:3)	1	4	6	7	1	1
	1972:1	*1972:2*	*1972:3*	*1972:4*	*1973:1*	*1973:2*
1970–72 recession (trough: 1971:4)	0	1	2	8	1	1

Source: The Bank of Japan, *The Japanese Economy in 1972.*

Table 28. *Change in Wholesale Prices of Goods Related to Public Investment,*
Residential Construction, and Plant and Equipment Investment
by Nonmanufacturing Firms, 1972–73[a]
Percent

Quarter	Goods related to			
	Public investment *(ten items)*	*Residential construction* *(twelve items)*	*Plant and equipment investment by nonmanufacturing firms* *(eight items)*	*Wholesale price index* *(all items)*
1972:1	2.5	3.8	7.4	0.1
1972:2	1.8	0.3	0.9	0.4
1972:3	2.1	6.6	4.5	1.4
1972:4	1.1	35.0	5.0	3.8
1973:1	2.9	4.9	4.8	5.1
1973:2	2.8	−2.6	3.6	2.7
1973:3	6.4	17.8	19.7	6.0
1973:4	8.3	11.3	3.5	12.7

Source: The Bank of Japan, *Wholesale Price Indexes Annual.*
a. Rates of increase over the previous quarter. The prices of goods in each group are weighted by the weights in the WPI.

Table 29. Actual and Estimated Components of the Increase in the Consumer Price Index, 1971–73[a]

Percent

Component	1971	1972	1973 Total	1973 1st quarter	1973 2nd quarter	1973 3rd quarter	1973 4th quarter
Consumer prices for all commodities and services							
Actual	6.1	4.5	11.7	2.7	5.3	2.9	4.5
	(100.0)	(100.0)	(100.0)	(100.0)	(100.0)	(100.0)	(100.0)
Estimated	5.5	5.1	10.6	2.1	5.3	3.0	4.6
	(90.2)	(113.3)	(90.6)	(77.8)	(100.0)	(103.4)	(102.2)
Price changes in manufactured goods and services							
Influence of wholesale prices of manufactured goods	0.3	-0.1	3.7	0.7	1.2	1.4	3.4
	(4.9)	(-2.2)	(31.6)	(25.9)	(22.6)	(48.3)	(75.6)
Changes in labor costs in retail trade and service industries	2.4	2.3	1.5	-0.2	2.3	0.3	0.4
	(39.3)	(51.1)	(12.8)	(-7.4)	(43.4)	(10.3)	(8.9)
Increases in private consumption (real)	1.9	2.4	2.4	0.6	0.5	0.5	0.3
	(31.1)	(53.3)	(20.5)	(22.2)	(9.4)	(17.2)	(6.7)
Price changes in agricultural, fishery, and live-stock products (actual)	0.5	0.4	2.6	0.9	1.2	0.5	0.4
	(8.2)	(8.9)	(22.2)	(33.3)	(22.6)	(17.2)	(8.9)
Price changes in publications (books, periodicals, and newspapers) (actual)	0.4	0.1	0.4	0.1	0.1	0.3	0.1
	(6.6)	(2.2)	(3.4)	(3.7)	(1.9)	(10.3)	(2.2)
Consumer prices of manufactured goods							
Actual	6.3	3.7	12.3	2.4	5.4	2.9	7.4
Estimated	4.7	4.8	10.9	1.4	5.9	3.7	6.4
Influence of wholesale prices	0.6	-0.3	7.9	1.5	2.6	3.1	5.8
Changes in labor costs in retail trade	2.5	2.9	1.0	-0.5	3.0	0.1	0.3
Increases in private consumption (real)	1.6	2.2	2.0	0.4	0.3	0.5	0.3

Consumer prices of services

Actual	6.9	7.1	9.6	2.0	4.3	2.5	1.9
Estimated	7.2	7.5	7.8	1.1	4.2	1.8	1.4
Changes in labor costs in service industry	3.6	3.0	3.2	0.0	2.8	0.9	0.8
Increases in private consumption (real)	3.6	4.5	4.6	1.1	1.4	0.9	0.6

Source: The Bank of Japan, *The Japanese Economy in 1973*.

a. Figures in parentheses are percentages of total increase. Increases in consumer prices of manufactured goods and those of services are broken down by the following regression analysis; for those of agricultural, fishery and livestock products, and publications, actual values were used because of their irregular fluctuations; the total of the four was based on their weights in the CPI.

1. Consumer prices of manufactured goods (period covered, April–June 1966 to July–September 1973).

$$CPIM = 1.0017\sum_{i=0}^{4} W(i)WPIM_{-1} + 12.7423ULCR + 0.0008C - 29.0201$$
$$(5.95) \qquad\qquad\qquad (5.94) \qquad\qquad (4.73)$$

$[W(i)\ (i = 0, \ldots 4)\ 0.2824, 0.2565, 0.2153, 0.1587, 0.0871]$
$\qquad\qquad (4.22)\ (6.51)\ (4.40)\ (3.03)\ (2.36)$

The *W*s are Almon weights (second degree polynomials).

$\bar{R}^2 = 0.9925$; Durbin-Watson statistic = 0.9166; *t*-values in parentheses.

2. Consumer prices of services (period covered, April–June 1965 to July–September 1973:

$$CPIS = 33.7826ULCS + 0.0018C + 29.8950$$
$$(14.69) \qquad\qquad (29.13)$$

$\bar{R}^2 = 0.9988$; Durbin-Watson statistic = 1.0198; *t*-values in parentheses.

$CPIM$ = Consumer prices of manufactured goods (1970 = 100, seasonally adjusted)
$CPIS$ = Consumer prices of services (1970 = 100, seasonally adjusted)
$WPIM$ = Wholesale prices of manufactured goods (1970 = 100, seasonally adjusted)
$ULCR$ = Labor costs in retail trade
$ULCS$ = Labor costs in service industries (ratio of nominal wage per employee to labor productivity, seasonally adjusted, based on financial statements of corporations)
C = Personal consumption in real terms (seasonally adjusted, National Income Statistics)

$$\text{labor productivity} = \frac{1}{\text{number of employees}} \times \left(\frac{\text{general consumer price index}}{\text{sales}}\right)$$
$$- \frac{\text{nominal expenses for buying materials}}{\text{wholesale price index of consumer goods}}$$

Expenses for buying materials are calculated by deducting value added from sales (both are in nominal terms).

Table 30. *Annual Change in Wages, Labor Productivity, and Labor Costs in Manufacturing Industries, 1965–73*

Percent

Year	Wages	Labor productivity[a]	Labor costs[b]
1965	8.6	1.6	7.1
1966	11.7	12.7	−1.4
1967	13.2	16.2	−2.7
1968	14.9	10.9	3.3
1969	16.3	12.2	3.4
1970	17.6	9.8	7.5
1971	13.9	2.0	12.1
1972	15.6	9.5	5.3
1973	23.6	17.4	3.7

Sources: Ministry of Labor, *Monthly Labor Survey*; Japan Productivity Center, *Quarterly Journal of Productivity Statistics*.
a. Ratio of production index to employment index.
b. Ratio of nominal wage index times employment index to production index.

Table 31. *Negotiated Wage Hikes and ex post Annual Increases in Wages, 1965–74*

Percent

Fiscal year	Negotiated wage hike[a]	Ex post wage increase	
		Total	Nonregular payments[b]
1965	10.6	9.4	7.6
1966	10.6	9.8	11.1
1967	12.5	13.1	18.5
1968	13.6	11.7	10.4
1969	15.8	13.7	5.1
1970	18.5	15.7	9.8
1971	16.9	14.6	11.5
1972	15.3	16.1	14.0
1973	20.3	19.5	26.6
1974	32.9	n.a.	n.a.

Source: Ministry of Labor, *Monthly Labor Survey*.
n.a. Not available.
a. The average rate of increase in wages agreed upon each spring (261 corporations).
b. Primarily bonuses and overtime payments.

Comments by Lawrence B. Krause

THE PAPER on Japan by Ryutaro Komiya and Yoshio Suzuki is an excellent study of inflation in that country. I am hard pressed to find points to criticize, although there is always room for different interpretations of economic forces and events. I will attempt to extend their analysis of a couple of points and in the process indicate some of the complexities of the Japanese economy that may not have been fully reflected in the paper.

In order to come to a judgment about how much inflation in Japan is imported, it is important to analyze indexes of import and export prices along with the CPI and WPI. During most of the 1960s (period I in the Komiya-Suzuki paper), Japanese export prices actually fell slightly while the Japanese WPI was rising slightly, thus indicating that the competitive environment in which Japanese exports were sold was contributing to price stability in Japan, not inflation. In periods II and III, the same restraint is seen except that the comparison was between a rising export price index and an even faster increase in the WPI. On the import side the story is much the same. Japan imports chiefly primary commodities (although in recent years manufactures have risen greatly). During period I, Japan's import price index was stable despite steadily rising Japanese demand. The stability of import prices thus made a contribution to price stability by keeping raw material costs down. Import prices did advance during period II, but as Komiya and Suzuki point out, much of the rise was due to a sharp increase in Japanese demand, partially of a speculative character and made possible by the excess liquidity of the Japanese economy. Thus Japan did not import inflation during period II, and may actually have exported some. In period III, Japan's import prices did rise rapidly as a result of the oil crisis and other external factors. But because Japanese import demand is price-inelastic, the inflationary consequences of rising material costs was offset in part by the deflationary impact of having to pay the higher import bill. Thus, only in period III was the direct price transmission from abroad an inflationary factor, and even then it might not have been a major determinant of the inflation.

Komiya and Suzuki's discussion of the divergence of the CPI and WPI in Japan points to a link between domestic inflation and other countries not mentioned elsewhere. It was noted that the CPI rose more than the WPI, in part because unit labor costs for producing the goods and services with heavy weights in the CPI rose more than those for goods alone (with heavy WPI weights) due to differentials in productivity advance. Productivity growth in manufacturing (with relatively heavier WPI weights) was advanced by the inflow of technology from abroad. Thus foreign technology, by increasing productivity differentials, added to the rise of the CPI in Japan. This factor was of greater importance in the earlier postwar period than today because Japan has essentially caught up with other industrial countries in its advanced technology.

The authors make the point, obviously correctly, that prices in Japan have exhibited more downward flexibility than in other countries, and they cite a number of reasons to explain the phenomenon. While I agree with them that some labor market characteristics of Japan contribute to this result, I think this explanation has been overemphasized. It is true that Japanese firms utilize a great deal of overtime work at premium wages during booms, so that when a recession occurs and total hours per worker are reduced, average hourly wages decline since a higher percentage of compensation is paid at straight-time rather than at overtime rates. But this same adjustment is made in other industrial countries and thus cannot contribute very much to the explanation of the difference in behavior between Japan and other countries. Also, the Japanese system of paying bonuses twice a year will contribute to wage flexibility only if the bonuses are calculated in relation to firm profitability. While this is true in part, bonuses are also calculated as a multiple of the standard monthly wage and are a subject of contract bargaining between firms and their unions. Thus bonuses often cannot be adjusted because of an unanticipated decline in sales so cannot be much of an element in the reduction of labor costs. Furthermore, one of the aspects of Japan's lifetime employment system works in a counter direction. Since firms are hesitant to take on permanent employees during periods of rapid growth for fear of having too many of them during recessions, they make extensive use of subcontractors whose employees are not guaranteed employment by the producing firm. The employees of the subcontractor are paid lower wages than the employees of the producing firm even though they may be doing identical work and working side by side. When slowdowns of business activity occur, firms reduce their subcontracting to maintain employment for their own employees, but because of their higher wage scales, average labor costs are increased because of the change in mix of employees.

In their discussion of the Japanese business cycle before 1970, Komiya and Suzuki make the point that the signal to the authorities to tighten money, which brought about recessions, was the worsening of the balance of payments. Since the balance of payments began to deteriorate when the WPI rose, targeting monetary policy on the balance of payments led to stability of the WPI but still permitted the CPI to rise, and it was argued that if the

CPI were stabilized, then Japan under fixed exchange rates would have developed balance of payment surpluses as it did in 1970–73 when monetary policy was directed toward restraining domestic inflation. But this need not have been the case. Japan accepted a fixed exchange rate in 1949 and it soon became evident that the ¥360 to the dollar rate overvalued the yen. In order to maintain the overvaluation, Japan exercised stringent trade and capital controls. It was only after the yen overvaluation was overcome during the mid-1960s that Japan really began the process of trade liberalization begun much earlier by other industrial countries. If instead the CPI had been stabilized by monetary policy and the WPI had followed a downward track, then the improved international competitiveness of Japan could have permitted liberalization much sooner rather than appearing as balance of payment surpluses.

Furthermore, Komiya and Suzuki pay very little attention to international capital movements, although monetary policy was the principal instrument of stabilization policy. Japan, of course, did exercise stringent exchange controls until recently, and still does not permit free entry into the foreign exchange market. Nevertheless, foreign monetary conditions did influence liquidity conditions in Japan. If money was tight in Japan, Japanese business firms and agency banks were able to borrow abroad to ease the strain, even with the controls (though some of the borrowing and repayment was hidden in the leads and lags of payment for international trade). Thus it cannot be ignored. International capital movements will be even more important in the future, not only because exchange controls have been eased, but also because so many more Japanese firms now have direct investments abroad, which make existing controls less effective.

Japan's policymakers might be criticized—which Komiya and Suzuki did not do—for failing to use fiscal policy as an anti-inflation device. In their study of taxation in Japan, Pechman and Kaizuka point out that the structure of Japanese taxes was very elastic so that revenue rose rapidly with higher money incomes.[7] Japan might have utilized these revenues to fight inflation (by running a budget surplus) but chose not to do so because of a long-standing policy of giving taxpayers an annual tax reduction about equal to the excess of revenues over expenditures. Thus, while the Japanese budget was not a cause of inflation, neither was it the counterinflationary force it might have been.

In conclusion, it should be noted that Japan would have to be given a

7. Joseph A. Pechman and Keimei Kaizuka, "Taxation," in Hugh Patrick and Henry Rosovsky, eds., *Asia's New Giant: How the Japanese Economy Works* (Brookings Institution, 1976), pp. 317–82.

rather high grade for its stabilization policy if one were to grade on a curve, considering the spectacular failures of other countries. Nevertheless, Japan could have done better if it had paid more attention to stabilization, as it will have to in the future. Japan is obviously affected by what happens abroad, but with respect to inflation it has been master of its own fate. Both for its own sake and for that of the smaller countries dependent on it, Japan will have to become more inflation conscious. I doubt that Komiya and Suzuki would disagree with me.

General Comments

ALEXANDER SWOBODA noted that one possible symptom of imported inflation is that prices of traded goods rise more rapidly, in relation to the prices of nontraded goods, than the difference in their rates of productivity growth would suggest (though such a test would be difficult to apply). If productivity grows at different rates in traded goods and in nontraded goods, however, the meaning of imported or exported inflation becomes ambiguous. Gottfried Haberler has argued that even though the U.S. price level was relatively stable in the late fifties and early sixties, the United States could still be said to have been exporting inflation under fixed exchange rates to the extent that it set the world price of traded goods, and productivity growth in the traded-goods sector abroad was higher than in the United States. In those circumstances, the price of foreign nontraded goods (and, hence, the general price level abroad) would had to have risen to maintain payments equilibrium under fixed rates.

Such an interpretation of exported inflation is questionable because it tends to confuse changes in relative prices with changes in the general price level, but the argument does raise the question of what kind of exchange rate regime a country such as Japan should want if it wishes to stabilize at some overall price level. If it chooses fixed exchange rates, it will have a higher rate of inflation than the rest of the world because of its more rapid rate of growth (as pointed out by Balassa, McKinnon, and others). The Japanese authorities could, in theory and in the short run, have stabilized the consumer price index, but only at the cost of a lower rate of investment and employment, and this policy would also have implied a larger balance of payments surplus. This raises the question of whether Japan can, in practice and in the longer run, stabilize the consumer price index and maintain a stable exchange rate. To offset the effect of the surplus would be very difficult, especially since it arises from the trade account rather than capital movements.

Komiya and Suzuki are correct in saying that inflationary pressure through rising prices of imports may be much more important than the pressure through rising prices of exports, but this statement may be true only of a particular historical episode. In any event, such a situation is really caused by a change in relative prices rather than a general change in the price of traded commodities or of all goods (though this is not to deny that additional difficulties for macroeconomic policy arise from the adverse change in the terms of trade and the fact that Japan is a heavy importer of the raw materials whose prices have risen most).

Gerhard Fels noted that an increase in consumer prices is a means of lowering real wages in the export industries, and the combination of stabilization of wholesale prices and increases in domestic prices is intended to promote exports. Also, the yen, probably undervalued in the late sixties, has been known all over the world as a cheap currency, and this had to do with the policy employed to maintain the dual price system.

Joseph Pechman thought that the papers on Japan and the United States indicate that up to the end of 1972 there had been no inflation problem; in fact, Japanese wholesale and consumer prices had risen in 1972 at a lower rate than in eight of the preceding dozen years, while in the United States the increase of prices in 1972 was also less than it had been for a number of years. Inflation began subsequently in the two countries, but the reasons for this were quite different. In Japan it was a gross miscalculation of the effect of changing the value of the yen; appreciation had been expected to cause a recession or depression, so the government had pursued an expansionary domestic policy. In the United States, on the other hand, the mistake was the decision in early 1973 to relax wage and price controls; as a result, prices and then wages had begun to rise. From table 1 of the Komiya-Suzuki paper, one is forced to conclude that Japan had been a stabilizing element in the world economy up to 1972, as had the United States. It is commonly said that rate of inflation has increased little by little over a long period and is now out of control, but it appears doubtful that this is factually correct.

Alexander Swoboda warned against inferring from the stability of a country's wholesale price index that it is contributing to world stability. That might be a useful first approximation, but since wholesale price indexes in various countries are tied together to some degree, one must inquire whether the Japanese wholesale price index is stable because of an active Japanese fiscal and monetary policy or because the exchange rate is fixed and the United States is stable. In analyzing transmission and the contributions of various countries to international inflation, the only intellectually satisfactory approach is one of general equilibrium. The concepts of imported and exported inflation catch only bits and pieces of that general equilibrium framework. Future research should try to tie the countries together before it appraises specific contributions to inflation or instability.

Ryutaro Komiya noted that the balance of payments had been a major constraint on Japanese growth until 1967 or 1968; the monetary authorities had tightened policy whenever the balance of payments turned into deficit, while continuing to supply additional money to the economy at other times. The yen had been overvalued during the 1950s and the first half of the 1960s; in fact, until the middle of the 1960s it had been much overvalued, with many restrictions on current-account payments and measures that artificially stimulated imports. During the 1960s the yen had become less and less overvalued as a result of faster inflation abroad, and restrictions on imports were gradually removed. By 1968, the overall balance of payments was approximately in equilibrium and the period of increasing surpluses began. As to the labor market, at least until 1973 or 1974, a big wage increase could not occur when the economy was stagnant. Wage increases were quite sensitive to business profits and the general business outlook. The unions knew that if companies promised too large wage increases they would get into difficulty; and the demand-supply situation in the commodities markets was a very important factor in determining wages. Large-scale industries were less competitive than small-scale, traditional industries in Japan, but up to the last recession, even the modern sector was highly competitive. There was always a strong pressure in Japan to reduce taxes, and the government had difficulty avoiding tax reductions every year. The inflationary effects of rising import prices were especially hard to combat because they involved a decrease in the real GNP.

JOHN D. PITCHFORD

Inflation in Australia

Tables

Figures

John D. Pitchford, Australian National University, Canberra, is particularly indebted to
Lindy Spence for valuable research assistance and to Ted Sieper for stimulating discussion on this topic. The editors' comments helped in revision of the first draft.

THIS PAPER DESCRIBES the nature of Australian inflation and the course of inflation-related variables since the 1950s, with particular emphasis on inflation in the 1970s, and attempts to identify the type and source of the inflation experienced. Three main questions are addressed. First, to what extent has recent inflation been imported rather than domestically induced? Second, what role have wage claims played in determining the rate of inflation? Finally, has the underlying mechanism of inflation changed in recent years so that the type of inflation being experienced in the 1970s is fundamentally different from that of the 1950s and 1960s? While the first two questions seem sufficiently well defined to justify leaving their further elaboration until the body of the paper, discussion of the third question here should help clarify one of its main themes.

Inflations may differ for two reasons. Suppose the operation of the economy could be described by a system of equations with certain variables exogenous, such as the money supply, the exchange rate, and the levels of export and import prices.[1] First, from one inflationary episode to another the mix of movements in the exogenous variables may well be different so that one inflation is, for instance, largely imported and another is largely the result of domestic budgetary policy. (Such issues, however, are dealt with in relation to the first two questions.) The second source of difference is that the structural equations through which the exogenous influences work may have altered. In particular, it is often suggested that people have become more responsive to inflation in the sense that because of adverse past experience they now try harder to anticipate and offset the effects of inflation on their activities. Apart from this expectational aspect, the underlying inflationary mechanism may alter for a variety of other reasons; for example, as changes in the composition of output, of activity, and in institutions cause shifts in the type and responsiveness of the markets that make up the economy.

These are complex issues, and it would be pretentious to suggest that a brief paper can do more than indicate tentative answers.

To begin with a brief description of salient features of the Australian econ-

1. These are examples only. Devotees of particular theories should substitute their own lists.

omy, consider first the degree to which the economy is open to international economic influences. In 1972–73[2] exports formed 17 percent of gross domestic product, the principal components being wool, 17.5 percent, other primary products, 33.5 percent, minerals, 22.9 percent,[3] and manufactured products, 13 percent. Thus not only is dependence on foreign trade considerable, but the sorts of commodities exported (especially agricultural products and minerals) are particularly subject to price fluctuations. On the other hand, imports consist mainly of manufactured products for both producer and consumer use, and their prices, though reflecting world trends, are relatively more stable than export prices. Since for most traded commodities Australia's share in world makets is small, it is reasonable and customary to assume that export and import prices are (apart from the influence of local tariffs and subsidies) essentially determined abroad.

Over the last ten years or so an important change in the export situation has been the considerable increase in both the value and the share of minerals (particularly iron ore). On the import side, discovery and use of petroleum and natural gas deposits has considerably reduced the dependence of the economy on imported petroleum. Generally exports have fallen short of imports in value, for Australia has traditionally been a capital-importing country, but failure to adjust the exchange rate to the above-mentioned trends caused a reversal of this tendency in the early 1970s.

Australia operates a fixed, periodically adjusted exchange rate system, which until recently was tied to the U.S. dollar. This makes it vulnerable to considerable short-term capital movements when the market perceives the Australian dollar as under- or overvalued.

The other notable feature of Australia's trading position is the tariff. It is part of a wide system of protection for industry, which extends to such things as home-price-support schemes for some rural exportables. If only imports bearing a duty of 12.5 percent or more are taken into consideration, the average level of the tariff on those items in 1973–74 was 26 percent.

In addition to the openness of the economy, a feature that commands considerable attention in discussions of Australian inflation is the method of determining wage awards. From relatively simply beginnings this process has evolved into an intricate system of federal and state wage courts, boards, and

2. The Australian fiscal year is from July 1 to June 30 of the subsequent year. In this paper the form 1972–73 is used for the fiscal year, and 1972/73 refers to the two calendar years 1972 and 1973.

3. This figure includes partly processed minerals. The source of these data is *Quarterly Summary of Australian Statistics,* no. 289 (Canberra: Australian Bureau of Statistics, September 1973).

tribunals. Despite the apparent complexity of both the institutions and the concepts involved in wage awards, their determination by and large follows a fairly straightforward pattern. Approximately once a year the Australian Conciliation and Arbitration Commission hands down a decision on future wage rates after hearing submissions from employees, employers, and the governments. This event is known as the National Wage Case. The substance of the decision is not only applied to those under federal awards but also usually adopted by state and other tribunals. The type of judgment made varies considerably from year to year as the judges seek a formula that will be appropriate to current economic and political circumstances. Sometimes, for instance, a particular percentage increase is granted to all relevant award wages while at other times the decision involves a uniform absolute increase. Besides the National Wage Case there are a large number of hearings on award wages for various groups such as metal workers, air pilots, public servants, and academics, and the judgments made in these cases may apply instead of, but more usually in addition to, those from the National Wage Case. Agreements reached by collective bargaining outside the arbitration system may be registered as "consent agreement" awards. Of course, employers are free to pay above-award wages.

A prominent feature of Australian wage awards in recent years has been the movement toward raising rates for females relative to those for males on the principle of "equal pay for equal work." (The effect of this on wage relativities is examined below.)

The minimum wage used to be subject to automatic quarterly "cost of living" adjustments, but this process was suspended in 1953, presumably on the grounds that it added to inflationary pressures.[4]

Causes of Inflation in Australia

This section provides a general description of what has happened to the Australian economy, relevant to inflation, since 1950, and then examines the period since 1970 in detail, contrasting where possible the 1973/1974 and the 1950/1951 experiences. The behavior of such variables as consumer prices, unemployment and job vacancies, rates of change of import and export prices, and movements in the money supply and balance of payments is first outlined.

4. The 1975 National Wage judgment has moved tentatively toward the reintroduction of quarterly wage indexing.

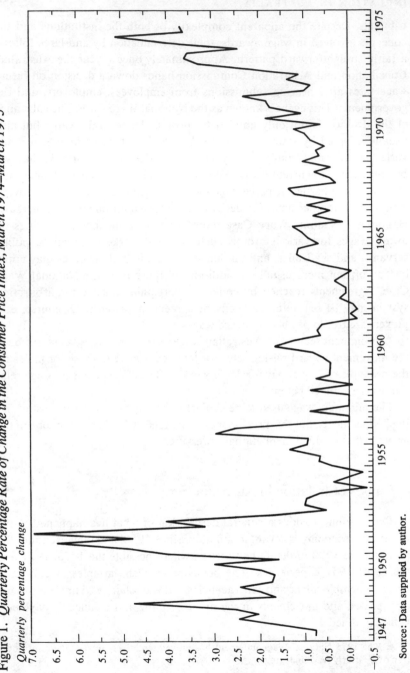

Figure 1. *Quarterly Percentage Rate of Change in the Consumer Price Index, March 1974–March 1975*

Source: Data supplied by author.

Behavior of the main variables

Figure 1 depicts quarterly percentage rates of change in the consumer price index from 1947 to 1975. Inflation was rapid from 1947 to 1950, this being a period of postwar shortages and adjustments. The largest price increases, as noted earlier, occurred in the 1950/1951 (wool boom) period. Since then identifiable inflationary periods have been roughly 1955/1956, 1960, 1964/ 1965, 1970/1971, and 1973/1974. During the 1960s, however, inflation rates were moderate, rarely exceeding 4 percent a year, and there is no evidence that inflation accelerated in the 1960s, as it did in many industrial countries. More recent inflation rates were 4.8 percent in 1970, 7 percent in 1971, 4.4 percent in 1972, 13.2 percent in 1973, and 16.3 percent in 1974.

Variables can be identified that give a picture of the state of excess demand and supply and that can therefore be used to check on another aspect of inflation. For Australia a readily available measure is the difference between vacancies and unemployment as a percentage of the work force (figure 2). Before commenting on these figures it is worth noting that the aggregate data conceal some significant sectoral differences. Figure 3 shows the metropolitan and nonmetropolitan breakdown of these measures and reveals the very different behavior of vacancies outside the metropolitan areas.[5] It seems plausible that in smaller towns and country areas vacancies are not reported as consistently through the Commonwealth Employment Service as in the larger cities. On the other hand, the benefits paid to those unemployed should ensure that reporting is comparable in both areas. Hence the aggregate figure may not be a completely satisfactory measure of the market situation. It is also plausible that the wage-setting markets are predominantly those in the big towns, so that a better picture of the state of the labor market relevant to inflationary pressures may be gained by examining metropolitan vacancies and unemployment. Unfortunately, this can only be done for the period since 1959, the earliest year for which these figures are available.

From figure 2 and the upper section of figure 3 1950/1951, 1954/1955, 1960, 1964 (June)/1965, 1969/1970, and 1973/1974 (June) emerge as periods of "excess demand" for labor, when vacancies exceeded unemployment. It can be seen that the earlier identified periods of inflation and excess demand in the labor market correspond closely, with a tendency for the periods when prices rose to lag somewhat behind labor demand conditions.

The relation between price movements and excess demand for labor is shown in figures 4 and 5. Figure 4 gives data for the whole period, using a lag

5. Metropolitan vacancies and unemployment cover the six state capital cities and include about 54 percent of the work force.

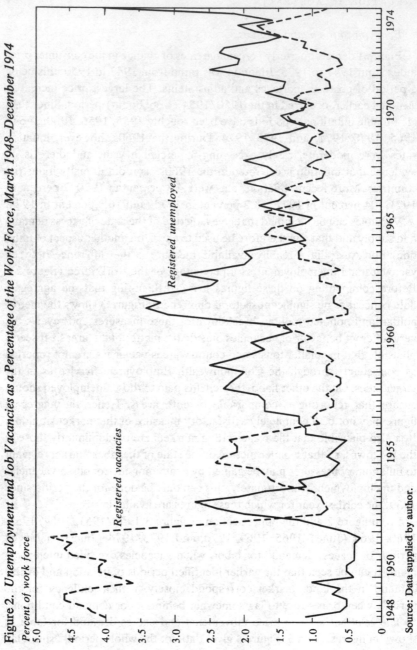

Figure 2. *Unemployment and Job Vacancies as a Percentage of the Work Force, March 1948–December 1974*

Percent of work force

Registered unemployed

Registered vacancies

Source: Data supplied by author.

Figure 3. *Unemployment and Job Vacancies as a Percentage of the Work Force, Metropolitan and Nonmetropolitan Areas, June 1959–December 1974*

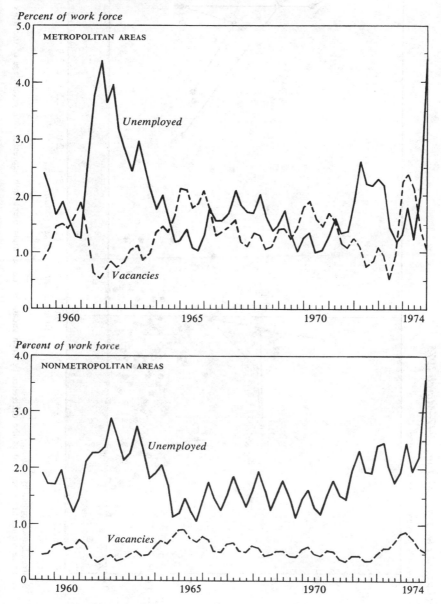

Source: Data supplied by author.

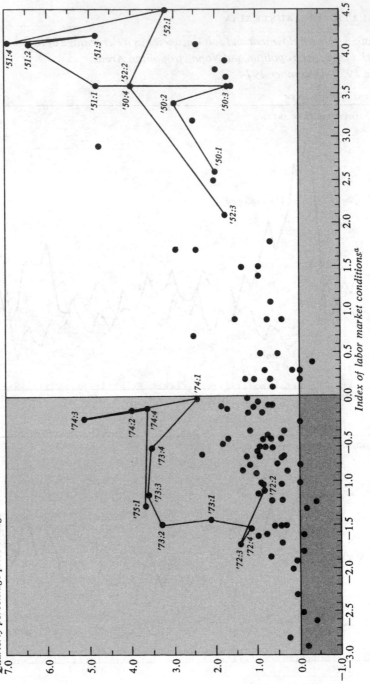

Figure 4. *Quarterly Percentage Price Changes in Relation to Labor Market Conditions (Lagged Two Periods), June 1947–March 1975*

Quarterly percentage price change

Index of labor market conditions[a]

Source: Data supplied by author.

a. These values are computed as the difference between vacancies and unemployment both expressed as a percentage of the work force.

Figure 5. *Quarterly Percentage Price Changes in Relation to Labor Market Conditions, Metropolitan Areas Only (Lagged One Period), March 1969–March 1975*

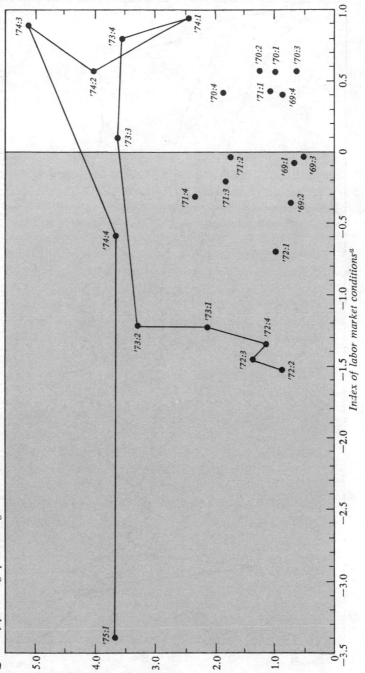

Source: Data supplied by author.
a. These values are computed as the difference between vacancies and unemployment both expressed as a percentage of the work force.

Figure 6. *Quarterly Consumer, Import, and Export Price Indexes, December 1947–December 1974*

Index (1952/53 = 100)

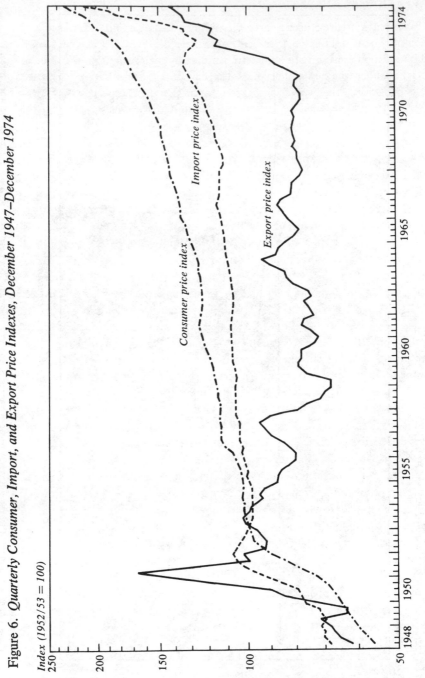

Source: Data supplied by author.

of six months; figure 5 uses a three-month lag and metropolitan vacancy and unemployment data since 1969 only. Further, the 1950/1951 and 1973/1974 inflation episodes are shown by connecting the relevant points. I leave it to the reader whether an inverse relation can be detected. Certainly in figure 4 the behavior of the two variables seems related in the classic way for 1950–52. The 1972–73–74 cycle seems to involve the standard direction of movement, but is located in a region of low excess demand.

Figure 6 shows the consumer, export, and import price indexes on a semilog scale, the two trade price indexes being measured in Australian currency. A striking feature of these data is the rapid rise in export prices that occurred before and during each of the severe inflations of 1950/1951 and 1973/1974. From the beginning of 1950 to the end of March 1951 export prices rose by 95 percent and from the end of September 1972 to the end of March 1974 their increase was 46 percent. Such large movements in export prices in an open economy of the Australian type must have had significant effects on the rate of increase of domestic prices. Another feature to note is the effects of the revaluation of the Australian dollar by 7 percent in December 1972, which can be seen in the Australian currency export and import price series and which thus resulted in a smaller rise in export and import prices than would otherwise have occurred. Moreover, because of exchange rate movements in other currencies and a further 5 percent revaluation in September 1973, the trade-weighted Australian dollar exchange rate appreciated by 20 percent between June 1972 and June 1974.[6] Unlike export prices, import prices were relatively stable until 1974, but during that year the index rose by over 60 percent. Some part of this was due to substantial rises in the price of "fuels and lubricants," but even when this item is excluded, the index shows a rise of almost 40 percent over the year.

Figure 7 illustrates movements in the money supply (M_3) and in gross domestic product at current and constant prices. During the latter part of the 1960s the annual growth rate of M_3 was close to 8 percent, but it can be seen that much more rapid growth was achieved in 1972 and 1973 (approximately 20 percent in each year). By contrast, 1974 shows a reversal of this trend, except for the last quarter, when the restrictive monetary policy of late 1973 to mid-1974 was dramatically reversed. Over the whole year the rise in M_3 amounted to 8.9 percent. (The reasons for and effects of these movements are discussed in the next section.) The growth in constant price gross domestic product averaged about 6 percent in the 1960s and has averaged 5 percent since then.

6. Reserve Bank of Australia, *Report for Year 1972–73* (Canberra: Government Printer of Australia, 1973), p. 17. The Australian dollar was devalued by 12 percent in September 1974.

Figure 7. *Changes in Money Supply and in Gross Domestic Product, Current and Constant Prices, March 1950–December 1974*

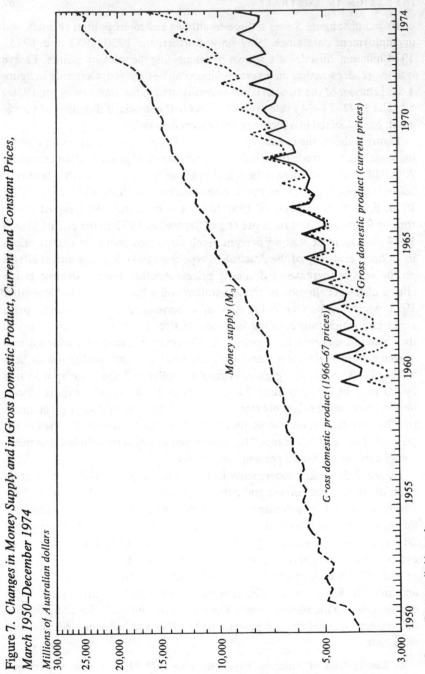

Millions of Australian dollars

Money supply (M₃)

Gross domestic product (1966–67 prices)

Gross domestic product (current prices)

Source: Data supplied by author.

Inflation since 1970

The foregoing discussion confirms that since 1970 the rate of inflation has been high and rising (except for a brief period following the deflationary budget of 1971). To analyze this experience it is convenient to treat it under four headings: *External influences, Local influences and responses (other than through wages), Wages and salaries,* and *Comparison with 1950/1951.*

EXTERNAL INFLUENCES. To understand the generation of recent inflation it is important to appreciate certain changes in the structure of the Australian export and import sectors that have had a considerable impact on the balance of payments. The discovery and exploitation of minerals and oil through the 1960s and in the 1970s has greatly strengthened Australia's balance of payments position. Another trend that helped to strengthen the balance of payments (and also to reduce dependence on agricultural and pastoral products) was that a larger proportion of Australia's exports have been manufactured goods. Despite the downward drift of export prices in the late 1960s and early 1970s (figure 6), the current-account deficits to the financial year 1968–69 remained fairly steady in money terms. Australia has been, and is likely to continue to be, a capital-importing country; thus when the current-account deficit fell to $760 million in 1969–70[7] and remained at the low figure of $872 million in 1970–71 it might have been expected that a revaluation of the exchange rate was in order. Unfortunately, the good performance of minerals and oil was accompanied by deteriorating prices for one of the major exports, wool.[8] From a level of 103 in 1966–67 the wool price index fell steadily to a low of 67 in 1970–71, and the value of wool exports declined from $67.2 million to $45.3 million. On the other hand, the deficit in the balance of payments declined from $1,144 million in 1967–68 to $872 million in 1970–71. These low levels of wool prices and incomes were causing woolgrowers, particularly those with smaller holdings, considerable difficulty, and with the coalition Liberal–Country party government in power in Canberra appreciation of the exchange rate was not undertaken.

Starting early in 1971 a substantial inflow of capital occurred, which

7. It was in 1970 that Australia's oil discoveries began to be exploited at a rate that substantially affected the balance of payments. By 1972 a Bureau of Mineral Resources index of Australia's "self-sufficiency" in various commodities showed a figure of 67 (out of a maximum of 100) for crude oil.

8. In 1972–73 wool exports amounted to 18.5 percent of the value of total exports. Actually, in the years of low wool prices, 1970–71 and 1971–72, ores and concentrates exceeded wool exports in value.

resulted in Australia's previously stable foreign reserves rising by 80.1 percent in 1971 and 72 percent in 1972. If the Australian dollar was not to be appreciated this inflow could have been prevented from affecting the domestic money supply only through sterilization by open market operations or budget surpluses. Table 2 below shows that the total actual deficits rose from $10 million in 1970–71 to $134 million in 1971–72 and $709 million in 1972–73. Hence, the burden of offsetting the capital inflow was thrown on open market operations.[9] These were substantial in 1971, and the growth in the money supply (M_3) was 8.6 percent for that year, which was not much greater than the average increase in the last part of the 1960s. However, with the considerable rise in unemployment during 1971 and an election in prospect at the end of 1972, the government not only reduced open market sales but also presented an expansionary budget. The result was an increase in the money supply of 18.2 percent in 1972 and 22.1 percent in 1973. It does appear that the money supply was substantially uncontrolled in these years, with the authorities pursuing other aims such as expanding employment and public expenditure. The restrictive actions of the monetary authorities in the last part of 1973 and most of 1974 (described later) were successful in bringing the rate of growth of M_3 back to 8.9 percent.

Since Australia's export prices can be regarded as largely exogenously determined, when looking for causes of inflation in a regime with a managed exchange rate it is important to examine their behavior in detail. Between the start of the recent export price boom (approximately September 1972) and December 1974 the overall export price index rose by over 59 percent. Table 1 shows the main components of the index on dates chosen to illustrate turning points in the boom. Despite the diverse behavior of different items, all experienced substantial price increases in the period. Wool prices, at particularly low levels in 1969–70, 1970–71, and 1971–72, rose from May 1972 to May 1973 by 137 percent but subsequently fell back considerably; meat prices rose from May 1972 to May 1973 by 37 percent and in the next four months by 10 percent and have since declined below the May 1972 level; prices of both dairy products and sugar fell between May 1972 and May 1973, contradicting the trend in all other items, but in 1974 both items (in particular sugar) rose substantially. The price index of metals and coal in the two years from May 1972 increased by 73 percent and continued to rise considerably; and gold prices followed the same general trend. Clearly the rise in export prices was broadly based and thus substantially affected items such as meats and cereals, which directly enter local consumption and

9. See, especially, Reserve Bank of Australia, *Report for Year 1971–72*, pp. 22–32, for a discussion of this sterilization process.

Table 1. *Main Components of the Export Price Index, 1972–74*
1959–60 = 100

Month and year	Wool	Meats	Dairy products	Cereals	Dried and canned fruits	Sugar	Hides and tallow	Metals and coal	Gold	All items
May 1972	87	150	146	98	103	148	108	141	141	110
September 1972	120	161	126	98	100	135	132	139	184	118
May 1973	206	205	113	99	118	130	142	152	210	144
September 1973	193	225	109	138	135	139	163	167	224	152
May 1974	144	163	110	256	172	208	169	244	374	173
December 1974	120	135	129	262	183	528	138	262	446	188

Source: Australian Bureau of Statistics, *Monthly Review of Business Statistics*, various issues.

hence the consumer price index. For some items (particularly wool and meats) the evidence that the boom faded is contained in the index. For others, such as metals, sugar, and dairy products, increases continued through 1974.

The import price index did not rise significantly in 1973 but increased by 63 percent in 1974. Part of this rise is directly attributable to the increase in "mineral fuels and lubricants," whose price rose by 203 percent that year. Australia's dependence on imported fuels had been considerably reduced from 1969 to 1974, so the item is greatly overvalued in this base-weighted index. However, if the item is excluded, the rise in the index was 39 percent, with, for instance, "machinery except electric" (weight 20.5) rising 35 percent, and "textiles" (weight 8.9) rising 22 percent. It should be noted that the import price index does not reflect changes in the Australian tariff.

LOCAL INFLUENCES AND RESPONSES (OTHER THAN THROUGH WAGES). The behavior of the building industry and that of imports offer good examples of the effects of the boom and its associated easy liquidity. As an industry particularly sensitive to economic conditions, it would seem that private building and construction should be greatly stimulated and experience rises in activity, costs, and prices. Between December 1971 and December 1972 the number of building approvals issued for private dwellings (seasonally adjusted) increased 25 percent and in the following year—to September 1973 —by 17 percent; but thereafter they declined. Imports, responding not only to the tariff and exchange rate cuts but also to domestic excess demand, started to rise about May 1973 and by April 1974 had risen by 60.6 percent in value. In interpreting this increase it should be recalled (figure 6) that the import price index had remained relatively steady until 1973.

Consider now the actions of government authorities (which were partly in response to inflationary conditions), in order to determine whether such actions produced any substantial stimulus to inflation. I have already mentioned certain government measures that could be considered anti-inflationary: the deflationary budget of 1971–72; the sterilization of short-term capital inflow in 1971; the appreciations of the exchange rate of 7 percent in December 1972 and 5 percent in September 1973, which, together with devaluations of other currencies, meant a 20 percent appreciation of the trade-weighted Australian dollar exchange rate between June 1972 and June 1974; and the 25 percent general tariff cut in July 1973.

Notable among other measures taken were the monetary restrictions of 1973 and 1974. In response to the inflation, the Reserve Bank of Australia increased the statutory reserve deposit ratio in August 1973,[10] requested trading and savings banks to reduce their new lending, and revised bank overdraft rates from 7.75 percent to 9.50 percent in the same month. But the tightening of credit came in the first half of 1974 with the large increase in imports and higher tax payments, both inflation-induced.[11] Even so, bank loans continued to grow rapidly, despite the reduced liquidity of banks. Later, rising unemployment (1.8 percent in June 1974, 2.4 percent in September, and 3.4 percent in December, seasonally adjusted) and falling activity, particularly in the private housing sector, brought an easing of credit, releases from statutory reserve deposits were made, and additional credit for housing loans became available. This reversed the downward trend in deposits and advances. Thus seasonally adjusted trading bank deposits increased by $685 million in the fourth quarter of 1974 though they had declined by $480 million in the third quarter, and their total loans, seasonally adjusted, rose by $500 million in the fourth quarter in contrast to a decline of $63 million in the preceding three months.

Having included in its electoral platform of 1972 a promise not to increase income taxes, the Labor government's anti-inflation measures in the 1973 budget were restricted to raising indirect taxes. While it is true that indirect taxes can help curb demand, the prices of many commodities received a direct upward push. Furthermore, high indirect taxes may well have a long-

10. Trading banks are required to keep certain deposits with the Reserve Bank specified as a ratio to the trading bank's current level of deposits.

11. See Reserve Bank of Australia, *Report for Year 1972–73,* for a detailed discussion of financial conditions in this period.

Table 2. *Australian Federal Budget, 1970–75*
Amounts in millions of Australian dollars

| Financial year | Domestic surplus | | Total surplus | | Increase in expenditure over previous year (percent) | |
	Budgeted	Actual	Budgeted	Actual	Budgeted domestic expenditure	Actual total expenditure
1970–71	530	460	4	−10	12.4	11.4
1971–72	630	387	−11	−134	13.1	13.1
1972–73	−60	−215	−630	−709	19.9	11.0
1973–74	−162	211	−687	−293	16.5	20.2
1974–75	23	−1,949	−570	−2,567	34.9	32.4

Sources: *Budget Speeches,* Parliamentary Papers (Canberra: Government Printer of Australia), various issues; and *Quarterly Summary of Australian Statistics* (Canberra: Australian Bureau of Statistics), various issues.

term effect on cost structures that adds to the rate of inflation.[12] Because the 1972 elections left Labor without a working majority in the Senate, it dissolved both Houses of Parliament and called for a new election in May 1974. The Opposition chose to fight the election on the issue of inflation and had considerable success with this tactic. Labor was returned to power, but with an apparently tougher attitude toward inflation and its control.[13] Although a number of experiments to control the rate of price increases have since been suggested or tried, none were particularly effective. These included a prices justification tribunal, which, by holding inquiries into reasons for proposed price rises, may have had some effect in slowing down the rate of price increases, and exhortations to unions to observe "wage restraint." However, the most effective influence in curbing demand seems to have been the monetary measures previously mentioned.

It is likely that the Australian government's budgetary policy contributed significantly to raising demand in 1972–73 and 1973–74, although the budget of 1971–72 was deflationary. Table 2 sets out the main features of the federal budget in recent years, although something should first be said about the difference between the domestic surplus and the total surplus (or deficits) and the relevance of the two concepts. The domestic surplus excludes inter-

12. This point is further discussed in John D. Pitchford and Stephen J. Turnovsky, "Income Distribution and Taxes in the Inflationary Context," *Economica,* vol. 42 (August 1975), pp. 272–82.

13. At the time of the May 1974 election, an unsuccessful attempt was made to change the constitution to give the federal government power to control prices and incomes.

national receipts and outlays of the government, the main difference for Australia for the years covered being on the outlay side. It was implied earlier in looking back at the effect of budgetary policy on the money supply, that the actual total surplus was the relevant figure. On the other hand, to gauge the expected impact of government policy on domestic demand the budgeted domestic surplus and the rate of change in expenditure seem most significant since it is the impact on domestic activity that is sought and the domestic concept seems to capture this best. It is evident that the 1971–72 budget was designed to be deflationary—the budgeted domestic surplus rose by $100 million over the previous financial year whereas the rate of increase of budgeted expenditure was similar to that of previous years. Because the labor market (see figures 2 and 3) was showing definite signs of reduced demand by the time the budget was announced, it seems probable that this budgetary action accelerated the tendency toward recession. As unemployment rose the government attempted to offset the deflationary impact by additional expenditure. For both the 1972–73 and 1973–74 financial years, the government budgeted for a deficit and for increases in expenditure that were larger than usual. In the 1974–75 budget, although a small surplus was budgeted, expenditure was estimated to increase by 35 percent. Macroeconomic theory suggests that such a large increase in government expenditure would have an expansionary impact. (The reasoning is analogous to that which attributes to a balanced budget a positive multiplier effect.) There seems little doubt that, starting with the 1972–73 Liberal budget and subsequently under the Labor government, budgets have been expansionary. This has reflected Labor's goals of expanding public service, increasing outlays on welfare plans, and becoming more involved in activities that were previously the preserve of private industry.

It should be noted that the inflation of 1973–74 together with the progressive personal income tax structure resulted in an actual domestic surplus although a deficit had been budgeted. The tax response thus provided some offset to the expansion in expenditure.

WAGES AND SALARIES. Both in the government and among academic economists the view that recent inflation is partly or largely due to "excessive" wage increases seems widespread. It is interesting to examine the basis for these opinions. First, by what means can it be decided whether or not wage increases are excessive? This is a complex issue, and I have examined it at length elsewhere.[14] Moreover, it can sometimes be the case that an "excessive" wage leads to unemployment rather than inflation. A simple-

14. John D. Pitchford, "The Usefulness of the Average Productivity Wage Adjustment Rule," *Economic Record*, vol. 47 (June 1971), pp. 255–61.

minded approach is to look at the increase in average earnings and pronounce it excessive if it seems high by reference to earlier experience. If the inflation is due to large excess demand for goods and labor, a large money wage increase could be expected to be induced by this rather than to be an initiating factor.

To decide whether a particular nominal wage is excessive and hence may have contributed to inflation, it is necessary to ask whether the real wage it represents at the current or expected price level is consistent, other things being equal, with an equilibrium in the labor market and simultaneously a zero rate of inflation. If it implies excess supply of labor the *real* wage is excessive because equilibrium in the labor market can only be achieved by using demand management to make prices rise and so to force down the real wage.[15] Thus an excessive real wage means either unemployment or inflation, or (for a range of inflation rates) both.

Despite the operational limitations of this concept, it nevertheless makes one suspect that large real wage increases over a short period of time lead to a (partly or wholly) wage-induced inflation. Real wage changes, however, must be compared with labor productivity changes (on the order of 0.5 percent a year for all industries, but 3.6 percent a year for secondary industries in the five years ending June 1974), for these can offset the effects of wages on costs and hence on labor demand.[16]

Unfortunately figures for average hourly earnings are not available for Australia. In analyzing the contribution of wages, average weekly earnings (with their overtime component) and average weekly rates are the best data that can be used in an aggregative study. Table 3 shows real wage earnings per male equivalent unit (that is, variations between the earnings of males and females are eliminated insofar as the data will allow).

First, note the 4.8 percent increase for the first quarter of 1971. This can be accounted for by the National Wage Case of late 1970, which awarded a 6 percent increase in all award wages and which thus applied generally throughout the economy. (Despite this large rise the annual rate of increase in real wages turned out to be of the same order of magnitude as that for 1969, 1970, and 1972.)

Second, the annual rate of change of earnings in 1969–72—between 4.1

15. How long the reduction in the real wage persists depends on the duration and degree of expansionary policy and the relative speeds with which prices and wages are adjusted.

16. There are two approaches to this comparison of productivity and real wages. Markup pricing requires it as a condition that the real-wage cost per unit of output remain constant, whereas marginal productivity theorists require it for equilibrium in the labor market. In the former case it is average productivity, in the latter case marginal productivity that enters into the comparison.

Table 3. *Annual and Quarterly Changes in Real Wages, 1969–74*
Percent except as noted

	Average weekly earnings per equivalent male unit			Change in real wages	
Year and quarter	Seasonally adjusted (Australian dollars)	Change	Change in consumer price index	Quarterly	Annual
1969:1	71.50	1.85	0.66	1.19	
2	72.30	1.12	0.75	0.37	4.57
3	74.00	2.35	0.56	1.79	
4	75.40	1.89	0.84	1.05	
1970:1	76.80	1.86	1.01	0.85	
2	79.10	2.99	1.28	1.78	4.14
3	80.40	1.64	0.63	1.01	
4	82.20	2.24	1.88	0.36	
1971:1	87.00	5.84	1.05	4.79	
2	88.60	1.84	1.74	0.10	4.37
3	90.20	1.81	1.88	−0.07	
4	91.70	1.66	2.35	−0.69	
1972:1	94.10	2.62	0.98	1.64	
2	95.20	1.17	0.89	0.28	4.66
3	98.00	2.94	1.37	1.57	
4	100.10	2.14	1.19	0.95	
1973:1	102.00	1.90	2.11	−0.21	
2	106.30	4.22	3.30	0.92	1.66
3	111.90	5.27	3.64	1.63	
4	115.00	2.77	3.58	−0.81	
1974:1	119.10	3.57	2.42	1.15	
2	126.30	6.05	4.05	2.00	11.49
3	140.10	10.93	5.13	5.80	
4	146.90	4.85	3.77	1.08	

Sources: *Monthly Review of Business Statistics*, various issues.

percent and 4.7 percent—is larger than the 0.5 percent average productivity change for the whole economy, but not significantly greater than the annual 3.6 percent increase in secondary industry productivity. Since secondary industries employ a large proportion of the work force and are regarded as having a substantial effect on wage setting in Australia, it is not possible to brand these wage increases as excessive with any degree of assurance.

Third, when the recent inflation began in earnest in March 1973, the real wage fell initially and then registered the unusually small increase of 1.7 percent for the whole of 1973. Indeed, even by the second quarter of 1974 the real wage increase for the previous eighteen months was not far out of line

Table 4. *Average Hourly Wage Rates, 1969–74*
Percent

Year and quarter	Males		Females	
	Change from previous quarter	Annual change	Change from previous quarter	Annual change
1969:1	0.87		1.66	
2	0.52		0.68	
3	0.63	3.71	1.18	6.13
4	1.65		2.49	
1970:1	2.46		3.35	
2	0.44		0.63	
3	1.36	6.26	0.73	6.75
4	1.88		1.91	
1971:1	7.41		8.19	
2	0.78		1.26	
3	2.62	13.83	4.16	18.46
4	2.47		3.81	
1972:1	1.29		2.43	
2	2.88		3.50	
3	2.44	8.87	2.34	10.89
4	1.99		2.20	
1973:1	2.33		2.04	
2	5.35		7.92	
3	4.33	14.59	4.97	21.83
4	1.89		5.40	
1974:1	1.89		3.76	
2	15.23		14.87	
3	7.90	31.4	13.05	41.53
4	5.10		4.84	

Sources: Australian Bureau of Statistics, *Minimum Wage Rates, Wage Rates and Earnings*, and *Wage Rates Indexes*, various issues; ABS data supplied to author.

with that of previous years. It certainly looks as if the inflation began as a traditional demand inflation with wages rising less rapidly than prices at the outset.

Fourth, the increase in real wage earnings of almost 6 percent in the third quarter of 1974 changed this pattern entirely, producing an 11.5 percent increase in real earnings for that year and a 13 percent increase over the two years 1973 and 1974. Table 4 shows that this followed the 15.2 percent increase in average hourly wage rates for males in the second quarter. Whether this sequence was a market response or an autonomous "excessive" increase is difficult to determine, but there is a strong presumption that the 12 percent real earnings increase in 1974 must have imposed problems for both the stability of prices and the rate of unemployment.

Figure 8. *Working Days Lost[a] per Work Force Member as a Result of Industrial Disputes, December 1947–December 1974*

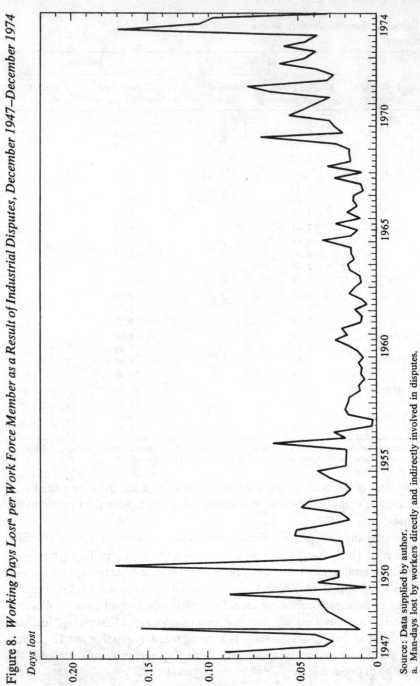

Source: Data supplied by author.
a. Man-days lost by workers directly and indirectly involved in disputes.

So far the wage variable has been related to male employees. Table 4 compares average hourly wage rates for males and females. There is no need to compute relevant real wage variables, as comparison of the nominal rates for males and females clearly illustrates the recent tendency for females' real wages to rise faster than those for males. Only in 1970 was there an increase of rates for males similar to that for rates for females. However, 1974 is outstanding as a move toward "equal pay." Females' money rates increased 10 percent faster than males' money rates in that year and females' *real* wage rates rose by 25.3 percent. Irrespective of the social worth of equal pay, the possibility of absorbing such a rapid change without additional inflation and/or unemployment seems slight.

An important aspect of the labor market is illustrated in figure 8, which shows working days lost because of industrial disputes as a proportion of the whole work force—that is, days lost per employee. A notable feature is the spike in the first quarter of 1974. This occurs approximately a year after the inflation rate began to increase and probably coincides with the time in which many wage agreements were up for renewal. In the next quarter the average hourly wage rate for males climbed 15 percent, no doubt reflecting the strike settlements. It seems reasonable to suppose that the rapid inflation of 1973 was induced by export price increases and domestic demand pressures, resulting in an unusually small rise in real wages that year. This in turn led to a high level of industrial disputes and to wage increases that (even if the female wage component is omitted) more than compensated for the increase of 1973, which was small in comparison with the 1970–72 real wage increases.

COMPARISON WITH 1950/1951. Now consider briefly the points of comparison between the 1950/1951 and 1973/1974 inflations. Both were associated with world commodity booms, and so with considerable increases in export prices. Although the 1950 export price rise was bigger than that for 1972/1973, the latter encompassed a wider range of exported commodities. In 1950/1951 large increases were mainly confined to wool and to metals (which were much less important exports then). For instance, from June 1950 to June 1951, wheat, meats, butter, and sugar showed modest increases compared with the rise of 143 percent in wool prices from June 1950 to February 1951. Further, unlike the earlier period, measures were taken in 1972 and 1973 to offset the external effects by appreciation and tariff cuts. In 1950/1951 import prices also showed a substantial rise, but this was not so marked for most of 1973/1974. One aspect in which experience differed considerably is that before 1950 there had been a long spell of excess demand for labor, whereas 1972 was a year of excess supply of labor. In both periods a considerable rise in imports occurred with about a year's lag after the initial acceleration of inflation.

Real wage behavior was also similar in the two booms. The real wage (as measured in table 3) had fallen for five quarters before it rose in the third quarter of 1950 by 2.8 percent. It fell again in the fourth quarter by 4 percent, and this was the period in which industrial unrest reached its peak (see figure 8). Following this, the real wage jumped by 7 percent in the fourth quarter of 1951. The similarity to the 1973/1974 experience seems clear.

The Mechanism of Inflation

The preceding section was concerned with the factors that initiate inflation rather than the mechanism through which it works. This section attempts to discover whether the mechanism has changed. The following discussion takes as its starting point a model I tested in 1968.[17] There have been a number of other such analyses since then, which have been the subject of various survey papers.[18]

The object of the model was to explain the quarterly rate of change in the consumer price index as a function of lagged values of variables that could reasonably be termed exogenous. Thus the equation tested could be regarded as a reduced form derivable from structural equations in which the chosen exogenous variables appeared. There was no attempt to infer anything about the underlying structural equations, mainly because for the data period 1947–

17. John D. Pitchford, "An Analysis of Price Movements in Australia, 1947–68," *Australian Economic Papers*, vol. 7 (December 1968), pp. 111–35.

18. See the surveys by C. G. F. Simkin, "Inflation in Australia and New Zealand: 1953–71," *Economic Record*, vol. 48 (December 1972), pp. 465–82, and N. R. Norman and John P. Nieuwenhuysen, "Australia's Inflationary Babel," in J. E. Isaac and J. R. Niland, eds., *Australian Labour Economics: Readings* (Melbourne: Macmillan, 1974). These surveys include discussion of econometric investigations such as John D. Pitchford, "An Analysis of Price Movements in Australia, 1947–68"; John P. Nieuwenhuysen and N. R. Norman, "Wages Policy in Australia, Issues and Tests," vol. 9, *British Journal of Industrial Relations* (November 1971), pp. 353–70; W. E. Norton and J. F. Henderson, "A Model of the Australian Economy, A Further Report," Occasional Paper 3G (Sydney: Reserve Bank of Australia, 1972); John W. Nevile, *Fiscal Policy in Australia: Theory and Practice* (Melbourne: Cheshire, 1970); C. I. Higgins, "A Wage Price Sector for a Quarterly Australian Model," in A. A. Powell and R. A. Williams, eds., *Econometrics of Macro and Monetary Relations* (Amsterdam: North-Holland, 1973; distributed in the United States and Canada by American Elsevier); P. D. Jonson, K. L. Mahar, and G. J. Thompson, "Earnings and Award Wages in Australia," vol. 13, *Australian Economic Papers* (June 1974), pp. 80–98; and Michael Parkin, "The Short-Run and Long-Run Trade-offs between Inflation and Unemployment in Australia," *Australian Economic Papers*, vol. 12 (December 1973), pp. 127–44.

68 the additional information available to test such equations did not seem adequate for the purpose. The prime virtue of this period is that it includes the rapid inflation of the late 1940s and early 1950s.

The equation tested relates the quarterly proportional change in the consumer price index, Y_t, to a linear combination of lagged values of quarterly rates of change for import prices, X_{1_t}, export prices, X_{2_t}, a wage pressure variable, X_{32_t}, and the excess demand for labor measured by vacancies *minus* unemployment as a ratio to the work force for Australia as a whole, X_{4_t}. The wage pressure variable requires explanation. As noted, wage rates in Australia are set by a variety of judicial bodies; one of these is the Arbitration Court. Although economic conditions are taken into account in these decisions, it seems probable that the rates arrived at contain a fairly considerable nonmarket element. Hence, there is some justification for using the rate of change of nominal hourly wage rates, X_3, in the construction of an independent variable to explain consumer price movements. In the original paper[19] a number of alternative wage pressure variables were constructed, the logic of the exercise being that it was the extent to which the rate of change of nominal wage rates exceeded (or fell short of) some productivity increase variable that measured its contribution to inflation. The most satisfactory version of this, X_{32}, was arrived at by subtracting an allowance for changes in "external productivity" (arising from changes in the terms of trade).[20] The validity of internal productivity figures for 1947–68 for Australia is subject to considerable doubt, so that for this element it was assumed that decision-makers took a constant growth of internal productivity as a datum. This constant is not included in the construction of X_{32} but may be inserted when interpreting the results. Various equations were tried with quarterly data for 1946–67, and the most satisfactory result was:[21]

19. John D. Pitchford, "An Analysis of Price Movements in Australia, 1947–68."

20. To see the meaning of external and internal productivity in this context, suppose y represents gross national product per capita, x the output per capita of exports (price, p_x), and z the output per capita of nonexports, all measured in constant prices. If the import price index is p_m, productivity is said to be measured by

$$y = z + xp_x/p_m.$$

On the assumption that z and x grow at the same rate, it follows that

$$\frac{dy}{dt}\left(\frac{1}{y}\right) = \frac{dz}{dt}\left(\frac{1}{z}\right) + \frac{xp_x}{zp_z}\left[\frac{dp_x}{dt}\left(\frac{1}{p_x}\right) - \frac{dp_m}{dt}\left(\frac{1}{p_m}\right)\right].$$

In other words, the rate of growth of productivity is the sum of the rate of growth of internal productivity, $(dz/dt)(1/z)$, and the movement in the terms of trade weighted by the term xp_x/zp_z. The justification for the first equation above is that the ultimate value of exports is the imports they can purchase.

21. Data revisions for the period would produce slightly different values for the coefficients. All equations reported were fitted by ordinary least squares.

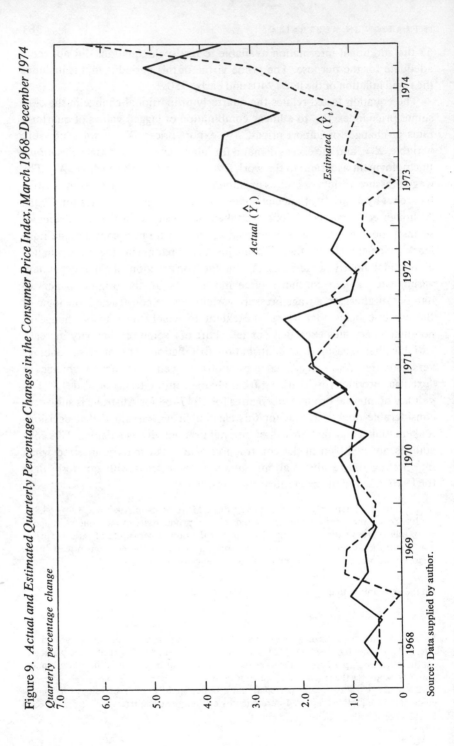

Figure 9. *Actual and Estimated Quarterly Percentage Changes in the Consumer Price Index, March 1968–December 1974*

Source: Data supplied by author.

(1)
$$Y_t = 0.44 + 0.33 \ X_{4_{t-2}} + 0.16 \ X_{1_{t-3}}$$
$$(3.66) \quad (5.76) \qquad (2.66)$$
$$+ \ 0.03 \ X_{2_{t-3}} + 0.15 \ X_{32_{t-1}} + 0.12 \ X_{3_{t-2}}$$
$$(2.82) \qquad (3.66) \qquad (3.08)$$
$$R^2 = 0.77; \ \text{Durbin-Watson statistic} = 1.82.$$

The t-statistics are shown in parentheses, and there is no evidence of multi-collinearity among the explanatory variables. At this stage it is sufficient to note that all variables are significant and in particular that excess demand for labor lagged six months was found to explain a good deal of the variation in prices.[22]

For later reference it should be noted that equations including the lagged value of prices, Y_{t-1}, were tested for this 1946–68 period, but were generally unsatisfactory.

The next step is to see how well equation 1 predicts inflation outside the estimation period. This is shown in figure 9 where it can be seen that until 1971/1972 the correspondence between actual quarterly change in the consumer price index, Y_t, and estimated quarterly change, Y_t, is reasonably close. In fact, the annual change in prices is underestimated by about 1 percent in each of the years 1968, 1969, 1970, and 1971. During and after 1971 the difference between actual and estimated prices becomes quite marked, and it is clear that equation 1 fails to account for the inflation of 1972, 1973, and part of 1974. Undoubtedly part of the reason for this failure is that rates of inflation of the magnitude experienced in this period have usually been associated with high levels of excess demand for labor, but in 1972/1974 excess demand was low and sometimes negative.

This last observation suggests that metropolitan excess demand, X_4^*, might give a better explanation of the current inflation. But the value of using it is limited because the series only goes back to 1959. A number of equations with a variety of lag forms were estimated for the 1959–74 period; the best of these are:

(2)
$$Y_t = 0.30 + 0.59 \ Y_{t-1} + 0.15 \ X_{4_{t-1}}^*$$
$$(2.72) \quad (7.09) \qquad (2.42)$$
$$+ \ 0.05 \ X_{1_{t-1}} + 0.05 \ X_{2_{t-1}} + 0.09 \ X_{3_{t-1}}$$
$$(2.07) \qquad (3.29) \qquad (2.2)$$
$$R^2 = 0.82; \ \text{Durbin-Watson statistic} = 2.14; \ h\text{-statistic} = -0.067.$$

(3)
$$Y_t = 0.16 + 0.79 \ Y_{t-1} + 0.13 \ X_{4_{t-1}}^*$$
$$(1.33) \quad (11.8) \qquad (2.03)$$
$$+ \ 0.06 \ X_{2_{t-1}} + 0.13 \ X_{10_{t-1}}$$
$$(3.27) \qquad (2.24)$$
$$R^2 = 0.79; \ \text{Durbin-Watson statistic} = 2.38; \ h\text{-statistic} = -1.77.$$

22. For detailed discussion, see ibid.

New variables X_3 and X_{10} are included in equations 2 and 3 and their meaning is given below. The following can be noted:

a. The lagged value of the dependent variable is the most significant variable in both equations. (With the inclusion of this variable the appropriate statistic for testing autocorrelation is h, which in each case, being less than 1.96 in absolute value, does not support the hypothesis of autocorrelated residuals.)[23]

b. The rate of change of import prices was not significant in various versions of equation 3 and hence was dropped as an explanator in that equation.

c. The lags on excess demand, export prices, and import prices (equation 2) are now only one period in length.

d. Better results are obtained with the variable X_3, which is simply the rate of change of minimum hourly wage rates, than with X_{32} (from which an allowance for external productivity movements is subtracted).

e. The variable X_{10} also gives satisfactory results. It is, in fact, the variable calculated in table 3 (except that X_{10} does not involve seasonal adjustment of earnings) and discussed there as a possible source of inflationary pressure. It is derived by subtracting the percentage change in the consumer price index from the percentage change in average weekly earnings. Thus from equation 3 the changes of approximately 4.2 percent in real wages in 1970 and 1971 would have contributed 0.5 percent to the rate of inflation *in the short run*. Long-run coefficients for each variable are found by setting $Y_t = Y_{t-1}$, in which case the coefficient of X_{10} is raised to 0.6 and the 4.2 percent real-wage increase implies 2.52 percent extra inflation. This exercise can be performed for each of the coefficients in equations 2 and 3. Actually, because X_{10} contains an element involving $-Y_{t-1}$, it is not possible to discriminate between a hypothesis that would replace X_{10} with average weekly earnings and the formulation in equation 3. However, this means precisely what it says; that is, the formulation in equation 3 is no better than, though not inferior to, the alternative mentioned.

I am somewhat hesitant about using X_{10} as an explanator in these equations. The difficulty arises because average weekly earnings must surely contain some element of market determination, and so should more correctly appear as a dependent variable in a larger system. To put this another way, X_{10} probably contains both demand and wage-push elements.

Further work on this model would require building a multiequation system in an attempt to sort out where the changes in inflationary behavior have taken place and to test competing theories. However, it can be tentatively

23. The Durbin h-statistic is distributed asymptotically as a standard normal variable.

concluded that recent Australian inflation has involved more rapid responses to exogenous changes than was the case in the past. Further, the significance of the lagged value of the dependent variable in equations 2 and 3 may be accounted for by a feedback mechanism that was previously weak or non-existent. Also, it is possible that this variable reflects a growing importance of expectational elements, tending to cause inflation to feed on itself.[24]

Summary

The paper began with three questions about recent inflation: the extent to which it was generated externally or internally; the related issue of the contribution of wage settlements to inflation; and whether the mechanisms through which it is produced have changed. The analysis indicates that the inflation of 1970–74 was mainly caused by external factors, particularly so in 1973–74, but that these were exacerbated by a failure to offset their effects and by both expansionary domestic fiscal policy and rising wages. Moreover, the experience of recent years suggests that the economy has become more responsive to inflationary influences either because of more rapid adjustment to past or present developments or because of a growing tendency to try to anticipate future rates of inflation.

A problem arises in deciding whether an inflation is imported or internally generated: almost always the effects of external factors could have been partially or wholly offset by domestic action, provided the authorities had been willing to accept the consequences of such offsetting action. But it seems reasonable to regard external influences not offset as external causes of inflation, even though in some sense they were failures of domestic policymakers.

To summarize earlier sections briefly: in the early 1970s Australia's balance of payments improved as a result of mineral and oil exploitation. The government at the time was unwilling to appreciate the exchange rate (mainly because of the adverse position of wool exports) so that a rapid increase in foreign exchange reserves occurred in 1971 and 1972. This was substantially sterilized by open market operations in 1971, but in 1972 rising unemployment led to an expansionary budget and to reduced open market sales, with the result that the money supply increased by about 20 percent in 1972 and again in 1973. The high levels of liquidity and the expansionary budgets of

24. A recent study claiming to have established the importance of expectational factors in Australian inflation is that by Michael Parkin, "The Short-Run and Long-Run Trade-offs between Inflation and Unemployment in Australia."

1972–73, 1973–74, and 1974–75 combined with the export boom of 1973 and 1974 and the rapidly rising prices of imports of 1974 to produce inflation rates of 13.2 percent in 1973 and 16.3 percent in 1974. The authorities tried to offset the effects of rising export prices in several ways, partly by acting to appreciate the Australian dollar and by not preventing the appreciation that occurred in the last few months of 1973 as a result of the Australian dollar's being tied to the U.S. dollar, and partly by tariff cuts (later negated by quotas and other forms of protection). However, restriction of demand was largely confined to a tight monetary policy from late 1973 to mid-1974 and to the passive practice of letting the personal income tax rise rapidly because of the progressive tax structure.

On the wage side average real wage increases for males of between 4 and 5 percent a year occurred from 1969 to 1972. While these were not excessive in relation to average productivity growth in secondary industries, for the economy as a whole they far exceeded productivity increases. Since secondary industries certainly exert considerable influence on wage setting in Australia, "reasonable" wage increases established in that sector could cause difficulties for industries with low productivity growth.

The rapid wage rise of 1974 (see table 3) does not seem so great when an average of 1973 and 1974 increases is taken, and it must have been, at least partly, inflation-induced. There may be doubt about the contribution the increases in the earnings of males made to inflation, but there can be little disagreement that the 1974 increase in wage rates for females (table 4) must have accentuated the inflation and unemployment of 1974 and 1975. The 1974 rise in females' wage rates is unusually large, whatever basis is used for comparison.

Comments by W. Max Corden*

BEFORE 1972 there does seem to have been some relation (if not a stable one) between excess demand for labor and the inflation rate. As Pitchford says of 1946–67: "excess demand for labor lagged six months was found to explain a good deal of the variation in prices." The 1952–53, 1961–62, and 1972 episodes stand out. In all three cases there was a sharp drop in the rate

---

* I am indebted to Peter Jonson, Richard Snape, and especially Donald Stammer for their comments.

of inflation associated with a significant increase in unemployment. But there is certainly nothing steady or regular about a possible Phillips curve.

The brief 1972 interlude is particularly interesting because it was, in effect, a break in the inflation acceleration which began in 1969–70.

While the figures for unemployment and job vacancies imply that 1973 was not a year of excess demand in spite of the high rate of price inflation, there is some indication of a structural shift, suggesting that these figures should not be taken at face value. First, average overtime hours worked in manufacturing rose throughout 1973 to reach an all-time high late in 1973. Then there were many reports of shortages of goods. Finally, registered unemployment may have risen because the ratio of unemployment benefits to the minimum wage rose substantially under the new Labor government and because the residence and skill requirements for remaining on the unemployment register were modified. For these reasons 1973 clearly seems to have been a year of excess demand.

Beginning in 1972 there was a great *monetary expansion,* which was fueled by capital inflow (and to a lesser extent the export surplus) and the inflationary budgets of 1972 (Liberal government) and 1973 (Labor government). This created excess demand and obviously affected wage demands. The generous pre-election budget of August 1972 was designed to reduce unemployment, but actually the unemployment figures turned down in that very month. It should be noted that the share of government budgetary expenditure in gross domestic product did *not* increase over the period. While this does not mean that governments failed to exert undue pressure on resources, it suggests that the monetary expansion originating externally was a more important stimulus than the inflationary budgets.

The *commodity boom* of 1973 improved Australia's terms of trade but directly contributed to price increases by raising the prices of some exportables sold domestically, especially meat, as well as some imports.

There was an *autonomous element* in wage increases, in the sense that they were not wholly related to excess demand or to changes in the cost of living brought on by the commodity boom. Essentially the autonomous element can be attributed to the Labor government—this surely explains a great deal of the wage explosion since June 1973. There was a large rise in civil service salaries and expensive improvements in civil service conditions. In addition, the first stage in the process of achieving equal pay was implemented. Early in 1973 the Australian Conciliation and Arbitration Commission made generous decisions, which were supported by the government. It is argued below, however, that there was an external influence on these wage decisions, so perhaps they were not wholly "autonomous."

These events were affected by the appreciation of the Australian dollar shortly after the Labor government took office in December 1972 and by several appreciations since then. By September 1974 the appreciation on a trade-weighted basis was 20 percent above the level of June 1972. The crucial decision was the 7 percent revaluation in December 1972, but it came too late to prevent the capital inflow of 1972, which led to the monetary expansion. Direct measures to discourage capital inflow also came rather late. In addition, there was an across-the-board 25 percent tariff cut in 1973. The beneficial effects on trade of the appreciation and the tariff cut were not felt until 1974, when the flood of imports they appear to have generated was not so welcome and, in fact, provoked a depreciation.

All three of the above factors have been reversed. There is a monetary contraction, stimulated to some extent by the turnaround in the balance of payments, the commodity boom is at an end, and the government is trying to discourage wage demands. The spiral is kept going by the familiar expectational process.

This inflationary spiral may have been helped along by the devaluation in September 1974, which was motivated by protectionist considerations, and increases in the real tax burden resulting from high tax progressiveness (insofar as unions bargain for after-tax real wage levels); but devaluation and tax increases alone do not explain the continuation of the inflation. Furthermore, some tax rates for the lower- and middle-income groups were reduced to mitigate the inflation-progressiveness effect. In 1973 the government share in GDP did not increase, but it did in the following two years.

It would be useful to know what happened to profits. Presumably they have been squeezed severely. But one might have expected the share of profits to have increased significantly in the latter part of 1972 and in 1973 if one believes that there was a demand inflation caused by monetary expansion. On the other hand, it seems likely that there were two different effects in 1973, with profits in the nontraded sector (such as finance and building) increasing but profits in the import-competing sector declining owing to the appreciation and the wage increases. Furthermore, wage increases based on confidence in the demand situation may have preempted benefits that would otherwise have gone temporarily to profits.

The central issue is whether, in some sense, wage increases are a "cause" of the inflation. It might be argued that in 1974, when money wages rose rapidly and well ahead of prices, they obviously were the cause (or, at least, whatever makes wages rise was the cause), but that 1973 is another matter. Yet the fact is that monetary expansion in Australia has been strongly motivated at various times by a fear of unemployment or a desire to reduce unemployment, notably in 1972. The intention has been to validate the wage level. If wages responded more flexibly to the labor market situation it would be possible to conduct monetary and fiscal policy aimed at a stable price level. In that sense, wage increases—and sometimes the failure of wages to decrease—are *the* cause of inflation even when wages lag behind prices. Once one agrees on the primary motive for aggregate demand policy, it is irrelevant whether real wages are increasing faster or more slowly than productivity.[25] This view must be qualified by considering the possible role of inflationary government spending designed to attract real resources to the government without apparent cost, but this motive has probably not had a significant influence on Australian policy other than in 1974 and 1975.

A last point about wages is that changes in wage differentials may be important. Even if the real wage *on average* rose very little in 1973, for example, it is possible that the excess demand brought on by the monetary expansion caused *some* real wages to rise while others lagged or even fell. Thus differentials were upset. For some reason, there appears to have been an explosion of the wages of white-collar workers (retail clerks, bank officials, civil servants) in 1972 and 1973. Perhaps some of the real wage increases represented greater realization of bargaining power in some sections. Subsequently, in 1974, some of the laggards sought to catch up while the gainers of 1972–73 tried to hold onto their gains. It would be useful to have some information about changes in differentials for the period 1972–74.

Finally, Pitchford recognizes, as do many others, that external influences stimulated, and perhaps caused, the Australian inflation. It is no coincidence that this inflation developed at the same time as that in most other countries in the Organisation for Economic Co-operation and Development. The channels through which inflation was "imported" are as follows:

1. *Export surplus.* The commodity boom created a surplus, thus increasing incomes and money supply.

2. *Capital inflow.* The abundance of funds on world markets combined with the expectation of appreciation (owing to the export surplus) led to a vast inflow of capital, which was one of the main reasons for the expansion of the money supply.

---

25. This could be translated into fashionable language. One might say that the trouble is that workers (unions) tend to keep the real wage at such a high level that the *natural level of unemployment* (which, broadly, equates the marginal product of labor to the real wage) rises above that which has been politically acceptable. The "cause" of inflation is either the high real wage (which can be temporarily reduced) or the political objective of trying to reduce unemployment below the natural rate through expansionary monetary and fiscal policies (which can be temporarily achieved).

3. *Higher food prices* as a result of world shortages brought about some rise in the domestic cost of living. As domestic prices were not always determined by world prices, this effect was less important than in food-importing countries, but it did apply to meat.

4. *Profits in manufacturing.* Higher prices of imports and, more important, shortages of some imported goods meant that import-competing industries could realize good profits and were willing to pay higher wages.

These represent the channels of *direct* import of inflation. By far the most important factors operated through the money supply, principally through the capital inflow. But just as important, or even more so, were two *indirect* effects:

5. *Balance of payments constraint and wages.* It is traditional in Australia for the Arbitration Commission to take into account the balance of payments situation in deciding whether the country can "afford" higher wages. No doubt the large foreign exchange reserves in 1972 and 1973 made the wage authorities more permissive. Similarly, the Labor government's encouragement of wage increases (and improved civil service conditions) must have been influenced by the absence of a balance of payments constraint.

6. *Balance of payments constraint and stabilization policy.* The generous budgets of 1972 and 1973 and the easy money policies of late 1972 must have been influenced by the balance of payments situation. To some extent the payments surplus directly increased the money supply (points 1 and 2 above). But also there were the creation of domestic credit and the financing of fiscal deficits (as well as larger budgets) designed—perhaps subconsciously—to avoid further balance of payments surpluses. It seems reasonable to suppose that if foreign exchange reserves had been lower even the Labor budget would have been tighter.

In this broad sense the inflation was "imported." Of course, Australia need not have imported it. Earlier appreciation of the exchange rate, less generous monetary and fiscal policies, and refusal to raise money wages just because the balance of payments was favorable could have avoided it. But what actually happened can be understood—though not excused—in terms of influences that came from outside.

None of this is really new to students of Australian economic history. Recent events bear a striking resemblance to the Korean boom and slump episode. In general, Australia's business cycles have been externally generated, so that the country has been described as a "dependent economy." It has also been recognized for some time that award wage decisions of the Arbitration Commission are influenced by the balance of payments and, more specifically, by income changes in the export sector, and thus cannot be regarded as wholly exogenous.[26]

There is not a great deal that is special about the Australian inflation; its timing and characteristics have been so much like those everywhere else. But three features might be noted.

First, as an exporter of commodities, Australia was one of the beneficiaries of the commodity boom. Perhaps world inflation is a bad thing, but at least Australia's terms of trade improved. There were national gains that *could* have been appropriated to compensate domestic losers. Appreciation is not as painful as depreciation, so a great opportunity was missed. A country that suffers a real national loss because of its terms of trade may find adjustment difficult, since there are *real* problems, not just problems of monetary management. But Australia experienced a real gain. Only truly bad politicians could despoil the economy of "the lucky country."

Second, the rise in commodity prices had very little effect on the cost of living in Australia, at least much less than in most other OECD countries, and there was less reason for it to set off a wage-price spiral. Chiefly this is because agricultural marketing devices separated home prices from export prices, originally to yield home prices higher than export prices for the benefit of producers, but in this circumstance benefiting consumers. Domestic wheat prices did rise, but only after a lag. The important exception to all this is meat, which is sold domestically at world prices.

Australia produces two-thirds of its crude oil needs and the price paid to domestic producers, having been somewhat above world prices before October 1973, was *not* increased as a result of the world price rise. Therefore, the average price paid by refiners only doubled and the price to consumers rose much less.

Third, in view of the first and second features, it is really surprising that Australia in 1974–75 had one of the highest rates of inflation among the

26. On all this, see A. M. C. Waterman, *Economic Fluctuations in Australia, 1948 to 1964* (Canberra: Australian National University Press, 1972); P. D. Jonson, K. L. Mahar, and G. J. Thompson, "Earnings and Award Wages in Australia," *Australian Economic Papers,* vol. 13 (June 1974), pp. 80–98; and P. F. Barry and C. W. Guille, "The Australian Business Cycle and International Cyclical Linkages," paper prepared for the Fourth Conference of Economists, August 1974; and for a summary of Australian wage policy and foreign trade until 1967, see W. M. Corden, "Australian Economic Policy Discussion in the Post-War Period: A Survey," *American Economic Review,* vol. 58, pt. 2 (June 1968), pp. 94–96. During most of the 1960s the Australian business cycle lagged behind the external business cycle, but in the late 1960s and early 1970s it became more closely synchronized with the external cycle. Also, award wage decisions are much influenced by past price changes.

OECD countries. The proximate explanation consists of exceptionally permissive wage and fiscal policies. The fundamental answer is political. At a crucial time in economic history—December 1972—there was a radical change of government. After twenty-three years of Liberal–Country party government, the Labor party came into power, eager to catch up on things left undone by the previous government (many of which required extra government spending), suspicious of advice from the notoriously conservative treasury, and just plain inexperienced in the business of running a country.[27]

General Comments

MICHAEL PARKIN had no disagreement with anything that had been said about Australia but wanted to add a few things on the basis of his own work. It is clear that Australia has been an importer of inflation not just recently but in the late sixties as well. Take the work done by Peter Jonson and others, for example, who constructed a model in which the National Minimum Award Wage provided the major cost-push and set the tone for everything else, and convincingly explained the award wage as determined by previous movements in consumer prices and in productivity.[28] They could not explain one award wage, however, and sought to find out how that wage had affected the inflationary course of the economy. Their investigation, based on a complete model of the economy, showed that the effect was washed out almost completely over a period of three or four years. They also asked what would have happened if Australia had appreciated the dollar earlier than it did and found that doing so would have had a powerful and persistent effect on the inflation rate. The results showed that Australia had been an importer of inflation but that it need not have been.

With regard to the Phillips curve in Australia, all the recent studies indicate that if there is any trade-off it is so steep that for all practical purposes it does not exist. There is a clear and reasonably well-determined Phillips curve in the short run, but only then. One problem is that Australia has been operating within a fairly narrow band of unemployment; only two observations in the postwar sample involve very substantial unemployment, and this lack of variability in the unemployment rate makes it impossible to get a well-

27. This was not like a change of government from Conservative to Labour in Britain. For Americans, imagine twenty-three years of Goldwater, and then McGovern.
28. P. D. Jonson, K. L. Mahar, and G. J. Thompson, "Earnings and Award Wages in Australia."

determined relationship. But nobody has found any satisfactory econometric explanation of the various Australian price indexes based on the movement of the factor prices and excess demand. There is no problem over a medium run; the difficulty is in explaining the timing on a quarterly basis.

John Pitchford agreed that Australia's inflation has been mainly, in fact almost wholly, imported, although the Labor government during 1974–75 feared that much of the inflation was due to wage-push. One of the tables in his paper suggests that that was not altogether the case; it is paradoxical that a Labor government should have concluded, on so little evidence concerning the movement of money wages, that wage-push was a major factor. Parkin's work has not yet adequately established that the Phillips curve in Australia is almost vertical or that there is a natural rate of unemployment for Australia.

ANTONIO C. LEMGRUBER

Inflation in Brazil

Tables

Antonio C. Lemgruber, Brazilian Institute of Economics, Rio de Janeiro, Brazil, wishes to acknowledge the many valuable comments made by Bennett McCallum, Arnold C. Harberger, Marc Nerlove, José L. Carvalho, José J. Senna, and Claudio Haddad, who are not, however, responsible for any errors that remain. Parts of the paper were also discussed with a group of economists from the University of São Paulo, Brazil. Comments by the participants of the Brookings Conference on World Inflation— particularly the editors of this volume—were extremely useful in revising the paper.

IN SPITE of a secular inflation going back at least to the beginning of the nineteenth century (1822), when the country became politically independent,[1] Brazil has faced its highest rates of inflation in the postwar period: the average annual rate of inflation from 1952 to 1973 was 30.4 percent.[2]

Between 1952 and 1958 the average inflation was 16.3 percent, ranging from 11 percent to 23 percent. There was a substantial acceleration of inflation from 1959 to 1964, with an average for this period of 51.6 percent. In 1964 the rate of inflation reached its peak of 87.8 percent.[3]

1. It is surprising that so few articles and books have been published (in English and in Portuguese) about inflation in Brazil. This is specially the case for work on the impact of external developments. Most of the relevant work done is mentioned in this paper. This situation is unlike that in other countries such as the United States and the United Kingdom, for example, where there has been "an inflation of articles about inflation."

It might be useful to provide some basic information about Brazil here. In 1973 Brazil had a population of 101 million and a gross domestic product estimated at 1973 market prices at Cr$389 billion, or $63.5 billion (U.S.), resulting in a per capita gross domestic product of approximately $629. The annual rate of population growth has been 2.9 percent. Urban population constitutes 58 percent of the total. In 1973 manufacturing represented 31.8 percent of total output and agriculture, 14.8 percent. Primary products make up approximately 69 percent of Brazilian exports, but there has been a large increase in the share of manufactured products (see table 5, note a). Coffee accounted for 20 percent of total exports in 1973. The ratio of exports to GDP is low by international standards, but it has increased substantially in recent years, attaining 9.8 percent in 1973 (table 5, note a). In 1973 oil imports amounted to 11.3 percent of total imports. The role of the public sector in the economy is extensive, involving direct controls, production activities, public enterprises, and national development plans. The relation of total taxes to GDP was 26 percent in 1973 (see table 4 for the federal government).

2. The GDP implicit price deflator is the price index used in this study. Averages for other price indexes are shown in table 1 where it can be seen that the average inflation rates as measured by different price indexes are remarkably similar. Besides the implicit deflator, a comprehensive index in the table is the general price index, a weighted average of the wholesale price index (0.6), consumer price index (0.3), and construction cost index (0.1). The econometric results reported in the third section below refer to the implicit deflator, but similar results are obtained with the general price index, as might be expected because of the high correlation of the two.

3. In the 1952–73 period, the highest twelve-month rate of inflation—94.2 percent—was attained between July 1963 and July 1964, and the lowest—3.9 percent—between January 1957 and January 1958. The monthly data are based on the general price index. Average annual inflation rates with this price index are given in table 1.

The rate of change of the price level decreased after 1965, decelerating from the 1964 peak of almost 90 percent to 15.5 percent in 1973. The average for 1965–73 was 27.1 percent. Deceleration was very rapid from 1965 to 1967: the rate was 32 percent in 1965, 17 percent in 1966, and 11 percent in 1967—a total decline of 60 percent from the peak of 1964 to 1967.

After 1967 price deceleration was much slower, but it did continue, with the rate of inflation reaching 15.5 percent in 1973. The 1968–73 average was 20.5 percent, with small deviations. It could be said that between 1967 and 1973 the country had an almost steady rate of inflation.

The lowest twelve-month rate of inflation for the 1960s and 1970s— 14.0 percent—occurred between September 1972 and September 1973. After September 1973 a rapid acceleration peaked in May–June 1974. As a result of the inflationary spurt of the first half of 1974, the rate of inflation was 34.0 percent.

Table 1 presents several ways of measuring inflation for the period 1951– 74.[4] In spite of some differences for particular years, the averages for longer periods show that these differences are negligible. Changes in the minimum wage are also reported in the table, although they are not analyzed until the next section.

From 1952 to 1973 the annual average rate of growth of real output in Brazil was 7.1 percent—a good performance measured by international comparisons. As the annual rate of population growth was roughly 2.9 percent in this period, per capita real income grew at approximately 4.2 percent a year, and it more than doubled between 1952 and 1973. Table 2 presents annual rates of growth of nominal output, total real output, agricultural output, and industrial output, as well as the percentage gap between potential and real output.[5,6]

4. To round out the picture, below are some measures of inflation in Brazil before 1952. Annual average rates were 1.5 percent (1829–87), 8 percent (1887–96), −1.5 percent (1897–1900), 0.1 percent (1900–14), 8 percent (1914–27), −2.5 percent (1927–33), 7 percent (1933–39), 15 percent (1939–46), and finally 10.5 percent (1947–51). The best sources for these estimates are O. Onody. *A Inflação Brasileira— 1820–1958* (Rio de Janeiro: APEC Editora, 1960), and Mário Henrique Simonsen, *Brasil 2001* (Rio de Janeiro: APEC Editora, 1969). Inflation rates before 1939 were measured through indirect, incomplete, and unsatisfactory data. The average rate for 1952–58 (table 1) is practically the same as the average for 1939–58, around 15 percent. The inflationary jump to higher plateaus started in 1959 and exploded in 1962–64. See also Simonsen, *A experiencia inflacionária no Brasil* (Rio de Janeiro: Instituto de Pesquisas e Estudos Sociais [IPES], 1964).

5. The results of the 1970 census in Brazil indicated the need for substantial revisions in the Brazilian national accounts. Since revisions are available in published form for only the 1970–73 period and for selected years before 1970, the pre-census basis is used for the current- and constant-price gross domestic product and implicit gross

The years 1952 and 1954 were good ones and 1953 and 1956 bad for growth of output. In all these cases, the performance of the agricultural sector was an important factor, since more than one-quarter of total output came from that sector at that time.

The period 1957 to 1961 was one of above-average real growth—8.3 percent, peaking at 10.3 percent in 1961—in which the manufacturing sector grew rapidly. Clearly 1961 was a year of full capacity utilization, as indicated by the closing of the output gap in that year (table 2, last column).

In contrast, rates of real growth were low from 1962 to 1967, averaging only 3.7 percent. Particularly in the years 1963–65 the country faced a "growth recession," with an average real growth rate of only 2.4 percent. Although the stagnation of 1962–64 might be related to political problems and that of 1965–67 to the austerity of the new stabilization program,[7] as shown in table 2 the whole 1962–67 period was one of increasing output gaps. In 1967 the gap was 17.1 percent—an indicator of the stagnation and unemployment during the previous five years.

In more recent years—1968–73—the output growth rate jumped to an annual average of 10.1 percent. The large gaps of 1962–67 made this economic recovery possible, with high rates of economic growth between 1968 and 1973 through a growing utilization of productive capacity. In fact, if the following identity (valid for logarithmic changes) is used: actual rate of change of real output equals potential rate of change plus variation of the output gap; then one can say that the 10 percent growth in the six years from 1968 to 1973 corresponds to a 7 percent potential growth plus the output gap of 1967 (17 percent) recovered in six years (approximately 3 percent each year).

In 1973 the country had nearly returned to its "potential output line," closing the gap from 17.1 percent in 1967 to 1.3 percent in 1973 (table 2). In that year, Brazil obtained the highest rate of growth of real output in its recent history: 11.4 percent. The virtual elimination of the output gap, however, suggests a slowing of the growth process in the next years. In 1974 the rate of real growth was 9.5 percent—a very favorable result if one considers

---

domestic product price deflator series presented in this paper. It should be noted that while the new post-census basis yields substantially higher levels of nominal and constant-price GDP, the differences between the old and new series in terms of annual rates of change appear to be marginal.

6. The gap corresponds to (potential output − actual output)/potential output. The potential output series follows the trend-through-peaks method, with a constant rate of growth of 7 percent and a zero gap in 1961. The average gap for 1952–73 is 6.9 percent.

7. The Brazilian political system was thoroughly modified in 1964.

Table 1. *Inflation Rates, Selected Price and Wage Indicators, 1951–74*

Period	General price index[a]		Wholesale price index[b]	Consumer price index[b,c]	Construc-tion cost index[b,c]	Implicit price deflator (GDP)[d]	Minimum wage[d,e]
	Annual average	December to December					
	Annual rate of change (percent)						
1951	16.5	11.9	17.4	10.8	12.8	12.0	0.0
1952	11.8	12.9	9.4	20.4	7.1	13.2	215.8
1953	14.8	20.8	25.0	17.6	12.6	15.3	0.0
1954	27.0	25.6	22.3	25.6	31.8	21.4	50.0
1955	16.4	12.4	15.9	18.9	8.5	16.8	33.3
1956	19.9	24.4	26.2	21.8	28.0	23.3	24.2
1957	14.2	7.0	3.8	13.4	6.4	13.2	27.5
1958	13.0	24.3	35.1	17.3	28.1	11.1	0.0
1959	37.8	39.5	36.0	51.9	20.8	29.2	57.9
1960	29.2	30.5	34.5	23.8	40.8	26.3	10.0
1961	37.0	47.7	53.2	42.9	42.9	33.3	57.8
1962	51.6	51.3	45.5	55.8	55.3	54.8	29.2
1963	75.4	81.3	83.2	80.2	64.4	78.0	56.3
1964	90.5	91.9	84.5	86.6	104.2	87.8	83.3
1965	56.8	34.5	31.4	45.5	43.4	55.4	61.0
1966	38.0	38.8	42.1	41.2	35.1	38.8	30.6
1967	28.3	24.3	21.2	24.1	41.3	27.1	25.3
1968	24.2	25.4	24.8	24.5	32.7	27.8	21.6
1969	20.8	20.2	18.7	24.3	12.3	22.3	19.2
1970	19.8	19.2	18.7	20.9	18.7	19.8	20.1
1971	20.4	19.8	21.3	18.1	12.7	20.4	20.4
1972	17.0	15.5	16.1	14.0	19.8	17.0	19.5
1973	15.1	15.7	15.6	13.7	20.8	15.5	17.0
1974	28.7	34.5	35.2	33.7	31.8	34.0	20.4
	Average rate of change (percent)						
1952–73	30.9	31.0	31.1	32.9	31.2	30.4	44.5
1952–58	16.7	18.2	19.7	19.3	17.5	16.3	50.1
1959–64	53.6	57.0	56.2	56.9	54.7	51.6	49.1
1965–73	26.7	23.7	23.3	25.1	26.3	27.1	26.1
1968–73	19.6	19.3	19.2	19.2	19.5	20.5	19.6
	Level (1965–67 = 100) or cruzeiros						
1973	373	397	392	398	424	388	Cr$298 a month

Source: Fundação Getulio Vargas, *Conjuntura Econômica* (Rio de Janeiro: Instituto Brasileiro de Economia), selected issues.

a. The general price index is a weighted average of the wholesale price index (0.6), consumer price index (0.3), and construction cost index (0.1).

b. End of period (December to December).

c. Based on cost indexes calculated for Rio de Janeiro.

d. Annual average.

e. Based on wage rates established in the region of Guanabara.

Table 2. *Growth Rates of Gross Domestic Product,*
by Major Output Measures, 1951–74

Period	Gross domestic product		Real agriculture output[b]	Real industrial output[c]	Output gap[d]
	Nominal income[a]	Real output			
	Annual rate of change (percent)				
1951	18.6	6.0	0.7	6.4	2.2
1952	23.1	8.7	9.1	5.0	0.6
1953	18.2	2.5	0.2	8.7	4.8
1954	33.6	10.1	7.9	8.7	2.1
1955	24.9	6.9	7.7	10.6	2.2
1956	27.1	3.2	−2.4	6.9	5.7
1957	22.3	8.1	9.3	5.7	4.8
1958	19.7	7.7	2.0	16.2	4.1
1959	36.4	5.6	5.3	11.9	5.4
1960	38.4	9.7	4.9	5.4	3.0
1961	47.3	10.3	7.6	15.0	0.0
1962	62.9	5.3	5.5	7.8	1.7
1963	80.5	1.5	1.0	0.2	6.6
1964	93.4	2.9	1.3	5.2	10.2
1965	59.7	2.7	13.8	−4.7	13.8
1966	45.9	5.1	−3.2	11.7	15.3
1967	33.1	4.8	5.7	3.0	17.1
1968	39.7	9.3	1.4	15.5	15.3
1969	33.3	9.0	6.0	10.8	13.6
1970	31.2	9.5	5.6	11.1	11.7
1971	34.0	11.1	11.4	11.2	8.1
1972	29.2	10.4	4.5	13.8	5.2
1973	28.7	11.4	3.5	15.0	1.3
1974	46.7	9.5	8.5	8.2	−1.0
	Average rate of change (percent)				
1952–73	39.2	7.1	4.9	8.8	6.9
1952–58	24.1	6.7	4.8	8.8	3.5
1959–64	59.8	5.9	4.3	7.6	4.5
1965–73	37.2	8.1	5.4	9.7	11.3
1968–73	32.7	10.1	5.4	12.9	9.3
	Millions of cruzeiros or level (1949 = 100)				
1973	Cr$389,090	504	289	745	...

Source: *Conjuntura Econômica*, selected issues.

a. For a discussion concerning the national accounts series used in this paper, see note 5.

b. Agriculture as a percentage of total output: 1953, 26.1; 1963, 19.8; 1973, 14.8. Fishing and forestry are also included.

c. Manufacturing as a percentage of total output: 1953, 23.7; 1963, 26.8; 1973, 31.8. Construction, mining, and utilities are also included, but manufacturing represents 90 percent.

d. Output gap corresponds to (potential real output − actual real output)/potential real output in percentage terms. The potential output series has a constant rate of growth of 7 percent and is equal to actual real output in 1961.

not only the full capacity utilization but also the international recession. It is expected, however, that with the recovery process completed and with the economy hitting the moving ceiling of potential output with zero gaps, Brazil will grow again at its potential or natural growth rate of 7 percent.

It is argued that the high growth rates of 1968–73 seemed to reflect a natural readjustment process of the economy. This recovery, however, was accompanied by no acceleration in the rate of inflation, in spite of growing capacity utilization.

Recent theories of inflation suggest a negative relation between the acceleration of inflation and the output gap: the larger the gap between potential and actual real output, the smaller is the acceleration of inflation.[8] Phillips curves that take into account price expectations imply precisely such a relation.

In Brazil more evident confirmation of this hypothesis is found in the years 1964–67: the deceleration of inflation was accompanied by a growth recession with large and increasing gaps. The same relation between acceleration and the gap may also be observed for the 1950s and early 1960s.[9] The reduction of the gap after 1968, however, should have led to an acceleration of inflation, but this did not occur until 1974. On the contrary, there was a slow but visible deceleration.[10]

A simple commodity market Phillips curve for Brazil for the whole period 1952–73 (annual data, ordinary least squares) shows a satisfactory performance:[11]

$$\dot{P} = 0.8870 \, \dot{P}(L) - 0.9247 \, H(L) + 10.8313,$$
$$\quad (7.65) \qquad\qquad (2.44)$$

$R^2 = 0.756$; $\bar{R}^2 = 0.744$; standard error = 10.8; Durbin-Watson statistic = 1.57; h-statistic = 1.21.

8. The acceleration can of course be negative. This theory is incorporated in the more formal model of inflation presented in the second section below. Notice that, because of the presence of expectations in a Phillips curve, the inflation-unemployment trade-off is replaced by an acceleration-unemployment trade-off. The output gap is used instead of unemployment in the above analysis, and this replacement is valid because of Okun's law. There is some evidence that for countries with high or steady rates of inflation, the expectational factor is very strong in a Phillips curve. See Antonio C. B. Lemgruber, "A Study of the Accelerationist Theory of Inflation" (University of Virginia, 1974; processed).

9. In fact, the Phillips curve presented here suggests that the relation can be observed for the whole 1952–73 period.

10. This analysis is informal; the regression fails to reject an expectational or accelerationist Phillips curve for Brazil when one takes into account lagged effects and so forth. It is true, on the other hand, that the predicted values of inflation for 1971, 1972, and 1973 are greater than the actual values.

11. The figures in parentheses are t-statistics.

where $\dot{P}$ is the percentage rate of inflation (GDP implicit price deflator), H the percentage output gap, and (L) a one-year lag. However, as suggested in the previous paragraph, this commodity market Phillips curve predicts more inflation—or a greater acceleration—for the more recent years (1971–73) than was actually observed.

One can certainly find some "ex post" explanations for the overestimation of the inflation rate in the 1970s, even though they might not be entirely satisfactory. For example, it is possible that the government was able to overcome inflationary expectations through "announcements" of lower expected inflation, so that anticipations were modified in the downward direction. Consequently, the implicit hypothesis of the above Phillips curve about expectations, based on past rates of inflation, leads to some overestimation for recent years.

Brazilian economists have been doing some theoretical work on the question of announcement effects and inflationary expectations.[12] Although this is not the place to discuss their research, some points should be mentioned. In their model, the expected rate of inflation is a weighted average between a historical component (past inflation) and an "announcement" component, where the weights depend on a certain credibility coefficient. It is argued that the announcement can be useful to break inflationary expectations since major price increases have to be submitted to a price council, but its credibility will depend on its consistency with future monetary and fiscal policy.

Clearly, the frontier between announcements to break price anticipations and repressed inflation is not well defined. In this sense, one might simply say that inflation was partly repressed in the early 1970s, leading to a postponement of inflationary pressures.[13]

The inflationary explosion of 1974, with its rapid acceleration of inflation,

12. A. C. Pastore and R. D. Almonacid, *Gradualismo ou Tratamento de Choque—Considerações em torno dos custos da estabilização* (Universidade de São Paulo, Instituto de Pesquisas Econômicas, 1974).

13. From 1968 on, there was an increasing institutionalization of price controls, with the supervision of the Price Council (Conselho Interministerial de Preços, CIP). Firms have to obtain permission from the CIP for price increases. Basically, firms are allowed to increase prices proportionally to their cost increases, but they need the approval of the CIP. The system, however, is not a rigid one of price controls and price freezes. The price increases proposed by the firms are simply reviewed by the CIP. Apparently, such controls were useful between 1968 and 1970 as part of the announcement effect strategy, when there was no excess demand in the economy and expectations had to be depressed. But with the increase of capacity utilization in the 1970s, the continuing use of these controls has led to some shortages and retail queues, especially in 1973 and 1974.

Table 3. *Growth Rates of Monetary Aggregates, 1951–74*

Year	Money supply (M_1)[a]	Monetary base	Domestic credit[b]	International reserves[c]	Loans from commercial banks and monetary authorities to the private sector
			Annual rate of change (percent)		
1951	16.4	13.0	25.8	−22.4	28.4
1952	15.4	17.3	22.3	2.3	18.6
1953	19.3	16.4	21.2	170.9	17.6
1954	23.7	22.5	25.3	10.0	26.7
1955	16.4	14.9	13.0	23.0	12.5
1956	21.9	22.0	25.1	22.8	19.9
1957	32.1	35.2	31.6	−20.0	24.4
1958	23.0	17.0	19.6	65.8	22.4
1959	42.9	36.8	28.5	−4.0	28.5
1960	38.8	40.9	43.4	13.8	40.9
1961	52.5	61.8	42.4	95.0	38.2
1962	64.1	62.1	60.1	−13.5	60.6
1963	64.6	69.9	61.7	14.3	55.1
1964	81.6	86.2	79.1	146.4	80.3
1965	79.5	66.6	49.2	193.9	57.5
1966	13.8	26.4	27.5	2.9	33.6
1967	45.7	25.2	57.2	−43.8	55.9
1968	39.0	46.5	56.7	64.8	64.8
1969	32.5	29.9	33.6	206.4	43.2
1970	25.8	19.4	32.0	103.9	34.4
1971	32.3	34.2	37.3	69.3	45.5
1972	38.3	25.6	33.7	168.9	45.1
1973	47.0	42.7	46.7	58.4	45.3
1974	34.0	32.9	54.5	−3.4	53.6
			Average rate of change (percent)		
1952–73	38.6	37.2	38.5	61.4	39.6
1952–58	21.7	20.8	22.6	39.2	20.3
1959–64	57.4	59.6	52.5	42.0	50.6
1965–73	39.3	35.2	41.5	91.6	47.2
1968–73	35.8	33.0	40.0	112.0	46.4
			Level (millions of cruzeiros)		
1973	90,490	42,710	125,628	39,317	111,872

Sources: *Conjuntura Econômica*, International Monetary Fund, *International Financial Statistics* (IMF), and Banco Central do Brasil, *Boletim do Banco Central do Brasil*, various issues.

a. Currency in the hands of the public plus demand deposits.

b. Monetary authorities plus commercial banks. See *International Financial Statistics*.

c. International reserves (held by the monetary authorities) in cruzeiros.

seems to confirm the Phillips curve–accelerationist approach. However, the presence of the external effects of world inflation, especially for the more recent years and for 1974 in particular, should not be neglected. (Later in this paper, the emphasis is on the external variables.)

Inflation and the output gap are related to nominal policy variables, such as monetary and fiscal aggregates, that affect nominal aggregate demand. The growth of nominal income is presented in table 2. Tables 3 and 4 show the evolution of some monetary and fiscal variables in the period. Since this paper deals with the effects of external factors as well as the effects of domestic policy on inflation, growth rates of international reserves and domestic credit are presented within the monetary aggregates. I have followed the classification of the International Monetary Fund, which divides the money supply and the monetary base between domestic credit and foreign assets. Although the evolution of domestic credit is not disaggregated between the government and the private sector, the fiscal data in table 4 give some indication of the relative importance of government budget deficits.

The effects of these policy and external variables on aggregate nominal demand, and consequently on prices, are presented theoretically and empirically later in the paper. It may be useful, though, to make a few comments about the numbers in tables 3 and 4.

Confirming the long-run validity of the quantity theory, the average rate of growth of the money supply (M_1) in Brazil was 38.6 percent (30 percent inflation plus 7 percent real growth plus a small residual). With the rapid development of money substitutes in recent years (see the next section), broader definitions of the money supply have been used by some researchers, but they will not be included here because differences in their rates of change have been reasonably predictable and the main monetary policy variable continues to be M_1.

The balance of payments effect on the monetary base may be seen through the evolution of international reserves. It must be emphasized that the substantial increase of international liquidity between 1968 and 1973 from $257 million to $6,416 million was a result of overall balance of payments surpluses. The increase in international reserves has made the money supply— or the monetary base—a policy variable more difficult to control. In 1974 the balance of payments effect was contractionary, leading to a discrepancy between the rates of expansion of money and of credit (34 percent as against 54 percent).

In contrast to the greater importance of foreign assets as a component of the money supply or the monetary base, the importance of government credits has greatly diminished. This can be seen in the last column of table 4: the

Table 4. *Federal Government Receipts and Expenditures, 1951–74*

Period	Receipts	Expenditures	Receipts as percent of GDP	Expenditures as percent of GDP	Deficit as percent of GDP
		Annual rate of change (percent)			
1951	40.38	11.67	9.0	8.3	0.7[a]
1952	12.67	13.43	8.3	7.7	0.6[a]
1953	24.32	69.74	8.7	11.0	2.3
1954	22.98	5.23	8.0	8.7	0.6
1955	17.69	19.52	7.6	8.3	0.7
1956	25.84	51.62	7.5	9.9	2.4
1957	30.07	40.35	8.0	11.4	3.4
1958	35.81	17.52	9.0	11.1	2.1
1959	37.46	36.41	9.1	11.1	2.0
1960	36.76	46.34	9.0	11.8	2.8
1961	50.04	57.01	9.2	12.6	3.4
1962	52.37	66.40	8.6	12.9	4.3
1963	85.86	83.80	8.8	13.0	4.2
1964	102.53	83.64	9.2	12.4	3.2
1965	83.50	57.48	13.3	14.9	1.6
1966	51.27	44.38	11.0	12.1	1.1
1967	15.30	23.74	9.5	11.2	1.7
1968	50.80	43.08	10.3	11.5	1.2
1969	35.79	27.88	10.5	11.1	0.6
1970	37.56	28.71	11.0	11.4	0.4
1971	40.57	46.06	11.5	11.8	0.3
1972	39.87	38.34	12.5	12.7	0.2
1973	40.08	37.42	13.6	13.5	0.1[a]
1974	45.30	38.73	13.5	12.8	0.7[a]
		Average rate of change (percent)			
1952–73	42.2	42.6	9.7	11.4	1.8
1952–58	24.2	31.0	8.2	9.7	1.7
1959–64	60.8	62.3	9.0	12.3	3.3
1965–73	43.9	38.6	11.5	12.2	0.8
1968–73	40.8	36.9	11.6	12.0	0.5
		Level (millions of cruzeiros)			
1973	52,863	52,568	...	...	...

Source: *Conjuntura Econômica*, various issues.
a. Surplus.

government budget deficit as a percentage of gross domestic product declined from 4.3 percent in 1962 to 0.3 percent in 1971. In 1973 and 1974 the government budget showed surpluses, which had not happened since 1952. The same table reveals a stable percentage of federal government expenditures with respect to GDP, around 12 percent, in contrast to a growing percentage for government receipts. A tax reform and an administrative reform in 1966–67 helped accelerate the growth rate of revenues and decelerate that of government expenditures. Moreover, with the success of purchasing power bonds (see the next section), the remaining deficits of the late 1960s and early 1970s did not have to be financed through monetary expansion.

The analysis of external effects on the Brazilian inflation is undertaken more formally in the following sections. Tables 5 and 6 present the basic data on the external sector of Brazil, including the balance of payments, the exchange rate, and export and import prices, as well as some indexes of world inflation and world production.

The greater openness of the Brazilian economy during the 1970s can be seen in table 5. It was only after 1968 that the external sector began to grow rapidly, at higher rates than the rest of the economy. While the dollar value of exports and imports in 1966–67 was equal to or even smaller than this same value in 1951–52 (less than $2 billion), from 1968 on high rates of change in exports and imports have altered the picture completely. The relation of exports to GDP grew from 6.1 percent in 1967 to 7.2 percent in 1970 and 9.8 percent in 1973. This happened in a period when the growth rate of real output was also very high. Another relation that indicates the greater openness—international reserves to money supply—went from 3.7 percent in 1967 to 16.2 percent in 1970 and finally to 43.4 percent in 1973 (see also table 3).

Clearly, in this new situation the evolution of the world economy—especially that attributable to the main commercial partners of Brazil—had more important effects on the country, favorable or unfavorable. More than half of the external trade of Brazil is carried on with only five industrial countries: the United States, the United Kingdom, Japan, West Germany, and France. The economic performance of these countries—especially the growth of their real output, prices, and interest rates—is now more relevant for Brazil. Table 6 presents some simple proxies for world inflation and world production, based on weighted averages of the price indexes and production indexes of these five countries.

Historically, the Brazilian balance of payments has shown deficits in the current account and surpluses in the capital account. Before 1968 the sum of these two results alternated between overall deficits and overall surpluses in the balance of payments. Between 1968 and 1973, however, the capital-account surpluses more than compensated for current-account deficits, leading to impressive overall surpluses, which reached more than $2 billion in 1972 and again in 1973.[14]

---

14. A new exchange rate system—the trotting peg—was introduced in 1968. Its effects on the external sector are discussed in the next section.

Table 5. *Balance of Payments and Related Measures, 1951–74*[a]
Millions of U.S. dollars except where percent is indicated

Year	Trade balance	Exports (FOB)	Imports (FOB)	Current-account balance	Net capital movements	Balance of payments surplus	International liquidity	Change from preceding year (percent)	
								Exports[b]	Imports[b]
				Level					
1951	41	1,771	1,730	−403	−11	−291	517	30.3	82.3
1952	−286	1,416	1,702	−624	35	−615	529	−20.0	−1.6
1953	424	1,540	1,116	55	59	16	605	8.8	−34.4
1954	148	1,558	1,410	−195	−18	−203	483	1.2	26.3
1955	320	1,419	1,099	2	3	17	491	−8.9	−22.0
1956	437	1,483	1,046	57	151	194	611	4.5	−4.8
1957	107	1,392	1,285	−264	255	−180	476	−6.1	22.8
1958	65	1,244	1,179	−248	184	−253	465	−10.6	−8.2
1959	72	1,282	1,210	−311	182	−154	367	3.0	2.6
1960	−23	1,270	1,293	−478	58	−410	345	−0.9	6.8
1961	113	1,405	1,292	−222	288	115	470	10.6	−0.1
1962	−89	1,215	1,304	−389	181	−346	285	−13.5	0.9
1963	112	1,406	1,294	−114	−54	244	219	15.7	−0.8
1964	344	1,430	1,086	140	82	4	245	1.7	−16.1
1965	655	1,596	941	368	−6	331	484	11.6	−13.4

1966	438	1,741	1,303	54	124	153	425	9.1	38.5
1967	213	1,654	1,441	−237	27	245	199	−5.0	10.6
1968	26	1,881	1,855	−508	541	32	257	13.7	28.7
1969	318	2,311	1,993	−281	850	549	656	22.9	7.4
1970	232	2,739	2,507	−562	1,015	545	1,187	18.5	25.8
1971	−341	2,904	3,245	−1,307	1,846	530	1,746	6.0	29.4
1972	−244	3,991	4,235	−1,489	3,492	2,439	4,183	37.4	30.5
1973	7	6,199	6,192	−1,680	3,680	2,179	6,418	55.3	46.2
1974	−4,562	7,968	12,530	−6,882	5,666	−1,216	5,203	28.5	102.4
Average									
1952–73	138.5	1,958.0	1,819.4	−374.2	589.8	246.9	961.2	7.0	8.0
1952–58	173.6	1,436.0	1,262.4	−173.8	95.6	−146.3	522.8	−4.4	−2.9
1959–64	88.2	1,334.7	1,246.5	−229.0	122.8	−91.2	321.8	2.8	−1.1
1965–73	144.9	2,779.5	2,634.7	−626.9	1,285.4	778.1	1,728.3	18.8	22.6
1968–73	−0.3	3,337.5	3,337.8	−971.2	1,904.0	1,045.7	2,407.8	25.6	28.0

Sources: *Conjuntura Econômica* and *Boletim do Banco Central do Brasil*, selected issues.

a. The structure of the external sector is as follows:

	Coffee exports as percent of total exports	Manufactured exports as percent of total exports	Total exports as percent of GDP	Oil imports as percent of total imports	Wheat imports as percent of total imports
1965–73	34.8	24.2	7.4	10.7	6.6
1973	20.1	31.3	9.8	11.3	5.6

b. Exports and imports in U.S. dollars.

Table 6. *Change in Price Indexes of International Trade,*
World Output, and the Exchange Rate, 1951–74

Annual percentage change, except exchange rate level (in U.S. dollars)

	Price index			World real output index[b]	Exchange rate (cruzeiros per U.S. dollar)[c]	
Year	Export[a]	Import[a]	World[b]		Level	Annual change
1951	21.5	20.2	9.5	10.1	0.019	0.0
1952	−1.9	2.7	3.6	3.0	0.019	0.0
1953	−2.9	−13.0	0.7	8.0	0.045	136.8
1954	17.0	−33.0	1.0	−1.0	0.062	37.8
1955	−20.6	18.0	0.5	11.9	0.075	21.0
1956	−4.3	−11.4	2.3	5.5	0.074	−1.3
1957	2.2	11.5	2.8	4.1	0.076	2.7
1958	−7.6	−9.0	3.6	−2.9	0.129	69.7
1959	−16.2	−1.7	1.3	9.7	0.157	21.7
1960	−1.9	−2.5	1.8	6.5	0.190	21.0
1961	5.0	1.7	2.2	4.0	0.272	43.2
1962	−12.8	0.8	2.6	6.1	0.388	42.6
1963	−0.4	2.4	2.7	5.8	0.577	48.7
1964	19.7	−3.1	2.2	9.0	1.271	120.3
1965	1.0	1.3	2.8	6.4	1.891	48.8
1966	−4.2	2.1	3.5	6.9	2.216	17.2
1967	−0.2	2.2	2.7	3.2	2.662	20.1
1968	−1.3	2.9	3.8	7.8	3.396	27.6
1969	2.9	−1.9	4.8	8.7	4.076	20.0
1970	13.0	1.9	5.6	2.7	4.594	12.7
1971	−3.5	3.8	5.5	1.9	5.287	15.1
1972	12.8	7.3	4.5	6.4	5.934	12.2
1973	37.4	24.8	7.4	10.2	6.126	3.2
1974	22.0	54.4	13.5	−1.0	6.790	10.8
Average						
1952–73	1.5	0.1	3.1	5.6	1.796	33.7
1952–58	−2.6	−4.9	2.1	4.1	0.068	38.1
1959–64	−1.1	−0.4	2.1	6.8	0.476	49.6
1965–73	6.4	4.9	4.5	6.0	4.020	19.6
1968–73	10.2	6.5	5.3	6.3	4.902	15.1
Level (1963 = 100)						
1973	221	139	152	184	...	...

Sources: *Conjuntura Econômica, International Financial Statistics,* and *Boletim do Banco Central do Brasil,* various issues.

a. Export and import prices in U.S. dollars. Series for 1951–59 were linked to series for 1959–74.

b. Weighted averages of consumer price indexes and industrial production indexes, with the following weights: the United States, 0.5; the United Kingdom, 0.1; France, 0.1; West Germany, 0.2; Japan, 0.1.

c. The exchange rate is taken from annual averages published by the central bank.

In 1974 this favorable situation changed completely, with imports more than doubling in value from those of 1973. Although the oil crisis was a major contributor to the unsatisfactory results of the Brazilian external sector in 1974, it was not the only disturbing factor. Below, the results of recent years—particularly 1974—are considered in some detail.[15]

As I have indicated, the period 1968–73 was characterized by economic recovery with rapid growth and an almost steady rate of inflation. In the external sector, after the introduction of the trotting peg (small and frequent changes of the exchange rate) combined with many incentives to export manufactured products, the balance of payments was favorable, with high growth rates for exports, huge net capital inflows, and substantial overall surpluses.[16]

Even without new elements such as the oil crisis, one could argue that all these favorable results would certainly not be obtained over the next few years. Both the huge balance of payments surplus with its monetary effects and the declining output gaps generated by the high growth rates were exerting excess demand pressures on the economy and threatening the steadiness of the inflation rate. The government attempted to neutralize these effects through announcements about expected inflation, compensatory open market operations, contractionary fiscal policy, and restrictions on external loans,[17] but these pressures finally exploded in 1974.

Since the economic boom of Brazil was partly based on export promotion and other external elements, including huge capital inflows, it would certainly also be affected by the external economic situation of late 1973 and 1974, particularly the world inflationary explosion, the oil crisis, and reces-

15. The analysis in the following paragraphs is based on the model described in the second section of this paper. A more formal regression analysis, covering 1952–73, is presented in the third section.

16. Again, the overall surpluses were obtained in spite of current-account deficits caused by chronic deficits in the services account and a high growth rate for imports. The financing of the current-account deficit through external savings, especially in the form of medium-term loans, evidently led to an increasing external debt, reaching $12 billion in 1973, which corresponds roughly to one year of exports plus international reserves in 1973.

17. The central bank in Brazil uses three basic instruments to control (or decontrol) external loans and reduce (or increase) capital inflows and consequently international reserves: compulsory deposits, minimum terms, and taxes. Such restrictions (or incentives) can always be roughly translated into an increase or reduction of the differential between Brazilian interest rates and world interest rates. In 1973, to reduce the growth of international reserves, the restrictions were applied, with increases in all three control instruments. When the balance of payments turned from surplus to deficit in 1974, all the restrictions were eased, with reductions of the compulsory deposit, the minimum term, and the taxes. Apparently, capital movements in Brazil are sensitive to interest rate differentials.

sions in the industrialized countries. The oil crisis, the internal boom, and world inflation caused imports to grow at a rate of 102 percent in 1974, more than doubling in dollar nominal values, whereas export growth slowed to 28 percent as a result of recessions in the industrialized countries as well as specific difficulties in some commodity markets such as coffee. Dollar export prices grew by 22 percent and import prices by 54.4 percent (see table 6), whereas quantity indexes increased 31.1 percent for imports and only 5.4 percent for exports.

Under the trotting peg system, the exchange rate was devalued eleven times in 1974, amounting to a total change of 19.6 percent for the year, roughly the difference between the internal and the external inflation rates (34 percent minus 14 percent). It should be pointed out that in 1973 there was a slight deviation from the trotting peg system, with less devaluation than a purchasing-power–parity rule would imply. I have suggested that as a consequence there was a greater neutralization of imported inflation in 1973, but on the other hand, there were also lagged effects in 1974, with slow growth of exports, acceleration of imports, a huge current-account deficit, and an overall deficit.

Despite the inflation and the balance of payments performance, which was as poor as or even poorer than in other industrialized or developing countries, Brazil continued to grow at high rates in 1974. There was, however, a clear slowing down of the growth process, especially in the manufacturing sector. The elimination of output gaps has not only provoked price acceleration—at least partially—but has also begun to depress output growth rates.

There is a strong argument against the use of a deflationary shock treatment in Brazil that seems to have been important even in 1974, in spite of the inflationary acceleration. A tight monetary policy was applied in the first half of 1974, substantially reducing real balances, but it was replaced in the second half by a reflationary policy. For the next few years, one can derive from official announcements the likelihood of a "gradualist" monetary and fiscal policy,[18] designed not to eliminate inflation but to decelerate it to the previous steady plateau of 1968–73 (averaging 20 percent), without provoking high stabilization costs in the form of a growth recession.

18. The expressions "gradualist policy" and "shock treatment policy" are frequently used in Brazil. Their precise meaning and differences are not well defined, but one can attempt to differentiate between them with the following example. Applied to the 1974 situation (34 percent inflation and 9.5 percent growth) and concentrating on monetary policy (34 percent money supply growth in 1974), one possible "gradualist" monetary policy approach to decelerate inflation would be 30 percent in 1975, 25 percent in 1976, 20 percent in 1977, down to 10 percent. A shock treatment could be exemplified by an immediate 10 percent money growth rate in 1975 and the maintenance of this steady

Monetary Correction and the Trotting Peg

From 1964 on, many indexation mechanisms were introduced in Brazil to reduce the effects of inflation on the economy. There was evidence that, in spite of an at least partly anticipated inflation, institutional obstacles created a situation in which price changes subsidized debtors in the capital and money markets and discouraged saving. Furthermore, fictitious nominal profits were taxed, investments were misdirected, the mortgage market atrophied, and balance of payments disequilibria were frequent.[19] Under the general name of "monetary correction," indexation methods were then systematically applied in many areas—savings, loans, debts, rents, assets, insurance, interest, wages, housing, and the exchange rate. Nowadays, after twelve years of monetary correction, it is suggested that inflation has been almost neutralized in Brazil and that the country has learned how to live with an anticipated annual rate of price change of two digits. Hence 25 percent inflation in Brazil would be a smaller problem than 10 percent inflation in an industrialized country without an indexation system.[20]

Imagine the absence of monetary correction in an inflationary situation— 30 percent inflation, for example, the Brazilian average of the last twenty years. It is certainly correct to assume that, even without monetary correction, in a free competitive market with no money illusion, wage, interest, and exchange rates would naturally adjust upward because of inflationary expectations. The general increase in prices and nominal income would create excess demand in the markets, which would lead to these upward adjustments.

The truth is, however, that this abstraction does not occur in the real world. Market distortions and imperfections, partial money illusion, fixed exchange rates, and institutional obstacles such as usury laws[21] do not allow this natural process of indexation to happen fully. In fact, one might argue

rate thereafter. Supposedly, the stabilization costs (loss of real output) of the second policy would be greater than the costs of the gradualist one, but it must be emphasized that these results are still being discussed (as in the work cited in note 12).

19. An analysis of the effects of inflation in Brazil before 1964 can be found in Mário Henrique Simonsen, "Inflation and the Money and Capital Markets of Brazil," in Howard Ellis, ed., *The Economy of Brazil* (University of California Press, 1969).

20. The welfare cost of inflation—the tax on real cash balances—still exists in Brazil, since monetary correction (or at least payment of interest) does not go as far as the money stock (demand deposits plus currency). Thus, inflation is not entirely neutral in Brazil, if only because of this welfare cost.

21. The usury law in Brazil (1933) forbids nominal interest rates above 12 percent a year.

that with a steady rate of 30 percent inflation and no monetary correction, the institutional interferences with market processes could delay but not impede the operation of the market forces. But inflation rates are variable: a *high* rate can be anticipated, but *rising* or *falling* rates leave at least part of the inflation unanticipated. The institutionalization of indexation—that is, the widespread use of escalator clauses with contracts in real terms—leads not only to adjustments that would occur anyway in a steady anticipated inflation but also, and most important, to adjustments resulting from variable inflation rates that would not occur otherwise. Besides, the official monetary correction itself leads the public to form more realistic expectations about inflation, thus reducing the costs of inadequate information that make inflation less neutral.[22]

As pointed out, before indexation was instituted, the rising inflation between 1957 and 1964, for example, subsidized debtors and borrowers. Negative real rates of interest in Brazil in the early 1960s provide an example of this distortion.[23] With low nominal interest rates, there was excess demand for funds and the supply was discouraged. In contrast to an atrophied capital market, the government could raise revenue from inflation: higher income taxes based on nominal incomes moving to higher tax brackets, borrowing at low interest rates, and deficit financing through monetary expansion as a tax on cash balances. As shown below, monetary correction permitted a remarkable development of capital markets and reduced government revenue from inflation.

In 1964–65 the adoption of a gradualist policy designed to decelerate the rate of inflation made necessary the introduction of monetary correction to neutralize the effects of the remaining inflation. A "shock treatment" to eliminate inflation completely and quickly was not considered practical because of its costs in recession and unemployment. The gradualist program included orthodox measures such as the reduction of budget deficits through tax increases and expenditure cuts, credit restrictions, tight monetary policy, incomes policy, and correction of previous price distortions.[24] Progress in reducing inflation from the 87.8 percent peak of 1964 was steady—55.4 per-

22. Brazil is far from having a steady, fully anticipated, and neutral rate of inflation, with the economy working as if there were price stability. See also footnote 20.

23. These negative real rates are found by using any plausible measure of inflationary anticipations for the period. Evidently, many extra commissions and service charges paid by the borrowers in that period are difficult to measure empirically. But see Antonio M. Silveira, "Interest Rate and Rapid Inflation: The Evidence from the Brazilian Economy," *Journal of Money, Credit, and Banking,* vol. 5 (August 1973).

24. See, for example, Alexandre Kafka, "The Brazilian Stabilization Program, 1964–66," *Journal of Political Economy,* vol. 75 (August 1967), pp. 596–631.

cent in 1965, 38.8 percent in 1966, and 27.1 percent in 1967[25]—because of the gradual character of the program and the corrective price adjustments in the period, designed to eliminate distortions of previous years.

The basic legislation for monetary correction was passed between 1964 and 1966. For the calculation of the "monetary correction coefficients," the wholesale price index, which is computed by a private research institution (the Getulio Vargas Foundation), was selected. Table 1 presents the annual variations of the WPI as well as the GDP implicit deflator and the general price index.

The use of the WPI refers to the so-called a posteriori, post-fixed, or ex post monetary correction. On the other hand, especially for short-term bills, an ex ante, pre-fixed, or a priori correction was developed, with a future anticipated inflation instead of actual past rates of price change, as in the case of a posteriori indexation.

In the securities market, the pre-fixed, or ex ante, correction is valid for certificates of deposit, bills of exchange, and time deposits.[26] The post-fixed, or ex post, indexation is used for treasury bonds (ORTN), housing bills, and savings accounts, as well as for some forced saving mechanisms.

One- or two-year treasury bonds are corrected monthly based on a quarterly moving average of the WPI, with a lag of four months (that is, the July coefficient refers to the average of January, February, and March). Real rates of interest vary between 5 percent and 7 percent. The ORTN coefficients are the basis for the whole indexation mechanism of the ex post variety.[27]

The counterpart of the monetary correction of savings is naturally the indexation of loans. As with the saving instruments, pre-fixed correction is

25. GDP implicit price deflator is used. With the general price index, the rates were 90.5 percent in 1964, 56.8 percent in 1965, 38.0 percent in 1966, and 28.3 percent in 1967. See also table 1.

26. In practice, the pre-fixed correction represents a semantic method of allowing nominal interest rates to be higher than the maximum imposed by the usury law. It could almost be classified as a new distortion designed to circumvent old ones.

27. In 1973 some modifications in the correction of treasury bonds introduced mixed elements of the pre-fixed and post-fixed methods, with substantial changes in the indexation system. The monetary correction coefficients were then obtained on the basis of a five-month moving average: the actual quarterly average plus an official estimate for two months. Two new terms were therefore included so that past rates and expected future rates could be taken into account simultaneously. The objective of the modifications was to diminish the possible feedback effects of indexation on inflation (discussed later). In the previous scheme, the lag and the ex post aspect of the indexation were supposedly creating obstacles to the deceleration of inflation. In 1974, however, the indexation of treasury bonds returned to a strict ex post basis.

generally used for short-term loans and post-fixed correction for long-term loans. Besides treasury bonds, the main long-term loans with post-fixed indexation are related to the financing of housing, involving savings passbooks and housing bills.

The ex ante correction mechanism (bills of exchange, certificates of deposit, and time deposits) can be regarded as an institutionalization of the Fisher hypothesis for interest rates, to the extent that it makes explicit the division of the nominal return between real interest and a pre-fixed premium that represents the anticipated inflation for the period. In contrast to the ex post method, where the nominal interest rate is variable or floating, the pre-fixed method continues to imply a fixed interest rate.

In 1974 there were some attempts to introduce post-fixed correction for certificates of deposit, bills of exchange, and time deposits in cases where these financial assets corresponded to longer-term loans (more than two years). The result was a mixture of pre-fixed and post-fixed indexation, with a fixed nominal interest rate but a variable term for the loan. For example, in the case of monthly payments, the value of the payments is fixed but the number of payments is variable, whereas under strict ex post indexation, the number of payments is fixed but the value of each payment is variable.

Table 7 shows the annual nominal return in recent years for different securities with pre-fixed and post-fixed correction. It should be mentioned that the nominal interest provided by the pre-fixed system has been subject to controls in recent years. Besides, there are differences in taxation between ex ante and ex post correction; however, except for the controls, there tends to be a market compensation, with adjustments in the nominal returns of the different securities. One further remark can be made about the table: monetary correction rules are being applied in conjunction with many distortions in the capital market, including interest rate controls.

The ORTN coefficients are also used to adjust tax debts, insurance premiums, social security pensions, and rents. In other sectors, especially the construction industry, more specific price indexes are used to promote readjustments along the same lines. The minimum wage is also used for indexation purposes as an alternative to the wholesale price index in some cases related to the financing of housing.

The monetary correction of wages is basically made through the annual fixing of the minimum wage as well as the publication of monthly guidelines for collective wage negotiations and labor court awards. These rates of change are also used for the readjustment of government employees' wages and as a yardstick in private negotiations between labor and business. In practice they work as minimum, or floor, rates of change in money wages;

Table 7. *Comparison of Nominal Yield of Selected Brazilian Securities and Increase in the Price Index, 1966–74*

Percent per year

	Yield[a]			
	Post-fixed indexation		Pre-fixed indexation, bills of exchange[d]	Increase in general price index[e]
Year	Treasury bonds[b]	Housing bonds[c]		
1966	46.2	46.3	n.a.	38.8
1967	29.9	36.5	33.2	24.3
1968	43.3	33.4	31.8	25.4
1969	22.8	27.1	30.3	20.2
1970	24.0	28.7	30.5	19.2
1971	27.1	32.7	30.3	19.8
1972	19.6	25.1	28.1	15.5
1973	17.1	19.7	24.1	15.7
1974	39.5	38.4	22.0	34.5

Source. *Boletim do Banco Central do Brasil*, selected issues.

a. December rates.

b. The annual real interest rate was 6 percent for paper issued before July 20, 1967, and 4 percent for issues after that date for a maturity of twelve months until January 1974. After February 1974, a two-year-maturity treasury bond was adopted, with 5 percent real interest and reinvestment of received interest.

c. Housing bonds carry a three-year maturity and an annual real interest rate of 8 percent with monetary correction and interest paid quarterly. For the purposes of this table, reinvestment in other housing bonds was taken into account. After March 1972, the interest rate is 6 percent a year.

d. Bills of exchange of six-month maturity, taken at an annual rate. After 1971 maturity considered is 360 days.

e. The increase in December over previous December.

these rates can be higher depending, of course, on excess demand in a specific labor market.

The wage adjustment formula takes into account past and anticipated inflation as well as productivity increases. In other words, there are three basic components: past real wages, future inflation, and future productivity increases. More specifically, the formula attempts to make the expected real wage for a certain period equal to the average real wage of the previous twelve months, with an adjustment for productivity.[28] Although the actual average real wage for the period may differ from the expected one if the anticipated inflation coefficient is different from the actual inflation in the period, this eventual discrepancy between anticipated and actual inflation is corrected in the next adjustment. The evolution of the minimum wage is

28. See Mário Henrique Simonsen, "Política Antiinflacionaria," in C. Pelaez and M. Malta, eds., *Ensaios sobre Café e Desenvolvimento Econômico* (Rio de Janeiro: Instituto Brasileiro do Café [IBC], 1974).

shown in table 1.[29] It should perhaps be pointed out that, in the case of minimum wages, the productivity component of the formula is not taken into account, supposedly in order to avoid unemployment. There is evidence that in recent years minimum wages have directly "affected only unskilled labor in the less-developed regions of Brazil."[30]

Post-fixed correction of the balance sheet of firms is another feature of the Brazilian indexation system. Fiscal legislation before 1964 allowed the taxing of nominal fictitious profits, but monetary correction laws of that year determined that firms should make an annual readjustment of their fixed assets, working capital, and depreciation allowances, based on variations in the wholesale price index. Firms can deduct from taxable profits an amount corresponding to the maintenance of working capital, which is monetarily corrected. In 1967 there was an attempt to introduce indexation of all accounts in the balance sheet, but it was not implemented because of its complexity. There is some evidence that the partial indexation of balance sheets has permitted firms to maintain their real capital in spite of inflation.[31]

Besides the indexing of fixed capital assets, depreciation allowances, and working capital, which substantially changed the corporation income tax, the personal income tax is also monetarily corrected in Brazil, with annual escalator clauses for the personal exemption, the deductions, and the limits of the tax brackets.

Monetary correction since the mid-sixties has led to a remarkable increase in the number of nonbank financial intermediaries and a great diversification of financial assets held by the public, with increases in financial savings in nominal and real terms. Before 1964, the financial system consisted almost entirely of commercial banks. Government bonds with purchasing power clauses (ORTN) were successful, allowing the government to finance its budget deficits without monetary expansion and at the same time to conduct open market operations on a large scale. The growth of the capital and money markets, however, must be attributed not only to monetary correction but also to many parallel fiscal incentives, which in practice have represented higher interest rates.[32] One might say that the effects of monetary correction

29. In May 1974 the new minimum wage was Cr$377, or $57, a month. It represented an increase of 20.8 percent over the previous minimum wage (May 1973). In table 1, the rates of change are derived from *annual averages* of the minimum wage.

30. Alexandre Kafka, "Indexing for Inflation in Brazil," in *Essays on Inflation and Indexation* (Washington, D.C.: American Enterprise Institute for Public Policy Research, 1974), p. 89.

31. See P. Auberger, *Le modèle brésilien de lutte contre l'inflation, 1964–1973* (Paris: La Documentation Française, 1974).

32. There are many tax exemptions and deductions designed to promote saving. In general, one can deduct from the income tax certain amounts corresponding to specific percentages of investments made in some financial instruments or in some

were favorable to saving not only because of the higher level of nominal interest rates but also because it greatly reduced uncertainty as to the real rate of interest.

Even though monetary correction may have neutralized the damaging effects of inflation on saving and investment, it has probably had its own new effects on the economy. On the one hand, there is the argument that indexation, by more rapidly transmitting inflationary expectations through-out the economy, might paradoxically facilitate the ending of inflation by reducing stabilization costs. In other words, a Phillips curve would be verti-cal even in the short run.[33] The evidence of the Brazilian economy does not wholly favor this hypothesis. On the other hand, there is the opposite argu-ment that indexation might have introduced feedback mechanisms into the economy from past inflation to present inflation. Believers in cost-push mechanisms, including wage-push, interest-push, and exchange-push, might argue that indexation would perpetuate inflation. For example, under a decelerating inflation, the correction of wages and interest would be based on inflation rates higher than those prevailing at that moment, and this feed-back might lead to a new acceleration of inflation. But even with no monetary correction, the feedback mechanisms from past to present inflation would occur. Recent models of inflation emphasize the powerful effect of antici-pated inflation, based on past price changes, on present inflation, with or without indexation.

If monetary correction does not seem to be of great help in ending infla-tion, it also does not seem by itself to impede that painful process. The point is that, given the high costs of anti-inflationary policies, monetary correction is a necessary evil to neutralize the damaging effects of a two-digit inflation rate and hence to reduce the harm done by inflation.

An additional comment can be made. If one neglects the inflation tax on cash balances, widespread indexation like that of Brazil seems to neutralize inflation. Why, then, bother with inflation? It must be emphasized that in-dexation involves substantially high transaction costs. It would be "far bet-ter to have no inflation and no escalator clauses. But that alternative is not currently available."[34]

In the external sector, a new exchange rate system with small and fre-quent changes in the rate was adopted in August 1968. In practice, the new

---

sectors of the economy. One is also allowed to forgo payment of a certain percentage of income tax to purchase share certificates in the capital market. Furthermore, capital gains taxation is favorable.

33. See Milton Friedman, "Monetary Correction," in *Essays on Inflation and In-dexation* (American Enterprise Institute for Public Policy Research, 1974), pp. 25–61.

34. Ibid., p. 35.

mechanism represented the application of a purchasing power clause (used internally since 1964 under the name of monetary correction) to the price of foreign currency. Evidently, both the domestic price level and the external price level are taken into account in making the necessary adjustments of the exchange rate, as is the general position of the balance of payments. But the interval of the changes, though always small, is not known precisely. The name suggested by Machlup, the trotting peg, is probably appropriate for the Brazilian experience—a compromise between fixed and flexible rates, similar to the crawling peg.[35]

In the postwar period Brazil has tried many exchange rate systems. From 1947 to 1953 there were strong mechanisms of exchange controls and import restrictions (the licensing system). In 1953 an exchange auction system with multiple exchange rates was introduced, with a variable auction premium equivalent to a fluctuating tariff on the import side and variable bonuses on the export side.[36] In 1955 there were at least twelve different exchange rates. The system continued until 1961, when a process of unifying the rates was initiated. Other trade and exchange regulations were introduced in the late 1950s, expanding the protection schemes of the country, with a deliberate process of import-substitution industrialization.[37]

From 1961 to 1968 the country had a pegged rate. Large and sudden changes in the rate were periodically announced (one a year, in general). Between two changes, the exchange rate lagged well behind internal inflation, leading to instability of exports and imports. Since 1968, when the trotting peg was adopted, at varying but frequent intervals the central bank has issued simple communiqués stating the new selling and buying rates in relation to the U.S. dollar. On the average, the central bank has announced a 1 percent devaluation of the cruzeiro every forty days. The timing and size of the exchange rate changes have varied, respectively, between ten and seventy days and from 0.5 percent to 2.5 percent.[38] Table 5 indicates the evolution of the annual *averages* of the exchange rate from 1951 to 1974.

35. See Fritz Machlup, *On Terms, Concepts, Theories, and Strategies in the Discussion of Greater Flexibility of Exchange Rates,* Reprints in International Finance 14 (Princeton University Press, International Finance Section, 1970).

36. See Alexandre Kafka, "The Brazilian Exchange Auction System," *Review of Economics and Statistics,* vol. 38 (August 1956), pp. 308–22.

37. Parallel to import substitution, it has been argued that there was a discouragement or at least neglect of exports, with overvalued exchange rates and export restrictions. See, for example, Nathaniel H. Leff, "Export Stagnation and Autarkic Development in Brazil, 1947–1962," *Quarterly Journal of Economics,* vol. 81 (May 1967), pp. 286–301. The data in table 5 in fact indicate instability and no growth of exports between 1952 and 1964.

38. With one exception (February 1973, revaluation of 3 percent), the exchange rate has always been devalued in relation to the U.S. dollar under the trotting peg.

The problems of the previous exchange systems of Brazil—multiple rates and fixed but abruptly adjustable rates—are well known. Before 1968, when the average interval between changes in the exchange rate was twelve months, exports became expensive between adjustments and were held back, awaiting a new devaluation with more favorable rates; on the other hand, imports became cheaper and were subsidized, with a decline of effective tariff protection. Financial transactions involved high speculation, with sudden exceptional profits made possible by the fixity of the rate for long periods and continuous internal inflation. Before an expected devaluation, there was a great outflow of capital from the country, and soon after a big devaluation there was a huge inflow of foreign short-term capital. Such cyclical pressures and crises in the financial system, with scarcity of credit before the expected change in the rate and excess of credit after the devaluation, "made the task of monetary management extremely difficult."[39]

The new system of small and frequent changes made it possible to avoid the problems inherent in abrupt changes in the exchange rate. Although the boom experienced since 1968 by the country in the whole economy and in the external sector in particular cannot of course be solely attributed to the new exchange rate system, there is some evidence that the new system was able to remove bottlenecks in the external sector, avoiding disequilibria in the balance of payments resulting from rapid growth and domestic inflationary pressures. The remarkable improvements in the balance of payments (see table 5) since 1968 were in exports and the capital account.

The introduction of the trotting peg was a necessary prerequisite for the use of fiscal, credit, and administrative incentives—tax exemptions, special financing schemes, subsidized interest rates—to stimulate exports of manufactured goods in that it maintained the profitability of the export sector throughout the year by avoiding oscillations between profits and losses caused by variations in the real exchange rate. For trade, the trotting peg has guaranteed a permanently satisfactory exchange rate that provides continuous competitive conditions for Brazilian products in international markets.

There is also evidence that the trotting peg favored the capital account and eliminated speculation from the foreign exchange market (see table 5). The new system seems to have reduced speculation not only because of the routine character of the changes, but also because devaluations have been in general less than or equal to the difference between domestic and external nominal interest rates. In fact, for the financial sector, the trotting peg can be

39. See P. H. Lyra, "Cruzeiro: o Preço Exato da Moeda," *Jornal do Brasil* (March 26, 1971).

seen as a necessary complement of the indexation system. As an indexed economy in an unindexed world, Brazil has had huge surpluses in the capital account of its balance of payments because of very large nominal interest rate differentials. Normally, the trotting peg system would eliminate such differentials, which should be roughly equal to the inflation differentials, but this has not happened because interest rates abroad have not wholly reflected the world inflationary explosion.

Another benefit is that the emotional and political problems related to exchange rate changes, which before 1968 were considered an affront to national dignity and a taboo, have been eliminated. This change in attitude toward exchange rate changes, with a depoliticization of devaluation, is one of the most interesting practical results of the new exchange system. Apparently, the level of international reserves replaced exchange rate changes in political debates.

When the trotting peg system was introduced, the monetary authorities emphasized that it was to a great extent a consequence of the inflationary process in Brazil.[40] Given the existence of an inflationary process, the trotting peg was considered a suitable mechanism to make inflation easier to live with, since a gradualist policy would not eliminate it completely.[41] As I have pointed out, the trotting peg can be considered an application of the monetary correction clause to the external value of the currency. There are, however, no precise rules for exchange rate changes and even though inflation differentials are certainly very important elements in determining the changes, they are not the only ones.[42] In 1973, for example, a strong balance of payments led the government to promote much less devaluation than

40. Both the monetary correction and the trotting peg have sometimes been accused of adding to the very problem they are designed to ease—inflation—via feedback.

41. The main arguments against the use of freely floating rates (another alternative) in a country like Brazil are generally related to the thinness of the foreign exchange market and the absence of organization in this market that might lead to unnecessary fluctuations of the daily exchange rate. Besides, freely floating rates lack the political virtue of acceptability, and the unrealistic nature of a policy of hands-off is emphasized because the monetary authorities would always intervene in the market. In spite of the attempt to imitate the workings of a floating rate with small and frequent changes, it is clear that the Brazilian system is much closer to fixed but adjustable rates than to freely floating exchange rates.

42. Evidently, in the case of the depreciation of the currency, other factors such as the specific evolution of export and import prices, the balance of payments performance, the behavior of the interest rates, and international reserves have also to be taken into account, leading to less rigid monetary correction. But the inflation differential—the difference between inflation rates at home and abroad—has certainly been a more important factor in the changes. In this sense, the parallel between monetary

would be suggested by the difference between external and domestic inflation.

On the other hand, it is true—and the data in tables 1 and 6 provide evidence for this—that the variations in exchange rates since 1968 are following the purchasing-power–parity rates closely, suggesting that the rate changes can be roughly obtained as the difference between domestic inflation and an average of inflation rates of Brazil's main commercial partners, especially the United States. Suppose internal inflation is 35 percent and external inflation 15 percent a year. The trotting peg policy would suggest a 20 percent devaluation at short intervals; that is, a 35 percent devaluation minus a 15 percent revaluation.

A Model of Imported Inflation

In this section, I summarize the theoretical framework for the analysis of imported inflation that served as the basis for some simple econometric tests concerning the recent Brazilian inflationary experience. (Some regression results are presented in the next section.) Clearly, external factors play an important part in this model. The channels of transmission of world inflation get special emphasis, with many external variables being included among the main determinants of domestic inflation. A more detailed mathematical formulation of the structural macromodel used in the following analysis is presented in appendix A. This model can be described as a combination of IS-LM and Phillips curve analyses of an open economy, and both aggregate demand and aggregate supply factors are taken into account.

It is clear from the model in appendix A that there is a system of equations designed to determine many important endogenous, or dependent, macroeconomic variables such as the price level (and the rate of inflation, naturally), real output (and hence its growth rate), the interest rate, the wage rate, the balance of payments surplus (or deficit), and so on. In this section, I concentrate on the determination of the price level, since this is basically an analysis of price inflation, with emphasis on external factors.

In the language of the econometricians, I have derived from a large structural model a reduced form for the price level. In other words, I derived, from some basic hypotheses about the behavioral structural equations (demand-for-money function, import function, production function, and the

---

correction and the trotting peg is clear. As I have suggested, they are in fact complementary, with the exchange rate "indexation" being necessary to compensate for domestic indexation—that is, to isolate it from abroad.

like), the effects of the exogenous, or independent, variables on the price level. Interest is clearly concentrated on the signs of the multipliers, or partial derivatives, of the reduced form for the price level (and thus the rate of inflation).

The reduced form for the price level can be written as follows:[43]

$$P = F(Wy, ER, WP, G, B, f_o, P^a, Wi, y^+),$$

where

P = domestic price level

Wy = world real output

ER = exchange rate (domestic currency per unit of foreign currency)

WP = world price level (in foreign currency)

G = nominal government expenditures

B = nominal monetary base

f_o = exogenous real imports

P^a = anticipated domestic price level

Wi = nominal world interest rate

y^+ = potential real output.

The nine variables within the parentheses correspond to the group of exogenous, or independent, variables of the model that make the whole system, including the price level, move. There are five external variables: the exchange rate, the world price level, the world real output, the nominal interest rate, and exogenous imports. The exchange rate is supposedly a policy variable under the control of the government.[44] The other four external variables are determined exogenously, outside the domestic economy. Exoge-

43. Formally, some lagged endogenous and exogenous variables should also enter this reduced form, but they are less important for the following analysis. See also appendix A and the next section.

44. In the above analysis, exchange rates are assumed to be exogenous and international reserves "endogenous." Implicitly, a system of fixed but exogenously adjustable exchange rates is being considered rather than freely floating rates. Under floating rates, the roles should be reversed, with the exchange rate endogenous and the change in international reserves exogenously equated to zero (balance of payments equilibrium). The Brazilian trotting peg system does not seem to fall into either of the two cases. In fact, from the discussion of the previous section, one might argue that the exchange rate in Brazil has been, at least since 1968, endogenously determined by the difference between domestic inflation and external inflation. As a consequence, the exchange rate would disappear from the list of independent variables and the multiplier for WP, the world price level, would tend to be zero. I prefer, however, to maintain the exchange rate among the independent variables because I feel that it continues to be a variable under the control of the Brazilian government. Future research, however, should certainly take into account a "policy reaction function" for the exchange rate rather than treating it as an entirely exogenous variable.

nous imports are included merely to capture effects such as the oil embargo; the remaining four variables are the monetary and fiscal policy proxies—government expenditures and the monetary base—plus a predetermined variable designed to represent price expectations, P^a,[45] and finally a long-run element, potential output, y^+.

In view of the controversy related to the exogeneity and controllability of the above fiscal and monetary variables, the nominal government deficit, D, and nominal domestic credit, DC, should also be used in the analysis as alternative proxies for fiscal and monetary actions, respectively. The former —government expenditures minus receipts—should eliminate somewhat the endogeneity of taxes, and the latter could be a more appropriate monetary policy indicator for an open economy because of the endogenous effect of international reserves on the monetary base and the money supply. Nominal domestic credit here is the money supply minus net foreign reserves. The alternative reduced form would then be

$$P = F(Wy, ER, WP, D, DC, f_o, P^a, Wi, y^+).$$

In this section, the main purpose is to show the channels of influence from these nine independent variables—especially the external variables—to the domestic price level. Simple estimates of the reduced form for the price level (as well as for nominal income) are reported in the next section.

The reduced form for the price level with the corresponding *signs* for the multipliers is

$$P = F(Wy, ER, WP, G, B, f_o, P^a, Wi, y^+).$$
$$+ \quad + \quad + \quad + \ + - \quad + \quad - \ -$$

Needless to say, G and B, the fiscal and monetary variables, could be replaced by D and DC, government deficit and domestic credit, with the same expected positive signs.

The model therefore suggests that an increase in world real income, the exchange rate, the world price level, government expenditures (or deficit), the monetary base (or domestic credit), or price anticipations leads to an increase in the domestic price level—that is, inflation. In contrast, an in-

---

45. In general, price expectation models are based on past prices and past inflation, and this is why P^a is treated as an exogenous (more precisely, predetermined) variable. Note that wages are endogenously determined in the model, which contains a labor market (see appendix A). However, some readers might prefer to regard P^a—especially in view of the Brazilian wage indexation system—as a "proxy" for exogenous wages or for "wage policy." Data for wages in Brazil are poor.

crease in exogenous imports, the world interest rate, or potential output leads to a reduction of the domestic price level.

The derivation of the signs of these multipliers—that is, the direction of the effects of these nine independent variables on prices—is set out below.

Initially, the influence of "external prices" on the price level is examined. In the model, the effects of an increase in the exchange rate are assumed to be exactly equal to the effects of an increase in world prices in foreign currency. In fact, the exchange rate simply translates the world price increases in foreign currency into a price increase in domestic currency. Therefore, a devaluation of the exchange rate has exactly the same effects as a world inflation, and a revaluation corresponds to a world deflation.[46] In mathematical terms, it is assumed that the partial derivative F_{WP} is exactly equal to the partial F_{ER}. Hence, "external price" here will be the terminology used for ER times WP, that is, world prices in domestic currency.[47] Moreover, it is assumed that the terms of trade are constant—that an increase in the external price affects export and import prices equally.

The model indicates three basic channels of influence through which the external price might affect domestic inflation: the trade balance effect, the overall balance of payments effect, and the direct supply effect.

An increase in the external price will affect export volume positively and import volume negatively, improving the trade balance. This greater trade balance will directly affect aggregate demand. If full employment is assumed, the increase in aggregate demand resulting from the *trade balance effect* will lead to a higher price level. Without full employment, the effect will be divided between higher real output and a higher price level.

The *overall balance of payments effect* is related to the monetary consequences of the balance of payments surplus caused by the improvement in the trade balance.[48] As a consequence of the overall surplus, international reserves would increase, leading to an endogenous monetary effect on aggregate demand (analogous to the exogenous effect of B or DC, discussed later) and provoking higher domestic prices.

46. This clearly indicates that an increase in world prices can always be offset by a revaluation of the exchange rate, and vice versa.

47. Under eternally fixed rates this qualification would be unnecessary, since ER, the exchange rate, would be, by definition, a constant. At the other extreme—freely floating rates—ER would have to be treated as an endogenous variable. See also note 44 above.

48. A possible opposite effect in the capital account is neglected: the external price increase might reduce the nominal interest rate differential and decrease the overall surplus somewhat.

Finally, if it is assumed that imported materials enter the production function, there will also be a *direct supply effect,* or cost effect, from the external price increase. The more expensive imported inputs will negatively affect aggregate supply, leading to domestic price increases. In other words, the higher external prices will represent higher costs, forcing a reduction in supply, that is, lower output and higher prices. It is interesting to note that this supply effect goes in the same direction as the demand effect in the case of prices, but in the opposite direction for real output. Consequently, the multiplier for *ER* or *WP* in the reduced form for real output—not discussed here—is certainly ambiguous as to sign.

A fourth external price effect could, for the sake of completeness, be included in a more comprehensive model, where it could be assumed that external prices influence domestic price expectations and/or that real imports enter the demand-for-money function along with real income. In this case, an increase in external prices will, because of lower imports and higher interest rates as a result of higher inflationary expectations, reduce the demand for money.[49] Once more, another additional monetary effect would occur, causing excess supply of money and hence domestic price increases.

The multiplier effects of the other external variables are now considered in less detail. An increase in *world real output* should also lead to domestic price increases through two channels analogous to the ones for external prices: a trade multiplier (higher exports) and an overall balance of payments multiplier with the surplus leading to endogenous monetary impulses through higher international reserves.

An increase in the other two external variables—world interest rates and exogenous imports—would have, in contrast, deflationary effects. A higher *world interest rate* would reduce the capital-account surplus of the balance of payments: thus provoking a reduction of international reserves and a fall in aggregate demand. An increase of *exogenous imports*—for example, the end of an oil embargo—would negatively affect aggregate demand (trade balance and overall balance effects) and positively affect aggregate supply, leading to an unambiguous fall in the price level.

Monetary and fiscal policy effects are captured in the model through *B* or *DC* (monetary base or domestic credit) and *G* or *D* (government expenditures or deficit), respectively. An increase of the exogenous *monetary variable* will cause an excess supply of money that will tend to be eliminated by

---

49. There would also be an additional supply effect through price expectations. See the paragraph where P^a is analyzed.

higher prices and lower interest rates (plus higher real output). Furthermore, the lower interest rates will affect private expenditure positively, contributing to higher prices too. The *fiscal policy variable* also has a direct positive effect on aggregate demand through higher expenditures, provoking higher prices and real output. But the pure fiscal policy will increase interest rates, and this deflationary effect might reduce somewhat the positive fiscal influence on inflation.

Finally, there are the price expectation variable, P^a, and potential output, y^+. The former is not precisely exogenous but simply represents past price history—a predetermined variable. In the model, P^a affects interest rates (and thus the demand for money) and wage rates (through the labor supply or, correspondingly, the Phillips curve). This latter effect is entirely analogous to the presence of price expectations in a wage Phillips curve, and it might be regarded as a proxy for a "wage indexation policy."[50] An exogenous increase of price expectations leads to higher interest rates and higher wages because of indexation or market forces. Consequently the demand for money is reduced (or velocity rises), the capital account of the balance of payments improves, and aggregate supply is also reduced. All these aggregate demand and supply effects act in the same direction, leading to higher prices.[51] As far as *potential output* is concerned, an increase of y^+, by shifting the aggregate supply positively, is naturally deflationary.

Another interesting reduced form is the one for nominal income, Y. As pointed out above, all the aggregate demand effects of ER, WP, Wy, DC or B, D or G, P^a, Wi, and f_o, are divided between price effects and real output effects, depending of course on the level of capacity utilization, that is, on the position of the aggregate supply function or the Phillips curve. In the reduced form below for nominal income, aggregate demand effects are consequently the same as the ones for prices (and real output). Aggregate supply effects from ER, WP, P^a, f_o, and y^+, however, are ambiguous because they work in

50. See note 45 above.

51. A parenthetical remark should be made here to relate the aggregate supply analysis to the Phillips curve analysis of the introductory section. If external factors are omitted, the aggregate supply shown in appendix A could be rewritten as $y = G(y^+, P, P^a)$, where y is domestic real output, the other symbols are as already defined, and the signs for the derivatives are, respectively, plus, plus, and minus. This equation is basically equivalent to a Phillips curve type of equation such as $\dot{P} = R(\dot{P}^a, H)$, where H is the output gap ($[y^+ - y]/y^+$), a dot indicates percentage change, and the signs of the derivatives of R are, respectively, plus and minus. This last equation was the one used in the first section, with $\dot{P}^a$ approximated by past inflation. See also appendix A.

opposite directions for P and y. This is the reason for the question mark below the sign for some of the independent variables:[52]

$$Y = Y(Wy, ER, WP, D, DC, f_o, P^a, Wi, y^+).$$

$$+ \quad + \quad + \quad + \quad + \quad - \quad + \quad - \quad -$$

$$? \quad ? \qquad\qquad ? \quad ? \qquad ?$$

Some econometric tests of these reduced forms for prices and nominal income are presented below.

Some Econometric Results

Regression results for the period 1952–73 of the model of imported inflation described in the preceding section are analyzed here. But more detailed results, including estimation methods, are presented in appendix B. The regressions, although very simple, satisfactorily explain the variations in inflation and nominal income in Brazil.

The inflation model contained the following basic exogenous variables in the reduced form: the exchange rate, world inflation, a fiscal variable, a monetary variable, a proxy for domestic inflationary expectations, and world real output.[53] The estimation, except for world real output, confirms the significant effects of these variables on the Brazilian domestic inflation. For internal factors, the monetary variable seems to be the most powerful and stable explanatory variable. For external factors, the exchange rate variable seems to be the most important one. This is the case for both inflation and the rate of change of nominal income.

The variation of inflation in Brazil from 1952 to 1973 had a standard deviation of 20.3 percent, and the variation of nominal income changes of 18.9 percent (see table 8). The reduced form regressions explain about 85 to 90 percent of these variations, which is a very satisfactory result since percentage rates of change, not levels, are used. Moreover, there is no indication of significant autocorrelation problems in the regressions. Multicollinearity has clearly lowered the t-scores, but the estimates are generally significantly different from zero, with the correct signs.

52. The reader should perhaps recall the identity $Y = P \times y$, where Y is nominal income, P is the price level, and y is real income (or output).

53. Other exogenous variables are world interest rates, exogenous imports, and potential output. Since percentage changes are used, potential output disappears because it will be a constant by definition. World interest rates and exogenous imports were not considered for the empirical application; see appendix B.

Here each of the independent variables is discussed (see also tables 9 and 10).

The fiscal variable—government expenditure changes—has a significant positive effect on inflation and nominal income, although this influence is more reduced in some variants, especially when the monetary base or the lagged dependent variables—past inflation and past nominal income changes —are taken into account simultaneously.

The effect of world real output is insignificant, probably because of the relative small variation of this variable, but the estimated sign is correct in four cases out of seven.

World inflation and exchange rate devaluation are included separately in some cases and combined into a single variable in other cases. When they are separated, the world inflation variable has the correct expected sign but it is not significant,[54] whereas exchange rate devaluation is generally significant (with two exceptions, discussed in the next paragraph). When they are combined to make a single variable—the variation of the exchange rate plus the world inflation in foreign currency, that is, the variation of external prices in domestic currency—this single variable has the correct positive sign and is significant. But one can deduce from the separate estimates that its significance must be attributed more to the exchange rate than to world inflation.

A few comments on the effects of external prices should be made. First, the minor world inflation effect could simply be attributed to the changes in this variable in the period 1952–73, which was relatively small compared, for example, to exchange rate devaluations in Brazil. On the other hand, its small significance could also be related to the exchange rate policy applied in Brazil, especially after 1968, of devaluations based on the differential between domestic and world inflation. As pointed out in the preceding section, such a policy might lead to a zero multiplier for world inflation. This seems to be confirmed by the finding that the exchange rate (or the sum $E\dot{R}$ + $W\dot{P}$) is less significant when past inflation is also included in the regression— the "exceptions" mentioned above. Past inflation might be neutralizing or absorbing the external price effect because of multicollinearity among the independent variables.[55]

54. The higher (relative to all the other explanatory variables) estimated coefficient for world inflation is merely a consequence of the very low mean of that variable. See also table 8.

55. Note that in the regressions in appendix B the exchange rate and world inflation enter with a one-period lag. A parenthetical L indicates a one-period lag. Evidently, if $E\dot{R}(L)$ is based on the difference $\dot{P}(L) - W\dot{P}(L)$, the inflation differential, the sum $E\dot{R}(L) + W\dot{P}(L)$ is highly correlated with $\dot{P}(L)$. Thus, when $\dot{P}(L)$ enters the regression, the external price variables seem to lose their significance.

The monetary variables—either the monetary base or domestic credit—have powerful positive effects on inflation and nominal income. The regressions with domestic credit variations have greater explanatory power than the regressions with monetary base changes.

The lagged dependent variable—past inflation—in the inflation reduced form is significantly positive, reflecting both the importance of inflationary expectations and lagged effects of the exogenous variables. In contrast, the lagged dependent variable in the reduced form for nominal income changes is less satisfactory, but its sign is correct and it improves at least marginally the R^2 or standard error statistics.

Finally, the lagged output gap has a correct negative sign in the reduced form for inflation, but it has low significance, probably because of multicollinearity.

All in all, the results are satisfactory, especially if one takes into account the simplicity of the model and the small number of degrees of freedom provided by annual data. It is true that domestic factors—especially money supply changes and past inflation—are the main determinants of inflation in Brazil. But external factors—mainly exchange rate variations—certainly cannot be neglected in the explanation of domestic price inflation in Brazil. It should also be emphasized that domestic monetary changes are often influenced by external developments through changes in international reserves.

If one had to choose two of the ten reduced form variants in tables 9 and 10, one would select 9F and 10D. For these specific equations, inflation is adequately explained by fiscal actions, monetary actions, past inflation, past output gaps, and by "external inflation" (exchange devaluation plus world inflation). Nominal income changes are explained by monetary and fiscal actions as well as external inflation.

Conclusions

The average annual rate of inflation in Brazil for the period 1952–73 was 30 percent, with a standard deviation of 20 percent. The average rate of change of nominal income was 39 percent and the standard deviation, 19 percent, as a result of an average rate of growth of real income of 7 percent with a standard deviation of 3 percent. In 1974 inflation was 34 percent and real growth, 9.5 percent.

Econometric tests of a textbook type of model of imported inflation satisfactorily explain these variations in inflation and nominal income. The inflation reduced form model contains the following basic independent variables: the exchange rate, world inflation, a fiscal variable, a monetary variable, a proxy for inflationary expectations, world real output, domestic potential output, and other external variables.

The theoretical analysis indicates three channels through which world inflation affects domestic inflation: the trade balance multiplier, the balance of payments or monetary effect, and a direct price effect through the supply side.

The econometric application, with estimation of reduced forms for inflation and nominal income changes, suggests that external factors—especially exchange rate variations—had a significant effect on the Brazilian domestic inflation in the 1952–73 period.[56] On the other hand, internal factors seem to be relatively more important for the determination of changes in the price level and in nominal income, including monetary and fiscal variables as well as inflationary anticipations based on the past history of inflation.[57]

More intensive empirical research on the Brazilian inflation should be done. Needless to say, the econometric exercise presented here is very simple. Future tests of alternative specifications for the inflation model of the third section would undoubtedly provide interesting results, particularly if alternative measures for price expectations, world inflation, and potential output were used. In the case of expectations, for example, it should be useful to study carefully the policy option of "announcement effects" as well as to introduce some new theoretical developments such as the rational expectations hypothesis. Moreover, attempts should also be made to estimate the model with quarterly or even monthly data and to analyze more complicated lag structures. My model contains one important characteristic as far as economic policy decisions are concerned—simplicity.

Appendix A

The reduced forms discussed in the second section are derived from a structural macroeconomic model. In this appendix, the equations that form this simple but complete macromodel are given.

56. It must be pointed out that external developments, including exchange rate variations, will also affect real output. Although such effects are neither discussed nor tested in this paper, they could be easily derived from the model in appendix A. For example, the sign of the multiplier for the exchange rate is ambiguous because demand and supply effects go in opposite directions. When a policymaker is analyzing the option of exchange rate adjustments, he must keep in mind both price and real output effects.

57. Another interesting result is that the so-called output gap is significantly and negatively related to the acceleration of inflation, according to an expectational, or accelerationist, Phillips curve type of equation that presented a satisfactory performance for Brazil.

Let

B = nominal monetary base

bps = real balance of payments surplus

D = nominal government deficit

ER = exchange rate (domestic currency per unit of foreign currency)

e = real internal private expenditure

f = real imports

f_o = exogenous real imports

g = real government expenditures

G = nominal government expenditures

H = output gap, $(y^+ - y)/y^+$ (percent)

i = nominal interest rate (percent)

k = real capital-account surplus (balance of payments)

L = employment (man-hours)

M = nominal money supply

M^d = nominal money demand

P = domestic price level

PX = export price level (in foreign currency)

PF = import price level (in foreign currency)

P^a = anticipated domestic price level

Q = real capital stock

R = nominal net foreign reserves

r = real interest rate (percent)

s = real net foreign reserves

T = nominal government receipts

t = real government receipts

U = unemployment rate (percent)

W = nominal wage level

Wi = nominal world interest rate (percent)

WP = world price level (in foreign currency)

Wy = world real output

x = real exports

y = domestic real output

Y = domestic nominal output

y^+ = potential real output

Z = labor force (man-hours)

γ = technical progress.

With the exceptions explicitly indicated in the above list, all variables are considered in domestic currency (constant or current domestic prices). In the model below, a *dot* over the variable is used to indicate its percentage rate of change. For example, $\dot{P}$ is the symbol for the rate of inflation, and so forth. The hypothesized signs of the partial derivatives are represented by a plus or minus sign below the appropriate symbol.

First, the goods market:

$$y = e + g + x - f \qquad \text{I: market equilibrium}$$

$$e = \underset{+\ -\ -}{E(y,\ r,\ t)} \qquad \text{II: private expenditure function}$$

$$g = G/P \qquad \text{III: definition}$$

$$t = T/P \qquad \text{IV: definition}$$

$$G = T + D \qquad \text{V: government budget constraint}$$

$$T = \underset{+\ +}{T(y,\ P)} \qquad \text{VI: tax function}$$

$$x = \underset{+\ +\ +\ -}{X(Wy,\ ER,\ PX,\ P)} \qquad \text{VII: export function}$$

$$f = \underset{+\ +\ -\ -\ +}{I(f_o,\ y,\ ER,\ PF,\ P)} \qquad \text{VIII: import function}$$

$$PF = PX = WP \qquad \text{IX, X: constant terms of trade.}$$

After the natural substitutions, these ten equations can be reduced to one equilibrium function—an *IS* type of equation:

$$(1) \qquad \underset{-\ -\ -\ +\ +\ -\ +\ +}{J(y,\ r,\ P,\ Wy,\ D,\ f_o,\ ER,\ WP)} = 0.$$

The fiscal variable G could replace D in equation 1.

Second, the money market:

$$M^d = \underset{+\ +\ -}{M(P,\ y,\ i)} \qquad \text{XI: money demand function}$$

$$i = r + \dot{P}^a \qquad \text{XII: Fisher hypothesis}$$

$$M^d = M \qquad \text{XIII: market equilibrium}$$

$$M = \underset{+\ +}{N(B,\ i)} \qquad \text{XIV: money supply function}$$

$$M = R + DC \qquad \text{XV: sources of money supply}$$

$$R = s \times P \qquad \text{XVI: definition.}$$

Again, after some substitutions, an equilibrium *LM* type of equation can be derived from the six equations above:

$$(2) \qquad \underset{+\ -\ +\ -\ -\ -}{L(y,\ r,\ P,\ s,\ DC,\ \dot{P}^a)} = 0.$$

The monetary variable B could replace DC in equation 2.

The next step is the balance of payments.

$bps = x - f + k$ XVII: overall surplus

$x = X(Wy, ER, PX, P)$ VII: export function
$$+ \quad + \quad + \quad -$$

$f = I(f_o, y, ER, PF, P)$ VIII: import function
$$+ + - - +$$

$PF = PX = WP$ IX, X: constant terms of trade

$k = K(i, Wi, \dot{ER}, P)$ XVIII: capital-account surplus
$$+ \quad - \quad - \quad -$$

$i = r + \dot{P^a}$ XII: Fisher hypothesis

$\dot{s} = bps$ XIX: international reserve increases

The dot over s actually represents an absolute change, but it is unnecessary to establish any distinction between linear (absolute) and logarithmic (percentage) first-differences. The three new equations plus the five repeated equations lead to a balance of payments equilibrium equation:

(3) $S(y, r, P, \dot{s}, \dot{P^a}, Wy, f_o, ER, WP, \dot{ER}, Wi) = 0.$
$$- + - - + + - + + - -$$

Finally, the supply side is included:

$y = A(Q, L, f, \gamma)$ XX: production function
$$+ \quad + \quad + \quad +$$

$L = B(W, P, y)$ XXI: labor demand function
$$- + +$$

$L = C(W, P^a, Z)$ XXII: labor supply function
$$+ - +$$

$f = I(f_o, y, ER, PF, P)$ VIII: import function
$$+ + - - +$$

$PF = WP$ IX: constant terms of trade

$y^+ = D(Q, Z, \gamma)$ XXIII: potential output.
$$+ + +$$

Import supply is of course assumed to be given, with WP exogenous. An aggregate supply equation can be derived from this final group of equations after a few substitutions:

(4) $P(y, y^+, P, P^a, ER, WP, f_o) = 0.$
$$- + + - - - +$$

In perhaps more familiar terms, one could derive a commodity market

Phillips curve for an open economy to "close" the model, which would be basically equivalent to equation 4. For example, from

$$\dot{P} = Q(\dot{P}^a, U, \dot{ER}, \dot{WP}) \qquad \text{(Phillips curve)}$$
$$\quad\; + \;-\; + \;\; +$$
$$U = U(H) \qquad\qquad\qquad \text{(Okun's law)}$$
$$\quad\; +$$

and

$$H = (y^+ - y)/y^+ \qquad\qquad \text{(definition)}$$

one can derive the implicit equilibrium function

$$P'(y, y^+, \dot{P}, \dot{P}^a, \dot{ER}, \dot{WP}) = 0.$$
$$\quad\; -\; +\; +\; -\; -\; -$$

Except for the implicit presence of some lagged variables (caused by the rates of change) and the absence of exogenous imports, f_o, this final Phillips curve type of equation is equivalent to the aggregate supply function (equation 4).

Equations I to XXIII form a system of structural equations with twenty-three endogenous variables: y, e, g, t, G (or D), T, x, f, PF, PX, r, i, M^d, M, B (or DC), R, bps, k, s, P, L, W, and y^+. Equations 1 through 4 represent a "semistructural" or "quasi-reduced" form of the larger structural model, with a more manageable and equivalent model of four endogenous variables: the price level, P, real output, y, real interest rate, r, and real foreign reserves, s.

In fact, even the smaller structural model can be further reduced to a two-equation model. Equations 1, 2, and 3 can be combined to produce the aggregate demand equation:

$$(5) \qquad E(y, P, DC, \dot{P}^a, Wy, D, f_o, ER, WP, Wi, \dot{ER}) = 0.$$
$$\qquad\quad -\; -\; +\; +\; +\; +\; -\; +\; +\; -\; -$$

The variables r and s are eliminated. As before, DC and D could be replaced by B and G, respectively.

Aggregate demand (equation 5) and aggregate supply (equation 4) form a system of two equations to determine the price level, P, and real output, y. Some economists prefer to regard aggregate demand (equation 5) as determining nominal income, $Y = P \times y$, and use equation 4 (or the Phillips curve) to explain the short-run division of nominal income between prices and real output.

One could work with the system of internal equations I–XXIII, equations 1–4, or alternatively with 4–5, and the list of exogenous or independent variables in the corresponding reduced forms would contain precisely the same variables. In the above model, these independent variables are the following: Wy, ER, WP, D (or G), DC (or B), f_o, P^a, Wi, Q, Z, and γ. These last three supply long-run variables can be replaced by y^+ (potential output) in the list. Moreover, there are also some lagged variables such as past foreign reserves, past price expectations, past exchange rates, and the like, that should enter the reduced forms because of the presence of variables such as $\hat{s}$, $\dot{P}^a$, ER, and so on, in the model.

In the third section, the analysis is concentrated on the reduced forms for the price level. It should be pointed out that the signs of the partial derivatives or multipliers of these reduced forms will be exactly the same if one starts from any one of the three analogous systems of twenty-three equations, four equations, or only two equations:

$$P = F(Wy, ER, WP, D, DC, f_o, P^a, Wi, y^+).$$
$$+ \quad + \quad + \quad + \ + \quad - \ + \quad - \ -$$

With the alternative monetary and fiscal variables, one has

$$P = F'(Wy, ER, WP, G, B, f_o, P^a, Wi, y^+).$$
$$+ \quad + \quad + \ + \ + \quad - \ + \quad - \ -$$

These signs are easily derived after some conventional comparative-static analysis using inversion of matrices and Cramer's rule. In the third section, an attempt is made to describe the channels of influence from the independent variables to the price level. The signs of the multipliers for the other twenty-two endogenous variables could also be derived, but they are of less interest here and many will certainly be ambiguous. One reduced form that seems to be of some interest is the one for nominal income, $Y = P \times y$ (this identity would of course be the twenty-fourth equation of the model):

$$Y = Y(Wy, ER, WP, D, DC, f_o, P^a, Wi, y^+).$$
$$+ \quad + \quad + \ + \ + \quad - \ + \quad - \ -$$
$$? \quad ? \qquad\qquad ? \ ? \qquad\quad ?$$

This provides an example of ambiguous signs (which do not occur in the case of P). The independent variables with a question mark affect prices and real output, through the supply side, in opposite directions. A stronger effect on prices is assumed.

Simple econometric estimates of these reduced forms for P, the price level, and Y, nominal income, are presented in the fourth section and appendix B.

Appendix B

Detailed results of linear stochastic formulations of the reduced forms are presented in this appendix. The analysis covers 1952–73 and is based on annual data. The technique used in the estimation process is ordinary least squares (OLS).

Table 8 presents a list of the symbols used in the regression equations and means, standard deviations, and coefficients of variation of selected variables for the period. In the regressions, rates of change are in percent and a dot over the variable indicates percentage change. For example, $\dot{P}$ is the rate of inflation and $\dot{y}$ is the rate of growth of real output. More precisely, all variables with a dot over them correspond to a percentage change, that is, $\dot{Y} = 100 \ \{[Y(t)/Y(t-1)] - 1\}$. The variable H (GDP output gap) is calculated as $100 \times$ (potential output $-$ actual output)/potential output (see table 2 above). The potential output series has a constant rate of growth of 7 percent, and it is assumed that potential output equals actual output in 1961.

Regression results are shown in tables 9 and 10. Figures in parentheses are t-statistics, and h is the Durbin statistic designed to test for serial correlation in the presence of a lagged dependent variable. The R^2 statistic is reported as well as the R^2 adjusted for degrees of freedom ($\bar{R}^2$). The constant term of the regressions is not reported, but it was included in all the cases. The basic sources for the raw data used in this study are *Conjuntura Econômica*, *Boletim do Banco Central do Brasil*, and *International Financial Statistics*; and all the figures used in the regressions are shown in tables 1 to 6 above.

The tested reduced form equations clearly involve simplifications. For example, one can easily imagine alternative specifications for them, especially for the distributed lag structures. Since annual data with twenty-two observations are being used, these lag structures had to be extremely simple. To avoid severe multicollinearity problems, loss of degrees of freedom, and nonlinear estimation, either no lags or one-period lags (L), rather than more complicated distributed lag models, were used.

Tables 9 and 10 present estimates of reduced forms for inflation and nominal income. The reduced forms of the second section:

$$P = F(Wy, ER, WP, G, B, f_o, P^a, Wi, y^+)$$

and

$$Y = Y(Wy, ER, WP, G, B, f_o, P^a, Wi, y^+)$$

Table 8. *Mean, Standard Deviation, and Coefficient of Variation for Selected Variables in Reduced Form Equations Used in the Model of Imported Inflation*
Percent

Variable[a]	Mean	Standard deviation	Coefficient of variation
$\dot{Y}$	39.2	18.9	48.2
$\dot{P}$	30.4	20.3	67.0
$\dot{WP}$	3.1	1.7	53.9
$\dot{W}y$	5.6	3.5	62.5
$\dot{ER}$	33.7	34.8	103.4
H	6.9	5.1	73.6
$\dot{G}$	42.6	20.8	48.8
$\dot{B}$	37.2	19.8	53.5
$\dot{DC}$	38.5	16.3	42.3
$\dot{y}$	7.1	3.1	43.4

Sources: Annual data for 1952–73 from *Conjuntura Econômica, International Financial Statistics,* and *Boletim do Banco Central do Brasil.*
a. Y = nominal output (GDP at current prices); see table 2 above;
     P = general price level (GDP implicit price deflator); see table 1;
     WP = world price level (weighted average of consumer price indexes); see table 6;
     Wy = world real output (weighted average of industrial production indexes); see table 6;
     ER = exchange rate (cruzeiros to U.S. dollars); see table 6;
     H = GDP output gap (percent), 100 × (potential output − actual output)/potential output; see table 2;
     G = nominal government expenditures; see table 4;
     B = nominal monetary base; see table 3;
     DC = nominal domestic credit; see table 3;
     y = real output (GDP at constant prices); see table 2.
A dot over the symbol indicates percentage change.

were transformed in percentage changes:

$$\dot{P} = F(\dot{Wy}, \dot{ER}, \dot{WP}, \dot{G}, \dot{B}, \dot{f_o}, \dot{P}^a, \dot{Wi}, \dot{y}^+)$$

and

$$\dot{Y} = Y(\dot{Wy}, \dot{ER}, \dot{WP}, \dot{G}, \dot{B}, \dot{f_o}, \dot{P}^a, \dot{Wi}, \dot{y}^+).$$

Again, D and DC are alternative fiscal and monetary variables to replace G and B.

For the econometric tests, the percentage changes, $\dot{Wi}$ and $\dot{f_o}$, were neglected. Of course, f_o (exogenous imports) cannot be measured, and its rate of change is certainly not well defined. The percentage change, $\dot{y}^+$ (the rate of growth of potential output), is by definition a constant. The rate of inflation for the previous year was used to approximate inflation anticipations; that is, $\dot{P}(L) = \dot{P}^a$. In other words, a very simple hypothesis for anticipations has been adopted: the expected inflation, $\dot{P}^a$, for period t is the actual inflation of period $t - 1$. After some experimentation, a one-period lag was

Table 9. *Estimates of Reduced Form Equations for Inflation (Dependent Variable, $\dot{P}$), Ordinary Least Squares, 1952–73*

Variable and statistic	Reduced form variant					
	9A	9B	9C	9D	9E	9F
Explanatory variable[a]						
$\dot{G}$	0.3922	0.4957	0.4807	0.2420	0.2358	0.2454
	(2.29)	(3.82)	(4.10)	(1.38)	(1.61)	(1.85)
$\dot{W}y(L)$	0.2517	0.0758	...	−0.1813	−0.3202	...
	(0.42)	(0.13)		(0.31)	(0.63)	
$H(L)$	...	...	...	−0.2974	−0.6374	−0.6104
				(0.79)	(1.84)	(1.86)
$\dot{W}P(L)$	0.7772	0.6428	...	0.5273	0.4572	...
	(0.63)	(0.55)		(0.47)	(0.46)	
$\dot{E}R(L)$	0.1697	0.2239	...	0.0814	0.1104	...
	(2.25)	(3.48)		(1.04)	(1.63)	
$\dot{P}(L)$	...	...	...	0.4149	0.4272	0.4016
				(2.31)	(2.77)	(2.85)
$\dot{D}C$	...	0.5266	0.5377	...	0.4708	0.4698
		(3.24)	(3.57)		(2.98)	(3.13)
$\dot{B}$	0.5068	...	...	0.3564	...	...
	(2.77)			(2.01)		
$\dot{W}P(L) + \dot{E}R(L)$	...	...	0.2147	...	...	0.1086
			(3.84)			(1.81)
Statistic						
Standard error	9.860	9.315	8.823	8.909	7.912	7.541
R^2	0.8288	0.8472	0.8458	0.8777	0.9035	0.8999
$\bar{R}^2$	0.7885	0.8112	0.8295	0.8288	0.8649	0.8763
Durbin-Watson	1.8560	1.8996	1.9064	2.0247	2.0433	2.0682
h	...	...	...	−0.1075	−0.1471	−0.2131

Source: See text for explanation.

a. For explanation of the symbols, see appendix A. Numbers in parentheses are t-statistics. (L) indicates a one-period lag.

chosen for the external variables—exchange rate, world price, and world output percentage changes. The actual reduced forms were therefore

$$\dot{P} = F[\dot{W}y(L), \dot{E}R(L), \dot{W}P(L), \dot{G}, \dot{B}, \dot{P}(L)]$$

and

$$\dot{Y} = Y[\dot{W}y(L), \dot{E}R(L), \dot{W}P(L), \dot{G}, \dot{B}, \dot{P}(L)].$$

In some cases, $\dot{D}C$ replaced $\dot{B}$. Another natural variant was to consider $\dot{E}R(L) + \dot{W}P(L)$ as a single variable, as suggested in the discussion in the main text.

Note that $\dot{P}(L)$ not only reflects the presence of inflationary expectations, but in the inflation equation may also account for lagged effects of the other

Table 10. *Estimates of Reduced Form Equations for Nominal Income*
(*Dependent Variable,* $\dot{Y}$), *Ordinary Least Squares, 1952–73*

Variable and statistic	Reduced form variant			
	10A	10B	10C	10D
Explanatory variable[a]				
$\dot{G}$	0.2183	0.3806	0.2983	0.3643
	(1.48)	(3.24)	(2.37)	(3.42)
$\dot{W}y(L)$	0.1971	0.0119	−0.1482	...
	(0.38)	(0.02)	(0.29)	
$\dot{W}P(L)$	0.8179	0.7120	0.5232	...
	(0.77)	(0.67)	(0.51)	
$\dot{E}R(L)$	0.1312	0.2045	0.1554	...
	(2.03)	(3.51)	(2.39)	
$\dot{D}C$	...	0.5996	0.5043	0.6095
		(4.08)	(3.25)	(4.46)
$\dot{B}$	0.6370	...	...	...
	(4.06)			
$\dot{Y}(L)$	...	...	0.2241	...
			(1.50)	
$\dot{W}P(L) + \dot{E}R(L)$	...	...	...	0.1931
				(3.80)
Statistic				
Standard error	8.464	8.442	8.128	8.019
R^2	0.8543	0.8551	0.8740	0.8529
$\bar{R}^2$	0.8200	0.8209	0.8347	0.8374
Durbin-Watson	2.1406	2.2524	2.1859	2.2589
h	...	...	−0.6115	...

Source: See text for explanation.

a. For explanation of the symbols, see appendix A. Numbers in parentheses are t-statistics. (*L*) indicates a one-period lag.

variables, as can be seen, for example, in a simple Koyck type of transformation. Analogously, the one-year lagged rate of change of nominal income, $\dot{Y}(L)$, was also included in one variant of the nominal income reduced form to reflect the possibility of longer lags for the effects of the independent variables.

Finally, some variants of the reduced form for inflation also included $H(L)$, the lagged value of the GDP gap, suggested by a Phillips curve such as the one presented in the introductory section of this paper—that is, a Phillips curve that contains $H(L)$ as an explanatory variable. Again, a reduced form may include not only exogenous variables but also lagged exogenous and *endogenous* variables—all these variables are predetermined for period t.

The regressions in tables 9 and 10 are variants of the two reduced forms shown above. The variations, as already indicated, involve the use of $\dot{B}$ or

$\dot{D}C$—monetary base or domestic credit changes—the inclusion or exclusion of the lagged endogenous variables $H(L)$, $\dot{Y}(L)$, and $\dot{P}(L)$—past output gap, past nominal income changes, and past inflation—and the use of $\dot{W}P(L)$ + $\dot{E}R(L)$ as one single variable—external inflation in domestic currency. To avoid multicollinearity the lagged endogenous variables $\dot{P}(L)$ and $\dot{Y}(L)$ are not included simultaneously in any single regression.

It must be emphasized that this reduced form inflation model is perfectly compatible with quantity theory of money models of inflation, Phillips curve models, and the like. In fact, it could be seen precisely as a reduced form of a simple demand-for-money plus Phillips curve structural model, since it is in fact a reduced form of an aggregate demand plus aggregate supply structural model. Therefore, there is no inconsistency between the reduced form model and the estimated Phillips curve in the introductory section. The latter presents a structural relation between two endogenous variables, while the former contains a relation between an endogenous variable and all the exogenous or predetermined variables of the model.

According to the theoretical framework presented in the second section, the expected signs for the above reduced form equations are as follows:

$$
\begin{array}{ccccccc}
& \dot{W}y(L) & \dot{E}R(L) & \dot{W}P(L) & \dot{G} & \dot{B} \text{ (or } \dot{D}C) & \dot{P}(L) \\
\dot{P} & + & + & + & ++ & & + \\
\dot{Y} & + & +? & +? & ++ & & +?
\end{array}
$$

The question mark for nominal income is discussed in the second section, where it is suggested that the signs are not entirely unambiguous.

As mentioned above, some variants have also included $H(L)$—past output gap—for the $\dot{P}$ equation, and $\dot{Y}(L)$ for the $\dot{Y}$ equation. Their expected signs would then be minus and plus, respectively. Finally, note again the variant $\dot{E}R(L) + \dot{W}P(L)$, whose expected sign is evidently positive.

Comments by Edward S. Shaw

BRAZIL'S economic experience of the past two decades provides an exciting puzzle for economists. Some of its intricacies are suggested by a small sample from Lemgruber's data (table 11).

In the earlier, pre-miracle period there was real growth, with high capacity utilization and a near-doubling of the inflation rate. In the later period there was sensational real growth, with rising capacity utilization, and the inflation rate was reduced by more than one-half. What is even more startling

Table 11. *Some Brazilian Macromagnitudes, Selected Periods, 1953–73*
Percent

Period	Average growth rate		Average output gap
	General price index[a]	Real output	
Pre-miracle			
1953–55	19.4	6.5	3.0
1959–61	34.7	8.5	2.8
Miracle			
1965–67	41.0	4.2	15.4
1971–73	17.5	11.0	4.9

Sources: Tables 1 and 2.
a. Based on annual percentage changes in annual average general price index.

is that the pre-miracle experience occurred in a time of diminishing world inflation and the miracle coincided with accelerating world inflation.

Following conventional procedures of macromodel-building and econometric legerdemain, Lemgruber derives and tests six equations in search of an explanation for the Brazilian rates of inflation from 1952 to 1973 and four equations that attempt to discover the reason for the growth rate of Brazilian nominal income. From the potentially relevant independent variables, he selects some nine to concentrate on. Four survive tests of significance: growth in domestic real income (as measured by the GDP gap), the lagged rate of domestic inflation, and the expansion rate of either the monetary base or domestic credit. The first of these bears a negative sign in the price and income equations because of course it stimulates growth in real money balances demanded. The lagged rate of domestic inflation emerges with the positive sign that is expected: inflation in one year tends to maintain the momentum of inflation in the preceding year, and both reflect earlier policy mistakes. The explanatory power of the monetary base and domestic credit makes it clear that Brazilian inflation has been monetary, a matter of growth rates in nominal money supply exceeding growth rates in real money demanded. The junk heap of discarded variables includes several that figure prominently in some theories of inflation.

The power of monetary impulses in Brazil and their proximate source are suggested in tables 12 and 13. Table 12 discloses the relative effects on Brazilian money supplies, in recent years, of growth in Brazil's international liquidity and of growth in the monetary system's portfolios of domestic credit.

In 1967–70, Brazil shared with other "small" countries a shower of dollars from the balance of payments of the United States. The flow to Brazil

Table 12. *Reserves and Money in Brazil, Selected Periods, 1967–73*

Money in millions

Period	International liquidity (dollars)	Net foreign assets (cruzeiros)	Reserve money (cruzeiros)	Domestic credit (cruzeiros)	Money (cruzeiros)	Marginal money multiplier[a]
Level[b]						
1967	199	1,101	8,218	16,851	15,004	...
1970	1,187	4,979	18,503	46,563	35,920	...
1973	6,417	34,890[c]	44,215	125,673	93,784	...
Increase[b]						
1967–70	988	3,878	10,285	29,712	20,916	2.03
1970–73	5,230	29,911	25,712	79,110	57,864	2.26

Source: *International Financial Statistics*, various issues.
a. This is the ratio of increments in the money stock to increments in reserve money.
b. Based on end-of-year figures.
c. Third quarter, 1973.

accounted for one-third of growth there in reserve money—the monetary base. Still, by restraint on the part of the Brazilian monetary authority, growth in money and reserve money was slowed, and the inflation rate declined. Then in 1970–73 the shower of dollars became a flood. The Brazilian monetary authorities did neutralize Cr$4.2 billion of the dollar inflow by reductions in its domestic credits, but other components of the monetary system were permitted to increase the money multiplier. The balance of payments and lax Brazilian monetary policy combined to raise money's growth rate from 26 to 47 percent between 1970 and 1973 (see table 3).

Table 12 looks at the source of the shower and the flood of international reserves to Brazil and other "small" countries. Fiscal deficits of the United States and their monetization by the Federal Reserve System spilled "international reserves" into central banks the world over—including Brazil's, whose experience was not unique. The deficits were relatively small during 1967–70, and nearly one-third of the debt issues that financed them were acquired by other than monetary authorities. The deficits nearly tripled during 1970–73, and monetary authorities bid the prices of U.S. government debt high enough to draw net sales from other holders.

Lemgruber is correct in his conclusion that external inflation had a significant effect on Brazilian price levels. American fiscal and monetary policy must be the culprit he means. However, the culprit might have been thwarted. While Brazil raised the cruzeiro price of dollars only 26 percent from 1970 through 1973 as against 82 percent from 1967 through 1970, even that was too much. Its indexing formula for the cruzeiro-dollar rate opened wide the

Table 13. *U.S. Fiscal Deficits and Official Reserves, Selected Periods, 1967–73*

Billions of dollars

| Period | Fiscal deficits | Change in government securities held by | | | Official reserves |
		Federal Reserve System	Other monetary authorities[a]	Others[a]	
1967–70	24.8	12.0	5.6	7.2	− 5.5
1970–73	60.7	20.9	43.0	−3.2	−45.9

Source: *International Financial Statistics*, various issues.
a. As computed by commentator.

coffers of the monetary base to the inflow of deficit dollars from the United States.

When one looks back at table 11, the anomalies there are not so bewildering after all. In 1953–61 the inflation tax was imposed with increasing severity, by means of accelerating growth in the monetary base, and financed a significant part of economic growth. During the miracle the inflation tax was imposed with decreasing severity as it was being supplanted by other techniques of resource mobilization. The sequel to the miracle is a new burst of inflation to finance resource mobilization in both the United States and Brazil. This monetary error is in part the result of "monetary correction" of the cruzeiro-dollar rate of exchange. This conclusion is a dissent from Lemgruber's judgment that the trotting peg has guaranteed a permanently satisfactory exchange rate.

Nothwithstanding Lemgruber's lucid essay in praise of monetary correction, my own enthusiasm for the device is dimming. One can be fervently in favor of eliminating monetary falsifications such as ceilings on nominal rates of return to public utilities and on nominal deposit and loan rates, fixed foreign exchange rates, and the like. At the same time, one can be cautiously against those "corrections" that seem to have their own biases toward market distortion.

General Comments

WILLIAM CLINE considered that Shaw's general interpretation of world inflation, although correct for most of the world, did not apply as fully to the inflation in Brazil; the rampant increase in Brazilian monetary reserves was related to many things other than Brazil's share of the U.S. deficit. Lemgruber's paper is useful, especially his statement that indexation has made a 25 percent inflation in Brazil less serious than a 10 percent inflation in the United States. This goes to the heart of the question—namely, what is the harm of inflation? The major harm results from uncertainty, and indexing has removed the uncertainty about the expected value of future earnings. But Lemgruber's choice of a Keynesian structure and the concept of the Phillips curve is less useful in a situation like that in Brazil where the unemployment rate has very little meaning. The paper pays too little attention to the formation of real capital, which is what drives developing countries such as Brazil, and too much attention to the type of macromodel used to represent the U.S. economy, which is inappropriate to the Brazilian case. The emphasis on imported inflation, both in the paper and in Shaw's comment, is strained. The crucial period of Brazilian inflation was from 1959 to 1964. Since that was a period of stable prices in the United States, it is difficult to argue convincingly that Brazil's inflation was imported at that time. It can be regarded as imported only for the year 1974; and Lemgruber's econometric results, notably the low significance of the coefficient on prices in the rest of the world, bears out this view. Important lessons can be learned from Brazil's method of dealing with inflation, however, and that has not been fully brought out in the paper. One lesson is that gradualism is preferable to shock treatment; this was discovered during Brazil's experience in 1965–67, when it was found that suddenly cutting off the business sector's access to circulating capital reduced real output. That led Brazil to shift to a more gradual policy. A second important lesson is that indexing does decrease the uncertainty that goes with inflation. It remains an open question, however, whether the effect of indexing in aggravating the inflationary spiral does or does not swamp the benefits from the reduction of uncertainty. Finally, what happened in Brazil shows that it is possible to isolate an economy from imported inflation by using flexible exchange rates and that it is easier to do so if the country is experiencing faster inflation than other countries.

Antonio Lemgruber considered that the Keynesian and Phillips curve approach used in the paper explains Brazilian inflation very well. Although the formation of real capital is not specifically taken into account in the model, it is implicit in the assumption that the potential growth rate was 7 percent, which presumably is explained by the formation of real capital. The paper does not discuss the issue explicitly because its primary theme is inflation. Imported inflation is stressed because of the international focus of the volume; but it is true that the basic explanation of Brazilian inflation is domestic monetary growth in excess of output growth. One would need more than an equation for the demand for money to explain it; one would also need the Phillips curve to explain the growth of real income and the rise of prices.

Edward Shaw observed that the effect of development enters the model through the variable representing the growth rate of potential real income and that this emerges as a powerful deflationary force in Lemgruber's model, having a high regression coefficient and a very high *t*-statistic, thereby illustrating the deflationary effects of growth on the demand for real money. Similarly, the growth rates of domestic credit and of the monetary base, which can be treated as alternatives, have high means, substantial regression coefficients, and high *t*-statistics. The change in the world price level has little influence, on the average, because the mean rate of world inflation is very low.

Robert Gordon questioned the statement that evidence of imported inflation is weak, since the paper finds the elasticity of domestic to world inflation to be between 50 and 77 percent. However, the model does not clearly explain the deceleration of inflation from the 20 percent rate of 1967 through 1970 to the 15 and 14 percent rates of the last two years, respectively, before inflation of commodity prices began.

Richard Cooper said that the striking thing about Brazil's experience is that it is the first country to change its exchange rate frequently and yet increase its reserves by a factor of 30 between 1967 and 1974. Was there during this period any discussion in Brazilian policy circles of whether the rule by which the exchange rate was changed should be revised? Brazil began its variable rate policy by using a purchasing-power parity rule to determine variations of the rate; however, it should have learned from the experience of Japan that for a rapidly growing economy it is inappropriate to apply that rule to the consumer price index, since in such an economy there is a discrepancy between the consumer price index and the wholesale price index, and Brazil is, like Japan, a rapidly growing economy. The purchasing power comparison that they are using is obviously the wrong one from the point of view of both the balance of payments and price stability.

Antonio Lemgruber said that the rule had been revised in 1973 because of the immense reserve increase that resulted from following the monetary correction formula precisely. From December 1972 to December 1973 the rate of devaluation was zero even though the inflation rate differential was 10 or 15 percent. Brazil is no longer using an automatic rule.

In relation to the deceleration of inflation in the past few years, the model may overstate the rates of inflation for 1972 and 1973, although not by much. The reason it fails to catch the deceleration that actually occurred is probably that it assumes that expectations of future inflation are determined by past rates of inflation, whereas the Brazilian government is trying to influence expectations by announcing what the future rate of inflation will be and is announcing lower rates than those that prevailed in the past. This might have made expected rates lower than the model assumed in those years. It is very difficult to include announcement effects in such a model but a more sophisticated variable for determining expected inflation rates might better explain the deceleration in the years 1971 through 1973.

Charles Maier questioned how political or group conflict is mediated in determining the method and degree of indexation, and in what sense the Brazilian indexing system depends on the authoritarian character of the government. Does the government make choices among the various interest groups? Is that done through one ministry? Do a number of different bureaucratic groups participate in the decisions? Here is a whole range of questions that need to be answered.

WYNNE A. H. GODLEY

Inflation in the
United Kingdom

Tables

WAGES and the cost of imported materials (insofar as wage inflation at home did not affect them) have been the proximate determinants of prices in the United Kingdom since World War II. In the inflationary process the role of demand has been virtually confined to its effect on costs and does not appear to have altered the relationship between costs and prices.

A satisfactory general theory of wage determination applicable to the United Kingdom has yet to be proved; so has any reasonably successful attempt to model wage inflation in the country econometrically over any period that includes 1969–72. The increase in wages accelerated in 1968 because of a large increase in import prices, the notorious further acceleration of 1969–70 occurred at a time when the price rise was not accelerating and unemployment was relatively high and, if anything, tending to increase.

Exogenous changes in import prices of materials have usually been the result of fluctuations in world activity, although occasionally and spectacularly of special situations such as the Korean and the 1973 Arab-Israeli wars. Much of the change in import prices has been the consequence rather than the cause of domestically generated inflation, and whereas import prices have sometimes temporarily and to a limited extent been checked by defending an unrealistic exchange rate, the check has probably always been fully reversed after the devaluation occurred.

The net effect so far of incomes policies, which have occasionally been efficacious for short periods, has probably been counterproductive in the sense that wages have reached a higher level than they would have in the absence of such policies.

It is sometimes held, mainly because of the possible role of internationally traded goods, that inflation is essentially an international phenomenon. Apart from the existence of theoretical grounds for expecting convergence of rates, the fact that all countries have suffered from faster rates of inflation since about 1965 than in previous years by itself suggests that any explanation other than an international one is implausible.

But international comparisons of inflation rates are not so uniform as to strongly suggest a common cause. It is surely inappropriate, for the estimation of convergence, to take retail or other final prices as the indicator of in-

451

flation rates inasmuch as these include a large common component in the form of primary input prices; for instance, there is nothing significant or interesting in the present context about the element of price inflation, common to all countries since 1974, caused by the rise in oil prices. For the purpose of making international comparisons, therefore, the appropriate measure would be value added per unit of output in manufacturing industry.[1] The nearest approximation to this that I have been able to assemble relates to average hourly earnings in manufacturing in seven countries, in each case divided by a productivity trend appropriate to the country in question.[2] Analysis of this data tends to refute the convergence hypothesis. For instance, the annual average increase in unit costs between 1964 and 1969 was 2.3 percent with an average standard deviation of 1.7 percent; in the subsequent four years the average inflation rate rose to 6.7 percent and the average standard deviation rose to 3.4 percent. Comparable figures are not yet available for the more recent period but it appears that the standard deviation will have risen as well as the rate of cost inflation, particularly in 1975.

An analysis on which I have been engaged for some years of U.K. statistics of costs and prices at a relatively disaggregated level suggests strongly that, at least during the last fifteen years, the domestic wholesale price of manufactures has not been significantly influenced by international trade other than by exogenous changes in the prices of imported materials. British manufacturers appear to have been astonishingly impervious in their domestic pricing policies to foreign competition whereas earnings relativities in the private sector appear to be almost completely rigid both in the short- and medium-term.

1. An alternative would be to compare gross domestic product deflators but comparisons based on these would be vulnerable to the large differences between countries in the share of output taken by agriculture and primary commodities.

2. Earnings data were taken from Organisation for Economic Co-operation and Development, *Main Economic Indicators: Historical Statistics,* various issues, and OECD, *Main Economic Indicators,* monthly issues, for Germany, Japan, France, Canada, and the United States; from the International Labour Organization *Bulletin,* for Italy; and from Department of Employment and Productivity, *British Labour Statistics: Historical Abstract, 1888–1968* (London: Her Majesty's Stationery Office, 1971), and the *Department of Employment Gazette* (London: Her Majesty's Stationery Office), various issues, for the United Kingdom. The data are for average hourly earnings in manufacturing for all countries other than Japan, where the data are for monthly earnings, and for France, where the data are basically for wage rates, with adjustments for wage drift to bring the data in line with census values. The data would be improved by inclusion of fringe benefits, but I have not been able to obtain adequately comparable figures for these. The trend annual productivity growth rates (in percent) are as follows: Canada 3.9, United States 2.9, France 5.8, Germany 4.7, Italy 5.7, United Kingdom 3.2, Japan 9.2.

The conclusions of this paper as regards policy recommendations are neither emphatic nor optimistic. It follows from the argument that fiscal and monetary policy if taken to extremes in either direction will lead to accelerating or decelerating inflation. But it is unclear what level of unemployment would be necessary to bring about any significant deceleration.

Recent Trends

Table 1 shows annual changes in the retail price index, in hourly earnings, and in import prices between 1949 and 1974 together with the average level of unemployment expressed as a percentage of the labor force. There was a rise in retail prices of just over 9 percent between 1950 and 1951 and again between 1951 and 1952. Prices and wages rose far less rapidly in the next two years and the inflation trend (as measured by a four-year moving average) slowed down right through the fifties although the unemployment rate was on average very low. The trend rate of inflation rose again in the early sixties from about 2 percent a year to about 3½ percent; but this was still significantly less than on average between 1954 and 1960 and also in the 1950s as a whole. From the mid-sixties inflation accelerated further, to 6 or 7 percent a year. The beginning of 1970 saw a rapid acceleration; after the fall of 1973 a further major spurt brought the inflation rate to 16 percent in 1974 and well over 20 percent in 1975.

This paper attempts to amplify the bare recital given above of recent inflationary progress, by an analysis of the data gathered. The evidence presented here, however, seems inconsistent with the view that the acceleration of inflation has been the result of an attempt by the government to keep unemployment below some natural rate. There was no general tendency for the inflation rate to accelerate over the seventeen-year period 1950–67 although the unemployment rate was (almost) continuously lower throughout this period than in the 1967–74 span when a major acceleration did occur.[3]

What is the explanation of the course of inflation since 1950?

The rise in retail prices between 1950 and 1951 and again between 1951 and 1952 was primarily the result of the rise in commodity prices because of the Korean War, but it was partly caused by a rise in wage rates as a reaction

---

3. It is generally accepted that the unemployment rate corresponding to a given pressure of demand for labor has risen since the fifties though the reasons are not fully understood. Nevertheless the pressure of demand was probably somewhat higher in the earlier period than later.

Table 1. *Annual Rate of Change in Selected Economic Indicators and the Employment Rate, United Kingdom, 1950–75*

Percent

			Change from preceding year								
			Hourly wage rates		Unit value Index numbers		Money supply[b]				
Year	Gross domestic product implicit deflator	Retail price index[a]	Manu-facturing	All industries and services	Imports	Exports	M_1	M_3	Wholesale prices[c]	Average hourly earnings[d]	Unemployment rate[e]
1950	0.7	3.2	1.9	2.2	17.1	1.1	...	...	6.9	3.5	1.4
1951	7.5	9.2	9.1	8.6	33.1	16.8	...	...	16.8	10.1	1.1
1952	9.1	9.1	8.7	8.2	-3.0	5.1	0.8	2.8	2.4	7.7	1.6
1953	3.0	3.0	4.6	4.7	-11.7	-2.4	2.5	3.1	-1.9	5.6	1.4
1954	2.0	2.0	4.2	4.3	-1.0	-1.0	3.9	3.0	0.2	6.7	1.1
1955	3.7	4.4	6.6	7.0	2.9	1.0	-0.9	-2.8	3.2	8.1	0.9
1956	6.2	4.9	7.7	8.1	1.8	3.2	0.7	1.0	4.4	7.7	1.1
1957	4.1	3.7	5.1	5.0	0.8	5.4	-0.9	2.6	3.9	6.3	1.4
1958	4.5	3.1	3.3	3.8	-7.1	-1.1	2.1	2.9	1.2	3.2	2.3
1959	1.6	0.5	2.6	2.7	-1.0	-1.0	5.9	6.3	0.7	3.7	2.1

Year											
1960	1.9	1.1	5.2	4.5	0.0	2.1	−1.8	1.8	1.5	8.3	1.6
1961	3.3	3.4	6.0	6.4	−1.9	0.1	−0.1	2.6	2.8	6.9	1.7
1962	3.3	4.3	3.3	4.3	−1.1	−1.0	2.8	2.7	1.4	4.2	2.5
1963	2.2	1.9	3.0	4.0	4.1	5.0	8.1	6.5	1.1	4.2	2.3
1964	2.5	3.2	5.1	5.1	3.0	1.6	2.1	5.2	1.9	7.9	1.7
1965	4.3	4.8	6.1	6.1	0.1	2.6	4.2	7.8	2.6	9.8	1.3
1966	4.0	3.9	6.4	6.6	1.6	3.7	−0.4	3.4	2.6	5.9	1.7
1967	2.7	2.5	4.3	4.1	0.2	1.5	8.6	10.0	0.8	4.8	2.3
1968	3.5	4.7	7.9	6.8	12.0	7.9	4.0	7.3	3.9	7.1	2.3
1969	3.7	5.4	5.6	5.5	3.1	3.3	0.2	2.7	3.1	7.8	2.4
1970	7.9	6.4	10.1	10.3	4.6	7.5	9.5	9.5	7.5	14.9	2.5
1971	10.3	9.4	12.5	13.2	4.7	5.6	8.4	12.4	8.8	12.7	3.7
1972	10.2	7.1	13.8	14.1	4.8	5.2	13.9	25.8	6.3	15.0	3.4
1973	9.0	9.2	12.9	14.0	27.3	13.4	6.5	28.7	8.0	12.7	2.2
1974	15.4	16.0	17.2	17.4	56.0	29.1	11.0	12.7	24.6	20.2	2.7
1975	28.4	24.2	29.9	29.6	12.7	22.0	13.6	7.8	n.a.	n.a.	5.0

Sources: The data are from the publications cited below: gross domestic product implicit deflator, Central Statistical Office, *National Income and Expenditure* (London: Her Majesty's Stationery Office), various issues; retail price index, wage rates, and earnings, Department of Employment and Productivity, *British Labour Statistics: Historical Abstract, 1886–1968* (HMSO, 1971), and *Department of Employment Gazette* (HMSO), various issues; unit values, Central Statistical Office, *Monthly Digest of Statistics* (HMSO), various issues; money supply, *Bank of England Statistical Abstract, 1970* (London: Bank of England, Economic Intelligence Department, 1971), and *Bank of England Quarterly Bulletin*, various issues; wholesale prices, *Trade and Industry* (HMSO), various issues; unemployment, *British Labour Statistics: Historical Abstract, 1886–1968*, and *Department of Employment Gazette*, various issues.

n.a. not available.

a. All items.

b. First of year. M_1 = notes and coin in circulation plus private-sector deposits in current sterling accounts in banks and National Giro; M_3 = M_1 plus other private-sector bank and National Giro deposits, plus private-sector deposits with discount houses, plus public-sector deposits.

c. Nonfood manufacturing (home sales).

d. For full-time male manual workers, aged twenty-one and over, in all industries and services; data are for October of each year.

e. Percent of total employees; excludes school leavers and adult students; data are for last quarter of the year.

to Stafford Cripps's freeze, which ended in 1950. In 1952 and 1953 the inflation rate slowed down very markedly because commodity prices fell absolutely and substantially. The underlying rate of inflation (as measured by a four-year moving average) continued to slacken during the fifties (possibly because of a progressive improvement in the terms of trade) although the pressure of demand was on average very high. There were, however, cyclical fluctuations in the rate of cost increase, probably associated with cyclical fluctuations in demand and output, which were, in turn, caused by stop-go fiscal and monetary policies. From about the beginning of 1960 the inflation rate speeded up, but in absolute terms by only the small amount of from about 2 percent a year to about 3½ percent a year. This was probably because import prices relative to domestic incomes rose a little instead of falling, though until 1967 the domestic price level was artificially protected by the determination of successive governments to maintain a fixed exchange rate through a period when sterling was becoming progressively overvalued. In 1966 the domestic price level was probably also temporarily checked by income and price policies.

The rate of price and wage inflation accelerated markedly in 1968 and 1969, reaching 6 to 7 percent a year, and this was probably the direct and indirect consequence of the overdue devaluation of sterling at the end of 1967. The spurt in wage increases that took place in 1970 is at first a little difficult to explain because there was no preceding acceleration of retail prices and the pressure of demand for labor was relatively low and falling. The chief reason for this development, I maintain, was that a kind of backlash occurred as the result of the holding down of pay increases of the main groups of public-sector workers, by means of the incomes policy started in 1966. When this policy finally disintegrated, very large increases of almost unprecedented size were awarded to public sector groups that had fallen behind, producing a contagious effect which made the net result of the entire venture perverse. In 1973 there was a sizable further acceleration in prices caused by a very large increase in world commodity prices including that of oil. (The rise in oil prices was induced partly by the simultaneous expansion of real demand and output in all industrial countries.) Between April and December 1974 a final turn of the screw was applied, as a result of the coming into operation of a system of "threshold agreements" under which a large group of employees obtained up to about 1 percent additional earnings for every 1 percent increase in the retail price index above 6 percent, compared with October 1973. That the threshold was triggered eleven times probably directly caused basic wage rates to rise at least 13 percent compared with what would otherwise have happened.

Causes of Inflation in the United Kingdom

It is a basic argument of this paper that with insignificant and temporary exceptions the rate of price inflation in the United Kingdom (whether measured by retail prices or the domestic wholesale price of manufactures) has been proximately determined (with a lag) by factor prices.[4] More specifically price inflation is determined by:

1. The rate of change in the cost of imported materials and food.

2. The rate of increase in the cost of labor defined as the cost of an average hour's work at a normal rate of capacity utilization. Changes in the cost of labor so defined will be determined by national or plant bargaining or by statutory regulation, together with a long-run trend for earnings to rise in relation to basic rates, and are to be distinguished from changes resulting from seasonal or cyclical movements that cause short-term fluctuations in actual average earnings (mainly) through overtime payments. Interindustry shifts in the pattern of employment have not significantly affected changes in average earnings in the United Kingdom.

3. The trend (as opposed to the cyclical) rate of growth of productivity.

The validity of this first contention is, for two reasons, of strategic importance to the development of the argument of this paper. First, if it is correct it will be necessary and sufficient to confine the investigation of the causes of inflation to consideration of how factor prices as defined above are determined; an international transmission mechanism, to the extent that one exists, is only to be discovered in the context of input prices. Second, although the contention in no way prejudges the issue of whether or not demand or the money supply influences the final price level, the implication is that, if they do so, it is through their influence on factor prices. The view that either demand or the money supply enters independently as an agent governing the *relationship* between costs and prices is therefore excluded.

Empirical Work on Domestic Prices and Normal Costs

The evidence necessary to test the premise on normal pricing is not easy to assemble. Fluctuations in demand clearly do have a marked positive effect on observed average earnings through overtime payments and on observed

4. For completeness the effect of indirect taxes should be added. Price inflation could have been modified if owing to a slower growth in public expenditure indirect taxes could have been reduced, but there is nothing here that bears significantly on the question: why did price inflation accelerate from about 2 percent at the end of the fifties to 20 percent in 1975?

labor productivity, principally because of overhead labor and through more efficient use of labor not paid as piecework.

To test whether demand influences retail and wholesale prices other than through factor prices as defined above—normal unit labor costs and import prices—it is necessary to correct observed unit costs for cyclical influences. This is easier to do for the United Kingdom than for most other countries because the official statistics clearly separate both weekly wage *rates* (minimum weekly rates determined statutorily or by national bargaining) and the standard working week (for hours in excess of which overtime rates are payable) determined in the same way, from actual average weekly *earnings* and hours. Although matched data relating to retail prices are virtually impossible to assemble for the reasons given below, U.K. official series for wholesale prices of materials and fuel purchased by the manufacturing industry and of domestically sold output are particularly suitable for examining pricing behavior.[5] The prices both of inputs and outputs are measured free of duplication, on a net sector basis, in effect treating manufacturing industry as though it were a single firm. Purchases are defined as purchases by manufacturing industry as a whole from outside manufacturing and sales are comparably defined.

The preliminary results of a new examination of the hypothesis were published in 1972 in "Pricing in the Trade Cycle."[6] The study gave a precise set of rules for calculating normal unit labor costs for the manufacturing industry as a whole and produced quarterly estimates over the period 1955–69, all the relevant data having been assembled.

In abbreviated form, the procedure was to estimate the relationships:

$$(1) \qquad H = a_0 + a_1 HS + a_2 \frac{X}{Xn} + a_3 t$$

5. It can be convincingly established that the quotations that make up the wholesale price index are not "shaded" in recession (and vice versa) in the manner described by George J. Stigler and James K. Kindall in *The Behavior of Industrial Prices* (Columbia University Press for the National Bureau of Economic Research, 1970). (See William D. Nordhaus and Wynne Godley, "Pricing in the Trade Cycle," *Economic Journal,* vol. 82 [September 1972], pp. 876, note 2, and 877.)

6. Ibid. The present paper is a summary and the reader is invited to read the original article before reaching opinions about detailed questions of econometrics and data. There were several previous studies of which the most careful was that of R. R. Neild, *Pricing and Employment in the Trade Cycle: A Study of British Manufacturing Industry, 1950–61* (Cambridge: Cambridge University Press, 1963). The main defect of this study is that Neild assumed without econometric testing that $b_3 = 1$ and $b_4 = 1\frac{1}{2}$, which are values significantly different from those I obtained. The normalizing procedure is critical to the story—if it is wrong, spurious demand effects (positive or negative) will turn up in the price equation. For this reason Neild's study and interpretations of his data by other people must be regarded as having been superseded.

and

(2) $\ln AWE = b_0 + b_1 t + b_2 \ln BHR + b_3 \ln [HS + b_4(H - HS)]$,

where

      ln denotes logarithms

      H = observed hours of work

     HS = negotiated standard weekly hours above which overtime is worked

      X = real output

     Xn = trend of output

  AWE = average weekly earnings

  BHR = basic hourly rates

      t = a time trend mainly representing the long-term increase in the number of part-time workers which, other things being equal, reduces average hours.

Then customary hours (HC) may be inferred by setting $X/Xn = 1$ and calculating

(3) $HC = (\hat{a}_0 + \hat{a}_2) + \hat{a}_1 HS + \hat{a}_3 t$,

where the circumflex denotes estimated values. Normal earnings ($AWEN$) may be inferred by substituting HC for H, using estimated values of coefficients in equation 2, thus:

(4) $\ln \widehat{AWEN} = b_0 + b_1 t + b_2 \ln BHR + b_3 \ln [HS + b_4(HC - HS)]$.

Comparable corrections were applied to observed changes in labor productivity and a quarterly series on normal unit labor costs was inferred.

A large number of tests were then carried out to ascertain whether the relationship between final prices and normal costs had been influenced by demand.[7] The results indicated that it had not, although it should be reemphasized that no presumptions were established at this stage about the effect of demand on the cost components themselves.[8]

7. The cost series, unlike those used in previous studies, comprised not only the normal unit cost of manual operatives (including employers' national insurance and other contributions) and the price of materials and fuel, as the Neild study did, but included also the cost of salaried employees, purchased services, and certain indirect taxes such as local authority rates.

8. In the study by Nordhaus and Godley distributed lags corresponding to historical cost pricing were inferred from stock output ratios and imposed on costs, the components of which were added up using input-output weights. The resulting "predicted price" series, having been constructed without any reference whatever to actual prices, was confronted with the latter and the residual, unconstrained by any fitting procedure,

Since this preliminary study was undertaken, a great deal of further work has been carried out. The results, in my opinion, have been to establish conclusively, at least for manufacturing industry in the United Kingdom and for the period 1957–72, that final price changes behaved as if they were governed by factor price changes, and that demand affected final prices only through any effect it may have had on factor prices. (A forthcoming study by W. D. Nordhaus, K. J. Coutts, and Godley is to present this work.)

Additional evidence of the effect of demand on prices derives mainly from the examination contained in the new study of individual industry groups; some criticisms of the preliminary study have also been dealt with, particularly those concerning the lag specification and the precise manner in which the tests for demand effects were specified. Quarterly matching series on all the elements of labor costs and the price of inputs and outputs (including services and indirect taxes and always by the use of a net sector approach) were constructed for each of the seven major manufacturing industry groups and a common set of normalizing procedures applied to each. Predicted price series were again constructed using alternative assumptions about time lags; a uniform battery of tests was then applied to discover whether, through a variety of specifications, any influence of demand could be detected. Notwithstanding cyclical fluctuations for individual industries far greater than for manufacturing industry as a whole, the coefficients of the demand variables were without exception extremely small and although about 10 percent of these coefficients were significant at the 5 percent level (4 percent at the 2.5 percent level), over half of these bore a negative sign.

This disaggregated study has a particular relevance to the question of how an international transmission mechanism might work. There are no appropriate official statistics relating to the unit values (inclusive of import duties) of those imports that are competitive with each of the seven industry groups under consideration. Annual series were therefore constructed from the trade and navigation accounts. In the tests then carried out it was discovered that in every case domestic prices were closely related to lagged normal costs, and that this relationship was unaffected by the often highly vagrant path of the index of market prices of imports of the same categories.[9]

---

tested for demand effect. A more conventional approach, in which the time lags were estimated by maximum likelihood, was applied to our data by H. Pesaran, "A Dynamic Inter-Industry Model of Price Determination—A Test of the Normal Price Hypothesis," *Quarterly Journal of Economic Research* (University of Tehran), vol. 9 (Summer and Autumn 1972), pp. 88–123. His conclusion about the effect of demand agreed with ours.

9. Evidence and full justification for these results await publication of the monograph by Nordhaus, Coutts, and Godley.

It might be insisted that the different movement of import prices must be affecting the average price at which things are sold in U.K. markets even if they do not affect prices of domestically produced goods. But the share of total domestic expenditure on imports of manufacturers has been so small—well under 10 percent—that their direct impact cannot have been a major factor in the inflationary process.

A further objection might be that foreign competition could have worked through the agency of differential pressure on wages. But here again the data appear to rule this out. Increases in earnings have been remarkably uniform across individual manufacturing industries. For instance, between 1963 and 1974[10] average earnings in manufacturing rose 175 percent. The clustering around this figure for the fourteen component industries was extraordinarily close. Earnings in ten of them rose by an amount not greater than a 2 percent difference from 175, and one in the range 2.1–3 percent. The largest divergence was in shipbuilding (one of the U.K. manufacturing industries in which the labor force has declined fastest owing to foreign competition) where earnings rose 191 percent, or 9.2 percent *more* than the average. The relative uniformity of earnings increases was striking even on a year-by-year basis, as seen in table 2.

Some further confirmation of the normal pricing hypothesis worth mentioning here because it covers *retail* prices (of services as well as goods, but not of rent, local authority rates, or the products of nationalized industries—all heavily influenced by direct government intervention—or the prices of seasonal foods like fresh fruit or vegetables) is to be found in a short study by K. J. Coutts.[11] This study was carried out for the limited purpose of forecasting retail prices in 1974 as part of the annual review by the Department of Applied Economics of the British economy. The data could not be matched satisfactorily inasmuch as no import price or earnings figures exist that are exactly appropriate to an analysis of the price of consumer goods and services. For this reason, and because the normalization exercise was therefore not possible, Coutts took as his explanatory variables the all-industry series for hourly wage rates, the average price of imports of all goods and services, and indirect tax rates applicable to consumer goods. A reasonable result was ob-

---

10. Figures from the monthly inquiry of earnings by all employees. For 1974, figures are taken for March to October; January and February are excluded because working weeks of three days and other restrictions were in operation.

11. K. J. Coutts, "Prospects for Economic Management 1973–77" (Cambridge: University of Cambridge, Department of Applied Economics, January 1974; processed), chap. 9. The study was revised and brought up to date (without the conclusions having been changed) in *Economic Policy Review* (University of Cambridge, Department of Applied Economics), no. 1 (February 1975), chap. 2.

Table 2. *Earnings in Manufacturing, by Industry Group, 1963–74*

Industry group	1963	1964	1965	1966	1967	1968	1969	1970	1971	1972	1973	1974
						Index of average earnings						
All manufacturing	100.0	107.6	115.0	122.1	126.0	136.9	147.8	166.5	185.3	209.2	235.6	275.5
						Earnings index as percent of all manufacturing[a]						
Food, drink, tobacco	100.0	98.6	98.9	99.6	101.3	100.7	100.3	100.7	103.3	102.3	101.6	100.5
Chemicals and allied industries	100.0	99.4	100.3	100.7	101.3	100.6	101.4	102.7	104.3	102.8	100.7	101.1
Metal manufacture	100.0	101.5	101.6	100.2	100.3	99.9	100.6	100.9	95.6	97.8	99.4	99.1
Engineering and electrical goods	100.0	100.0	99.4	99.2	99.2	98.3	98.8	99.2	98.7	98.4	98.5	98.7
Shipbuilding, marine engineering	100.0	103.0	106.5	108.9	106.7	107.5	111.0	109.5	110.2	106.2	108.5	109.2
Vehicles	100.0	110.7	99.4	98.5	97.5	99.1	99.6	101.2	101.0	102.7	100.7	98.3
Metal goods, not elsewhere specified	100.0	100.8	100.7	100.1	100.3	99.7	100.5	99.7	98.3	98.1	98.6	99.6
Textiles	100.0	98.6	98.6	99.3	99.9	101.0	99.7	97.6	99.2	98.9	99.0	100.7
Leather, leather goods, fur	100.0	95.9	95.8	94.1	92.3	92.8	90.5	89.7	92.1	93.0	91.2	93.4
Clothing and footwear	100.0	98.8	98.9	100.4	99.9	99.2	96.4	94.8	94.5	93.7	93.9	95.2
Bricks, pottery, glass, cement, etc.	100.0	101.0	100.8	101.2	101.8	101.3	100.3	100.4	101.0	100.5	101.4	100.7
Timber, furniture, etc.	100.0	100.0	99.6	98.2	100.6	99.8	96.9	95.4	97.0	96.4	99.3	98.3
Paper, printing and publishing	100.0	99.2	99.4	99.6	99.1	99.4	100.0	99.6	97.7	99.1	98.9	97.7
Other manufacturing industries	100.0	99.0	99.7	99.4	99.6	99.5	99.0	97.6	97.9	97.4	98.4	99.7

Sources: *British Labour Statistics Historical Abstract, 1886–1968* and Central Statistical Office, *Monthly Digest of Statistics*, various issues.

a. Calculated from indexes based on 1963 = 100.

tained for forecasting purposes, but the point of interest in the present context is that the inclusion of a demand term in his equations always proved insignificant so that he felt able to conclude that *given the movement of basic wage rates and import prices* "with reasonable confidence one may forecast the [retail] price index without prior knowledge of the state of consumer demand."

The view put forward is not applicable, as remarked above, to fresh food prices or to rents[12] and the prices charged by nationalized industries which have been heavily influenced by government legislation and decision. It is factually the case, however, that prices of this group of items, which, in any case, account for only about one-quarter of the retail price index, have diverged from other retail prices by something like a trend that, if not smooth, shows no cyclical variation.

Determination of Factor Prices

On the assumption that the foregoing argument is correct, consider how the costs of materials and food and also of labor have been determined.

Materials and food

It is notable that the cost of basic materials and food to the United Kingdom is substantially governed by import prices (even where the United Kingdom is itself a producer), whether or not these are determined by supply and demand in world markets, as, for example, are grain or meat; by some kind of international commodity agreement, as has generally been the case with sugar; or by any other means.

Regarding import prices, I subscribe to the view put forward by John Llewellyn, although it is conceded that the econometrics of his study are at a level of excessive aggregation which leaves much further work to be done.[13] His argument may briefly be stated as follows. Taking the world as a whole, import prices of primary products are governed by long-run demand and supply considerations that may be approximated by a trend. But fluctuations about the trend are likely to be caused by fluctuations in world activity. And it is improbable that the terms of trade between manufactures as a whole and primary commodities (determined by the market) will be substantially

12. Or to the price of land and houses. These do not enter the retail price index, but it is conceded that such prices are indeed determined by supply and demand.
13. G. E. J. Llewellyn, "The Determinants of United Kingdom Import Prices," *Economic Journal,* vol. 84 (March 1974), pp. 18–31.

or permanently affected by the inflation of industrial wages in the world as a whole. Therefore, if all developed countries were lumped together, the expectation would be that the price of their imports from other countries would be determined as:

$$(5) \qquad \ln M_P = c_0 + c_1 \ln XW + c_2 \ln L + c_3 t,$$

where

M_P = import prices of primary products
XW = world industrial production
L = domestic costs per unit of output

and the coefficient on time, t, represents the long-term response of supply to demand. The expectation is that c_1 would be positive and c_2 nearly equal to unity.

Llewellyn maintained that if U.K. unit costs rose faster than those of other countries without any exchange rate adjustment then U.K. import prices of primary products would also rise faster (if only because the United Kingdom is such a large market for certain commodities (such as tea), although not to the full extent of the excess. On the other hand, a relative increase in U.K. unit costs accompanied by an equal appreciation in the sterling price of foreign currencies would probably effect an increase in import prices measured in sterling to a fully equivalent extent. These considerations led to the formulation:

$$(6) \quad \ln M_P^{UK} = c_0 + c_1 \ln XW + c_4 \ln L^{UK} + c_5 \ln L^F + c_6 \ln RX + c_7 t,$$

where the superscripts UK and F make L refer, respectively, to the United Kingdom and other industrial countries, and where RX is the exchange rate between sterling and the currencies of those countries. The expectation was that $(c_4 + c_5) \approx (c_4 + c_6) \approx 1$.

It was argued next that import prices of finished manufactures are also likely to be determined by relative costs at home and abroad (measured in own currency), by the rate of exchange, and by the change in primary product prices. The rise in import prices at the point of devaluation would be unlikely to be fully as large as the percentage appreciation in the sterling price of foreign currencies because quotations get shaded. Since this hypothesis yields an equation identical in form and subject to the same expectations about the sums of pairs of exponents as equation 6, the two may be aggregated.[14]

14. A disaggregated study cannot be carried out without much further work because the cost of basic materials is a large component of the cost of imported manufactures.

The coefficient on ln XW now represents the impact of demand on primary product prices both directly and indirectly as they are embodied in imported manufactured goods; and so on. The results come out rather neatly: the unconstrained coefficients on[15]

ln XW being 0.14
            (1.87)
ln L^{UK} being 0.37
            (3.63)
ln L^F being 0.60
            (3.28)
ln RX being 0.63
            (10.06)

The standard errors of these coefficients, although they conform broadly to expectations, are also clearly consistent with results that would have fitted the hypothesis less elegantly.

It has already been noted that a reduced form import price equation of this kind can do no more than establish apparent presumptions and that most of the work remains to be done. Furthermore, preliminary calculations for other countries suggest that the functional form used is too restrictive; that the hypothesis is rather clearly inappropriate for items which, although they are primary commodities, such as oil, are not market-determined; and that the equation quite seriously underestimates the growth of U.K. import prices during 1974 (it does, however, "forecast" a very large increase) partly because of the oil situation and possibly also because there was an exceptionally important speculative element in that particular commodity boom. Its results would also produce poor conditional predictions for the period when the Suez Canal was closed, accommodated in Llewellyn's empirical work by dummy variables. These make only a brief appearance, however, so that the results are fully consistent with a post-Suez decline as large as the previous increase had been.

The main conclusions to emerge from this argument and analysis are:

1. Import prices have on the whole and in the long term operated to damp down price inflation slightly; between 1954 and 1972 the United Kingdom's terms of trade improved about 10 percent.[16] But there have been certain

15. The figures in parentheses are t-statistics.
16. Measured by the ratio of the national income deflators for exports and imports of goods and services.

periods, for example, during the Korean and 1973 Arab-Israeli wars and in the Suez crisis, when import prices have moved sharply for reasons independent of the business cycle or cost inflation in industrialized countries. Generally upward movements of this kind have subsequently been fully reversed.

2. Fluctuations in world activity and trade have generated perceptible fluctuations (compared with what otherwise would have happened) in import prices. But these fluctuations have not been very large, and taken by themselves have not had much impact on final prices. Although this seems a clear case of real demand "having an effect" on prices, it is quite unclear, because the business cycles have all been of short duration, whether the effect would have generated a change in supplies sufficient to induce an automatic reversal had demand remained high or low relative to trend. Moreover, the United Kingdom is not a large enough market to make feasible opting against an increase in commodity prices generated by a world boom by the pursuit of disinflationary policies out of step with other industrialized countries.

3. If, as seems the correct neutral assumption, every 1 percent addition to the relative growth of domestic costs (everything else being given) eventually generates a 1 percent additional appreciation of foreign currencies in terms of sterling, it will probably also generate a 1 percent addition to sterling import prices (compared with what otherwise would have happened). By this argument, import prices may not be considered a natural damper on the movement of final prices in relation to domestic costs. If U.K. costs were rising faster than those of competitors the exchange rate could for a time be defended, so temporarily damping the inflation rate and allowing the terms of trade to improve. But this position would become progressively untenable, because either an intolerable loss of foreign exchange or a continuous rise in unemployment would ensue. On the other hand, according to the same argument, it *is* possible to prevent an increase in import prices generated by a cost inflation abroad more rapid than at home simply by allowing sterling to appreciate in terms of other currencies.

4. A depreciation of sterling may be brought about by a deficit in the U.K. balance of payments caused by factors other than the relative movements in domestic unit costs; a deficit like this may occur because of overexpansionary fiscal policy, lack of competitiveness for reasons other than relative cost movements, or capital movements. Such a depreciation of sterling will give rise to an increase in import prices, although on a proportionately somewhat smaller scale than the depreciation.

Between 1971 and the beginning of 1974 the deflator for imports of goods and services rose 64.8 percent. Under the Llewellyn system, the increase may be apportioned between the various causes as follows:

Factors contributing to rise in import deflator	Percent change, 1971–early 1974	Contribution to total movement (percent)
World production (deviation from trend)	5.1	1.2
Domestic unit costs	24.2	24.2
Depreciation other than that generated by relative costs	5.0	3.3
Oil embargo and subsequent price rise	213.9	20.3
Long-run trend	...	−2.2
Residual	...	18.0
Total	...	64.8

In making these attributions the assumption is that the rise in domestic relative to foreign unit costs caused sterling to depreciate by an equal amount compared with what would otherwise have occurred. Hence, the contribution of the 24.2 percent rise in domestic costs is not 24.2 times 0.37;[17] it would be so only if the exchange rate had not responded to the change in domestic costs. Because of the assumed effect of that change on the exchange rate, import prices are affected equal to the full 24.2 percent; this also explains why foreign costs do not figure in the list.

Labor costs

There is, in my opinion, no valid *general* theory—at least one applicable to the United Kingdom—that defines a set of forces governing wage inflation; there is no equilibrium rate of increase in wage rates. This indeterminacy is the result of collective bargaining pushing on costs with more or less urgency and the strong tendency noted above for rates of increase in wages in private industry to be uniform across the board. Individual employers become unable, or are insufficiently motivated, to resist wage demands, and employers collectively have no motive for resisting them at one rate of increase rather than another. Before exchange rates were floating some manufacturers, engaged in substantial export business or competitive with imports, were motivated to resist excessive wage increases. Their impulse was weakened, however, by the government's commitment to maintain a high level of employment, if necessary by stimulating home demand. But, as indicated above, the evidence on wage differentials in private manufacturing industry between 1963 and 1974 discounts this as an important factor.

17. The estimated coefficient c_4 in equation 6 is 0.37.

What can be said about the probable outcome in terms of what the rate of increase of wages will actually be in this indeterminate world? One proposition that can be made is that the average and nearly uniform rise in pay in the private sector is likely to be, to some extent, serially correlated. If employees receive the same money increase this year that they did last (whatever that may have been), this will usually be the necessary condition for them to obtain, simultaneously, a normal increase in their real income compared with what it was at the time of the previous award. The presumption is that prices will have risen less than the previous award by an amount equal to the normal average increase in productivity. The size of the change in real wages being bargained for sets limits to the indeterminacy of the extent to which the rate of inflation can change.[18]

My suggestion is that the rate of wage inflation will be changed, quite simply, whenever there is widespread pressure to change it. The going rate has only a weak inertia that may readily be shoved from one position to another. Pressure may be generated by a number of different factors and the whole process probably cannot be modeled econometrically. Nevertheless, some of these factors may be listed.

In the first place, exogenous changes in import prices will sometimes change the rate of price inflation, which affects most people's actual real income and either their expectations or knowledge of the money increases necessary to maintain or improve their standard of living.

Second, pressure may also vary with the pressure of demand for labor, especially if this tends to be positively correlated with profit shares. A noteworthy point, however, is that while econometric studies of the postwar period up to 1969 all showed clear evidence that the pressure of demand for labor influenced wage inflation, this evidence does not survive in any study I know of covering the period 1969–73.[19] It is the rapid acceleration in wages that took place in 1969–70 at a time when retail prices were not accelerating and the pressure of demand for labor was relatively low and tending to fall that calls into question all strong theories about the effect of demand on wage inflation.

18. The change in real wages is defined here as the change in money wages compared with what they were at the previous award in excess of the change in prices over the same period.

19. See, for instance, Michael Parkin, Michael Sumner, and Robert Ward, "The Effects of Excess Demand, Generalized Expectations and Wage-Price Controls on Wage Inflation in the UK: 1956–71," in Karl Brunner and Allan H. Meltzer, eds., *The Economics of Prices and Wage Controls,* Carnegie-Rochester Conference Series on Public Policy, vol. 2 (Amsterdam: North-Holland, 1976; distributed in Canada and the United States by American Elsevier), pp. 193–221. This econometric study (in its unconstrained version) yields a coefficient on unemployment insignificantly different from zero.

Table 3. *Increases in Weekly Earnings of Manual Workers in Manufacturing and in the Public Sector, 1963–73*[a]

Percent

Sector	1963–69		1969–73		1963–73	
	Six-year increase	Annual average compound rate of increase	Four-year increase	Annual average compound rate of increase	Ten-year increase	Annual average compound rate of increase
Manufacturing	49.3	6.9	62.5	12.9	142.6	9.3
Public	41.2	5.9	75.2	15.0	147.1	9.5
Coalmining	36.9	5.4	79.8	15.8	146.2	9.4

Source: *Department of Employment Gazette* (HMSO), various issues.

a. The data are for manual workers only and are derived from a different survey from that used in table 1 for the comparison of earnings in manufacturing, which does not have adequate coverage of the public sector. Earnings for each year are calculated by averaging recorded levels in October of the year in question, the year before, and the year after.

As a third factor I suggest that the main significance of differentials in the inflationary process is not so much that people are always trying to change them as that they insist on restoring them if they alter, except in the very rare cases where a relative change has generally been accepted by the community.[20] If this interpretation is right, an important agent of change in the general rate of inflation may be the making of an individual settlement which is right out of line with the going rate and which then has a contagious influence. Key settlements do appear to have occurred, almost invariably in the public sector.

During the sixties, when many attempts were made to institute an effective incomes policy, the government was more successful in holding down the pay of its own employees than pay in the private sector. When the incomes policy was discontinued the restoration of differentials effected very large individual increases which were probably unseen or accepted as "catching-up" awards. The period following 1969 when the Labour government's incomes policy finally disintegrated may be a case in point, and may provide an explanation of the general acceleration in 1970.

Consider table 3, which compares changes in earnings of manual workers in manufacturing industry with manual workers employed in the public sector over a ten-year span. The figures show that all public-sector employees

20. For instance, the increase in women's pay relative to that of men's which has been in progress for some years appears to be accepted.

particularly the coalminers fared badly during the 1963–69 period. Most of the other main groups also did considerably less well than manufacturing industry. Much of the deterioration in the relative position of the public sector appears to have been the result of the way in which the Labour government's incomes policy was operated. That the ground was fully made up and more in the subsequent four years, however, is evident from table 3.

The manifestation of the catching-up process, in each case following strikes, was a succession of startling individual settlements: for example, nearly 17 percent was awarded to local authority manual workers in 1970, 20 percent to electrical supply workers in 1971, and 25 percent to the coalminers in 1972.

Although it cannot be proved, my strong impression is that these increases in the public sector largely affected the outcome of other negotiations taking place at that time and subsequently. The net result of holding down public-sector pay for a period of many years was ultimately to increase average pay (of public and private sectors together) compared with what otherwise would have happened. This view implies that the response of the private sector to public-sector settlements was asymmetrical; when public settlements were being held down it was not generally known that this was the case. The enormous settlements in 1969–70 were perhaps seldom recognized and accepted as a catching-up process.

Furthermore, although there were from 1969 to 1972 discernible reasons for very large increases to be awarded, the awards may have occurred for *no* substantial reason. It was then widely supposed, for instance, that the "out-of-line" award made to the railwaymen in 1956 was quite unnecessary in that it was larger than what they had expected or were prepared to accept. The outcome of bargaining in these cases was not one of inevitability. After all, some determined attempts to obtain particularly large settlements, notably the busmen's strike in the late fifties and the postmen's strike in the early seventies, had failed. And there is more than a suspicion that some of the major capitulations by the government would never have occurred had negotiations been more skillfully handled.

Conclusions for Policy

Fiscal and monetary policies influence the domestic inflation rate through any effect they may have on the relation between supply and demand for those primary products that have a market clearing price. This is not a strong mechanism, however, for an individual small country such as the United Kingdom, which does not absorb a large share of the total market. The same might not be true for the United States providing, as it does, a market large enough to influence world prices; nor would it be true if all countries operated disinflationary policies in concert.

The evidence supports, although only weakly, the view that the pressure of demand for labor influences the rate of change in money wages in both the short and the long run. (But the postwar period contains no evidence as to what would happen if unemployment were allowed to exceed one million [4 percent] for any length of time.)

Through their effect on the balance of payments and ultimately on the exchange rate and sterling import prices, fiscal and monetary policies must inevitably influence the domestic inflation rate. The manifestation may be slow in evolving, however, particularly if, as often happened in the past, the exchange rate is protected by the use of reserves or by foreign borrowing.

There is no distinctively monetarist solution to inflation. Alternative ways of managing fiscal and credit policy work on inflation, if at all, only through the mechanisms described above. Compare two situations, differing only in that in one a general wage increase is conceded, in the other it is not; and suppose further that fiscal policy is the same in each case. If an attempt is made to contain the consequent inflation by control of the money supply with no change in fiscal policy, the wage and price increases are not thereby directly affected. Rather there would be an indirect effect on the inflation rate through the same means of lower real demand, employment, and so on, as a change in fiscal policy, although the incidence would be different.

Concern in the present context is with inflation; wage differentials and the distribution of income are of interest only insofar as they have a relevance to this problem. There is a body of opinion that holds that the desire to change wage differentials is one of the key agents of inflation and that the way an incomes policy should work is to establish criteria for differentials that command such acceptance that this key factor would be removed.

It is possible that the main cause of inflation is the desire of many groups of workers continuously to improve their relative positions. But this is an implausible view given that differentials are, in practice, so stable; variations in the rate of inflation can then only be explained by variations in the desire to alter them. It is improbable that the sense of injustice aroused by the seemingly rigid hierarchy of differentials fluctuates very much.

Even if this were an important mechanism, however, the use of incomes policy to set criteria (presumably through some scheme of national job evaluation[21] that will determine a new hierarchy) will fail unless the criteria are

21. Another even more pernicious idea, which never quite dies, is that wage increases in particular industries should be related to productivity increases in those same industries.

accepted to the extent that those who lose relatively do so willingly. Indeed, unless a redistributive incomes policy were to command such extremely unlikely support, it would very emphatically have a counterproductive effect on the general rate of inflation inasmuch as the desire of those who lose relatively to restore their position would make them determined to obtain money increases equal to the maximum awards. If some means of doing this could be found, the object of an anti-inflationary incomes policy should be specifically to refrain from interfering with differentials, and to deduct whatever single and common percentage each year from all money incomes would keep final prices reasonably stable.[22] This happens for a short while when the government introduces freezes. In the United Kingdom, freezes or near-freezes, such as those the Conservatives initiated in 1962 and 1972, and Labour in 1966, have all been successful temporarily and have approximated to the criteria suggested above because, for these very short periods, no great violence was done to the hierarchy of differentials that would have obtained had the freeze not been introduced.

If, however, a substantial control over money pay is exercised for any length of time—probably anything more than a year—hard cases will appear and accumulate. A process of adjudication on such cases will have to take place, with policy becoming more and more concerned with exceptions and the attempt to establish acceptable criteria for admitting them. In other words, the longer an incomes policy continues the more it becomes a policy about the distribution of income; it loses sight not merely of the objective of controlling inflation but becomes itself a most powerful agent of inflation.

In short, the best that can be expected from an incomes policy is that, by means of a temporary intervention, the going inflation rate is nudged down a step. The possibility of the effectiveness of such an intervention is harmonious with the views about wage determination set out earlier in the first paragraphs of the section on labor costs.

A successful intervention must be very carefully devised and timed. The first stage of that policy is bound to damage temporarily the real income of those whose wages or expenses were about to increase. It is essential, therefore, that a moment be chosen when as few as possible are left behind in the race. Insofar as a wage round can be identified, it should be complete when the intervention is made. The time chosen should also be one when fresh food prices and, to a lesser extent, other raw materials prices are not going to rise for external reasons: the import content of food sold in the shops is so high

22. This is the idea behind the logically quite sound scheme proposed originally by Peter Elkan for using the direct tax system to control inflation. For a restatement of this proposal see Maurice Scott, *The Banker* (London), vol. 124 (April 1974).

that it is impossible for distributors to absorb these cost increases even in the most rigorous period of freeze.

In the second stage of the intervention, the main objective is to withdraw from the first stage without allowing its effects to be reversed by forces generated by the freeze itself. Because there is normally a time lag between a rise in wages and the consequential rise in prices, a slowdown in the growth of money wages is likely to result in some once-and-for-all loss of real wages as prices continue to rise in response to the previous wage increases. At the end of a successful freeze period, therefore, stored-up cost changes will exist, which occurred before the freeze was imposed. Consequently, the chief aim in the second stage of an anti-inflationary exercise should be to ensure that there is no significant (once-and-for-all) loss of real wages if an attempt is made to pass on these stored-up cost increases.

At the beginning of the third stage of the policy, a slower rate of price increase will have occurred without a comparable, and possibly without any, loss of real income. This condition should be sufficient for the new rate of inflation to be permanently lower than it otherwise would have been.

Appendix: A Note on Michael Parkin's Empirical Studies

Michael Parkin claims to have successfully modeled wage changes in the United Kingdom through the period 1956–71 by using as explanatory variables indicators that measure the demand for labor and price expectations.[23] A critique of his work by Angus Deaton[24] makes the following major points:

1. Parkin, Sumner, and Ward (PSW) maintain that their results "give strong support for the model. . . . In particular the evidence denies the existence of a long-run trade-off between inflation and unemployment." In his note Deaton sketches confidence ellipses around the unconstrained estimates of coefficients of the independent variables and finds that the point at which, according to the PSW model, the Phillips curve is vertical lies just outside the 95-degree ellipse. It follows, according to Deaton, that there is a "wide range of points implying the existence of a long-run trade-off which are better supported by the evidence than the point which denies such a proposition."

23. Parkin and others, "The Effects of Excess Demand" (see note 19 for full citation).
24. "Notes on the Parkin-Sumner-Ward Tests of Wage Inflation" (Cambridge: Cambridge University, April 1975; processed). This critique would have been impossible had Michael Parkin not generously provided the data on which his study was based.

2. In the unconstrained version, which, according to (1) above, there are no grounds to reject, the coefficients on the variables representing the demand for labor are insignificantly different from zero and therefore do not support the view that there is even a short-run trade-off between inflation and unemployment.

3. The PSW "fit" derives almost entirely from the behavior of *employers'* expectations about *domestic* prices. None of the other coefficients are significantly different from zero in the unconstrained version. It is surely more likely that employers' expectations are the result rather than the cause of wage increases currently being negotiated.

4. PSW emphasize that the coefficients on the incomes policy variable are derisory, that is to say, small and statistically insignificant. The principal element of the 1966 policy, introduced toward the end of July of that year, was that there was to be no change in wage rates for six months, followed by a further six months of restraint. As may easily be ascertained, however, the wage rate index was *completely unchanged for the whole period of the freeze*. If the regression analysis rejects the effectiveness of this freeze it must be misspecified. It is clear from the data that employers' expectations were doing the work of the dummy variables purporting to represent policy.

Additional points not touched on in Deaton's paper are: (a) The econometric results are good by the standard of wage equations but extremely poor by other standards: not nearly good enough to settle the main question at issue, namely, whether or not wage determination in the United Kingdom can be modeled at all. If fitted to data for the period 1956–69, the model fails to predict the acceleration in 1970 and 1971 given the actual movement of the independent variables in those years. (b) The choice of basic weekly rates as the dependent variable is not appropriate as a measure of wage or price inflation because they refer only to the *minimum* weekly rates which emerge from national bargaining or which are determined by statute. Between April 1956 and October 1971 basic weekly rates rose 115 percent. But during the same period weekly *earnings* rose 169 percent.

Comments by Michael Parkin

WYNNE GODLEY has produced a useful and accurate summary of the facts concerning U.K. inflation and related economic developments in the postwar years. He has also presented a clear and coherent statement of what might be called the "British conventional wisdom" explanation of those facts and its policy implications. He has also directed criticism at an alternative explanation—a minority view in the British context with rather widely accepted concurrence outside Britain—which was developed largely by members of the Manchester University Inflation Workshop.[25] That explanation may be summarized as the expectations-augmented Phillips curve monetarist view.

In this comment I first restate as briefly and accurately as possible, Godley's explanation of Britain's inflation and point out what I regard as its major weaknesses. At each stage of this criticism an alternative explanation is offered. That alternative is finally brought together and summarized.[26]

The British conventional wisdom on inflation

In his explanation of U.K. inflation Godley sets forth the following propositions:

1. Prices are independent of excess demand and determined only by "normal costs."

2. Normal costs depend on trend changes in wages, import prices, and productivity.

3. Import prices depend on world prices and the exchange rate.

4. World prices depend on world demand factors.

5. The exchange rate is determined in part by policy and in part by the state of the balance of payments.

6. Wages are to some extent responsive to excess demand but to too little an extent to be useful. On the whole, wage change displays a great deal of inertia but may easily be given a push in one direction or another, most typically upward, by a variety of *noneconomic* factors.

7. Aggregate demand is determined by monetary policy and fiscal policy, by world demand, and by movements in wages and prices in the domestic economy. The monetary policy component of all this, however, is passive in the sense that it permits the movements of wages and prices determined in propositions (1) and (6) without leading to recession.

25. A Social Science Research Council research program on "Inflation: Its Causes, Consequences and Cures," directed by David Laidler and Michael Parkin.

26. It is not possible in the space available here to give a completely detailed argument supporting my own interpretation and explanation of U.K. inflation. Instead the reader is referred to Michael Parkin, "The Causes of Inflation: Recent Contributions and Current Controversies," in Michael Parkin and A. R. Nobay, eds., *Current Economic Problems, Proceedings of the Conference of the Association of University Teachers of Economics, 1974* (Cambridge: Cambridge University Press, 1975), chap. 12; and David Laidler and Michael Parkin, "Inflation: A Survey," *Economic Journal*, vol. 85 (December 1975), pp. 741–809.

Criticism and reconstruction

PRICE DETERMINATION. Godley hypothesizes that wholesale prices of manufactures respond only to "normal costs" and are not affected by demand pressures. The evidence he cites arises partly from Godley and Nordhaus[27] and partly from other, as yet unpublished work, which has been done in Cambridge. The proposition that price changes are not affected by demand pressures in the goods market is in line with the earliest empirical work on U.K. price determination by Klein and Ball, Dicks-Mireaux, Neild, and Godley and Rowe.[28] All these earlier studies postulated that price changes were determined by changes in wages, import prices, and productivity. The precise way in which Godley and Nordhaus attempted to establish the independence of price change from excess demand was, superficially at least, very thorough. First, they attempted to measure normal costs by decycling factor price and productivity changes and building up an appropriately decycled cost change variable that they defined as normal costs. They then used ten alternative measures of excess demand and specified ten alternative forms of the price equation—one hundred equations in all. Using their normal cost variable along with the ten demand pressure variables in the ten alternative specifications of the price equation, they found only *one* significant positive coefficient on excess demand. This result led them to favor the normal cost hypothesis against the hypothesis that excess demand has an independent role to play in the determination of prices.

The conclusion, like that of the literature of the late 1950s and early 1960s, unfortunately stands in rather strong contrast to the results emerging from work done in the late 1960s and early 1970s. Rushdy and Lund, McCallum, Solow, and Brechling all found positive and statistically significant coefficients on a variety of alternative excess demand variables in price equations.[29] Rushdy and Lund and McCallum used the famous Dow and Dicks-

27. William D. Nordhaus and Wynne Godley, "Pricing in the Trade Cycle," *Economic Journal*, vol. 82 (September 1972), pp. 853–82.

28. L. R. Klein and R. J. Ball, "Some Econometrics of the Determination of Absolute Prices and Wages," *Economic Journal*, vol. 69 (September 1959), pp. 465–82; L. A. Dicks-Mireaux, "The Interrelationship between Cost and Price Changes, 1946–1959: A Study of Inflation in Post-War Britain," *Oxford Economic Papers*, new series, vol. 13 (October 1961), pp. 267–92; R. R. Neild, *Pricing and Employment in the Trade Cycle: A Study of British Manufacturing Industries, 1950–61* (Cambridge: Cambridge University Press, 1963); W. A. H. Godley and D. A. Rowe, "Retail and Consumer Prices, 1955–1963" *National Institute Economic Review*, no. 30 (November 1964), pp. 44–57.

29. F. Rushdy and P. J. Lund, "The Effect of Demand on Prices in British Manufacturing Industry," *Review of Economic Studies*, vol. 34 (October 1967), pp. 361–73; B. T. McCallum, "The Effect of Demand on Prices in British Manufacturing: Another

Mireaux index of excess demand.[30] Solow employed the Paish capacity utilization index[31] and Brechling his own excess demand variable defined as the difference between real national product and a quadratic trend. In the light of these studies it seemed well established by the time Godley and Nordhaus came on the scene that excess demand did exert an upward pressure on prices independently of changes in costs.

The conflict apparent between the conclusions of Godley and Nordhaus and the other recent studies makes it natural to pose the question: who is right? Fortunately, a straightforward reconciliation can be offered. One major reason for the lack of any correlation between excess demand and price change in the Godley-Nordhaus studies arises from their specification of the *rate of price change* as depending on the *change in excess demand*. This is an incorrect specification as it is at odds both with the theory of price setting and with those earlier empirical studies that had found that the *level* of excess demand was the important factor. In the ten equations that correctly specified price change as depending on the level of excess demand, positive coefficients are found in all the goods market excess demand variables. Furthermore, the *t*-statistics are greater than 1 (but less than 2) in each case. The remaining equations, which had negative excess demand coefficients, used a variable representing demand pressure in the labor market rather than in the product market. Aside from its inappropriateness as an excess demand factor one would expect a priori that excess demand in the labor market, other things being equal, would lower the markup, not raise it. Hence, the Godley-Nordhaus results are entirely in line with the view that excess demand does affect prices.

But the argument may be taken further. As is well known, *actual* unit cost changes are countercyclical in that they tend to fall in the boom and rise in the recession. Prices, however, are less cyclical and this presents a fundamental identification problem. Prices may be regarded as affected by decycled costs and not by demand or, alternatively, as affected by actual costs along

View," *Review of Economic Studies,* vol. 37 (January 1970), pp. 147–56; R. M. Solow, *Price Expectations and the Behavior of the Price Level* (Manchester: Manchester University Press, 1969); Frank P. R. Brechling, "Some Empirical Evidence on the Effectiveness of Prices and Incomes Policies," in Michael Parkin and Michael T. Sumner, eds., *Incomes Policy and Inflation* (Manchester: Manchester University Press, 1972), pp. 30–47.

30. J. C. R. Dow and L. A. Dicks-Mireaux, "The Excess Demand for Labour: A Study of Conditions in Great Britain, 1946–56," *Oxford Economic Papers,* new series, vol. 10 (February 1958), pp. 1–33.

31. Frank W. Paish, *Studies in an Inflationary Economy: The United Kingdom, 1948–1961* (Macmillan, 1962).

with demand. This basic identification problem is one which will not be solved by the running of one hundred regressions and comparing of standard error and *t*-statistics.

There are two further areas where demand pressures could be present but are missed in the Godley-Nordhaus procedure. The first concerns excess demand pressures, which are, on the average, positive. It is at least possible to argue that in the postwar British economy excess demand has been persistently positive, hence imparting the persistent upward trend to the rate of inflation. The precise Godley-Nordhaus results indicate that this may be an important point. Their regression equations estimating the relation between price change and normal cost change should, if the normal cost hypothesis is correct, yield an intercept of zero and the slope coefficient on normal cost change of unity. In fact, there is a significant positive constant in most regressions and the slope coefficient on the normal unit cost changes significantly less than one. Although this is consistent with the hypothesis that there is, on the average, positive excess demand forcing up prices, it is inconsistent with the normal cost hypothesis advanced by Godley and Nordhaus. A second source of demand pressure, which would be missed by the Godley-Nordhaus procedures, is that arising from world demand. The kinds of goods that enter into the prices of the British index of manufactures would typically be highly internationally tradable. It would therefore be anticipated, by the law of one price (international arbitrage), that domestic prices would not diverge too far from world prices. Furthermore, world, and therefore domestic, price movements might be expected to respond to world excess demand pressures rather than to specifically domestic excess demand pressures.

On the basis of the study by Godley-Nordhaus, then, the conclusion certainly cannot be that excess demand has no effect on prices. On the contrary, their study points to at least some possibility that demand pressures do indeed exert an independent influence on prices. Of course, excess demand pressures can affect the rate of inflation in two ways: by direct pressure on the markup and by indirect pressure through their effects on factor prices. Godley purports to have shown that such pressures do not affect the markup. Regarding these conclusions, I have tried at least to raise a question. The effects of demand pressures on factor prices will now be considered.

DETERMINANTS OF WAGE INFLATION. It is here that my disagreements with Godley are strongest. "There is . . . no valid *general* theory," Godley states, "—at least one applicable to the United Kingdom—that defines a set of forces governing wage inflation; there is no 'equilibrium' rate of increase in wage rates. This indeterminacy is the result of collective bargaining 'pushing' on costs with more or less urgency and the strong tendency . . . for rates of increase in wages in private industry to be uniform across the board. . . . One proposition that can be made is that the average and nearly uniform rise in pay in the private sector is likely to be, to some extent, serially correlated." It is impossible to deny that there is a problem about understanding the movements of money-wage rates in the U.K. economy in the period after 1966. Until that year nearly every student of wage determination in the United Kingdom would have supported some kind of Phillips curve hypothesis. The basic curve fitted by Phillips[32] to the data of the nineteenth and early twentieth centuries predicted the 1950s and early 1960s almost exactly. By 1966, however, that relationship began to crumble and by 1969 it collapsed completely as an adequate explanation of wage change. Reactions to this breakdown of the Phillips curve relationship varied. Most people, like Godley, invoked a variety of sociopsychological "push" hypotheses centered upon labor union behavior and collective bargaining. Others, noting the erratic behavior of the relation between wage change and unemployment in the 1920s,[33] and also bearing in mind the theoretical contributions of Friedman and Phelps,[34] suggested that the behavior of inflation expectations is a major factor in the shifting of the Phillips curve in the northeasterly direction (rising inflaton and rising unemployment) in the late 1960s and 1970s. Furthermore, it has been suggested that the behavior of inflation expectations is not independent of the behavior of the foreign exchange rate and international price movements.[35] To be more specific, PSW derived a simple wage equation for the United Kingdom in which the rate of wage change depended on excess demand, on the expected rate of inflation of retail prices, domestic wholesale prices, and export prices, as well as on expected rates of change of income tax and social security taxes. Strong a priori restrictions were derived from the theory con-

32. A. W. Phillips, "The Relations between Unemployment and the Rate of Change of Money Wage Rates in the United Kingdom, 1861–1957," *Economica*, new series, vol. 25 (November 1958), pp. 283–99.

33. Michael Parkin, "The Phillips Curve: A Historical Perspective, Lessons from Recent Empirical Studies and Alternative Policy Choices," in H. G. Johnson and A. R. Nobay, eds., *The Current Inflation* (London: Macmillan, 1971), chap. 11.

34. Milton Friedman, "The Role of Monetary Policy," *American Economic Review*, vol. 58 (March 1968), pp. 1–17; Edmund S. Phelps, "Money-Wage Dynamics and Labor-Market Equilibrium," *Journal of Political Economy*, vol. 76 (July/August, pt. 2, 1968), pp. 678–711; amended and reprinted in Edmund S. Phelps and others, *The Microeconomic Foundations of Employment and Inflation Theory* (Norton, 1970), pp. 124–66.

35. Michael Parkin, Michael Sumner, and Robert Ward, "The Effects of Excess Demand, Generalized Expectations and Wage-Price Controls on Wage Inflation in the UK: 1956," in Brunner and Meltzer, eds., *The Economics of Price and Wage Controls*, pp. 193–221 (see note 19).

cerning degree one homogeneity in nominal magnitudes, so that the predicted long-run Phillips curve becomes vertical. Estimation of this equation, using the best available direct measures of expected rates of inflation based on surveys of the Gallup Poll and the Confederation of British Industries showed that, on a t-test, one could not reject the hypothesis that there was no long-run trade-off between inflation and unemployment.[36] As Deaton subsequently demonstrated[37] and as Godley reports, however, a more comprehensive significance test shows that the "no long-run trade-off" result of PSW (page 194) is on the edge of the 95-degree confidence ellipse rather than being centrally placed in that ellipse. If one accepts the strong a priori presumption that there is no long-run trade-off, a result that is on the edge of the 95-degree confidence ellipse does not seem disquieting. If one is prepared to impose the restriction of no long-run trade-off, then it is possible to derive a significant inverse short-run relation between the rate of wage change and unemployment. The exercise conducted by PSW extends to 1971. Subsequent work attempting to continue that analysis into the 1970s proved unsuccessful and for an apparently straightforward reason. During the late 1960s and 1970s, the ratio of unemployment compensation to average earnings net of tax has been increasing substantially. Theory would predict that such an increase would raise the rate of voluntary unemployment consistent with the absence of demand pressure in the labor market. It would not seem, however, that a simple relationship was active here, for when workers voluntarily leave their jobs the compensation they receive is poorer than that deriving from involuntary layoffs. The expectation therefore would be that the effects of the improved unemployment compensation would be distributed over time and in a somewhat cyclical fashion over the period of the last two years of the 1960s and the 1970s. Allowing for this process, Gray, Parkin, and Sumner (GPS)[38] have estimated a modified expectations-augmented Phillips relation for the United Kingdom (see appendix) with the following characteristics: (1) there is a very well-determined short-run trade-off between wage inflation and unemployment; (2) the coefficient on the expected rate of inflation is 1.07 and not significantly different from unity; (3) unemployment compensation substantially affects the position of the short-run trade-off between wage change and unemployment as it does equally the natural rate of unemploy-

36. John A. Carlson and Michael Parkin, "Inflation Expectations," *Economica*, vol. 42 (May 1975), pp. 123–38; Parkin and others, "The Effects of Excess Demand."

37. Angus Deaton, "Notes on the Parkin-Summer-Ward Model of Wage Inflation" (Cambridge: Cambridge University, April 1975; processed).

38. M. R. Gray, Michael Parkin, and M. T. Sumner, "Inflation in the U.K.: Causes and Transmission Mechanisms," Discussion Paper 7518 (Manchester: University of Manchester, SSRC Programme on Inflation, 1975; processed).

ment. In round figures, the British natural unemployment rate which, up to the mid-1960s, was somewhere around 2 percent, is now a little under 4 percent as a result of the improved unemployment compensation.

Provided these findings withstand scrutiny, far from a lack of an econometric wage equation for the United Kingdom there is apparently a very sensible equation on a priori considerations. It is one displaying no long-run trade-off, a well-defined but deteriorated short-run trade-off as a result of improved unemployment compensation benefit rates relative to wage rates.

Godley's view, stated in his appendix, that the PSW wage equation is best interpreted as indicating that firms form their price expectations on the basis of wage changes—that is, the reverse of PSW's hypothesis that wage changes are determined (in part) by the expected rate of inflation—is not easy to deal with on the basis of work that has already been done. It is worth noting, however, that, in the context of an analysis that explains both wage change and inflation expectations, PSW found that an adaptive expectations mechanism tracks the evolution of inflation expectations rather well. In contrast to this finding, experiments with equations in which the expected inflation rate is determined by wages add little or nothing.[39] Furthermore, the expected inflation rate used in the GPS paper is that of retail prices and Godley's interpretation, therefore, does not apply in that case.

Finally, work that was attempted explicitly to find a role for wage-push factors, the hypothesis preferred by Godley, has failed to find any convincing explanation.[40]

IMPORT PRICES. I do not quarrel with Godley's remarks about the determinants of import prices and the analysis by Llewellyn on which he draws.[41] I would simply emphasize that here is an area where Godley and I agree; there is room for excess demand factors to affect costs and therefore to affect prices. This condition occurs when excess demand leads to a lack of competitiveness and the depreciation of the exchange rate.

INFLATION EXPECTATIONS. In the above discussion of wage determination, the expected rate of inflation is a central issue. The omission of a systematic discussion of the determination and influence of inflation expectations is a major shortcoming of Godley's paper. Although a generous reading of the paper makes clear that Godley does believe expectations to be important, he fails to give them nearly the central role they deserve.

39. Carlson and Parkin, "Inflation Expectations."
40. Parkin and others, "The Effects of Excess Demand" (see note 19).
41. John Llewellyn, "The Determinants of U.K. Import Prices," *Economic Journal,* vol. 83 (March 1973).

Work done in the Manchester inflation program that bears directly on this problem is relevant and worth noting here. Carlson and Parkin have shown how direct observations of inflation expectations may be obtained from survey data.[42] Monthly surveys of consumer expectations and quarterly surveys of business firms' expectations of domestic wholesale and export prices have been processed. An analysis of the way in which these expectations affect the actual rate of inflation has been conducted through studying the determination of wages and prices. In general, expectations are important factors and appear to affect actual inflation with a coefficient of unity as predicted by standard economic analysis.[43]

In addition to the study of the effects of expectations, a variety of hypotheses have also been examined concerning the factors that influence them. The hypothesis tentatively indicated to be best is a modified version of "adaptive expectations" or "error learning," the modifications being of two types. First, when the rate of inflation is accelerating, both the size of the error and its rate of change appear to be important determinants of the amount by which expectations are revised. Second, the adjustment of the exchange rate by devaluation in November 1967 put a large-step jump into inflation expectations. No evidence was found that large and highly publicized wage settlements such as those that came after prolonged strike activity or major press and television publicity materially affected expectations. Nor was it evident that wage-price controls affect expectations about inflation.

An alternative explanation

An attempt must now be made to bring together the discussion so far and to fill in some gaps in order to provide a coherent alternative to Godley's explanation of Britain's inflation. Godley's view of the interaction of prices, wages, and related factors is that prices are determined by costs, costs are determined by foreign factors and by wages, and wages are determined by an autoregressive process augmented by unspecified "push" forces. The burden of the above exposition has been to argue that prices are determined by costs and by excess demand; that changes in foreign prices, being translated into domestic prices by the exchange rate, are also subject to domestic demand influences; and that wages respond to demand pressures as well as to inflation expectations. Inflation expectations are themselves determined by the

42. Carlson and Parkin, "Inflation Expectations."
43. Parkin and others, "The Effects of Excess Demand"; Gray and others, "Inflation in the U.K."; and Graham W. Smith, "The Determinants of U.K. Price Expectations" (Manchester: University of Manchester, April 1975; processed).

previous inflationary history of the economy. When these propositions are brought together, the rate of inflation is seen to be proximately determined by the history of excess demand over some previous period, as well as by the current level of excess demand in both labor and goods markets. This broad perspective is consistent with the greater part of the empirical literature on British inflation. It stands in sharp contrast to the view presented by Godley, which, despite its support by only a handful of studies whose defects have been pointed to above or in the longer works cited, is widely believed in Britain.

The alternative view places excess demand at the center of the story and makes it necessary to explain how that variable is determined. This is a further major omission of Godley's analysis.

Knowledge of the factors determining aggregate demand in the U.K. economy has not been so well researched and extensively studied as that concerning the proximate determinants of prices, wages, and expectations. What I write here therefore is in part based on informed hunch as much as on serious research. In my view, throughout the 1960s and especially in the latter part of the decade, the economy was run with too low a level of real interest rates and too low an unemployment rate. Godley is clearly right to point out that the unemployment rate in the 1960s was high compared with what it had been in the 1950s. As I have suggested above, however, the natural unemployment rate has almost doubled since 1966; during this period fiscal policy has been persistently expansive and monetary policy permissive. The result has been a tendency for inflation to accelerate. It is true that cycles have been superimposed upon these trends and for the most part these cycles can be identified with electoral management of the economy.

The behavior of the balance of payments over the 1960s and 1970s seems to be consistent with this interpretation: there was a trend deterioration in the current-account balance up to the devaluation of 1967, a fact entirely in accord with the modern monetary analysis of balance of payments.

But a complete picture of the behavior of British inflation requires that the British economy be put into its world setting. When this is done, many things that look puzzling no longer appear to be so. A series of papers that have emerged from the Manchester project, the SSRC Research Programme on Inflation,[44] have developed a simple aggregate world (Group of Ten)

---

44. Nigel Duck, Michael Parkin, David Rose, and George Zis, "The Determination of the Rate of Change of Wages and Prices in the Fixed Exchange Rate World Economy, 1956–71," in Michael Parkin and George Zis, eds., *Inflation in the World Economy*, (Manchester: Manchester University Press; Toronto: Toronto University Press, 1976), pp. 113–49; M. R. Gray, R. Ward, and G. Zis, "The World Demand for Money Func-

model of inflation for the period 1958 to 1971 that determines the average movements of Group of Ten prices as functions of excess demand and inflation expectations.[45] Excess demand is generated by movements in real money balances and inflationary expectations are determined by a simple process of learning by error. That model fits the world aggregates remarkably well and suggests that the rate of increase in world inflation through the 1960s was caused by repeated increases in the world rate of monetary expansion. The Group of Ten world was in a state of excess supply in the late 1950s through 1961. During this period the rate of inflation was falling. From 1961 to 1969 the world went into excess demand, and inflation gradually increased. In 1969–70, excess supply reemerged for a short period and, as a consequence, the inflation rate began to fall in 1971. By 1972–73, however, the world had gone back to a state of strong excess demand and a renewed rise in inflation rates. These developments of the world economy alone shows a broad trend for the rate of inflation in the fixed exchange rate world of the 1960s. British inflation was being swept along by that current but deviating from it with movements that, on the whole, resulted from Britain's overly expansive domestic credit policies. There were, however, some years when Britain was swimming very strongly *against* the tide. The best example, and that which has proved most puzzling to some scholars, is the period of 1966–67. The introduction of a very tight budget in July 1966 drove up the unemployment rate through late 1966 and early 1967. Nevertheless, British inflation continued to accelerate: a trend that, seen against the backcloth of developments in the world economy, is no mystery but looked at in isolation seems most peculiar.

The sizable literature I have cited and attempted to summarize presents a view of the generation of inflation in the United Kingdom very different from that developed by Godley. He emphasizes a mechanical link between prices and costs and an autoregressive process, influenced by various random-push factors, generating wage changes. I have given weight to the role of monetary and fiscal policies as generators of excess demand and of an expectations-augmented excess demand mechanism generating wage and price changes.

---

tion: Some Preliminary Results," in ibid., pp. 152–81; Michael Parkin, "The Causes of Inflation" (see note 26); Michael Parkin, "International Liquidity and World Inflation in the 1960's," in Michael Parkin and George Zis, eds., *Inflation in Open Economies* (Manchester: Manchester University Press; Toronto: Toronto University Press, 1976); and Michael Parkin, Ian Richards, and George Zis, "The Determination and Control of the World Money Supply under Fixed Exchange Rates, 1961–1971," *Manchester School*, vol. 43 (September 1975), pp. 293–316.

45. The availability of data led the Manchester team to define the world as the Group of Ten. The countries are Belgium, Canada, France, Italy, Japan, Netherlands, Sweden, West Germany, United Kingdom, and United States.

Moreover, I have tried to emphasize the openness of the U.K. economy and the importance of the role of world inflation in analyzing U.K. inflation, especially in the prefloating exchange rate period of the sixties.

Appendix: Determinants of the rate of change of money wages in the United Kingdom

The wage equation in Gray, Parkin, and Sumner is set out fully in this appendix.

The basic hypothesis is that:

$$(7) \qquad \Delta w = \alpha' X_L + \Delta P^e \qquad \alpha' > 0$$

where

Δw = rate of change of money wages, percent a year
ΔP^e = expected rate of change of prices, percent a year
X_L = proportionate excess demand for labor.

$$(8) \qquad X_L = f(U, B^*) \qquad f_1 < 0, f_2 > 0$$

$$(8a) \qquad 0 = f(U^*, B^*)$$

where

U = unemployment rate in percent
B = *effective* ratio of unemployment compensation to wages net of tax
$B^* = B$ if $\Delta U > O$.

($B^* = B_{ik}$, where k is the number of years since $\Delta U > 0$, and where B is the actual ratio of unemployment compensation to wages net of tax.)

Equations 7 and 8 combine to give an expectations-augmented Phillips curve, the position of which depends positively on B^*:

$$(9) \qquad \Delta w = \alpha' f(U, B^*) + \Delta P^e.$$

The *effective* unemployment compensation/wage ratio is defined to reflect the fact that when workers leave their jobs voluntarily they are not entitled to the improved compensation rates related to earnings.

The specific functional form used for $f(U, B^*)$ was:

$$(10) \qquad f(U, B^*) = a + bU^{-2} + c(B^*)^3,$$

so that the empirical wage equation becomes:

$$(11) \qquad \Delta w = \alpha' a + \alpha' b U^{-2} + \alpha' c (B^*)^3 + \Delta P^e,$$

or, with obvious reparameterization,

$$(11a) \qquad \Delta w = \alpha + \beta U^{-2} + \gamma (B^*)^3 + \delta \Delta P^e.$$

This equation was estimated on *annual* data for 1952–74 and gave the following:[46]

(12) $\Delta w = -1.5 + 4.9U^{-2} + 16.0(B^*)^3 + 1.06\,\Delta P^e.$
                   (2.2)   (4.8)   (6.4)   (9.0)

$\bar{R}^2 = 0.949$;   Durbin-Watson statistic $= 2.160$.

The largest residual, of $+1.90$ percentage points, is for 1972. The dependent variable used in this empirical work is the most comprehensive measure of wages available, namely, total income from employment divided by the number in employment. The annual percentage rate of change of this series is set out in table 4 and compared with the rate of change in the series for hourly wage rates index reported by Godley. It is clear that our series behaves very similarly to the movements in hourly wage rates.

General Comments

WYNNE GODLEY noted that by far the most important question at issue is whether or not the acceleration of wage inflation in the United Kingdom has been caused by excess demand, a result, in turn, of overly expansive fiscal and monetary policy. Notwithstanding the emphasis Michael Parkin brings to his conclusion, the evidence he provides does not support his case. Parkin concedes that the model he presents in collaboration with Sumner and Ward has broken down for the years of greatly accelerated inflation and record unemployment since 1971. It has already been pointed out that even for the period prior to 1971 the significance of the negative coefficient on unemployment in the wage equation is entirely conditional on the imposition of an a priori constraint that the evidence comes close to rejecting; even with the constraint imposed, the coefficient is small and poorly determined. Parkin's empirical case that wage inflation is caused by excess demand now rests entirely upon a new equation prepared in collaboration with Gray and Sumner, and described in "Inflation and the United Kingdom."

The success of the GPS equation turns entirely on the inclusion of a new term in unemployment compensation relative to post-tax pay, B^*, in the sense that if this term is dropped, thus making wage inflation dependent on unemployment and price expectations only, the coefficient on unemployment is *positive,* although insignificant. Accelerated wage inflation, notwithstanding

---

46. Figures in parentheses are *t*-statistics.

Table 4. *Annual Rates of Change for Hourly Wage Rates and Employment Income, 1952–74*
Percent

Year	Hourly wage rates	Employment income per worker
1952	8.2	6.3
1953	4.7	5.2
1954	4.3	5.3
1955	7.0	8.0
1956	8.1	7.7
1957	5.0	5.1
1958	3.8	4.4
1959	2.7	4.3
1960	4.5	5.8
1961	6.4	6.7
1962	4.3	4.1
1963	4.0	4.5
1964	5.1	7.4
1965	6.1	6.7
1966	6.6	6.2
1967	4.1	4.8
1968	6.8	7.7
1969	5.5	7.7
1970	10.3	11.4
1971	13.2	12.7
1972	14.1	10.8
1973	14.0	12.5
1974	19.8	18.1

Sources: Hourly wage rates, Wynne Godley, table 1 above; employment income per worker, M. R. Gray, Michael Parkin, and M. T. Sumner, "Inflation in the United Kingdom: Causes and Transmission Mechanisms," Discussion Paper 7518 (Manchester: Manchester University Inflation Workshop, 1975; processed).

much higher unemployment, cannot be statistically, or in plausibility, identified as having been caused by higher unemployment compensation. (With a rerun of the GPS equation, substituting for B^* on the one hand a jump dummy worth one for 1968–70 and two for 1971–74 and, on the other hand, a time trend covering 1968–74, I obtained results similar in other respects to those reported by GPS.) Moreover, the amount of work the variable has to do makes its quantitative implications (on the GPS interpretation) extremely implausible. Thus the raising of unemployment compensation was by itself enough—given unemployment and price expectations—to add, it is implied, about 50 percent to wage inflation between 1967 and 1974. If one allows for a feedback to price expectations, there would probably, on the GPS model, have been no wage inflation at all, and a falling price level since 1967, had unemployment compensation not been raised and had output and thus unemployment been as they actually were.

Furthermore, the policy implication was quite at variance with Parkin's statement. It is not that fiscal policy has been too expansionary. The entire inflation since 1967 on the GPS model has been generated by this one factor—the progressive rise in unemployment compensation—and inflation could now be immediately reduced by about 10 percent a year if the 1967 position were restored. But for the rise in unemployment compensation, fiscal and monetary policies could have been *more* expansionary than they had been and Britain could still have had the best performance of any country in the inflation league!

With respect to Parkin's criticisms of the Godley-Nordhaus studies on the normal price hypothesis:

1. The studies Parkin cites, which find significant excess demand variables in price equations, have many unsatisfactory features, but it is sufficient refutation to point out that Solow does not normalize unit labor costs at all, Rushdy and Lund and McCallum use a rule of thumb (that overtime hours are paid at time and a half) not based on econometric analysis, whereas Brechling omits wage costs altogether. The accurate elimination of the cyclical components of costs is absolutely essential for a valid test of the normal price hypothesis. If costs are inaccurately purged of cyclical influences spurious demand effects will be picked up in test equations.

2. There is no good reason for rejecting labor market indicators of excess demand to test the normal price hypothesis, as they are closely correlated with the business cycle. Parkin is inconsistent on this issue, as he accepts the use of a labor market indicator, the famous Dow and Dicks-Mireaux index, by those investigators (Rushdy and Lund and McCallum) who find positive coefficients on it.

3. Parkin claims that the only correctly specified test equations in the Godley-Nordhaus article are those that relate price *changes* to the *level* of excess demand (and that show, the article maintains, that they are not). Parkin seems here, and elsewhere, to have forgotten that the Godley-Nordhaus hypothesis concerns not price changes as such but the relationship between price changes and cost changes. The only equation Parkin accepts implies that, if the demand term were significant, any level of excess demand would cause prices *relative to costs* (that is, gross profit margins) to rise forever, even if current high demand had fallen. The implied hypothesis, al-

though not wholly implausible, is rather less so than that tested in other specifications by Godley-Nordhaus that prices rise or fall relative to normal costs
in response to changes in demand. In this connection Parkin suggests that "in
the postwar British economy excess demand has been persistently positive,
hence imparting the persistent upward trend to the rate of inflation" and that
the Godley-Nordhaus results are consistent with this, or even confirm, it. To
be relevant to the Nordhaus-Godley work the expression "rate of inflation,"
as pointed out above, has to be understood as referring to the relationship
between prices and costs, that is, gross profit margins. But the data immediately indicate that gross profit margins had fallen continuously over the whole
period studied so that no part of the inflation was caused by prices rising in
relation to costs.

4. In any case, even if one accepts the specification preferred by Parkin
and eliminates the tests using labor market indicators of demand (where the
coefficients are negative), the positive coefficients are all statistically insignificant. They are also very small, effectively ruling out the possibility that the
role of demand (given costs) has been important.

5. Parkin states that the "regression equations estimating the relation between price change and normal cost change should, if the normal cost hypothesis is correct, yield an intercept of zero and the slope coefficient on normal cost change of unity." This is not correct; a zero constant and a slope
coefficient of unity would not necessarily be obtained if the normal price hypothesis were correct unless there were no errors in variables or omitted
variables and no autocorrelation of disturbances. Errors in the variables are
likely to have been large. The Godley-Nordhaus paper has imposed a constant gross markup on costs; it has also imposed a distributed lag based on
a priori considerations. These procedures have certainly introduced substantial errors—for one thing, as was known from the start, there has been a large
secular decline in gross profit margins—and these tend to bias the coefficients
downward. Our argument is that, however imperfect the normal price prediction, the normal price hypothesis (insofar as it relates to short-run behavior) would be confirmed if the residual between the prediction and actual
prices exhibited no cyclical properties.

6. Parkin's "fundamental identification problem" does not arise on his
own favored specification. If his contention is that the level of demand
changes price relative to cost, this should be easy to identify because the
Godley-Nordhaus work has purged cost changes by reference to changes in
demand. On the other hand, it is a matter of complete indifference to the
Godley-Nordhaus argument, whether or not the fact that prices are fixed as

though they were related to normal costs comes about as a compromise between cyclical forces on actual costs and the markup operating in opposite directions. However, there is no good reason to suppose that the two forces should be such as to offset one another exactly; the normal price hypothesis is the most economical one.

Robert Gordon referred to the statement in Godley's paper that if more fundamental agents of inflation operate by affecting only factor prices and not the markup of goods prices over factor costs, a monetarist interpretation of inflation has only limited applicability. This condition has no such implication: the idea that it reflects a basic misunderstanding of how money influences prices in the framework of a Phillips curve incorporating generalized expectations. This cannot be seen if one eliminates the wage equation entirely by writing the model in a reduced form. If wages are a function both of excess demand for goods or labor and of expected inflation, one can simply add an equation that says prices are a function of wages and thereby connect prices with the determinants of wages, eliminating wages from the equation completely and making prices a function of excess demand and expected inflation. If one then allows that monetary factors have any influence on excess demand for products, money becomes part of the process of setting prices. Moreover, it does not matter how large or small the coefficient on excess demand is in the wage or price equation; an increase in the money supply will raise the excess demand for products and that excess demand can be eliminated only by a rise of prices. In Britain demand pressure does not affect only the rate of change of wages; it also affects the price of imports because Britain is a major customer for many of its imports. Thus excess demand for products will work through both import prices and wages and thereby affect the general rate of inflation. There is no need for the emphasis Godley has put on the determinants of the markup of prices over factor costs. Also in question is the method used to test the equation explaining this markup. If one regresses a price index on factor costs and then looks for a correlation between the residuals and excess demand, the resulting estimate of the influence of demand pressure on prices will be biased toward zero if the price level and excess demand are positively related. The appropriate method is a multiple regression analysis in which both factor costs and excess demand are independent variables. This would avoid the econometric bias of a two-step method. Work has already been done on the cyclical behavior of the relation between transaction prices and list prices in the United States that might be relevant to the United Kingdom because all the price indexes used in the econometric models (not only Godley's) are list prices. It has been found that in the United States a recession is accompanied by a drop of 4 to 5 percent in transactions prices of durable goods relative to their list prices. If list prices are used, the relationship between excess demand and prices will be biased toward zero.

Wynne Godley responded to Gordon's comments by pointing out that if an increase in demand raised prices of manufactured goods independently of factor prices, control through demand management would be much easier. That is central to the paper's argument. Demand does operate both on the demand for labor and the cost of materials and the point about list prices is very important. The Godley-Nordhaus paper deals with this last point by constructing two different estimates of the gross output of nonfood manufacturing (free of duplication) and confronting them. On the one hand the wholesale price index for each year between 1954 and 1968 inclusive is multiplied by the corresponding index of production (1963 = 100 for both indexes) and the product is, in turn, multiplied by the value of gross output in 1963. The resulting value figures appear reasonably reliable because they agree closely with the figures recorded in the only other two years (1954 and 1968) when a census of production could provide a check. Next, estimates of the value of gross output for each year between 1954 and 1968 are built up by the use of estimates of all the elements of cost: wages and salaries, profits (excluding stock appreciation), materials, purchased services, and indirect taxes. Some of these estimates of cost (incomes and profits) can be obtained directly from the national income statistics whereas others have to be inferred from cost and production indexes; but once again the figures for census years provide a check that the estimating is reasonably accurate. The two estimates of gross output are confronted in the belief that, if price shading occurs, the first of the two should move procyclically in relation to the other. In the event, it is found that the residual is small and, rather surprisingly, if anything, it is *anticyclical*. The analysis, therefore, appears to rule out any significant shading of list prices in recession, and vice versa.

The criticism relating to the tests of the effect of demand on the relation of prices to normal costs is based on a misunderstanding. The residual between costs and prices used for this test is not a regression residual. The procedure was to forecast final prices with no reference at all to actual prices by constructing estimates of the individual elements of unit cost, imposing distributed lags on these derived a priori from stock-output ratios and adding up the cost components using input-output weights. The residuals tested for the effect of the demand are those between lagged unit costs so constructed and observed final prices, and are quite unconstrained by any prior fitting procedure.

In the Godley model import prices depend on factor costs in the rest of the world, but the paper omits any reference to a contribution of changes in factor costs in the rest of the world to price changes in Britain. That omission should be made good, because anything that happens to net aggregate monetary demand in the rest of the world will affect foreign costs and thereby the British price level. The effect of the omission has been to play down one element in the mechanism of international transmission. That mechanism is also understated by considering only import prices. The demand for domestic output depends at least partly on exports, and the prices of some manufactured exports are determined in world markets, which depend partly on world demand. The price index for goods in the domestic economy should therefore be a function not only of domestic excess demand but of world excess demand.

LARS CALMFORS

Inflation in Sweden

Tables

Figures

Lars Calmfors, Institute for International Economic Studies, Stockholm, was assisted in his work on the regression equations by Jan Herin, who also gave much valuable advice on the presentation. Lars Calmfors is indebted to Eva Hamberg, Jan Häggström, and Felix Nordström for research assistance, and would also like to thank William H. Branson, Stephen LeRoy, Assar Lindbeck, Erik Lundberg, Rudolf Rhomberg, Don Roper, Richard Snape, and the editors for helpful comments. He is grateful to Caroline Burton and Edda Liljenroth for their patience in typing a number of versions of the manuscript.

THE INTENTION of this paper is, first, to provide empirical data on Swedish inflation, with a focus on its increasing rate in the early 1970s; and second, to give an analytical interpretation of that data with emphasis on international dependence.

I shall not try to illuminate the Swedish experience from all possible points of view but rather to give an account of the "conventional wisdom" on inflation in Sweden. Because Swedish economists' opinions on the causes of inflation differ in certain respects from economists' ideas in other countries, especially in the United States, I believe that a survey of Swedish views may be valuable in introducing an approach to the analysis of inflation somewhat different from the usual one.

Wage and Price Movements, 1956–75

Sweden, like most Western countries, has had a marked increase in the rate of inflation during the early seventies. This is seen in figure 1, where changes in some price and wage indexes for Sweden are shown. Both prices and wages have increased at much faster rates since 1969–70. Whereas the average annual rate of increase of consumer prices was 3.9 percent between 1960 and 1969, it was 8.1 percent between 1970 and 1975. During the 1960s, hourly wages in industry increased by 8.7 percent a year, whereas the corresponding figure for 1970–75 was 14.5 percent.[1]

Figure 1 also shows a fairly normal business cycle pattern for Swedish inflation, with price increases reaching a peak (trough) around the upper (lower) turning point of the cycle. In 1972–73, however, the pattern was broken with unusually large price increases at the end of an unusually deep recession. This probably reflected the sharp acceleration at that time in international inflation, which gave rise to very significant export and import price increases.

That there is a close covariation between export and import prices on the

1. Wages have been calculated inclusive of all social costs and fees paid by employers.

Figure 1. *Annual Percentage Changes in Selected Swedish Price and Wage Indexes, 1956–75*

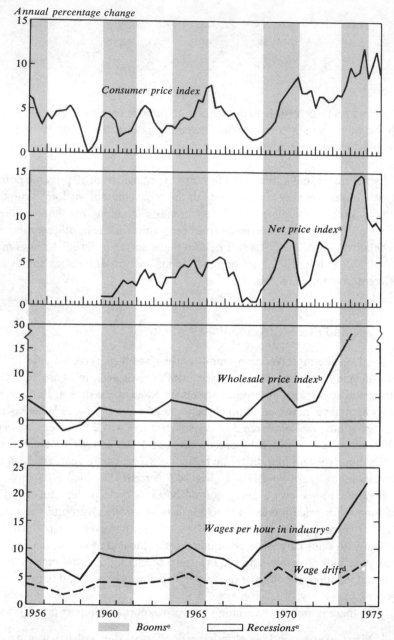

Sources: Data for the consumer price and net price indexes are from SCB [the Central Statistical Office], *Statistika Meddelanden*, various issues. Data for wages are from SAF [the

Figure 1 (*continued*)

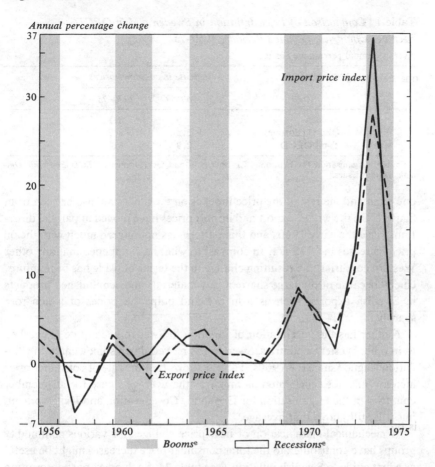

Annual percentage change

Import price index

Export price index

Booms[e]   Recessions[e]

Swedish Employers' Confederation], *Det ekonomiska läget* [*The Economic Situation*] and *Konjunkturläget* [*The Swedish Economy*], various issues. Data for the wholesale, export, and import price indexes are from *Konjunkturläget*, various issues.

Note. The percentage changes for the consumer and net price indexes are percentage differences between each quarterly average and the quarterly average of the previous year. For all other indexes the percentage differences are between each annual average and the annual average of the previous year.

a. Consumer price index net of indirect taxes and government subsidies.

b. Industrial commodities.

c. Calculated inclusive of all social costs and fees paid by employers.

d. Defined as the difference between ex post registered wage increases and the wage increases agreed upon in the central negotiations.

e. Booms and recessions are defined on the basis of the labor market situation. Booms are considered to have started one or two quarters after every lower turning point in labor market conditions (difference between the numbers of vacancies and unemployed) and to have ended one or two quarters after every upper turning point. The classification is taken from Assar Lindbeck, "Is Stabilization Policy Possible?—Time-Lags and Conflicts of Goals," in Warren L. Smith and John M. Culbertson, eds., *Public Finance and Stabilization Policy* (Amsterdam: North-Holland, 1974; distributed in the United States and Canada by American Elsevier), pp. 269–309.

Table 1. *Comparison of Price Inflation in Sweden and in OECD Member Countries, Selected Periods, 1960–75*
Average annual percentage change

	Increase in consumer prices	
Area	1960–69	1970–75
Sweden	3.9	8.1
OECD (Europe)	3.5	8.9
Total OECD	2.9	8.1

Source: Organisation for Economic Co-operation and Development, *OECD Economic Outlook*, various issues.

one hand and the rest of the price indexes on the other can also be seen from figure 1. On the whole, export and import prices have moved in parallel directions since the early 1960s and this pattern has not altered much with the oil price increases in 1973–74. In contrast to what has happened in many other Western countries, the resulting change in the terms of trade has been minor, chiefly because of the large share of raw materials and semifinished products in Swedish exports, such as iron ore and pulp, the prices of which rose sharply in 1973–74.

Neither has the acceleration of inflation in Sweden been quite as marked as in other Western countries. Sweden has moved down somewhat in the "inflation league" since the 1960s. Table 1 shows that the rate of consumer price increase has not accelerated as much as the average figure for all member countries of the Organisation for Economic Co-operation and Development, but it is still above that average.

A mechanical classification of how price changes for various commodity groups have contributed to the total consumer price increases might be useful as a first guide to Swedish inflation (see table 2). Such an ex post description of inflation is made annually by the Swedish National Bureau of Economic Research (Konjunkturinstitutet). The increase in the consumer price index is broken down as follows: changes in agricultural prices, changes in housing costs, changes in public fees, a trend deviation for perishables, changes in import prices, changes in indirect taxes, and an unexplained residual. This residual is calculated as the difference between the total increase of the consumer price index and the consumer price increases accounted for by the other components. It mainly represents price increases for domestically produced goods (exclusive of agricultural products and the regulated prices of housing and the services of the public sector).

This method of breaking down consumer price increases is not intended to provide a causal explanation of inflation since all indirect causations and mutual interdependences between the components are disregarded. For in-

Table 2. *Contributions of Various Components to Total Consumer Price Increases, Selected Periods, 1960–75*

	Average change (percentage points per year)[a]		
Component	1960–75	1960–69	1970–75
Indirect taxes	1.0	1.0	1.1
Import prices	1.0	0.2	2.3
Agricultural prices	0.3	0.3	0.3
Housing costs	0.8	0.6	1.0
Public fees	0.3	0.2	0.4
Trend deviation for perishables	0.0	0.0	0.1
Residual	2.0	1.5	2.8
Total consumer price increase	5.3	3.9	8.1

Sources: *Konjunkturläget* [*The Swedish Economy*] (Stockholm: Liberförlaget), various issues.

a. The figures in the table were calculated by multiplying the observed price increases for the various categories by their weights in the consumer price index. Since the categories are mutually exclusive, the figures for the components in the columns should add up to the total increases in the consumer price index. All discrepancies are due to rounding.

Beginning with 1971 automatic price increases due to the existence of ad valorem indirect taxes were added. Earlier, the residual took account of this factor. Here, it has been included in the residual for 1970–75, too, to get comparability with the earlier period.

stance, it is assumed that international price increases influence the consumer price index only through the immediate effects on prices of imported goods. Factors apparently not considered are that it becomes possible for import-competing firms and firms selling both on export and home markets to raise their domestic prices as well, that import and export price increases may give rise to wage increases leading to further price increases, and the like. Moreover, it is assumed that changes in indirect taxes are completely shifted onto prices. Obviously, then, too much importance should not be attached to the classification in table 2, but it nevertheless serves as an introduction to the analysis.

Table 2 shows, in fact, that the residual, the increases in indirect taxes, and the rises in import prices contributed most to Swedish price increases during the 1960–75 period. If the highly inflationary 1970–75 period and the earlier 1960–69 period are compared, nearly all components appear to have contributed to the higher rate of inflation. Although this method of breaking down increases underestimates the importance of price changes on the world market, the faster international inflation has plainly been the most important element. Import price changes directly contributed only about 0.2 percentage point to total consumer price increases during the 1960s. In 1970–75, however, they contributed about 2.3 percentage points. The residual, that is, mainly larger price increases for most domestically produced goods, was also important. During the 1970–75 period the residual's average annual value was more than 1 percentage point higher than in the 1960s. The public sector also contributed to the increased rate of consumer price increases in the 1970s because indirect taxes and public fees were raised at a faster rate than in the 1960s. To some extent this was the result of larger increases in the prices of goods and services purchased by the government, but a shift from direct to indirect taxation also played a role.

Effects of International Prices: The Aukrust-EFO Model

It seems by now to be generally recognized that, at least in the long run, the rate of inflation in a small open economy (like that of Sweden, in which exports and imports each constitute about one-quarter of gross national product) cannot deviate very much from the rates of inflation in other countries under a system of fixed exchange rates. Since the "bookkeeping" classification above indicates only the immediate effects on consumer prices of changes in import prices, a more comprehensive discussion of this international dependence is needed.

The literature on international inflation distinguishes between the following major channels for transmission of inflation between economies under fixed exchange rates:

Direct price influences. These are usually taken to include the effects on consumer prices of price changes not only for imports but for all tradables, that is, all commodities that are exposed to foreign competition. The effects on the prices of import-competing goods and goods sold both on domestic and foreign markets are thus included. Furthermore, price changes for tradables may affect wages because they influence profits, affect inflationary expectations, and trigger claims to compensate for a higher cost of living. Price changes for nontradables, that is, commodities that are sheltered from foreign competition, can be induced by such wage changes. (It seems customary to include these secondary effects under this heading as well.)

Keynesian income effects. Increased exports can set off a Keynesian multiplier process driving up aggregate demand to a new level that will then affect prices and wages. The Swedish business cycle seems mainly to be a consequence of such variations in exports.

Monetary liquidity effects. If there is a surplus in the balance of payments, the foreign component in the domestic monetary base will increase. Unless completely offsetting sterilization measures are taken, the domestic money supply will consequently increase, entailing a rise in aggregate demand that will raise the rate of inflation.

Direct effects on wages. Inflation abroad may influence wage increases directly through effects on inflationary expectations, if these are affected by price and wage increases in other countries. Moreover, the behavior of trade unions can be influenced by wage increases obtained by trade unions in other countries by means of so-called demonstration effects.

Because the above effects are often intertwined, it is hard to distinguish between them, either in theory or practice. For a satisfactory treatment, a complete model of the Swedish economy would probably have to be developed. The aim of this paper is more limited; only one of these influences, namely, the direct price links and their compatibility with aggregate demand conditions will be discussed. Direct price effects have been stressed most by Swedish economists when trying to explain the increase in the rate of inflation in recent years.[2] It should be obvious that Keynesian income effects or monetary liquidity effects working by means of aggregate demand did not cause the acceleration of Swedish inflation in the early 1970s since it coincided with an unusually deep recession. Indeed, it will be argued in this paper that the major part of the increase in the Swedish rate of inflation can be explained by direct price links.

The so-called Aukrust-EFO model is an attempt to elaborate these direct price links. The model was developed almost simultaneously by the Norwegian, Odd Aukrust,[3] and by a group of Swedish economists—Gösta Edgren, Karl-Olof Faxén, and Clas-Erik Odhner—in the EFO report.[4] In the model the economy is divided into two sectors: one producing tradables, exposed to foreign competition, and the other producing nontradables, sheltered from foreign competition.

If input-output relations between the two sectors are disregarded, and it is assumed that export and import prices move in parallel directions—apparently a good approximation for Sweden—the propositions of the model are the following:

1. A small open economy meets an infinitely elastic excess demand (or supply) for tradables on the world market, which means that the rate of price increase for tradables in this economy has to equal the rate of price increase

2. See, for example, Lars Calmfors and Erik Lundberg, *Inflation och arbetslöshet* (Stockholm: Studieförbundet Näringsliv och Samhälle, SNS [The Business and Social Research Institute], 1974); or Erik Lundberg, N. Lundgren, L. Matthiessen, and G. Ohlin, "Kris eller konjunkturuppgång?" Konjunkturrådets rapport 1974/75 (Stockholm: SNS, 1974; processed).

3. Odd Aukrust, "Wage-Price Interdependencies in Open Economies" (Oslo: Statistisk Sentralbyrå [Central Bureau of Statistics], 1972; processed). See also Aukrust, "Inflation in the Open Economy" (the Bureau, 1974; processed).

4. Gösta Edgren, Karl-Olof Faxén, and Clas-Erik Odhner, *Wage Formation and the Economy* (London: Allen and Unwin, 1973). The EFO report derives its name from the first letters in the authors' surnames.

on the world market under fixed exchange rates. The sector producing tradables is thus a price taker on the world market.

2. The rate of wage increase in the sector producing tradables is equal to the rate of increase in the value of average labor productivity, that is, approximately the sum of the rates of increase of price and productivity in this sector.

3. Because the sector producing tradables acts as a wage leader, the rates of wage increase in the two sectors have to be equal. Both market forces and the "solidaristic wage policy" of Swedish trade unions, that is, their attempts to raise wages uniformly in the whole economy, work in this direction.[5]

4. Prices in the sector producing nontradables are determined by a constant markup on unit labor costs, meaning that the rate of price increase in that sector can be obtained approximately as the difference between the rates of wage and productivity increase. Because productivity increases are smaller for nontradables their prices will increase more than prices of tradables.

5. The total rate of increase in consumer prices is finally arrived at as a weighted average of the rates of price increase for the two types of commodities. From the mathematical derivation below, it can be seen that the total rate of consumer price increase may be expressed as the sum of the rate of price increase for tradables (equal to the rate of price increase on the world market) and the difference between the rates of productivity increase in the two sectors, this difference being multiplied with the weight of nontradables in the consumer price index. According to this model, a more rapid world inflation as well as a greater difference between productivity increases in the two sectors will thus be inflationary.

If

p_T = the rate of change of the price of tradables

p_w = the rate of change of world market prices

w_T = the rate of change of wages in the sector producing tradables

q_T = the rate of change of labor productivity in the sector producing tradables

w_N = the rate of change of wages in the sector producing nontradables

p_N = the rate of change of the price of nontradables

q_N = the rate of change of labor productivity in the sector producing nontradables

5. In the Swedish wage negotiation round, agreements are generally made first for industry, and other sectors then follow suit. The wage leadership of industry—the major part of the sector producing tradables—has also been established empirically by Lars Jacobsson and Assar Lindbeck in "On the Transmission Mechanism of Wage Change," *Swedish Journal of Economics,* vol. 73 (September 1971), pp. 273–93.

p_c = the rate of change of the consumer price index
e_T = the weight of tradables in the consumer price index
e_N = the weight of nontradables in the consumer price index,[6]

the propositions of the Aukrust-EFO model can be written as follows:[7]

$$p_T = p_w$$
$$w_T = p_T + q_T$$
$$w_N = w_T$$
$$p_N = w_N - q_N$$
$$e_T + e_N = 1$$
$$p_c = e_T p_T + e_N p_N = (1 - e_N)p_w + e_N(w_N - q_N)$$
$$= (1 - e_N)p_w + e_N(p_w + q_T - q_N) = p_w + e_N(q_T - q_N).$$

The Aukrust-EFO model undoubtedly gives a simple and elegant description of important aspects of inflation in a small open economy like Sweden's. The model, however, presents several analytical problems; it is a partial model that is not intended to present a complete picture of the inflationary process. Most of these problems will be dealt with only in passing. The emphasis will instead be on the relation to explanations of inflation stressing the demand side, which is not explicitly taken into account in the model. Demand necessary to validate price and wage increases determined from the supply side is assumed as always forthcoming, which is unsatisfactory. Furthermore, the relation of the Aukrust-EFO model to the framework stressing the role of price expectations in the inflationary process needs to be examined.

Indeed, the behavioral assumptions about price and wage setting of the Aukrust-EFO model do not yet seem to have been shown satisfactorily to fit the empirical facts. Because this must be done, if the model is to be used for explaining inflation, I examine the evidence on price and wage formation in Sweden more closely to determine whether the assumptions of the model are supported. Regressions are made on both price and wage changes and on the basis of these regressions a simple model showing the interdependences between prices and wages in the Swedish economy is derived. The results are compared with the Aukrust-EFO model, and it is argued that this model should be interpreted as applying to the long run, whereas it cannot very well explain short-run variations in the rate of inflation.

6. Because there are only two types of goods in the model, e_N and e_T must, of course, add to one.
7. As a general rule, rates of change are denoted by small letters, whereas capital letters show levels of the same variables. Sectors will be indicated in subscript; time indexes, when necessary, in superscript.

Price Formation

Price formation for tradables and nontradables is examined in this section. The same classification as in the EFO report is used, that is, tradables will broadly correspond to manufactured goods and nontradables to nonmanufactured goods.[8] Since little work has been done on price formation in Sweden, some new regression equations are estimated.

Nontradables

In examining price formation for nontradables the basic hypothesis is that this market does not clear instantaneously, because prices adjust slowly to pressures of excess demand or excess supply. The rate of price change in such disequilibrium situations is assumed to be affected by demand-pull, cost-push, and expectations variables, the influences of which are studied. Demand-pull factors are measured by the level of current excess demand, or supply. The reason for including expectations and cost-push variables besides the level of excess demand is that these are thought to affect the rate of price increase not only indirectly, because changes in them shift the demand and supply curves in the market (that is, change the level of excess demand), but also directly. These variables are thus assumed to have an influence on price setting by firms that is independent of currently prevailing market conditions. The influence of cost-push factors could be explained by the rule-of-thumb method (for example, because market conditions are difficult to judge), such as applying a markup to unit labor costs. In the Aukrust-EFO model this markup is assumed to be constant; in that case the rate of price increase for nontradables would equal the difference between the rates of increase of wages and labor productivity. According to the new microeconomics, price

8. The following kinds of economic activities are included in the sector producing tradables: (1) forestry and logging, (2) fishing, (3) mining and quarrying, (4) manufacturing, except sheltered food manufacturing and manufacture of beverages and tobacco, and (5) transport between Sweden and other countries.

Included in the sector producing nontradables are: (1) agriculture, (2) sheltered food manufacturing, (3) manufacture of beverages and tobacco, (4) production of electricity, gas, and water, (5) construction, (6) wholesale and retail trade, restaurants, and hotels, (7) inland transport and storage, (8) communications, (9) financing, insurance, real estate, and business services, and (10) community, social, and personal services.

The shares in GNP are approximately one-third for tradables and two-thirds for nontradables.

expectations should influence price setting independently of current demand and supply conditions, because price changes are costly and made at discrete time intervals. It is worthwhile for a firm, therefore, to try to take into account the anticipated future course of prices when pricing decisions are made.[9]

The above hypotheses were tested by regressing the rate of change in the price of nontradables (p_N) on the following variables.[10]

1. The rate of change of unit labor costs in the sector producing nontradables. This factor was approximated by the difference between the rates of increase of wages and labor productivity in the sector, $(w_N - q_N)$.[11]

2. The level of excess demand for nontradables. As a proxy for this variable the gap between actual GNP (Y) and potential GNP (Y_f) divided by potential GNP was used.[12]

3. The expected rate of price change for nontradables. As a proxy the rate of price change for nontradables during the previous year $\left(p_N^{t-1}\right)$ was used.[13]

4. The rate of change of world market prices (p_w). The index used was

9. See David Laidler and Michael Parkin, "Inflation—A Survey," *Economic Journal*, vol. 85 (December 1975), pp. 741–805. The influence of cost-push factors on the rate of price increase in a disequilibrium situation could perhaps also be explained with reference to price expectations if, for example, the rate of change of unit labor cost is taken to determine the expected rate of price increase. To investigate this possibility, survey data on actual price expectations held seems necessary. However, this question is not particularly interesting except from a terminological point of view.

10. Data on p_N, p_T, q_N, q_T, w_N, and w_T have been taken from the EFO report up to 1968, and from calculations made by the Swedish Confederation of Trade Unions (Landsorganisationen i Sverige, LO) for 1968–73. Price and productivity data refer to values added at factor cost.

11. It should be noted that the figures used for changes in labor productivity are the observed figures, which have not been corrected for cyclical deviations from the trend. Constructing a measure of standard productivity was tried, but this gave a lower coefficient of correlation in the regression equation than the uncorrected figures.

12. Unfortunately, it was not possible to construct separate measures of excess demand for tradables and nontradables. Potential GNP has been calculated by fitting a trend to the actual values of GNP.

13. Time indexes are shown in superscript. For the expected rate of price increase, an adaptive error-learning mechanism was tried:

$$\pi_N^t = \pi_N^{t-1} + \lambda\,(p_N^{t-1} - \pi_N^{t-1})\quad 0 \leq \lambda \leq 1$$

where π denotes the expected rate of price increase. Although different values of λ were tried, the highest coefficient of correlation for the regression equation was obtained by setting $\lambda = 1$, which gives

$$\pi_N^t = p_N^{t-1}.$$

an export price index for manufactured goods from market economies,[14] a variable included to test the sector division made in the EFO report and to account for changes in input prices.

The following equation was estimated for nontradables on the basis of annual data on rates of change:[15]

$$(1) \quad p_N^t = 0.65 + 0.39(w_N^t - q_N^t) + 0.41\, p_N^{t-1} + 0.19\, p_w^t + 0.06\, \frac{Y^t - Y_f^t}{Y_f^t}.$$
$$ (2.66) (2.31) \phantom{p_N^{t-1} +} (1.71) (0.35)$$

Estimation period, 1956–72: $R^2 = 0.77$; $\bar{R}^2 = 0.69$; Durbin-Watson statistic = 2.08.

Equation 1 shows that changes in unit labor costs and expected price increases both proved to be significant at the 5 percent level. Changes in world market prices and excess demand were not significant, however, even at the 10 percent level.[16] The result for price changes on the world market could be taken to support the reasonableness of the distinction between tradables and nontradables made in the EFO report. It might be considered more surprising that excess demand did not prove to be significant. This result did not change, even when different lag structures were experimented with. One explanation might be that the proxy for excess demand is not a good one. It has also been concluded, however, in many empirical studies for other countries, that excess demand in commodity markets does not seem to exert strong direct

14. The source for this index is United Nations, *Yearbook of International Trade Statistics*. In the index the various countries are weighted by their shares in world trade. It would have been preferable to have a price index in which the countries are weighted by their shares in the foreign trade of Sweden. The index used, however, can serve as an approximation. It should be noted that if p_w is regarded as a proxy for changes in input prices, the coefficient for this variable could be negative in the equation, because the price index for nontradables is an index for value added in this sector. The reason that the variable could be negative is that an increase in input prices might simultaneously cause an increase in the price of final output and a decrease in the price of value added. If changes in input prices are completely shifted onto output prices, the price of value added should not, of course, be affected.

15. All rates of change in the regression equations are changes from one annual average to another in percentage points unless stated otherwise. Thus, for example,

$$p_N = \frac{\Delta P_N}{P_N} \times 100,$$

where P_N is the price of nontradables and p_N the rate of change of this price. The values in parentheses under the coefficients in the equations are t-values.

16. It should be noted that the inclusion of the lagged dependent variable as one of the independent variables means, strictly speaking, that the usual significance here is not quite appropriate. However, it has been concluded that the bias arising from this is very small and "that no serious error is committed if we apply the usual methods conceived for regression models to the treatment of autoregressive models." (See Edmond Malinvaud, *Statistical Methods of Economics* [Amsterdam: North-Holland, 1966; distributed in the United States and Canada by American Elsevier], p. 456.)

influences on commodity prices.[17] But this does not mean that aggregate demand conditions are unimportant for inflation. It might be that prices adjust slowly in response to excess demand pressures. An increase in aggregate demand would then lead primarily to an expansion of output and thus to increased demand for labor with consequent wage increases, which then feed back on commodity prices by means of a markup process. These results may also be explained by the fact that excess demand for nontradables in an open economy spills over swiftly onto the world market and causes increased imports of tradables instead of rising prices for nontradables.

Reestimated without the nonsignificant terms equation 1 becomes:

(1a)
$$p_N^t = 0.23 + 0.53(w_N^t - q_N^t) + 0.41\,p_N^{t-1}.$$
$$\quad\quad\quad\quad\quad (4.70) \quad\quad\quad\quad (2.72)$$

$$R^2 = 0.64; \; \bar{R}^2 = 0.59; \; \text{Durbin-Watson statistic} = 2.32.$$

Thus it appears that both changes in unit labor costs and price expectations influence price changes for nontradables.[18] That the sum of the coefficients for these two variables is close to one means that the rates of change of unit labor costs and prices are approximately equal, when price changes are perfectly anticipated. This is easily seen if p_N^{t-1} is set equal to p_N^t. The following is then obtained (if time indexes are omitted):

(1b)
$$p_N = 0.23 + 0.53(w_N \quad q_N) + 0.41\,p_N$$
$$p_N = 0.39 + 0.90(w_N - q_N).$$

Because the constant term is close to zero[19] and the coefficient for changes in unit labor costs is close to unity, it can be concluded that markup pricing seems to be a fair description of pricing behavior in the sector producing nontradables in a long-run steady state, when price increases are perfectly anticipated.

Tradables

In the case of price formation for tradables the basic hypothesis regarding this market is that there is an infinitely elastic foreign excess supply (demand) so that all discrepancies between domestic supply and demand for

17. Compare, for example, William D. Nordhaus and Wynne Godley, "Pricing in the Trade Cycle," *Economic Journal*, vol. 82 (September 1972), pp. 853–82.

18. Because the lagged dependent variable appears as an independent variable, the coefficient for P_N^{t-1} has a somewhat downward bias. I have not tried to correct for this bias because it is very small and because such a correction might create other statistical problems (increasing the mean squared error). (See J. Johnston, *Econometric Methods: Second Edition* [Tokyo: McGraw-Hill–Kogakusha, 1972], pp. 305–07.)

19. All rates of change in the equations are measured in percentage points.

tradables are filled by net imports (exports). This market is thus assumed to clear at a price determined on the world market under fixed exchange rates, neglecting all impediments to trade. The rate of change of the Swedish price of tradables would then have to equal the rate of change of world market prices, as is assumed in the Aukrust-EFO model. This hypothesis is examined below.

In the equation for nontradables, the influences of domestic demand-pull, cost-push, and price expectations variables were also studied. These factors should not be expected to affect the rate of price increase for tradables according to my hypothesis. To make as fair a test as possible, however, the role of these variables for price formation in this sector, too, are examined. Consequently, the rate of price change for tradables, p_T, was regressed on the same variables as before,[20] but with the difference that the rate of change of unit labor costs and the expected rate of price increase would then refer to the sector producing tradables.[21] This gave the following equation:

$$(2) \quad p_T^t = -0.47 + \underset{(4.36)}{0.88\, p_w^t} - \underset{(1.39)}{0.40\, p_T^{t-1}} + \underset{(1.38)}{0.21(w_T^t - q_T^t)} + \underset{(0.41)}{0.12} \left(\frac{Y^t - Y_f^t}{Y_f^t} \right).$$

Estimation period, 1956–72: $R^2 = 0.73$; $\bar{R}^2 = 0.64$; Durbin-Watson statistic = 2.13.

Equation 2 seems to support the hypothesis that only price changes on the world market exert an important influence on price changes for tradables. Price changes on the world market are significant at the 1 percent level. The GNP gap and changes in unit labor costs have the expected signs but are not significant even at the 10 percent level. Expectations of future price increases enter with a negative sign but are also not significant at the 10 percent level. If the equation is reestimated without the nonsignificant terms, the result is:

$$(2a) \qquad\qquad p_T^t = -0.45 + \underset{(5.15)}{0.78\, p_w^t}.$$

$R^2 = 0.64$; $\bar{R}^2 = 0.62$; Durbin-Watson statistic = 2.32.

The constant term is close to zero and the coefficient for changes in world market prices is not significantly different from one on the 5 percent level.[22]

---

20. The price index used for tradables refers to domestically produced tradables only and not to imported goods.

21. As before, the rate of change of unit labor costs is approximated by the difference between the rates of change of wages and labor productivity ($w_T - q_T$). The rate of price increase for tradables in the previous years, p_T^{t-1}, is used as a proxy for the expected rate of price increase. A scheme of adaptive expectations was tried here, too, but the specification above gave the highest coefficient of correlation for the regression equation.

22. An exact correspondence, of course, could not be expected since the index for prices of tradables refers to the value added in this sector, whereas the index for world market prices is for final manufactured goods.

The hypothesis that prices of tradables in Sweden have to rise at about the same rate as world market prices for industrial commodities therefore appears consistent with the data.

Summary

If results regarding price formation in the Swedish economy are summarized, the following seems to hold:

1. Price changes for nontradables (using the same definitions as in the EFO report) seem to be determined by changes in unit labor costs and expected price increases. No significant influences from excess demand on the commodity market or from changes in world market prices could be traced. When price changes are perfectly anticipated, price increases seem to be approximately equal to changes in unit labor costs.

2. Price changes for tradables seem to be determined by price changes on the world market for industrial commodities. No significant influences from domestic excess demand, price expectations, or changes in unit labor costs could be found.[23]

Wage Formation

The principal hypothesis regarding wage formation is that the sector producing tradables acts as a wage leader. I first attempt, therefore, to explain wage changes in this sector and then to link to them wage changes in the sector producing nontradables.

Previous studies

Much work has been done in Sweden on wage formation, and I shall begin by briefly describing some of these earlier findings. The emphasis has been

23. The above results could be compared with some preliminary findings of Franz Ettlin and Johan Lybeck, "A New Econometric Model of Sweden: Some Main Features of the Step 1 Model" (Stockholm School of Economics, Economic Research Institute, 1974; processed). They have estimated regression equations for prices in manufacturing and nonmanufacturing. According to them, prices in manufacturing depend on prices in the United Kingdom and West Germany (the two main competitors of Sweden on the world market), past prices in manufacturing, and the rate of growth of international trade. Prices in nonmanufacturing are explained by current and past unit labor costs and the rate of change in output in that sector. The steady-state solutions of their equations are, however, very similar to my results. In such a situation, price increases in nonmanufacturing approximately equal increases in unit labor costs, and price increases in manufacturing approximately equal price increases in the United Kingdom and West Germany, if exchange rates are fixed.

on wage changes for workers in industry, broadly corresponding to the sector producing tradables. The traditional approach has been to split wage changes into negotiated wage changes and wage drift (each contributing about half of total wage increases), which are explained separately.[24] This is the method used by Lars Jacobsson and Assar Lindbeck.[25] The distinction is made because there are probably somewhat different mechanisms determining wage drift and negotiated wage increases: the former the result of market forces, that is, employers bidding for labor, and the latter the result of a centralized bargaining process. Wage drift may also be taken to respond faster to various impulses, inasmuch as it involves continuous changes, whereas wage negotiations give rise to step-wise changes. Because centralized wage bargains often span fairly long periods (from one to three years), negotiated wage increases for a given year other than the first year of a bargain period are probably uninfluenced by current conditions.

Jacobsson's and Lindbeck's basic hypothesis is that the labor market normally is in a state of disequilibrium, and that the rate of wage change therefore depends on the level of excess demand, or supply, in the market. They also find that various proxies for demand and supply conditions give a rather good explanation of both wage drift and negotiated wage increases in the 1950s and the 1960s, the period of their study. They do not find significant influences from profits, changes in productivity, or changes in prices, if these are included besides labor market variables in the regression equations.[26] As a measure of the labor market situation, the difference between the numbers of vacancies and unemployed (that could be taken as a direct measure of excess demand on the labor market) proved better than unemployment alone. This might be explained by the effect on the relation between wage changes and unemployment of the dispersion of unemployment between different labor submarkets. Because of the curvature of the Phillips curve (relating wage changes to unemployment only), a higher rate of wage increase should be expected for a given total unemployment rate, the more unevenly unemploy-

24. Wage drift is calculated as the difference between ex post registered wage increases and the wage increases agreed upon in the central negotiations.

25. See Lars Jacobsson and Assar Lindbeck, "Labor Market Conditions, Wages and Inflation—Swedish Experiences 1955–67," *Swedish Journal of Economics,* vol. 71 (June 1969), pp. 64–103, and Jacobsson and Lindbeck, "On the Transmission Mechanism of Wage Change," *Swedish Journal of Economics,* vol. 73 (September 1971), pp. 273–93.

26. In their 1971 article, however, they do not reject the hypothesis that unusually large price increases might affect wage setting.

ment is distributed between submarkets.[27] The relation between wage changes and the difference between the numbers of vacancies and unemployed ought to be less affected by changes in the dispersion of unemployment, since an increased unevenness in the distribution of unemployment should increase the number of vacancies as well.

Current analysis

In figures 2 and 3 the relations between wage increases in industry and the difference between the numbers of vacancies and unemployed for the period 1956–75 are shown. The results obtained by Jacobsson and Lindbeck for the 1950s and 1960s seem to be confirmed. It is obvious that wage drift could be explained well by an ordinary Phillips curve up to the end of the 1960s.[28] From 1970 onward, however, the observations lie significantly above the regression line for the earlier period. Inasmuch as there are no theoretical reasons for expecting the earlier positive partial derivative of wage drift with respect to the difference between the numbers of vacancies and unemployed to have disappeared, it seems plausible to assume that the earlier Phillips curve has shifted upward. Although the number of observations for the 1970s is small, the drawing of a new and higher regression line seems indicated.

A somewhat similar pattern may be traced for negotiated wage increases. Because the number of observations is small, care should be taken in drawing conclusions, but it appears that the difference between the numbers of vacancies and unemployed explains rather well negotiated wage increases up to the end of the 1960s. The observations for 1971–73 and 1975–76, however, lie far above the earlier regression line.

Obviously, then, the earlier observed Phillips curve seems to have broken down because it cannot explain the wage increases in the early 1970s. This is, of course, not solely a Swedish phenomenon; the same observations have been made for almost every developed Western country. It seems necessary to try to arrive at new explanations of wage formation in Sweden.

A suitable extension of the Jacobsson-Lindbeck analysis would be to include inflationary expectations along with a measure of excess demand for labor in the wage equations, as has been done in many empirical studies for

27. Compare also George L. Perry, "Changing Labor Markets and Inflation," *Brookings Papers on Economic Activity*, 3:1970, pp. 411–41.

28. The Phillips curve in the following text relates wage changes to the difference between the numbers of vacancies and unemployed.

Figure 2. *Wage Drift in Relation to Labor Market Conditions, 1956–75*

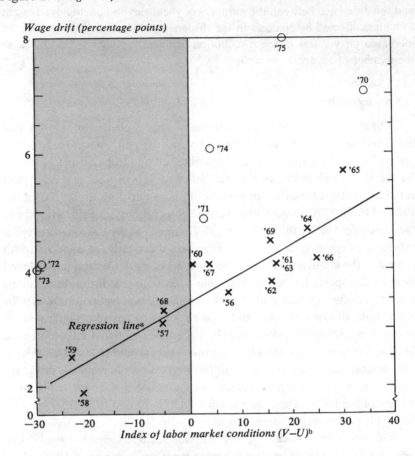

Wage drift (percentage points)

Index of labor market conditions (V−U)[b]

Sources: The wage data are based on calculations by the Konjunkturinstitutet [National Bureau of Economic Research]. The number of vacancies and unemployed were calculated from data supplied by the AMS [Labor Market Board], *Arbetsmarknadsstatistik.* A more detailed description of the derivation of the data is given in Lars Calmfors and Erik Lundberg, *Inflation och arbetslöshet* (see note 2 for full citation).

a. The equation of the regression line is:

$$w_D = 3.45 + 0.05 \ (V-U).$$
$$(7.35)$$

Estimation period, 1956–69; $R^2 = 0.82$; $\bar{R}^2 = 0.81$; Durbin-Watson statistic $= 2.28$; the number in parentheses is the t-value.

b. Difference in thousands between numbers of vacancies and unemployed $(V-U)$. The following weighting system for $V-U$ in year t has been used:

Year	Second quarter	Fourth quarter
year $t-1$	0.125	0.375
year t	0.375	0.125

Figures for the first and third quarters are not included because variations in winter weather and summer vacations render them difficult to interpret.

Figure 3. *Negotiated Wage Increases and Labor Market Conditions, 1956–76*

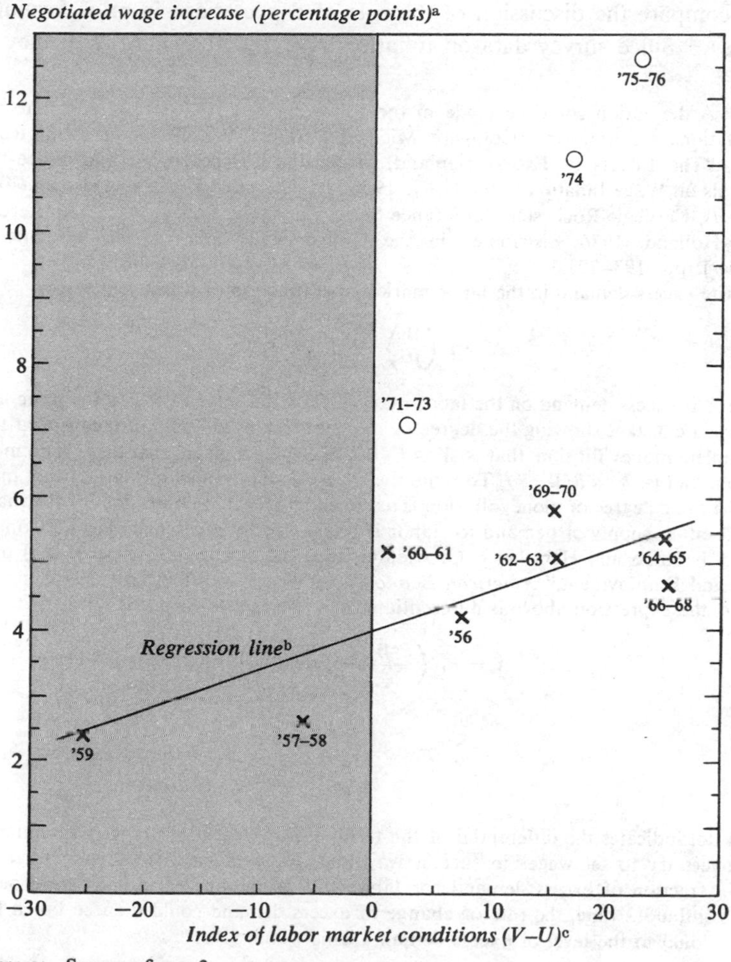

Negotiated wage increase (percentage points)[a]

Index of labor market conditions $(V-U)$[c]

Sources: Same as figure 2.

a. The negotiated average annual wage increase for each wage agreement has been treated as *one* observation. Increases in social costs and other fees paid by employers known at the time of the bargain have been included in negotiated changes, since these increases in labor costs could be considered as being deducted from the "room" for wage increases.

b. The equation of the regression line is:

$$w_A = 3.98 + 0.06\ (V-U)$$
$$(3.38)$$

Estimation period, 1956–70; $R^2 = 0.66$; $\bar{R}^2 = 0.63$; Durbin-Watson statistic $= 1.95$; the number in parentheses is the t-value.

c. Difference in thousands between numbers of vacancies and unemployed $(V-U)$. The difference for a given bargain period has been calculated as the average of the figures for the fourth quarter of the year before and the second quarter of the year in which the agreement was made (see also figure 2, note b).

other countries. These expectations are thought to influence wage changes independently of prevailing supply and demand conditions in the labor market (compare the discussion of the role of expectations in price formation above).[29] Since survey data on inflationary expectations are rare, they are

29. A derivation could be made in the following way, if it is assumed that price expectations are uniform. (Compare Michael Parkin, Michael Sumner, and Robert Ward, "The Effects of Excess Demand, Generalized Expectations and Wage-Price Controls on Wage Inflation in the U.K.: 1956–71," *The Economics of Price and Wage Controls,* Carnegie-Rochester Conference Series on Public Policy, vol. 2 [Amsterdam: North-Holland, 1976; distributed in the United States and Canada by American Elsevier], pp. 193–221.)

Write excess demand in the labor market as a function of wages and prices:

$$X = F\left(\frac{W}{P^\alpha}\right) \qquad 0 \leq \alpha \leq 1$$

where X is excess demand on the labor market, W is the wage rate, P is the price level, and α is a constant showing the degree of money illusion. If $\alpha = 0$, it means that there is complete money illusion, that is, $X = F(W)$; if $\alpha = 1$, it means that there is no money illusion, that is, $X = F(W/P)$. To write the excess demand functions in this way means that the same degree of money illusion is assumed to prevail on both sides of the market or that either supply or demand for labor is unaffected by prices and wages. (Compare Robert J. Barro and Herschel I. Grossman, "A General Disequilibrium Model of Income and Employment," *American Economic Review,* vol. 61 [March 1971], pp. 82–93.) If the expression above is differentiated with respect to time it is:

$$\dot{X} = F_1 \cdot \left(\frac{P^\alpha \dot{W} - \alpha \dot{P} W P^{\alpha-1}}{P^{2\alpha}}\right),$$

where

$$F_1 = \frac{\delta F}{\delta\left(\dfrac{W}{P^\alpha}\right)},$$

and a dot indicates the differential of the term with respect to time. Now, assume that employers try to set wages in such a way that, for a given rate of price change, a certain fraction of excess demand for labor will be eliminated in each time period. With continuous time, the rate of change of excess demand could then be taken to be proportional to the level of excess demand. This would give:

$$\dot{X} = -\lambda X,$$

where λ is a constant and

$$-\lambda X = F_1 \cdot \left(\frac{\dot{W}}{P^\alpha} - \frac{\alpha \dot{P} W}{P^{\alpha+1}}\right).$$

This might be rewritten as:

$$\frac{\dot{W}}{W} = -\frac{\lambda X}{F_1 \cdot \left(\dfrac{W}{P^\alpha}\right)} + \alpha\left(\frac{\dot{P}}{P}\right).$$

If it is assumed that F_1 and W/P^α are single-valued functions of X, the rate of wage

usually derived in some way from past price changes.[30] This procedure, however, raises problems, since it is not at all clear that a relation between wage
increases and past price increases reflects only the influence of price expectations. It may well be that past and current price increases affect the relation
between wage changes and excess demand directly and not only because of
expectations. In my view, the role of inflationary expectations in wage formation has probably been somewhat exaggerated in recent literature on inflation
at the expense, for example, of claims for compensation for earlier or current
unanticipated changes in consumer prices and claims for a fair share of past
or current profit increases, which are the result of unanticipated increases in
producer prices. In interpreting a relation between wage and price increases
it often seems safe merely to conclude that such a relation exists, without
specifying whether or not the mechanism works because of expectations. This
is the approach to be followed here.

Although Jacobsson and Lindbeck could not find much empirical support
for including price increases in the wage equations, they point out that it is
possible that the rate of inflation did not vary enough in the period examined
to give statistically significant results. A rather stable rate of inflation might
have been built into the Phillips curve of the 1960s. With the higher rates of
price increases in the early 1970s, however, there ought now to be a greater
possibility of detecting the influence of price increases.

Tradables

What type of prices should be included in the wage equation is an important question. It is usual to use consumer price changes, because wage earners
are thought to compensate themselves for increases in the cost of living. But

---

increase might be rewritten as a function only of excess demand for labor and the rate
of price increase, thus:

$$\frac{\dot{W}}{W} = G(X) + \alpha \left(\frac{\dot{P}}{P}\right),$$

where

$$G(X) = -\frac{\lambda X}{F_1 \cdot \left(\frac{W}{P\alpha}\right)}.$$

The next step is then to interpret $\dot{P}/P$ as the expected rate of price increase. As indicated
in the text, however, this interpretation is not the only one possible.

30. In some studies on wage formation, expected wage increases are included instead
of expected price increases (compare, for example, Stephen J. Turnovsky, "The Expectations Hypothesis and the Aggregate Wage Equation: Some Empirical Evidence
for Canada," *Economica*, new series, vol. 39 [February 1972], pp. 1–17). But a general
result seems to be that wage expectations perform worse than price expectations in the
wage equations.

it is not clear that consumer prices constitute the relevant price variable. It may be that the price increases influencing wage formation are more connected with employers' ability to pay. If this is so, wage increases in an open economy like that of Sweden, where the sector producing tradables acts as a wage leader, ought to be heavily influenced by price increases for tradables or, possibly, by price and productivity increases in this sector (as the Aukrust-EFO model assumes). Another reason for the importance of price changes in this sector, touched upon in the discussion of international transmission of inflation, could be that inflationary expectations—whether referring to consumer or to producer prices—in an open economy may, to a large extent, be determined by inflation abroad, for which increases in prices of tradables should be a good proxy, at least under fixed exchange rates. This seems to be a plausible hypothesis for Sweden, since a general opinion among businessmen and trade union officials holds that the Swedish rate of inflation is very dependent on export and import prices.

To test the above hypotheses on wage formation in an open economy, wage changes in the sector producing tradables (w_T) were regressed on the difference between the numbers of vacancies and unemployed ($V - U$) and on price and productivity changes in this sector (p_T and q_T, respectively). Because it was not possible to decompose my figures on wage changes into wage drift and negotiated wage increases, only one equation for total wage changes was estimated.[31] The following equation was found to give a good fit:[32]

$$(3) \qquad w_T^t = 6.25 + \underset{(3.53)}{0.08(V - U)} + \underset{(2.44)}{0.31\, p_T^{t-1}} + \underset{(2.13)}{0.18\, (p_T^t + q_T^t)}.$$

Estimation period, 1958–73: $R^2 = 0.70$; $\bar{R}^2 = 0.63$; Durbin-Watson statistic $= 1.98$.

It thus appears that wage changes in the sector producing tradables can be explained by a weighted difference between the number of vacancies and un-

---

31. The same wage data as in the section on price formation were used. The figures thus refer to wage increases for all persons employed in the sector producing tradables, whereas the figures of Jacobsson and Lindbeck were for workers in industry only.

32. $V - U$ for year t was calculated using the following weighting scheme:

Year	Second quarter	Fourth quarter
$t - 2$	0.125	0.125
$t - 1$	0.250	0.250
t	0.125	0.125

The first and the third quarters are excluded for the same reasons as in figures 2 and 3. The labor market situation is believed to affect total wage increases with a fairly long lag, because wage negotiations often concern a period of several years. $V - U$, as before, is measured in thousands.

employed, the rate of change of prices during the previous year, and the sum of the current rates of change of prices and productivity in the sector.[33] Since price changes for tradables were earlier shown to be determined by international price increases, these evidently exert an important influence on wage changes apart from their effect on demand and supply conditions on the labor market. But price—and productivity—increases for tradables affect wage formation much less, according to equation 3, than could be expected from the Aukrust-EFO model. Elimination of the lags in the equation gives coefficients for these variables that are far from unity, the value predicted by that model.

Nontradables

In regard to wage formation in the sector producing nontradables the hypothesis is that the rate of wage change there, w_N, follows that in the sector producing tradables. To test the hypothesis equation 4 was estimated:

$$(4) \qquad w_N^t = 0.22 + 0.92\,w_T^t.$$
$$(5.07)$$

Estimation period, 1956–72: $R^2 = 0.63$; $\bar{R}^2 = 0.61$; Durbin-Watson statistic $= 2.18$.

The equation is consistent with the hypothesis. Moreover, it seems that wage increases in the two sectors have to be approximately equal, as they should be according to the Aukrust-EFO model. If the expression for w_T in equation 3 is inserted into equation 4, this could be rewritten in the following way:

$$(4a) \qquad w_N^t = 5.97 + 0.07(V - U) + 0.29\,p_T^{t-1} + 0.17\,(p_T^t + q_T^t).$$

Noneconomic factors

An important feature in both equations 3 and 4a is the presence of a large constant term that could be taken to indicate a strong element of autonomous wage-push in wage increases. Variations in this factor probably account for a large share of the unexplained variance of wage increases. It may be that especially negotiated wage increases are much affected by noneconomic factors that are hard, or impossible, to catch in a regression equation, a plausible

33. The inclusion of consumer price changes was tried—during the previous year in order to avoid simultaneity problems—in equation 3, but this variable turned out to be insignificant even at the 10 percent level, a surprising result in view of the strong role played by claims for compensation for increased costs of living in the arguments of trade unions. One explanation could be that claims for compensation of this kind are important only when some critical value for the rate of consumer price increase is exceeded.

explanation in view of the political character of centralized wage bargaining. A short digression, therefore, on the importance of such factors seems appropriate.

During the last few years, in many countries, a growing awareness of income differentials is apparent and a mounting feeling prevails that the present distribution of income is unfair, thereby causing a kind of wage-wage spiral —where successful attempts of one group to improve its relative pay position provoke claims for compensation from other groups, and so on (compare, for example, the United Kingdom).[34] This process was obvious in Sweden in the late 1960s and early 1970s, with heavy political emphasis on increased equality in those years. The struggle between different labor market organizations for relative wages was pronounced in the wage negotiations leading to the 1969–70 and 1971–73 wage agreements. In these negotiations, the Swedish Confederation of Trade Unions (LO) managed to secure substantial wage increases for their low-income groups and this provoked further claims from white-collar workers and high-income groups. These income-distribution conflicts were reinforced by a highly progressive tax system, through which increases in real disposable income for all wage earners were held down, thus diminishing the room for redistribution of real disposable incomes between different groups. The conflicts over income distribution during these years contrast rather sharply with earlier years, when there seemed to have been something of a tacit agreement on how to distribute the total wage increases between various groups. It is possible that an increased degree of wage-push contributed to the increased rate of wage increases in the early 1970s. This assumption is supported by the fact that my wage equations underestimate wage changes in 1970–73 (as is shown in figure 4). In the wage negotiations for the 1974 and 1975–76 bargains these income-distribution struggles were much less apparent, owing probably to the fact that income tax adjustments were coupled with wage negotiations.

By admitting the existence of autonomous wage increases of this sort I do not deny that for a continuous wage-push inflation to be possible, there must be a validating economic policy—monetary and/or fiscal policy—so that aggregate demand is maintained. Because of the political priority given to the goal of full employment, trade unions may, however, expect the necessary validation of cost-push increases to be forthcoming through an endogenously determined economic policy. This should especially be the case after a long period of successful employment policies such as that of the

34. See Stephen Marris's statement in the panel discussion of world inflation in Emil Claassen and Pascal Salin, eds., *Stabilization Policies in Interdependent Economies* (Amsterdam: North-Holland, 1972; distributed in the United States and Canada by American Elsevier), pp. 303–06.

Figure 4. *The Phillips Relation and the Aukrust-EFO Conditions for Wage Formation*

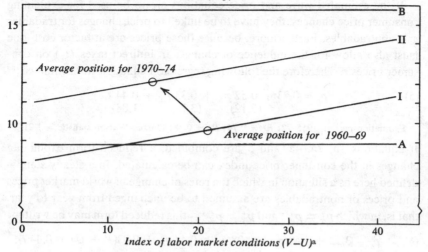

Percentage wage change, tradables sector (W_T)

Index of labor market conditions ($V-U$)[a]

Sources: Text wage equation 3 and the Aukrust-EFO model described in text. See note below.

a. The difference, in thousands, between the numbers of vacancies and unemployed.

Note. The two Phillips relations in the diagram (lines I & II) have been calculated by inserting mean values for p_T^{t-1} and $(p_T^i + q_T^i)$ for the 1960–69 and 1970–74 periods in wage equation 3. The results are the following two equations:

$$w_T = 0.08 \ (V-U) + 7.95 \ (1960\text{–}69)$$
$$w_T = 0.08 \ (V-U) + 10.7 \ (1970\text{–}74)$$

A comparison with table 4 indicates that the wage equation underestimates average wage increases for 1970–74 somewhat. However, this does not change the main arguments. Lines A and B represent "room" for wage increases, the exogenously determined sum of price and productivity increases in the sector producing tradables, for the 1960–69 and 1970–74 periods, respectively.

1960s in Sweden, which probably weakened the "unemployment ghost" as a factor restraining trade unions. Greater insight into the inflationary process could probably be gained by giving more attention to the question of how economic policy responds to wage-push disturbances.

Wage-Price Interdependences and the Aukrust-EFO Model

Price and wage formation are discussed separately above, but here wage and price equations are analyzed together to highlight wage-price interdependences and the influences of international price increases on Swedish consumer prices. The results are compared with the Aukrust-EFO model, the interpretation of which is further discussed in light of the empirical findings.

If the estimated wage and price equations are to be used for explaining consumer price changes, they have to be linked to price changes for tradables and nontradables. Furthermore, because those prices are at factor cost, one must also allow for the influence of changes in indirect taxes (t_i) on consumer prices.[35] Therefore the following regression equation was estimated:[36]

$$(5) \qquad p_c = 0.73 + 0.52\ p_N + 0.33\ p_T + 0.44\ t_i.$$
$$\qquad\qquad\qquad (3.12)\qquad (3.14)\qquad (1.88)$$

Estimation period, 1955–72: $R^2 = 0.74$; $\bar{R}^2 = 0.68$; Durbin-Watson statistic $= 1.91$.

If equations 1a, 2a, 4a, and 5 are combined, a reduced form explaining changes in the consumer price index can be calculated. In a steady state—defined here as a situation in which the rates of change of world market prices and prices of nontradables are assumed to be unchanged from year to year, that is, in which $p_w^t = p_w^{t-1}$ and $p_N^t = p_N^{t-1}$—this reduced form may be written:

$$(6) \qquad p_c = 3.52 + 0.43\ p_w + 0.08\ q_T - 0.47\ q_N + 0.03(V - U) + 0.44\ t_1.$$

The results, according to the equation, could be summarized as follows:

1. The large constant term in the equation seems to indicate that there is an important autonomous component in price increases. This component emanates mainly from the wage equation for the sector producing tradables.

2. There is a strong influence from price changes on the world market. The coefficient for this variable, however, is far from unity, which is the value predicted by the Aukrust-EFO model.

3. Productivity increases in the production of tradables have a small positive influence, because wage increases are affected, but this influence is also smaller than predicted by the Aukrust-EFO model.

4. Productivity changes in the sector producing nontradables exert a

35. The term t_i is defined as the product of the rate of change of indirect taxes and their weight in the consumer price index.

36. Another possibility would have been to calculate the weights of tradables and nontradables in the consumer price index. Exact calculations are hard to make, however, since the classification of commodities in the national accounts cannot be carried over directly to the consumer price index. Estimating the weights in a regression equation was therefore preferred. The estimations seem to square reasonably well with the shares in GNP (one-third for tradables and two-thirds for nontradables).

It should be noted that my price index for tradables refers to domestically produced exportables and importables and thus does not measure import prices. The regression therefore rests heavily on the close covariation between changes in export and import prices observed for Sweden. Including price changes for imported fuels and raw materials in the equation was attempted, but these proved not to be significant even at the 10 percent level.

strong downward pressure on consumer prices, because they tend to hold down the rate of increase of unit labor costs in that sector.

5. The labor market situation—measured as the difference between the numbers of vacancies and unemployed—is of great importance because of a Phillips curve for wage changes. This difference can change by about 100,000 from the bottom of a recession to the top of a boom, which means a change in the rate of increase of consumer prices by 3 percentage points.[37]

Equation 6 can be used for highlighting differences in inflation between the 1960s and the early 1970s. If average values for the exogenous variables in the two periods are inserted, steady-state values for the rate of consumer price change can be calculated. The steady-state values need not of course correspond to the actual values, but do nevertheless give a good indication of the importance of the various factors. In table 3 it is shown how each of such exogenous variables has contributed to the calculated steady-state rates of inflation in 1960–69 and 1970–74.

Table 3 makes it clear that the increased rate of international inflation has been by far the most important variable in the acceleration of Swedish inflation. It accounts for an increase in the predicted rate of change of consumer prices by 4.5 percentage points, a figure that should be compared to the actual increase of 4.2 percentage points. Changes in the other variables do not seem to have been of great significance. It is particularly noteworthy that aggregate demand pressures, caught by the labor market variable, have not contributed to the increase in the rate of inflation according to my equation. Whereas the difference between the numbers of vacancies and unemployed accounted for 0.6 percentage point of average annual consumer price increases in the 1960s, as table 3 shows, the contribution in the early 1970s was only 0.4.

In comparing the above results on price and wage formation with the Aukrust-EFO model, the assumptions of the model regarding prices seem to be supported by my findings. Prices of tradables seem to change at approximately the same rate as world market prices, and prices of nontradables do change at about the same rate as unit labor costs, when price increases are perfectly anticipated. But the regression equations on wage formation show price—and productivity—increases in the sector producing tradables to have much smaller influences than in the Aukrust-EFO model. This explains why the coefficient for the rate of change of world market prices in equation 6 is only 0.43, a figure significantly different from unity, which is the value predicted by the Aukrust-EFO model. I found instead that the labor market situation was important for wage determination and, consequently, for price

---

37. $V - U$ is measured in thousands in equation 6.

Table 3. The Contribution of Various Variables to the Average Annual Rate of Change of Consumer Prices, 1960–69 and 1970–74[a]

Period	Constant	World market prices, p_w	Labor productivity (tradables sector), q_T	Labor productivity (nontradables sector), q_N	Vacancies minus unemployed, $V - U$	Indirect taxes, t_i	Consumer price index	
							p_c, steady state	p_c, actual
1970–74	3.5	5.2	0.5	−1.5	−0.4	0.5	8.6	8.1
1960–69	3.5	0.6	0.7	−1.8	0.6	0.5	4.1	3.9
Difference	0.0	4.6	−0.2	0.3	−0.2	0.0	4.5	4.2

Source: Text equation 6.

a. The inserted average values for the exogenous variables during the two periods are:

	p_w	q_T	q_N	$V - U$	t_i
1970–74	12.0	6.7	3.1	14.8	1.2
1960–69	1.4	8.4	3.8	20.2	1.2

formation as well. Demand effects of this type are missing in the Aukrust-EFO model.

Can my results be reconciled with this model? It will be argued here that they can be, if due allowance is made for the interrelation between the labor market situation and price and productivity changes in the sector producing tradables, and if the Aukrust-EFO model is taken to apply to the long run. This also seems to be the interpretation of Aukrust himself, whereas the Swedish authors of the EFO report seem to vacillate between different interpretations of the model.

One method of reconciling the Aukrust-EFO model with explanations relating inflation to demand is provided in a paper by Henryk Kierzkowski,[38] who shows that under certain, rather specific assumptions the Aukrust-EFO conditions emerge from a general equilibrium analysis in which all resources are assumed to be fully employed if price changes for tradables and technical progress in the two sectors are determined exogenously. The interpretation here is somewhat vaguer, although perhaps a little closer to reality. In my view there are strong inherent factors in an open economy like Sweden's that tend to hold the profit share in the sector producing tradables fairly constant over longer periods, that is, that force wages to increase at about the same rate as prices and productivity in this sector. At least three forces tend to make wage-push and demand pressures adjust to levels compatible with the Aukrust-EFO conditions:

1. A more or less constant long-run profit share may be a reasonable compromise for both employers and trade unions to accept in the wage bargainings, even if this was not caught in the regression equations. It may be that such forces start to work only after some critical values have been exceeded or after very rapid changes in profits.

2. Aggregate demand is affected by profits. If the rate of price increase for tradables goes up, causing the share of profits in this sector to increase, production and investment will probably rise, inducing an expansion of aggregate demand in the whole economy.[39] Demand for labor will increase, affecting especially wage drift, which seems to be very responsive to the labor market situation. This effect will tend to counteract changes in the share of profits in the sector producing tradables.

---

38. Henryk I. Kierzkowski, "Theoretical Foundations of the Scandinavian Model of Inflation" (London: London School of Economics, International Monetary Research Programme, September 1974; processed).

39. I would venture the guess that expansionary effects of price increases for tradables of the type mentioned above are much more important than the real-balance effects working in the opposite direction, which are stressed so often in monetary theory.

3. A more or less constant share of profits could be an important aim for economic policy. To a large extent, fiscal and monetary policies may be endogenous because "the nation manages its macroeconomic policy with one eye on the external balance."[40] The share of profits in the sector producing tradables may be an important determinant of "the international competitiveness" of a country. If prices of tradables start to increase faster than unit labor costs in this sector, it seems likely that the external balance will improve under fixed exchange rates. If, because of the surplus in the balance of payments, monetary and fiscal authorities allow aggregate demand to increase and excess demand for labor to rise, wages will start to increase at a faster rate, forcing the share of profits in the sector producing tradables down again.[41] Balance of payments considerations may thus mean that economic policy is managed in such a way that the long-run profit share in this sector remains more or less constant.[42] But other factors too may be at work. The government may, on the one hand, try to avoid increases in the profit share because of income-distribution considerations and, on the other hand, try to avoid decreases in the profit share because of investment (and thus long-run economic growth) considerations. Such reasoning appears to have played some role in Sweden.

To summarize the arguments above, the estimated equations show that the Aukrust-EFO conditions for wage formation do not hold in the short run. Thus there is scope for short-run changes in the share of profits in the sector producing tradables. In the long run, however, aggregate demand in the economy may adjust, partly because of automatic effects and partly as a result of an endogenously determined economic policy. Over longer periods, then, wages will increase at about the same rate as the sum of prices and productivity in the sector producing tradables, if this result is not arrived at directly through the wage bargaining process. The Aukrust-EFO conditions for wage formation may then be said to determine the point on the Phillips curve where the economy will be in a long-run equilibrium, in which prices and productivity in the sector producing tradables increase at constant rates, and the share of profits is constant from period to period. This point could be shown as the intersection of the Phillips curve—for given price and productivity increases—and a horizontal line showing the sum of price and productivity

40. Richard E. Caves, "Looking at Inflation in the Open Economy," in David A. Belsley and others, eds., *Inflation, Trade, and Taxes* (Ohio State University Press, 1976), pp. 75–95.

41. It seems probable that the reactions of policymakers to disequilibria in the balance of payments are much more important than the automatic monetary effects.

42. The argument should be even more forceful in the case of decreases in the share of profits in the sector producing tradables since, under fixed exchange rates, deficits in the balance of payments could force the government to adopt contractive policies.

increases (see figure 4). An acceleration of the rate of price increase for tradables would mean upward shifts of both the Phillips curve and the horizontal line. But because the coefficient for the rate of increase of prices of tradables is significantly smaller than unity in the steady-state solution of wage equation 3, the Phillips curve would shift less than the horizontal line indicating the room for wage increases. Consequently, a larger number of vacancies and a smaller number of unemployed will be compatible with the new long-run equilibrium in which prices and unit labor costs in the sector producing tradables increase at the same rates. A change in the rate of price increase for tradables will thus mean both a shift of the Phillips curve and a movement along it (figure 4). With this interpretation there is no contradiction between the Aukrust-EFO model and the Phillips curve. Indeed, the existence of a Phillips curve, that is, a positive partial derivative of wage increases with respect to excess demand on the labor market, seems to be necessary for this interpretation to hold.[43]

If the Aukrust-EFO conditions for wage formation are conceived of in this way, it is possible to sketch a simple interpretation of some important aspects of Swedish economic development in the 1960s and early 1970s. This interpretation, while not the only one possible, should perhaps best be regarded as an illustration of the factors that I, and probably most Swedish economists, feel have been important.

Table 4 shows that annual average wage increases in the 1960s exceeded the sum of price and productivity increases in the sector producing tradables, thus squeezing the profit share in this sector. This could be interpreted as a

---

43. The above interpretation of the relation between the Aukrust-EFO model and the Phillips curve seems similar to Aukrust's described in this volume. It can also be compared with that of William Branson and Johan Myhrman in "Inflation in Open Economies: Supply-Determined versus Demand-Determined Models," *European Economic Review*, vol. 7 (January 1976), pp. 15–34. According to them, the rate of inflation is determined by a Phillips curve relationship for the whole economy:

$$p = f\left(\frac{Y - Y_f}{Y_f}\right),$$

whereas the Aukrust-EFO equation

$$p = p_T + e_N(q_T - q_N)$$

determines the share of nontradables (and thus of tradables, too) in total production. Instead, my interpretation is to regard the shares in production of the two sectors as fixed and to let the Aukrust-EFO equation determine the long-run rate of inflation, which means that the long-run level of excess demand (on the labor market, in my model) is determined by the Phillips curve. To introduce variable shares of tradables and nontradables in production into the analysis (which I have not tried to do) is a valuable extension of the Aukrust-EFO model. But if this is attempted, it seems more natural to relate these shares to relative prices, as Branson and Myhrman do in another part of their paper.

Table 4. *Average Annual Price, Productivity, and Wage Increases in the Swedish Tradable Sector According to the Aukrust-EFO Model, Selected Periods, 1960-74*

Percent

Description	1960-69	1970-74	1960-74
Price increase	0.5	9.1	3.3
Productivity increase	8.4	6.7	7.8
Room for wage increase	8.9	15.8	11.1
Actual wage increase	9.7	12.2	10.4

Source: See page 505, note 10.

consequence of demand-pull factors working during that period. In terms of a Phillips curve, it might be said that, as an average in the 1960s, the labor market situation was so tense as to give wage increases according to the Phillips curve of that period (line I in figure 4) considerably in excess of the exogenously determined sum of price and productivity increases in the sector producing tradables. (This "room" for wage increases is shown by line A.)

It is probably reasonable to say that the government welcomed this squeeze of profits for income distribution reasons. For a long time the depressive effects on employment of falling profits could be counteracted by an expansion of the public sector. But toward the end of the 1960s it became apparent that there might be a serious conflict of goals between income distribution and balance of payments considerations. Deficits on the current account appeared both in the boom years of 1965–66 and 1969–70. These deficits seem mainly to have been caused by too slow an expansion of capacity in the sector producing tradables in relation to demand for tradables, because of the profit squeeze in this sector and the development of relative prices. These thoughts predominated in a report of a government committee drawing up policy guidelines for 1971–75, in which a long-run expansion of investment in this sector was set up as a primary goal.[44]

The current-account deficit in 1969–70 seems to have been regarded by government politicians as a symptom of a serious balance of payments crisis, a crisis met not by a devaluation of the Swedish crown but by restrictive monetary (mainly in 1969 and 1970) and fiscal policies (especially in 1971). These contractive policies evidently made the 1971–73 recession very much more severe, in comparison both with contemporary developments in other countries and with earlier Swedish experiences.

Instead, to sustain full employment, a more expansive economic policy than usual in a recession would have been called for because special depres-

44. *Svensk ekonomi 1971–1975 med utblick mot 1990,* Statens offentliga utredningar (SOU) 1970:71 (Stockholm: Finansdepårtmentet, 1970).

sive factors, such as a heavy dampening of investment demand from municipal authorities (due to financing problems), a drastic cut in housebuilding (as a result of earlier overproduction), and an unexpected increase in household savings, would have had to be counteracted. To some extent the restrictive policies can probably be explained by misjudgments of the situation; nevertheless, it is hard to escape the conclusion that the political authorities attached a greater value to the maintenance of a fixed exchange rate than to keeping down unemployment.

The 1971–73 recession could be shown in figure 4 as a movement to the left (a smaller difference between the number of vacancies and unemployed). But because of the increased rate of international inflation, the Phillips curve, as well as the line indicating the room for wage increases, shifted upward in the early 1970s (to the lines marked II and B, respectively). Since the economy was rather far to the left on the new Phillips curve, however, wage increases during 1970–74 did not fill up the room. Consequently, the profit share in the sector producing tradables increased again, which can be seen from table 4. As it should be expected, the current account also improved considerably from 1970 to 1973 because of the low level of aggregate demand and because prices of tradables increased at a faster rate in relation to prices of nontradables and wages than in the earlier period. The deterioration in 1974 was due almost exclusively to the oil price increases.

With fixed exchange rates, price increases for tradables are determined only by price increases on the world market. But today only about 40 percent of Sweden's foreign trade is with countries like itself that participate in the deutsche mark bloc. With more flexible exchange rates, price increases for tradables (in Swedish crowns) would no longer be determined only by price changes on the world market, but by exchange rate changes, too. A continuous appreciation of the Swedish crown against an average of other currencies at an unchanged rate of price increase on the world market would, for example, mean downward shifts of both the Phillips curve and the horizontal line in figure 4 indicating the room for wage increases. Problems in this connection are discussed in the following section, where the possibility of using exchange rate variations as a means of fighting inflation is examined.

Policies against Inflation

Below is a brief assessment of policy measures taken against inflation, followed by a review of some of the ways of fighting inflation suggested by the Aukrust-EFO model.

Since World War II,[45] fiscal policy has been used for counteracting business cycle fluctuations. Especially during the period 1955–63 there was a very pronounced countercyclical pattern. Generally speaking, however, policy measures often seem to have been undertaken somewhat too late. Expansionary policies, initiated in recessions, have been abandoned too late in the upswings, thus contributing to inflationary pressures, particularly in the 1964–65 and 1969–70 booms. Sometimes restrictive actions aiming at counteracting booms have also been cut off very late in the downswings. The most obvious example is the above-mentioned deflationary policy in the recession year of 1971. The timing of fiscal policy measures, on the whole, seems to have deteriorated somewhat during the last ten years compared to the late 1950s and early 1960s.

The rate of growth of money supply shows a countercyclical pattern, too. It reflects both the countercyclical fiscal policy (with budget deficits increasing the money supply in recessions, and budget surpluses reducing it in booms) and a countercyclical monetary policy. A similar pattern for monetary policy can also be found from variations in interest rates.[46] In general, it seems as though monetary policy has reacted with somewhat shorter lags to changes in the business cycle situation than fiscal policy. It is probably correct to say that countercyclical fiscal and monetary policies have smoothed the fluctuations in the rate of inflation and counteracted serious internal inflationary pressures. As shown above, however, the trend rate of inflation seems to have been determined mainly by the rate of international inflation.

With respect to the growth of money supply, the long-run association implied in a crude version of the quantity theory fits the facts well as table 5 shows, although the association implies nothing as to the causality. If 1960–69 and 1970–75 are compared, the difference between the average growth rates of money supply and real output approximates very well the actual rate of consumer price changes for both periods. Without a discussion of the causal relation implied by table 5, it can probably be concluded that long-

45. Fiscal policy in Sweden has been analyzed thoroughly by Assar Lindbeck in his book, *Swedish Economic Policy* (University of Califorina Press, 1974), and in his chapter, "Is Stabilization Policy Possible?—Time-Lags and Conflicts of Goals," in Warren L. Smith and John M. Culbertson, eds., *Public Finance and Stabilization Policy* (Amsterdam: North-Holland, 1974; distributed in the United States and Canada by American Elsevier), pp. 269–309. See also Lars Matthiessen, "Finanspolitiken som stabiliseringspolitiskt instrument," in Erik Lundberg, ed., *Svensk finanspolitik i teori och praktik* (Stockholm: Aldus/Bonnier, 1971).

46. See Assar Lindbeck, *Swedish Economic Policy,* or Johan Myhrman, *Kreditmarknad och penningpolitik* (Stockholm: SNS [The Business and Social Research Institute], 1974), for a more detailed account of Swedish monetary policy.

Table 5. *Money Supply and Inflation, 1960–69 and 1970–75*
Average of annual percentage change

Variables	1960–69	1970–75
Growth in money supply[a]	8.5	10.2
Growth of real GNP	4.3	2.8
Actual consumer price change	3.9	8.1
Hypothetical consumer price change[b]	4.2	7.4

Sources: Prices, see table 1; money supply, Konjunkturläget [*The Swedish Economy*], various issues; GNP, the national accounts.

a. Cash balances of the public, plus demand and time deposits in commercial banks, savings banks, the farmers' savings associations, and the Post Office Bank (M_3).

b. Difference between first and second rows.

run increases in money supply seem at least to have been compatible with the inflation that has taken place.

These two periods present a contrast in that between 1960 and 1969 most of the increase in money supply seems to be accounted for by domestic credit creation, whereas between 1970 and 1975 most of the increase comes from growing foreign exchange reserves. This is implied by table 6, where the contributions to the growth of the monetary base of the domestic and foreign components are shown. The increases of foreign exchange reserves in the latter period were chiefly the result of the swing to considerable surpluses on the current account in 1971–73. This development, however, came to an abrupt end in 1974, when the current account turned into a deficit because of the oil price increases.

Although the authorities adopted countercyclical fiscal and monetary policies, it is probably fair to say that they attached much more importance to the goal of full employment than to the goal of price stability in the 1960s, even though, on several occasions, they acknowledged the need to reduce the rate of inflation. This policy of full employment was particularly successful in the early 1960s, during which there were no serious balance of payments problems. The expanded activities of the Labor Market Board (such as retraining programs, relief works, incentives in order to increase labor mobility, and the like) may perhaps be seen as an attempt to mitigate the inflation-unemployment trade-off, but these attempts were not enough to counteract the upward shift of the Phillips curve.

In fact, it seems as though an inflation rate of some 4 percent a year was regarded as an unavoidable price for high employment in the 1960s. Such a rate of inflation might also be claimed to be optimal for the government from other points of view. On the one hand, it was not high enough to cause general resentment. On the other hand, it provided easy financing for the expan-

Table 6. *Contribution of Foreign Exchange Reserves and Domestic Credit to the Growth of the Monetary Base, 1960–69 and 1970–75*
Average of annual percentage changes

	Average per year	
Variables	*1960–69*	*1970–75*
Growth of monetary base[a]	6.0	13.4
Growth of foreign exchange reserves	3.9	23.4
Growth of foreign exchange reserves weighted by the share of foreign exchange reserves in the monetary base[b]	1.9	9.1
Growth of domestic credit	9.7	7.7
Growth of domestic credit weighted by the share of domestic credit in the monetary base[b]	4.1	4.3

Source: *Sveriges Riksbank 1975, arsbok* [The 1975 Annual Report of The Swedish National Bank] (Stockholm: the Bank, 1976).

a. The monetary base is defined as the sum of outstanding notes and demand deposits of the commercial banks at the central bank. Since changes in money supply mostly have correlated well with changes in the monetary base, it seems plausible to draw conclusions concerning the influences on money supply from a discussion of the monetary base. In 1974, however, there was a very large increase in the domestic component of the monetary base because of open market operations in connection with the raising of reserve requirements of commercial banks. The table, therefore, significantly overestimates the contribution of domestic credit creation to the increases in money supply for 1970–75 (domestic credit actually contracted in 1970–73).

b. The shares of domestic credit and foreign exchange reserves in the monetary base are measured as of the beginning of each year.

sion of the public sector because of the progressive tax system.[47] Moreover, inflation probably facilitated the attempts to obtain a more equalized wage structure, which was an important goal for the Social Democratic government at the end of the 1960s. It was probably easier for high civil servants, for example, to accept real income decreases, when nominal wages still increased. The government showed that it was prepared to accept more inflation in exchange for a more equitable income structure when, in the 1970–71 wage negotiations, it offered its low-income employees very substantial wage increases, which had an inflationary impact on the whole economy.

It was not until the acceleration of inflation in the early 1970s that the fight against inflation became a priority. The comparatively restrictive stabilization policy in the 1971–73 recession seems to have been motivated mainly by a concern for the balance of payments, but to some extent it could perhaps also be seen as an attempt to hold back inflation. It did in fact slow the rate of inflation compared with that in other countries.

Attempts have also been made at some kind of incomes policy, though not so comprehensive as, for example, in the United Kingdom and the United States. From the end of 1970 to the end of 1971 there were almost complete

47. Compare the analysis of the effects of a progressive tax system below.

price controls. Through these price controls, the government hoped to influence the 1970–71 wage negotiations by reducing expectations of price increases. But since price increases due to negotiated wage increases were allowed, it probably did not have much dampening effect. In 1973–74 selective price controls (for example, for food) were in effect. The government body for price surveillance (SPK) also became more active. Price increases were also held down significantly through the subsidizing of food prices.

That no attempts at directly regulating wage increases were made was presumably because of the close ties between the governing Social Democratic party and the trade unions. Starting in the fall of 1973, however, a policy for influencing wage negotiations in an indirect way was initiated. Wage earners obtained increases in disposable incomes through reductions of personal income taxes in exchange for restraint in wage negotiations. The policy was supposed to be neutral with respect to the government budget deficit (surplus), since employer fees were raised to make up for the expected loss of tax revenues.

If used properly, this device can be a very powerful weapon against inflation, at least in the short run; large groups of wage earners have moved up into tax brackets where the progressiveness is so high that it is, in fact, impossible to obtain increases in real disposable incomes through increases in nominal wages only.[48] These effects can be illustrated by a few formulas.

Let

t_m = marginal tax rate

t_a = average tax rate

w = the rate of change of nominal wages before tax

x = the rate of change of nominal wages after tax

p_c = the rate of change of the consumer price index

$\bar{y}$ = the rate of change of real wage income after tax

p_N = the rate of price change for nontradables

q_N = the rate of change of labor productivity in the production of nontradables

e_N = the weight of nontradables in the consumer price index

p_T = the rate of price change for tradables

q_T = the rate of change of labor productivity in the production of tradables

e_T = the weight of tradables in the consumer price index.

48. First to point to effects such as these was Erik Lundberg in *Business Cycles and Economic Policy* (Harvard University Press, 1957). See also Lars Matthiessen, "Index-Tied Income Taxes and Economic Policy," *Swedish Journal of Economics,* vol. 75 (March 1973), pp. 49–66, or Lars Calmfors and Erik Lundberg, *Inflation och arbetslöshet.*

Then the following relation must hold:[49]

$$\bar{y} = x - p_c = \left(\frac{1 - t_m}{1 - t_a}\right) w - e_T p_T - e_N p_N.$$

If it is assumed that prices of tradables are determined on the world market and thus exogenously given to the economy and that prices of nontradables are determined by a constant markup on unit labor costs—assumptions that are supported by my price equations, if the influence of expectations on price changes for nontradables is disregarded—then:

$$\bar{y} = \frac{1 - t_m}{1 - t_a} w - e_T p_T - e_N(w - q_N)$$

$$= w \left[\frac{1 - t_m}{1 - t_a} - e_N\right] - e_T p_T + e_N q_N.$$

It is obvious that the value of $[(1 - t_m)/(1 - t_a)] - e_N$ is critical. If $[(1 - t_m)/(1 - t_a)] > e_N$, the expected result will follow that the larger the increase in pretax nominal wages, the larger the increase in after-tax real wage income. However, if $[(1 - t_m)/(1 - t_a)] < e_N$, the paradoxical result obtained is that the larger the increase in nominal pretax wages, the smaller the increase in real after-tax wage income. The reason is that nominal wage increases give rise to tax and price increases that are more than offsetting.[50]

49. $(1 - t_m)/(1 - t_a)$ is the elasticity of after-tax income with respect to pretax income. If an income earner gets a wage increase in crowns before tax of ΔW, his wage increase in crowns after tax will be $(1 - t_m)\Delta W$. If his previous pretax wage income was W, and thus his previous after-tax wage income $(1 - t_a)W$, the rate of increase of after-tax wage income will be

$$x = \frac{\Delta X}{X} = \frac{(1 - t_m)\Delta W}{(1 - t_a) W} = \frac{1 - t_m}{1 - t_a} w.$$

The elasticity $(1 - t_m)/(1 - t_a)$ can be taken to measure the progressiveness of the tax system. If it is progressive, $0 < (1 - t_m)/(1 - t_a) < 1$, and the lower the value the higher the progressiveness. If $(1 - t_m)/(1 - t_a) = 0$, a wage earner would not get any increase in after-tax income from pretax income increases. If $(1 - t_m)/(1 - t_a) = 1$, it is implied that $t_m = t_a$, which means that the tax system is proportional.

50. The most clear-cut case, of course, is for a closed economy. Then $e_N = 1$ and $e_T = 0$, which means that the expression above becomes:

$$\bar{y} = w \left[\frac{1 - t_m}{1 - t_a} - 1\right] + q_N.$$

Then larger nominal wage increases before tax will always give rise to smaller real wage income increases after tax, if the tax system is progressive. Because of the markup hypothesis, prices will always rise in the same proportion as wages, whereas taxes will rise more than proportionally. Real wage income after tax will increase as long as

$$q_N > w \left[1 - \frac{1 - t_m}{1 - t_a}\right].$$

It is then possible to be in a situation where significant increases in nominal wages before tax give rise to decreases in the real wage income after tax.

Because of the high tax progressiveness and rapid inflation, Sweden now seems to be in a situation where it is not possible for the majority of wage earners to obtain increases in real wage incomes after tax unless systematic revisions of the tax system are undertaken, as a numerical example illustrates. The marginal tax rate for an average wage earner (receiving a housing allowance dependent in size on his income) is about 60 percent, whereas the average tax rate is approximately 20 percent. Assume that the annual rate of price increase for tradables is 6 percent and the annual rate of productivity increase in the sector producing nontradables 3 percent. If $e_N = 0.6$ and $e_T = 0.4$ and the above values of t_m, t_a, p_T, and q_N are used in the equation above, then:

$$\bar{y} = -0.1\,w - 0.6.$$

This means a negative relation between nominal wage changes before tax and real wage income changes after tax. Indeed, all wage increases will give rise to decreases in real incomes after tax in the absence of revisions of the system of taxes and allowances. A 10 percent increase in nominal wages before tax will give rise to a 1.6 percent decrease in real wage income after tax. A 20 percent increase will mean a 2.6 percent fall in real wage income after tax. Consequently, if the tax system is not adjusted, wage earners taken as a collective would benefit from wage decreases,[51] as prices would then fall and the government would be cheated on tax incomes. But it does not seem very probable that wage earner organizations would try to lower wages, a move necessitating concerted action. Only then would there be incentives to hold wage increases down. Such cooperation between wage earner organizations does not seem possible, however. The effects, then, of the combination of high tax progressiveness and rapid price increases for tradables will be to frustrate the desire for increases in real incomes after tax, which may provoke excessive wage claims and contribute further to inflation.[52] Thus a progressive tax system, stabilizing though it may be from the demand side, may be very destabilizing from the cost side.[53]

51. If prices are as flexible downward as upward.

52. It should be recognized that the above analysis is in a sense very partial, since no account is taken of the increases in public consumption that are made possible because of the tax increases. If people were indifferent between increases in public and private consumption, effects such as those mentioned would not arise. But people are very much concerned about the allocation of their consumption.

53. In the analysis, wage increases are regarded as determined autonomously. In the long run, however, wages should increase at about the same rate as the sum of prices and productivity in the sector producing tradables, that is, $w = p_T + q_T$, accord-

The above relations form the background for the use of changes in tax rates in order to influence wage bargains. It seems that the government plans to use this instrument frequently in the future as a means of holding down the rate of inflation. The policy has been implemented in connection with the wage negotiations for both 1974 and 1975–76. Even if it is possible, however, to reduce wage increases in the short run by these methods, they do not provide any long-term solutions in a world of rapid inflation, unless they are combined with other measures. According to the above interpretation of the Aukrust-EFO model, wages will have to increase in the long run at the same rate as the sum of prices and productivity in the sector producing tradables. Short-run deviations from this long-run rate are possible, but will set forces in motion that bring wage increases back to the path indicated by the Aukrust-EFO conditions. If wages increase at a slower rate than prices and productivity in the sector producing tradables, the share of profits will increase with expansionary effects as a result, which will drive up the rate of wage increase. The best method to counteract this development seems to be successive appreciations of the Swedish crown, in order to hold down the rate of price increase (in domestic currency) for tradables. An arithmetical example may help to illustrate the reasoning.

Assume that the average long-run rate of annual price increase for tradables (determined on the world market) will be 8.0 percent in the future. If the annual average rate of productivity increase is 7.0 percent in the sector producing tradables and 3.0 percent in the sector producing nontradables, consumer prices will then increase by 10.4 percent as an annual average according to the Aukrust-EFO model[54] (see the first column in table 7). If, however, the crown is appreciated by, say, 6.0 percent annually, and the rate of price increase for tradables in Sweden has to equal the rate of price increase on the world market, because Sweden is a price taker, the rate of price increase for tradables in Swedish crowns would be brought down to

---

ing to my interpretation of the Aukrust-EFO model. Inserting this in the formula above and using the identity $e_N + e_T = 1$ gives:

$$\bar{y} = \left[\frac{1 - t_m}{1 - t_a} - 1\right] p_T + \left[\frac{1 - t_m}{1 - t_a} - e_N\right] q_T + e_N q_N.$$

The condition for increases of real wage income after tax in the long run, if tax rates are held constant, is then:

$$e_N q_N > \left[1 - \frac{1 - t_m}{1 - t_a}\right] p_T + \left[e_N - \frac{1 - t_m}{1 - t_a}\right] q_T.$$

It follows that there is a great risk that this condition will not be met if q_N and $(1 - t_m)/(1 - t_a)$ are small, whereas e_N, p_T, and q_T are large.

54. The weights of tradables and nontradables in the consumer price index are set at 0.4 and 0.6, respectively, in this example, too.

2.0 percent.[55] The result would be to reduce the rate of wage increase to 9.0 percent and the rate of price increase for nontradables to 6.0 percent. Consequently, the rate of consumer price increases could be lowered to 4.4 percent a year, which ought to be regarded as a tolerable level (see second column).

Table 7. *An Arithmetical Example of the Effects of Exchange Rate Changes in the Aukrust-EFO Model*
Percent

Change	No appreciation	Appreciation of 6 percent
1. Price increase for tradables in foreign currency	8.0	8.0
2. Exchange rate adjustment	0.0	6.0
3. Price increase for tradables in Swedish crowns (line 1 minus line 2)	8.0	2.0
4. Productivity increase in the production of tradables	7.0	7.0
5. Wage increase (line 3 plus line 4)	15.0	9.0
6. Productivity increase in the production of nontradables	3.0	3.0
7. Price increase for nontradables (line 5 minus line 6)	12.0	6.0
8. Consumer price increase	10.4	4.4
9. Real wage change before tax (line 5 minus line 8)	4.6	4.6

Source: Author's calculations.

If the appreciations work out in the way indicated above, they should be completely neutral with respect to the trade balance in the long run. This is because, according to the model, neither the development of real wages and the development of the relative price between tradables and nontradables nor the profit shares in the two sectors would be affected. Nor would the capital account have to be influenced by the appreciations, if monetary policy were adjusted to the lower rate of inflation. This would mean a smaller rate of domestic credit creation and a lowering of the annual nominal interest rate (properly defined) by as many percentage points as the crown is appreciated annually.

The indicated policy of appreciations could, of course, only be expected

55. In the calculation in table 7, it is assumed that an appreciation of the crown by a certain number of percentage points means a lowering of the rate of price increase for tradables in Sweden by the same amount. But since there is no exact correspondence between changes in world market prices and changes in Swedish prices of tradables according to equation 2a, this assumption should probably be seen as an approximation. The arithmetical example ought, therefore, only to be taken to indicate orders of magnitude.

to work in combination with some kind of incomes policy. According to the estimated wage equations, a lowering of the rate of price increases for tradables in Swedish crowns by a certain number of percentage points would not automatically reduce the rate of wage increase—or consequently the rate of price increase for nontradables—by the same amount in the short run, because the Phillips curve would not shift down sufficiently to give this result at an unchanged level of excess demand on the labor market (see figure 4). In that case the share of profits in the sector producing tradables would go down, and the relative prices of nontradables and real wages would increase more than they might have otherwise. The consequence would probably be a deficit in the trade balance and presumably a deficit in the balance of payments, too, unless interest rates were raised enough to attract an offsetting capital flow. The political authorities would then have to choose between abandoning the policy of appreciations and thus accepting a higher rate of inflation, and pursuing a very restrictive economic policy that would increase the rate of unemployment and in this way induce a lower rate of wage inflation.

To avoid the dilemma, some kind of stabilization agreement or indirect incomes policy seems required to make wage increases adjust rapidly and completely to the policy of appreciations. This would not mean any drastic change in the present system because, as described above, the high tax progressiveness has already made government intervention necessary, at least indirectly, in the wage negotiations. This policy might be implemented by the government declaring its firm resolution to achieve a given target for the rate of inflation and to adjust the exchange rate to obtain this result in return for lower wage increases. In view of the centralized structure and the tradition of cooperation between employers and trade unions in Sweden, it should be easier to carry out such a policy in that country than in most other countries. Moreover, the highly progressive tax system should give trade unions little choice other than to participate in this cooperation, inasmuch as they cannot achieve increases in real wage incomes after tax without tax rate changes. The government thus has a very strong bargaining position. To make this policy more acceptable to wage earners and safeguard against failures, however, it might perhaps also be wise to build index clauses into the wage agreements, and to use temporary price controls to smooth the transition to a lower rate of inflation.

But it does not appear that the Swedish government will try the policy sketched here. Discretionary exchange rate changes to achieve officially stated targets for the rate of inflation seem to be regarded as too adventurous. Instead, the officially proclaimed aim is to peg the krona to the German mark.

In practice this could approximate the results of the proposal above, mainly owing to the low rate of inflation in Germany enabling the mark to float up against most other currencies. The authorities prefer this alternative to setting their own priorities, presumably, because participation in a currency area is regarded as a kind of insurance in case of a balance of payments crisis. Pegging to the mark, however, may create exactly those problems mentioned earlier, if wage negotiations are not influenced vigorously enough by incomes policy measures, and if it is not realized by trade unions that, in practice, this policy means that the Swedish rate of inflation is pegged to the German one. If this fact is not understood, a choice may have to be made between a restrictive economic policy creating unemployment and devaluations against the mark with a continued high rate of inflation.

Successive appreciations of the Swedish crown seem to be a necessary condition for a low rate of price increase in Sweden, if the present world inflation continues. Problems created by revaluations could, in my view, be overcome by the use of an indirect incomes policy exchanging tax cuts for wage restraint. If such a policy were to succeed, it would be neutral with respect to the trade balance. Because Sweden seems to be a price taker on the world market, Swedish export prices in foreign currency should also be virtually unaffected. If this combination of successive revaluations and indirect incomes policy were used in a proper way, the charge could not be made that Sweden was exporting its inflation abroad. The use of exchange rate variations as a means of fighting inflation would mean only protection against foreign inflationary shocks and refusal to share in the inflation of others.

Comments by Rudolf R. Rhomberg*

I WOULD LIKE to comment on three aspects of Calmfors's paper, namely, on the character of the inflationary impulse in Sweden in the 1970s, on the international transmission of inflationary effects, and on possible remedies.

In the context of recent experience in Sweden, the inflationary impulse to be considered is the one leading to the acceleration of inflation in the 1970s. The material presented by Calmfors suggests that the major causes were imported inflation, the sharp rise in indirect taxes, and the wage-push, the latter possibly exacerbated by very high marginal income tax rates even at the level of wage earners' incomes.

* The views presented here are those of the author and not necessarily those of the International Monetary Fund.

The large contribution (1 to 1½ percent a year) of the rise in indirect taxes to the increase in consumer prices is remarkable. It is a reflection of the rapid expansion of indirect taxes in Sweden, as in several other European countries, during the period under review, and especially during the years of accelerating inflation, 1970–73. Indirect taxes, which can be reimbursed to exporters, were for reasons of export competition substituted for direct taxes, which cannot be reimbursed. The resulting price increases may be called "inflation" only in a very technical sense. Apart from the rise in indirect taxes, by far the largest contributing element among the identified factors was the advance of internationally determined prices. As Calmfors points out, this contribution is no doubt severely underestimated, since it covers only the direct effects on the consumer price index whereas the indirect effects are reflected in the residual, which also hides the wage-push element.

Calmfors considers the international transmission of inflation from two aspects: the direct influence of foreign on domestic price changes and the influences working through monetary channels. He estimates a wage-price model in which prices of tradable and nontradable goods are separately examined. In his model proportionate changes in foreign prices are estimated to cause proportionate changes in Swedish prices of tradables with a coefficient of 0.8, which moreover is not significantly different from unity. Furthermore, the equation explaining price changes in the sector of nontradables is compatible with the notion of a constant markup on unit labor cost. Both effects seem to confirm part of the mechanism underlying the Aukrust model, although it should be pointed out that the class of tradable goods is not necessarily identical with the output of the exposed sector of the economy.

Calmfors's model differs, however, from Aukrust's analytical framework in its system of wage determination. Calmfors tests Phillips curve relations for wage changes in the tradable sector; he finds—not surprisingly, in view of recent findings for other industrial countries—that wage increases during the 1970s exceeded the amounts one might have expected in relation to the 1960s. He adduces several possible explanations, including that of expectations of higher international price increases in the 1970s than in the earlier decade, but seems unwilling to consider the simple Aukrust explanation of large international price increases in the 1970s affecting wages directly, even apart from the influence that these price increases might have had on expectations, initially in the exposed sector and later in the rest of the economy.

Calmfors's reluctance may be based on two considerations. First, during the period from 1960 to 1969 wages in fact rose somewhat faster than they would have risen in accordance with the Aukrust hypothesis, whereas the opposite was true from 1970 to 1973. These slight differences (of about 1 percentage point a year in either case) seem, however, to call for marginal adjustment of the Aukrust hypothesis—for example, to allow for lags— rather than for its abandonment. Second, the complete Aukrust model appears to predict more price inflation during both subperiods than has in fact occurred, and Calmfors obtains better results with steady-state solutions of two versions of his model, in which international price changes have less, and domestic labor market conditions have more, influence on wage formation. It seems, however, that Calmfors's better results are not necessarily explainable by any superiority of his wage determination model; the Aukrust hypothesis not only performs rather well in this area but also deviates from actual results for the 1960–69 period in the "wrong" direction, that is, it predicts smaller wage increases than have actually occurred and, to that extent, less inflation. In correctly predicting smaller increases in consumer prices than the Aukrust framework, Calmfors's model may benefit instead from weaker reactions of tradable prices to world prices and of nontradable prices to unit labor costs. More analysis is needed to ascertain whether there is a systematic shortfall of these coefficients from the value of unity implied in the Aukrust theory or whether special circumstances operating in Sweden during the period under study reduced these coefficients temporarily.

In a much shorter section on the role played by monetary factors in the acceleration of inflation in Sweden, Calmfors shows that the rates of change of prices, output, and money in the two subperiods are consistent with the quantity theory and that monetary expansion during the 1970s resulted mainly from the sharp increase in external reserves. This section could contribute more than it does if it were integrated with the discussion of price and wage determination that precedes it.

I now come to the topic of policies against inflation. There is a growing popularity in countries with centralized wage negotiations of the so-called social contract approach, under which income tax and perhaps other fiscal concessions are made by the government in return for restraint in wage demands. Calmfors does not anticipate that this approach will counter inflation in the long run, and I tend to agree with him. Nevertheless, at times of acute inflationary pressure any available counterinflationary measures must be used even if their long-term effectiveness is subject to doubt. The real question is whether the government, through granting repeated income tax concessions, is giving away the powerful anti-inflationary weapon of the progressive income tax schedule. As Calmfors has estimated, a nominal wage increase for all wage earners in Sweden may in present circumstances result in a reduction of real wages after taxes. The trouble with this weapon is that it cuts real wages after taxes so effectively under conditions of rapid inflation that its use becomes politically impracticable.

In the long run, Calmfors thinks, inflation in Sweden is largely imported, and he advocates "currency appreciation as an anti-inflationary device," to use a phrase that forms the title of a paper by Randall Hinshaw, published almost twenty-five years ago.[56] In present circumstances, I would draw a distinction between two ways of using exchange rate policy to counter inflation. Under the first approach, the authorities would combat inflation at home perhaps through monetary, fiscal, and incomes policies, and allow the exchange rate to float up so as to counteract the effect of inflation abroad on the prices of tradables. By preventing erosion of the domestic program through price pressure coming from abroad, this passive use of exchange appreciation may be a useful supplement to a successful counterinflationary policy. There may not be much scope for this approach within the framework of Scandinavian models of price and wage determination, except to the extent that wages respond after some delay to an increase in the prices of tradables, so that appreciation can, as it were, fill the temporary wedge between foreign prices of tradables and domestic wages.

Under the second approach, which is the one Calmfors appears to advocate, exchange appreciation would be a more active weapon. The exchange rate would be pushed up through market intervention so as to reduce the room for wage increases in the exposed sector of the economy. There are two problems with this policy: first—and this was pointed out by Hinshaw twenty-five years ago—unless the country has an external surplus to begin with or large reserves, or both, it may have to abandon this policy before it has become fully effective; second, all countries cannot simultaneously appreciate, and this policy will, therefore, tend to be less effective the more popular it may become among a given group of trading partners.

General Comments

FRED BERGSTEN expressed concern about two aspects of the recommendation that exchange rates be used as a major policy instrument for achieving domestic price stability. First, that recommendation cannot be followed by all, or even most, countries because the effort to do so would result in conflict among countries as to appropriate exchange rates. Second,

56. Randall Hinshaw, "Currency Appreciation as an Anti-Inflationary Device," *Quarterly Journal of Economics,* vol. 65 (November 1951), pp. 447–62.

exchange rates are actually being set with different purposes in mind. Although the recommendation seems to be especially applicable to Sweden and Norway, these countries are members of the deutsche mark zone and peg their currencies to the mark; they maintain greater fixity of exchange rates than most other countries. Evidently their policies are directed to some target other than price stability. That suggests that some of the insights resulting from an analysis of optimal currency areas would be helpful. Ronald McKinnon's view of optimal currency areas suggests that Sweden and Norway might gain price stability by pegging to the mark, importing price stability from Germany instead of letting the rate float. The logical implication of the analyses by Aukrust and Calmfors is that the exchange rate should be allowed to float freely, which would avoid importation of inflation but sacrifice whatever anti-inflationary benefits would result from tying to the currency of a bigger country with price stability. Whether the theory of optimal currency areas would provide insights into the operation of small open economies is a question requiring further research.

Assar Lindbeck thought that there was no risk that all countries would try to change their exchange rate in the same direction because some countries are leaders and others laggards in inflation. The inflation leaders will usually not try to avoid imported inflation; they usually devalue. Inflation laggards, such as West Germany, Norway, and Sweden, can very well revalue their currencies without being followed by the rest of the world. Countries that appreciate, of course, are helping to bottle up inflation in the countries having the fastest inflation rates, but there is nothing wrong with the laggards insisting that they want to lag and saying to the more inflationary countries, "You should pay the price of your own inflation. Don't shovel it onto us." The situation becomes complicated, of course, if a country has both a low rate of inflation and a deficit in its current account. If it revalues and in the short run increases its trade deficit, it is borrowing resources from the outside world to keep down its own rate of inflation. But it is difficult to accept the idea that a country like West Germany, with a low rate of inflation and a trade surplus, should import inflation instead of revaluing.

Alexander Swoboda believed it important to recognize that a once-and-for-all revaluation is not an anti-inflationary policy; it is a policy concerning the *level* of prices. In an inflationary world the revaluation merely creates a discontinuity in the inflation rate although some time may elapse before the old inflation rate is resumed. But, unless a country revalues continuously, its rate of inflation will pick up once more. Furthermore, revaluation and floating exchange rates are two entirely different animals. If a country revalues, it must make its exchange rate stick and it would have to use monetary policy to do that. With a floating rate, such a country need not fix its exchange rate and it can therefore use monetary policy for some other purpose. As to the argument that all countries cannot revalue together, that depends on what they revalue against. If they all revalue against gold, then they are devaluing the outside reserve asset in the system and that results in a certain anti-inflationary effect by taxing money balances. Finally, there is nothing in the Aukrust and Calmfors models to indicate what the rate of inflation would be under a floating exchange rate system. That fact points to one omission from these models: there is no explanation of aggregate demand. It may be possible to dispense with that in describing a fixed-rate system but not in describing a floating-rate system.

With respect to the possible usefulness of applying analysis of optimal currency areas, what currency areas are feasible depends in part on the relationships between the rates of inflation preferred in the countries concerned. One could perhaps argue that until 1967 the OECD, excluding the United Kingdom and West Germany, was a feasible, if not an optimal, currency area.

Assar Lindbeck, observing that many contributors were saying that the Phillips curve relationship has "broken down," considered it very important to know what they meant when they said this. One meaning is that the *level* of the curve has become more unstable either because wages have fluctuated more as a result of greater fluctuations of causative factors other than conditions in the labor market, or because these other factors have bigger coefficients attached to them than before (even though they may not actually be fluctuating any more than they did previously). That would mean that the Phillips curve was less useful than was at one time believed for predicting future wage and price developments on the basis of forecasts of the situation in the labor market only. However, another meaning is that the *slope* of the curve, that is, the partial derivative of the rate of wage change with respect to the change in employment, has become unstable. That would be even more serious. As long as the slope is unchanged, the Phillips curve can be used to predict the *effects* of changes in the labor market situation, other factors being unchanged; that is what is important for policy purposes. But if the slope is unstable it cannot be used even for predicting the effects of a change in the labor market.

Governments try to induce labor unions to accept wage increases smaller than they otherwise would by offering tax reductions or other bribes. This had been done in Sweden. The result had been a lower rate of wage increase than had occurred in other countries in 1973 and an increase of about 5 percent in the real disposable income of employees. Although this policy has been very successful, it involves two problems. One, mentioned by Calmfors, is that with fixed exchange rates and rising world market prices, wage costs would go up very little so that profit margins would keep increasing over time. Unless profits taxes are continually raised, workers would come back for wage increases because of the reduction in their relative shares. The other problem has to do with labor union members becoming discontented with their leaders when wage increases are no greater than price increases and, although the tax reductions may raise their real incomes after taxes, they would not believe it. In 1974, the year after the Swedish labor unions got the biggest raise in their real disposable income that they had had since the war, they were asking for a 20 percent wage increase.

William Branson, by way of emphasizing the profit consequences of this kind of social contract, noted that its effect would be to shift some income from the government budget to profits because it would reduce gross wages while holding prices constant. In effect, it is merely a sneaky way of cutting profits taxes. Of course, if policymakers cut the tax rates a little bit more, they would be giving something to the workers that would more than offset the price rise, but the greatest gains would be made in profits, which would get the first part of the tax cut.

Johan Myhrman, pointing out that Calmfors finds no evidence of excess demand in the price behavior of the sheltered sector but finds evidence for price expectations and unit labor costs, thought that the excess demand probably shows up in unit labor costs. If so, one could not say that excess demand did not affect price behavior in the sheltered sector. In the general policy picture presented Calmfors barely mentions monetary factors. Observation of the Swedish economy—and also the description in Calmfors's paper— seems to indicate that a monetary approach cannot be ruled out as irrelevant. It has not been tried, but it seems consistent with the facts.

Alexander Swoboda thought that the conclusion that the Aukrust model shows a close correlation between wages in the sheltered and the nonsheltered industries suggests that perhaps the model is not needed to explain the determination of the price level. The Aukrust model is interesting mainly because it explains divergences in rates of inflation among countries by divergences in productivity growth. To the extent that these divergencies are not explained, then for some purposes a simpler model might be equally satisfactory.

Lars Calmfors noted that his finding that there is lower sensitivity of Swedish price increases to the increases of international prices than the Aukrust model cannot depend on the absence of lags because his reduced form equation is based on equations that include lags. The reason his equations are, or could be, compatible with the Aukrust model is that in the long run the difference between vacancies and unemployment, which is used in his equation, adjusts to the Aukrust conditions, so that the two models are compatible in the long run. As to the effect of appreciation of the Swedish currency and whether it involves the export of inflation to other countries, appreciation should not be considered as an isolated measure but as one accompanied by a package of other policies (fiscal, monetary, and incomes policies) to reduce internal inflationary pressures. In that case, it would be very misleading to talk about export of inflation in connection with a policy of revaluations.

PASCAL SALIN
GEORGES LANE

Inflation in France

545

Tables

Figures

Pascal Salin and Georges Lane, Centre Universitaire Dauphine, Paris, wish to thank Emil Claassen and the editors for their many useful comments and suggested improvements.

THIS PAPER describes and attempts to interpret French inflation during the years 1963 to 1974. The period was chosen mainly for statistical reasons; before 1963 reliable data, especially quarterly data, are difficult to obtain for some important variables. Moreover, 1963 was the year of the "Plan de Stabilisation," and marks the beginning of a time of relative stability and only mild inflation. It was not until 1968 that inflation accelerated (shown in figure 1).

A striking feature of French inflation at this time is how closely its pattern resembles that of "world" inflation (see, for example, the countries compared in table 1). A possible approach to a study of French inflation would therefore be to regard it as one national example of a more general phenomenon: to examine the French situation in isolation would be difficult and would provide only a partial interpretation of the inflation problem.

In comparing France with other countries, however, it must be remembered that France is a medium-sized country. It has a lower ratio of tradable to nontradable goods than the smaller countries and is therefore less vulnerable than they are to outside influences, especially in the long run. Inflation

Table 1. *Percentage Increase in Consumer Prices, Selected Industrial Countries, 1961–74*

| | | Annual increase | | |
Country	Average increase, 1961–71	1971–72	1972–73	September 1973– September 1974
United States	3.1	3.3	6.2	12.1
France	4.3	5.9	7.3	14.8
Germany	3.0	5.5	6.9	7.3
United Kingdom	4.6	7.1	9.2	17.1
OECD, total[a]	3.7	4.7	7.7	14.1
OECD, European members[a]	4.2	6.5	8.7	14.7

Source: Organisation for Economic Co-operation and Development, *OECD Economic Outlook* (Paris: OECD, December 1974).

a. The following are the European members of OECD: Austria, Belgium, Denmark, Finland, France, Germany, Greece, Iceland, Ireland, Italy, Luxembourg, the Netherlands, Norway, Portugal, Spain, Sweden, Switzerland, Turkey, and the United Kingdom. Other members are Australia, Canada, Japan, New Zealand, and the United States.

Figure 1. *Consumer and Industrial Price Indexes, Annual Averages, 1963–74*

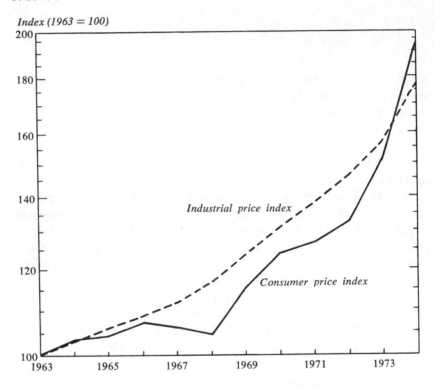

Index (1963 = 100)

Sources: Consumer price index, table 3; industrial price index, table 9.

in France could, in fact, have domestic as well as foreign roots.[1] On the other hand, France cannot exercise the same freedom in its pricing policy as, say, the United States and other large countries that are far less influenced by world price trends.

In this paper we evaluate the various approaches to the study of inflation in France and its transmission process; determine whether it was largely domestic or foreign in origin; and in the light of French experience, examine the relation between exchange rates and the rates of inflation, with particular reference to recent experience under a flexible-rate regime.

1. See, for example, E. M. Claassen, "The Role of Economic Size in the Determination and Transmission of World Inflation," in Helmut H. Frisch, ed., *Inflation in Small Countries*, vol. 119 of *Lecture Notes in Economics and Mathematical Systems* (Springer-Verlag, 1976), pp. 91–119.

Figure 2. *Relation of Inflations in France and its Partner Countries, 1960–74*

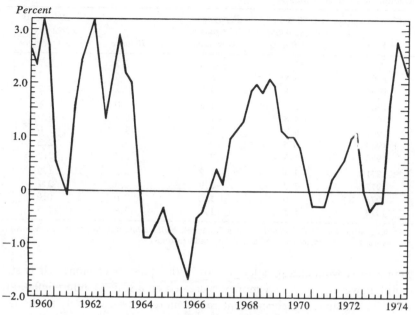

Percent

Source: Derived from data in Institut National de la Statistique et des Etudes Economiques, *Les indicateurs associés au 6ème Plan,* 1974:4 (Paris: INSEE). The authors computed the index by the following formula:

$$\frac{\text{French index, quarter T, year n}}{\text{French index, quarter T, year n-1}} - \frac{\text{composite foreign index, quarter T, year n}}{\text{composite foreign index, quarter T, year n-1}}$$

The composite foreign index was obtained by taking an average of the consumer price indexes of six countries (Belgium, Germany, Italy, the Netherlands, the United Kingdom, and the United States), with weights proportional to the exports of industrial commodities to OECD countries. Changes in exchanges rates are not included in these indexes.

Social and Political Background

The French inflation rate is generally one of the highest in the industrialized world (see table 1 and figure 2). Therefore, although inflation is now regarded as essentially an international phenomenon, conditions and attitudes must exist in France that make it particularly vulnerable. Some of these are described below.

Growth in money supply

A common tendency, particularly in France, is to claim that inflation is brought about solely by conflicts among social and economic groups that force up wages and prices. But in France, as in any other country, inflation

Table 2. *Budget Deficits and Surpluses, 1963–74*

Amounts in billions of francs

Year	Ordinary receipts minus expenditures	Repayments minus new loans	Balance	Balance as percentage of net receipts
1963	−7.3	−1.0	−8.3	8.7
1964	3.8	−5.4	−1.6	1.7
1965	4.4	−4.2	0.2	0.2
1966	3.7	−5.8	−2.0	1.8
1967	−4.8	−1.5	−6.3	5.0
1968	−6.4	−3.1	−9.5	7.0
1969	−0.5	−2.8	−3.4	2.2
1970	6.5	−2.8	3.7	2.3
1971	−2.3	−1.2	−3.5	1.9
1972	7.2	−2.9	4.3	2.2
1973	1.0	−1.0	0.0	0.0
1974	5.5	−1.6	3.9	1.7

Source: Ministère de l'Economie et des Finances, *Notes d'information* (Paris: the Ministry, various issues). Figures are rounded and do not add to totals.

cannot exist without a parallel growth in the quantity of money. It is still useful, however, to ask *why* money is created on a scale to induce inflation: why, for example, the government reacts more or less passively to the demands of the different sectors.

One reason for such a high rate of money creation may be the government's concept of economic policy. For a long time it has relied upon— and still may rely upon—a rather shallow and oversimplified Keynesianism that assumes aggregate demand should be systematically increased. Budget deficits play their part in this policy, since governments automatically apply the so-called Keynesian recipe of increasing budget deficits to ward off unemployment. At the same time, money is generally easy.

Nonetheless, the focus and instruments used have changed. Since 1970 the French government has followed more orthodox procedures and attempted to present balanced budgets or even budgets with a surplus. Since 1969, in fact, ordinary receipts have exceeded expenditures, except in 1971 (see table 2). Moreover, the Banque de France has changed its mode of operation. Before 1969, it used the discount rate as its main instrument, but since 1969 it has resorted more and more to open market operations and to shifts in reserve requirements (defined, according to the period, by deposits or credits in terms of levels or increments).[2]

2. People like Jacques Rueff deplore the changeover. He believes that an open market system puts pressure on the central bank from banks needing monetary re-

The Banque de France generally pays more attention to the level of interest rates than to the quantity of money available. In "normal" periods, credit is not "rationed." However, in 1974, a more restrictive policy was decided upon; banks were not permitted to expand credit by more than a certain percentage over the previous year or stipulated number of months. There were some exceptions, such as those for export credits.

It must be remembered that the government has always been primarily concerned with unemployment, not inflation. It is dealing with a population that is occupationally and geographically immobile and that is unwilling to relocate as the job market changes. The unemployment problem is consequently aggravated at a time when structural changes in industry eliminate certain types of jobs. Neither entrepreneurs nor wage earners want to face up to this situation, and inflation has been one escape route; it has allowed activities to continue that would otherwise lapse. Such activities survive thanks to the expansion of credit and low interest rates that, combined with inflation, act as subsidies. Public and semipublic organizations provide loans with a whole series of preferential interest rates ostensibly because such activities accord with the objectives of the current five-year plan, but often because of requests from private pressure groups or even public agencies.

Such social rigidity and such sensitivity to the employment problem makes the handling of anti-inflationary policy even more difficult. Although the French government decided upon quite a restrictive credit policy during the summer of 1974—not without a considerable number of exceptions—it would seem that the "préfets," who represent the central power in provincial "départements," did not hesitate to telephone the banks (most of which are nationalized) to ask them to allow larger credit allowances to firms that might get into difficulties and that might be obliged to reduce their staff as a result of this anti-inflationary policy.

The primacy of the goal of full employment made inflation socially acceptable because the Phillips curve relationship was thought to exist; that is, in order to dampen inflation, some unemployment would have to be accepted. It should be noted, however, that unemployment never appeared high during the period studied. But even that may have been an illusion because of the paucity of data available (as explained in a later section).

---

sources, which, with more or less validity, use the threat of bankruptcy. A discount rate system, on the contrary, is much less personal and applies to all banks, which makes them more careful about granting credit. We could therefore see more than mere coincidence when inflation accelerated in France at the same time as this "monetary reform." But we should also point out that under a discount rate system, the central bank can always decide which categories of assets are eligible or ineligible for discount.

The five-year plans

Another set of factors certainly played a role in the definition of economic policy. Since the war, the fulcrum of public action has been a series of five-year plans. These are supposed to define the medium-term (five-year) economic objectives, to outline a plan of action, and to make longer-run forecasts. Because the growth rate, prices, and the like have been prescribed for periods of five years, it has led policymakers to accept a somewhat fatalistic attitude and distracted their attention from short-term stabilization policies. If developments in the short run have not corresponded to a specific forecast it seems obvious that this was due to some unforeseeable or external factor over which policymakers had no control. This is why a slowdown of economic activity or a rise in prices is often explained away in France by the level of economic activity in Germany, the rise in the prices of raw materials, a particularly cold winter, and so on.

In the fifth five-year plan, a system of warning "signals" ("clignotants") was initiated. Indicators of short-term economic developments would "light up" when policy decisions had to be made. It could be considered that these indicators were intended to bridge the gap between short-range and medium-range planning. In fact, it seems that the official role of these indicators was not to draw attention to short-term fluctuations, but rather to possible divergences between the desired and the probable evolution of the economy within the five-year period. Disparities between a plan's forecast and reality have led to modifications of the plan. According to the Institut National de la Statistique et des Etudes Economiques, the use of these indicators made clear that unfavorable short-term developments were registered much too late, but also the targets of the Plan were not necessarily endangered when the indicators "lit up."[3]

It is characteristic of this approach that price stability was not in itself an objective—in the form, for example, of a monthly inflation rate that should not be exceeded. In fact, the price "warning signal" was to "light up" if, for three successive months, the consumer price index had risen by at least 1 percent more than the average index of France's principal trading partners. The indicator was, of course, related to the balance of payments.[4]

3. Institut National de la Statistique et des Etudes Economiques, *Les indicateurs associés au 6ème Plan*, 1974:4 (Paris: INSEE).
4. The working of this indicator is not so automatic in the period of the sixth five-year plan because the 1 percent threshold no longer exists. However, the price level objective is still to maintain relative parity with France's trading partners. (This "relative price index" is given in figure 2.)

Nonanalytical approach to policy

In France, economic forecasting and thinking are generally viewed from the accountant's perspective. Rather than analyzing functional relationships within the economy, French policymakers tend to base their forecasts on analyses of past trends, modified to ensure accounting consistency.

An econometric model, Fi-Fi, now serves as the planning tool. It is based on national accounting techniques and has between 2,000 and 3,000 equations.[5]

In fact, the Fi-Fi model depends on the distinction between "secteurs exposés" (competitive sectors) and "secteurs protégés" (sheltered sectors). This difference is very close to the one between tradable and nontradable goods in the Scandinavian models.[6] However, quite surprisingly, there is nothing in the Fi-Fi model to induce prices of the sheltered sectors to converge toward prices of the competitive sectors, even within the five-year horizon of the 1970–75 plan. Moreover, there is no econometric test of relationships, which seem to be a priori assumptions regarding the behavior of the main variables.

The importance of foreign prices in determining French prices in the Fi-Fi model may partly explain the bad forecasts for French inflation in the 1970–75 period, since the first hypothesis is a fairly stable outside world. No matter what the reason, all publications produced by the administrators of the French plan have severely underestimated the rate of inflation, which may have dulled the government's sensitivity to inflation, given the degree of blind confidence it retains in the plan's objectives.

The fight for shares

Because of their belief in the Phillips curve relationship, monetary authorities in France have been forced to create enough money to validate the inflation trends. Aggravating the situation is the strong antagonism between entrepreneurs and wage earners (in part reflected by the importance of the left-wing parties and by the communist trade union which is the biggest trade union in France). Appeals to "civism," or civic duty, have no impact on either side in spite of constant references in political and economic language

5. Fi-Fi stands for "physico-financier." Simulation exercises using a series of seemingly realistic hypotheses even led the authors of a quasi-official document to forecast for 1975 an inflation rate of between 2.10 and 4.56 percent!

6. See the paper by Odd Aukrust in this volume.

to "social cooperation" (of which economic planning is supposed to be an example). Successful demands for wage raises put constant pressure on costs. Moreover, inflationary expectations are formed all the more quickly because of France's long experience with inflation since the Second World War. (France has never known hyperinflation, even though inflation rates have often been high.) Wage demands are met because of the tendency of the monetary authorities to give credit easily to avoid unemployment.

Wage earners are motivated in one of two ways. First, they may anticipate a continued rise in wages made possible by cutting profits. This attitude can be interpreted as the result of a "bad" economic education (and typically French). Second, they may have been ideologically conditioned in the Marxist philosophy: the pressure to increase wages should reduce exploitation and lead to the confiscation of the surplus, or profits. At the same time there is a "destructive" element (no doubt prevalent in union headquarters), whose purpose is to hinder the working of a market economy so that the capitalist system will "wallow in its own contradictions."

In fact, aggressive unionism has never managed to change the distribution of incomes in the long run.

Social and economic barriers to mobility

The splitting up of French society into rigid occupational and regional groups that in part correspond to class differences may also have played a part in fostering inflation. Equal treatment within the group is regarded as more important than moving from one group to another. In a dynamic economy, such as the French, which includes very progressive and very backward sectors (such as in agriculture), increases in productivity vary among groups. But the emphasis on equality and "justice" rather than efficiency leads to demands for income parity—among firms, among economic groups, among regions, and among all income earners generally—that tend to raise all incomes. Public opinion in France accepts as a fact that everyone has the right to a job in the place where he lives at the "normal" wage rate. Population mobility is much lower than in the United States, for instance, or in most other developed countries, and this could intensify inflation trends for the reasons explained above.

In addition, there is the political price the French government pays to its small, rapidly decreasing, yet still disproportionately powerful agricultural lobby. France is still putting pressure on its partners in the European Community to maintain high prices for agricultural products.

Table 3. *Consumer Price Index, Quarterly and Annual Averages, 1963–74*

Year	Quarterly averages, 1963 = 100				Annual average	
	1	*2*	*3*	*4*	*1963 = 100*	*1966 = 100*
1963	98.2	99.2	100.7	101.7	100.0	...
1964	102.4	102.6	103.4	104.1	103.1	...
1965	104.7	106.0	106.2	106.7	105.9	...
1966	107.6	108.4	108.9	109.7	108.7	100.0
1967	110.6	111.0	111.8	113.4	111.7	102.8
1968	115.0	115.7	117.1	119.4	116.8	107.5
1969	121.5	123.1	124.5	126.4	123.9	114.0
1970	128.9	130.4	131.8	133.3	131.1	120.6
1971	135.2	137.3	139.1	141.1	138.2	127.1
1972	142.9	144.9	147.6	150.8	146.6	134.9
1973	152.1	155.1	158.9	163.3	157.4	144.8
1974	169.3	176.2	182.0	187.8	178.9	164.6
1974a	155.7	162.1	167.4	172.8	...	...

Sources: 1963 = 100, International Monetary Fund, *International Financial Statistics*, 1973 Supplement and vol. 28 (June 1975); 1966 = 100, authors' computations.
a. 1966 = 100.

Price Movements in France, 1963–74

Price movements in France between 1963 and 1974 had three distinct characteristics. First, prices moved steadily upward during a period of constantly accelerating inflation. Second, French prices increased more rapidly than elsewhere in the industrial world. And third, price indexes varied among categories of goods and services, rising at differing and not always consistent rates.

Inflationary trend

The numbers in tables 3 and 4 and figure 1 demonstrate that, in regard to the annual average consumer price index, there was almost continual acceleration throughout the period.[7] There were thresholds in 1968 and 1974

7. The general opinion of French statisticians is that the index of prices of gross domestic product (GDP) is not very reliable in France and it does not give a good idea of the real evolution of prices. Therefore, we shall not use the GDP price index; the consumer price index will be our inflation indicator, and since there is no wholesale price index (except for certain sectors) we have to assume that the price index of industrial products is a good proxy for the wholesale price index.

Table 4. *Quarterly and Annual Rates of Change in Consumer Price Index,*
1963–74

Percent

Year	Quarterly rate[a]				Annual rate[b]
	1	2	3	4	
1963	1.7	1.0	1.5	1.0	...
1964	0.7	0.2	0.8	0.7	3.1
1965	0.6	1.2	0.2	0.5	2.7
1966	0.8	0.7	0.5	0.7	2.6
1967	0.8	0.4	0.7	1.4	2.8
1968	1.4	0.6	1.2	2.0	4.6
1969	1.8	1.3	1.1	1.5	6.1
1970	2.0	1.2	1.1	1.1	5.8
1971	1.4	1.6	1.3	1.4	5.4
1972	1.3	1.4	1.9	2.2	6.1
1973	0.9	2.0	2.5	2.8	7.4
1974	3.7	4.1	3.3	3.2	13.7

Source: Table 3.
a. Rate of change from previous quarter.
b. Rate of change from previous year's annual average.

that show up more clearly in the quarterly data. Industrial prices (shown
in figure 1) indicate a more irregular pattern; they rose continuously but at
accelerated rates beginning in 1968 and 1973.

Comparison with other countries

The relation between French and foreign prices is best understood if three
series of data are compared: an index of French relative to foreign consumer
prices (figure 2); an index of import prices (table 5); and an index of
effective exchange rates of the French franc (figure 3).

RELATIVE FRENCH AND FOREIGN RETAIL PRICES. Figure 2 compares the
French price index with the composite price index for six other countries—
Belgium, Germany, Italy, the Netherlands, the United Kingdom, and the
United States—some of its main trading partners. The increase in French
consumer prices has nearly always been higher than in the other countries.
The exceptions are the 1964–66 period and two minor periods in 1971 and
1973. This appears to substantiate the theory that domestic factors have
played a role in French inflation. However, figure 2 also shows that acceleration took place at the same time in France as in the other countries.

Figure 3. *Index of the Effective Exchange Rate of the French Franc, 1967–74*

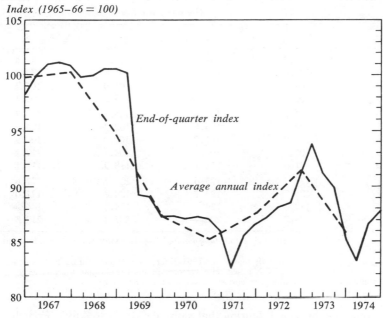

Index (1965–66 = 100)

Source: Computed by the authors; see text for explanation.

IMPORT PRICES. These prices have been much more volatile than other prices in France (tables 5 and 6). During the period 1963–68 increases and decreases were such that the average import price index was only 101.6 in 1968 (1963 = 100). In the following period, there were four years (1969, 1971, 1973, and 1974) with high rates of increase. The 18 percent increase in 1969 can be partly attributed to the French devaluation of 11.5 percent in August 1969.

EFFECTIVE EXCHANGE RATES OF THE FRENCH FRANC. This was computed from the exchange rates between the franc and the currencies of those countries that each contribute more than 1 percent to French trade (with weights modified from year to year).[8] The index is plotted on figure 3.

The effective exchange rate was quite stable until 1969 when in August

8. Trade includes exports and imports. The trade with oil-producing countries, which is chiefly in dollars, is added to the trade with the United States. The other countries are Belgium, Canada, Germany, Italy, the Netherlands, Switzerland, and the United Kingdom.

Table 5. *Import Price Index, Quarterly Averages, 1962–74*
1963 = 100[a]

Year	Quarterly average			
	1	2	3	4
1962	98.7	99.0	97.9	99.5
1963	101.6	100.1	101.8	102.0
1964	102.0	101.4	102.0	104.7
1965	103.0	103.7	103.5	103.3
1966	104.6	106.4	105.1	105.9
1967	104.1	105.6	102.3	104.2
1968	102.9	101.7	100.7	100.9
1969	102.5	103.3	108.7	119.1
1970	121.0	121.1	118.9	119.1
1971	122.5	123.6	122.7	127.6
1972	125.2	123.2	124.8	127.0
1973	129.4	129.4	134.3	144.5
1974	183.2	200.9	207.4	210.8

Source: International Monetary Fund, *International Financial Statistics*, 1973 Supplement and vol. 29 (March 1976).

a. The average of the quarterly figures for 1963 differs from 100 even though 1963 is the base year because the annual figure is based on a larger sample of trade than the quarterly figures, and because of the method used to correct seasonal variations.

the franc was devalued. During that same period (1963–69), French consumer prices appeared to move independently of import prices. Year-to-year changes were not in step. For instance, French prices increased more than foreign prices in 1967–68, whereas import prices were decreasing. In 1966, import prices were increasing, but French prices increased less than foreign prices. However, in 1973 and 1974 import prices appeared to exert a positive influence on consumer prices.

In the period from 1969 to 1974, the effective exchange rate was most unstable, and there is a close relation between import prices and changes in effective exchange rates (except in 1973 when increases, or decreases, in import prices occur simultaneously with the depreciation, or appreciation, of the franc). Moreover, the extent to which simultaneous or prior increases in French consumer prices exceeded, or fell short of, those of its trading partners appears to explain the depreciation, or appreciation, of the franc.

From this short-period experience, one might conclude that, except in 1973, a "higher-than-average" increase in French consumer prices was followed, or paralleled, by a relative depreciation of the franc and an increase in import prices. As persistent higher-than-average increases in French prices preceded depreciations in the French effective exchange rate and

Table 6. *Quarterly and Annual Rates of Change in Import Prices, 1963–74*

Year	Quarterly rate[a]				Annual rate[b]
	1	2	3	4	
1963	2.1	−1.5	1.7	0.2	2.5
1964	0.0	−0.6	0.6	2.6	2.6
1965	−1.6	0.7	−0.2	−0.2	−1.3
1966	1.3	1.7	−1.2	0.8	2.5
1967	−1.7	1.4	−3.1	1.9	−1.6
1968	−1.2	−1.2	−1.0	0.2	−3.2
1969	1.6	0.8	5.2	9.6	18.0
1970	1.6	0.1	−1.8	0.2	0.0
1971	2.9	0.9	−0.7	4.0	7.1
1972	−1.9	−1.6	1.3	1.8	−0.5
1973	1.9	0.0	3.8	7.6	13.8
1974	26.8	9.7	3.2	1.6	45.9

Source: Table 5.
a. Rate of change from previous quarter.
b. Rate of change from previous year's fourth quarter.

increases in import prices, it seems that a French inflation of domestic origin caused changes in effective exchange rates and import prices, rather than the other way around, during the period of exchange rate instability from 1969 to 1974.

Another measure of the relation between French and foreign prices is given in figure 4. One curve plots the weighted index of consumer prices in the major trading partners of France: the United States and oil-producing countries, Belgium, Canada, Germany, Italy, the Netherlands, Switzerland, and the United Kingdom, corrected for the effective exchange rate (given in figure 3). The other curve plots the index of French consumer prices. It appears that the 1969 devaluation of the franc shifted the world curve (as exemplified by France's trading partners) significantly above the French curve, but that, little by little, both curves tended to converge, at least until 1973. The 1969 devaluation, which was necessary to correct for the previous more rapid increases in French prices, may have overestimated the difference in price changes between France and the other countries.

Comparison of price indexes

Quarterly and annual data for various price indexes indicate that the rates of increase differ and are not necessarily consistent. When indexes are compared over longer periods, as in table 7, the rate of inflation appears to in-

Figure 4. *French and "World" Consumer Price Indexes,*
Quarterly Averages, 1966–75

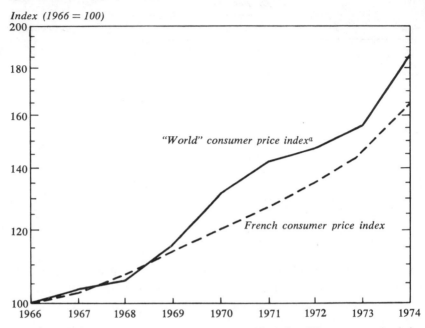

Index (1966 = 100)

"World" consumer price index[a]

French consumer price index

1966   1967   1968   1969   1970   1971   1972   1973   1974

Sources: French consumer price index, see text, table 3; "world" consumer price index, computed by the authors.
a. Denominated in terms of francs; see text for explanation.

fluence their relative rates of increase, that is, when inflation is rising slowly, consumer prices tend to increase more rapidly than industrial prices. But as the rate of inflation climbs so does the industrial price index; thus when inflation rises steeply (as in 1973–74), the industrial price index overtakes the consumer price index.

In the long run (for instance, between 1963:1 and 1974:4) the rates of increase are about the same for consumer and industrial prices: 5.7 percent and 6.0 percent respectively.[9] Moreover, also in the long run, French industrial prices appear to be considerably influenced by world prices; the curve for industrial prices generally lies in the corridor between the curves for import and export prices (figure 5).[10]

9. In fact, industrial prices increased more than consumer prices, but the very exceptional increase from 1973:4 to 1974:4 introduces a strong bias in the data; it can be argued that consumer prices could not rise fast enough in such a short period. There is also a relative price effect.

10. Whereas the 1969 devaluation affected industrial prices, import prices, and export prices, it had much less—or no—effect on consumer prices (tables 3 and 4).

Table 7. *Average Annual Percentage Changes in Selected Price Series, 1963–74 and Subperiods*

	Rate of change				
Price series	*1963:1– 1967:4*	*1963:1– 1972:4*	*1967:4– 1972:4*	*1972:4– 1974:4*	*1963:1– 1974:4*
Consumer	3.1	4.5	5.9	11.6	5.7
Industrial	1.7	3.5	5.2	19.7	6.1
Gross domestic product deflator	3.0	2.1	5.3	1.1	3.8
Import	1.1	2.6	4.0	28.8	6.7
Export	1.3	3.3	5.3	19.9	6.0

Sources: Institut National de la Statistique et des Etudes Economiques, *Tendances de la Conjoncture,* selected issues; International Monetary Fund, *International Financial Statistics,* various issues, tables 3, 5, and 9.

The comparison of import prices with consumer and industrial prices confirms our previous conclusion, namely, that French inflation rates although not independent of world inflation rates have developed their own momentum. A rise in import prices is not immediately reflected in an upsurge of domestic prices. Superficially, it would seem that, when import prices rise slowly, there may be a more rapid increase in industrial prices and an even more rapid increase in consumer prices. But when import prices rise rapidly, domestic prices react slowly to change.

However, it must be remembered that the higher rate of increase in consumer prices in France than in its main trading partners led, in the 1969–74 period, to a depreciation of the effective exchange rate, which in turn raised import prices measured in francs. Rather than referring to the price system as dampening the effect of rising import prices, one could refer to the aggravation of import price increases caused by an exchange depreciation that took place after French prices had increased at a higher-than-average rate.

Whatever the explanation, the French policies do have some independent effects on prices, at least in the short run.

In fact, the divergences among the price series can actually confirm the existence of nontradables (especially services), protected markets (such as those for government purchases), and the like. They can also confirm the existence of a closely related problem in connection with the composition of indexes: the import price index, the consumer price index, and the industrial price index each include different kinds of commodities and services. If, for example, the prices of imported commodities increase, the prices of domestic import-competing commodities also rise, as well as the prices of

Figure 5. *Quarterly Percentage Changes in the French Export, Import, and Industrial Price Indexes, 1963–74*

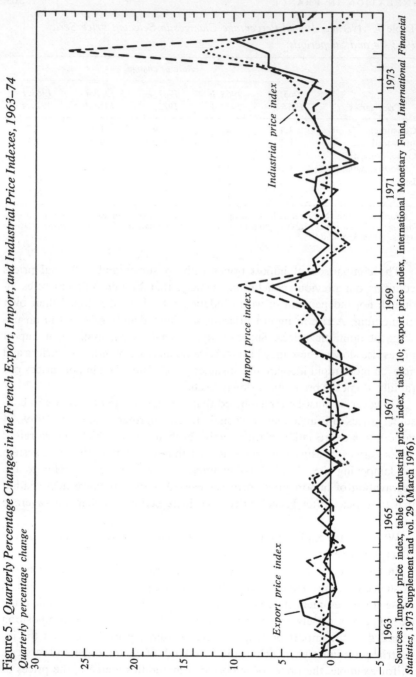

Quarterly percentage change

Sources: Import price index, table 6; industrial price index, table 10; export price index, International Monetary Fund, *International Financial Statistics,* 1973 Supplement and vol. 29 (March 1976).

factors of production. But, as technology advances more slowly in the service sector, the prices of services rise more rapidly than those of commodities.[11] As the various indexes mentioned above do not give the same weights to services and commodities, they do not change in the same way. McKinnon mentions this difficulty.[12] He points out that the divergence between import and consumer prices is greater the higher the real rate of growth. This relationship may be explained by the fact that in countries with rapid growth the income elasticity of demand is higher—and productivity growth lower—for services than for tradables.

The determination of consumer prices, which certainly include a high proportion of nontradables, may be much more independent of import price levels than those of industrial goods. The latter include imports, exports, and only certain nontradables. Import prices are dependent on world rates, but the prices of exports, which are more "specialized" goods, can be more independently arrived at. And to this extent, industrial prices can move relatively freely although not to the same extent as consumer prices.

French Inflation: A Further Look at the Facts

The preceding section presents a general description of price movements, the divergences and similarities among the main price indexes, and possible links with foreign price developments. Below is a more detailed study of French inflation. It is divided into three different periods of differing inflationary tendencies. This is followed by a discussion of the relations between inflation and other important macroeconomic variables such as employment, wages, and economic policy.

The stages of an accelerating inflation

The three periods of differing inflation rates indicated by French price indexes are 1963–68, a period of relatively mild inflation; 1968–73, one of

11. Similarly, the increases in import prices, much higher than the rise in national prices, may reflect a symmetrical phenomenon: for exogenous reasons, the relative prices of certain raw materials rose in the world in 1973–74, and national indexes, which give a lower weight to these commodities than import price indexes do, show less increase.

12. Ronald I. McKinnon, "Monetary Theory and Controlled Flexibility in the Foreign Exchanges," in Emil Claassen and Pascal Salin, eds., *Stabilization Policies in Interdependent Economies,* Proceedings of the conference held at the University of Paris-Dauphine, March 25–27, 1971 (Amsterdam: North-Holland, 1972; distributed in the United States and Canada by American Elsevier), pp. 3–32.

Table 8. *Average Annual Percentage Changes in Selected Indicators of Long-Term Inflation, 1963–74 and Subperiods*

	Prices		Gross domestic product			Money stocks	
Period	Con- sumer	In- dustrial	Real	Nom- inal	Re- serves	M_1	M_2
1963:1–1968:1	3.2	1.1	6.9	10.0	9.2	7.6	11.1
1963:1–1966:3	3.0	2.3	7.1	10.2	13.3	10.0	11.2
1966:3–1968:1	3.7	−1.8	6.3	9.7	0.3	2.2	10.8
1968:1–1972:4	5.9	6.0	5.8	12.0	8.1	10.4	15.0
1968:1–1970:1	5.9	9.4	5.6	11.8	−22.7	4.1	9.7
1970:1–1972:4	5.9	3.7	6.0	12.1	38.0	15.2	19.0
1972:4–1974:4	11.6	19.7	5.4	12.7	−6.0	12.5	16.5

Sources: Tables 3 and 9; INSEE, *Tendances de la Conjoncture*; International Monetary Fund, *International Financial Statistics*; various issues.

slightly accelerating inflation; and 1973–74, when the inflation rate rose precipitously (as shown in table 8).

THE PERIOD FROM 1963 TO 1968. In the first year the rate of increase of consumer prices was rather high (5.2 percent), which was primarily caused by the increase in the first quarter of 1963 (1.7 percent); this induced the authorities to adopt the "Plan de Stabilisation."

In the following four years the annual rate of increase in consumer prices was in the region of 2 to 3 percent (table 4). Quarterly rates from 1963:1 to 1968:2 show an increase that was always 1.2 percent or below, except during 1963, and in the last quarter of 1967 and the first quarter of 1968.

Prices of industrial products were much more volatile (table 9). Table 10 and figure 5 show quarterly rates of change that were even negative. Annual rates of change fluctuated between −0.9 percent in 1967 and 3.6 percent in 1964.

This period can be divided into two subperiods (1963:1–1966:3 and 1966:3–1968:1), taking external variables into account. During the first subperiod, the rate of exchange of the French franc against the dollar remained stable and reserves grew at the high annual rate of 13.3 percent (table 8). The rate of growth in the quantity of money (both M_1 and M_2) was below that for the rate of growth in reserves. In turn, all three growth rates were slightly above the growth rate of nominal GNP.

In the second subperiod the rate of growth of consumer prices and

Table 9. *Industrial Price Index, Quarterly and Annual Averages, 1963–74*
1963 = 100

Year	Quarterly averages				Annual average
	1	*2*	*3*	*4*	
1963	98.8	99.7	100.4	101.1	100.0
1964	102.5	103.4	104.0	104.5	103.6
1965	104.1	104.3	104.1	105.1	104.4
1966	106.5	109.0	107.0	106.7	107.3
1967	106.9	105.6	105.7	107.0	106.3
1968	104.2	102.6	104.3	107.2	104.6
1969	111.0	113.5	117.1	121.4	115.8
1970	124.7	125.7	124.0	123.3	124.4
1971	125.2	127.0	127.7	128.4	127.1
1972	129.6	131.4	133.0	137.7	132.9
1973	143.2	147.8	154.3	164.7	152.5
1974	186.6	202.7	201.3	197.2	196.9

Source: International Monetary Fund, *International Financial Statistics*, 1973 Supplement and vol. 29 (March 1976).

nominal incomes were about the same as in the first subperiod, but reserves grew at a much lower rate (0.3 percent), whereas the price of the dollar increased slightly (as shown in figure 6). Moreover, the annual rate of growth of M_1 fell from 10.0 percent to 2.2 percent, which implies that, in the short run, there is no rigid relation between nominal income and the quantity of money, at least as far as M_1 is defined.

The following facts are of interest. From 1966:3 to 1968:1 prices were relatively stable in France, the real rate of growth was relatively high (6.3 percent a year on average), but the growth in the quantity of money (M_1) was low, whereas international reserves were stagnant. In other words, given the rate of growth of nominal GDP, the balance of payments did not produce the expected inflow of money.

On the other hand, both these subperiods are not fundamentally different if one looks at the growth of either the nominal or the real GNP, the inflation rate, or the growth of M_2. Table 8 shows a close link between the rates of growth of nominal income and M_2 in both subperiods.

THE PERIOD FROM 1968 TO 1973. The quarterly rates of increase of consumer prices were generally higher than 1.2 percent, and fell below that rate only in 1968:2, 1969:3, 1970:3–4, and 1973:1 (as shown in table 4). The annual rate of increase rose from a level of 4.6 percent in 1968 to 6.1 percent

Table 10. *Quarterly and Annual Rates of Change in Industrial Prices, 1963–74*
Percent

	Quarterly rate[a]				
Year	1	2	3	4	Annual rate[b]
1963	0.9	0.9	0.7	0.7	...
1964	1.4	0.9	0.6	0.5	3.6
1965	−0.4	0.2	−0.2	1.0	0.8
1966	1.3	2.3	−1.8	−0.3	2.8
1967	0.2	−1.2	0.1	1.2	−0.9
1968	−2.6	−1.5	1.7	2.8	−1.6
1969	3.5	2.3	3.2	3.7	10.7
1970	2.7	0.8	−1.4	−0.6	7.4
1971	1.5	1.4	0.6	0.5	2.2
1972	0.9	1.4	1.2	3.5	4.6
1973	4.0	3.2	4.4	6.7	14.7
1974	13.3	8.6	−0.7	−2.0	29.1

Source: Table 9.
a. Rate of change from previous quarter.
b. Rate of change from previous year's annual average.

in 1972 (with slight declines in 1970 and 1971). In terms of consumer prices, therefore, inflation accelerated slightly over the period.

The increase in the prices of industrial products was less steady: the rate was high in 1969 (10.7 percent), which might be explained both by the lagged effect of the increases in wages in 1968 and the devaluation of the franc in August. This rate then fell to 2.2 percent in 1971 and rose to 4.6 percent in 1972.

Two subperiods can also be distinguished in this second period, using criteria relating to external variables. First, during the subperiod from 1968: 2 to 1970:1, reserves rapidly decreased at an average yearly rate of 22.7 percent. The French franc was devalued in August 1969, but reserves (excluding borrowing from the IMF) went on decreasing until 1970:1 (a possible lag effect of the devaluation).

This subperiod provides an interesting example of an exogenous increase in costs, in the form of an increase in nominal wages, at a rate of roughly 11 percent decided by the Grenelle agreements of June 1968. These were signed by the government, the workers' trade unions, and the professional associations after the political events of May and June that included a general strike. It is therefore a typical case of cost-push inflation of domestic origin.

If monetary policy had been restrictive, producers would have been able to bear this rise in costs in the face of foreign competition only by cutting

Figure 6. *Rate of Exchange of the French Franc for the U.S. Dollar,
1963–75*

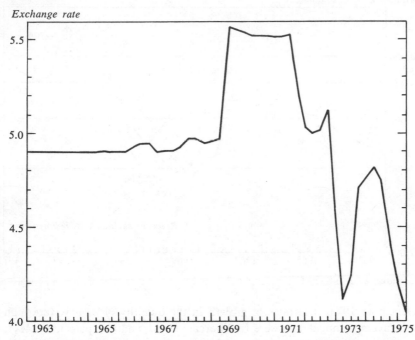

Exchange rate

Source: International Monetary Fund, *International Financial Statistics*, 1973 Supplement and vol. 29 (March 1976).

production and increasing unemployment. To avert this, the monetary authorities decided on an extremely expansive monetary policy. The deficit in the balance of payments increased, but it is difficult to assess whether this was the result of relative price changes—French prices having increased more than foreign prices—or whether there was a spillover of excess liquidity to foreigners. Both the trade account and the capital account were in deficit. The fact that the deterioration of the capital account was greater than that of the trade account could have been explained by either the 1968 import quotas or speculation. Speculation against the franc definitely accentuated the deficit, but the exchange controls decided on in the summer of 1968 were obviously ineffective.

During the second subperiod from 1970:1 to 1972:4 reserves increased rapidly and steadily at an average annual rate of 38.0 percent (table 8 and figure 7), in spite of the increase in the price of the French franc in terms of the dollar (figure 6) because of the parity adjustments decided upon in

Figure 7. *French International Reserves, 1963–75*

Millions of U.S. dollars

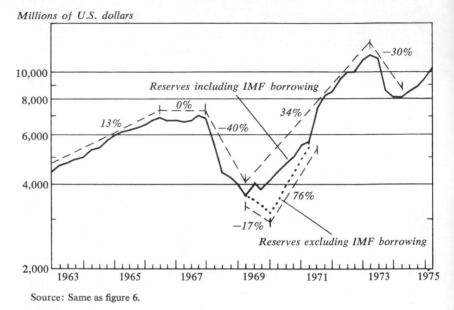

Source: Same as figure 6.

December 1971. The rates of growth in the quantity of money were high (the average annual rates were 15.2 percent for M_1 and 19.0 percent for M_2).

Until the end of 1971, the level of the world price index calculated by the Institut National de la Statistique et des Etudes Economiques was declining.[13] French industrial prices increased by 7.4 percent in 1970 and only 2.2 percent in 1971; but consumer prices increased by 5.8 percent and 5.4 percent, respectively.

THE PERIOD FROM 1973 TO 1974. This is the period of bursting inflation: consumer prices gained 7.4 percent in 1973[14] but rose by 13.6 percent from 1973:2 to 1974:2. This high rate can be partially explained by the government's reluctance to impose too restrictive a monetary policy and thereby cause more unemployment during an election period. A new National Assembly was elected in March 1973 and a new President of the Republic in May 1974. The only policy that was supposed to be anti-inflationary was the reduction of the value added tax at the beginning of 1973. The pro-

13. This index has been calculated from Reuter and Moody's indexes in dollars for raw materials, weighted according to French imports. Therefore it does not take account of exchange rate changes, and it is not an index of French import prices.

14. The low increase in 1973 can be explained by a decrease in the rate of the value added tax, decided upon before the March general elections.

Table 11. *Annual Rates of Growth of Real Gross Domestic Product, 1963–74*
Percent

Year	Rate	Year	Rate
1963	5.8	1969	7.7
1964	6.6	1970	6.0
1965	4.7	1971	5.5
1966	5.6	1972	5.4
1967	5.0	1973	6.1
1968	5.0	1974	4.7

Source: INSEE, *Tendances de la Conjoncture*, various issues.

gressive limitation of the rate of growth of credits given by banks was only decided upon at the beginning of 1974.

Growth and employment

The rate of growth of real income was quite high and remarkably stable during the whole period; the full employment target was reached. Moreover, it appears, as already indicated, that the real rates of growth and unemployment are quite independent of the rate of inflation, so that the opinion, widespread in France, that a "minimum" inflation would be necessary to support growth is unwarranted.

Table 8 indicates that the average annual rate of growth of the real national income was 6.9 percent in the first period from 1963:1 to 1968:1, 5.8 percent in the second period, 1968:1 to 1972:4, and 5.4 percent in the third period, 1973–74. Thus the relation between growth and inflation, if any, would be an inverse one.

The stability of the growth rate is apparent from table 11 (annual data) and figure 8 (quarterly data): the annual rate of growth of real GDP was below 5 percent only in 1965, and the only trough was caused by the 1968 events, which did not prevent a 5 percent growth rate for the whole year. However, the anti-inflationary policy caused economic activity to slow down in the first half of 1975.

On the other hand, economic activity was exceptionally high in 1969, which certain people attribute to the increase in wages, but which can be explained by a very high level of investment and foreign demand. The reason for the high level of investment might well have been that some investment projects had been deferred from 1968 to 1969 because of the uncertain economic climate.

Unemployment figures remained low and can be explained by demographic rather than short-term economic factors. Unemployment fluctuates

Figure 8. *French Nominal and Real Gross Domestic Product, 1963–74*

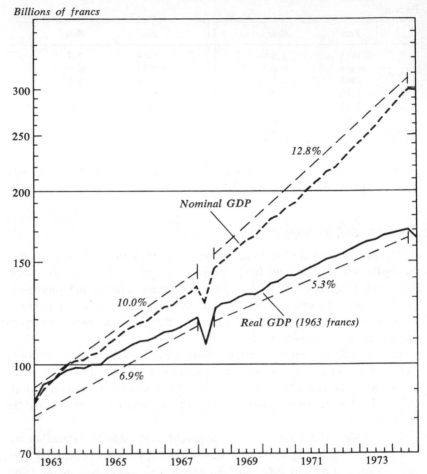

Billions of francs

Source: INSEE, *Tendances de la Conjoncture*, various issues. The percentages are average annual rates of growth over the periods indicated.

with the changing number of newcomers on the labor market. It varies depending on the age pyramid or special events such as the arrival of repatriates from Algeria in 1962[15] and the reduced length of military service after the Algerian war. And, over all, it varies according to long-term factors affecting the labor market (the natural rate of unemployment).

15. The people repatriated from Algeria and looking for a job have only been considered as unemployed since 1965, which may explain the rise in the number of workers in search of jobs from 1964 to 1965 (table 12).

Table 12. *Number of Unemployed and Unfilled Vacant Positions, 1963–74*
Thousands

Year	Number of unemployed	Number of unfilled vacancies
1963	97	54
1964	98	45
1965	142	30
1966	148	38
1967	196	32
1968	254	36
1969	223	78
1970	262	93
1971	337	126
1972	383	166
1973	394	252
1974	498	205

Source: INSEE, *Tendances de la Conjoncture*, various issues.

Both the number of workers looking for a job and the number of vacancies have been continuously increasing, as shown in table 12. It would therefore be wrong to interpret the increase in the number of unemployed as proof of a rising rate of unemployment. Both phenomena may indicate that workers have lengthened their search time in order to find better jobs. In other words, there has been a continuous rise in the natural rate of unemployment.[16] The fluctuations around the trend are not very important.

There is therefore no apparent Phillips curve relation in France, since the rate of unemployment has increased as inflation has increased. For instance, Spitäller finds a trade-off between the rate of change of the GNP deflator and the rate of unemployment in France only for the period 1956–68 and with a weak explanatory power.[17]

16. In 1967, a new official institution, l'Agence Nationale pour l'Emploi, was created to take care of employment problems. Due to its higher compensation rates, a larger number of people declared themselves unemployed. This institution also improved employment statistics. However, it is considered that adequate statistics of the number of unemployed are not available for the period before 1972. Therefore part of the rise in unemployment between 1966 and 1972 may be due to a progressive improvement in statistical methods (it has been said that previous data for unemployed people ought to be multiplied by 1.6 to give comparable figures). But the mere fact of a long-run increase in both excess supply and excess demand for labor remains. It is also not surprising that the OECD got a good fit by explaining the rate of unemployment only by time and a business cycle indicator (see Organisation for Economic Co-operation and Development, *Economic Surveys: France* [Paris: OECD, February 1974]).

17. Erich Spitäller, "Prices and Unemployment in Selected Industrial Countries," *IMF Staff Papers*, vol. 18 (November 1971), pp. 528–69.

Figure 9. *Annual Percentage Changes in the Consumer Price Index in Relation to Labor Market Conditions, 1963–74*

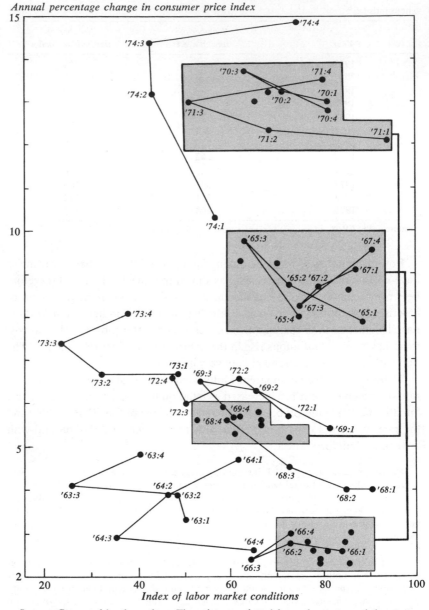

Annual percentage change in consumer price index

Index of labor market conditions

Source: Computed by the authors. The points are plotted for each quarter and the quarters for each year are joined by solid lines. For the years 1965, 1967, 1970, and 1971, see inserts. Rates of change are percentage differences between each quarter and same quarter of previous year. The index of labor market conditions is calculated as: [(registered job searchers − declared unfilled vacancies)/(registered job searchers)] × 100.

Figure 9 relates the rate of change of consumer prices to an index of labor market conditions.[18] It is striking that the three periods defined above that differ in rates of inflation are clearly delineated in figure 9. For each period there is a short-run trade-off between inflation and unemployment, but from one period to another the Phillips curve shifts upward as inflation accelerates. There is no apparent trade-off in the long run.[19] Similar relations can be found by connecting nominal wage changes and unemployment.

In the private sector wages are negotiated every year, usually for each sector, between the representatives of firms and the major trade unions. Collective agreements very often include "provisions for expected price increases"; similar procedures exist in the public sector, for public firms and for the civil service.

If the price increase is higher than expected, there is an a posteriori adjustment of wage rates in order to reach the collectively agreed target for real wages. But wage earners are induced to negotiate on the basis of high expected rates of inflation, since they will get the nominal wages decided in collective agreements even if the increase in prices is lower. This system has inflationary effects, which are very different from the effects of a system of a posteriori indexation.

Wages are often considered as responsible for a cost-push inflation. In fact, it is difficult to gauge the precise role of increases in nominal wages in the process of inflation, since both follow about the same path and the data do not themselves indicate which variable—inflation or wage increase—adjusts to the other.

In order to assess how nominal wages affect inflation it is first necessary to find out by what proportion increases in nominal wages have exceeded the rate of change of labor productivity. Unfortunately, statistics for labor productivity changes in France are not very reliable. From computations made by INSEE, it seems that net changes in labor productivity[20] have occurred at a fairly constant rate of 3 percent a year.

Taking this rate into account figure 10 shows that nominal wages did not contribute to the mild inflation of the period 1963–67. The year 1968 offers a typical example of an abrupt and exogenous change in cost conditions. Wage increases in 1968 certainly influenced the upswing of inflation begin-

18. See figure 9 for explanation of how this index is derived.
19. The use of the index defined in figure 9 eliminates the possible influence of the long-term growth of the natural rate of unemployment.
20. Defined as the excess of the rate of change in production over the rate of change of hours worked (calculated as the sum of working hours plus the number of working hours incorporated in investments and imports).

Figure 10. *Annual Percentage Changes in Nominal Wages,*
1964:1–1974:4

Annual percentage change

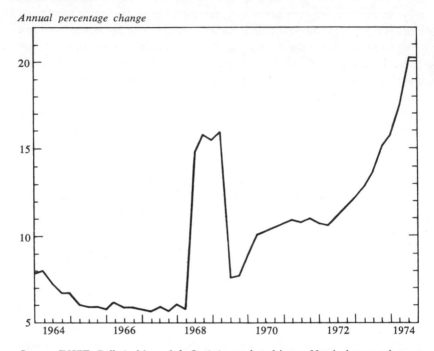

Source: INSEE, *Bulletin Mensuel de Statistique,* selected issues. Nominal wage values are
based on an index of workers' wage rates. Rates of change are percentage differences between
each quarter and same quarter of the previous year.

ning in the late sixties. It was not until late 1973 through 1974, however,
that wage earners succeeded in imposing similar increases in nominal wages.
In fact, as seen in figure 11, the increase in real wages in 1969 was much
lower than in any other year, which means that workers were not compensated for the price inflation caused by the excessive nominal increases in
1968. This indicates that real wages cannot be determined autonomously,
except in the special social and political conditions characteristic of 1968
when the government both accepted an exceptional increase in wages and
adopted a very liberal credit policy—or when, maybe, everyone took it for
granted that monetary and credit policy was very expansionary.

These and other developments led to an income distribution that remained
unchanged throughout the whole period from 1963 to 1971 (table 13). The
proposition that inflation stems from the continuous efforts of wage earners
to get a larger slice of the pie is debatable, since a drastic decrease in the *rate*

Figure 11. *Annual Percentage Changes in Real Wages, 1964:1–1974:4*

Annual percentage change

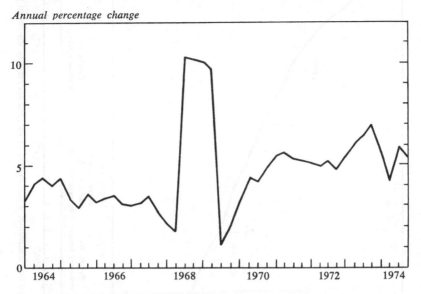

Source: Same as figure 10. Real wage values are based on an index of workers' wage rates, deflated by the consumer price index. Rates of change are percentage differences between each quarter and the same quarter of the previous year.

of change of nominal wages was accepted in 1969. That was a time of restrictive monetary policy, which may have dampened wage increase demands. However, as figure 11 illustrates, the quarterly rates of increase in real wages were higher after 1969 (1970–74) than before (1964–67).

Economic policy

Figure 12 plots the curve of consumer prices (given in figure 1) and indicates the main economic measures taken between 1963 and 1974 to regulate both price and monetary policies.

At different times, the government decided on various forms of price control:

1. In September 1963, price increases were forbidden for industrial products.

2. At the beginning of 1965, "contrats de stabilité" were instituted; price rises were possible for some products if compensated for by decreases in prices for other products; prices of industrial goods could increase in proportion to the rise in the cost of raw materials.

Figure 12. *Price Control Measures, Monetary Policy, and the Consumer Price Index, 1963–74*

Consumer price index (1963 = 100)

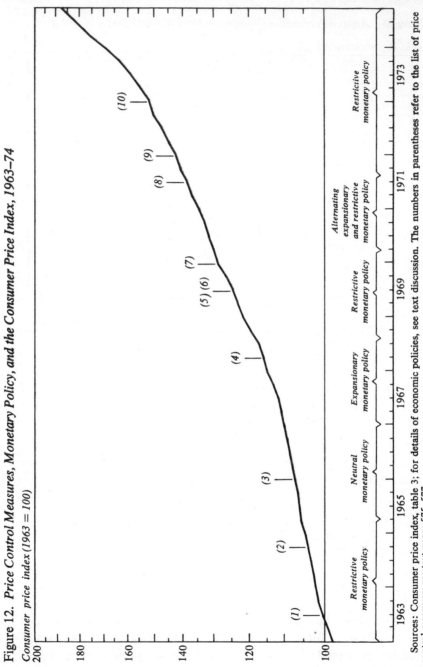

Sources: Consumer price index, table 3; for details of economic policies, see text discussion. The numbers in parentheses refer to the list of price control measures; see text pages 575, 577.

Table 13. *Ratio of Total Wages to National Income, 1963–74*
Percent

Year	Ratio	Year	Ratio
1963	61.5	1969	61.1
1964	61.9	1970	61.5
1965	62.2	1971	62.5
1966	61.9	1972	65.5
1967	61.6	1973	65.9
1968	61.8	1974	67.0

Source: INSEE, *Rapports sur les Comptes de la Nation*, various issues.

3. In March 1966, producers who signed agreements with the government on exports, productivity, wages, and prices could regulate the prices of their own industrial goods.

4. In 1968, prices of industrial commodities were not allowed to rise more than 3 percent during the second half of the year.

5. Between August and September 1969, no price increases were allowed.

6. In September 1969, the government requested one month's notice of any price increase.

7. In February 1970, firms were free to raise prices provided they signed a "contrat de programme" with the government.

8. In September 1971, producers agreed not to raise industrial prices more than 1.5 percent in six months.

9. In April 1972, small firms and firms in competition with foreigners were free to raise prices, but other firms had to sign agreements with the government agreeing not to raise them more than 3 percent a year ("contrats de programmation annuelle").

10. In April 1973, the government instituted the "programmation annuelle des prix industriels," the ceiling on the average rise in industrial prices was 3.6 percent from April 1973 to April 1974. These "contrats" were renewed in 1974. Traders agreed to limit their trade margins.

When the proposed targets of these various and imaginative policies are compared with their insignificant results, one cannot but regret the tremendous waste of energy on the part of civil servants and businessmen.

The Organisation for Economic Co-operation and Development outlines several stages in the development of French monetary policy:[21]

• March 1963 to June 1965, restrictive policy;
• July 1965 to February 1967, neutral policy;

21. OECD, *Monetary Policy in France*, Monetary Studies Series (Paris: OECD, 1974), especially pp. 41–47.

Figure 13. *The Money Supply in France, 1963–74*

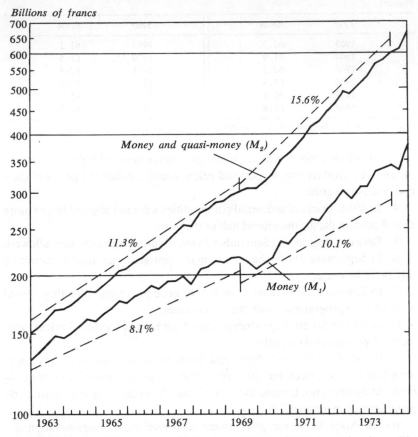

Source: International Monetary Fund, *International Financial Statistics*, various issues. The percentages are average annual rates of growth over the periods indicated.

- March 1967 to November 1968, expansionary policy;
- November 1968 to June 1970, restrictive policy;
- July 1970 to October 1972, expansionary policy with periods of restriction;
- After November 1972, a steadily more restrictive policy.

In fact, if the quantity of money is taken as an indicator of expansionary policy, it can be seen from figure 13 that there was only one period of really severe monetary restraint: between 1969 and 1970, when monetary balances (M_1) did not increase. This stage was one of "stabilization" in that the inflation rate did not increase, although it remained in the vicinity of 5 percent (table 4). But, at the same time, the sum of the quantity of money and quasi-money (M_2) increased at about the same rate as before.

In each of the periods before and after 1969–70, the rate of growth in the quantity of money was more or less constant, with a higher average value in the period after 1970.

Interpretation[22]

Any explanation of world inflation in recent years (and especially in 1973 and 1974) must deal with the relationship between exchange rates, both fixed and flexible, and the rate of inflation. Undeniably, significant changes in exchange rates have taken place at times of exceptional rates of inflation. Take the case of France, for instance. August 1969 marks the changeover from a fixed, and fairly stable, regime to one of variable rates (see figures 3 and 6). Inflation rates were much higher thereafter. However, in our opinion, it is going too far to infer a causal relation between the two. For one thing, the period of exceptionally high inflation rates (1973–74)—or even the longer period of floating exchange rates (1969–74)—is too short to indicate any such relationship. Second, even if the one-time rise in raw material prices did not generate inflation (that is, cause prices to continually increase), it did have a short-term impact in that prices were higher than they would otherwise have been. The rise obviously affected industrial prices, but it occurred independently and was not associated with the floating of the exchange rate. Our third rationale for not placing too much credence as yet in the argument that floating exchange rates transmit inflation is because we believe it reasonable to assume that the recent upsurge in world inflation logically follows the increase in inflation in previous years that began under a system of fixed rates and that was transmitted across national borders. It is normal for inflation to accelerate if policies are not sufficiently restrictive. External disequilibria necessarily follow that lead to parity changes and exchange floating.

It should also be pointed out that when a currency depreciates, prices of imports, import-competing goods, and finally nontradables rise, following

22. We restrict ourselves in this section to the evaluation of inflation as it affects France and the transmission of inflation to that medium-sized country. We use the monetary approach to support our interpretation of the French situation. Both the monetary approach to the balance of payments and the Keynesian theory are discussed in detail elsewhere in this volume (see the papers by William H. Branson and Alexander K. Swoboda).

Table 14. *Ratio of Imports to Gross Domestic Product, 1963–74*
Percent

Year	Ratio	Year	Ratio
1963	11.8	1969	14.1
1964	12.3	1970	14.9
1965	11.6	1971	14.9
1966	12.4	1972	15.3
1967	12.0	1973	16.5
1968	12.4	1974	22.7

Source: INSEE, *Tendances de la Conjoncture*, various issues.

substitution effects. The price of the franc in terms of the dollar and other currencies has certainly gone down since 1973:2 (figure 3), but this fall came after a steep climb that might have been excessive.

The period considered, in fact, is too short for a clear-cut judgment to be made on the relationship between exchange rates and inflation. In the specific case of France, exchange rate changes can be considered rather as a consequence of inflation than a cause, nor was inflation only imported. World inflation began under fixed rates and, later, floating rates may have played a permissive role in French inflation.

We attempt below to evaluate in which respects the characteristic features of the monetary approach are present in French inflation.

Price arbitrage

Price arbitrage implies that the country under review is in a competitive situation with the outside world. Table 14 shows that the ratio of imports to gross domestic product slightly increased between 1963 and 1973, that is, the French economy became more open. However, the table does not give a satisfactory picture of the arbitrage mechanism. Price arbitrage is likely to play an important role in the transmission of inflation if tradables as well as imports have a large share of the national income. One therefore needs to know the degree of competitiveness and the degree of substitutability between imported and domestic goods, which no doubt can only be evaluated on an a priori basis, that is, after deciding that such-and-such a category should be included among the tradables or nontradables. A classification of this sort cannot be satisfactory. Actually, in examining the facts, it is not obvious that price arbitrage played much of a role at all. The index of import prices in terms of francs (table 5) remained relatively constant until the third quarter of 1969 at a time when there was noticeable inflation in France and in the world. Table 7 shows that the index of import prices rose

Table 15. *Velocity of Money, End-of-Quarter Rates for M_1 and M_2, 1963–74*

	Quarter							
	1		2		3		4	
Year	M_1	M_2	M_1	M_2	M_1	M_2	M_1	M_2
1963	0.65	0.56	0.66	0.58	0.66	0.58	0.65	0.57
1964	0.68	0.59	0.67	0.59	0.65	0.57	0.64	0.56
1965	0.66	0.57	0.66	0.57	0.66	0.56	0.65	0.56
1966	0.66	0.56	0.65	0.55	0.65	0.55	0.65	0.54
1967	0.67	0.55	0.66	0.54	0.67	0.53	0.67	0.52
1968	0.72	0.54	0.62	0.47	0.70	0.52	0.70	0.53
1969	0.73	0.53	0.73	0.54	0.75	0.54	0.78	0.54
1970	0.84	0.56	0.84	0.56	0.84	0.55	0.79	0.53
1971	0.82	0.53	0.80	0.52	0.82	0.52	0.80	0.50
1972	0.83	0.51	0.79	0.48	0.79	0.48	0.78	0.48
1973	0.83	0.50	0.81	0.48	0.63	0.48	0.80	0.47
1974	0.82	0.48	0.84	0.48	0.90	0.49	0.78	0.44

Source: Based on data for figures 8 and 13.

by an average annual rate of 1.0 percent from 1963:1 to 1967:4, whereas the index of consumer prices rose at a rate of 3.2 percent. In the following period, the gap was smaller, since imports rose at a 4.3 percent annual rate between 1967:4 and 1972:4 and consumer prices at a 5.8 percent rate. (The divergences between import prices and industrial prices were slightly less.)

One might be tempted to conclude therefore that the price arbitrage mechanism does not operate with the precision attributed to it by those favoring the monetary approach to the balance of payments. At least it operates with a time lag so that many other elements may play a role in the international transmission mechanism during the price adjustment period. Import and domestic price movements differ for a variety of reasons; and it still remains a fact that all indexes accelerated at about the same time.

In the period of variable effective exchange rates (1969–74), French prices and world prices (corrected by the changes in effective exchange rates) moved closely together, giving some support to the purchasing-power–parity doctrine.

Stability of the real demand for money

The monetary approach to the balance of payments can be valid only if there is a stable demand for real balances, without any liquidity trap. Data on the velocity of money in France (table 15) confirm that such a stable function exists, at least if it is not defined according to the very strict quantity theory approach, and total income *and* the inflation rate are also considered as explanatory variables of the demand for money. The table shows that the velocity of M_1 clearly increased at the beginning of the most inflationary period (late 1968): from a value averaging 0.66 before 1968, it rose to an average value above 0.80 in 1970 and thereafter. But it is fairly constant within each homogeneous period, that is, when inflationary expectations can be assumed to be constant. In contrast, the velocity of M_2 decreased after 1970, which reflects the growing importance of quasi-money. During inflation, there is greater preference for quasi-money, since it provides income as well as liquidity.[23] Econometric studies have also confirmed that the demand for money is stable in France.[24]

The supply of money and the role of reserves

Verification of the monetary approach also implies a stable function for money supply. In fact, if it is possible to define a monetary base in such a way that the money multiplier is stable, it is possible to find out if the demand for money is satisfied by domestic money creation or by a change in the level of international reserves. Unfortunately, it is difficult to do this for France because, first of all, there is no satisfactory model to explain the supply of money, and, second, the preceding factual analysis produces somewhat mixed reactions. We noted when describing the first period (1963–68) that during both subperiods distinguished the real rate of growth remained roughly the same, whereas international reserves increased during the first subperiod and remained more or less constant during the second. The quantity of money, M_1, increased less during the second subperiod. Can it be said that the changes in the quantity of money are a consequence of fluctuations in the accumulation of reserves or that monetary policy was more restrictive in the first subperiod so that entrepreneurs and the like had to export more? Obviously, it is difficult to decide which of these interpretations is valid. However, the computations in table 16 support the idea that the changes in international reserves more or less compensated for the changes in the rate

23. The definition of M_2 in France can be criticized for it includes, for example, savings for housing in special accounts, which cannot be used for four years.

24. J. Melitz, "La demande de monnaie en France: tentative d'explication," *Statistiques et études financières*, no. 11 (1973), pp. 21–48; A. Chaineau and others, "Etude économétrique de la thésaurisation française (1952–1966)," *Banque* (June 1968), pp. 1–8; J. M. Grandmont, "Sur la demande de monnaie de court terme et de long terme," *Annales de l'INSEE* (January–April 1972), pp. 65–86; J. P. Dalloz, "La fonction de demande de monnaie—La France de 1920 à 1968," *Revue économique* (1969), pp. 468–96.

Table 16. *Rates of Growth of M₂ (Money Plus Quasi-Money),*
International Reserves, and Other Banking Sector Assets,[a] *1963–74*
Percent

| Year | | Rate of growth | |
	M_2	International reserves	Other bank assets[a]
1963	14.1	21.2	11.6
1964	9.8	16.6	7.4
1965	10.9	10.8	8.9
1966	10.6	6.1	9.8
1967	13.1	3.9	14.7
1968	11.6	−39.9	0.3
1969	7.1	−8.8	18.0
1970	15.2	29.4	20.8
1971	18.2	66.4	15.2
1972	18.6	21.3	18.5
1973	14.9	−14.8	13.9
1974	18.1	3.8	19.8

Sources: *International Financial Statistics*, various issues; Banque de France, *Bulletin trimestriel*, various issues.

a. These are all assets—except international reserves—of the consolidated banking sector (Banque de France and the commercial banks).

of growth of other components of the quantity of money, M_2 (no similar data exist for M_1). But any further study would imply knowing the rate of growth of the world quantity of money.

A recent econometric study also lends support to the monetary view. It finds that a 1 percent rise in credits of a domestic banking asset leads to a 0.7 percent decrease in international reserves in the period 1964–70, if the exchange rate and foreign prices are held constant.[25] In his paper, Alexander Swoboda also suggests an indicator to evaluate the existence of a monetary approach mechanism: a higher rise in the consumer price index than in the industrial price index (or the import price index) may be an indication of an autonomous—nonimported—national inflation.[26] Meanwhile, there ought to be a balance of payments deficit.

We have found a higher rise in the French consumer price index than in other indexes throughout the period 1963–72. But the balance of payments was in deficit only from 1968 to 1970 and was more or less in equilibrium

25. R. Archer and C. Bordes, "Les mouvements de réserves publiques dans l'économie française: une tentative d'explication par l'approche monétaire de la balance des paiements," *Banque* (May and June 1975), pp. 491–99 and pp. 595–604, respectively.

26. See pages 9–51.

between 1966 and 1968. There was a surplus in 1963–66 and 1970–72.[27] However, there are many reasons that may explain the possible divergence between the behavior of the indicator (relative price rises) and the balance of payments, which are not consistent with the monetary approach: the effective exchange rate has been variable since 1969; and, as we have already pointed out, there may have been changes in relative prices between tradables and nontradables due to real rather than inflationary factors, as was the case in 1973.

Comments by Helen B. Junz

SALIN AND LANE quite correctly begin by asking the relevant questions: (1) the extent to which French inflation has differed from the rate of inflation in the rest of the world; (2) why such a difference may have arisen; and finally (3) whether inflationary tendencies in France were mainly of internal or of external origin. In evaluating the various facts that might reveal the answers to these questions the authors say that they are attempting to test the validity of both the Keynesian and the monetary approach to the question of inflation. The conclusions drawn after a lengthy discussion of factual data imply that the main source of inflationary tendencies in France has been of internal origin and that changes in exchange rates have generally followed "above-average" increases in internal prices.

The conclusions drawn may well be correct. However, it would be hard to arrive at a decision regarding their validity from either the facts or the discussion presented in the paper. Salin and Lane make a commendable attempt to arrive at some overall conclusions, but they base these conclusions on a very simple examination of statistical series of retail prices, so-called export and import prices, exchange rates, and various policy variables. The actual circumstances giving rise to the changes in the statistical series are ignored as is the enormous complexity of the interrelationships between the variables presented; a complexity that has become especially apparent over the past several years when the evolution of the international monetary system toward greater exchange rate flexibility was being tested by high inflation rates and worldwide recession.

As to the general background, Salin and Lane state that, as measured by

27. The reverse happened in 1973: import prices and industrial prices rose more than consumer prices, but there was a fall in reserves instead of the possibly expected rise; we know, however, that the rise in relative prices (import or industrial prices to retail prices) was due to real factors—the price increases for oil and raw materials—and not a certain process of transmission of inflation.

changes in retail prices, French inflation rates for the period 1963 to 1974 have generally tended to accelerate and on the whole have been above price rises recorded in other industrial countries. This description, however, does not appear quite to accord with the facts as shown. For the subperiod 1963 to 1969, chosen by the authors, the French retail price index increased at annual rates that, on average, about equaled those in other European OECD countries. In the early seventies, French retail prices actually increased somewhat less than the European OECD average. Part of the confusion that might be created by a superficial analysis of these price data lies in the choice of the periods examined. Thus in the years before 1963 price pressures in France definitely were higher than those in other European OECD countries. This was largely the result of an excessive increase in consumer demand associated with the end of the Algerian conflict and with a very fast rise in incomes from employment. Consequently, a stabilization program was introduced in the fall of 1963. The choice of the starting point of the period reviewed thus coincides with the starting point of a stabilization program, which brought about a moderation of increases in retail prices to a stable, rather than an accelerating, rate of increase until early 1968. The policy environment during this period is rather different, therefore, from that pictured by the authors: the rate of expansion of gross domestic product at a relatively stable 5 percent a year was on average somewhat higher than those in neighboring countries, but was not sufficient to fully absorb productive resources—in particular, labor. Unemployment rose continually over the period, partly reflecting demographic changes. Hence, the commitment, or overcommitment, of the authorities to full employment that, according to Salin and Lane, led to excessively easy monetary policies, appears not to have been quite as strong as implied in the paper. It is true that the repatriation from Algeria and lower military recruitment after the end of the Algerian war may have given rise to a greater degree of mismatches between the demand for labor and the supply of it than existed earlier. There may have been shortages in particular categories of skilled labor—seen in the rising vacancy rates—at the same time as overall unemployment rose. Nevertheless, the 1963–68 period cannot easily be characterized as a period of excess demand, as Salin and Lane appear to do.

The inflation following the strikes of 1968 clearly was of a wage-push nature. But the strikes themselves appeared to be more a reflection of sociopolitical unrest rather than of strictly economic conditions. After the strikes, the authorities admittedly pursued very loose monetary and budgetary policies that were adopted explicitly to help the private sector accommodate to the higher wage costs, without creating significant strains on the liquidity position of medium-sized and small companies or measurably raising unemployment. Indeed, output made a strong recovery, but the accompanying increase in productivity could not prevent a very substantial rise in unit labor costs. Consequently, price pressures were considerable during that period. The accompanying inflationary expectations, the rapid rise in economic activity in France after mid-1968, and the still subdued demand situation elsewhere combined to bring about a deterioration in the external position of the French economy. This, in turn, resulted in speculation against the French franc, which was given further impetus by the growing expectations that an upward valuation of the deutsche mark would be inevitable. These circumstances brought about the devaluation of the franc in 1969.

During the period 1969 to 1974, except for the adjustment of the internal price level to the devaluation, inflationary pressures in France and the preceding cost increases do not appear to have been significantly greater than in other countries. In 1974, the rate of inflation clearly is strongly associated with the differential effect of the increase in oil prices on the French economy and the policy response of the French authorities, which was less restrictive than that in a number of other industrial countries. Thus it is hard to characterize the entire 1963–74 period in as homogeneous a fashion as the authors appear to do.

More troublesome than their rather broad-brush analysis of the period as a whole is the simple relationship between some of the relevant variables that the discussion appears to imply. For example, a higher rate of increase in retail prices compared with those of other countries is taken to be an indication of a loss in international competitiveness leading to devaluation. Clearly, the existence of higher-than-average retail price increases is not an a priori symptom of the need for exchange rate adjustment. In fact, since the French economy over the period grew at a rather faster rate than did those of neighboring countries, a higher rise in retail prices might have been expected and would not necessarily indicate a loss in competitiveness. It may even be that the steady rate of growth of output at relatively high rates of capacity utilization may have conveyed some competitive advantage to the French economy over those economies that suffered the effects of stop-go policies over the period. It should also be remembered that, abstracting from cyclical effects, the French trade balance was in surplus during the entire period, and official holdings of international reserve assets were increasing significantly. The question might be asked, therefore, whether a certain amount of internal inflation may not have been generated by a commitment to an undervalued rate of exchange and a buildup of international reserves over that period.

Second, throughout most of the discussion in the paper, a relatively simple relationship between changes in import prices, changes in retail prices, and changes in exchange rates is implied, although the exact nature of the causal chain is not quite clear. Apart from the arguments for and against purchasing-power–parity concepts, the rather simple statistical comparisons drawn may actually be misleading. The problems attaching to comparisons of unit value indexes, used as a proxy for price measurements in foreign trade, and internal price series based on transaction prices and fixed weights, are well known. They relate to the fact that unit value indexes reflect changes in the composition of trade and quality changes as well as price changes, whereas the internal price series attempt to isolate only price changes. In the case of France, these problems may all but invalidate the comparisons drawn, in part because of the considerable change in the structure of French foreign trade that occurred during the period under review. For example, the share of manufactured goods in French imports rose from 47 percent in 1963 to 63 percent in 1971. Under the assumption that the unit value of manufactured goods tends to be higher than that of other products, there would have been an upward tendency in the unit value index of French imports over that period. However, this upward tendency would have been tempered by the reduction in tariffs among the countries of the European Community and the more general tariff cuts following the Kennedy Round.

Perhaps more important than the statistical problems that tend to impair the "price" comparisons made in the paper is the analysis of the relationship between exchange rate changes, import prices, and domestic prices. The causal relationships implied appear to be based on a chain of events that runs from devaluation to a rise in import prices leading to a rise in the domestic price level. Interpretation of the relationships of interacting variables of this sort is always ambiguous and therefore cannot be undertaken in a vacuum. An exchange rate change presumably occurs because of the prior existence of a disequilibrium; the nature of the existing disequilibrium and the remedial policy actions accompanying the exchange rate change will determine the effects such a change will have on pricing decisions and on demand and supply conditions. Hence, the only generalized and simple statements that can be made in this context are that, in the absence of appropriate policy actions, inflation tends to breed inflation and that changes in both domestic prices and exchange rates reflect changes in domestic economic conditions and policies relative to those in other countries.

The fact that the conclusions that can be drawn from the type of examination employed in the current paper are necessarily tentative and nebulous points to the considerable complexity of the questions asked. In that respect Salin and Lane provide a valuable insight as to the direction of future research.

GERHARD FELS

Inflation in Germany

Table

Figures

Gerhard Fels, Kiel Institute of World Economics, wishes to thank those of his colleagues at the Kiel Institute who discussed various aspects of this paper with him, in particular, Klaus-Werner Schatz for doing the calculations, Frank Weiss for many valuable suggestions, Carolyn Ambler for improving the presentation, and Eva Maria Banerji for typing the draft several times.

INFLATION in West Germany since World War Two has posed a dilemma because it has been considered too high domestically but at the same time has been much below world levels. Since the remedy of permitting the deutsche mark to appreciate was for a long time taboo, external inflationary pressure was exerted by the international commodity, capital, and money markets. Thus the history of anti-inflation policy has been one of a succession of domestic efforts thwarted by an international inflationary trend, and balance of payments surpluses have been generated by resisting adjustment. Policymakers have learned something about inflation management, but the challenge to them has grown with the acceleration of world inflation and the sharpening of the causes of inflation at home.

This paper is a historical assessment of inflationary development and antiinflationary policy in West Germany. It reviews the general conditions under which inflation took place and which might have influenced its magnitude, analyzes the inflationary process from a cyclical point of view, and deals with the debate on the sources of inflation and to what extent it was imported from other countries. The roles of monetary, fiscal, and incomes policies are also outlined, and policy conclusions drawn from the postwar experience.

General Conditions

The conditions determining rates of inflation are supposed to have been more benign in Germany than in most other industrialized countries. Though precise knowledge of these conditions is hardly attainable, one can hypothesize some that may have had a moderating influence. Among them—though their influence seems to diminish with time—the most important appear to be the following:

1. Experience of the open hyperinflation in 1923 and of the suppressed hyperinflation after the Second World War made German public opinion extremely sensitive to rising prices. Hence, the goal of a stable price level had highest priority in economic policy.

2. Unemployment was high in the early fifties and the supply of labor re-

591

mained ample even after full employment was achieved, first, through the influx of refugees from East Germany and, later, through the influx of foreign labor from southern Europe.

3. The trade unions showed a high sense of responsibility toward the overall economic goals of employment and price stability. An indication of the relatively harmonious wage-policy scene is Germany's strike statistics, among the best for member countries of the Organisation for Economic Cooperation and Development.[1]

4. Fiscal demand management was not used to stimulate the economy before 1967; although depreciation allowances and other programs were employed during the fifties to encourage private investment, public budgets as a whole were in surplus—as it later turned out through accident rather than policy.

5. In the course of general liberalization rounds and the founding of the European Community, West Germany went ahead in reducing tariffs and other trade barriers. Revaluations of the currency also led to more competition from imports.

6. Entrepreneurs seem to have pursued long-term rather than short-term profit maximization; there is some evidence that, due to underutilization of capacity and an elastic supply of labor, real output expansion, "Mengenkonjunktur," was their objective more frequently than higher prices and thus price changes were in response to costs rather than demand.[2]

Of course, these factors have not worked independently of each other, in either an economic or a political sense. In 1967 and the following years, conditions so changed as to constitute a qualitative difference. In the recession of 1967, six years after a similar change had taken place in the United States, a form of modified Keynesianism superseded the earlier fiscal laissez-faire and monetary powerlessness. Restrictive monetary policy, though often tried, became effective only in 1966 when foreign economic conditions favored it. As a result, the German economy drifted into a real recession for the first time since the war. In the winter of 1967 economic policy was faced with a typical Keynesian discquilibrium. The gap between potential and actual gross national product amounted to 30 billion deutsche marks, or about 6

---

1. See Klaus-Werner Schatz, "Wachstumsbedingungen der Bundesrepublik Deutschland im internationalen Vergleich" [Growth Conditions of the Federal Republic of Germany by International Standards], *Die Weltwirtschaft,* vol. 1 (Tübingen: J. C. B. Mohr [Paul Siebeck], 1971), p. 213.

2. Sachverständigenrat zur Begutachtung der gesamtwirtschaftlichen Entwicklung, *Stabilisierung ohne Stagnation,* Jahresgutachten 1965/66 [Expert Council on Overall Economic Development, *Stabilization without Stagnation,* 1965/66 Annual Report] (Stuttgart and Mainz: W. Kohlhammer-Verlag, 1965), p. 147.

percent of GNP; more than one million jobs had been lost since the beginning of the downswing; and the rate of inflation was below 2 percent. It was at this time that the new government of the Grand Coalition launched an anti-recession program to reduce unemployment by increasing public spending, mainly on investment goods. The program was supported by the Bundesbank, which had accelerated money supply growth in the second half of 1966, and, despite previous reluctance, in the first half of 1967 it lowered its discount rate and financed additional public spending. The economy recovered through a domestic upswing in the summer of 1967 that was reinforced by strong export demand in the fall.

Fiscalists and monetarists disagree as to the forces that generated the upswing. Although there is much ground for controversy, public opinion ascribes the success of the antirecession policy to fiscal measures, which were widely understood as applied Keynesianism. Contrary to the predictions of the opponents of the new policy, the rate of inflation declined in the course of expansion. One year after the downturn had been reversed, the economics minister was able to claim that "inflation is as dead as a doornail."

The recession also brought about an improved legal framework for stabilization policy. In 1967 the Bundestag passed the bill on the promotion of stability and growth of the economy, which both formulates the objectives of overall economic policy and suggests the tools to be employed. Stable prices, a high level of employment, and external equilibrium were the overall objectives of the federal and state governments, along with steady and appropriate economic growth. Since the law does not attach priorities to these objectives, priority was given, in practical policy, to that goal, which was furthest from fulfillment at the particular time.

The law committed and empowered the federal administration inter alia to take the following measures:

1. To change income taxes and depreciation rates, investment premiums and public debt operations in the management of anticyclical policy.

2. To offer quantitative guidelines that would facilitate the so-called concerted action of public authorities, trade unions, and entrepreneurial associations in achieving any of the unrealized goals.

3. To employ existing economic policy tools to maintain external equilibrium, if international coordination processes did not function sufficiently well.

Although the Stability and Growth Law marks a promising new start for stabilization policy as far as the formulation of objectives is concerned, it never attained great importance in practical policy. In critical situations the government often did not offer guidelines, obviously because it feared that any individual guideline consistent with overall goals would not be obeyed. While anticyclical measures were implemented several times by legislative acts, the tools of existing law were used only in a few cases.

But these events and policies were only a part of the changes in sight. Probably those occurring during and after 1969 when the Grand Coalition was superseded by the Social-Liberal Coalition were more essential. They included:

1. More flexible exchange rates. After 1969 there were two periods of floating and three revaluations before the deutsche mark was allowed to float vis-à-vis most currencies in 1973. This meant that the Bundesbank, after a period of massive inflows of money, had to a great extent regained control of the money supply.

2. Unprecedented wage increases. In 1970 wages rose nearly 15 percent and in 1971 nearly 12 percent. The annual rate of increase had been about 8 percent between 1960 and 1969. This development was surely not independent of the wildcat strikes that occurred in the fall of 1969. In 1973 wildcat strikes flared up again, and two-digit wage increases of 12 percent occurred in both 1973 and 1974.

3. Full employment goal. The federal government in 1970 emphasized its employment goal in such a manner that it was widely understood as a guarantee.[3] Only recently, in a time of tight money and rising unemployment, had leading government officials stressed that trade unions share responsibility for full employment.

4. Public sector expansion. Since 1969 the public sector has become one of the most expansionary parts of the economy; from 1969 to 1973 its value added increased at an annual rate of 16 percent, whereas that of the private sector at only 11 percent.

5. Less foreign labor inflow. In 1973 the government slowed the influx of foreign workers, mainly by prohibiting recruitment from countries outside the European Community.

Apart from the currency float and regained monetary control since 1973, most conditions seem to have acted against stability. Although West Germany's actual inflation rate has accelerated significantly since 1970, it has remained low by international standards. And although the international

3. For instance, both the *Frankfurter Allgemeine Zeitung* of April 27, 1970, and *Der Spiegel* of May 4, 1970, refer to statements by Chancellor Willy Brandt. According to *Der Spiegel* the chancellor declared that "it is regrettable that we have to live with too high a price level for some months but it would be far worse, if—like in 1966—we had to fear a risk of jobs."

value of the deutsche mark rose significantly, much to the surprise of many experts, export surpluses increased. (Both these striking incidents are examined more closely in a later section.)

The Inflationary Process

In order to gain insight into the West German inflationary process, it is useful to break it down into two components: cycle and trend. The cycles of the general price level have followed the cycles of overall economic activity, in accordance with historical and international experience. Expansionary forces from abroad often generated the upswing, whereas domestic stabilization measures employed during the boom triggered the downturn. Domestic cycles of both production and price level have not always been synchronized with the cycles abroad due to lags in adjustment, and disharmony in anti-inflationary policies among countries. This is why, in the short run, inflation often seemed to be largely independent of foreign influences, and subject to control by domestic measures—which, however, would create balance of payments surpluses.

But study of the trend reveals that it closely followed the international inflationary trend when one took into account the revaluations of the deutsche mark. The interactions between domestic and foreign cycles and the balance of payments effects created by them often obscured the interdependence between national and international price developments in an open economy like that of West Germany. It is useful, therefore, to separate the cyclical behavior of inflation from the trend.

Figure 1 provides a picture of the cyclical variations of industrial production, labor productivity, hourly wages and salaries, unit labor costs, and the prices of industrial products from 1958 to 1974. The numbers are seasonally adjusted and expressed as percentage deviations from the trend. The industrial production cycle, which corresponds rather closely to the cycle of overall economic activity, was chosen as the reference cycle, the upper and lower turning points of which are supposed to represent the peaks and troughs of the business cycles.

The four business cycles of the German economy since 1958, including the cycle that began in 1972, are clearly indicated. (The curves of the cycle that peaked in 1955 and that of the Korean boom in 1951 cannot be shown because of inadequate data.) During the postwar period there were five booms—1951, 1955, 1960, 1965, and 1970—and two marked recessions—

Figure 1. *Cycles in West German Industry, 1958–74*

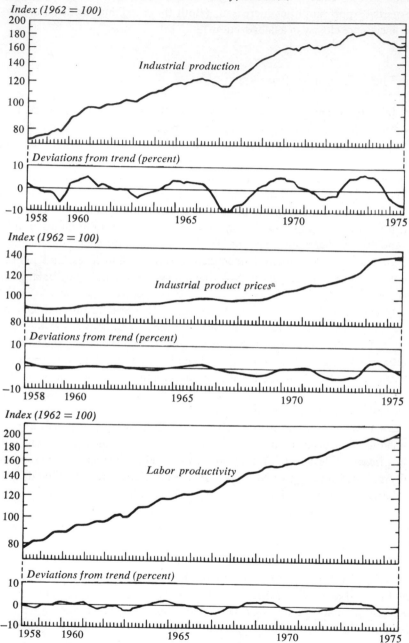

Figure 1 (*Continued*)

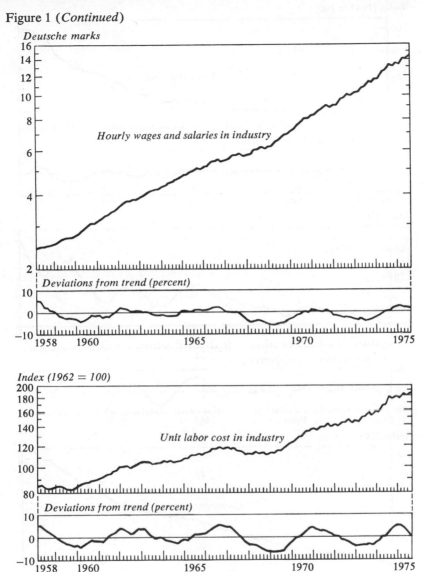

Deutsche marks

Hourly wages and salaries in industry

Deviations from trend (percent)

Index (1962 = 100)

Unit labor cost in industry

Deviations from trend (percent)

Source: Data supplied by author, converted to six-month moving averages. The trend was calculated using a thirty-period moving average on bimonthly data and extrapolated to include the final observations. Simultaneously, the percentage deviations from trend were seasonally adjusted. These deviations were further smoothed using a three-period moving average.

a. Excluding turnover taxes.

Figure 2. *West German Price Indexes, 1955–74*

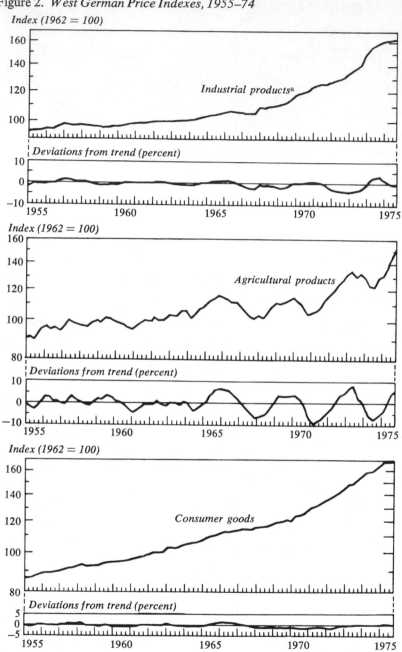

Index (1962 = 100)

Industrial products[a]

Deviations from trend (percent)

Index (1962 = 100)

Agricultural products

Deviations from trend (percent)

Index (1962 = 100)

Consumer goods

Deviations from trend (percent)

Source: Data supplied by author, converted to quarterly averages. The trend was calculated using a sixty-period moving average on monthly data (see figure 1, source).
a. Including turnover taxes.

1958 and 1967. (Troughs in 1953, 1963, and 1972 were not very significant.) The upswing that started in 1972 turned down early in 1973 when the central bank launched restrictive monetary measures under the regime of floating rates and the federal government implemented a fiscal stabilization program.

The cycles of unit labor costs and prices lagged behind the production cycle. The shortest lag was in unit labor costs. This is the consequence of cyclical changes in labor productivity, on the one hand, and the wage lag, on the other. Labor productivity, measured by output per employee, is highly sensitive to changes in total output, mainly due to the reluctance of entrepreneurs to displace labor in the downswing. There are many reasons for the wage lag, but the two most important are that unions need time to assess the business situation and that wage contracts are usually concluded for at least twelve months. These lags cause the cost wave to peak at a time when capacity utilization, as well as the cycle of industrial prices, is already declining. The widespread coincidence between the unit labor cost and the price cycle would indicate that the price behavior of the individual firms was determined by cost rather than demand, but one must not forget that the cost cycle itself is determined by the demand cycle.[4]

Figure 2 presents the indexes and deviations from trend for German industrial prices, agricultural prices, and consumer prices. The cyclical pattern of industrial prices is similar to that of consumer prices, although agricultural prices (which often have their own cycle) and rents and service prices are of great importance in the consumer price index. Rents developed rather independently of the general cycle since they were either administered by public regulations or the time of their increase was determined by the removal of these regulations, which took place successively during the sixties. The cycle of service prices seemed to be greatly influenced by the overall business cycle.

Altogether, industrial and consumer prices lagged behind the activity cycles by one or one and one-half years. Hence, the price peak lagged behind the activity peak, but occurred before the activity trough. In such situations the government has not known whether to promote price level stability or less

4. A recent econometric study on price determination in Germany demonstrates that entrepreneurial price behavior depends, not only on current wage increases, but on the long-term development of productivity. (See Rainer Schmidt and Torsten Tewes, *Stabilisierung in der Marktwirtschaft* [*Stabilization in Market Economies*] [Berlin: Duncker und Humblot, 1975].) This result corresponds to the findings of Eckstein and Brinner on the U.S. economy. (Otto Eckstein and Roger Brinner, *The Inflation Process in the United States,* Prepared for the use of the Joint Economic Committee, 92:1 [Government Printing Office, 1972].)

unemployment. The dilemma seemed to emerge because there was good reason to assume that disinflationary actions could accelerate the downturn of the activity cycle immediately, but price-restraining pressures would occur only after a lag. The situations in 1957–58 and in 1962–63 were less dramatic by current standards because the medium-term inflationary trend was below 3 percent and entrepreneurs were not inclined to dismiss workers, because their expansionary expectations remained unbroken by the then temporary decline in capacity utilization. But in 1966 the first sharp conflict arose when the rate of inflation exceeded 4 percent during the downturn largely because of an agricultural price peak. Restrictive monetary and fiscal policy lowered the inflation rate at the expense of employment, bringing about the first real recession since the war.

The next such conflict came in 1972 when the rate of inflation exceeded 5 percent; but the government with its parliamentary base could not decide on stringent anti-inflationary measures. In that year, the new economics and finance minister declared that an inflation rate of 5 percent was less troublesome than an unemployment rate of 5 percent. An upswing began in late 1972 that was arrested by tough monetary and fiscal stabilization measures in 1973 and by the oil crisis: inflation accelerated and unemployment increased. Early in 1975, the government was confronted with both a 5 percent unemployment rate and an even higher inflation rate.

The Sources of Inflation

In the early fifties the experience of excessive money creation by public deficit spending during and after the war suggested one cause of inflation. During the fifties, however, public budgets showed surpluses, so other explanations for rising prices gained ground. In 1956 a balance of payments surplus led to an undesired swell of liquidity, highlighting for the first time the problem of inflation imported by foreign exchange inflows. But the external surpluses soon vanished. Attention was then directed (not independently of the cost-push debate in the United States) to a wage theory of inflation, referring to the increase in unit labor costs that occurred after the boom of 1955. Proponents of this theory argued in terms of a wage-price spiral, their opponents in terms of a price-wage spiral. The chicken-egg problem became a matter of serious controversy.

The boom of 1960 and the balance of payments surpluses associated with it revived the theory of imported inflation. Full convertibility had been introduced in 1958 and now when the Bundesbank tried to counteract excessive demand by tightening money supply, it found it had become powerless, as each countermeasure attracted more money from abroad. The Bundesbank gave up its monetary restraints in the fall of 1960 for balance of payments reasons, and the first revaluation in March 1961, which launched the downswing of the business cycle, brought the discussion on imported inflation to a temporary close.

In the course of the downswing, when double-digit wage increases were granted, the old wage theory of inflation came back into favor. It was in this situation that Parliament in 1963 passed a bill creating an independent Expert Council on Overall Economic Development. Apart from analyzing and forecasting the overall economic situation, the council's task was to investigate how, in the framework of a market economy, price stability, high employment, and external equilibrium could be realized and combined with steady and adequate growth—the same formulation of the "objective function" that became part of the Stability and Growth Law of 1967.

The council began its work early in 1964 and was first confronted with imported inflation. Its consequent plea for a flexible exchange rate, though refused by the federal government "without hesitation," has been considered to have triggered the long-lasting and vehement discussion on imported inflation that finally led to much greater exchange rate flexibility and less restraints on monetary policy in the seventies. Discussion then focused on the routes by which foreign inflation infiltrates the economy, and it has given valuable insights into the mechanism of the international transmission of inflation to an open economy like West Germany's. The council has also presented new concepts of anti-inflationary and anticyclical policy. In 1965, when the cycle had passed its peak and a conflict over the Phillips curve relation emerged, the council pushed the idea of "stabilization without stagnation" by means of coordinated action among the institutions and social groups that can influence the overall economic process and hence share responsibility for it. This "concerted action" has developed into a permanent forum of economic policy. Since 1966 representatives of the federal government, the trade unions, the employers' and producers' associations, the central bank, and the expert council have been meeting together—normally twice a year—to try to arrive at a common assessment. Public budgets also had to be reconsidered in light of the stabilization policy. During and after the recession of 1967 it became obvious that the traditional ways of measuring the cyclical effects of public revenue and expenditures were inadequate. The council introduced the concept of a neutral budget to be measured against the actual budget.

These three topics—imported inflation in combination with monetary policy, concerted action, and budget policy—constitute the main themes of the anti-inflation debate, amended recently to include certain monetaristic ideas. The analysis below follows the same course.

Imported Inflation

Discussion of imported inflation since the fifties has focused on balance of payments effects, whether in the real or the monetary sphere. On one side is a Keynesian school that claims inflation is introduced via the export multiplier or income effects, and thus relies on the current-account balance variation as an indicator of whether inflation is being imported or exported. The school advocating the quantity theory of money, on the other hand, emphasizes the money supply or liquidity effects originating from the foreign exchange balance, and consequently links imported inflation to an increase of money caused by an overall balance of payments surplus. In practice, the two schools are not mutually exclusive because the multiplier effects and the quantity of money effects have often worked hand in hand. In addition, both believed that imported inflation is a problem only as long as foreign demand improves Germany's balance of payments.[5] Accordingly, in periods when foreign balances were deteriorating, many Germans thought that stability and not inflation was being imported.

It is quite in harmony with this balance of payments theory that the problem of imported inflation was appreciated only in 1956, 1960, 1964, and 1968–69 when increasing surpluses emerged and suggested revaluation. Linking exchange rate adjustments to a balance of payments indicator was also in harmony with the "fundamental disequilibrium" philosophy of Bretton Woods. Vagueness as to what is "fundamental" was a permanent source of argument and could serve to exonerate the government for having failed to revalue in time—or at all. But even if the government had employed the exchange rate tool in the way that balance of payments theory dictates, one must doubt whether it would have met the demands of a fairly perfect isolation from foreign inflation. The doubts are based on the hypothesis that in an open economy highly integrated with other open economies, the transmission of inflation from abroad will be a permanent process rather than a more or less accidental disturbance associated with the emergence of a

5. An improvement of a nation's balance of payments can also, of course, occur in a domestic recession when import demand is weak and export efforts are especially strong. But this has always been recognized as having nothing to do with imported inflation.

balance of payments surplus. According to this school of thinking, the international markets of goods and services act as the main transmitters, because competition does not permit long-lasting price differences among identical or similar commodities. The hypothesis refers to the mechanism of commodity arbitrage as observable in the market for highly competitive goods. With regard to noncompeting imports the method of transmission is obvious and undisputed among the different schools: a rise in the price of noncompeting imports alters the cost level or prices of consumer goods directly. But most imports into Germany compete with domestic products.

Following classical economic thinking, Angell and Haberler formulated a theory of international prices in the interwar period, suggesting that for a small open economy, a foreign trade price standard is quasi-automatically established by the mechanism of international markets and the interaction between the international and domestic sectors.[6] The two crucial assumptions of the hypothesis are, however, subject to empirical testing. First, one has to check whether competition in international markets for heterogeneous manufactured goods, which dominate foreign trade today, is workable enough to equalize prices, as the arbitrage model suggests. Second, one has to examine to what degree prices of domestic goods and services are related to international prices in an economy beset by many rigidities. If price adjustments in international markets or between international and domestic markets are incomplete or take place after a long lag, balance of payments feedbacks are likely to occur, thus forming the connecting link between both theories. Such feedbacks may also be the consequence of an adjustment lag between international prices and domestic wages that makes production of exports and import substitutes more attractive than is the case in other countries. The closer the direct price and wage interdependence, the smaller are the balance of payments effects that tend to equalize prices indirectly. Of course, one cannot assess the strength of price interdependence from actual balance of payments variations because they are subject to other influences as well.

The theory of direct price interdependence has become important in Germany's stabilization discussion since Stützel made a point of it in the revaluation debate of 1960.[7] The council adopted the theory in 1964 and

6. James W. Angell, *The Theory of International Prices: History, Criticism, and Restatement* (Harvard University Press, 1926), chap. 15; Gottfried von Haberler, *The Theory of International Trade with its Applications to Commercial Policy* (London: Hodge, 1936), chap. 4.

7. Wolfgang Stützel, "Ist die schleichende Inflation durch monetäre Massnahmen zu beeinflussen?" ("Can creeping inflation be influenced by monetary measures?"), Supplement, *Konjunkturpolitik*, vol. 7 (1960).

substantiated the policy implications in its annual report of 1966.[8] The main implication is that there is a permanent need for revaluations to neutralize totally or partly foreign inflationary trends if Germany is to reach a goal of either price stability or less inflation than its trading partners. Most striking is the conclusion that inflationary pressure from abroad also has an effect when Germany's balance of payments position is deteriorating or in deficit.

The federal government and Otmar Emminger of the Bundesbank examined the different theories and pointed out that international inflation is transmitted in three ways: via the liquidity effects, via the income effects, and via the direct price effects.[9] The government stated that it would orient policy toward countering all three effects. Emminger argued that the three are different ways in which a country is affected by international inflationary tendencies.

While such prudent statements tried to account for all phenomena of imported inflation at the same time, they may have complicated the decision-making process in concrete situations, since the liquidity and income effects on the one hand and the direct price effects on the other were inconsistent. The prices of Germany's exports and import substitutes were subject to a cycle similar to those of its domestic goods, which deviate cyclically from the international inflationary trend. During the upswing, for instance, German export prices lagged behind foreign export prices, whereas the balance of payments position was improving, due partly to strong foreign demand and partly to the price lag itself. Slightly increasing (or even absolutely decreasing) export prices coincided with positive income and liquidity effects. Was inflation imported or not? Conversely, in the aftermath of the boom, when costs and prices adjusted to foreign prices, the balance of payments deteriorated. Again, the basis for decisionmaking seemed to be puzzling: the price effects were positive, but the income and liquidity effects negative. Several theoretical and empirical studies were undertaken to clarify the relationships.

In a study originally carried out on behalf of the council, I tried to find empirical evidence on the relative importance of the competing transmission

8. Expert Council on Overall Economic Development, *Stable Money—Steady Growth,* 1964/65 Annual Report (1964), p. 131, and *Expansion and Stability,* 1966/67 Annual Report (1966), p. 117.

9. *Stellungnahme der Bundesregierung zum Jahresgutachten 1966 des Sachverständigenrates zur Begutachtung der gesamtwirtschaftlichen Entwicklung. Beilage zu dem Jahresgutachten 1966/67* [*Comment of the Federal Government on the Economic Annual Report 1966/67 of the Expert Council on Overall Economic Development*] (1966); Otmar Emminger, "Stabilität ohne Absicherung nach aussen?" ["Stability without Safeguards vis-à-vis Abroad?"] *Frankfurter Allgemeine Zeitung,* December 3, 1966.

theories.[10] The study, which was completed in 1968, refers to the period from 1955 to 1967; its main findings were:

• In the medium run the development of German export prices followed rather closely the development of foreign export prices. In the short run, however, there were deviations from the international trend because of cyclical influences.

• Similar results were obtained in regard to the relation between the prices of import substitutes and imports.

• The deviations from the international price trend were associated with income and liquidity effects, which initiated domestic adjustment mechanisms, and linked foreign and domestic price movements more closely to each other.

• In addition, there was a close—but delayed—connection between price increases for traded (or international) and nontraded (or domestic) goods that, however, becomes apparent only after differences in productivity trends between the international and the domestic sectors had been accounted for.

• The income and liquidity effects played an important role in transferring inflation to the domestic sector.

• Because of the differences in productivity and cost increases between the domestic and international sectors, after 1960 an annual decrease of export and import substitute prices of 1.5 to 2.0 percent would have been required to have general price stability (measured in terms of the price level of net domestic product at market prices).

It seems a useful exercise to reexamine the key problem of price connections by extending the period of observation to the present.

The first question that arises is how both the cycle and the trend of Germany's inflation corresponds to price developments abroad. The simplest way to find the answer to this is to compare German with foreign prices—in particular, German export prices with foreign export prices, German industrial producer prices with the prices of competing imports, and consumer prices and gross national product deflators with those abroad. Since the available statistical information does not allow absolute price comparisons, the changes of price indexes have to be examined. Foreign price indexes are calculated as weighted averages of the national index figures of the ten most important trading partners. In order to obtain comparable figures, export prices, consumer prices, and GNP deflators are expressed in U.S. dollars; the

10. Gerhard Fels, *Der internationale Preiszusammenhang* [*International Price Interdependence*] (Köln: Karl Heymanns Verlag, 1969).

Figure 3. *Export Prices in West German and Foreign Markets, 1956–74*

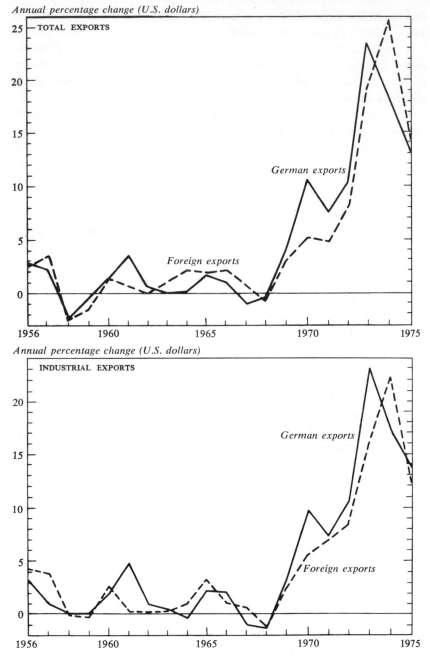

Annual percentage change (U.S. dollars)

TOTAL EXPORTS

German exports

Foreign exports

Annual percentage change (U.S. dollars)

INDUSTRIAL EXPORTS

German exports

Foreign exports

Source: Data supplied by author. The countries included in the foreign export price index are Austria, Belgium, Denmark, France, Italy, the Netherlands, Sweden, Switzerland, the United Kingdom, and the United States, using their 1970 share of world exports as weights.

prices of imports and import substitutes in deutsche marks. The results of the calculations are shown in figures 3, 4, and 5.

Between 1956 and 1974 German and foreign export prices (in figure 3), which could only be measured by unit values, differ from each other in the short run but show a broadly common pattern in the long run. The ups and downs of export price variations reflect the general domestic price cycle. The amplitudes of the German export price cycles are greater than those of corresponding foreign export prices. First, foreign prices derive from several countries and therefore the individual cyclical variations tend to cancel each other out. Second, the revaluations of the German mark in 1961, 1969, 1971, and 1973 caused outstanding upward deviations of German export prices (expressed in U.S. dollars). In general, price disparities in the one or other direction have been equalized by either market forces or exchange rate adjustments, although the latter are not always required to remove disparities. They seem rather to have substituted for more harmful adjustment inflation.

To make a long-term comparison of export prices, one has to start from an equilibrium situation in external exchange. There is, of course, enough grounds for arguing about what external equilibrium means and when it is realized. But to avoid immediate objections, I use here only the period after the international reintegration of the West German economy had been largely accomplished, which means, broadly speaking, the years after 1958–59. Between 1958–59 and 1974 there were only two years in which the balance of payments seemed to be in the "neighborhood of equilibrium," and in which great price disparities also seemed to be absent: 1962 and 1965. These years have therefore been chosen as base years for long-term comparisons. The results are shown in table 1. In 1972, the year before floating rates were introduced, the relationship between German and foreign export prices (each expressed in U.S. dollars) was the same as in 1962 and only slightly different from the relationship in 1965. In 1973 due to the strong upward movement of the deutsche mark German exports became relatively expensive for a time. But in the course of 1974 Germany regained its long-run competitive position in export prices.

The domestic markets of import substitutes are shown in figure 4. The prices of domestic import substitutes and import prices are represented by Laspeyres indexes, but comparisons are available only since 1958. The patterns shown by the variation of these indexes resemble those observed in the export markets. Subsequent to the revaluations of 1961, 1969, and 1971, imports became cheaper in relation to competing domestic products, and the anti-inflationary effect is visible. In 1973 and 1974 imports became relatively

Figure 4. *Import Prices in West German and Foreign Markets, 1959–74*

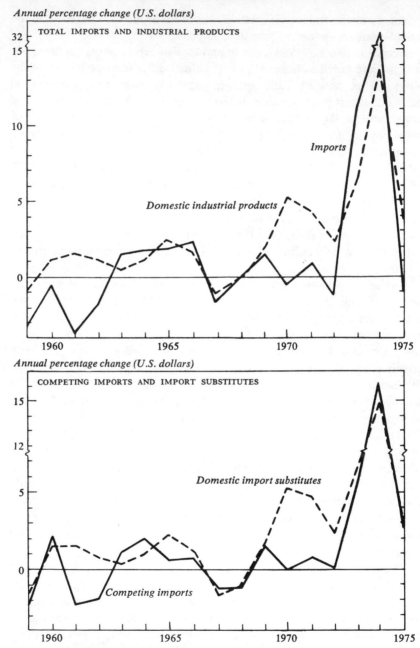

Annual percentage change (U.S. dollars)

TOTAL IMPORTS AND INDUSTRIAL PRODUCTS

Imports

Domestic industrial products

Annual percentage change (U.S. dollars)

COMPETING IMPORTS AND IMPORT SUBSTITUTES

Domestic import substitutes

Competing imports

Source: Data supplied by author. The import-competing sector comprises each of the eleven branches to which more than 1 percent of West German imports can be ascribed. But it excludes nonferrous metals and refined petroleum products, presumably noncompeting, and foods and beverages, which are highly regimented.

Table 1. *Price Developments in West German and Foreign Export Markets and German Import Markets, 1962–74*
Annual rate of increase (percent)

	U.S. dollar prices	
Period and market	German exports	Foreign exports
Total exports		
1962–72	2.6	2.8
1962–73	4.4	4.2
1962–74	5.5	5.8
1965–72	3.5	3.3
1965–73	5.8	5.2
1965–74	7.1	7.2
Industrial products		
1962–72	2.6	2.8
1962–73	4.3	3.9
1965–72	3.5	3.3
1965–73	5.7	4.8

	Deutsche mark prices	
	German import substitutes	German imports
Industrial products		
1962–72	2.1	0.7
1962–73	2.5	1.9
1962–74	3.4	4.1
1965–72	2.4	0.2
1965–73	2.9	1.9
1965–74	4.0	4.8
Manufactured products		
1962–72	1.9	0.5
1962–73	2.3	1.0
1962–74	3.3	2.2
1965–72	2.1	0.2
1965–73	2.7	0.9
1965–74	3.9	2.5

Sources: Author's calculations based on data from the United Nations and Statistisches Bundesamt. Beginning in 1970, underlying data used is from revised series (1970 = 100).

dearer again. From the annual rates of increase since 1962 or 1965 calculated in table 1, it can be seen that up to 1974 domestic industrial products and imports of industrial goods were subject to nearly the same price increases. The same comparison for manufactured products reveals a few sharper increases of import prices than of domestic prices. Altogether, there seems to be a fairly close connection between international and national prices in the long run.

German and foreign gross domestic product deflators and consumer price levels expressed in U.S. dollars show rather striking developments after 1969

Figure 5. *Inflation in West Germany and Foreign Countries, 1962–74*

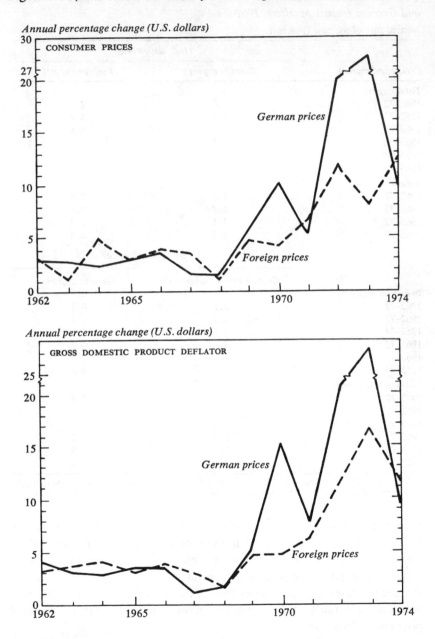

Source: Data supplied by author.

(figure 5). During the sixties no significant deviations occurred. But in 1970, 1972, and 1973, as a consequence of the revaluations, Germany's consumer prices and GDP deflator increased so rapidly in terms of the U.S. dollar that they are significantly different from foreign consumer prices and GDP deflators. It follows from this that Germany has become an expensive country for tourists and other people who earn their income abroad and spend it in Germany. But, as the analysis of price variations in the export and import markets indicates, Germany has maintained (or regained) her relative price position in the international markets, since the revaluations have corresponded to the relatively moderate increase of deutsche mark prices for exports and import substitutes. In other words, the disinflationary effects of the revaluations have not been fully transmitted to domestic markets. The lack of penetration also becomes obvious by comparing German overall price developments in terms of the mark with foreign price developments in terms of U.S. dollars: from 1969 to 1974 the mark was revalued by 27 percent, but in the same period consumer prices lagged behind foreign consumer prices by only 7 percent. This difference, which is sufficient to place Germany at the lower end of the international inflationary scale, shows that revaluation makes it possible for a country to have a lower rate of inflation than other countries, but it has not achieved the deflation expected by experts.

Since 1970 the difference in price development of exports and imports on the one hand and consumer prices and GDP prices on the other is likely to be linked with the working of the income and liquidity effects. As figure 6 indicates, since 1972 income effects have apparently occurred when, under the pressure of export demand or the domestic stabilization program of 1973, net exports have risen sharply. A massive inflow of foreign currency has taken place since 1970, initiated several times by the expectations of a revaluation. All this means is that, since 1970, balance of payments effects have also played an important role in the transmission of inflation. The liquidity inflows were a severe impediment for anti-inflationary monetary policy.

Monetary Policy before and after March 1973

Until March 1973 the scope of monetary policy was confined within narrow limits under the regime of fixed exchange rates and full convertibility. As long as the central bank was bound to buy dollars at fixed spot rates it was unable to control money supply. Only once was the central bank in a powerful position: when its 1966 credit tightening happened to be in line with

Figure 6. *Price Effects and Balance of Payments Effects in the International Transmission of Inflation, 1956–73*

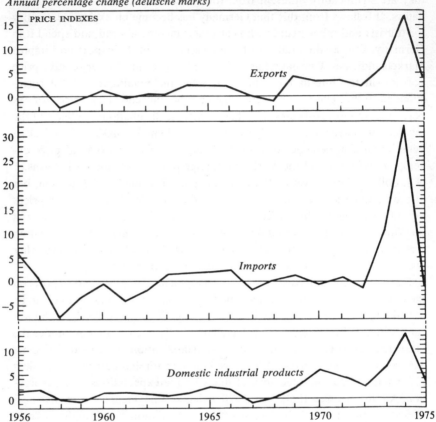

Annual percentage change (deutsche marks)

monetary restrictions abroad, it could pursue an effective anti-inflationary policy that apparently contributed to the succeeding recession. The central bank had often endeavored to neutralize undesired money inflows, and foreign deposits were subjected to especially high minimum reserve requirements and to an interest payment prohibition. But apart from these, there were no barriers to hinder access to foreign money markets. At best, some neutralizing effect was achieved within the banking system. When in 1972, notwithstanding the Smithsonian realignment, new speculative waves set in, administrative restrictions on money and capital transactions were introduced, first on transactions of commercial banks, and later also on trans-

Figure 6 (*Continued*)

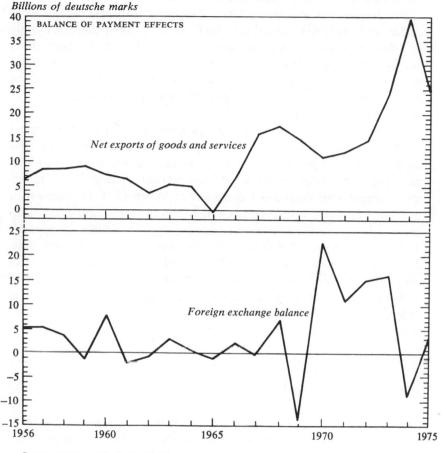

Billions of deutsche marks

BALANCE OF PAYMENT EFFECTS

Net exports of goods and services

Foreign exchange balance

Source: Data supplied by author.

actions of the nonbanking sector, including foreign trade credits. Full convertibility was withdrawn for capital inflows, and Karl Schiller, the dissenting economics and finance minister, resigned.

But even far-reaching restrictions could not stop the speculative inflows, which had taken routes previously unknown. Finally, in March 1973, the West German government, acting in coordination with other European countries, released the central bank from its intervention commitment vis-à-vis the dollar. An essential condition for the efficiency of monetary policy was created. It is presently limited only by its buying obligations toward other jointly floating European currencies (the Dutch guilder, the Belgian franc, the Danish krone, the Swedish krona, and the Norwegian krone).

The central bank also changed its technique for managing the volume of money; up to 1973 it controlled (or tried to control) volume rather indirectly by influencing the quantity of free reserves disposable in the banking system and by influencing their use through its interest policy. Several steps taken in the course of 1973 reduced the free reserves to a minimum, so that the central bank is currently able to control the money supply directly through open market operations.

As long as the "external flank" was open, the central bank often emphasized the government's responsibility for price stability, but since 1973 it has discovered its own power. It was no coincidence that monetaristic views became popular in the central bank.[11] As to actual policy, the growth of monetary aggregates has decelerated sharply since March 1973. In combination with the fiscal stabilization program, which worked mainly through tax disincentives for housing and other investment, a significant decline in capacity utilization was achieved. Pushed by the oil crisis, however, the prices of industrial products increased greatly. The rate of increase of consumer prices changed little, thanks to declining agricultural prices, but in the course of 1974 durable consumer goods in particular rose in price despite a decline in orders and production. All this leads to the conclusion that the anti-inflation policies introduced in 1973 were slow in taking effect.

Public Budgets and Inflation

To hold government's spending behavior mainly responsible for inflation has belonged to the ritual lament over the inflationary disease for a long time. The two hyperinflations that originated primarily from disastrous war financing created high public sensitivity to any kind of public deficit spending, and even public debt. Consequently, during the fifties, paternalistic principles guided budget management, often generating budget surpluses (the so-called Juliusturm), which were thought to be a kind of public nest egg. In the course of time, however, the public sector was faced with increasing tasks, especially in defense, road construction, education, and social security. The puritanical attitude had slowly to be modified. A spurt in public spending preceded the

11. H. Schlesinger, *Die Geldpolitik als Mittel der Inflationsbekämpfung* [*Monetary Policy as a Means of Combating Inflation*] Press Summary 54 (*Deutsche Bundesbank*, 1973).

1965 Bundestag election. After a temporary slowing down in 1966 and 1967, government budgets became one of the most expanding sectors of the economy.

After 1965 the central bank expressed concern several times about the inflationary impact of public budgets and so did the parliamentary opposition of the day. Confusion arose about the ways in which public budgets promote inflation and about the quantitative impact. The Expert Council on Overall Economic Development, which itself had strongly criticized expansionary budget management in 1965, met a wall of opposition from the central bank and public opinion when it stated during the recession of 1967 that the overall impact of public budgets was deflationary, although two recovery programs had been instituted in order to promote public investment.[12] The council argued that the contractive effects of the regular budgets were not fully offset by the expansionary effects of the recovery programs.

During the controversy on the role of public budgets the council refined its budget concept. It attempted to measure the net impact of public revenues and expenditures on overall capacity utilization.[13] Budget management was defined as neutral, expansionary, or deflationary if it led, respectively, to unchanged, higher, or lower utilization of overall production potential. The concept was supposed to be superior to the balanced budget concepts usually applied because it related both public revenues and public expenditures to potential output.

In the simple budget concepts there is no orientation toward potential output at all; the full employment budget concept only relates the revenue side to full employment outputs. The adjusted budget concept accounts, additionally, for structural changes in the share of the public sector, and for the various multipliers of different revenue and expenditure categories. Though a direct relationship between the budget and the rate of inflation remained unestablished, conclusions about inflationary effects became possible by assessing net budget effects in combination with the business cycle situation.

From a theoretical point of view the concept has matured sufficiently, although it is difficult to measure exactly the contractive effects of revenues and the expansionary effect of expenditures. Practical and methodological problems arise in particular with regard to (1) the choice of the base period during which public budgets can be considered neutral; (2) the rate of price increase for public goods and services to be assumed ex ante in order to

12. Expert Council on Overall Economic Development, *Stability and Growth*, 1967/68 Annual Report (1967), p. 85.
13. Ibid., *Alternatives of External Adjustment*, 1968/69 Annual Report (1968), p. 34.

Figure 7. *Cyclical Effects of Consolidated Public Budgets, 1960–72*

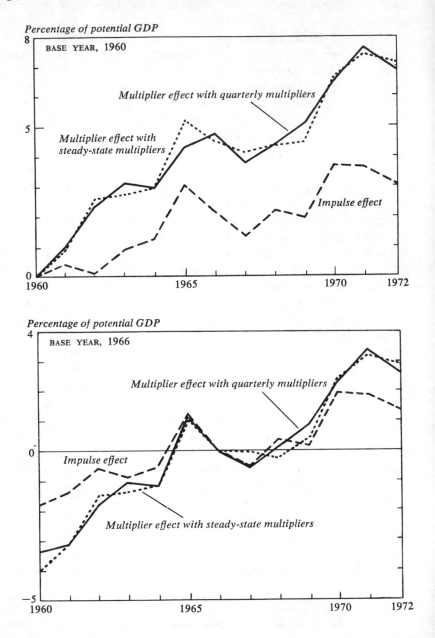

Source: Data supplied by author.

avoid an undesired decline in real expenditure; (3) the multipliers (and the lag structure of their impact), which have to be associated with different types of revenues and expenditures; and (4) the direct and indirect budget effects on the monetary sphere.

Despite these difficulties, a comprehensive effort was made by Biehl and others to calculate the cyclical effects of consolidated public budgets.[14] The results, which are given in figure 7 for the period 1960 to 1972, turn out to be sensitive with respect to the base year chosen and to the hypotheses on the multipliers. Though alternative base years and multiplier hypotheses lead to different magnitudes of annual cyclical effects, all curves show a somewhat common time pattern. First, the expansionary effect of public budgets reached its peak in 1965 and 1970–71 and its trough in 1967. Second, a strong upward trend in all curves shows the increasing expansionary impact of public budgets.

At first sight there seems a strong case for the presumption that fiscal policy has worked procyclically rather than anticyclically. The upward trend of the net expansionary effect indicates increasing participation of public budgets in the inflationary struggle for real resources.

In order to avoid misunderstandings, further explanation is needed. First, the reservation is made that the ex ante rate of inflation for the public sector is assumed to equal the overall ex ante rate of inflation. This means ignoring structural changes in price relations between public and private sectors, for instance, those caused by the different productivity trends of goods and services produced by the public sector and of those produced by the private sector. Hence, insofar as the public sector is faced with a sharper price increase than the private sector the results overestimate the expansionary effects. But as a matter of experience this overestimation may be limited. Second, the observations refer to a period of convertibility and fixed exchange rates (except the temporary floating rates of 1969 and 1972). As emphasized several times, the central bank was unable to control the money supply under these conditions and, therefore, also unable to counteract budget deficits financed by money creation. Although it is true that the public authorities financed expenditures not covered by tax revenues mainly through medium- and long-term credits or bonds, the private sector could easily substitute liquidity, which was absorbed from public budgets by borrowing in foreign markets. Thus public budget management has to be understood as an

---

14. Dieter Biehl, Günther Hagemann, Karl-Heinz Jüttemeier, and Harald Legler, "Schätzung konjunktureller Wirkungen öffentlicher Haushalte" ["Estimates of the Cyclical Effect of Public Budgets"] (Kiel: Kiel Institute of World Economics, 1973; processed).

increasing source of expansion and domestic adjustment to the international inflationary trend, regardless of the question whether these effects were brought about by the public expenditures themselves or by the monetary expansion going along with them. If the monetary hypothesis should turn out to be a more valid explanation of the inflationary process, however, the conclusions from measuring the budget position using the multiplier approach would have to be questioned.

Under the regime of floating exchange rates, the role of fiscal policy in stabilizing the economy may have become less important. If the central bank controls the volume of money, which in turn controls the price level (still a matter for research), public budget effects have to be assessed within the framework of overall monetary policy. According to the monetarists, monetary policy works by influencing the price relations between monetary and real assets. Fiscal policy can affect this relation by measures that change the profitability of private investments, that is, interest premiums, profit taxes, or other direct incentives and disincentives. The liquidity effects of the budget are only part of the overall liquidity effects controllable by the central bank. Of course, this statement is made on the assumption that the central bank is institutionally independent of the government, and in these circumstances fiscal policy means primarily a policy determining the allocation between the private and the public sector.

Concerted Action and Wage Policy

The basic concept of concerted action suggested by the council in 1965 covered more than just either incomes policy or wage policy.[15] It aimed at ex ante coordination of government and central bank policies and the behavior of unions, entrepreneurs, and other groups with the power to influence overall economic development—the rationale being that a mechanism was needed on the macroeconomic level to induce public authorities and powerful private groups to coordinate activities, much as the market mechanism operated on the microeconomic level. Of course, market forces can be and are used to run the economy on the macroeconomic level too, such as when restrictive demand management is used to slow wage and price increases. Adjustment in these cases in labor and capital markets may mean friction in the form of unemployment or overinvestment if the restrictive measures are

15. Expert Council on Overall Economic Development, *Stabilization without Stagnation,* 1965/66 Annual Report (1965), p. 109.

not anticipated by unions and entrepreneurs. Thus the concerted action procedure was designed to avoid such harmful ex post coordination of plans by harmonizing policy actions and the behavior of entrepreneurs and labor market participants.

In 1965 and the years thereafter, the council proposed rules for wage policy, fiscal policy, monetary policy, and exchange rate policy. Monetary policy rules were complementary to the exchange rate proposals, ranging from flexible exchange rates, to crawling peg mechanisms, and to peg adjustments used under the Bretton Woods system. Fiscal policy rules (discussed above) were developed step by step in the years after 1967. The council's concept of wage policy was oriented toward overall cost level neutrality, thus taking into account, inter alia, changes in labor productivity, unit capital cost, the terms of trade, as well as structural effects.[16] In practice, allowance had also to be made for price increases already in the pipeline or inevitable in the period under consideration. The unions, however, were reluctant to subscribe to the concept. They suspected that it would freeze income distribution among labor, business, and other social groups, although the rules tried to allow for the income effects of long-run changes in scarcity relations.

In the downswing of 1966 the council's ideas were not implemented successfully, although unions as well as employers were inclined to participate in balanced, simultaneous, and step-by-step action intended to reduce the rate of inflation to 2 percent. Chancellor Ludwig Erhard and the central bank went ahead unilaterally in employing strong fiscal and monetary restrictions, which induced the deep downturn of 1967. Nevertheless, concerted action became established in the form of an institutionalized round table conference, chaired by the economics and finance minister, at which representatives of trade unions, employers' and producers' associations, the central bank, and the council sit together two or three times a year to discuss the overall economic situation. This kind of institution has a legal basis in the Stability and Growth Law, but its existence has nevertheless been subject to endless critical debate among economists, public law experts, political scientists, and politicians.

It would be an exaggeration to maintain that concerted action has fulfilled the coordinating function originally intended. What took place at the conferences was an exchange of information. Sometimes the economics minister used the forum for moral suasion. The main impact that might be ascribed

16. Ibid., *Stable Money—Steady Growth,* 1964/65 Annual Report (1964), p. 136.

to it was an outstandingly long wage lag after 1967. But after wages had lost contact with sharply rising profits in the upswing of 1968 and 1969, the unions became more and more reserved about the concerted action procedure, and their militancy in 1970 and 1971 was surely not independent of their disappointing experience in 1968 and 1969. One is inclined to interpret the moderate wage claims up to 1969 as a kind of unilateral concession made by the unions in the expectation that fiscal and monetary demand management would fulfill its role. Indeed, neither the government nor the central bank was able to cope with the boom after 1967 spurred by the recovery programs and strong export demand. But, curiously, the real wage increase realized in 1968 was even less than the council had suggested as realizable in its guideline for 1968.[17] The unions, still shocked by the previous recession, refused to accept this guideline in the concerted action early in 1968, arguing on principle that it is the unions—and not the council—that should regulate wage policy (even a golden cage is a cage) and that no guidelines were set for prices and profits.

After the boom had reached its peak in 1969 and wildcat strikes had shaken the union organizations, the time was coming for the unions to change into a higher gear in wage demands. In 1970 and 1971 the overall wage increase amounted to 15 and 12 percent, respectively, bringing the economy onto a steeper wage and cost trend. This happened when the deutsche mark was revalued and both foreign and domestic demand were about to become sluggish. The downswing beginning in 1970 came to a close by mid-1972 when a period of export expansion set in. Again wage increases in the upswing were rather moderate. The unions, which trusted the government's optimistic price projections, were once more disappointed by the actual inflation rate and embarrassed by spontaneous and uncontrolled strikes in September 1973. The revaluations in the course of the block floating introduced early in 1973 and the strong domestic stabilization program launched by the middle of that year could not stop price increases in time and were soon overrun by the inflationary effects of the oil crisis. Thus conditions for wage negotiations at the beginning of 1974 were rather unfavorable. And the increases resulting from them were correspondingly high.

If one tries to summarize incomes policy since 1967, one has to point to a lack of harmony between overall wage policy and demand management, while admitting this was aggravated twice—in 1969 and 1973—by the strong pull of foreign demand. In this respect, concerted action never matched its

17. Expert Council on Overall Economic Development, *Alternatives of External Adjustment,* 1968/69 Annual Report (1968), p. 57.

function. But to ascribe accelerated cost and price increases to insufficient coordination of policies would be too abrupt an explanation, because an internationally determined inflationary trend was at work as well.

Concluding Remarks

In the course of this paper several policies and other factors, which may
have contributed to inflation in West Germany, have been discussed. The
analyis is not exhaustive; many areas had to be neglected for reasons of time
and scope (and will be touched on in the proposals for future research). The
analysis may be faulted for not trying to give a monocausal explanation of
the mainspring of inflation. But it has pointed out that the external inflationary trend seems to have determined the long-run development of Germany's
international prices and partly also that of its domestic prices.

The analysis has further demonstrated that there are various domestic inflationary forces, the relative importance of which changes over time. The
more a country is integrated into the world economy and the longer inflation
goes on, the more difficult it becomes to distinguish between external causes
and internal consequences. The more inflation is anticipated, the more it becomes a self-sustaining process. In an open economy and from a long term
point of view it would be a waste of time to seek responsibility for inflation
among domestic sectors of the economy or among different social groups.
From a policymaker's point of view this implies that one-sided actions of
anti-inflationary policy most probably will be as inadequate as one-sided explanations of the process. Consequently, only comprehensive policy actions
covering all important fields of stabilization policy—external as well as internal, demand management as well as cost control via incomes policy—seem
to be capable of success in defeating inflation. One-sided actions would tend
to bring about a substitution of one source of inflation for another. Besides,
one-sided actions are likely to have high costs in terms of unemployment and
structural distortions.

Since 1973 the stabilization scene in Germany has been changed fundamentally by the introduction of floating rates. If the central bank takes the
responsibility for anti-inflation policy—and it is about to do so—the trade
unions are responsible for maintaining full employment, whether they like it
or not. Therefore, simultaneous steps are necessary in order to avoid unemployment arising from the coincidence of restrictive monetary policy with
high nominal wage increases. Moreover, with regard to the immediate aim of
cutting down the inflation rate to a tolerable level of 3 to 4 percent, the most

important problem is to harmonize the inflationary expectation of the private sector with new monetary policy. One device, which has been suggested as helpful at least for passing through the transition period without creating additional distortions and friction, seems to be to permit indexation of all contracts.[18]

Comments by Assar Lindbeck

THIS IS a very useful exposition of the German experience. If one considers, first of all, the causes and transmission mechanisms of inflation, as outlined in Fels's paper, one finds the approach is eclectic. This is no criticism of eclecticism. The problem with this approach, however, is the risk that all factors are given, so to speak, the same weight. It is difficult to see what is important and what is less important when so many factors are considered at the same time.

Inflation is regarded as a complex phenomenon, with many—explicit or implicit—sources and mechanisms: direct international price influence, income and liquidity effects from abroad, excess demand variations for commodities and labor, differences in the rate of productivity increase in different sectors, struggles over income distribution, domestic financial and monetary factors, expectations, and so on. However, it is probably correct to say that the emphasis is on the transmission of impulses from abroad.

The West German cycle

The paper begins with a very useful description of the business cycle in Germany, including the leads and lags among the variables. The picture depicted is similar to those found in other West European countries, such as my own (Sweden), with volume fluctuations generated very much from the export sector, and with the volume component leading wages, and wages leading prices. Moreover, it is assumed in such analyses of open economies that downturns are largely generated by restrictive government policies. Thus there is a business cycle generated largely by the mixture of (1) foreign influences and (2) government policies. The outside world generates the upswings and the government generates at least the timing of the downswings

18. Herbert Giersch, "Indexklauseln und Inflationsbekämpfung" ("Indexation and Combating Inflation"), Kiel Discussion Paper, 32 (Kiel: Kiel Institute for World Economics, 1973; processed).

to counteract inflation when it becomes too strong. It is basically a stop-go cycle, where the "go" is always generated by foreigners and the "stop" by the government.

Why slow inflation?

In the section on general conditions, Fels lists the circumstances that, in his judgment, are typical of the West German scene, in the sense that they would explain why Germany has had less inflation than other countries.

At least three of these circumstances make a lot of sense to me. They are that (1) the previous experiences of hyperinflation in Germany have made anti-inflation policy politically acceptable in that country, not to say politically "necessary"; (2) until the early sixties there was a very elastic supply of labor because of the influx of refugees from Eastern Europe, mainly East Germany; and (3) Fels's probably correct assumption that the absence, until recently, of a Keynesian aggregate demand policy to stimulate economic activities tended to dampen the rate of inflation, as demand did not press against the capacity limits of the economy. It remains, of course, to explain why an expansionary fiscal demand management policy was not pursued. Perhaps the reason lies in the first point—the high preference for price stability.

I have, however, some difficulties in connection with Fels's other three points. He states that the unions show a high sense of responsibility toward overall economic goals. Perhaps he is correct, but one needs explanations for this. Why, for instance, was this not the case in other countries with fast rates of productivity increases, such as Italy and France? Is the explanation to be found in the political philosophy and aims of the unions?

Again, Fels's assertion that the tariff cuts partially explained West Germany's low rate of inflation needs clarification. Other countries have cut their tariffs too, quite as much as West Germany has. This could hardly explain why the long-term rate of inflation was different in West Germany from those in other countries.

In fact, an analysis of the effects of the tariff cuts is rather complicated. No doubt imports increased, and this would help depress the price level. Moreover, tariff reductions acted as a negative cost-push similar to reductions in indirect taxes on commodities. On the other hand, when other countries also cut tariffs they stimulated aggregate demand for West German products, with expansionary effects as a result.

Fels's last point—that entrepreneurs were interested in real output expansion rather than price increases—sounds very much like the second point

—that underutilization of capacity and an elastic supply of labor created a rather flat aggregate marginal cost curve for the West German economy. Then the issue perhaps reverts again to his assertion about low capacity utilization—that West Germany had been working on a rather flat range of the aggregate cost curve.

"Dilemmas"?

Time lags are frequently interpreted by Fels as causing "dilemmas" and "conflicts" in economic policy. Let me clarify by giving two examples.

First, Fels points to the following alleged conflict. Suppose there is a boom and it generates increased inflation, but because of time lags for prices and wages, the peak is in the next recession rather than the boom. I think this is normal. There is a time lag, usually I would suggest of between twelve and eighteen months, between the peak of the boom of the volume components and the maximum rate of price increase. That holds for most West European countries.

But why should this be regarded as a "dilemma"? It would perhaps appear so superficially to a government that sees unemployment rising at the same time as prices are going up. However, in a slightly deeper sense it is not really a dilemma at all. If it is true that the price increase in this situation is generated by previous excess demand for commodities and labor, then it will not necessarily be dangerous to expand aggregate demand, because it will not lead to any excess demand or much more inflation than if aggregate demand is allowed to fall further.

If policymakers realize that inflation in a recession is caused by excess demand in the previous boom, they will not perhaps be so afraid to stimulate additional demand in the recession. At least, the inflationary impact should be small. The problem for economic policy in this case is rather how to remove inflationary expectations from the system and prevent wages from catching up with inflationary expectations.

Second, suppose there is an expansion in exports due to an international boom and that prices of exports and imports go up. Suppose also that in West Germany a surplus is created on the current account, with Keynesian stimulation income effects, and that there is a balance of payments surplus, with "quantity theory" expansionary liquidity effects.

When analyzing this case, Fels asserts that the income effects and the liquidity effects are usually "inconsistent" with the price effect. What he really means is that the improvement in the current balance and balance of payments is immediate, but there is a time lag until price changes penetrate the system.

When analyzing the case, I think it is much clearer to say that the time lag for the price variable is longer than the time lag for the income and liquidity effects on output, generated by way of current balance and balance of payments. I know of no reason for seeing a "contradiction" in these different time lags.

Price effects, income effects, and liquidity effects

Fels as already indicated makes a distinction between three different types of influences from abroad: "direct" price effects, income (or current-account) effects, and liquidity (or balance of payments) effects. He also makes the point that the closer the direct price interdependence, the smaller are the balance of payments effects that tend to equalize prices indirectly. But this is not self-evident. It also depends on what happens to wages. There could be a situation in which foreign commodity prices substantially influence the West German commodity price level for tradables, at the same time as a very big balance of payments surplus occurs—especially if the trend for wage rates has not accelerated. If both commodity prices and wage rates go up as a result of the foreign impulse, Fels's point is more relevant, because price and wage increases are likely to make the balance of payments improvement small, or even zero. Thus it is important to specify *what* prices are being referred to: if he means commodity prices only, that is one thing, but if he includes labor prices as well, that is another.

Do revaluations work?

By comparing consumer price changes to alterations in the deutsche mark exchange rate, Fels gives the impression that the revaluations have not "worked," at least that they have not influenced consumer good prices. However, when I look at the OECD average for other countries' inflations compared with West Germany's, I find that between 1969 and 1973 there is a difference of 3.7 percentage points, a considerable amount. Moreover, in 1974 the difference in inflation rates between West Germany and OECD (excluding West Germany) is 6.6 percent. If the 3.7 and 6.6 percent are added, there is a difference in consumer good price increases in West Germany of 10.3 percent since 1969. I think this is quite consistent with the assumption that revaluations make it possible for a country to have a smaller rate of increase. (The development in 1975 and 1976 strengthens the point.)

Fels also makes some comparisons of prices for tradables in West Germany and other countries, or more specifically between prices of German exports and foreign exports. I do not know what conclusion can be drawn from this. Probably Fels wants to show—again—that the revaluations have not had the expected effects on West German prices. The conclusion that I would draw is rather that if there is a difference in the dollar price of West German exports and foreign exports over long periods, it is most likely that this partly reflects a change in the marginal rate of substitution on the demand side between West German export commodities and those from other countries, that is, a change in the relative price between two different baskets of commodities. Thus, a change in this relative price may partly have been caused by a change in the relative quality and composition of products from the various countries.

To summarize Fels's discussion about imported inflation and exchange rate policies, I cannot see that he has made a strong case for the proposition that the domestic price trend cannot be (much) influenced by exchange rate policies.

General Comments

WILLIAM BRANSON, referring to Fels's statement that in 1972 some measures had been taken that permitted the West German monetary authority to begin controlling the money stock, questioned why it could not always have been controlled. Fels has implied that monetary authorities cannot sterilize inflows of foreign funds, a view frequently advanced but recently disputed. There is econometric evidence that the German central bank had been controlling the money stock on previous occasions. Kouri and Porter have found coefficients for changes in the domestic credit base on the money stock in Germany significantly different from zero, and Herring and Marston have found that changes in the German international capital account did not induce equal changes in the German money stock.[19] Both findings indicate that the domestic money stock is not entirely dependent upon the international flow of funds. Why, then, if the German central bank was able to make changes in 1972 that permitted it to control the money stock, had it not made them earlier? If it had decided not to, it was hard to see how one could say that the central bank was actually unable to control the money stock, rather than that it was merely unwilling to do so.

19. Pentti J. K. Kouri and Michael G. Porter, "International Capital Flows and Portfolio Equilibrium," *Journal of Political Economy,* vol. 82 (May/June 1974), pp. 443–67, and Richard J. Herring and Richard C. Marston, "The Monetary Sector in an Open Economy: An Empirical Analysis for Canada and Germany," Working Paper 7-74, the Rodney L. White Center for Financial Research (Wharton School, University of Pennsylvania, 1974; processed).

Alexander Swoboda said that such econometric evidence applies only to what part of the money stock can be controlled in the very short run, that is, before the current account adjusts to the capital inflows. For example, Kouri and Porter treat the current account as exogenous, thereby excluding its adjustment to changes in the money stock. They do not support any further inferences as to the degree of central bank control over the money stock after the trade account adjusts. More generally, it is not surprising that Germany has some control over its money stock, so long as it does not try to exercise too much. A country's control over its money stock is related to the size of its economy compared with those of other countries, since its relative size influences how much of a policy-induced change in money supply will eventually be offset by capital or trade flows. Thus, although in an infinitesimally small country, one would expect an open market sale of securities to be entirely offset by a capital outflow or a trade deficit, "only" about 85 percent should be offset in a country such as Germany, which represents 15 percent of the relevant fixed-rate world. It is difficult to get convincing econometric evidence about the possibilities of sterilization; no one knows what will happen if a country really tries to maintain a level or rate of growth of its money supply widely different from what is compatible with equilibrium in the balance of payments. A country can maintain some independence, but it would be seen that such independence is limited if it tries to have its money stock grow at a very different rate from that of the rest of the world, and also tries to maintain a fixed exchange rate.

Gerhard Fels agreed that sterilization is possible only in the short run. Such sterilization as Germany has been able to achieve has been made possible by regulations in the money market, which have been introduced step by step since the early sixties and have operated by breaking up the money market to some degree. Although these measures may have given the central bank scope for some autonomy in controlling the money supply, it is only short-term autonomy; in the long run, income and price effects are dominant. There have been many cases in which the inflow of funds from abroad have thwarted domestic monetary restriction, despite efforts to regulate the money market.

Hendrik Houthakker asked why, despite all Germany's revaluations and relatively low rate of inflation, the current-account balance had continued to increase. Does that suggest that the Marshall-Lerner conditions do not hold for Germany or is there some other explanation of this peculiar behavior?

Weir Brown pointed out that, according to his best recollection, Germany's rate of inflation had been lower than those of other countries not only when the mark was appreciating but when it was not. Is there any significant difference in the rates of price increase during periods of appreciation compared with other periods? Germany might have been able to maintain current-account surplus during domestic booms as well as in times of domestic slack because it had greater supply flexibility than other industrial countries and therefore greater success in avoiding bottlenecks.

Helen Junz thought the greater mystery is the behavior of imports: why, with the relative price changes caused by revaluation of the mark, have imports failed to respond in the manner expected, even in the longer run?

Walter Salant observed that Germany's ability to increase its exports persistently, despite currency appreciation, would be no mystery if the growth of productivity in German manufacturing were rising much more rapidly than anywhere else or if it had accelerated when the currency appreciated; but a comparison of indexes of unit labor costs in manufacturing in several countries indicated that these had been rising fastest in Germany even when expressed in national currencies, and seemed faster still when expressed in a common currency, a fact which added to the puzzlement evoked by Houthakker.

Assar Lindbeck noted that the relationship between revaluation of the German mark and domestic inflation must be considered in conjunction with the question of revaluation's effect on the trade surpluses. There have been two extreme positions about this in the profession: one, that a change in the exchange rate causes domestic prices, including factor prices, to adjust accordingly, so that the country's competitive situation and its trade balance, although affected for a few months, revert to their customary positions; and two, that a change in the exchange rate does not influence prices in domestic currencies at all, the effect is entirely on the trade balance. West Germany appears to have been in an intermediate position; when it revalued, it got some reaction in the trade account compared with what would have happened otherwise, and some reduction in the rate of inflation compared with what it would have been otherwise. The exchange rate is an efficient instrument either for price stability or for the current-account balance, but it cannot be completely inefficient for both, as many people seem to argue; the two problems have to be treated simultaneously.

Michael Parkin noted that in a paper by Peter Jonson concerning the J-curve (that is, the tendency for the trade balance to get worse immediately after devaluation and to improve only after a lag) it is shown that the behavior of the British balance of payments following an exchange rate change is dominated by domestic credit policy.[20] It could either deteriorate or improve following a change of the exchange rate in either direction, depending upon the domestic credit policy followed. Perhaps the behavior of the German current account might be explained by Germany continuing a tight domestic credit

20. See P. D. Jonson and H. I. Kierzkowski, "The Balance of Payments: An Analytic Exercise," *The Manchester School*, vol. 43 (June 1975), pp. 105–33.

policy when the mark appreciated, thereby sustaining the process that supported a strong balance of payments.

Gerhard Fels agreed that the revaluation of the mark in 1973 had been accompanied by restrictive monetary and fiscal policies, which had forced German manufacturers to look to export markets. The net effect of these policies had been an appreciation of the mark that affected prices less than real incomes. To avoid the tremendous export surplus it would have been necessary to combine appreciation with expansionary domestic policy. Parkin's general argument on the importance of domestic policies in determining the effects of exchange rate changes on the current account is supported by the experience of Italy and France, which had devalued but had increased their domestic consumption and investment, thereby creating greater payments deficits. Earlier revaluations, such as those in 1969 and in 1972, had been accompanied by reductions in the trade balance; it was only the 1973 appreciation that had the paradoxical result. As to the effects on prices, appreciation of the mark had disinflationary effects on export and import prices. What was striking was the failure of this effect to communicate itself to domestic prices. There is no definite explanation for this; it may have been related to a structural shift between the export- and import-competing sectors on the one hand and the rest of the economy on the other, the two international sectors being restrained by the currency appreciation while the domestic sector had inflation, pushed by wage increases and supported by inflows of liquidity from abroad. This possibility, as well as alternative explanations—indeed, the whole field of interaction between international and domestic sectors of an economy—deserves further research. On most occasions West Germany had cut tariffs earlier than other countries, and that might have had a significant stabilizing impact.

The paper's hypothesis, which implied that businessmen marked up their prices only after unit labor and other costs had increased, was borne out by observation. That was their typical behavior until 1969–70. In 1969, however, industrial prices went up before costs increased. This has been recognized as a structural break. After 1970 price behavior became more aggressive; price policy had ceased to be defensive. In "conflict" situations it is difficult for the government to employ expansionary measures, and it had been right to be reluctant; what matters in such a situation is to break the inflationary expectations.

On the question whether an increase in the export surplus should be regarded as exogenous or endogenous, it would normally be endogenous, but the paper had concentrated on cases in which improvement in the current account was exogenous. Of course, endogenous increases in the current-account balance do not indicate imported inflation.

PART THREE

Future Research

A Supranational Approach
and
Specific Topics

WALTER S. SALANT

A Supranational Approach
to the Analysis of
Worldwide Inflation

THE CONCEPT of worldwide inflation implicitly underlying the organization of this book is that such inflation is the result of events in individual countries. This concept calls for examining the experiences of individual countries, selected either because they are large and therefore influence the level of world prices, or because they are believed to be representative of a number of small nations, and then trying to capture the mutual interactions among countries by examining the mechanisms that transmit inflationary influences from one to others. Although the study of national developments presumably takes into account both domestic and foreign influences, the latter are treated as mainly autonomous and, under past circumstances, of much less importance for large countries than domestic influences. Such an approach to the problem is a natural result of the dominant historical and institutional facts, namely, that economic integration has been greater within than among nations; that nations have separate monetary authorities; that data are collected on a national basis; and that cultural influences have encouraged the concept of the world as an aggregation of nations. This approach, if carried out with sufficient care, can lead to the correct answers; the study of national developments in large countries probably gives a good first approximation, and its amendment by incorporation of the mechanism of international transmission can refine this first approximation. The degree of refinement and the accuracy of the result will depend on the extent to which feedbacks are taken into account and on other refinements of the analysis.

This paper proposes, first, to point out what may be omitted or treated incorrectly in such a national approach to an analysis of world inflation, and then to suggest a global approach that, in its first approximation, concentrates more on supranational variables and gives less emphasis to some variables than one with a national focus. This alternative approach is the more appropriate the greater is the integration of the world economy. Insofar as this integration increases, so do the advantages of this alternative approach, and those of the national approach diminish. A forecast that such integration will, in fact, advance therefore implies that the proposed alternative may become increasingly the appropriate approach to the future study of worldwide inflation.

635

Limitations and Defects of a National Approach

The conventional national approach begins by looking for causes of inflation that are autonomous from the point of view of the country under consideration. Typical causes are domestic, such as increases in the government budget deficit, excessive creation of credit by the central bank, or demands for higher money wages per unit of output, depending on the theory assumed. Or they may be influences coming from abroad, such as increases in demand for exports and a consequent increase in the surplus of international transactions in goods and services (or reduction in the deficit), a rise in the world prices of traded goods, an inflow of monetary reserves. These variables, all autonomous from the point of view of the country under review, are then regarded as inducing further changes that, when inflation has actually occurred, have the net effect of aggravating the price rise, although some may have a dampening effect.

The induced inflationary effects on the domestic economy are part of a process of *intra*national transmission of inflation. When recipients of increased government spending increase their own spending on domestic output because their incomes have risen, for example, this induced effect on demand is part of the process by which increases of demand and inflationary pressures are transmitted within the country. So is the flow of bank reserves from the central money market to outer regions of the country that occurs when the national monetary authority purchases government securities from holders in the financial center. In contrast to these induced effects, which are part of the process of transmitting national or domestic inflation, increases of national expenditure on foreign goods and services and increases in tax revenues from higher incomes are both regarded as dampening factors because they limit inflation in the given country.

In an analysis of world inflation that begins with a national approach, the tax and import leakages are distinguished only at the next stage, when the process of international transmission is examined; then the increase in demand for foreign goods and services becomes part of this transmission process whereas the increase in tax revenues remains a leakage. Any feedback to the given country's exports induced by the expansion of its own imports is likely to be neglected until a third stage of refinement.

For analysis of inflation from a truly global point of view, the national approach has a number of practical dangers. First, the aggregation of national factors may result in neglect of supranational factors of current or future importance. For example, consideration must be given to the role of levels and changes in world monetary reserves (including the creation of special drawing rights [SDRs], a supranational factor that, although probably of slight consequence during the period under examination, should be incorporated in any theoretical framework and might later become significant) and the relationship of world monetary reserves to national balances of payments and monetary policies. Another supranational factor of importance in any interpretation that does not entirely discount monetary factors is the development of the Eurocurrency market. Eurocurrency deposits are not included in the reported data on national money supplies, even on a broad definition, but their amount, according to one measure, has risen from $37 billion at the end of 1969 to $145 billion at the end of 1974.[1] By omitting these deposits, the rise in the aggregate of national money supplies would understate the increase in the world money supply or at least in world liquid assets.[2]

A second danger in a national approach supplemented by an analysis of international transmission is that the very idea of transmission implies that the inflationary infection originates in one or a few countries and that the disease is then transmitted to other countries. This may very well be the case, but it should be a conclusion, not an initial assumption. That it is an assumption, even though only implied, becomes evident when it is recognized that it provides little room for, or distracts attention from, some hypotheses. For example, inflation could result from the coincidence of persistent expansions of demand in a number of countries, no one or two of which are sufficiently important to cause it by themselves, just as the price of a single commodity with a large number of buyers and sellers may be forced up as a result of their combined actions when the same actions by a fraction of their number would not have the same effect. In such cases, the result cannot be attributed to the action of a few.

That expansions of demand in a number of countries approximately coincide in time may be the result of the transmission of influences in one or a few identifiable countries to others, but it need not be. Simultaneous expansions of demand may be a common response to some change that influences many markets or government policies in the same direction in all countries rather than a change generated in merely one or two and spreading from them. They may be common responses to a single world cause, such as re-

1. These figures represent the estimated amounts of foreign currency credits channeled through reporting European banks, excluding amounts supplied by banks in the reporting European area. The data came from the *Annual Report of the Bank for International Settlements, Forty-fifth Annual Report, 1st April, 1974–March 31, 1975*, p. 141. There is a minor incomparability in the two figures given in the text.

2. See pages 224–26 for differences of views as to whether Eurocurrency deposits should be regarded as part of the money supply.

armament in reaction to increasing world political tensions (as in the world price boom of 1936–37); or they may be responses to national policy pressures common to many countries, such as the increased priority given to full employment, where any international transmission that has occurred has been of ideas, not market factors. Conceivably, if improbably, coincidence of expansion might even result from a conjunction of independent factors. When expansions that, individually, would have little effect on the price level of world-traded goods occur simultaneously in many countries, for whatever reason, the price level of those goods rises, but in the national approach that rise appears as a change coming from outside the national economy. What caused it? The analysis of international transmission does not answer that question. The main reason is that in the national approach there may be no explicit aggregation until a late stage of the analysis, and such analyses are not always or even often carried to that point. Morever, in many such cases external and domestic factors would both be present and it might be hard to identify the source of the inflation or to distinguish autonomous and induced changes.[3]

Another issue that perhaps belongs in this category because it raises questions not identifiable with any one country is the role of the international monetary system in world inflation. One feature of the Bretton Woods system as it developed, the use of the dollar as an international reserve, is perhaps as easily analyzed in the transmission analyses of the national approach as in a supranational approach. It involves what are in effect open market operations in dollar assets by non-American monetary authorities, operations induced by surpluses or deficits in the balance of payments that are not offset by opposite open market operations in the United States. Even here, however, the global approach is more straightforward (as explained in the following section).

A third danger of the national approach is that it begins by drawing the line between autonomous and induced factors in a way that is inappropriate to treatment of inflation as a world phenomenon. Variables that are auton-

3. It appears also that in efforts that have been made to join national models together, in Project LINK and other studies, the national models do not disaggregate the national economies into tradable and nontradable output and are therefore not well adapted to analyzing the effects on domestic general price indexes of changes in world prices of tradable output. This characteristic is not inherent in the national approach, however, and I do not adduce it as a defect of that approach. The economists working on Project LINK have recognized the need for models of the prices of world-traded commodities that transcend national boundaries and aggregate world supply and demand for a given product (see pages 207–10, 230–31).

omous from a national point of view may, from a world point of view, be induced. For example, increases in foreign demand for a country's exports or shifts in its domestic demand from imports to domestic output when an increase of foreign demand raises import prices are external developments. They are therefore autonomous from a national point of view, but from a world point of view they may be induced.

Similarly, in conventional analyses of national demand, increases in government or private expenditures appear as expansionary influences on domestic demand; insofar as they are spent abroad, however, as they are to an increasing extent, they have no direct influence on the domestic economy. In the national accounts, the lack of domestic effect emerges from the analysis in the form of an equal autonomous increase in imports, which offsets the increase in domestic expenditure, but in practice this increase is mixed in with induced changes in imports, making it difficult to separate the autonomous element in the import change. Moreover, the equal and offsetting autonomous changes in foreign expenditure of government and in imports, besides being part of total changes in government expenditure and in imports, appear in the national accounts as two independent events, although from the national point of view they are a nonevent. A disaggregated analysis must be made for the specific purpose of seeing whether the increases of expenditure and imports are associated and whether the autonomous change in domestic expenditure, which is in fact inflationary, has its induced effects in other countries or at home.

A corresponding problem arises in connection with financial transactions. In a world where capital markets are as integrated as they now are, it is probably of more serious proportions.

Finally, the division of the national approach into domestic effects and their international transmission gives an emphasis to the international aspect of transmission that, from a world point of view, is excessive relative to intranational transmission. It is excessive in the sense that from a world point of view transmission within large countries is just as important as transmission among countries. In this connection, it may be noted that the least populous Federal Reserve district in the United States, the Minneapolis district, with a 1970 population of 6.7 million, contains more people than seventy-five of the 135 members of the United Nations.

From the point of view of global inflation, these defects and dangers of the national approach may be regarded as falling broadly into two general classes. One is analytical: that the distinction between autonomous and induced forces will be drawn in a way that is inappropriate for the analysis of a global phenomenon. The other is statistical: that in the process of world aggregation of national data some variables will be double-counted or omitted from the count.

To make my general point vivid at the risk of overstating it, I would say that to study world inflation by beginning with analyses of national inflations and then studying international transmission is like studying inflation in the United States by first studying inflation in each of the twelve Federal Reserve districts, and then analyzing the process of transmission among them. It can be done, but with the degree of integration that exists in the United States, it is not the best approach.

This analogy may appear to be a caricature because the twelve Federal Reserve banks are not separate and uncoordinated policy authorities or controllers of the money supply, as are the monetary authorities of nations. But it is not caricature, because much of the coordination of actions by the various Federal Reserve banks is, in the last analysis, forced on them by actual or foreseeable responses caused by the high integration of the domestic capital market. Coordination of changes in their discount rates, for example, reflects the expected results of what market forces would do if the eleven Reserve banks outside New York did not keep in step with the New York bank; open market operations are conducted entirely in New York and affect other districts only through the actuality or anticipation of market-induced capital flows similar in nature, if not in volume, to those between countries. Integration of world capital markets has proceeded far enough to create similar interdependence among countries.

The analogy might also be objected to on the ground that the world differs from the United States in that its component nations, besides having formally independent monetary authorities, have independent and uncoordinated national treasuries. But in the United States there are fifty states that can raise and lower taxes and expenditures independently of the federal government and of each other, and any number of smaller local jurisdictions with taxing and spending powers. In 1973 state and local expenditures were 45 percent of the total $407 billion of all government expenditure in the United States and accounted for 47 percent of the $411 billion receipts.[4]

Let me repeat that I am not saying that the national approach cannot yield correct answers. It can if it is applied carefully and is refined enough.

---

4. In these figures, the $41 billion federal grants-in-aid to state and local governments are included in state and local but not federal expenditures, and are not included in state and local receipts. Figures come from U.S. Department of Commerce, Bureau of Economic Analysis, *Survey of Current Business,* vol. 54 (July 1974), tables 3.1 and 3.3, pp. 25, 26.

Nor am I ignoring the institutional fact that, in a world divided into countries, all developments, including policies affecting inflation, take place within them (although even here, a small exception must be made for international economic institutions such as the International Monetary Fund and the World Bank). What I am suggesting is, first, that the factors that may be left out of account in a national approach, unless it is carried to a great degree of refinement, may be more important for world inflation than those left unaccounted for in an equally refined global approach, and that the advantage of a global approach is greater the more integrated the world economy becomes. Second, a supranational approach forces the analyst to abandon the deeply ingrained habits of thought imposed from birth by the national character of institutions and by the whole culture. It therefore requires a radical reorientation of thinking, and this reorientation may be far more fruitful in yielding new insights than a continued treading along old paths. To this alternative approach I now turn.

A Proposed Supranational Approach

The basic characteristic of a supranational approach to world inflation is that, in its first approximation at least, it should begin by treating the world —or so much of the world as it considers—as integrated, paying no more attention at the outset to its division into countries than is paid to the division of a country into regions in the study of national inflations. This approach implicitly assumes, as a first approximation, that international integration is as great as intranational integration, and leaves international economic barriers to be taken into account in a later approximation. In that later refinement events in each country would be analyzed to see if one or a few countries were sources of infection and, if so, to discover how the infection spread.

A supranational approach also implies that the distinction between autonomous and induced changes is drawn from a world point of view. Some changes, such as export increases resulting from expansion of incomes in customer countries, are treated as induced, although from a national point of view they are regarded as autonomous. Correspondingly, induced changes include both those induced by globally autonomous factors and those intranationally or internationally transmitted. In principle, there are no import leakages, although in practice, some will occur if parts of the world have to be omitted from the analysis.

Furthermore, all national money variables are translated into a world unit of account and aggregated into a world total, or an appropriately weighted world average, at least during a period of generally stable exchange rates.[5]

These points suggest the need to study specific variables in a way that might otherwise not be pursued.

One of these variables is the relation of the level and changes of world monetary reserves to the world aggregate of "high-powered" or "reserve" money, and the world money supply. In data to be obtained for the supply of world money or near-money, Eurocurrency deposits would be taken into account. In aggregating national money supplies denominated in the countries' own currencies, the investigator need not be concerned about whether a given country's money supply should include holdings of its money by foreigners or holdings of foreign money by its residents (a neglected but growing problem in measurement of national money supplies); it would be sufficient to avoid omission and multiple counting of such cross-holdings.

The world total of reserve money would be divided between the portions consisting, on the asset sides of central bank balance sheets, of international reserve assets and holdings of loans and investments so that the source of changes could be assigned to changes in international reserves and changes in domestic credit creation. It would not at this stage be necessary to distinguish between domestic and foreign credit creation; it would be enough to know their sum because, in a supranational view, whether central banks extend credit to domestic or foreign residents does not matter. Whether, for the world as a whole, central bank credit creation is autonomous or is induced by increases in world monetary reserves, as contended, at least for the long run, by Harry Johnson and perhaps others,[6] is a question to be examined with the use of these data.

How much of the increase in high-powered money results, respectively, from the increase in international monetary reserves and from credit creation by central banks may be determined from data aggregating the changes in these two components of high-powered money. Some indication of their relative importance in the years 1968–72 is given in table 1, which shows the aggregate change in the total and in its two components for six major coun-

5. In a world of fluctuating rates the difficulty of translating national money variables into a common unit of account is not merely statistical; fluctuating rates raise a fundamental problem about the concept of world inflation itself. The ensuing problems are discussed in the appendix to this paper.

6. See Harry G. Johnson's comments on a paper by Richard N. Cooper in *International Reserves: Needs and Availability*, Papers and Proceedings, A seminar at the International Monetary Fund, 1970 (IMF, 1970), pp. 150–51. See also J. Marcus Fleming, "Reserve Creation and Real Reserves" in ibid., pp. 521–52.

Table 1. *Changes in Aggregate Reserve Money and in Its Domestic
and Foreign Components, Six Countries, 1968–72*[a]

Amounts in billions of currency units

Currency and component	Amount		Change	
	End of 1967	End of 1972	Amount	Percent
In dollars				
Total reserve money	129	215	86	66
International reserves	26	66	40	152
Net nonreserve assets	103	149	46	45
In deutsche marks				
Total reserve money	516	688	172	33
International reserves	105	211	106	101
Net nonreserve assets	412	477	65	16

Source: International Monetary Fund, *International Financial Statistics*, vol. 29 (May 1976).
Some figures are rounded and do not add to totals.
a. The countries are France, Germany, Italy, Japan, the United Kingdom, and the United
States.

tries (France, Germany, Italy, Japan, the United Kingdom, and the United
States), which are probably fairly representative of the change during that
period in the world as a whole. Table 1 expresses the aggregate figures in both
U.S. dollars and German marks. Total reserve money expressed in dollars
increased by 66 percent whereas when expressed in marks it increased by
only 33 percent. Similarly, when the levels are expressed in dollars, only 47
percent of the increase in the total consisted of the increase in the interna-
tional-reserves component, whereas when the levels are expressed in marks,
the change in that component accounts for 62 percent of the change in the
total. This difference between the two sets of figures, which of course is attributable to changes in exchange rates, brings out sharply one of the problems involved in aggregating national data.

To see how closely or loosely the world supply of money is connected with
the aggregate of world reserve, or high-powered, money, changes in their
relationship would be examined and analyzed into changes in national relationships and shifts in the distribution of reserve money between countries
with different ratios of money supply to reserve money. (Because the data
used would be measured for finite periods and the changes in these two
components might be large, the cross-products might also be a significant
component of the change in the aggregate ratio.)

To follow this monetary approach, a similar analysis would be carried
out of the relation between gross world product and world money supply.

Here again it would have to be recognized that changes in the aggregate world relationships could be the effect either of changes in the relationship in individual countries or of shifts in the world money supply among countries with different relationships.

Fiscal developments would require a comparable analysis. Again it is irrelevant, from a global point of view, in which country a government's expenditure is made or what country's residents are affected by its tax changes or where deficits are financed. In an era when governments can and do sell bonds to foreign as well as domestic central banks, commercial banks, and private investors, a national approach demands that foreign and domestic sources of financing be distinguished so that the foreign financing may be matched with the corresponding elements in the capital account of the balance of payments. A global approach, however, does not require making that distinction until a later stage of refinement. The main condition of a global fiscal approach is the aggregation of the high-employment budgets of all countries—or, to be more practical, of the major countries—to get the fiscal changes that are autonomous from a world point of view.

These monetary and fiscal data would provide the foundation for a first approximation in a macroeconomic approach to world inflation. When the next stage, analyzing induced effects, was reached, the national character of existing data would probably require taking into account the composition by countries of the location of changes in expenditure and taxation, as well as the effects of changes in high-powered money on the money supply, along the lines suggested by Goodwin and discussed by Chipman.[7]

In an analysis of increases in the prices of world-traded commodities, the temptation to concentrate on the national demands that have increased would be automatically avoided because one would be dealing with *net* changes in world demand. Indexes of world prices of internationally traded commodities and the quantities purchased would presumably be required in this analysis. It would capture information relevant to one aspect of the transmission that occurs directly through prices and at the same time capture the effects on world prices of independent expansions and contractions of national demands.

When an examination is made of the extent to which pressure on productive capacity affects prices of tradable goods it will presumably be found, in general, that pressure on world capacity is what counts, even for prices in individual countries. To this generalization the only exceptions, so far as substantial price changes are concerned, are cases in which trade barriers

7. See R. M. Goodwin, "The Multiplier as Matrix," *Economic Journal*, vol. 59 (December 1949), pp. 537–55, and the comment on it by John S. Chipman in ibid., vol. 60 (December 1950), pp. 753–63.

are high or are adjusted to offset price movements, as in the case of the European Community's variable levies on imports of agricultural products.

As international trade expands in relation to gross world product, this proposition becomes increasingly true of even the broader comparisons of the relation between actual and potential total output. A measure of the relation between *aggregated* actual and potential output, at least for a substantial group of economically important countries, would automatically capture the degree to which their expansions coincided and imply a comparison of the degrees of that coincidence between or among periods. It would also make easier a comparison among periods of the rates at which utilization of capacity increased, and the extent to which expansions in different periods began from different levels of such utilization. Furthermore, it could be directly compared with movements in indexes of the prices of world-traded commodities. If such a comparison did not show the expected relationships, that would suggest that disaggregation of the data on rates of capacity utilization, not by countries but by commodity sectors, might throw a guiding light on changes in the structure of demand unmatched by changes in capacity and on how the speed of such changes compared with their speed in earlier periods of expansion.

The mobility of labor, although far less than that of goods, has similar implications, especially within some groups of countries, such as continental Europe, where it is very great. Large proportions of workers in Germany and Switzerland have come from Italy, Spain, Greece, and other countries of southern Europe. This fact poses the question whether labor is much less mobile among some countries than it is within some countries. In any event, international labor mobility is greater now than it was, and in the absence of world recession the trend is likely to continue. The implications for a supranational approach are that the possibilities of developing a Phillips curve for the world or at least a large group of countries[8] should be examined.

Institutional factors may be responsible for increases in sectoral prices or costs. Autonomous increases in such prices and costs, some economists be-

8. After having written the above I learned that Nigel Duck, Michael Parkin, David Rose, and George Zis have attempted to develop a world Phillips curve in "The Determination of the Rate of Change of Wages and Prices in the Fixed Exchange Rate World Economy, 1956–71," in Michael Parkin and George Zis, eds., *Inflation in the World Economy* (Manchester: Manchester University Press; and Toronto: University of Toronto Press, 1976), pp. 113–43. P. D. Jonson in "Our Current Inflationary Experience," *Australian Economic Review*, no. 22 (2nd quarter, 1973), p. 21, says: "The resulting wage equations are highly promising, with unemployment and 'price expectations' highly significant and together explaining about two thirds of the variance in the rate of change of wages" (p. 22), but their results are severely questioned by M. J. Artis in Parkin and Zis, eds., *Inflation in the World Economy*, pp. 143–49.

lieve, can occur and force up the general price level; most economists hold that increases in sectoral prices or costs that are responses to increases in the prices of inputs do contribute to the transmission of inflation. Analysis of the role of such autonomous increases requires appraisal of changes in market power through changes in the concentration of sellers in the markets for goods and for labor. National measurements of concentration might show that the number of firms responsible for a given percentage of the market in each country was unchanged over a period of time, and therefore be interpreted to imply that the degree of concentration was unchanged. But concentration, although remaining unchanged in any one country, might have increased in the world as a whole. This would be the case if at the beginning of the period the dominant firms in one country were independent of those in other countries but during the period took over, or were taken over, by those in another country, or merged with them, so that the same firms became dominant in several or all countries. My impression is that this has actually happened.[9] Here again, measurement of sellers' concentration in world rather than national markets would avoid the risk of coming to a wrong conclusion.

The same problem arises in connection with concentration in the labor market, although here it is probably of smaller practical importance because the internationalization of labor unions is less advanced.

One difference between the national and supranational approaches to developments in a major sector may be partly illustrated by considering the effects of the increase in the price of oil in late 1973. A national view of the economically dominant countries leads to major emphasis on three aspects of this increase. First, for these countries, as for most of the world, a deterioration occurs in the terms of trade that forces a cut in the sum of domestic consumption and investment at given levels of output. Second, current-account deficits are increased for most of them, requiring external financing or stimulating efforts to reduce nonoil imports and to increase exports, efforts that are incompatible so long as the oil exporters have vastly increased current-account surpluses. Third, the increase in the price of oil directly and indirectly causes increases in the domestic price level which, although possibly of a once-for-all character, take time to work through the price system. The resistance of buyers to accepting the cut in absorption

9. Between 1962 and 1970, the number of mergers involving a controlling interest takeover grew from 173 to 612 in the original six-member European Community, and the rate of mergers between 1962 and 1966 was nearly doubled between 1966 and 1970. Concentration has reduced some sectors to only four manufacturers, and in others the number has been reduced by half. (See European Community Information Service, "Background Note No. 11/74" [June 21, 1974; processed], p. 1.)

forced by the deterioration in the terms of trade may set off an inflationary price-cost spiral. From a supranational point of view, the threat to the price level appears as an equally prominent effect, but the first and second effects look different. Assuming that residents of oil-importing countries do not maintain their total consumption by cutting their saving as much as their spending on oil products increases, the dominant macroeconomic effect of the shift of total consumption from domestic output to imports from the oil-exporting countries is an increase in the world propensity to save. That increase provides an opportunity to expand world investment. In the national view, the increase of imports is not so readily seen as an increase in saving.

Conclusion

Lest the suggestion of this paper be misunderstood, let me repeat that I recognize that the "truth" about world inflation may be approached from either direction: by beginning with national price levels and what influenced them and then examining their interrelations to arrive at a world picture, or by taking the world as a whole and then examining the parts. But the first procedure is very conventional and probably leads to little that has not been said before. The second procedure, on the other hand, may break new ground because it approaches the whole problem in a way that has not been adopted before and acknowledges that the world economy is integrated. Although its first approximation may exaggerate the degree of integration, the second approximation should correct that exaggeration. The novelty of the approach makes it likely to give more new insights than the national approach. Moreover, the effort to "think globally" provides a healthy corrective to the unconscious bias of American economists, who tend to think in terms appropriate to a large economy relatively little influenced by foreign trade and finance.

Even if authors do not need that corrective, the difference in approach would be a major influence on readers.

It may be true, of course, that even in a study with a truly global point of view most of the content would probably be devoted to developments in each country and might have to be organized on national lines. Departure from the conventional would be very slight, however, unless there were an initial chapter treating inflation from a world point of view and somewhere—perhaps in the first chapter or perhaps in the last, if the bulk were divided nationally—providing a world aggregation of the relevant variables. This is the minimum requirement in a contribution that really recognizes the global character of the subject and that paves the way for a global approach to anti-inflationary policy.

Appendix: A Statistical Problem in a Supranational Approach to World Inflation—the Common Unit of Account

A question that accompanies the study of global inflation is: what unit of account should be used to measure it? The question arises also in connection with the aggregation of national variables, which are expressed in national currencies. When all exchange rates, or at least those among major currencies, are fixed, the choice of a unit to use in aggregating national variables poses no problem; it makes no difference in what monetary unit their values are expressed. When relative values of currencies change, however, there is a problem, and it is especially severe when they are in a constant state of flux.

Consider, as one example, the aggregation of national money supplies. If the German supply of money is constant and the U.S. money supply is rising, while the deutsche mark is rising in relation to the dollar at the same rate as the U.S. money supply increases, the aggregate money supply of the two countries expressed in marks will be unchanged, but if it is expressed in dollars it will rise by the same percentage as the U.S. money supply and the dollar price of the mark.

Similarly, the degree of inflation of the world price level (if that is not too fictitious a concept to use) is influenced by the choice of the common unit of account, and so is the degree of its acceleration. The depreciation of one major currency has an inflationary effect in the depreciating currency's country but has an anti-inflationary effect in other countries. Suppose that the net result in the nondepreciating countries is stability of their general price levels. If the world price level is measured in one of their currencies, the inflation in the depreciating country may be fully or more than fully offset by the depreciation of its currency so that the average price level for the world is shown as stable, even though national price levels expressed in national currency units have risen on the average and have fallen in no country. If the world price level is measured in the currency of the depreciating country, however, it will reflect increases in all countries.

This dilemma may perhaps be avoided by confining the study to the period of relatively stable exchange rates. But to limit it in that way would mean cutting the study off before the period when inflation became most severe. That course should be rejected.

A possible solution of the problem of fluctuating currency relationships is to develop a global unit of account for measurement of all money values. This hypothetical unit of account might be defined as an average of the main national currency units weighted by the relative real gross national product of the countries that issue them. Still open is the question of whether these weights should be fixed or current.

Alternatively, it could be argued that even in a world of fluctuating exchange rates the selection of a single unit of account is not a problem if all or most countries are experiencing a rise of prices measured in their own currencies. From this perspective one might leave unanswered the question of what to do when some countries are inflating and depreciating and others have stable or even slowly falling prices and are appreciating. It may be said that no answer is necessary because that situation does not exist. This response is a practical one, although intellectually unsatisfying in its failure to explain whether such a situation is one of world inflation.

One may carry this second view further and argue that, although the world economy is highly integrated, under fluctuating exchange rates there is and can be no problem of world inflation in the sense of a depreciation of the goods-and-services value of a unit of world currency, inasmuch as no such currency exists. World inflation can occur in a world of fluctuating rates only in the sense that the real values of most or all national currency units are depreciating.

The implication of this point of view is that interest is focused not on the increase in the world's average price level (the weighted *average* of increases in national price levels) but on the frequency distribution of such national increases. A given rate of world increase is not of interest if it reflects extreme increases in one or two large countries combined with stability elsewhere, but only if it reflects a wide diffusion of inflation measured in the national currencies of the countries affected.

This position is essentially inconsistent with a view of the world as one integrated economy where national boundaries are relevant only insofar as they are responsible for barriers to the transmission of economic changes. A truly global approach does not distinguish between economic change of given amount that occurs in one or two big countries and one of equal average size that is distributed among many. Whether a given rise in the world average price level is widely distributed among countries or highly concentrated in a few is of no greater interest from the global standpoint than whether a given rise in the consumer price index in the United States results from widely diffused increases in its regional components or from an extreme rise concentrated in one or two regions with approximate stability in the others. That few citizens, if any, ask about the diffusion of inflation in the United States is probably the result of institutional statistical practice, which not only fails to confront them with the problem but conceals it, rather than of their considered view that it is not of interest.

For the purposes of a first study of world inflation, therefore, the decision about whether to aggregate during the period of fluctuating exchange rates —essentially, the choice between the national and truly global approaches— may best be based on what has made economists interested in the problem. They may find this out by asking themselves whether the rise of the average level of world prices would be of equal interest if, instead of being widely diffused over many countries, it were equal in amount but confined to a few countries, with others having a stable price level. If very few people regard this hypothetical situation as presenting a "world" problem, the appropriate inference is that there is little real interest in considering the world as one economy. The implication for the specific statistical problem here posed is that the attempt to find a global unit of account in a world of fluctuating exchange rates is a nonproblem. If, however, concern exists about the proportion of the world's transactions carried out at varying degrees of price rise in the currencies used, irrespective of the number of countries involved in these transactions, there should be interest in a world price level (in practice, derived as a weighted average of national price levels), and there is then a need to develop a world unit of account.

Comments by Harry G. Johnson

SALANT'S paper is obviously sensible and acceptable. Its main point is to show the shifts of emphasis that have to be introduced in the change from a unit, or individual, experiment basis to a market experiment basis and from a case study to a system view of the whole process of inflation. The only question I have is why Salant is so diffident. In the circles I have moved in during the past five years, it has been taken for granted that there is a world system linked by fixed exchange rates and that such a system behaves as a system. Refusal to accept that fact seems to reflect two things. One is that the world has emerged from some twenty-five years or so of depression, war, and postwar reconstruction economics during which there was an emphasis on national problems; many of the linkages that used to exist were not there, although they have since been restored. Second is the belief, which I think is methodologically wrong, that unless some very simple linkage is found between national economies, they are all special cases.

That belief, in turn, represents a fallacious point of view. If I insist that someone show me how something works, according to a system of logic that does not fit the facts, then obviously he will find it difficult to do so. I may say that I will not believe that money influences anything until it is demonstrated how it works its way through some central bank action from short-term rates to long-term rates to the equity market and decisions of entrepreneurs and their animal spirits. My contention is that this kind of sequential linkage is a very special imposed requirement and may not seem to work at all. It has led to much pointless argument in the domestic monetary field and now in the international monetary field. If people refuse to believe something unless it is proved according to a logical structure of relationships which itself is unproved and highly controversial, then nothing but argument will follow.

I was rather surprised by Salant's diffidence in suggesting that maybe there was an international system here that was capable of experiencing world inflation. But I have become convinced that there is a need for diffidence, if only to lead the still more diffident by the hand down the path to recognition that there may be a world system.

One situation encountered in this field is that some economists, rather than admit that there is a world system governed by economic logic—and for the last 200 years this logic has been available—fight desperately against admitting that there is such a system, and give interminable chronicles of day-to-day national history to disprove its existence.

This demonstrates another proposition: if one resolutely refuses to ask a scientific question, one will never get a scientific answer. But perhaps by standing still, these opponents may have become right for the time being because there is no international system any more, in principle. There is a floating-rate system. In that case it becomes true again in principle that there is no such thing as world inflation or world depression. There is simply a national choice. On that ground, I would concur in resisting the term "world inflation." But so far, everyone has chosen to support that resistance without understanding its dependence on floating rates.

One aspect of floating rates almost invariably overlooked by its advocates is the tremendous influence of habit and custom on the way in which national monetary authorities operate floating-rate systems.

In principle, there is no world inflation affecting individual countries at the present time, because it is in principle impossible for any country to be forced to import inflation with floating rates. But if each country thinks it must keep its interest rates in line with other countries, it is automatically guaranteeing that it will have an equivalent of a fixed rate with little if any flexibility and that it will have the same inflation as others. But that is a national choice; it is not the inevitable result of the exchange rate system.

That brings me to the appendix of the paper in which Salant worries about establishing a measurement of world inflation in a system where there is no world inflation. Clearly, a measure can always be found by imposing on the world the necessity of there being world inflation, by assuming that it exists, and by taking an average of some kind. Some countries will then be seen to have more, some less, according to how they use their floating rates, with the more inflationary countries depreciating and the less inflationary countries appreciating. And the existence of world inflation may be believable, because it is thought there are limits to how far individual countries will diverge from the policies of the rest.

For this purpose one must have some kind of index to set a standard for the "world average inflation rate." The closest parallel I can think of at the moment is the problem inherited from Adam Smith and Ricardo, the absolute standard of value, which gave way to an emphasis on relative prices. An absolute standard can always be found such that, if anything moves, one can say it went up or down by comparison with this standard, and thereby avoid being confined to a statement that one item has gone up or down relative to other things. Economists can always take, say, the United States or Germany as a standard, and define "world inflation" as inflation by everyone else relative to the United States or German price level. But a theory is needed to rationalize the choice of that particular country rather than another. There is no way around the problem of imposing world inflation on a world that does not exist, namely, a single world system with floating rates among the components. To tackle that problem, one has, first of all, to construct the problem, and then to construct the solution. And, when one has finished, maybe one is back where one started. But the problem seems pointless to me if one really believes in floating rates. In that sense, those who insist on the national nature of inflation may be right if they understand that it is a national choice to have inflation in a floating-rate system.

The notion of world inflation was valid under the fixed-rate system, but it is not valid now except as a matter of voluntary choice by the governments and publics concerned.

General Comments

ARTHUR OKUN expressed concern that an emphasis on the supranational approach and the transmission process might divert attention from the choices that countries actually have, and to varying degrees have failed to use, in coping with inflation. Relatively little attention has been paid in this study to the variability of exchange rates, for example. And exchange rates are one of a wide variety of possible instruments that might enable countries to assume greater control over their domestic inflation rates, rather than merely to place the blame on the worldwide inflationary process.

Johan Myhrman questioned Johnson's surprise that there is world inflation under a flexible exchange rate regime, since that system did not start afresh.

Harry Johnson responded that when a country floats its exchange rate it *is* starting afresh if it wants to; it can manage its exchange rate so as to be free of world inflation. Countries have chosen, however, not to use exchange rate flexibility to full advantage in order to eliminate inflation. For example, Canada and Germany have let their currencies appreciate only slightly. They have views on other matters, such as what their interest rates should be relative to interest rates elsewhere. As soon as a country places limits on its exchange rate or on its interest rates, it automatically ties its monetary policy up with other countries' monetary policies and, in effect, restores a fixed-rate system except for the slight flexibility provided by a nonfixed margin.

John Pitchford pointed to the need, given an imperfect world not free of inflation, to include in a supranational approach the examination not only of money but of a number of basic commodities such as fibers, cereals, metals, and fuels. The examination should aggregate these commodities across countries, and take account of the considerable autonomous supply shifts behind relative price changes. In an imperfect world the accommodation of money supplies to these shifts serves as an impetus to world inflation.

Assar Lindbeck noted that comments focused on the question of whether the usefulness of Salant's approach depends on which exchange rate system, fixed or floating, is involved. This distinction is important, but even in a floating-rate system an aggregated approach is necessary because prices of tradables are formed by some kind of demand-supply mechanism on the world market. Even if the price differs with different currencies when the exchange rate changes, still, in order to explain what happens to their prices in the various currencies, some kind of demand-supply aggregate is required. For this reason the usefulness of Salant's approach survives even in a floating system.

Rudolf Rhomberg questioned the view that there cannot be a world inflation problem under a floating system because all countries have a choice. Although it is true that every country, individually, has a choice, if all countries tried to appreciate they would not have the choice collectively and world inflation would still exist. If the standard against which a country's floating is measured is not other currencies but something else, such as gold, then a significant deflation, rather than inflation, would occur. If gold is dismissed as a standard, then the choice of standard would revert to some weighted average of currencies, as suggested by Salant. Defined in these terms, the problem of world inflation might still be said to exist and be subject to useful analysis.

Harry Johnson argued that price stability is stability of some index of commodity prices and if a country stabilizes domestic prices, what happens to exchange rates is a consequence of that stabilization and the policy of other countries. Price stability, it is now understood, is not achieved by fixing the exchange rate. The whole point of floating is to permit countries to pursue domestic policies. Once a country chooses to stabilize its currency with that of another country, or with SDRs, or with some commodity, then a different policy objective is involved and inflation results. Averting inflation is a question of stabilizing money prices of goods that enter into utility functions, appropriately weighted; it is not a matter of stabilizing exchange rates or the price of gold.

Michael Parkin suggested that there is a serious policy message in Salant's approach. In a fixed exchange rate world, the focus is on the fact that it is the world aggregate rather than individual national developments in money supply that are the primary driving forces on the price level. Attention, therefore, is drawn to the need for appropriate forms of international control and regulation of that particular aggregate. If one assumes the perspective of a fiscalist, rather than a monetarist, still there will be some aggregate which may be pinpointed for control. Study along these lines was undertaken by the University of Manchester. It involves a Group of Ten model, with an approach similar to Salant's, but developed specifically for a fixed-rate world. For the more-or-less, fixed-rate period of 1958–71 the model fits very well by conventional criteria.

Weir Brown raised the question whether there would be some agency or process that would somehow assume the role of world central bank in Salant's model. Or would the national central banks and fiscal authorities involved in demand management still have to be included as a necessary part of the system? The question of inflation as a world problem may be analogous to the problem in the medical field of distinguishing between contagion and epidemia, which involves a process of transmission of disease, or the simultaneous occurrence of a disease because of a common cause, as in the case of occupational diseases. A new approach might be made not on the basis of a choice between the aggregate and the individual approaches, but rather to include new elements in a qualitative sense, perhaps widening the horizon to encompass political, social, and psychological factors.

Rudiger Dornbusch argued that a systems approach is required with regard to flexible rates because the degree of independence afforded by that system is grossly exaggerated. Real disturbances will be transmitted even under flexible rates, and monetary disturbances are real disturbances; if they did not have real effects, changes in the money supply would not occur. Monetary disturbances are typically transmitted through changes in real interest rates, which produce real effects abroad on the price level and the inflation rate. Because there is capital mobility, a systems approach is required, particularly for flexible rates.

Odd Aukrust addressed the point that decisionmaking is national, not international. The study has shown that, although different models and perspectives are applied to national problems, still much common ground exists as to the causes and effects. The transmission process is an example; the weights attached to the various mechanisms might differ from one country to another, but there would be general agreement as to the list of mechanisms itself. Common ground therefore exists as to national policy options.

Edward Shaw questioned the concern about competitive appreciation. If all countries desired stable price levels, then stable price levels would be achieved, so there would be no temptation to appreciate. If in that situation a country did appreciate, there would be a tendency toward falling price levels, and if that were unacceptable then the authorities might turn around and depreciate. The relationships among changes in national price levels is an interesting world problem; it is useful to observe the world from a unitary point of view to see if it is one in which there are common monetary decisions and stable exchange rates or divergent monetary decisions and divergent exchange rates. Pressures extend beyond national boundaries and that affects relative real income levels. These mutual effects of a common demand for some good are worth tracing on a world level.

Walter Salant addressed the point that policy decisions are made on a national basis. While the first phase of the project is primarily concerned with analytical problems, policy conclusions are expected to receive attention. If the analysis shows that there is a world problem, then the policy implication would be that, although policy is determined at the national level, the problem at least calls for introducing a supranational element into the decisionmaking process. Existing policy mechanisms should not be taken as unchangeable. If supranational analysis were to indicate the need for a world central bank, then it would strengthen existing opinion to that effect. The analysis might also reveal the need for supranational institutions, or at least more international cooperation, in other fields than monetary, as well.

Fred Bergsten noted that there appears to be some movement in that direction already, in certain microeconomic areas, such as food and energy. The problem to be dealt with is the degrees of nominal and real sovereignty at the macroeconomic level and the extent of the sovereignty illusion in between.

RICHARD N. COOPER AND CONTRIBUTORS

Specific Topics

Introduction by Richard N. Cooper

THE STUDY of world inflation requires nothing less than an understanding of how the entire world economy functions. It incorporates the whole of macroeconomics and much of microeconomics, particularly the microeconomics of money. Moreover, the term inflation refers to a symptom that may result from a wide range of possible conditions. It will have to be defined more specifically.

Two themes that have recurred frequently during discussions point the direction for future research. One concerns the actions of economic policymakers, which ought to be considered rather more as endogenous to the system than as exogenous. For instance, in the past, political, psychological, and economic reasons—all of which need to be defined—have led monetary and fiscal authorities to resist exchange rate changes. In coping with inflation, policymakers have often preferred to rely on balance of payments arguments for restraint. The second concern is with the dynamics of the transmission process, which should assume greater importance in the study of world inflation. It is necessary to break away from the traditional comparative-statics approach and to concentrate on transmission itself and its various political, social, and economic components.

Since the ultimate aim of research is anti-inflationary policy, it may be necessary to place less emphasis on economic structure and to focus more on the target instruments used. The analysis of inflation could be divided into two parts: (1) issues related to, and instruments to deal with, the present high rate of inflation, and (2) a study of future inflationary impulses.

Immediate Issues

Problems associated with inflationary expectations and the nature of continuing inflation are among the immediate issues. One has to consider the effects of divergences between expected and observed rates of inflation. The means for dealing with widely expected inflation is a cost-benefit problem. It can be examined by defining the various policy instruments available to dampen inflation, and the costs and benefits associated with each of them.

659

One question that needs special attention because it has been neglected in the past is how to assess the benefits of reducing the rate of inflation; it is important to distinguish between the variability in inflation rates (and the resulting uncertainty) around a given long-run rate and the degree of certainty of expectations about a given rate of inflation. In appraising the long-run benefits of reducing a known rate of inflation, one should distinguish between reducing its variability and reducing its trend. The two are separate issues.

Future Inflationary Impulses

It is first necessary to define possible future inflationary impulses and to determine to what extent they are real and to what extent monetary. There is a tendency in continental Europe to view inflation as triggered largely by government actions and as essentially monetary in origin, whereas the Anglo-Saxon view generally sees it as arising from nonmonetary sources. However, as Dornbusch emphasizes, monetary impulses are real in the short run, and in a transmission-dynamics approach the distinction must be treated as to some extent artificial.

It is also important to determine for the individual countries to what degree such inflationary impulses are internal or external, and whether they are mutually offsetting, as many would be in a world of purely random events. The analysis might indicate that pooling economies in a common currency area might speed the transmission of mutually offsetting impulses and minimize real losses. Then it would be important to examine whether the covariance of inflationary impulses in the world had not increased. To the extent that impulses have become more correlated over time, the pooling benefit derived from uncorrelated impulses would be lost.

Specific Research Projects

One country-specific research project that might be undertaken relates to the issue of national responses to inflationary impulses: how, for instance, did the governments involved respond to the major external impulse from the United States during the late 1960s and early 1970s, induced by the increase in U.S. spending for the Vietnam War? Was the response primarily the relaxation of balance of payments restraint, as mentioned earlier, or rather was it the monetary effect—a failure or inability to resist an inflow of funds?

Another country-specific question involves currency changes: why have they not had the expected effects? Of particular interest is the impact of German revaluations and the difference between the effects of the French devaluations of 1958 and 1969 and those of the British devaluation in 1967.

A third important area is research on national policies to mitigate or alleviate the costs of inflation. It is necessary to aggregate the various mitigating influences (that is, different forms of indexation) in order to determine to what extent they have succeeded, jointly, in limiting distorting inflationary effects, and whether, through inflationary expectations, the devices themselves have aggravated the rate of inflation.

On a more general level, research might be undertaken on the importance of the effects of changes in real-money balances on expenditure. In principle, there is general agreement that such changes have some effects; the question to be resolved is their significance. The monetarist tends to place heavy emphasis on these real-balance effects, as illustrated in Swoboda's paper, whereas the nonmonetarist sees them as long run and not decisive.

A further general question is how to ascertain which markets clear fastest. Swoboda's paper makes certain assumptions concerning the relative speeds with which financial and money markets clear compared with goods markets. These relative speeds need to be specified more precisely to determine which markets clear fastest and what the implications are for the dynamics of adjustment to initiating impulses.

Finally, studies can be undertaken of world markets for key internationally traded commodities, treating both recent developments and future prospects. It would be useful to anticipate future impulses in these markets and to prepare for them in advance by defining appropriate policy instruments. The impulses may appear external to most countries, but in fact they reflect the confluence of global supply and demand, and it might be possible to outline appropriate measures to offset them. Global commodity market considerations, especially in markets for food, are likely to be important, at least over the next several years.

Comments by Contributors

General Issues

Assar Lindbeck. Since the international economy can change course rapidly, the question arises whether worldwide inflation is the best aspect of the world economy to study for several years. It might be better to ask the question: what are the stability properties of the world system, considering both volume fluctuations and price formation? There are certain interesting inter-relations between the cyclical changes of output, unemployment, productiv-ity, and price changes in various countries that might be overlooked by zero-ing in on inflation.

James Tobin. Characterizing inflation as the critical economic problem is itself an interesting political and social phenomenon because many of the difficulties confronting the various national economies would exist even if there were no inflation. People tend to associate inflation with deterioration in the terms of trade, environmental pollution, and the like, and to use it as a scapegoat.

Hollis Chenery. The inflation problem should be treated as one of objec-tives, instruments, and trade-offs. The reason some countries do not arrest inflation despite having the technical means to do so is that they do not feel able to pursue that objective without sacrificing others. Economists ought to study how easily adjustments can be made among competing goals, what controls are exercised by policymakers, and why these differ among coun-tries. Certain high-growth countries—such as Japan, Korea, Taiwan, and Brazil—seem to have been willing to accept high inflation rates in the past; some of these seem to have been able to take the recent and sudden shocks in their stride whereas others have not. The cases of Taiwan and Japan, for instance, where drastic measures were taken to reduce inflation, would sug-gest that they used additional instruments; whatever the reason, their systems appear more manageable than those of other countries. In any event, such differences ought to be investigated.

Dynamics of Inflation: Impulses and Responses

Frank Schiff. It is important to study the relationship between the magni-tude and speed of economic changes and the ability of individual economic and political systems to respond. Recent experience suggests that economic institutions often have the capacity to accommodate changes gradually with-out significant inflation but cannot do so in the case of sudden impulses. Analysis might yield some conclusions as to the relative flexibility of institu-tions in different countries. The relationship between inflation and real growth rates, as well as levels of capacity utilization in different economies, should also be examined. The relative usefulness, if any, of contraction as a countermeasure to inflation tends to differ among countries and at different levels of resource utilization, particularly when long-term effects on capital formation are taken into account.

Assar Lindbeck. From a policy point of view the mechanisms by which inflation is transmitted are significant because understanding the details of wage formation, cost-push, and other endogenous elements might indicate where to intervene in the transmission process. Once the chain of events in the transmission were more clearly defined, more policy options and perhaps new instruments might be revealed.

Monetary and Capital Market Aspects of Inflation

Hendrik Houthakker. Both the monetarist model presented by Swoboda and the Keynesian model presented by Branson should be further developed by applying more quantitative evidence to them. It is not difficult, on the basis of the monetarist model and using IMF data, to make a cross-country analysis of the influence of a variation in money supply on GNP and on the price level in a large number of countries. Branson's Keynesian model might be treated similarly, using national accounts data, although this is more difficult.

Second, the real-balance effect resulting from the change in the international monetary system from fixed to floating rates should be investigated. The first question to be addressed is the extent to which the recent worldwide inflation was a once-and-for-all adjustment of the world economy to a lower level of needed reserves, resulting from removing the obligation to intervene. Analysts also need to treat the relationships between international reserves and domestic money supplies for other countries in the way that Komiya and Suzuki have done for Japan. This leads to the next question of how international official reserves are transferred to private reserves and, in turn, to the domestic money supply.

Michael Parkin. The University of Manchester has been conducting a Social Science Research Council research program on "Inflation: Its Causes, Consequences and Cures." The program, which is now nearing completion, has been concerned with three broad areas: first, a subproject on the "world" (but defined as the Group of Ten countries for data purposes); second, a series of empirical studies on the process of transmission of inflation among countries; and, third, a series of more detailed papers on the United Kingdom. The model used for the world inflation project is monetarist in orientation and points to several areas in which further study is needed. First of all, it is important to expand the scope of concern beyond the Group of Ten to consider a group of countries that more adequately represents the world. One project that this expansion in scope suggests is developing a consistent base of data on prices, output, employment, and other key variables for such countries. The undertaking might be possible for a research group with more resources at hand than the one in Manchester.

A systems approach is necessary for a study of the flexible exchange rate system. This involves constructing a model to determine national exchange rates and other important variables in less aggregative terms. A monetarist Project LINK is desirable, that is, a link that focuses on the determination of exchange rates and differentials in inflation rates. It is difficult, however, to define such a link, and some theoretical work remains to be done in this area.

Rudolf Rhomberg. The LINK Project was initiated before the problems of inflation and the change to flexible rates developed. As a result, the LINK models are not fully adapted to the present situation and must be patched up to account for new developments. It might be more desirable for a monetary LINK project to start from scratch with a model better designed for that specific function and to use it alongside the existing Project LINK model, on which patching efforts would continue. This was the course adopted by the IMF, where an exchange rate model was constructed to assess the effects of simultaneous exchange rate movements on trade balances, for which there had been no appropriate existing LINK model at the time.

Bert Hickman. Developers of Project LINK envisage, among other studies of inflation, two specific areas in particular need of attention.

First, they would like to see models developed that take account of the extent to which individual decisionmakers in individual countries react to changes in reserves flows and the effects of such flows on the monetary base.

Another objective they have not yet realized is to interest analysts in modeling commodity markets. Their idea is to branch away from the established LINK structure in which international prices are determined from export prices set by individual countries on the assumption that those prices are determined by developments within those countries. This assumption is considered inapplicable for some of the large commodity markets. It would be desirable to overlay commodity market models on the LINK system so as to have demand-side models derived from aggregating demand in the national models and supply-side models of the principal commodity markets to determine the prices of those commodities. These prices would then be fed back into the national models to derive better specifications of price determination for such markets.

Edward Shaw. Economists tend to look on the bond market as redundant. Little is heard about the impact of inflation, floating exchange rates, or variance in inflation rates and exchange rates on capital markets, on maturity and risk structures, on feedbacks to saving, or on the selection of technological innovations. There is evidence that inflation has major effects on capital markets. The indexing of interest rates only partially inhibits these effects. And its importance is all the greater when there are oligopolies that can accumulate huge amounts of saving that capital markets are not equipped to handle. Although Project LINK is interested in capital flows, there is room for independent work in this area. An important question to consider would be whether the significant improvement in the efficiency of capital markets during the Bretton Woods period has been undermined by recent developments.

Hendrik Houthakker. Effects on the bond market is an important issue. Why, for instance, have real interest rates become negative in nearly all major countries? Was this an effect of world capital markets or perhaps of the surplus in world money arising from the changing international monetary system?

Walter Salant. The study of the relationship between stock and bond yields might provide valuable information about the development of inflationary expectations. In a world of stable prices and no real growth one would expect bond yields to be lower than yields on stocks. Expectations of inflation or real growth, or both, however, tend to reverse this relationship. To test the effect of expectations of inflation one would therefore have to adjust stock yields to eliminate the effect of expectation of real growth and then compare adjusted stock yields and yields on bonds to see if the changes in their relationship might reflect changes in expectations about the price level.

W. Max Corden. The most important single research topic is an analysis of national policies to avoid importing inflation. The focus should be on, first, appreciation of the exchange rate, and, as a second-best policy, neutralization of monetary flows. The topic requires detailed investigation of these mechanisms in the context of the political institutions within which they operate. Questions to be addressed include why countries have failed to appreciate—or adequately appreciate—exchange rates; what forces and issues lay behind such decisions; and what the institutional obstacles are. Also to be considered are possible institutional changes in certain countries that may reinforce resistance to imported inflation, and an extension of such an analysis to more countries than those discussed in the volume.

A comparative analysis of countries with low inflation, including but extending beyond Sweden and Germany, would be useful, as well as a case study of the 1950–52 episode. If such an investigation already exists, an analysis highlighting the similarities and differences between that period and the recent one would be a helpful addition.

Comparisons of the indexing experiences of different countries and shifts in the natural rates of unemployment (assuming for the moment that they exist) are needed. With regard to the latter, the analysis should focus on whether shifts have occurred as a result of changes in workers' aims in relation to real wages or because of shifts in marginal profit curves, which can occur as a result of changes in the international terms of trade and in the terms of trade of the wage earner.

A further research question concerns the relative desirability of an integrated fixed exchange rate world or a disintegrated world with flexible rates. One approach might be to divide all of the countries into two categories: those prone to imbalance, either in the form of inflation or excessive unemployment, and those that are generally in balance. The former need the discipline of, and would benefit from being a part of, an integrated world with fixed rates. The latter category, of which Germany is perhaps the best example, would be better off in a disintegrated world having flexible rates. Such a classification might help to define more clearly the differing interests of countries tending to move toward fixed or flexible rates.

Wage-Price Policies and Income Distribution

Wynne Godley. More attention needs to be given to the roles of trade unions, incomes policy, and the general structure of wage differentials. The structure of wage differentials is very difficult to analyze but it is clear that in the United Kingdom, at least, when the structure is artificially disturbed it tends to be reestablished. A comparative analysis of this and related questions is especially important in a study of inflation.

Walter Salant. U.S. economists with knowledge of labor relations place much greater emphasis on wage differentials than the more theoretical economists. It is desirable to make more explicit the theory of wage differentials implicit in Godley's paper and to develop empirical evidence that tests the theory. To do so it is necessary to find a way to express empirically the normal differential in the wage structure and disturbances of it in order to recognize when the normal structure has been restored, and to investigate what disturbs it and what reestablishes it.

Frank Schiff. An analysis of the impact of inflationary impulses on income shares might lead to two different solutions. In some instances the solution might lie in a real shift in income distribution or in resource allocation for an individual country (or perhaps at the international level). In others, it might be the restoration of traditional relationships. The former type of situation is likely to involve a significantly greater inflationary potential.

James Duesenberry. Another related phenomenon should be considered. The inflationary process not only leads to changes in the distribution of income but also, in some degree, resolves the inconsistencies and conflicts about the distribution that cannot be resolved through the political process. For example, the process of distributing the burden resulting from income transfers in the wake of the recent oil and agricultural price increases is being determined by inflation rather than political decision making. Economists should focus on how such conflicts might be resolved through the political process.

"Noneconomic" Aspects of Inflation

Leon Lindberg. Political scientists tend to view inflation as a mode of group bargaining, or as an expression of political power, and they are interested in the role of government as an actor in the inflationary process. A study of worldwide inflation is therefore of interest because it can reveal much about changes in the styles of group bargaining, in the patterns of political power, and in the nature of political conflict and political alignment. These perspectives suggest several questions that might be included in an analysis concerning noneconomic aspects of inflation. The first of these is why inflation has become so much more intractable in the 1970s than it was during the 1950s and 1960s. It would be necessary to examine both the "load" side of this question—how the nature of the problem has changed—and the "supply" side—the availability of resources, including policy instruments—to find answers.

Another area of investigation is determining the kinds of group coalitions that form in response to different solutions to the problem of inflation. Research might involve formulating a typology of such responses and associating various forms of response with different political coalitions. A related question is what policies to minimize inflation, or to mitigate its effects, would be both effective and most likely to be adopted, given the existing political alignments.

A further consideration related to the benefit-cost issue should be faced. It is important to define what kind of problem inflation is and for whom it is a problem. Inflation may serve certain functions for some groups in society. Identifying these groups might help to explain the ranking of the anti-inflationary objective among a government's priorities. Both the nature of inflation as a problem and the group for which it is a problem will vary with the various phases of the inflationary cycle.

Political scientists can accept a model in which decisionmaking about inflation would not be rational decisionmaking but would be carried out under conditions of uncertainty and rapid environmental change. Assuming that political systems are basically conservative in their responses to unanticipated shocks, if the changes in the external environment are significant, then the responses of the political system may lead to policy errors. Policy errors in turn lead to changes in the relative resources of the actors and may lead to changes in the policy orientation of the system and to a search for new solutions.

Joseph Pechman. It would be useful to compare the political forces at work in the inflationary process that obstruct efforts to combat depression with those that obstruct the fight against inflation.

James Duesenberry. Any review of the role of politics should be broadened beyond considerations of monetary and fiscal policy formulation to include, for example, the role of government regulation in limiting competition and promoting inflation. The role of trade union politics, both within and between unions, is also a consideration in the treatment of both wage bargaining and formulation of incomes policy.

Charles Maier. Several of the proposed research projects, especially those geared to institutional questions, point toward a broad social science investigation. For example, the issue of wage differentials raises questions about changes in relative deprivation and relative equality in the Western world over the past generation and how to measure them. It is said that the sense of community has been lost, that information about changes in pay differentials are transmitted in a way that is qualitatively different from a generation ago. How does one measure these and other variables that are said to have changed so that one can test these hypotheses? The roles of institutions, such as central banks and political parties, also need to be thoroughly examined. The nature of party loyalties is changing. Inflation has brought to light incompatible interests within parties that originally did not exist.

Henry Owen. The study of noneconomic causes of inflation should include the role of trade unions, changing attitudes toward consumption and investment, the growth or decline of egalitarian pressures, and the degree of willingness among different groups to bear the transitional costs of economic change. Although it may not be possible to treat these issues in quantitative terms, they should nevertheless be addressed explicitly, both on the national and the international levels.

John Pinder. From a sociologist's perspective, it would be helpful to address two key questions in any inflation study: the nature and courses of shifts in the Phillips curve and the nature of cost-push inflation. Surveys of both employed and unemployed workers can be undertaken in order to measure the impact of changes in workers' attitudes toward employment and compensation in a situation of rising inflation.

Contributors

ODD AUKRUST *Statistisk Sentralbyrå, Oslo, Norway*

GIORGIO BASEVI *University of Bologna, Italy*

C. FRED BERGSTEN *Brookings Institution, Washington, D.C.*

WILLIAM H. BRANSON *Princeton University, New Jersey*

WEIR M. BROWN *U.S. Department of the Treasury, Washington, D.C.*

LARS CALMFORS *Institute for International Economic Studies, Stockholm, Sweden*

HOLLIS B. CHENERY *International Bank for Reconstruction and Development, Washington, D.C.*

WILLIAM R. CLINE *Brookings Institution, Washington, D.C.*

RICHARD N. COOPER *Yale University, New Haven, Connecticut*

W. MAX CORDEN *Australian National University, Canberra, Australia*

RUDIGER DORNBUSCH *Massachusetts Institute of Technology, Cambridge, Massachusetts*

JAMES S. DUESENBERRY *Harvard University, Cambridge, Massachusetts*

GERHARD FELS *Kiel Institute of World Economics, Federal Republic of Germany*

WYNNE A. H. GODLEY *Cambridge University, United Kingdom*

ROBERT J. GORDON *Northwestern University, Evanston, Illinois*

BERT G. HICKMAN *Stanford University, California*

HENDRIK HOUTHAKKER *Harvard University, Cambridge, Massachusetts*

HARRY G. JOHNSON *University of Chicago, Illinois*

HELEN B. JUNZ *Council of Economic Advisers, Washington, D.C.*

RYUTARO KOMIYA *University of Tokyo, Japan*

LAWRENCE B. KRAUSE *Brookings Institution, Washington, D.C.*

GEORGES LANE *Centre Universitaire Dauphine, Paris, France*

ANTONIO C. LEMGRUBER *Brazilian Institute of Economics, Rio de Janeiro, Brazil*

ASSAR LINDBECK *Institute for International Economic Studies, Stockholm, Sweden*

LEON N. LINDBERG *University of Wisconsin, Madison, Wisconsin*

CHARLES S. MAIER *Harvard University, Cambridge, Massachusetts*

JOHAN MYHRMAN *Carnegie-Mellon University, Pittsburgh, Pennsylvania*

ARTHUR M. OKUN *Brookings Institution, Washington, D.C.*

HENRY OWEN *Brookings Institution, Washington, D.C.*

MICHAEL PARKIN *University of Western Ontario, Toronto, Canada*

JOSEPH A. PECHMAN *Brookings Institution, Washington, D.C.*

JOHN PINDER *Political and Economic Planning, London, United Kingdom*

JOHN D. PITCHFORD *Australian National University, Canberra, Australia*

RUDOLF R. RHOMBERG *International Monetary Fund, Washington, D.C.*

WALTER S. SALANT *Brookings Institution, Washington, D.C.*

PASCAL SALIN *Centre Universitaire Dauphine, Paris, France*

FRANK W. SCHIFF *Committee for Economic Development, Washington, D.C.*

CHARLES L. SCHULTZE *Brookings Institution, Washington, D.C.*

HAROLD T. SHAPIRO *University of Michigan, Ann Arbor, Michigan*

EDWARD S. SHAW *Stanford University, California*

YOSHIO SUZUKI *Bank of Japan, Tokyo, Japan*

ALEXANDER K. SWOBODA *Graduate Institute of International Studies, Geneva, Switzerland*

JAMES TOBIN *Yale University, New Haven, Connecticut*

THOMAS A. WILSON *University of California, Berkeley*

Index of Names

673

General Index